SEA HUNTERS OF INDONESIA

OXFORD STUDIES IN SOCIAL AND CULTURAL ANTHROPOLOGY

Oxford Studies in Social and Cultural Anthropology represents the work of authors, new and established, which will set the criteria of excellence in ethnographic description and innovation in analysis. The series serves as an essential source of information about the world and the discipline.

OTHER TITLES IN THE SERIES

Organizing Jainism in India and England
Marcus Banks

Society and Exchange in Nias
Andrew Beatty

The Heat of the Hearth
The Process of Kinship in a Malay Fishing Community
Janet Carsten

Global Migrants, Local Lives: Travel and Transformation in Rural Bangladesh
Katy Gardner

Contested Hierarchies: A Collaborative Ethnography of Caste among the Newars of the Kathmandu Valley, Nepal
David N. Gellner and Declan Quigley

The Culture of Coincidence: Accident and Absolute Liability in Huli
Laurence Goldman

The Female Bridegroom: A Comparative Study of Life-Crisis Rituals in South India and Sri Lanka
Anthony Good

Of Mixed Blood: Kinship and History in Peruvian Amazonia
Peter Gow

The Archetypal Actions of Ritual: A Theory of Ritual Illustrated by the Jain Rite of Worship
Caroline Humphrey and James Laidlaw

Shamans and Elders
Experience, Knowledge, and Power among the Daur Mongols
Caroline Humphrey with Urgunge Onon

The People of the Alas Valley: A Study of an Ethnic Group of Northern Sumatra
Akifumi Iwabuchi

Nuer Prophets: A History of Prophecy from the Upper Nile in the Nineteenth and Twentieth Centuries
Douglas H. Johnson

Knowledge and Secrecy in an Aboriginal Religion: Yolngu of North-East Arnhem Land
Ian Keen

Riches and Renunciation: Religion, Economy, and Society among the Jains
James Laidlaw

The Interpretation of Caste
Declan Quigley

The Arabesk Debate: Music and Musicians in Modern Turkey
Martin Stokes

Inside the Cult: Religious Innovation and Transmission in Papua New Guinea
Harvey Whitehouse

SEA HUNTERS
OF
INDONESIA

*Fishers and Weavers
of Lamalera*

R. H. Barnes

CLARENDON PRESS · OXFORD
1996

Oxford University Press, Great Clarendon Street, Oxford OX2 6DP

Oxford New York

Athens Auckland Bangkok Bogota Bombay
Buenos Aires Calcutta Cape Town Dar es Salaam
Delhi Florence Hong Kong Istanbul Karachi
Kuala Lumpur Madras Madrid Melbourne
Mexico City Nairobi Paris Singapore
Taipei Tokyo Toronto

and associated companies in
Berlin Ibadan

Oxford is a trade mark of Oxford University Press

Published in the United States by
Oxford University Press Inc., New York

British Library Cataloguing in Publication Data
Data available

Library of Congress Cataloging in Publication Data
Barnes, R. H. (Robert Harrison), 1944–
Sea hunters of Indonesia: fishers and weavers of Lamalera / R. H. Barnes.
Includes bibliographical references (p. ••) and index.
1. Lamaholot (Indonesian people)—Fishing.   2. Lamaholot (Indonesian people)—Economic conditions.
3. Lamaholot (Indonesian people)—Social life and customs.   4. Fishing villages—Indonesia—Lamalerap.
5. Textile fabrics, Lamaholot—Indonesia—Lamalerap.   6. Lamalerap (Indonesia)—Economic
conditions.   7. Lamalerap (Indonesia)—Social life and customs.   I. Title.
DS632.L33B37   1996 959.8'6—dc20   96-22391
ISBN 0–19–828070–X

1 3 5 7 9 10 8 6 4 2

Typeset by Best-set Typesetter Ltd., Hong Kong
Printed in Great Britain by
Biddles Ltd, Guildford and King's Lynn

I would like to dedicate this book to my parents.

PREFACE

This study has had a long and irregular gestation. I first had the privilege of visiting Lamalera briefly for a week in July 1970, during a break in research in the neighbouring Kédang culture on the east end of Lembata. Then in 1979 I had the opportunity to spend three months, from July to September, in the village as part of a team sent there by the World Wildlife Fund to investigate the conservation implications of the indigenous whaling industry. I was successful in leading a team to the village from July to December in 1982 to investigate economy and culture. In June and July 1987 I went to the village with a crew from Granada Television, Great Britain, for four weeks while we made a film of life in the village. Finally, I made an informal visit to the village for five days in July 1995, during a journey over two months (July and August) through the four islands of the East Flores Regency. These are the sum total to date, except for a week in Wailolong, East Flores, in 1970, and various brief travels, of my experiences in the Lamaholot-speaking region of eastern Indonesia, which I had intended to be the subject of my life work as an ethnographer and about which I wrote a master's thesis before undertaking my initial research in quite a different culture and language area. I have published a loosely articulated set of reflections on how this research came about as it did and do not intend to repeat much of it here (R. H. Barnes 1988a). Except for the discussion of the past, in this study the present is around 1979 to 1982, unless otherwise indicated.

My research in Lamalera, always rushed, has been undertaken in the medium of the national language Bahasa Indonesia, in which I have sufficient proficiency for the task. Most people in Lamalera are bilingual to some degree or another. I do not, however, speak Lamaholot. In 1969 my wife and I prepared for our own use a preliminary vocabulary of Lamaholot from published works, primarily those of Leemker and Arndt. Subsequently Gregorius Keraf published his invaluable grammar of the dialect of Lamaholot spoken in Lamalera. As a preliminary to writing this book, I prepared a very extensive set of Lamaholot vocabularies, drawing on Keraf's grammar, his counterpart report for the 1982 research trip, and on Oleona's recent account of the fishery. These have been a very great assistance. Nevertheless, the reader should be prepared for the limitations inherent in this book and judge them for himself.

Because of the circumstances in which this research was conducted, including the specialized focus of each of the trips, my data for some topics of general ethnographic interest, such as child rearing and star lore, are not as rich as those I have been able to publish for Kédang. I have attempted to make relevant references to what is known about Lamaholot ethnography elsewhere in the region throughout the book, but I have not attempted to pad out these thinner passages by simply adding information provided by other authors writing about other villages situated on other islands. Should I not have made it clear enough elsewhere in this book, then this is the place to stress that there is a very great deal of cultural variation within the Lamaholot region, only part of which is on record. It is unsafe to simply assume that information pertaining to, let us say, Solor applies on Lembata, despite the presence of widely shared themes and principles. I have tried to report what I know or have reasonable grounds to think is true, but I make no claims that the resulting ethnography is either free of error or complete.

My debts are many and various. Unfortunately, the period between initial contact with the community and present writing having been a long one, twenty-five years, my memory is inadequate to recall all of them. First of all, I must thank my wife and children, who were companions on the trips. Obviously, I have a large and enduring debt to our many friends and acquaintances in the village. The leader of the 1979 expedition and marine biologist, since deceased, was Durant Hembree and the counterpart was Saddon Silalahi, to both of whom I express my appreciation. My wife was formally part of the 1982 research project, and has since published a book and articles on the local textile tradition. I am also grateful to Gregorius Keraf, who was the counterpart, and whose counterpart report I have frequently cited in this study. Father Arnoldus Dupont has been persistently courteous and helpful to us, both during our visits and at other times, while we on the other hand have all too readily added to his many burdens. Many people have helped in providing leads to and even copies of obscurely published sources. Here I cannot possibly recall every debt over the many years. Nevertheless, James J. Fox, Penelope Graham, Stefan Dietrich, Janet West, and Rodney Needham have frequently guided me to information I would not have known about or helped me get publications that otherwise I might not easily have acquired. Paul Dresch has supplied me with guidance on Arabic usage. I should like to thank Rodney Needham, James J. Fox, Stefan Dietrich, and Ruth Barnes for their many comments and corrections. In addition to the many libraries in the University of Oxford, I have at one time or another used the library of the Koninklijk Instituut voor Taal-, Land- en Volkenkunde, Leiden, the University Library of the University of Leiden in the Netherlands, the library of the School of Oriental and African Studies in London, England, the Australian National Library and the library of the Australian National University, Canberra, Australia, the Fondren Library of Rice University, Houston, Texas, and the Graduate Studies Library of the University of Michigan, Ann Arbor, Michigan.

Research in 1970 was supported by the National Science Foundation of the United States. The World Wildlife Fund supported the 1979 expedition, while that of 1982 was supported by the Social Science Research Council of Great Britain (now the Economic and Social Research Council). In 1986, I was a visiting fellow of the Research School of Pacific Studies for three months, and part of my travel costs was met by a travel grant from the British Academy. For part of 1986 and 1987 I was very hospitably received by the Department of Anthropology, University of Michigan. A British Academy travel grant funded the visit in 1995. All research in Indonesia was carried out under the auspices of the Indonesian Institute of Sciences.

Portions of four chapters were published elsewhere. Thanks are due to the *Bulletin de l'École Française d'Extrême-Orient* for parts of 'Educated Fishermen: Social Consequences of Development in an Indonesian Whaling Community' (1986) included in the Introduction; to the University of Michigan Press for selections from 'Time and the Sense of History in an Indonesian Community' in *Time: Histories and Ethnologies*, ed. Diane Owen Hughes and Thomas R. Trautmann (1995) used in Chapter 2; the Royal Anthropological Institute for passages from R. H. Barnes and Ruth Barnes, 'Barter and Money in an Indonesian Village Economy' (*Man*, 1989) incorporated into Chapter 7; and Tempvs Reparatvm for material from 'Whaling Vessels of Indonesia' in *Sewn Plank Boats: Archaeological and Ethnographic Papers Based on Those Presented to a Conference at Greenwich in November, 1984*, ed. Sean McGrail and Eric Kentley (1985) now in Chapter 9.

September 1995

CONTENTS

List of Plates   xv
List of Figures   xvii
List of Maps   xviii
List of Tables   xix

Introduction   1
   Terrain   6
   Early Regional History   10
   Trade, Piracy, and Slavery in the Historical Background   13
   Population and Population Growth   20
   Governmental Structure   29
   Sources   31
   Language Note   33
   Note on the Spelling of Names   34
 1. The Village   35
   The Different Kinds of Lamalera   35
   The Upper Village   39
   The Lower Village   44
   Administrative Structure   46
   Recent Historical Background   47
   Communications   49
   Religion   51
 2. Disaster, Migration, Foundation, and History   54
   A Migration Charter and the Discovery of a New Home 55
   Genealogies   61
 3. Descent Groups   62
   Clans   65
   Clan Divisions   74
   Non-Descent Means of Acquiring Clan Membership   77
   Groups which have Disappeared   79
 4. Marriage Alliance   81
   Alliances between Descent Groups   81
   Relationship Classification   87
   Improper Unions   87
   Marriage   89
   Residence   96
   Kefina Muko Pukã   97
   Marriage Prestations   99
 5. Life, Development, Spirits, Faults, and Retribution   109
   Pregnancy and Birth   109
   Twins   109
   Babies   110
   Birth Control   111

Names	112
Hair Cutting	114
Baptism and First Communion	114
Constituents of the Person	115
Spirits and Witches	115
Healers	117
Faults	118
6. Death	121
Historical	121
Memories	124
Funerary Rites and Observations	125
Deaths at Sea	130
Injury and Illness	133
7. Cloth, Salt, and Markets	135
Weaving	135
Trade in Cloth	137
Salt and Lime Production	138
Markets and the Absence of Markets	139
The Market at Wulan Doni	141
Trading Journeys	145
8. Seasons, Winds, Tides, Currents, Celestial Objects, and Directions	150
Seasons	150
Winds	153
Tides	154
Currents	155
Moon and Stars	156
The Sun	158
Directions	163
Sailing Directions	166
9. Fishing	168
Shellfish Gathering, Traps, and Spearguns	168
Floats and Small Boats	171
Nets	173
Other Forms of Fishing	176
Bobu	177
10. Boat-Owning Groups	179
Corporations	179
Rights and Distribution	183
Whale and Porpoise	188
Ray	196
Turtle	199
Marlin and Shark	199
Sunfish	200
11. Large Boats	201
Background	201
Construction Principles	203
Lamalera Boat Construction Sequence	206

The Mast	219
The Sail	220
Weaving the Sail	223
Sail Decorations	226
Sections	226
Bow Decorations	229
Stern Decorations	238
12. Boat Construction Ceremonies	241
13. Harpoons, Ropes, and Other Gear in the Boats	250
The Principal Harpoon and its Attachment to its Rope	250
Harpoons	253
Harpoon Poles	255
Ropes	257
Rope Making	259
Kemité	264
Other Tools and Gear in the Boat	266
14. Open-Sea Fishing and Hunting	268
Annual Fishing Ceremony	268
Launching the Fleet	271
Hunting and Fishing	272
Hunting Ray	280
The Téti Heri Disaster	287
15. Hunting Whales and Other Cetaceans	289
The Hunt	289
Prohibitions	295
Luck	299
Returning Home	300
Boats Towed by Sperm Whales	304
Baléo	307
Dangers at Sea	307
The Results of Fishing and Hunting in Large Boats over Time	309
16. Fishing near Lobetobi and Pantar	313
Lobetobi	313
Pantar	320
17. Early Whaling and Contacts with Timor	323
Early Records	323
Whale Oil and Ambergris	325
Trips to Kupang	329
European and American Whaling in the Timor Strait	329
Possible Influence of Commercial Whalers on Indigenous Whaling	336
Indigenous Whaling in the Indian and Western Pacific Oceans	337
18. Lamalera Past, Present, and Future	341
Postcript (30 September 1995)	344
Appendix I. Relationship Terminology	346
Appendix II. Fish, Molluscs, and Turtles Known in Lamalera	355
Some Additional Lamalera Fish Names	360

Turtles	362
Squid and Octopi	362
Some Shells and Shellfish	362
Appendix III. Summary of Share Distribution in Boat Corporations in 1979	364
Appendix IV. Wood and Other Plants Used in Boat Construction and for Other Purposes	367
Other Useful Plants	368
Unidentified Plants	370
Appendix V. Identifying Characteristics of the Sails of Lamalera Boats	371
Appendix VI. Boat Measurements	372
Appendix VII. Whales and Porpoises	376
Notes	377
References	403
Name Index	431
Subject Index	437

LIST OF PLATES

1. Altar stone and iron dibble blades at the top of the Labalekang volcano   9
2. Lamalera seen from the sea   36
3. Lamalera beach and boat sheds with houses behind, seen from the East   36
4. The lower village, beach and boat sheds seen from the West   37
5. Statue of Father Bernardus Bode erected to commemorate '100 Years of Religion' in 1986   37
6. St Peter Chapel at *Ikã Kotã* (Fish Heads) marking the centre of the beach   45
7. Sun Plate, *Lāma Lera*   55
8. Lontar palm-leaf plates being distributed to women during a festival   93
9. Women attending a discussion of marriage prestations   94
10. A bride entering her husband's great house   95
11. Weaving with a back-strap loom   137
12. Women returning from a day's trading in the mountains. In the background is the great house of Téti Nama Papã sub-clan of Běliko Lolo clan   147
13. Collecting shellfish and edible seaweed   169
14. Killer Whale   189
15. Sperm Whale   189
16. Removing blubber from the torso of a Sperm Whale   190
17. Cutting up Sperm Whale in the surf   190
18. Cutting into the spermaceti reserve in head of a Sperm Whale   191
19. Slices taken from the tail of a Sperm Whale   191
20. Women preparing to carry meat from the beach   192
21. Whale and Manta Ray meat in a drying rack   192
22. *Téna* searching for game   202
23. *Holo Sapã* shifting its sail   202
24. Internal compression structure of a hull, including ribs, thwarts, stringers, and bindings   205
25. Preparing the keel   207
26. The *mādi* or decorated stern piece of a *téna*   209
27. *Guã gaté*, substitute marks on the hull of the *téna* intended to deceive Sperm Whale into thinking the hull has been built according to the proper pattern   212
28. *Fajo*, fastenings from palm branch skin being used to force planks tightly together   215
29. Weaving a section of the sail   221
30. Bow of the *Nara Ténã*   234
31. Bow of the *Kopo Paker*   235
32. Bow of the *Holo Sapã*   235
33. Bow of the *Horo Ténã*   236
34. *Temōto* of the *Nara Ténã*   239

35. A boat builder with a wooden tool box, *kĕlapa*   242
36. Bellows, *rokã*, used in manufacturing harpoons   252
37. A set of harpoons appropriate for a *téna*   254
38. Rolling the strands on to spindles, *bōpa*, prior to weaving the rope   261
39. Pulling the strands taut in rope weaving   262
40. *Kemité*, bindings securing the loop at the end of the main rope   265
41. *Korké Ikã* (Fish Temple) at *Fūka Léré*, just above Lamalera   269
42. Launching of a *téna*   272
43. Preparing to harpoon   283
44. Harpooning   284
45. Boats returning to shore while towing a Sperm Whale   302
46. Pulling a returned *téna* up the beach   303
47. *Téna*, fully laden on its return from Lobetobi   319
48. Dried fish and bamboos of fermented fish intestines brought back
    from Lobetobi   319
49. Harpoons of Western manufacture found by *Kéna Pukã* in a dead
    whale in the nineteenth century   337

LIST OF FIGURES

1. Descent groups of Lamalera   63
2. Marriage alliance ties among Lamalera descent groups according to
   Yosef Bura Bataona   82
3. An ideal pattern of marriage alliance among Lamalera descent groups   83
4. *Kefina muko pukā* of Lamalera descent groups   98
5. Relative values of different types of woven cloth in Lamalera, Lembata,
   in 1979 and 1982   138
6. Wind directions   154
7. The stages of the moon   157
8. Directions away from speaker   163
9. Directions toward speaker   164
10. Directions away from speaker showing intermediate directions   164
11. Directions toward speaker showing intermediate directions   164
12. Direction terms as used by a Lamalera boat in the bay in front of
    Lewoleba, Lembata   165
13. Sailing directions   167
14. Distribution of shares held in boat-owning corporations according to
    type of relationship   185
15. Share locations in Sperm Whale   193
16. Share locations in Manta Ray   197
17. Sections of the keel with stem and stern posts   206
18. Keel and planks   208
19. Decorated stern piece   210
20. The plank pattern   211
21. Top and base of the bipod mast   220
22. *Selaga*, frame for weaving sections of a sail   224
23. Extending a gebang palm-leaf strip while weaving a sail section   226
24. The Lamalera *téna*   227
25. Harpoon, *kāfé*   251
26. Attachment of harpoon leader and harpoon rope   252
27. Lamalera relationship terminology for a male Ego ordered for
    patrilineal descent and asymmetric marriage prescription   352
28. Lamalera relationship terminology for a female Ego ordered for
    patrilineal descent and asymmetric marriage prescription   353

LIST OF MAPS

1. South-East Asia   xx
2. East Flores and the Solor Islands   xxi
3. Lembata   xxii
4. Lamalera   40

LIST OF TABLES

1. Days of Rain in the Kecamatan Nagawutung, 1989 — 11
2. Population Changes, Lembata, 1931–1980 — 22
3. Comparison of Lembata Population 1980, 1990, and 1994 — 23
4. Lembata, 1980 Population Expressed as a Percentage of 1931 Population — 23
5. Population Changes 1931–1980 and 1980–1990 for Province, Regency, and Island — 23
6. Growth Rate 1971–1980 and 1961–1971 — 27
7. Sex and Age Ratios — 27
8. Population by Age and Sex, Lamalera (1979) — 27
9. Marriages of Men in Lamalera Descent Groups — 84
10. Marriages of Women in Lamalera Descent Groups — 86
11. Surnames of Lamalera Descent Groups — 113
12. Boats and Descent Groups — 180
13. Harpoon Head Measurements in *Menula Belolong* in 1979 — 254
14. Word Substitutes Used in the Presence of Whales — 297
15. Running Record of Annual Catch of Sperm Whale and Large Ray, 1959–1995 — 311
16. Lamalera Relationship Terminology after Gregorius Keraf (1978) — 347
17. Lamalera Relationship Terminology Used by a Male, after Petrus Bau Dasion — 349
18. Relationship Terminology, Male Ego (Reference and Address) — 350
19. Lamalera Relationship Terminology Used by a Female, after Maria Korohama, Maria Sura Belikololong, and Yosefina Sefai Keraf — 351
20. Relationship Terminology, Female Ego (Reference and Address) — 352

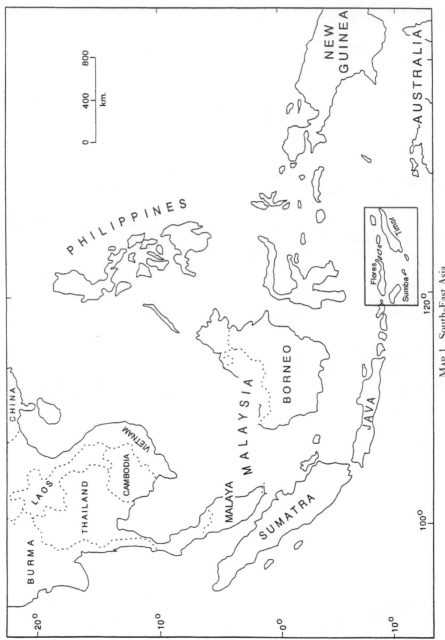

MAP 1. South-East Asia

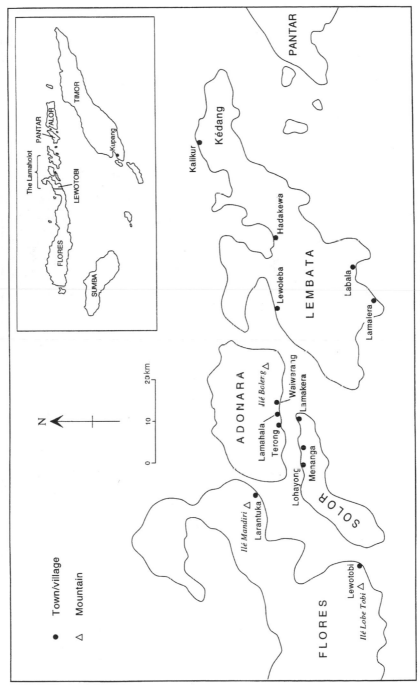

MAP 2. East Flores and the Solor Islands

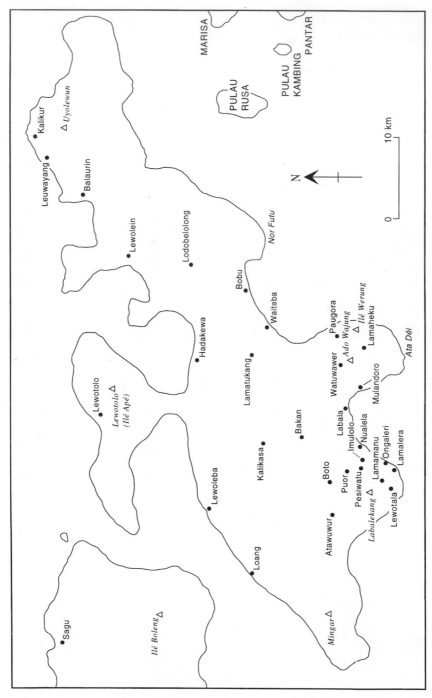

MAP 3. Lembata

Introduction

Lamalera represents an historically important variety of society in South-East Asia, one which by analogy with a usage introduced by Pigeaud and drawing on Malay for 'coastal regions' might be called *pesisir* societies. These societies are characterized by their links both to the interior and to the outer world. They are frequently at once isolated and involved in contacts far beyond their region. They are often remote communities, far from the centres of commerce and culture. At the same time they are in local perspective sophisticated mediators of external influences who maintain far-flung and even international contacts and commitments. This paradox has caused difficulties in understanding their characteristic place in South-East Asian life. Nevertheless every shore of every island and of every part of the mainland of Asia is lined with smaller or larger exemplars of this pattern, appreciation of which is essential for understanding both the past and the present in South-East Asian economy and society. They are the communities which look outward in an island world where to mention another historically important paradox many cultures are steadfastly landlocked and therefore relatively inward-looking. Some of the communities are tiny hamlets. Others are influential regional centres. Some at critical periods have grown to become internationally important emporia like Surabaya, Malacca, or Palembang.[1]

In the not so distant past these communities suffered from exposure to attack by local raiders or long-distance pirate fleets and from assault by skirmishers from the interior. They often had little or no land, except that on which their houses stood, and even that they may have held at the sufferance of the land-rich people of the interior. On the other hand they had the advantage of greater mobility and thus access to wider opportunities, and they too could engage in raids in the interior or further along the coasts. Their local history and legend is characterized by memories of events exemplifying all of these kinds of aggression. Their position also often permitted them to establish special trading ties with the peoples of the interior, involving systematic patterns of production specializations. Not infrequently they were able to secure political influence over the interior incommensurate with their marginalized relationship to the land.

There have been several studies of specialized fishing communities in South-East Asia. Among the more well known are Walter Grainge White's *The Sea Gypsies of Malaya* (1922), David E. Sopher's *The Sea Nomads* (1965), Raymond Firth's *Malay Fishermen: Their Peasant Economy* (1946 and 1966), and Thomas M. Fraser's *Rusembilan: A Malay Fishing Village in Southern Thailand* (1960). Also to be mentioned is Alexander Spoehr's *Protein from the*

Sea: Technological Change in Philippine Capture Fisheries (1980). The books by
White and Sopher concern geographically widely dispersed ethnic groups,
whose marginality is somewhat different from that of Lamalera, for they have
no political authority over and generally little influence on land-based peoples
(see also Verheijen 1986). Counter to this marginalization is the fact that language and culture links them to similar peoples thousands of miles away,
whereas Lamalera's language and cultural ties are entirely local. The studies
by Firth, Fraser, and Spoehr concern money-mediated commercial fishing
economies, in which fishermen deliver fish to brokers or wholesalers who in
turn supply markets. Some ranges of these fisheries may involve sophisticated
boats and equipment and deficit financing. In these respects, at least, these
studies provide no parallels to the situation in Lamalera, where the fishery is
largely unmediated by money, the equipment used is mostly traditional and
locally manufactured, and there are no middlemen. However, Lamalera sea-
hunting and fishing obviously resembles in scale and sometimes in techniques
other small-scale, subsistence, traditional, artisanal fisheries, to use a standard
list of characteristics (see Emmerson 1980: preceding p. i). It is not a commercial, large-scale, industrial or, yet, modern fishery. The distinction between
inshore and offshore is relative. Lamalera fishermen and whalers do not go
many miles from shore, but as well as fishing inshore, they also fish and hunt
in very deep water well away from the comfort and safety of the coastline. In
some respects, Lamalera's fishery more closely resembles that of the Trobriand
Islanders or that of the pre-contact Maori of New Zealand than that of Firth's
Malays (Malinowski 1922, Firth 1959, 1966).

There have been other studies of specialized subsistence communities in
eastern Indonesia, Ormeling's investigation of ecological degradation and agricultural underdevelopment on Timor being an important early case (Ormeling
1956), followed in inspiration by Fox's complementary study of the lontar palm
economy of Roti (Fox 1977). Also to be mentioned is Metzner's ecological
study of eastern Timor and his investigation of agriculture and population
pressure in Sikka, Flores (Metzner 1977, 1982). None of the works in this list
of books, of course, has anything directly to do with fishing, and in that respect
any parallels with Lamalera are indirect. Nevertheless, it has been argued that
the commonplace association of fishing traditions with hunters and gatherers
is one-sided and that 'for every one of the traits considered diagnostic of
fishing communities, there is a parallel or analogous trait in other agrarian
systems' (McCay 1981: 1–2). It is not necessary here to go into the question
whether the specific features McCay mentions apply to Lamalera (some of
them, rent, middlemen, perishability of the commodity, do not or do not fully).
The important point is that Lamalera's economy is systematically linked to
horticultural communities of the interior and that there are structural parallels of significance.

Lamalera is a community on the south coast of the eastern Indonesian island of Lembata in the province of Nusa Tenggara Timur or East Southeast Islands (formerly called the Lesser Sundas). Members of this community speak the Lamaholot language. In many ways they possess a unique way of life, unusual not only for the area but for South-East Asia as a whole. In other very important respects they exemplify significant themes, not only of local culture, but of Indonesia as a modern nation. In this book I wish to describe Lamalera's social organization and culture, focusing in particular on its economic organization and relating the community to its regional and national context.

Lamaholot is one of the many languages of eastern Indonesia. Its three principal dialects are distributed across four islands, from the eastern region of Flores in the west via Adonara and Solor to Lembata[2] in the east. To the west, this language grouping borders the Sikka language. In the east several minor dialectical variations are found on Lembata, all mutually intelligible versions of Lamaholot. An isolated population in Kédang at the extreme eastern end of Lembata speaks an entirely different, but related, language. A fourth dialect, usually called the Alor Language, which can be understood by speakers of Lamaholot, is found in small coastal enclaves on the north coast of Pantar and the west coast of Alor, to the east of Lembata.

There are many unifying cultural and historical features in the Lamaholot language area, but the language boundaries have never had any specifically political implications, nor have Lamaholot speakers ever regarded themselves as constituting a unified ethnic group with a common purpose. Nevertheless, Lamaholot speakers comprise the great majority of the population of the East Flores Regency.

Among distinctions within this population frequently noticed by early European observers is that between coastal dwellers and peoples living in the mountains.[3] According to Baron van Lynden (1851a: 321–2) in the mid-nineteenth century, the coastal-dwelling people lived entirely from trade and fishing, leaving agriculture to the mountain dwellers. Most of the former were foreign conquerors, who exercised a limited authority over the peoples of the interior. Curiously he denied that there were any foreign settlers on Lembata or that the distinction between shore and interior peoples existed, although he did remark that the inhabitants of coastal villages in Kédang and in Lamalera were less shy and more use to dealing with strangers. 'Lomblen', he wrote, 'is still very little known.' The name of Lamalera's head was also unknown. The village was 'heathen'. It is significant that he stated that it stood under *no* flag, that is, under neither that of the Portuguese nor that of the Dutch (van Lynden 1851a: 328).

His lack of familiarity with Lembata is not surprising given the circumstances of the time. Baron van Lynden was then the Netherlands Indies Resident stationed at Kupang, Timor. His report on conditions in the Solor Archipelago was the first comprehensive account of the region, written at a time when the Dutch were preparing to take over temporary (later to become permanent) control of the Portuguese holdings there, including Lembata. Just two years before Temminck (1849, vol. 3: 187) had written correctly that Lembata was then a completely unknown land, just a blank space on the map of the world. As late as 1856, Crawfurd could only describe 'Lombata' as 'The name of a considerable island lying between Floris and Timur' in his generally well-informed *A Descriptive Dictionary of the Indian Islands & Adjacent Countries*.[4] In 1882 Donselaar wrote that only the coastal regions of the Timor area were known to the Dutch, and that the interior of central Flores, of Alor, and of Lembata had not yet been visited by Europeans. What there was there and what went on there was unknown to them (Donselaar 1882: 272). During the greater part of the nineteenth century, the Dutch pursued a policy of political 'non-interference' in the parts of the eastern islands under their nominal control (Dietrich 1989: 1–4). Lulofs stated that nowhere else in the outer islands had this policy been taken to the extremes reached in the Timor Residency.

Abstinence from all interference was the watchword for the government officials. As a consequence the interior lands were pretty well *terrae incognitae*; to the point that under the skirts of government anarchy and barbarism ran rampant (Lulofs 1911: 281).

Van Lynden inadvertently touched on another distinction within the Lamaholot region. Villages on Solor and Adonara along the shores of the Solor Strait, as well as Larantuka on east Flores, entered very early into contact with Europeans. Portuguese traders appeared near the beginning of the sixteenth century, and Dominican priests established a mission and a fort at Lohayong, Solor in 1562. From then on villagers had continuous dealings with the Portuguese and later the Dutch, with the consequence that Dutch and Portuguese documents repeatedly mentioned affairs and events of the western part of the Lamaholot region. Despite repeated man-made or natural catastrophes involving the complete loss of houses and possessions, the greater number of communities named in the earliest Portuguese records still exist. In contrast, after brief Portuguese references to Lamalera in the early seventeenth century, as van den Windt (1936: 75) has commented, that village and the island of Lembata disappeared from history.

Neither effectively reappeared until the end of the nineteenth century, when the village of Lamalera on the rocky and inaccessible south coast of Lembata surprisingly became the portal through which Jesuit priests introduced Catholicism to the island. As hinted at by van Lynden, one of the concomitants of the distinction between mountain peoples and coastal peoples in eastern Indonesia is a differential distribution of subsistence occupations and craft specializations. At the time the Jesuits first encountered it in the 1880s, Lamalera was, in its own conception, a village of outside origin whose inhabitants exercised political dominance in a district of south Lembata. They were seafaring peoples surrounded by agriculturalists. Their women wove and dyed fine, resist-dyed cloths which were essential items of exchange in the marriage transactions of the whole region (see Ruth Barnes 1989), while some of the districts which they helped to supply with cloth observed a traditional prohibition on weaving and cloth production (Ruth Barnes 1987). The same women went into the mountains with loads of dried fish and meat, or salt and lime, which were the specialized products of the village economy and traded these goods in mountain villages for fruit and vegetable staples. The men were fishermen, hunters of large fish and mammals in the open sea. With some exaggeration, Captain Beckering (1911: 194) wrote that Lamalera lived exclusively from the fishery. In fact, Lamalera was, and still is, the only village in South-East Asia which routinely hunts large toothed whales, such as sperm whales and killer whales, as well as several varieties of porpoise and pygmy whales, not to mention giant manta ray.

Despite the many changes which Lamalera has experienced during the century since the first conversions to Christianity took place in the village, these dimensions of contrast still hold true, with the exception that the village retains no formal political superiority. The contrasts also provide points of comparison with other parts of the Lamaholot region and outside this region. They are the grounds upon which the claim may be based that Lamalera's very exceptionality makes it in many respects typical and representative of Lamaholot life and culture.

Today Lamalera is an entirely Catholic community of around 2,000 persons, about the same as Engbers's estimate in 1906 (Engbers 1906: 12). Behind this apparent demographic stagnation lies a mixed tale of relative success in adjusting to the demands of the modern world and in taking advantage of the opportunities that world has presented. From the point of view of anthropological categories, Lamalera could be described as having a mixed economy divided into subsistence and market-governed spheres, although of course the border between the two spheres is all too permeable. It could also be described paradoxically as experiencing economic dualism internally to its own economy. Whatever categories are applied to it, one side of village life which is deeply significant to villagers' self-identity and is therefore dear to them is gradually being supplanted by occupation patterns appropriate to the national and international economies. Similar tensions may be found in all sides of community life, including the religious, family, economic, and political. In many ways this situation makes the village representative of modern Indonesia. It is above all this set of counter-tending forces which will be central to this study. I intend to present here the standard features of Lamalera social life, and to show how these are being modified under pressure from the outer world. Given a loose sense of the terms, this book is therefore a contribution to the study of development and social change, although social change and development of whatever form are consequences of the situation being described and not my own primary focus or interest. Above all, I wish to describe what happens to be in many ways an exceptional way of life.

Terrain

Lembata belongs to the so-called inner arc of the Tertiary Sunda Mountain System. The outer arc of Timor, Roti, Savu, and Sumba are volcanically inactive and made up of generally older rocks and geological structures including igneous rocks of the pre-Tertiary, mainly Permian, and Tertiary age (Brouwer 1939: 3–4; Ormeling 1956: 31). The inner arc consists in a volcanically active series of faults and subduction zones that runs through Indonesia and belongs to the Alpine–Himalayan belt of volcanoes running from Europe to South-East Asia and terminates adjacent to the so-called 'ring of fire', a similar belt which eventually circles the Pacific Ocean (Bullard 1984: 446; Peter Francis 1993: 18, 20, 22). This inner arc is one of five arcuate sectors of the 7,000-kilometre-long Sunda Mountain System, each consisting of a volcanic inner arc, a non-volcanic outer arc, and a foredeep (van Bemmelen 1954: 154). In very remote geological times, a crystalline crust formed which produced an Indonesian Primeval Continent, which was eventually destroyed by two processes. The first was extensive subsidence, in which land made way for the ocean. The second was mountain-building cycles which ploughed through the primeval continent, producing a new continental area in the Sunda region of western Indonesia and causing the final breaking up and subsidence of the crust in eastern Indonesia (van Bemmelen 1954: 167). The specific geology of the Timor and Flores area is determined by the fact that the Australian Continental Crust is in the process of dipping down into the earth under the Timor Trough and the outer and inner arcs (Ollier 1980: 11, fig. 5).

According to Brouwer (1939: 8), in the northern row of islands no volcanic rocks older than the Upper Tertiary are known. There are, however, numerous recent volcanic formations. Brouwer also notes that Vatter (1932: 9) had recorded local legends concerning the disappearance of a land mass between Lembata and Pantar, from which the ancestors had to flee. These legends, which describe land subsidence and inundation from the sea, agree according to Brouwer quite well with the geological facts.[5] Lembata, like the other islands, consists of a mixture of volcanic structures and upheaved coral limestone and marine deposits. 'The submergence in the straits between the upheaved islands of the northern row may be connected with the continuation of stresses by which the straits were formed' (Brouwer 1939: 7). Using Brouwer's material, van Bemmelen (1949: 52 n. 1), however, concluded that it was impossible to decide whether such submergence of land was due simply to local crumbling along the edges of islands or whether it is part of a recent general sinking of this portion of the earth's crust.

Lembata lies between 123° 12′ 36″ and 123° 54′ 11″ east longitude and between 8° 10′ 18″ and 8° 35′ 14″ south latitude. It is about 1,266 square kilometres or 489 square miles in size. It lies diagonally, running from south–west to north–east and is 82.5 kilometres or 51.26 miles long. Its coast line is irregular, being indented with many bays between extended points and peninsulas. A spine of mountains runs up the centre of the island. These are old volcanic structures which have been strongly sectioned and denuded. Peripheral to this spine are low-lying plains and extinct or active volcanoes. The most spectacular of these is the Lewotolo or Wariran volcano on the north coast, the prominent sulphur-covered, smoking, and broken crater of which reaches 1,449 metres or 4,754 feet above sea level. The inactive Uyolewun in Kédang to the east stands 1,532 metres or 5,027 feet high. The tallest mountain on the island is the moderately active Labalekang volcano which at 1,643 metres or 5,391 feet looms over Lamalera on the south coast. The greatest volcanic activity is found in several newer volcanoes on the Lerek Peninsula to the east of Lamalera on the other side of the wide Labala bay.

The largest volcano on the Lerek Peninsula is the old Ado Wajung at 1,000 metres or 3,281 feet. Seawards of Ado Wajung is the 'New' volcano or Ilé Werung, once 500 metres or 1,640 feet high, which appears to have erupted around 1870 killing several people with hot ash in the village of Lamaheku. In March 1910, when Rouffaer visited it, the new volcano emitted a great deal of smoke (Rouffaer 1910; Beckering 1911: 185; Kemmerling 1929: 493). A gigantic catastrophe of unknown date caused the south-east section of Ilé Ado Wajung to collapse producing the depression later filled in by the Ilé Monyet crater (592 metres or 1,942 feet high).[6] According to villagers in 1870 this crater had a flat bottom with gigantic solfatara (vents). The 1870 explosion of Ilé Werung left a wall of rubble around the eruption which subsequently filled with lava. In 1928 lava broke through the dome on the south and west sides. This volcanic structure lies on a slippage fault which is in the process of splitting the whole island on a line which runs precisely north–south (Hartmann 1935: 824–31).

In September 1936 the land in the village of Watuwawer split open leaving two large holes, and a small volcano near the hamlets Merekpuka and Paugora began rumbling and threatening to explode (Bintang Timoer 1936: 96). In 1947 a new volcanic area appeared at the shore near Ilé Ado Wajung. In 1974 there was another eruption and a further volcano appeared under the sea 800 metres (2,625 feet) from shore. The new volcano at the shore has supposedly been named Ilé Petrus, while that at sea is Ilé Hobal.[7] The volcano at sea produced an island which appears, disappears, and reappears. There are also three or four other areas where the earth keeps pushing out as though there were a mountain in the making. People from Lamalera report that the two newest volcanoes constantly throw out earth and stones. From afar it looks like the spouting of a whale, but from close up, they see that it is earth. If they go ashore there, they find the earth is hot, even after being washed by waves. There appears to be a new peninsula in the making.

By 1976, the eastern part of the Lerek Peninsula was subjected to constant earth rumblings and rock falls. On 1 and 2 November 1978 an earthquake separated a hill on the side of the Benolo mountain, which slid five kilometres in the direction of the sea and would have covered the village of Waiteba had the landslide not been split in two and its direction altered by a hill behind the village. At the same time Ilé Werung pushed up to a height of 1,018 metres or 3,340 feet. The government initiated a programme to move members of the endangered villages in the area to Loang on the west coast of Lembata, but delays of various kinds prevented completion of the project. Then at 1.00 a.m. in the morning of 18 July 1979 a complex catastrophe took place in which the Belopor (Round) mountain collapsed destroying the village of Sarapuka and causing a tidal wave which wiped out the village of Waiteba. Over five hundred lives were lost, and the fatalities included fourteen people from Lamalera and Lewotala who had gone to the Waiteba market or who temporarily lived in the area.[8] The wave reached deep into the Labala bay on the opposite side of the peninsula and killed six people in the village of Labala. Its energy had dissipated by the time that it reached Lamalera and it did no damage there, although two people sleeping on the beach got a soaking.

The Labalekang volcano behind Lamalera has the shape of a sharp volcanic cone. Between it and Lamalera lies the half-crater of the parasitic Ilé Tebulele (also Mulu Keroko or Folo Keroko), in which the hamlet of Lamamanu is now situated. Hardened lava flows from this crater run through Lamalera to the sea. Ilé Tebulele is no longer active. Indeed the most recent lava flows from Labalekang were diverted by it, indicating that they were younger. There are traces on Labalekang of a recent lifting of the land from seven to twelve metres, indicated by upheaved coral and corrosion on stones caused by sea water. While the upper sides of Labalekang are almost bare, there are pleasant bushes and grass at the very top. Along the east side of the highest crater there are three small hot vents which produce sulphur deposits. Poisonous gases (H_2S and CO_2) cover the ground in places with a layer as thick as 40 centimetres. This is the only present evidence of activity. There is no historical record or local memory of eruption. Characteristic of all of the volcanoes of Lembata is the frequency of lava streams and the formation of lava cones. All of them are strato-volcanoes. It is possible to distinguish in each of them a period of growth, ending in a destructive phase in which a larger crater was formed. A third phase followed in which within this crater new craters and lava cones formed (Hartmann 1935: 831–5).

At the very peak of the Labalekang mountain there is a benchmark indicating the highest point. Near it is a flat stone surrounded by iron dibble blades and one file blade (see Plate 1). When I visited the site in 14 September 1979, companions from the village of Imulolo told me that these had been put there

PLATE 1. Altar stone and iron dibble blades at the top of the Labalekang volcano

by people from the village of Puor in ceremonies designed to keep the mountain from exploding. The lord of the land of Puor had placed them there when there had been earth tremors in order to hold the mountain firm. Elders from Imulolo still conduct ceremonies there. The crater becomes a lake during the rainy season, which if it gets too full threatens the villages of Boto and Atawuwur, who request priests from Imulolo to hold a ceremony there to make the lake recede. When I was at the site, it was dry, but there were signs that there had been water; it must be a quite large lake in an unusual year. This lake is the source of the various springs down the mountain. On our visit there were two (half-) coconut branches around the stone, from one of which dangled a dead baby chicken. This chicken had been hung live in a ceremony around April or May to bring the rains to a halt at the end of the growing period so that the lake would not overflow. This ceremony attempts to turn the clouds white and to stop the rain from descending.

Lembata shares the general monsoon patterns of eastern Indonesia. The climate of this area is influenced by Australia. From May to September the prevailing winds are from the east or south-east, bringing the dry season. October and November are a transition period of wind stillness and great heat. The rainy season of the west monsoon, upon which agriculture depends, begins in early December and lasts until March, when the rains gradually die out. The west monsoon is a product of the airflow from a semi-permanent low over Australia during these months. During the dry season, barometric pressure is low over Asia and high over Australia. During the wet season, these relationships are reversed (US Navy Hydrographic Office 1962: 24, 27, 42). Gebuis (1939: 264) estimated the average rainfall from December to March in the north coast regions of the archipelago as 1,000 mm., with a minimum of ±700 mm. Late March and April are another transition period marked by shifting gusty breezes and occasional light showers. January and February are characterized by continuous heavy rains and sometimes violent storms. July is in the depths of the southern hemisphere winter, and even though Lembata has a tropical climate, July evenings can be unpleasantly cold for the lightly dressed. The landscape during the rainy season shows the characteristics of a tropical rainy climate. On the timing and duration of the short and irregular rainy monsoon depends the success of the crops, the failure of which is a dreaded but common experience. The dry season produces near desert conditions. The steady east winds of May and June completely dry out the vegetation. Every year toward the end of the dry season great areas of open land and forest are burned over, either accidentally when fires in fields get out of control or intentionally to clear underbrush for hunting. These fires may burn for days and blacken thousands of acres. Partly because of mistreatment of the vegetation, the sides of hills and mountains are prone to erosion and dangerous flash floods in which boulders weighing hundreds of tons may be rolled toward the sea. One such flood wiped out a section in the centre of Larantuka, Flores on 27 February 1979. The atmosphere at the end of the rainy season, when the air has been washed by the rains, is crystal clear and visibility extends for many miles. Towards the end of the dry season, when the air becomes humid and filled with particles from fires, the sky can become quite hazy. Part of the dust and smoke in the air originates over Australia (US Navy Hydrographic Office 1962: 31). Visibility of course is much reduced during the rainy season, when heavy black clouds press down on the land and sea, but is generally clear when not obscured by rains or cloud cover. The first months of the rainy season, when food stocks are low and crops are not yet ready for harvest, are a period of hunger for mountain peoples.[9]

There are no meteorological records for Lamalera, but an indication of the normal pattern of rainfall may be found in Table 1.

Early Regional History

In the mid-sixteenth century the two clove-producing kingdoms of Ternate and Tidore, which stand opposite each other off Halmahera, were drawn into a four-way struggle between clove producers and exploiters by the Portuguese who approached them from the west and the Spanish from the east. The Europeans possessed superior military equipment and skill, but were outmatched in diplomatic ability by Sultan Hairun of Ternate. In 1565, by which

TABLE 1. *Days of Rain in the Kecamatan Nagawutung, 1989*

Month	Days	Total rain (in mm.)
January	17	196
February	17	280
March	15	191
April	10	240
May	7	62
June	2	14
July	1	16
August	1	3
September	5	32
October	4	65
November	10	167
December	5	179
TOTAL	94	1,405

Source: Kecamatan Nagawutung Dalam Angka 1989.[10]

time the Dominicans had succeeded in establishing their foothold on Solor at Lohayong and Lamakera, the troops of Sultan Hairun destroyed the Molucca mission by attacking and killing native Christians. In 1570 the Portuguese murdered the Sultan after concluding a formal treaty of friendship with him. His successor Sultan Babulah Datu Sah besieged the Portuguese in their fort, which he took in 1574.[11] At the peak of Babulah's power, seventy-two islands, according to contemporary mission accounts, recognized the sovereignty of Ternate. Babulah even planned to send *kora kora* with troops from Buru to attack the Dominican fort on Solor. The Solorese had sent envoys to Ternate requesting assistance, and even though the attack never came off the Sultan responded by returning some of his own kinsmen as his representatives (Hall 1966: 222–3; Anonymous 1956: 321–3). Within two decades the once Catholic villages of the Solor Strait fell away from Portuguese control. Catholic Lamahala was attacked by Muslims from neighbouring Terong and remained Muslim from that time on (Cácegas and de Sousa 1678: 350). The Dominicans accused the head of Lohayong of having 'the soul of a Moor' underneath a Christian exterior. He in turn plotted with the head of Lamakera to attack the Dominicans, and this scheme eventuated in a failed assault on the fort on 12 August 1598. The uprising came to an end seven months later on 24 March 1599 when a Portuguese fleet from Malacca razed and burned Lamakera. From this date on Lamakera has been staunchly Muslim (Cácegas and de Sousa 1678: 357–66). The Dutch arrived in the Indies at the end of the sixteenth century. Early in the seventeenth century they succeeded in ousting first the Portuguese and then the Spanish from the Moluccas, and turned their attentions toward Solor (for a recent summary of the sequence of events in the Moluccas see

Andaya 1993: 152–4). When they arrived at Lohayong to attack the Portuguese fort on 17 January 1613, they brought with them a *kora kora* and several troops from Ternate (Tiele and Heeres 1886: 13–18).

Later, when the Ternate connection was no longer convenient to them, the Dutch quickly forgot it. In 1675 Paduka Siri Sultan Kaichil Kibori, Prince Amsterdam, King of Ternate, wrote to tell the Governor-General of the Dutch East Indies Company that he intended to send a frigate to Solor to see what his subjects there were up to (van der Chijs 1903: 213). In 1679 a Ternatese Captain Groffola forced the Solorese to deliver tribute to Ternate. Having been defeated and imprisoned at Batavia by the Dutch in 1681, the Sultan of Ternate signed a treaty of 7 July 1683 in which the Company returned his empire 'on loan'. In this treaty the Company forced the Sultan to renounce his 'old, unfounded pretension' to Solor (Stapel 1934: 304, 310–11; Fruin-Mees 1928: 317; Leupe 1877: 481; for further discussion of the vicissitudes of Dutch and Portuguese relationships in the Solor Archipelago see Boxer 1947 and R. H. Barnes 1987). In 1682 representatives from Adonara (presumably including Lamahala) approached the King of Buton requesting protection (which they were not getting from the Dutch) from the Portuguese, who had done them damage in ten different places on Adonara, Solor, Pantar, and Alor.[12] The representatives are credited with saying that they had planned to make the affair known to the King of Ternate, but since he had been brought down, they decided to turn to Buton. From old, in the time of their ancestors, it had been their practice to go first to the King of Buton and then to the King of Ternate. This assertion may turn in part on the historical fact that Ternate derived its claims to Solor through its conquest of Buton in 1580 (Fruin-Mees 1931: 1207; Ligtvoet 1878: 31). In a later period, the official judgement was that the basis for Dutch supreme authority in Solor and Timor rested on the ancient rights of the Sultan of Ternate to the south-east section of the Indian Archipelago (Koloniaal Verslag 1850: 31). Heijmering was told by 'Solorese' that according to their traditions, their ancestors came from Ternate-Halmahera and brought Islam with them. They possessed an historical account written in Arabic characters, which Heijmering was never permitted to look at (Heijmering 1847: 10).

The Dutch referred to the Lamaholot peoples they were in touch with as Solorese. Their allies on Solor and Adonara provided supporting troops for various Dutch military adventures against the mestizos, so-called Topasses or Black Portuguese, who became for an extended period a dominant military and political power on Timor and whose origin was in Larantuka, Flores. When in 1655 Jacob van der Heijden, Commander of Solor and Timor, led a force including two hundred Solorese troops in an attack on Sonbai, Timor, many prominent nobles of Solor died in the ensuing débâcle. Van der Heiden himself died under the sword of António de Hornay, son of the former Dutch Captain of the Solor fort (Coolhaas 1968: 14–15). A punitive expedition of eight hundred Europeans led by Arnold de Vlamingh van Oudtshoorn was twice beaten by the Timorese and Black Portuguese under de Hornay in 1656. De Vlamingh blamed his defeat on the carriers, who ran off (Bor 1663: 256; van Dam 1931: 256–7), but the Queen of Solor lamented that de Vlamingh had ordered the evacuation of the Solor fort, then in a dilapidated state, even though the Solorese had carried the powder and balls, as well as bringing the wounded to the boats. 'It was also all children of sengajis and free people who all together were left [dead] on Timor with Jacob van der Heijden, and this only for the Company's cause, not for any affair of our own on Solor' (Boxer 1947: 5–6; Coolhaas 1968: 154; de Hullu 1904: 226–8). A pejorative name for these troops from Solor current in the 1640s is Groene Geuszen, Green Beggars (Tasman 1898: 57).

After 1613 the Dutch East Indies Company maintained diplomatic relations, underpinned by treaties, with the Muslim villages or petty principalities in the Solor Strait. The villages in question were Lohayong (which the Dutch records spell variously, a typical example being Lawajong) where the fort was located and Lamakera, both on Solor, Lamahala and Terong, on Adonara. They also had contact with a political entity on the north coast of Adonara, and with Labala on Lembata. These ties consisted in military and commercial alliances against the Portuguese and their allies in the islands. The heads of these villages bore the title *sengaji*, and the head of Lohayong, who was recognized as supreme, bore the title of *kaicil*, in the early seventeenth century. These titles are evidence of political relationships with the Sultan of Ternate, one of the famous spice islands in the Moluccas. In the Ternate scheme of government, *sangaji* was the title of a district head, while *kaicil*, pronounced *kaicili*, was the title of a prince or someone of princely descent (de Clercq 1890: 277, 294). *Naicil*, the origin of the name given the successive Queens of Solor in the seventeenth century, was the female equivalent of *kaicil* (Andaya 1990: 4).

Trade, Piracy, and Slavery in the Historical Background

Throughout the historical period, that is to say from about the beginning of the sixteenth century until sometime in the twentieth century, the abundant evidence available shows that trade, piracy, raiding, and slavery were complexly interlinked in South-East Asia, as elsewhere, with different nationalities and groups taking leading roles at different times and places and with Europeans fully participating from the earliest years of their presence in South-East Asian waters (cf. Warren 1981: xiv, xv). In Meilink-Roelofsz's judgement, in the period between 1500 and around 1630 (and it could be added before and after too), 'Because of the wide-spread practice of abduction, the slave trade flourished throughout the whole area of the Lesser Sunda Islands' (Meilink-Roelofsz 1962: 86). Müller stated concerning the period around 1829 that in the Timor area wars were undertaken with the exclusive purpose of capturing

slaves and plundering the countryside. After the slave trade had been prohibited in the Netherlands' possessions, the quarrels and feuds in the various districts noticeably declined (Müller 1857: 99). According to Hagenaar (1934:
106–7), during the whole period from the time the Dutch assumed control of
Portuguese possessions to the twentieth century, Flores was marked by numerous indigenous tiny wars, slave trading, piracy at sea, and raiding against
coastal settlements. Although we have an embarrassment of information
about such matters, we are short of systematic knowledge about the relationships of these factors with the workings of local societies beyond scholarly
surmise often based on anecdotal information. Sutherland, for example,
writes,

Looking back over the patchy information on the seventeenth and eighteenth centuries,
it is apparent that slaves were a very important element in the total trade pattern, and
that the trade must have had deep effects on many Indonesian societies. . . . Occasional
references to deserted coastal villages, or the high death rate which accompanied the
larger raids, suggests that this commerce had negative demographic effects, although
it replenished manpower in other areas. Moreover, the temptation to make enslavement
a more frequent punishment must have been great. Indications are that rulers in Nusa
Tenggara, for example, did tend to discover a number of wrongdoers liable for punishment by enslavement around the time that the trading *perahus* were due (Sutherland
1983: 271).

   Brumund (1853: 73) divided sea raiders in the east into three classes. They
were exclusive sea raiders who cruised through the whole of the archipelago;
raiders and fishermen, especially of trepang, or also traders; and finally coastal
troops who often attacked neighbouring villages and then on the next day
shoved off from their own shores as defenceless fishermen again. If this classification is accepted as an approximation of conditions in the region of Flores
and Timor, it is probably the second and third types which were of most persistent effect on local populations. In various centuries the waters of Flores
and Timor were visited by Javanese, Macassarese, Endenese, and Bugis pirates
(for a summary see Needham 1983: 1–2). Much feared in the Dutch East Indies
and elsewhere during the eighteenth and nineteenth centuries were the great
fleets of tens of ships and hundreds of men that set sail from the Sulu islands
in the Philippines on raiding expeditions lasting months or years, reaching as
far as Java, Sumatra, and western Malaysia and circling Celebes and Borneo.
These were the so-called Illanun (Iranun) and related (mixed) ethnic groups
from the small islands between Mindanao and Borneo (Warren 1981; Tarling
1963: 146–85).
   In 1838 the Dutch punished several villages on Flores including Larantuka
for suspected piracy on Timorese boats under Dutch flags. The Dutch had
complained several times to the Portuguese about piracy by the inhabitants of
Ende and Larantuka, including the overrunning of their post at Atapupu,

Timor, in November 1836. Having received no satisfactory answer from the Portuguese Governor at Dili, they sent the corvette of war *Boreas*, together with the brig of war *Siwa*, and several boats with ninety Savunese to Larantuka. Together with auxiliary troops from Solor and with the Resident of Timor present, they burned Larantuka to the ground, before setting out for Ende. This event led to diplomatic complications with Portugal which in the long run ended up in the sale to Holland of Portuguese claims to Flores and the Solor Islands. At the time of the attack, the Raja of Larantuka was at Dili, Timor, where he had taken fifty slaves with whom he purchased the title of Colonel from the Portuguese (Veth 1855: 170, 175–8; Needham 1983: 23; van Alderwerelt 1906; Anonymous 1850: 624; Hagenaar 1934: 106; Ezerman 1917: 870–2).

In the 1830s pirates were found all along the north coast of Flores. Toward the end of the east monsoon, the Illanun raided Salayer and the islands to the south of it and when the winds were favourable they plundered the north coast of Flores (de Groot 1847: 275, 321). On 9 May 1843, in a fairly famous incident, the English whaler *Sara and Elisabeth* put an undefended party ashore on the north coast of Timor to cut wood, when a fleet of pirates entered the bay and overran the wood cutters and subsequently the ship (de Groot 1848: 33–45). Two months later a small Danish schooner narrowly missed being taken on the north side of Timor by six or seven boats which attacked it during a calm (Jukes 1847: 374). In 1844 the Dutch steamship *Hekla* undertook an expedition against pirates on the north coast of Flores (Brumund 1853: 76–7). Near Palué, the *Hekla* captured three boats under a man described as a genuine Illanun. Stopping at the trading port Geliting in East Flores, they heard from the head of that village that a month previously the pirates in many boats had sailed along the north Flores coast toward the east (Brumund 1853: 128, 138).

Such fleets would of course have also passed the exposed coasts of the islands to the east of Flores, including Lembata. In 1861 the Dutch destroyed a pirate camp at Rium, Flores, thereby, so it was claimed, freeing the island of pirates ([May] 1864: 375). Whatever effects the depredations of long-distance pirate fleets may have had on coastal communities, local slave trading and slave raiding also added to insecurity. In the 1870s, according to Riedel, kidnapping and slave trading were carried on in a greater or smaller scale on Sumba, Flores, and on the Solor and Alor Islands; and kidnapping was always paired with headhunting and pillaging of villages (Riedel 1885: 5, 9). Whereas the great far-flung pirate raids may have struck mostly coastal communities, local raiding also exposed the peoples of the interior; and the opposition between coastal communities founded by outsiders and indigenous hamlets of the interior was marked by exploitation including slave raiding of the latter by the former. The Koloniaal Verslag for 1875 attributed tensions between coastal and mountain dwellers in the Solor and Alor Islands to several causes. Mountain peoples claimed to be the original inhabitants, while the coastal peoples were of a different origin and even (in some places, especially Alor and Pantar) spoke different languages. Through their dealings with foreign traders and seafarers, the Muslim coastal dwellers were more developed than the heathen mountaineers. Already at the first contact with Europeans (some three and a half centuries before the date of this comment), the leaders of the coastal communities presented themselves as the rulers over the mountain peoples, and, supporting their claim with the silent acknowledgement of their rule by the mountain people, they still regarded themselves as such. However, frequently the mountain people were not prepared to be obedient, leading to bloody clashes (Koloniaal Verslag 1875: 27).

Riedel thought that the export of slaves did not take place on the islands in areas close to the seat of government, but suspected that it did further away. Furthermore, traffic in slaves between one district and another continued without restraint, although in 1877 the Resident completed a treaty with the heads and chiefs of Solor and Alor in which they agreed to see to it that no more slaves were kept and that debt slaves were also freed unless they were registered within six months of signing the treaty (Riedel 1885: 10–11).[13]

In the region of Larantuka [and] on the Solor and Alor Islands there are four types of slaves, namely hereditary slaves, people captured in war, people guilty of theft and those held in slavery because of debt. War captives may nevertheless be ransomed by their relatives. It is also not unusual that in Larantuka men sell their wives and parents their daughters to the highest bidder. The number of slaves present on Sumba, Flores, Solor and Alor cannot be given even by estimation (Riedel 1885: 10).

Similar classifications are commonplace in the literature (Ruibing 1937: 1–28), although recent scholarship seems inclined to avoid the issue of categorization of slaves and other types of dependants. According to Reid (1988: 132), most South-East Asia terms which Europeans translated as slave could be rendered in other circumstances as debtor, dependant, or subject. Most, but not all. He also emphasizes that the absence of wage labour meant that bondage was the primary source of labour mobility. Also, 'It was dangerous if not impossible to accumulate capital unless one also accumulated bondsmen to protect and use that capital' (Reid 1988: 136). It was not uncommon for witnesses to comment on the astonishing freedom of movement accorded slaves and their lack of interest in escaping, as Beckering did in reference to Adonara and Lembata (Beckering 1911: 181, 198). In his secret political report for 1867, the Resident of Timor, J. G. Coorengel, gave a fairly complacent picture of slavery in the island.

Slavery is in full bloom here. Export of slaves from one island to another or from the Timor Archipelago can be said not to exist. An exception is Sumba, from where indeed formerly slaves were exported to Flores, but this has become more and more seldom.

A slave is regarded as being a kind of thing. In general the slave is conceded the right to buy himself free. A freeborn [person] can become a slave, for example if he cannot pay his debts. The creditor can publicly sell his debtor to the highest bidder. Putting western concepts of slavery aside and giving the matter benefit of its inner being, then it cannot be said that the slaves have a hard lot here; indeed there are places here where the slave is better off than the freeborn rabble. To try to end slavery through reasonable arguments sounds fine but may as well be omitted because the effort will have as much success as if in a European society someone were to preach: 'strip yourself of your possessions' (Coorengel 1867).

Among possibilities open to the slave were redemption by relatives or for a slave to buy his way free on the strength of his own earnings. De Castro (1862: 484–5) wrote that in Portuguese Timor if a slave managed to buy his freedom by payment of tribute to the king with permission of his owner, he became of the same class as his former owner. In this way, yesterday's slave could become today's aristocrat. The slave of a king, however, could not become a prince capable of succeeding to the throne.

This comment throws some light on events following the death of the second and last Queen of Solor, Injai Chili Muda, in 1686. In her place the nobles chose a certain Captain Poro. In the next year, however, the Dutch East Indies Company declared this appointment unlawful, having discovered that Poro was the Queen's former slave (Coolhaas 1975: 37, 118). De Castro said nothing about Solor, of course, but the nobility of Solor had close ties with Timor and commerce in slaves was one of the uniting factors. In Poro's place Sengaji Chili, the son of the Queen's sister and Sengaji Boli of Lamahala, Adonara, was chosen. When Sengaji Chili died without a male heir in March 1700, Poro again became head of Solor as provisional regent, which he remained until his own death in 1703 (Coolhaas 1975: 210, 284; 1976: 123, 155, 240).

Export trade in slaves had a different, harsher significance. 'Since slave export was almost invariably linked with internal disunity, the stateless societies and microstates of eastern Indonesia, New Guinea, Bali, and Nias were consistently among the exporters' (Reid 1988: 133). That slaves were not always content with their condition is shown by the number of occasions in which formerly free persons in the possession of Europeans ran amok (Fox 1983: 258–60; Abeyasekere 1983: 305–6). The role of the European powers in the slave trade can be followed in several works, among them Manguin (1983) and to some extent Boxer (1969) for the Portuguese and Fox (1983) and Boxer (1965a: 238–41) for the Dutch. Slavery was officially abolished in the Dutch East Indies on 1 January 1860, although practice was otherwise (Sutherland 1983: 274–5). The state of matters at the beginning of the twentieth century is indicated by the fact that cases of piracy were still being tried in 1905 and that in 1908 the Dutch East Indies government, 'discontinued the practice of cruising the eastern shipping routes of the archipelago to prevent kidnapping and the slave trade for the simple reason that the results did not come up to expectations' (Resink 1968: 333–4). In earlier years the Europeans were cheerful participants.

On 27 October 1627 Jan Pietersz. Coen, Governor-General of the Dutch East Indies Company, wrote to the Commander of the Solor fort, Jan d'Hornay (who was himself soon to defect to the Portuguese in Larantuka) to complain about the slaves recently sent to Batavia. They were in such a miserable and brutal condition that they were more beasts than men, so that they were of no use or service to the Company, indeed were not even worth the value of the rice they ate. If d'Hornay could find no better class of slaves, he should cease to purchase them. D'Hornay could not possibly send too many stout and capable people, but such brutal humans were useless (Colenbrander 1923: 196). In February 1646 the sengajis of Solor were instructed to sail to the inner and outer coasts of Timor and other nearby islands to collect as many slaves and as much wax and tortoiseshell as possible and to bring them to the commander of the fort on Solor, in order to lighten the costs of maintaining the fort (Tiele and Heeres 1895: 325). In 1648, without asking for a pass or so much as presenting his booty at the Solor fort for sale to the Company, the sengaji of Lamahala transported sixty slaves from Sabu, leaving the chagrined Netherlanders to guess where he had taken and sold them. The commander of the fort complained that the sengajis were a bunch of knaves. The slaves had been purchased with the Company's clothing, made available to them as such a 'civil price' according to contract, but instead of coming to the fort, they went by night to Larantuka, where they sold the slaves to Portuguese merchants (Tiele and Heeres 1895: 426, 428).

[In April, 1803, the Commander of the American ship *Hunter*] reported . . . that iron was still more valuable at Solor, Flores, and the neighboring islands, and that supplies of fresh provisions were more plentiful [than at Kupang]. The usual profits of trade here, seemed to be cent. per cent. upon every exchange; and this the commander of the Hunter proposed to make many times over, during his voyage. At Solor he had bought some slaves for two muskets each, which muskets he had purchased at the rate of 18s. in Holland, at the conclusion of the war; these slaves were expected to be sold at Batavia, for eighty, or more probably for a hundred dollars individually, making about thirty capitals of the first price of his muskets. If such advantages attend this traffic, humanity must expect no weak struggle to accomplish its suppression; but what was the result of this trading voyage? That the commander and his crew contracted a fever at Diely [Dili, Timor], and nearly the whole died before they reached Batavia (Flinders 1814: 256).

Dutch trade from their earliest years in Asia was carried on by means of war not only against local powers, but also against European rivals (van Leur 1967: 180–90). After taking the Spanish fort on Tidore in January 1613, the Dutch East Indies Company captured the Portuguese fort at Lohayong, Solor in April, promising themselves a rich return in sandalwood trade with Timor (R. H. Barnes 1987: 224). In 1617 the representatives of the shareholders of the

Company ordered that Spanish and Portuguese who fell into the hands of the Netherlanders should be thrown overboard at once, except for those who could be used as slaves (Biermann 1924: 24, n. 36). In September 1628 Governor-General Coen ordered that Chinese and other Asian ships trying to trade on Timor should be taken prize and the crews sent away, while English, French, or other European vessels should be headed off and forced to leave. As much damage as possible should be done the Spanish, Portuguese, and their adherents. Any goods captured from them should be used to the benefit of the Company, and persons taken should be used for heavy work as slaves (Colenbrander 1920: 429–33).

Needham wrote of Sumba, which had been long subject to slave raiding from Ende, Flores,

When I lived in Kodi, in the mid-[nineteen]fifties, the appearance of a strange vessel out at sea, or just the rumour of one, would provoke all the signs of a general panic; men looked fiercely serious, and screaming women dashed to pick up their children. The assertion that such apparitions were *penyamun*, robbers or marauders . . . was quite frequent, especially in the early months of the years. Contumacious children might be told that if they did not behave properly the marauders would get them (Needham 1983: 41).

In 1862 Semmelink found people in the vicinity of Larantuka, Flores (which of course had been flattened by the Dutch some years previously) were very frightened of Europeans. More than once it happened to him that when on patrol on horseback with the military commandant people near the path climbed trees from fear and only came down again once they had gone on a good distance or assured them that they need not be afraid (Semmelink 1864: 64). Similar stories can be easily repeated, either from experience or from the literature. An example further away in time and place occurs in an Arabic collection of tales from the tenth century about the Wāqwāq, who may, or may not, have been peoples of South-East Asia (Tibbetts 1979: 161, 175). The captain of ship was blown off course to the land of the Wāqwāq, where it stopped not far from a village. The inhabitants fled, taking all their possessions. After two days, a sailor fluent in the local language disembarked to search for the locals. Eventually he found a man hiding in a tree whom he befriended and persuaded to coax the villagers to return and enter into trade. Subsequently the village was attacked by another tribe, which the Arabs helped to drive off. Thereafter the village could not do enough for them. 'Deceiving them without ceasing, stealing their children, buying some of them from others with garments, dates and other trinkets, we soon had the ship full of a hundred slaves both small and large' (Tibbetts 1979: 162). Eventually their slaves rebelled and stole their ship, and they were left to construct another small boat to make their escape. A Captain Williams of the *Thames* who was with a fleet of six English ships bound from Europe to China which passed through the Flores Strait in

1797–8 recounted that, 'In attempting to land on Solor [the southwest coast], the natives were found hostile, firing some arrows from the bushes at the boats; but they *probably* believed the ships to be Dutch, who are said to carry away the inhabitants when opportunity offers, to sell as slaves at Batavia' (Horsburgh 1852: 716–17; for further examples of suspicions of kidnappings by Dutch officials and others see R. H. Barnes 1993*c*).

Until the twentieth century life in the islands was marked by dangers resulting from both long-distance and local raiding. Other negative factors included illness, theft of livestock, crop failure and resulting famine. Many a person gambled away his freedom by losing at dice. Several of these factors are still part of everyday life. As a consequence of the general lack of safety, villages were built on steep hilltops and other defensible heights, usually at a great distance from sources of fresh water, although rarely such locations actually brought them closer to springs than their present sites.[14] Hygiene and health were disadvantaged by the lack of ready access to free-flowing water, as is all too often still the case. One of the first things the Dutch military attempted after 1910 was to try to force villages to move down into regularly laid-out situations in the lowlands or on the coasts (Lulofs 1911: 285). The greater degree of security brought about by military and police measures in most of the twentieth century, as well as somewhat improved transportation and health measures, provided conditions for the substantial population increases which have also taken place since 1910. It is also true, and should be borne in mind, that features of social organization and measures for economic subsistence exist today in a very different context than was the case in the past. In particular, institutions of marriage alliance and ceremonial exchange today have no direct reference to the traffic in humans and the military insecurity which was part of their environment in the past and which must have affected their operations and meanings.

Population and Population Growth

E. Francis (1838: 391) estimated the population of Lembata in 1831 as consisting of 7,080 known persons and 8,000 unknown. Direct European control did not come to Lembata until 1910, when Captain J. D. H. Beckering and a company of troops visited the island to confiscate fire-arms and register the population—a rather late incident in the process of expansion and consolidation of Dutch East Indies possessions at the end of the nineteenth century and beginning of the twentieth. This intervention derived from general policy decisions of the Netherlands-Indies government and reflected no concrete interest in the region (see Dietrich 1989: 1–11). At that time the island was divided into various districts most of which were subject to the Raja of Adonara or the Raja of Larantuka, Flores. The Dutch maintained treaty relationships with minor principalities on Solor and Adonara from 1613. Their involvement with

Larantuka began in 1851, when in return for a loan of Dutch Fl. 80,000 to the government of Portuguese possessions on Timor they acquired the right to station a military garrison there. This loan led to a series of negotiations that eventuated in a treaty of 1859 in which Portugal ceded her possessions on Flores, Adonara, Solor, Lembata, Pantar, and Alor to the Netherlands-Indies.

The social geography of Lembata has changed greatly in the eighty years since Beckering arrived. Beckering estimated a population of 31,000 to 32,000 on the island of 1,266 km. sq., giving a population density of 25 persons per square kilometre (Beckering 1911: 184). By 1980 the island's population had increased to over 85,000. The 1980 census estimates the population density of this island as 67.4 persons per square kilometre. Beckering commented (1911: 189) on the strange fact that in 1910 a great proportion of the population lived on the slopes of the four highest mountains: Uyolewun in Kédang, Ilé Wariran or Lewotolo on the north coast, Ilé Mingar in the west, and the highest Ilé Labalekang in the south above Lamalera. The rest of the population lived on the high plateau above Labala on the Lerek peninsula to the east of Lamalera or in the mountains of Lewoleba. The extensive low plains that exist in various places were completely uninhabited. This distribution of population responded to the need to find easily defendable village sites. There were only a few villages along the coasts, among them Lamalera and nearby Labala to the east. The protected bays of the north with good harbours providing access by sea to low-lying and relatively flat and easily cultivable land did not at that time attract populations more concerned about exposure to attack and pillage by pirates from the sea and local enemies on land.

In 1910 the head of Lewoleba district in the north lived at the village Lewokukun, occupying a mountain redoubt of extremely difficult access. The original village of Lewoleba had once been situated closer to the sea, but had been completely laid waste by inhabitants of a village in the more northerly Lewotolo district that was subject to the Raja of Adonara (Beckering 1911: 188). Beckering moved the village of Lewokewe from the mountains down to the shore and renamed it Lewoleba, thereby founding what since World War II has grown into the governmental and commercial centre of the island and the principal establishment of the Catholic mission (Munro 1915). In Muslim Labala on the south of the island each of the clans lived enclosed within heavy palisades, made higher and strengthened with thorny *bambu duri* (*Bambusa blumeana* Bl. ex. Schult. f.). The complex of the Raja of Labala was similarly surrounded. Lamalera was not then palisaded (Beckering 1911: 188–90), though it had once been enclosed by fences of stone and cactus (van den Windt 1936: 75).

By 1980 the Lembata's population had increased to more than two and a half times the estimate of 1910. Between 1931 and 1980 the Regency and the province doubled, and the island nearly so, while the settlement (as opposed to

TABLE 2. *Population Changes, Lembata, 1931–1980*

District	1931			District	1980		
	Population	%	Males/100 females		Population	%	Males/100 females
				Labatukan	(7,701)	(9)	(107/100)
				Perwakilan Labatukan	(9,211)	(11)	(78/100)
Lewoleba	5,817	12	94/100	Labatukan	16,912	20	92/100
Labala	6,631	14	96/100	Ata Déi	11,397	13.5	71/100
LAMALERA	(7,420)	(16)	(93/100)				
Kawela	(2,896)	(6)	(94/100)				
	10,316	22	93/100	NAGAWUTUNG	13,852	16	80/100
Lewotolo	8,077	17	94/100	Ilé Apé	14,461	17	65/100
				Omesuri	(13,021)	(15)	(78/100)
				Buyasuri	(15,656)	(18.5)	(84/100)
Kédang	16,319	35	96/100		28,677	33.5	81/100
TOTAL	47,160	100	95/100	TOTAL	85,299	100	78.5/100

Sources: Biro Pusat Statistic 1981*b*; Seegeler 1931.

the district) of Lamalera added a mere 38 per cent of its 1931 size (see Tables 2, 3, 4, and 5). Over the same period the south of the island lost in relative numbers to the rapidly growing north. In contrast Lewoleba district, which contains the island's capital, grew to nearly three times its numbers in 1931 and comprised 20 per cent as opposed to 12 per cent of the island's total. Nagawutung (into which Lamalera and Kawela districts were consolidated) declined relatively from 22 per cent to a mere 16 per cent. In summary, during a half-century of substantial population growth for the district, the island, the Regency, and the province, Lamalera village virtually stood still. Also the dis-

TABLE 3. *Comparison of Lembata Population 1980, 1990, and 1994*

District	1980	1990	1994
Nagawutung	13,854	13,088	13,065
Ata Déi	11,397	10,062	9,144
Ilé Apé	14,461	14,006	13,204
Lebatukan	16,912	18,622	20,199
Omesuri	13,021	13,558	14,092
Buyasuri	15,656	15,584	15,630
Total Lembata	85,301	84,920	85,334

Sources: Kantor Statistik 1992, *Kecamatan Nagawutung Dalam Angka* 1994, *Kecamatan Atadei Dalam Angka* 1994, *Kecamatan Ileape Dalam Angka* 1994, *Kecamatan Lebatukan Dalam Angka* 1994, *Kecamatan Omesuri Dalam Angka* 1994, *Kecamatan Buyasuri Dalam Angka* 1994

TABLE 4. *Lembata, 1980 Population Expressed as a Percentage of 1931 Population*

District	%
Labatukan + Perwakilan	
Labatukan	291
Ata Déi	172
Nagawutung	134
Ilé Apé	179
Omesuri + Buyasuri	175
Total Lembata	181

TABLE 5. *Population Changes 1931–1980 and 1980–1990 for Province, Regency, and Island*

	1931	1980	1990	Annual growth rate 1931/1980	Annual growth rate 1980/1990
Nusa Tenggara Timur	1,343,000	2,737,166	3,267,919	1.46%	1.79%
Flores Timur	130,951	257,687	266,405	1.39%	0.33%
Lembata	47,160	85,299	84,920	1.22%	−0.04%

trict grew more slowly than the island, the island than the Regency, and the Regency than the province.[15]

This record might suggest a pattern of extreme backwardness, which by no means fits the facts in the village. Not only have persons from the village been exposed to elementary education for a century, but today schooling is available in Lamalera from kindergarten to junior high school. There is a large, modern Catholic church, built by funds donated by West German sources. A nurse and staff run a dispensary. Motor boats taking passengers to and from other islands call at the village twice a week. It is even possible for trucks and motorcycles to reach a village in the mountains under an hour's walk away from Lamalera. They have been recipients of development aid of various kinds, and in 1973–5 the Food and Agriculture Organization ran a project there intended to modernize the fishery (R. H. Barnes 1984).

Calculating the actual population size of Lamalera is complicated by the fact that the village census of the lower part of the village was incomplete during my visit in 1979 and by the fact that, as will be explained later, the two official villages of Lamalera, Lamalera A and Lamalera B, include hamlets which are historically and culturally distinct from it. Census records for Lamalera A, broken down by wards, show that there were 834 persons in that part of the village, of which 261 belonged to the mountain hamlet of Lamamanu, actually a distinct community. The size of Lamalera A proper was therefore 573. The census records for Lamalera B in 1979 were incomplete for the remote and historically unrelated Ongaona and Nualela, now included for governmental purposes in it. It is possible too that some wards in the new suburb of Futung Lolo were unavailable. The portion of the census available to me included 626 persons. If this is actually the whole of that part of the population belonging to historical Lamalera, then the total for the village excluding the outlying hamlets was 1,197. A published estimate by a son of the village is that Lamalera A and B together number more than 2,000 and the parish of Lamalera around 5,000 (Moses Beding 1982: 16). In 1931 the whole village of Lamalera numbered 1,056, although this figure probably included Lamamanu (Seegeler 1931: 9–18; Symons 1935: 3–9). Even allowing for the possibility that the number for 1979 is somewhat depressed and that for 1931 somewhat inflated, these figures indicate very moderate growth at best over that period.[16]

In 1855 and in 1866 the government of the Dutch East Indies twice rejected suggestions that it open schools in the Solor Archipelago, in the first instance because delicate negotiations with Portugal were still under way to acquire Portuguese holdings in the region and in the second because it did not want to divert scarce resources from Roti and Timor.[17] However, a Jesuit priest, G. Metz, started a school in Larantuka around 1865.[18] In 1871 it was still the only school in the islands north of Timor and catered for forty students, aged between 7 and 12, some of them from fairly far away from Larantuka. They were taught hymns, some reading, poor writing, but no arithmetic. The teacher, a native of Larantuka who served simultaneously as organist, was poorly trained and supported and had no idea even of what fractions were (Chijs 1879).

By 1886 there were already a couple of youths from Lamalera at the Jesuit school in Larantuka, which then catered for 160 boys and girls. On 8 and 9 June 1886 two Jesuits, J. de Vries and Cornelius ten Brink, returned to Larantuka from Kupang, Timor, via Lamalera, where they stopped having informed the government of their plan to do so (van den Windt 1936: 75; Greve 1886). They brought with them Don Lorenzo Oesi Diaz Vieira Godinho, Crown prince of Larantuka. His influence enabled the missionaries to baptize immediately two hundred and twenty children in Lamalera and perhaps a total of three hundred children in the region and to obtain permission to take three boys to their school in Larantuka (Heslinga 1891: 68–9; van den Windt 1936: 75). The baptismal book in the village actually shows that they baptized 104 on the 8th and 117 on the 9th.

On 30 September 1887 ten Brink returned to Lamalera for a longer stay. Since there was as yet no housing available for the missionary, the mission workshop at Larantuka prefabricated one to be sent after him. Meanwhile he slept in one of the boat sheds at the beach, at the back of which on a shelf the clan owning the boat then kept the skulls of its ancestors. Ten Brink returned to Larantuka at the beginning of December having increased the number of schoolchildren to ten and the number of baptized Christians to three hundred and sixty. The government discouraged a return in 1888 because of troubles in the Solor Strait. Lamahala, Adonara, and Lamakera, Solor had attacked the village of Boleng on Adonara, killing forty-seven people and capturing sixty-two. The Dutch gunboats *Prins Hendrik* and *Benkoelen* retaliated in November by bombarding Lamahala, Menanga (on Solor), Lamakera, *and* the victimized Boleng (Wichmann 1891: 264–5). During a visit of a little over a month in 1889, ten Brink baptized another one hundred and seven children. He died in 1890. The Jesuits lacked personnel to do anything more thereafter than make a few visits to the village. The school at Larantuka, however, continued to train Lamalera boys. They were educated as catechists, schoolteachers, and carpenters.[19]

When the Dutch moved into the island in 1910 therefore there were already educated persons from Lamalera, and by around 1913 a mission school had been established in the village (Munro 1915). Today Lamalera A has a kindergarden, a governmental elementary school, and a Catholic junior high school established around 1967. A government elementary school was opened about a kilometre or so east of Lamalera B in the late 1970s. In 1979 Lamalera A sent 36 children (15 boys and 21 girls) to the kindergarden, 117 children (75 boys and 42 girls) to the elementary school, and 84 children (46 boys and 38 girls) to the junior high school. Figures from Lamalera B were not available. In 1979, 5 per cent of adults of Lamalera A had no schooling at all, 8 per cent had not finished elementary school, 76 per cent had completed elementary school, 4.6 per cent had completed junior high school, 4.1 per cent had finished senior high school, and 2.3 per cent had completed teachers training school. In 1984 there were 137 children (67 boys and 70 girls) attending the government elementary school in Lamalera B and 136 children (69 boys and 67 girls) in the Catholic elementary school in Lamalera A.[20]

The local explanation for the relative stagnation of population numbers is that persons who have received education leave the village for jobs elsewhere. Indeed villagers often complain that modern youth would rather become government clerks than take up useful occupations or put their skills to the benefit of the village. The first jobs which drew men from the village were teaching, carpentry, and the ministry. For a period when the first schools were being introduced, most schoolteachers in the islands derived from Waibalun near Larantuka, Flores and from Lamalera. The first generation of teachers have now retired (see Piskaty 1964 for a history of education in the province). Some have returned to Lamalera, but others have permanently settled elsewhere. Itinerant employment as craftsmen and carpenters has been available equally long. Much of the building work in the Regency was carried out by Lamalera carpenters, and today they regularly contract such work, especially on the larger-scale construction projects now being introduced by the national government. Schoolteachers and workmen rarely completely cut their ties with the village, but their occupations entail extended absences from home, sometimes for years, leading to dual residences which easily shade into permanent settlement elsewhere. An élite has made its way into the professions. Lamalera has produced a university professor, a university lecturer in Japanese and South-East Asian languages, a medical doctor, a general, a publisher, as well as priests, nuns, newspapermen, businessmen, members of the state assembly, government clerks, and many schoolteachers.

The East Flores Regency was the only one in the province to register a decline in growth rate during the period 1971–80 (1.28 per cent per year compared with 1.71 over the years 1961–71). It had a growth rate of only 0.29 per cent between 1990 and 1991 (when Nagawutun actually declined by 0.45 per cent), compared with a growth rate for the province of 1.79 per cent and for the nation of 1.98 per cent (see Table 6). The Regency also shows a general loss of productive, young adult males—a situation which may be tied to its declining growth rate (see Table 7). There are somewhat more males than females under the age of 15 in the village, Regency, and province. Over age 15 the Regency shows a drastic drop in male numbers (64 males/100 females), quite out of keeping for the province. The part of the Regency most heavily affected in this respect is eastern Adonara around Ilé Boleng and northern Lembata around Ilé Lewotolo, where young men have left in large numbers to work as migrant labourers at Tawau, Kalimantan.[21] Lamalera is less sharply affected, although it participates in the pattern of declining numbers of adult

TABLE 6. *Growth Rate 1971–1980 and 1961–1971 (annual percentage)*

	1980–1990	1971–1980	1961–1971
Nation	1.98	2.32	2.10
Province (NTT)	1.79	1.95	1.57
Regency (FloTim)	0.33	1.28	1.71

Sources: Biro Pusat Statistik 1981*b*; Kantor Statistik 1992.

TABLE 7. *Sex and Age Ratios*

	Sex ratio (males/100 females)			Age ratio (%)	
	Under 15	Over 15	Total	Under 15	Over 15
Province (NTT) (1980)	107	94	99.6	42.3	57.7
Regency (Flotim) (1980)	106	64	80.0	42.2	57.8
Island (Lembata) (1980)	107	63	78.5	40.9	59.1
Distict (Nagawutung) (1980)	107	65	80.0	39.5	60.5
Village (Lamalera) (1979)	114	75	86.0	31.4	68.6

TABLE 8. *Population by Age and Sex, Lamalera (1979)*

	Under 15		Over 15		Total	
Males	200	36.2%	353	63.8%	553	46.2%
Females	176	27.3%	468	72.7%	644	53.8%
Total	376	31.4%	821	68.6%	1,197	100.0%
Sex ratio m/f	114/100		75/100		86/100	

males (75 males/100 females over 15) (see Table 8). Relative to the Regency and province, Lamalera has a somewhat higher percentage of persons over 15 (68.6). Lamalera has an ageing population which is not only losing males, but also females.

The relative lack of population growth in the village would appear therefore to result from success in the village in acquiring education and moving to modern occupations sooner than has been average for the Regency and to be explained by migration. Young men from Lamalera provide labour for extended periods at Tawau and other places as far away as Malaysia, but alternatives exist. The line between migrant labour and itinerant labour may be unclear, but men and women continue to find occasional employment within the Regency which keeps them from the village for only part of the year. Their movement is facilitated by the fact that many Lamalera households have permanently settled in other population centres, where typically they gather together in small wards of families with ties to Lamalera or other south Lembata villages. There were an estimated forty family heads of Lamalera descent living in Lewoleba in the early 1980s. An entire division near the beach around the Catholic church in Waiwerang, the modern commercial centre on Adonara, is inhabited by people from Lamalera. Lamalera families have lived for decades in Larantuka. The same pattern is taking place at the provincial capital, Kupang, and the national capital, Jakarta.

The village has benefited by the establishment in the village of a polyclinic in the *Puskesmas* (*Pusat Kesehatan Masyarakat*, Public Health Centre) programme during the 1970s, which provides various forms of medication, but the lack of electricity to refrigerate medicines, the cash poverty of villagers, and the distance from the nearest hospitals (at Lewoleba and Larantuka) means that many deaths occur which would not be necessary in more favourable circumstances. According to Corner (1991a: 191), the province recorded the highest decline in urban infant mortality rates during the 1970s and 1980s, but only a slight improvement in the rural rates. This discrepancy is hardly surprising, as such hospitals as exist are in the towns, and transportation to them from rural villages is generally difficult and time consuming. Furthermore, the distribution of doctors in the province is highly skewed in favour of the capital Kupang, although the distribution of health centres is more balanced (Corner 1991a: 197).

Corner (1991a: 179) comments that the two provinces of West and East Southeast Islands (Nusa Tenggara Barat and Timur) are among the poorest and most isolated as well as among the least developed provinces in Indonesia. During the 1970s Nusa Tenggara Timur experienced a fall in the relative importance of the agricultural contribution to domestic product, which was mostly due to the expansion of the government sector. Government investment, and the employment it created increased the monetization of the economy, leading to a transfer of activities from agriculture to the service sector (Corner 1991a: 184). In 1980 the province was ranked second in the nation for rural poverty, but only tenth for urban poverty. The Directorate-General of Agrarian Affairs in the Department of the Interior estimated in the late 1970s that 13 per cent of the regencies in the province were 'extremely poor', 45 per cent were 'poor', and 28 per cent were 'almost poor', leaving only 14 per cent which were fairly well off. Their criteria were that annual per capita incomes of Rp. 16,717 (*c*. US $40) and below indicated an 'extremely poor' regency, between that and Rp. 43,818 (US $104) 'poor', and from there to Rp. 70,110 (US $167) 'almost poor' (Corner 1991a: 202, 206 n. 31). Corner (1991b: 50) concludes gloomily that, 'The costs of social development in NTT are well beyond the resources (current or likely to be available in the immediate future) of the province'.

In 1979 the domestic product of the East Flores Regency was reported to be Rp. 11,559,549 (or US $17,330), an increase from Rp. 9,570,858

(US $14,349) in the previous year. The annual per capita income for all of Nusa Tenggara Timur Province in 1979 was reported to be Rp. 92,322 (or US $138); by 1986 it had risen to *c*. Rp. 228,000 (*c*. US $139). In 1987, 54 per cent of the population were reckoned to be below the poverty line (Statistical Office of the Province, Kupang, Timor; Barlow and Gondowarsito 1991: 20). I have no idea what faith should be placed in such figures. They are compatible with a poorly monetized economy, but I should have thought that the per capita income figure for the province would be considerably higher than, perhaps double, any reasonable figure for Lamalera. To the degree that these figures derive from reports by village administrators, they may be mythical, especially if the annual report of Lamalera A for 1978 is not exceptional. This report, dated 31 December 1978, stated that except for some fish caught by a few boats at Lobetobi, Flores, the village had captured no fish at all throughout the whole of 1978 and that as a result it was expecting a famine. In fact, by the time the report was written the village had taken fifteen sperm whales. There was no famine in 1979.[22]

Governmental Structure

In the past Lamalera constituted one of the Demon Lewo Pulu, ten Demon districts, which were subject to the Raja of Larantuka. The head of each such district bore the title *kakang*.[23] Directly subordinate to the Kakang of Lamalera were the village heads of the twenty-six villages in his district. To the west of Lamalera was Mingar district, subject to the Raja of Adonara, and to the east the independent rajadom Labala. The only other region on the island owing allegiance to Larantuka was Lewoleba. Each of the islands was divided into the lands attached to Larantuka, described as Demon, and lands under a loose alliance of petty rajas, including Adonara, designated Paji. Both Mingar and Labala were Paji areas. The Demon–Paji split is backed by legend and is documented by the first European visitors in the early seventeenth century (de Sá 1956: 484; Santa Catharina 1733: 792–3; Arndt 1938). It reflected military alliances and hostilities which were still active in 1910.

From the seventeenth century on, the Dutch maintained treaties and alliances with the so-called 'five coasts', *lima pantai*, five Muslim enclaves including Lohayong, Lamakera, Lamahala, Terong, and the holdings of the Raja of Adonara. They also had ties to Labala, Lembata, which claimed to be one of the original five. The Portuguese, who entered the region early in the sixteenth century, maintained links with the realm of Larantuka and with its allies and dependencies on Solor, Adonara, and Lembata. These ties were eventually transformed into claims to Portuguese suzerainty, which were maintained with greater or lesser practical reality until Portugal ceded its rights in the area to the Netherlands in 1859.

During the nineteenth century the Dutch pursued a hands-off or 'non-interference' policy in the Flores region, punctuated by occasional military incursions and gunboat assaults.[24] According to Dietrich there were two main reasons for this policy. Direct involvement was too expensive because of the military costs and those of maintaining an established colonial apparatus. Furthermore the area had no economic interest for them; the Timor Residency had always been a financial liability (Dietrich 1983: 39). There were also legal inhibitions, as noted by Resink. Had the Netherlands asserted a claim to sovereignty over all of the principalities in the archipelago not in the British, Portuguese, or German spheres of influence, 'it would have found its rights encumbered by too many responsibilities, for instance with regard to the interests and safety of subjects of other powers in Indonesian self-governing realms' (Resink 1968: 330). The Dutch shifted to a policy of active pacification and direct political control in the early years of the twentieth century (Dietrich 1989: 1–11). This change in policy only became possible after the end of the war in Aceh in 1898. The Netherlands-Indies economy grew 'immeasurably stronger' in the years 1884 to 1896, and with it the army (Reid 1969: 281). As a consequence of the Dutch move into the Flores area, the regional swirl in what Resink called a 'dust cloud of sovereignties' across the far-flung East Indies archipelago was transformed into subordinate and minor branches of the Dutch East Indies colonial state. In another telling phrase, Resink wrote that, 'Arching above this "dust cloud of sovereignties" in some parts of the archipelago was the thickening mist of Dutch suzerainty'. The image of a Netherlands at the end of the nineteenth century 'in a position to claim sovereignty over all Indonesia, can and should be turned all but completely upside down' (Resink 1968: 329–30, 334–5).

Effectively, Dutch sovereignty over Lembata arrived abruptly and late and lasted briefly. Historically, all that it achieved was to establish the groundwork for the eventual assimilation of Lembata into the bureaucratic apparatus of the Republic of Indonesia. In Dietrich's view the content of the traditional relationship of raja to *kakang* to village community had been minimal. The Dutch, however, transformed these relationships into true governmental administrative structures (Dietrich 1985: 288–9). In 1929 and 1931 the Dutch consolidated all of the territories in the Lamaholot region under the rajas of Larantuka and Adonara. They broke the historical pattern of alliances by annexing Lohayong to Larantuka in 1929 and Labala and Lamakera to Larantuka in 1931 (Symons 1935: 9–18).[25]

When the Dutch took over, Lamalera was in advance of the rest of the island in political standing with the Raja of Larantuka, relative sophistication, education, and experience with a world religion. Its rugged and rather isolated position made it unsuitable as a centre of administration, and the Dutch established their administrative centre at Hadakewa near the middle of the north coast. Hadakewa remained the government's capital for the island throughout the Dutch and Japanese periods.[26] Today it is little more than a village and a few stores. Lewoleba is now the site of principal government offices, the main mission station, a hospital, post office, and recently built market-place. There are daily motor-boat connections between Lewoleba and other islands, and the limited motor transportation on land originates there. There is also a small airport connecting Lewoleba with Larantuka, Flores, and Kupang, Timor. As a thriving town it attracts population from elsewhere on the island.

Sources

Lamaholot culture has been but imperfectly described, partly because of its variety and the distribution of its population. Other than passing comments by travellers, missionaries, and government officials of which there are quite a number containing useful information, the anthropological record begins with the eight-month visit of the museum ethnologist Ernst Vatter, who made a collection for the Ethnological Museum of Frankfurt, Germany. He travelled with his wife over the four islands of the Lamaholot region and beyond to Pantar and Alor. Most of the information he collected he presented in his book *Ata Kiwan* (Vatter 1932). His short visit to Lamalera is still remembered there. He was forced into retirement and then in 1939 emigrated from Germany to Chile, where after a difficult period he died in 1948. Most of his museum collection survived World War II. It has never been exhibited, however, and only recently has it been possible for work to begin on providing a catalogue. Those interested in the circumstances of Vatter's collection and experiences at the museum should consult Schare (1990) and Ruth Barnes (1993) (see also Holzinger 1970).

The second major figure in Lamaholot linguistics and ethnography was the Divine Word Society priest and anthropologist Paul Arndt. Although the major focus of his ethnographic work was elsewhere, particularly in central Flores, he still managed to produce a Grammar of Lamaholot (Arndt 1937), an important study of the ritual enmity between the Demon and Paji (Arndt 1938), a comparative study of the social organization of East Flores, Adonara, and Solor (Arndt 1940), and a study of the traditional religion of East Flores, Adonara, and Solor (Arndt 1951). His study of the religion is unmatched and unlikely to be matched given the changes which have since occurred in the area. His book on social organization is useful, but fails to cover several important topics. Arndt confined himself to parts of Flores, Adonara, and Solor. He never visited Lembata, and his publications contain no information about it. Arndt died on Flores at the age of 77 in October 1962 (see Anonymous 1963, which contains an account of his life and a list of his publications on Flores and neighbouring islands).

Two important articles were published by Cornelis Ouwehand, a colonial officer once stationed in Larantuka who went on to become a distinguished anthropologist of Japan. The first of these deals with social organization and landrights in East Flores (Ouwehand 1950) and the second with agricultural co-operation on Adonara (Ouwehand 1951). In 1949 and 1950 Raymond Kennedy, an American anthropologist, toured Indonesia including Flores. He was shot out of his Jeep and killed near Bandung, Java, before he could return home, but Harold Conklin edited his field notes, which contain important information on East Flores culture (Kennedy 1955). A secondary account of headhunting practices in the Lamaholot-speaking region was published by Downs (1955, reprinted 1977). Summaries of Lamaholot culture may be found in R. H. Barnes (1972 and 1993*b*).

More recently the Lamaholot region has attracted increased interest from anthropologists. Nancy Lutz (1986) has written a Ph.D. thesis on Adonara. Penelope Graham has produced an M.Phil. thesis and a Ph.D. thesis on East Flores, where she has done research in Lewotala (Graham 1985, 1991). Karl-Heinz Kohl has begun to publish the results of his research in Belogili, East Flores (Kohl 1986, 1988, 1989, 1990). Stefan Dietrich (1989) has produced an important study of colonial and mission relationships in Lamaholot life and has conducted research into the history and social organization of Larantuka, Flores. Ruth Barnes (1989) has published a study of Lamalera textiles and is preparing a catalogue of the Vatter collection at the Frankfurt Ethnological Museum. Useful material has been collected by local students supported by Indonesian government projects, examples of which are Leyn (1979, 1980, and 1981). Further collections of local culture include Anonymous (1978–9, 1979–80, and 1983).

A series of linguistic studies by scholars from the Regency have considerably increased our knowledge in that area, including those by Monteiro (1975) and Fernandez (1977, 1980, 1983–4, 1988). The first is a study of the special dialect of Malay spoken in Larantuka. Fernandez 1977 is a masters thesis on the Lamaholot spoken around the Ilé Mandiri in East Flores. Fernandez 1980 concerns Proto-Malayo-Polynesian phonemes in Lamaholot and Sika. Fernandez 1983–4 is devoted to the historical relationships among Flores languages, while Fernandez 1988 is a doctoral thesis which reconstructs the proto-language of Flores. Most important for this work is the scholarly description of Lamaholot grammar as spoken in Lamalera by Gregorius Keraf (1978). Apart from Ruth and R. H. Barnes, of all the students of Lamaholot life mentioned above, only Vatter and Keraf published information specifically dealing with Lamalera.

Vatter shot important footage of Lamaholot life, which Hermann Niggemeyer subsequently edited and which is now available from the Institut für den Wissenschaftlichen Film, Göttingen (Vatter 1963*a*, 1963*b*, and 1963*c*). Some of this film was made in Lamalera. Commercial television films have been made about Lamalera in Britain (Blake *et al.* 1988), Japan (NHK 1992), and Germany (von Matthey 1992).

There are any number of ephemeral publications about Lamalera in weeklies, newspapers, airline magazines, and so on, one or two of them heavily derived from or even lifted wholesale from my own publications. I have read quite a long list of these, but will cite, by way of example, only one, namely Anonymous (1944).

Language Note

Lamaholot, like neighbouring languages except for non-Austronesian languages on parts of Pantar, Alor, and Timor, belongs to the Central Malayo-Polynesian grouping of Central-Eastern Malayo-Polynesian. Central-Eastern Malayo-Polynesian is a section of Malayo-Polynesian. Malayo-Polynesian comprises all Austronesian languages outside of Taiwan (Blust 1980: 11–12; 1987: 30–1).

Lamalera dialect distinguishes itself from other Lamaholot dialects principally by pronunciation. Whereas Lamaholot generally has a *w* which verges on a *v*, Lamalera has an *f*. There are other systematic differences in vocabulary and pronunciation. For example, the Lamaholot *ona*, meaning interior, inner state, appears in Lamalera as *onã*, with a nasalized final vowel and in other south Lembata dialects as *or* or *ora*. Linguistic deviations from Lamalera habit begin immediately within a few hundred yards toward the interior from the village. This means that dialectal differences are experienced among friends and members of the same family.

Lamalera dialect has fifteen consonants: /b/, /d/, /f/, /g/, /h/, /j/, /k/, /l/, /m/, /n/, /ŋ/, /p/, /r/, /s/, and /t/. One consonant, /h/, appears only at the beginning of words except in one instance, *fakahaé*, 'all'. The consonants /b/, /d/, /g/, and /n/ may appear in first or medial position but never in final position. All other consonants may appear in first, medial, or final position (Gregorius Keraf 1978: 43–4). There are seven short vowels: /a/, /i/, /u/, /é/, /o/, /e/ and a nasalized *a*, /ã/. Keraf has chosen to deviate from the International Phonetic Alphabet in respect of the two *e*'s. I follow his conventions in all respects, for reasons of consistency, except for the nasalized *a*, where I follow his preference *ã*, rather than the solution he was forced to adopt, *â*, through technical limitations of the press. There are also weakened or silent *e*'s, which Keraf usually indicates as *e*, but, inconsistently, sometimes indicates by simply leaving the vowel out between consonants. I spell the words in full in all cases and indicate the silent *e*'s with *ĕ*, thus *bĕréun* ('friend'), rather than *bréun*. There are also at least six long vowels, the same set except for /é/. The last, i.e. *ē̆*, Keraf says is difficult to prove, but he does nevertheless use it. A long vowel is, following Keraf, indicated by placing a macron over it, as in *ō* (Gregorius Keraf 1978: 29–37). Some verbs, but not all, are conjugated. Verbs may also change the final vowel depending on whether the usage is transitive or intransitive (Gregorius Keraf 1978: 15). Possessive pronouns are attached to and modify the endings of some nouns (Gregorius Keraf 1978: 84–94).

Some adjectives with a final or penultimate *a* change to a nasalized final or penultimate *ã* in unemphasized usage. Those which already end in a nasalized *ã* in emphasized usage, add *ng* to it for unemphasized usage. Others mark the difference by changing the final vowel from *é* to *i*, *a* to *é*, or *a* to *o*. Others use infixed consonants to indicate the difference. The differences for some adjectives are hard to fit into any pattern. Finally, some adjectives undergo no change at all (Gregorius Keraf 1978: 109–11).

Note on the Spelling of Names

I have decided to separate the semantic units of personal, group, and place names except for surnames and the names of villages and towns, thus Bĕliko Lolo is the name of a clan, while Belikololong is a surname derived from this clan name, Futung Lolo (On the Point) is a location, while Lamabakan is a village. Furthermore, I use the conventional, rather than phonetic, spellings of surnames and village names, hence Keraf, rather than Kéraf, and Lamakera, rather than Lāma Kéra. As a happy consequence of these conventions, the spellings of the village name Lamakera distinguishes it visually from that of the clan name Lāma Kéra, although both are to be pronounced the same.

Generally speaking, I have given conventional spellings to Lamaholot names or words when the source or context is outside of Lamalera. The result may be most noticeable in names containing *w/f*. Thus, the market-place is at Wulan Doni, not Fulan Doni in conformity with Lamalera pronunciation, because the people closest to it so pronounce it.

1

The Village

Visitors like the early missionaries have often begun their accounts of Lamalera by describing it as it is approached from the sea. A small inlet lies at the foot of a very large volcano. The long rocky coast is accessible only at the small beach that lies at the inner edge of this inlet (see Plate 2). At the back of the beach stands a semicircle of thatched huts. These sheds house the boats. Behind them may be seen a stone wall about two metres high, providing protection from the sea on the one side and retaining the soil upon which the dwellings stand on the other. The houses stand four or five or six deep behind the boat sheds and restraining wall and are so close to each other that it is difficult to get past them. In the open places and along the sides of the houses are situated platforms for drying fish. The air may be made intolerable from the smell of fish and whale. The buildings in this semicircle comprise the lower half of Lamalera. To the west of the beach a steep and once very difficult climb leads to the upper half of the village (see Plates 3 and 4).

Formerly the upper village was surrounded by a wall of cactus and stones for defence. The difficulty of access to the upper village kept the first missionaries resident in the lower village, where a small hut was built for them and a storehouse which served as a church. Eventually their successors managed to construct a more spacious dwelling in the upper village and a church of sorts. However, lack of manpower in the Jesuit mission and the rigors of existence in Lamalera meant that no missionary settled permanently in the village until 1920 when the 35-year-old German Bernardus Bode of the Divine Word Society took up a residence which was to last until 1951, uninterrupted except for imprisonment by the Dutch during World War II (see Plate 5). Above all, the missionaries complained about the lack of fresh water, the only source being a pair of small tide-covered springs emerging from boulders at the shore below the upper village (Wintjes 1894a: 29; Engbers 1906: 11).

The Different Kinds of Lamalera

Lamalera must be viewed from three perspectives: the historical, the administrative, and the sociological. Historically, Lamalera identifies a location inhabited by descent groups with a common background and way of life. Quite early on, this community divided itself into two hamlets, that which lies higher on the stone plateau to the west, and that which lies lower and to the east behind the boat sheds at the beach. In Lamaholot these two sites are distinguished as

PLATE 2. Lamalera seen from the sea

PLATE 3. Lamalera beach and boat sheds with houses behind, seen from the East

PLATE 4. The lower village, beach and boat sheds seen from the West

PLATE 5. Statue of Father Bernardus Bode erected to
commemorate '100 Years of Religion' in 1986

Téti Lefo (up at the village) and *Lali Fata* (down at the beach).[1] This division
parallels the fact that these two regions are associated with two different 'lords
of the land', and it corresponds to further differences in the location of the
boat sheds along the beach and certain aspects of dividing whales once they
have been caught. Sociologically, it does not strictly mark differences between
descent groups, for sections of the same descent group may be located at either
place, and persons within the same descent-group segment may live in either
part of Lamalera.

Contrasted to the Lamalera identified by history, is the administrative
Lamalera. Today it is divided administratively into two independent government villages or *Desa* called 'Lamalera A' (for Lamalera Atas, Upper Lamalera)
and 'Lamalera B' (for Lamalera Bawah, Lower Lamalera). These two administrative villages approximate *Téti Lefo* and *Lali Fata*, respectively. They go
beyond the bounds of historical Lamalera, however. Lamalera A includes the
ancient mountain hamlet of Lamamanu (Lama Manuk, sometimes pronounced
Lamanu), while Lamalera B takes in the quite separate and fairly distant
hamlets of Ongalere and Nualela.

In addition to the administrative and historical Lamalera, there is also the
sociological one, that collection of villagers who at present derive their livelihood from the sea or whose relatives and ancestors did. The outlines of this
Lamalera correspond roughly with those of the historical Lamalera except that
it also takes in a new settlement called Futung Lolo (i.e. On the Point) located
about a quarter of a mile to the east of Lamalera B. Futung Lolo was founded
in this century by settlers from Lamalera who wished more room. They continue, however, to participate fully in village life and the fishery. For various
purposes the sociological Lamalera may also be taken to include an extended
number of offspring of the village living temporarily or permanently elsewhere
who maintain contact with family and friends in the village and who come and
go with varying degrees of regularity and frequency. Naturally, this group
fades out irregularly into those who were born and who live elsewhere but who
are regarded and who regard themselves in some sense or another still to be
part of the community.

Given these distinctions and divisions, some justification is required for
speaking of Lamalera as a unity. In this book, I intend to follow local usage and
employ 'Lamalera' to refer to the physical location of Lamalera A and B,
including especially Téti Lefo, Lali Fata, and Futung Lolo, but excluding
Lamamanu, Ongalere, and Nualela, to the people who live in this location, and
to the defining features of their history. References to 'the village' are usually
to be interpreted in this sense as well. There will always be a certain ambiguity about adjacent hamlets, particularly Ongalere and Lamamanu, and to a
degree the nearby village of Lewotala. It is not possible to provide a definition
which removes these ambiguities, because the causes of the ambiguities, as will
be seen, are also in part those factors which are constitutive of Lamalera's iden-

tity. Perhaps it is best to regard Lamalera as a focus of interest, rather than a clearly defined entity. In any case, an appeal must be made to the reader's patience and willingness to use context as a guide.

The Upper Village

The site of Lamalera is the broken down south side of a huge volcanic crater. Three hills behind it constitute the east and west lips as well as the central basaltic core of this crater, emerging from the flanks of the Labalekang mountain. The upper village sits on great lava flows which hardened into fantastic shapes when they plunged into the sea. Landward it rises up to the steep shanks of Labalekang. A sharply rising climb leads to the mountain hamlet Lamamanu. A path through fields to the west runs to the villages of Lewotala, Lamabakan, and beyond. A road of layered stone passable only on foot or horse which was built at the orders of the *kakang* in 1938 and 1939 runs east and west directly through the upper village, around a ridge to the east, past the polyclinic, to the steps which lead down to the lower village (see Map 4). There was once a large boulder on the ridge above this road which was used in ceremonies. As late as the 1910s, the lord of the land held a ceremony there when the fishing was bad. The name of this particular boulder has not been remembered. It was toppled to use in the road foundation when the road was built.

Just to the landward of this road in the centre of the site is the great house (clan temple) of the Lefo Tukã clan. In 1911 the *kakang* lived at this spot in a house that was somewhat larger than other dwellings. Near by was a shed where people gathered in the evening and where assemblies were held. Somewhat further along was the village temple (*korké*), called for reasons of history 'brought on the east current' (*olé mau*). In 1911 it served as barracks for travelling Dutch officials (Beckering 1911: 192). Seaward of the road is a small clearing or village plain, *nama*. This clearing is called *Nama Bau Lāngu*, the clearing below the banyan. There used to be a banyan (*bau, Ficus bengalensis*) there, but the head of the Téti Nama Papã section of Bĕliko Lolo clan planted a *budi* tree, which grows there now, to replace it because a *budi* tree's branches are broader, providing better shade, and there is not the problem with the air roots which if not carefully cropped will grow into the ground and turn a single banyan into a forest.[2] Around the square were placed stone seats, *belera*, for the head of all the clans, until the missionary Bode buried them along with other sacred stones in the foundations of his church. They were upright flat stones providing a place to sit and lean one's back on. They also had a religious significance. Each clan used to have one such seat there, on which an elder of the clan would sit when there was an assembly of elders to discuss affairs of the village. Now only one remains, which belongs to Bata Onã. On the east side of this clearing is the great house of Téti Nama Papã section of the clan Bĕliko

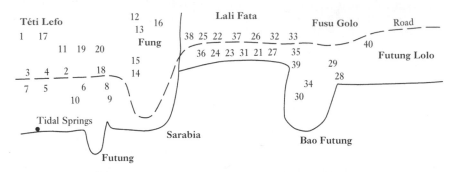

Great Houses of:

1. Tufa Onã	21. Perafi Langu, Lāma Kéra
2. Dasi Langu, Lefo Tukã	22. Musi Langu, Tapo Onã
3. Lima Langu, Lefo Tukã	23. Guna Langu, Tapo Onã
4. Kéda Langu, Lefo Tukã	24. Mana Langu, Tapo Onã
5. Béra Onã, Lefo Tukã	25. Sola Langu, Tapo Onã
6. Téti Nama Papã, Běliko Lolo	26. Kělaké Langu, Bata Onã
7. Lali Nama Papã, Běliko Lolo	27. Kifa Langu, Bata Onã
8. Haga Langu, Tana Kěrofa	28. Jafa Langu, Bata Onã
9. Laba Langu, Tana Kěrofa	29. Ola Langu, Bata Onã
10. Lāma Nudek	30. Kebesa Langu, Sula Onã
11. Ata Kéi	31. Kěloré Langu, Sula Onã
12. Sinu Langu, Léla Onã	32. Miku Langu, Bedi Onã
13. Bělaké Langu, Léla Onã	33. Muri Langu, Bedi Onã
14. Guma Langu, Ebã Onã	34. Kéda Langu, Bata Fo
15. Daé Langu, Ebã Onã	35. Kaja Langu, Bata Fo
16. Sita Langu, Ebã Onã	36. Olé Onã
17. Ata Folo	37. Lāma Nifa
18. Badi Langu, Lāma Kéra	38. Hari Onã
19. Lafa Langu, Lāma Kéra	39. Lefo Léin
20. Sinu Langu, Lāma Kéra	40. Ata Gora
	41. Lango Fujo

MAP 4. Lamalera

Lolo. This structure, which has been rebuilt in stages in the 1970s and 1980s of concrete and commercially purchased teak wood and has a tin roof with gables suggesting the shape of buffalo horns, is called *Balé Olé Mau*. It has therefore the same name as the former village temple, which used to be a separate structure for housing heirlooms of general village significance, but which Téti Nama Papã eventually combined with their *lango bélã* (great house). A *balé* is a meeting house or temple. *Olé mau* means to be swept along by an east current, and the name refers to the events which brought the ancestors to the present site after fleeing the catastrophe which struck them when they lived at Lapan Batan, east of Lembata. Near the steps which at present lead down from the road in front of this great house, there used to be a village sacred stone called the *nuba lefo*, which stood for the whole village and which used to be fed along with the other sacred stones during the annual ceremony marking the beginning of the season of large-scale fishing. *Nuba lefo* was a shiny coloured stone, brought from Lapan Batan.

Seaward of *balé olé mau* are the great houses of Tana Kĕrofa and, below it, that of Lāma Nudek. Immediately to the west of the clearing, just below the road is the house of the Béra Onã section of the Lefo Tukã clan. Near by are the houses of the Lali Nama Papã section of Bĕliko Lolo. The two sections of Bĕliko Lolo take their names from the village clearing, in that the first name means 'East of the Village Square', while the other means 'West of the Village Square'.[3] Lefo Tukã means 'Middle of the Village', which is precisely where their great house is located. Landward of this structure are the houses of Ata Kéi and of the descent group which has claims to being lord of the land for the upper village, Tufa Onã. There is doubtless some significance to the fact that the dwellings of the last group are to the landward and west of the site, for this clan also has members who live in the village of Lewotala, about half an hour's stroll to the west. Landward of the road, on the east side of the site, are the great houses of three sections of the Lāma Kéra clan, Badi Langu, Lafa Langu, and Sina Langu. Beyond them up a ridge on the east are the great house of Ebã Onã and of Léla Onã.

Of course there are many other individual dwellings belonging to these clans sheltering around the great houses. In most cases they are in appearance indistinguishable from the great houses, which are usually just ordinary dwellings. The only real exceptions are the great houses of Bĕliko Lolo (Téti Nama Papã) and Lefo Tukã (Dasi Langu). Immediately to the west may be found the foundations of a former church, now used as a basketball court. Behind it is the graveyard and to the landward the present church. The new church is a very large concrete structure with a shining tin roof which dwarfs all around it. It is prominently visible from miles away. Below the former church stands the elementary school and nursery. To the east and landward from the former church is the dwelling of the missionary. At the back of this compound the carpenter shop may be found. The junior high school stands above the upper village. On Fung, the ridge to the east, is the dwelling of the last *kakang* and that of his son. On either side of the steps of the *kakang*'s house are two cannon, *pésa*. One of these is an ornate Portuguese piece. Neither has ever been fired with a projectile in it. They have only been used to make a noise. They were given by the Raja of Larantuka, Raja Oesi, to Kakang Yosef Raja Muda to use to keep the peace. There had been two more, which have disappeared.[4] Below these houses is an ornate hexagonal wooden hut, which has served as a sort of office for the village government, and a clearing of irregular shape which the *kakang* had the village construct in 1943–4 as a gathering place for governmental purposes. Where an individual dwelling is situated is often a matter of private interest, but for those who know village history, the physical location of especially the great houses is of considerable significance. They serve, as it were, as silent witnesses to the truth of that history.

Further down the ridge, where the road bends around in a horseshoe-shaped curve before descending to the lower village, the village government has constructed a *balai desa*, that is a simple structure which serves as a government office, just above the road. Opposite, seaward, is the polyclinic which was erected in the 1950s on a site inhabited by spirits or witches. It was picked out by a German woman doctor on the grounds that being on a point, the wind would blow the germs to sea on either side. Only one person has died there, a Muslim woman from Labala, buried below near the sea. People, however, have been reluctant to go to the polyclinic in the past because of the witches, but this worry does not now seem to inhibit many.

At the shore below the upper village is a point of raw lava extending into the sea called *Futung* (point) and also known by one of its uses as *Lodo Ikã*, To Unload Fish. Small boats of people who live in the upper village returning from fishing trips often unload here because it is closer than the beach. On the rocky shore to the east of the village are the two small springs which used to be the sole source of fresh water for both halves of the village, the higher and the lower spring, *Fai Bĕlolo* and *Fai Léré*. These springs are only exposed at low tide and do not produce a very great volume of water, which in any case is very brackish. The village owes *Fai Bĕlolo* to the ancestor of the clan Ebã Onã, who was brought to Lamalera on the back of a whale. When the whale stopped at the shore to let him land, the ancestor dropped a bamboo containing water, which shattered, leaving the spring behind.

The poor water supply was a daunting factor for the first missionaries. Wintjes (1894a: 32) described the water as being very bad and usable by Europeans only for washing and bathing. It made the missionaries sick. The mission smith, brother van Hoek, went to work with some boys from Larantuka in an effort to dig a proper well. Two attempts failed, and they gave up on the third when once again at a depth of four or five metres they came upon huge stones which could only have been moved with dynamite (Wintjes 1895: 61). Nowadays running water is brought to the two halves of the village through water pipes from an excellent spring above Lewotala. There is a cistern and an open stand for collecting water in both parts of the village. Twice a day the water is turned on so that women and girls can collect it in buckets and bamboos. The water from these pipes, organized by the mission and financed by German sources, has been exceptionally beneficial for village health and well-being. However, the pipes are also a cause of friction between Lewotala and Lamalera, and a constant frustration for the missionary who has to keep after the village authorities to repair damage, often the result of human malice or carelessness, which periodically dries up the pipes and threatens to ruin the cisterns. In the 1950s before these pipes arrived, the *kakang* organized a system of piping water from the spring by the use of several miles of split lontar palm trunks, but of course this arrangement was even more prone to damage.

To the west of the village at the shore are two small caves, called *Betu Liang* (Betu's Cave). Villagers once stored lumber there for building boats. In these and other caves, people hid valuables during the Japanese occupation. Near by, where there are lontar trees for tapping, there are the remains of stone walls. These were once built to protect the people tapping from attack by Lewotala. Cactus was planted on top. There were several rows of such walls circling the village. The wall around the lontar palms was a kind of forward line of defence. Lewotala was the principal threat. When Beckering pacified the island in 1910 Lamalera was not palisaded as were Labala and the mountain villages above it (Beckering 1911: 190, 192). Nevertheless the upper village was once surrounded by this wall of cactus, prickly pear, of which there are still remnants. The cactus was a nuisance until a missionary brought in chemicals to kill it off in the 1950s. Oddly, the villagers were unaware that the fruit is edible until I showed them. Through this wall was an opening to the south-west, which at one time was blocked by a village gate. A member of the Lali Nama Papā section of the Běliko Lolo clan named Solé ordered it to be closed every day at sunset. People from Lewotala could not come through after that and everyone had to be in the village by then. This entrance was called Solé's gate, *Solé Bafalofě*.

There is a path just to the east of the great house of Lefo Tukā, past which the torrents run during the rainy season. It eventually leads to a ravine near the point (*Futung*) called *Anu Fanga* which floods with run-off water. Near by is the site of a sacred stone called *Nuba Siola*. The path must not be blocked up or closed, apparently because this flooding is the meeting (sexual union) of a shark of the variety *bungkari* with *Nuba Siola*. Bode buried *Nuba Siola* along with the other stones in the church foundations, but apparently the elders hid *Nuba Lefo*, and its present whereabouts is unknown. He replaced *Nuba Siola* with a sculpture, *Nuba Lefo* with a cross, neither any longer there. The location of the graveyard and the new church as well as the mission residence is an area that used to be sacred and of which villagers were afraid. The location of the graveyard is *Kěrongo Arakian* (Arakian's thicket). The new church is at *Fatu Boli Ama* (Boli Ama's Stone).

Connecting the upper village to the lower village to the east is a set of fairly comfortable stone steps descending a steep drop. These steps were constructed in 1917 when the Resident of Timor visited the village and found that he could not get up to the upper village. He then sent a workman from Pohon Sirih, Larantuka, together with dynamite and other materials to build a proper way up. The name of the location of these steps is *Géripé*, derived, at least in local folk etymology, from *géri*, to climb, and *pé*, to grab, since before the steps were built people going up had to grab hold of a rock to get past a large over-hanging projecting boulder. This particular obstruction was called *Belugus* from *lugu*, to stoop, because people had to bend down to get under it. If they were carrying anything on their heads, they had to take it off. Before the steps were built, this difficult entrance was part of the village defences. Wintjes (1894*a*: 32) warned his readers that in an eternity they would never be able to climb it, but if they succeeded they would never get down again, or would do so much too quickly. Hoeberechts (1913: 151) also wrote of the fright his readers would have if they tried.

The Lower Village

Like the upper village, the lower village was once surrounded by cactus walls, even at the beach. Every once in a while the waves uncover and then recover the base of a post well toward the sea which might have been a post for a former boat shed. Anciently the sheds were apparently much more forward. Where they are now located supposedly *kĕroko* trees (*Calotropis gigantea*) grew. Estimates have been made locally that the beach recedes 1 cm. per year. A road runs through the lower village and out to the east. It is just possible to ride a motor cycle into the lower village, as the male nurse used to do, but this is the only motorized land transportation which can get within a few miles of the village, and this road is essentially confined to foot and very occasionally horse traffic. At present villagers seem to prefer keeping things that way. Midway through the lower village there is a small clearing surrounded by dwellings, including the great houses of various descent-group segments.

The several entrances to the lower village are also called rather grandly village gates, *bafalofé*, although at present most of them are just paths from the beach and none is blocked by a gate. In the past when a clan great house was built, they would hold a ceremony in which, among other things, a large tray of rice would be taken to four doors of the village. Rice would be dropped on the ground at each and spread along the ground as they walked from door to door. The first gate visited was the door *Bafalofé Bélã*, the great gate, which is to the east and is the most exposed entrance to the lower village. The second was *Bafalofé Leföléin*, a beach access near a house belonging to the small descent group Lefo Léin, and the third was at *Bafalofé Méi Larã*. This name translates as the 'Gate of the Path of Blood'. The entrance in question is a modest beach access, the main path from the beach to the central clearing. The explanation for the gruesome name is that in the past if they killed someone from, for example, Labala with whom they used to be at war, he could not be brought into the village through the *Bafalofé Bélã*, to the east, but had to be brought around to this third one. The fourth door was the beach path leading to the centre of the beach at *Ikã Kotã* (Fish Heads) where the St Peter chapel now stands, replacing a small hut marking the border between the territories of the two lords of the land (see Plate 6).

PLATE 6. St Peter Chapel at *Ikã Kotã* (Fish Heads) marking the centre of the beach

Kifan, the ancestor of a man whose house is adjacent to the path of blood, once killed a man from Lewuka, who had been sitting at the beach. They began joking and he made a jocular remark about their boat, *Sili Tënã*. Kifan killed him and then hung him from the tree in the central clearing, hooking him through the eye. Later they took his body down to the beach via *Bafalofë Méi Larã* to be thrown away at sea. I do not know if this incident was behind the report that in the past if the village was at war with others and managed to kill someone, they would take the body down this entrance (presumably after having first taken it into the village) to be thrown away at sea.

Immediately to the east of the beach is a point of raised coral sticking into the sea called *Bao Futung*. The village has grown east of this point, and eventually has expanded into the new site at Futung Lolo. The short stretch of dark sand beach is why Lamalera is situated where it is.[5] It is the only such break in the rocky shoreline for miles on either side. Since there is no serviceable anchorage there, villagers only use boats which may be brought to shore. The boat sheds and the sand around them is a social area where people gather and work, taking advantage of the shade provided by the palm-leaf roofs of the sheds. When large animals, such as whales or manta ray, are landed, great crowds may assemble there, where the men carve up the meat and women carry it off in pans or turtle shells balanced on their heads. Passenger boats pick up and land passengers there, and it can become a bustling place of departures and returns. The sea is not only a source of livelihood and a surface over which transportation travels, it is also a cleanser, a dumping place for rubbish, filth, excrement, and dead animals. There are sea spirits, just as there are land spirits, and those at the shore on the boundary between the sea and the land are particularly troublesome.

A characteristic sight is that of many children playing in the surf. They stand on small logs and support themselves on poles, while the surf lifts the logs a few inches up the beach. Another game is to throw the logs down the beach during high tide and to spear them with the poles as the tide brings them up the beach. Among the characteristic sounds of Lamalera are the constant wash of the waves, which of course become thunderous during the heavy storms of the rainy season, but are still quite loud when conditions are right during the dry season. The day is filled with the sounds of children crying, roosters crowing pointlessly, dogs fighting, and pigs squealing. All of this goes on constantly. Of smells, the acrid scent of whale meat is most characteristic. Although I never found it either very bad or especially strong, except on the beach when an animal is being cut up, other outsiders, including those from Lamakera, typically do.

Administrative Structure

As official government *desa*, Lamalera A and B each has its own village government, representing the bottom rung of national governmental bureaucratic structure. Village government consists in a village head (*kepala desa*), secretary (*secretaris*), *mandor* or herald, and three *pamong* or assistants to the village head. Of the *pamong*, one each is contributed by Lamamanu, Ongalere, and Nualela. Each village is divided into wards or mutual assistance associations, called by the Bahasa Indonesia name *rukun tetangga* (RT), household associations, and family associations, *rukun keluarga* (RK). These RT and RK were set up by order of the Bupati or regent. The head of the RT organizes communal work such as help in erecting a building. The house owner contacts the head of the RT, who then orders its members to help. The owner provides food and materials, but labour otherwise is unpaid; even the carpenter goes without wages. The head of the RK is supposed to help maintain domestic tranquillity. If there is some small disagreement in a family or between neighbours it may be taken to him first, before (if unsettled) going up to the *pamong*, and perhaps as far as the village head. There are six RT in Lamalera A, plus a further three in Lamamanu. There are three RK in Lamalera A, plus another one in Lamamanu. There are nine RT in Lamalera B, plus another at Ongalere and another at Nualela, making eleven in all. There are three RK in Lamalera B, plus another at Nualela, for a total of four.

Recent Historical Background

In 1909 the Kakang of Lamalera Dasi Dasi, sometimes known as Yosef Raja Muda, died (Beckering 1911: 200). He had been given the title of Raja Muda, a sort of second raja, by Lorenzo Oesi Vieira Godinho, who on 14 September 1887 had succeeded as Raja of Larantuka. Lorenzo, or Raja Oesi (Usi), as he was known locally, was described by the Resident of Kupang at the time as a pet of the mission, more interested in getting his subjects to church regularly, than in government (Villeneuve 1888). Lorenzo had a turbulent reign, which ended 1 July 1904 when, at least in local interpretation, as a consequence of executing the head of Pamakayu, Solor, by having him tied to a chair and sunk at sea, he was arrested by the Resident in Larantuka and later imprisoned in Yogyakarta, Java, where he died in 1910 (Eerde 1923). Before the Dutch arrived on Lembata in the same year, Dasi Dasi led a successful war in defence of the mountain village Puor. The offending villages were plundered and burnt, and many of the inhabitants were killed. Many children were captured and taken to Lamalera as slaves.[6] Dasi Dasi was succeeded by his son Mikael Molan or Molan Dasi, a former student in the mission school. Misunderstanding local history, Beckering divided Lamalera district into two kakangships in 1910, Lamalera and Nualela. The Dutch set this mistake right in 1911 when they recognized Mikael Molan as head of the district. They also ordered the captive children returned to their villages.

Munro (1915: 5) described Mikael Molan as lacking energy, being almost lazy. In 1912 the Dutch held him prisoner in Ende, Flores, for repeatedly failing to carry out orders. At Ende he made known his desire to give up his post as *kakang*. The reason for his being sent to Ende, as memory in the village has it, was that Mikael Molan sent a Dutch soldier to the village of Lewotala to get him palm wine. The soldier returned without the palm wine, but with a rifle, which he had confiscated. The Dutch were, after all, attempting to disarm the population. Mikael Molan got angry, and the soldier reported the incident to his superior. At Ende Mikael Molan was placed in charge of guarding a policeman's wife. One day another policeman came and molested the woman. Mikael Molan alerted the husband. With this aid, the culprit was captured, and the Dutch returned Mikael Molan to Lamalera, but not to office. However, according to Munro, the only suitable replacement was his nephew Johannis Mura, who did not want to accept the office, since to do so would be a violation of custom. So long as the *kakang* was alive he should remain in office. Mikael Molan therefore remained in office, but, without officially holding the post, Johannis Mura exercised real power in the district. He gave orders, and his authority was much greater than that of Mikael Molan. Mikael Molan was satisfied with this arrangement and left the burden of carrying out government orders to his nephew. Perhaps it was because of the tension inherent in this arrangement that Johannis Mura chose to live in a house at the beach, rather than in the centre of the upper village where other *kakang* had their residences. Mikael Molan's term officially came to an end in 1917, when Johannis Mura replaced him. Johannis Mura served until 1934. He was replaced by Petrus Bau, Mikael Molan's son, who assumed office in 1935 and held it until 1962.

Prior to becoming *kakang*, Petrus Bau served as a governmental clerk in Hadakewa, the centre of Dutch administration on the north coast of Lembata from 1929 until 1934. During that period he travelled with Dutch officials all over Lembata, Adonara, and East Flores. On East Flores he had the opportunity to ride in the Raja of Larantuka's Ford, the first automobile in the area. Petrus Bau was 57 years old when he was replaced by his son Tomas Kifan, who served during a transition period for five years until 1967, when the post was abolished by the Indonesian government.

Successive *kakang* were required to travel through the villages of their district three months in the year, leaving them only five days a month at home. According to Hens, in 1916 the Kakang of Lamalera was paid Dutch Fl. 25 per month (Hens 1916: 136). Petrus Bau remembered having been paid only Rp. 24 per month, which meant that he needed another source of income, which he derived from a coconut plantation at Wulan Doni. Hangelbroek, who was Controleur in Larantuka in 1937–8, later wrote that he did not have the impression that the district heads had very great authority in their regions or that they could expect services and tribute from the inhabitants. He confirmed that they received only a small salary from the regency treasury (Hangelbroek 1977: 146–7). In 1931 the Kakang of Lamalera had a nominal salary of Dutch East Indies Fl. 40 per month, but such officers had to wait on their salaries because there was not enough money in the treasury, due to poor tax-collecting (Seegeler 1931: 89). The coconut plantation in question was located near the boundary between the districts of Lamalera and Labala. In 1928, during the reign of Petrus Bau's predecessor, the plantation, which had previously been a school plantation, became the occasion for a small war between Labala and Lamalera (Bintang Timoer 1928*b*).

In the traditional scheme of Larantuka government, the head or Kakang of Lewoleba held more prestige than the Kakang of Lamalera. However, the Kakang of Lewoleba was killed at the village Lewo Lera on 25 September 1914, when villagers attacked a Dutch patrol which he was accompanying (Java-Post 1914: 734–5; Munro 1915: 7; Koloniaal Verslag 1915: 44–5). Since his legal successor Atala was then a minor, and no one else who was acceptable existed, the Dutch turned to Lamalera and chose a stepbrother of Mikael Molan, Laurensus Koli Sinu, to serve as acting Kakang of Lewoleba. From this step probably derives the origin of the community of families with Lamalera descent who now live in Lewoleba.

At the time of district reorganization in the 1960s, the former districts of Lamalera and Kawela at the western end of Lembata were consolidated into a new *kecamatan* (subdistrict) called by the romantic name Nagawutung (Dragon Point), after the rugged peninsula at the extreme south-west tip of the island. The district head, *camat*, is appointed by the government and normally comes from outside. The administrative offices of the subdistrict was located at a new town called Loang on the north-west coast. The boundaries of the Kecamatan Nagawutung no longer reflect the division between the former realms of Larantuka and Adonara, nor the traditional division between Demon and Paji. There is no direct passenger communication between Lamalera and Loang. The only way to get to Loang is by a day's walk, or by travelling on a passenger boat to Lewoleba on the north coast and then back west to Loang. By this development, Lamalera became even more remote and isolated than it had been made by the Dutch. Today Lamalera is not just cut off physically, it has also lost its political influence in the hinterland.

Communications

Beckering observed that anchorage in front of Labala is poor because of the rough surf. For the same reason Engbers (1906: 12) said that steamboats could not be used to reach Lamalera. Traffic in and out of these coastal locations was entirely by means of boats small enough to be pulled ashore. The possibility of reaching Lamalera from the north by cutting across the island had not yet been explored by 1906, although even then there was a network of footpaths leading from village to village across the island. In the 1930s van den Windt (1936: 77) commented on the extraordinary difficulty of working on Lembata. In particular the south was completely mountainous and then lacked roads. He described travel over the trails, sometimes impassable even to horses, as requiring constant jumping from boulder to boulder. At that time there was a good road along the north coast, suitable for motor cycles, which was begun in 1920 and completed in 1935. However, since the bridges could not be maintained, there were no automobiles. Mountain farmers cut down trees and burned off the hill sides causing flash floods which wiped out the bridges. In the 1960s this road was mostly disused, but it now carries motorized traffic and has been blacktopped with support from the World Bank. Nevertheless in the 1930s the north was still very thinly populated. It was the south which was most heavily settled, and villages were never separated by more than an hour's walk.

A telephone link from Ende, via Maumere, to Larantuka, Flores, was started in 1913 and completed in 1914 (Koloniaal Verslag 1913: 34; 1914: 30). By 1931 there was a telephone for official use in Lewoleba, Wai Jaran, Hadakewa, and Kalikur on the north coast of Lembata and in Lamalera and Labala on the south. It was possible to telephone from Labuan Bajo, Flores, through to Labala (Bintang Timoer 1931: 96; Hagenaar 1934: 3). This arrangement did not long survive World War II. In 1960 the Indonesian government gave a telephone system to Lamalera, but people ruined it by cutting down the wires. During the aftermath of the tidal wave at Waiteba and Sarapuka in July 1979, when the government commandeered local shipping for disaster relief for a week, it was impossible to get any messages out of the village, except by walking them out. By 1987 the government had supplied the head of Lamalera A with a shortwave telephone.

For many years the only electricity in Lamalera was from a small generator which supplied electricity to the missionary's residence and to a few adjacent houses in the upper village. By 1982 both Lamahala and Waiwerang, Adonara, had been electrified. At night they looked quite bustling when seen from the sea. Lamakera, Solor, had a generator supplying fifty houses, but at the time it was broken down. There was excitement in Lamalera in 1982 because of a rumoured government plan to bring electricity to Balaurin on the north coast and to Lamalera. There was to have been a head tax of Rp. 500 per family. Nothing came of this plan. By 1987 a privately operated generator in Lamalera B supplied electricity for a single dim neon bulb per house to several houses in Lamalera B. The generator operated for a fixed period in the evening and cost Rp. 1,000 per month. However, the fixtures had no switches, so the bulbs could not be turned off. Around 1980 the government gave each of the halves of Lamalera a television and kerosene-powered generator. They worked very well, villagers said, until the kerosene ran out. Privately owned radios were common and provided a source of information about external news. Especially popular was a late afternoon broadcast from Kupang of personal messages sent in by people living far from home. More than once, the first news of a death or personal tragedy arrived in the village by this means.

Since 1910 Lembata has experienced the same major political upheavals that have influenced the rest of Indonesia. Following consolidation of Dutch military and government control, there were the world influenza epidemic of 1918 which cost many lives in Lamalera, the world economic depression of the 1930s which may have had little effect locally, the Japanese invasion in 1942 and military control of the island until 1945, the attempt of the Dutch to return and establish a federation of puppet states, the successful Indonesian revolution, and the violent coup of 1965 and its aftermaths.

Reminiscing, one villager spoke of the Dutch period, which he did not remember directly. Things were cheap then. A tin (twenty litres) of unhusked rice was 25 cents (Dutch), a cloth (*lipa*) 5 cents, an elephant tusk perhaps a ringgit (2½ rupiah). Few people had money. A family that stored a ringgit was rich. The boats would go to Lobetobi to fish and have to bring their catch back in two boats. But before the boats reached the shore, the gong would sound calling the boatmen to come and pay their tax. These trips made it possible for some in the village to save up some wealth.

In those days, only a few children were given education. They were selected by the government. Before daybreak the herald would go through the village telling individual children to get ready to leave for Larantuka the next morning to start school. Only a few were sent. There were no motor boats. The village boats would have to take them. Dutch government was strict, but it brought changes. The Japanese were even more firm. Everyone had to have a field. Anyone who did not obey was beaten with green bamboo until he passed out. Then he was woken up and told to go to work. All along the sides of the road people raised cassava. Pigs of course were penned (which they are not today, despite repeated government orders to do so). If a pig ran loose, the Japanese killed it and took it for their own.

Religion

Looking back, it may seem strange that the earliest mission interest focused on the fairly inaccessible south coast village of Lamalera. Relative population density was not at first a consideration. Both Lewoleba and Lamalera owed allegiance to the Catholic Raja of Larantuka, which had been an ancient locus of the religion from the sixteenth century.[7] Naturally Larantuka was also the principal base of the late nineteenth-century mission. With its fine harbour, Lewoleba might have appeared the natural staging-post for the mission on Lembata, but its villages were inaccessibly located in the mountains and the present site of Lewoleba was then uninhabited, which might have made Lewoleba less appealing to the undermanned Jesuit mission. Even in 1913 there was little there except a few houses and the carpenter's shed of the pearl fisher- man Captain Kock (Hoeberechts 1913: 160).[8] An attraction of Lamalera was that the villagers were seamen with their own boats who periodically visited Larantuka and at one time also Timor. Mission attention would have been drawn to Lamalera when in October 1883 one of its boats (*Sili Téná*) carrying tribute to the Raja of Larantuka was attacked in the Solor Strait and eleven of its occupants killed by people from the Muslim village Lamakera—a village which in the sixteenth century had been Catholic (Hagestein 1883).

The Dutch deposed Raja Bai Palembang of Lamakera and his lieutenant or *temukung* Melang from office in January 1884 and exiled them to Kediri and Malang, Java, respectively. In the same year missionaries announced their intention to extend their activities to Lamalera (Greve 1884). In 1886 two mis- sionaries accompanied by the Crown prince of Larantuka made their first visit to Lamalera, and the events followed which were described above. After World War I, the new Divine Word Society replaced the Jesuits and quickly expanded in numbers and activities.[9] Bernardus Bode, who had been a missionary in Togo, Africa, where the English made him a prisoner of war, arrived in Lamalera in 1920, where he was to be permanently stationed. There were then already three hundred adults and four hundred children who were Christians. Within three years Bode expanded the number of Christians on the island to one thousand two hundred. He also expanded his activities to include other villages on the south of the island. By 1925 Bode claimed only a single 'heathen' remained in the village (Bode 1925: 113). The mission erected a new house for the missionary and a large church in 1920.

The first building for religious services was a bamboo construction in the lower village which soon had to be dismantled. For a time thereafter a storehouse, which had previously served as a Chinese store, was pressed into service. From 1915 until 1920 services were held in a school building in the upper village. In 1920 craftsmen from the mission station at Larantuka, Flores, erected a church with walls made of earth mixed with lime. This structure, however, proved unsound, and in 1928 Bode announced plans to build another. The former *kakang* Mikael Molan donated an elephant tusk belonging to his clan and worth 700 to 800 rupiah to cover a large part of the costs of the new building (Bintang Timoer 1928*a*: 282). In 1931 this building was struck by a typhoon, causing the walls to lean and forcing its demolition. It was pulled down in 1932 (Bintang Timoer 1932: 208). The villagers erected a more substantial structure with cement walls and a tin roof, which was still in use when I first visited the village in 1971. In 1963 they commenced work on a much larger church, which was consecrated in 1975, the older church then being torn down (Alex Beding 1986*a*: 42–3).

Bode built chapels in various parts of the village, buried the ancestral skulls, and dug up the holy stones, *nuba nara*, which he buried in the foundations of his new church. These activities provoked opposition. Villagers claim that the leading men insisted the fish would flee, if Bode moved the stones. Apparently threats were made against his life. Fortunately for him on the first day after the stones were moved every boat caught something. Bode wrote (1925: 130) that some of his converts continued to make offerings on the stones when they were unsuccessful in fishing. To provide an alternative, Bode held a mass at the beach and solemnly blessed a boat. However, the boat then failed to catch anything for the next four days, and the native priests (three men who had been among the children baptized in the 1880s) renewed their efforts to get the villagers to return to their older form of worship. Thereafter the boats spent two months at Lewotobi, Flores, and returned heavily laden with fish. Bode announced in church that from then on anyone who was guilty of idolatry or heathenish superstitions would no longer be allowed to participate in the Holy Sacraments. He called all men in the church to the altar and made them swear to give up all heathenry. Without exception, they did so. The catch that year was especially good, which made an impression on the villagers. The fifty to seventy non-Christians in the village, including old men, allowed themselves to be converted. By 1923 two of the three native priests had converted. Bode brought an end to blood offerings and got the women to wear blouses. In 1926 he received a chaplain as assistant. In the same year the second mission station was opened at Lewoleba. According to Gregorius Keraf (1978: 2), religious teaching on Lembata in the early years was carried on in the dialect of Lamaholot spoken in Lamalera. Sermons were preached in this language throughout Lembata. In 1937 a collection of religious texts was put together in a book called *Soedoe Hormat* used in all the churches of the island. This book was also composed in the Lamalera dialect. For some decades, therefore, this dialect enjoyed the status of being the official language of religion, until it was supplanted by Malay and modern Indonesian.

In the intervening years circumstances have changed greatly. Schooling and mission activities in the Flores region expanded steadily prior to World War II, answered by a somewhat weaker response from Islam. The 1980 census does not even allow declaration of religious persuasion other than Muslim, Catholic, other Christians, Hindu, or Buddhist. The discrepancy of nearly 3,700 (nearly all in Ilé Apé and Kédang on Lembata) between the total population of the East Flores Regency and the total declaring religious allegiance should not be regarded as a true indicator of the strength of traditional orientations. Around Lamalera, even native priests who perform essentially pagan ceremonies are at least nominally Catholic and do attend church. Nevertheless in 1980 22 per cent of the island's population was reported as Muslim, 73 per cent as Catholic, less than one per cent as Protestant, while 4 per cent were undeclared, which means implicitly acknowledged as traditionalists or 'pagans'. Lamalera is entirely Catholic. In 1986 it celebrated '100 Years of Religion', for which occasion many hundreds of outsiders travelled to the village. For this anniversary Alex Beding prepared a pamphlet (Alex Beding 1986b), complete with tables and photographs, setting out the history of the Catholic Church on Lembata.

2

Disaster, Migration, Foundation, and History

Lamalera means 'sun plate', a definition I have heard hotly defended when someone was so rash as to suggest that it actually means a plate made from the leaves of the *lera* tree. The leaves of this tree allegedly are small and of no consequence, whereas the distinguished history of the people of Lamalera makes them worthy to live in a village named for the sun or to be, as Wintjes (1895: 57) dubbed them, children of the sun. Difficulties with interpreting this name begin with the fact that *lāma* has two highly relevant, but contrasting meanings. The first of these is place, region, or community. This meaning seems to be the active one in the name of the Lamaholot language, *nuã lamaholot*. Gregorius Keraf (1978: 7) suggest that *holot* in this name is the word which means 'to stick together'. The other meaning of *lāma* is plate.

With one meaning or the other the word is used in the names of many villages, Lamahala, Lamalere, Lamakera, Lamabakan, Lamadua, and so on. A species of tree is called *hāla*, and some have told me that Lamahala means a plate made from the leaves of this tree. I do not know what the people of Lamahala say about the matter, however, although Leemker (1893: 442) derives the name from *hala*, meaning not, and interprets it as meaning no divisions. Although Leemker says that the meaning of Lamakera is a division from the shoots of the cabbage tree (*mōtong, Moringa oleifera* Lam.), *lāma kéra* are plates or food containers made from the leaves of the lontar palm, and the people of both Lamalera and Lamakera say that Lamakera refers to these plates. Lamakera legend about the founding of that village says that the ancestors were brought to the site by being pulled behind a baleen whale. They then purchased land at the shore and gave a feast for the indigenous population whom they served with food in such plates. I have often been served myself with such plates at feasts in Lamalera. Characteristically Leemker has it that Lamalera means sun division.

It may be suspected that folk etymology plays a role in many or all of these interpretations of Lamaholot toponyms. According to the preferred interpretation in Lamalera, the proper name of the village should be Lefohajo, after the ancestral village on Lapan Batan, but the founder of the village, Korohama, chose to name it Lamalera after an heirloom he brought with him on the flight from a disaster which struck the homeland. This heirloom, the Sun Plate, was said to be in the possession of the leading elder of Běliko Lolo clan together with other clan treasures, but I was not shown it on my first three visits to the village on the threadbare excuse that the only key to the trunk it was kept in

PLATE 7. Sun Plate, *Lāma Lera*

was in Larantuka. However, in 1987 I was allowed to see and photograph it (see Plate 7). It is a bowl with a red gold glaze, which looks to be of recent manufacture. The nuances of the village name relate to the fact that the Lamaholot for God is *Lera Fūla*, Sun Moon. A sun plate therefore is an heirloom of sacred significance.

A Migration Charter and the Discovery of a New Home

The clans of Lamalera, like those of so many other Lamaholot-speaking villages, may be divided into those whose ancestors migrated to the village following a natural disaster at Keroko Pukan or Lapan Batan to the east of Lembata, those whose ancestors emerged on Lembata itself, and a residual category of clans whose ancestors came to Lamalera from elsewhere at different times in the past. Obviously, clans of this last group have individual histories which stand by themselves. However, the legend which serves as what Malinowski (1926: 29) called the charter myth for much of the village relates the flight of a group from Lapan Batan.

This legend resembles Trobriand myths in which according to Malinowski (1926: 44–5) 'the very foundation of such mythology is flagrantly violated'.

This violation always takes place when the local claims of an autochthonous clan, i.e. a clan which has emerged on the spot, are overridden by an immigrant clan. Then a conflict of principles is created, for obviously the principle that land and authority belong to those who are literally born out of it does not leave room for any newcomers. On the other hand, members of a subclan of high rank who choose to settle down in a new locality cannot very well be resisted by the autochthons. . . . The result is that there come into existence a special class of mythological stories which justify and account for the anomalous state of affairs.

He also comments (1926: 57–8) that myths serve to cover certain inconsistencies created by historical events, rather than to record these events exactly and that myths cannot be sober history, since they are always made *ad hoc* to glorify a certain group, or to justify an anomalous status.

The anomalous status of the core clans of Lamalera lies in precisely this claim to rank coupled with dependency on autochthonous peoples for land.[1] The central legend does glorify and justify to an extent the leading clans, although there are references to humiliations. Above all it accounts for the relative positions of various village groups. It also belongs to a widely spread cycle of migration legends, about which Vatter (1932: 71) wrote that 'despite their mythological garb and many purely fairy tale features, the stories . . . nevertheless almost always reveal an historical core'.

History begins in Luwuk-Bélu, which is generally placed on Sulawesi (possibly Luwuk facing the Peleng Strait and overlooking the Banggai Archipelago on the eastern arm of Sulawesi, rather than the former Bugis state on the coast of central Sulawesi at the top of the Bay of Bone), although the pairing may combine both Luwuk and the Belu or Tetun regions of Timor (Andaya 1981: map 3; van Fraassen 1991). Upon leaving Luwuk the ancestors sailed east to Ambon and Seran and then down through the south Moluccas back west until they reached Lapan and Batan (in Lamalera pronunciation Lepã-Batã), which today survive as two tiny islands in the strait between Lembata and Pantar.[2] The stopping places after Luwuk-Bélu were Sérã-Gorã (the islands of Seram and Goram), Abo-Muã (Ambon and Moa), Fato Bélã (the Watu Bela Archipelago), Kĕroko Tafa-Tĕria Géré (where the Kĕroko tree (*Calotropis gigantea*) grows and the Tĕria (a kind of wild gourd) rises), and finally Lepã-Batã (Lapan and Batan between Lembata and Pantar).

Bataona (n.d.) identifies Muã as the Moa Archipelago. Perhaps he means the Leti Archipelago just east of Timor, the largest island of which is Moa. It could be, as Bataona speculates, that Bélu is a geographical name near Luwuk, which someone with an intimate familiarity with the area could identify. By the same token, Moa might be a toponym appropriate to the Ambon surroundings. However, I think that the opposite interpretation cannot be ruled out, namely that the paired names do not refer to adjacent locations and that Belu might well refer to Timor and Muã to the island of Moa (see van Fraassen 1976: 296 and Dietrich 1984: 320).

A possible significance of the itinerary of islands touched at before arriving at Lepã-Batã is that it retraces the eastern part of the old trade route between the Moluccas and Spice Islands in the east and Java in the west (see Cortesão 1944: lxxxiii, n. 1).

As for Kĕroko Tafa-Tĕria Géré, my sources have it as a stop-off before Lapan Batan, but there are reasons to interpret both as in general the same place. Many clans on the various islands of the Lamaholot language area have a tradition of coming from Keroko Pukan, and often these accounts refer to a disaster involving a flood. A particularly relevant version from Pamakayu, Solor, is given in Arndt (1940: 216–18). When asked where Keroko Pukan was located, people of these clans always answered to the east, beyond Lomblem (Lembata), which is certainly compatible with an identification with Lapan Batan. Many people of the area identify Keroko Pukan with Lapan Batan and place it to the east of Lembata (Vatter 1932: 71; Arndt 1938: 24; Leyn 1979: 12, 20). For example, the clan Hayong in Menanga, Solor, derives from Lapan and Batan, 'also called Keroko Pukan Kemahan Niron' (Leyn 1979: 34). Vatter wrote (1932: 9–10, 71) that he was able to establish with certainty that Keroko Pukan was identical with Lapan Batan. Further conviction as to the identity of Keroko Pukan with Lapan Batan is added by the knowledge that in 1907 the Kakang of Lamalera (Yosef Rajamuda) told Couvreur that he descended from emigrants from Keroko Pukan who struck up friendship with the inhabitants of Lembata and received their permission to settle (Couvreur 1907).

Also common to groups that claim to have come from Lapan Batan is an association with the toponym Lewo Hayon, sometimes abbreviated as Lohayon. Generally the legends of such groups relate difficulties in their journeys as they failed to be received with hospitality at places where they wished to come ashore, until finally they were accepted in their present location. Acceptance also often meant having their own claims to rank recognized. The earliest mention of this tradition which I have come across concerns the 'Second' Raja of Larantuka, Flores, who lives in the Larantuka ward called Lohayon and descends from refugees from Keroko Pukan who were given the position of 'Second' Raja by the ancestors of the Raja of Larantuka (Heynen 1876: 73, 77–8; Couvreur 1907; Seegeler 1931: 80; Dietrich 1984: 321). Arndt (1940: 56, 58, 59, 81–3, 85, 87, 163, 167–8) mentions such groups in eastern Flores and Adonara. In Pamakayo, Solor, the clan Lewo Hayong came from Keroko Puken (Arndt 1940: 216–18). The village of Lohayong, Solor, was the site of a Portuguese/Dutch fort which played a central role in local politics from the mid-sixteenth century (Boxer 1947; R. H. Barnes 1987). Although its present clans appear to have lost the Keroko Pukan tradition (being later comers from the Moluccas), the tradition lives on in the closely linked neighbouring village of Menanga (Leyn 1979: 28–9, 34; Dietrich 1984: 320, 324 n. 13).

On Lepã-Batã an old, childless woman found an eel when gathering shellfish at the shore which she brought home and raised until it was grown, whereupon it disappeared into a hole in a tree in the forest. Every day when the adults went to work, the eel came out and ate a child. Eventually the adults discovered the eel and killed it by sticking a red-hot iron rod into the hole. When this happened sea water began to rise, inundating the village. Those who survived fled. Most of the refugees came west in the boat named *Kebako Pukã* (which also carried the unfinished boat named *Bui Pukã*)[3] until they reached Kédang on the eastern end of Lembata, where they went ashore and stayed briefly. The old woman who had caused the disaster followed on land.

The refugees sailed further along the south coast of Lembata, while the old woman followed along the shore crying. They did not stop for her because they were angry (Gregorius Keraf 1978: 236–7).[4] When they came to the peninsula marked on some modern maps as Bela Galeh, but locally referred to as Gafé Futuk, Lefo Kumé, or Nor Futu, the currents were too strong, so they threw overboard a golden bench named *Kuda Belaung* (Golden Horse) in order to 'buy' the currents and wind (*hopi enã angi*).[5]

Having calmed the sea, they rounded the peninsula and approached the shore at Bobu. There they requested of people who were in the tops of lontar palms (i.e. tapping palm wine) permission to come ashore and settle. These people answered that there was no more room, the place was full, the land packed, 'just look at us who have to live in the tops of palms'.

Tricked in this way they sailed on until they came to the Ata Déi (Standing Person) peninsula, where again their safety was endangered by winds and currents which prevented them from passing.[6] A young woman named Somi Bola Deran (wife of the ancestor who later assumed the name Korohama) gave birth to a son in the boat. The baby cried very much, so they decided again to 'buy' the wind and the current and threw a chain of gold links (*Sora Kai*) into the sea. The wind and current became calm again and the party sailed through and anchored at Luki Lewobala (the village Labala and the Luki Point in the Labala Bay). *Sora Kai* was swallowed by a porpoise, which was subsequently harpooned and the chain recovered. I have seen this object. At Ata Déi, the old woman who had been following them on shore turned to stone, giving the peninsula its name (Keraf 1978: 236). She can still be seen there.[7]

They went into the mountains above Labala[8] and settled in a hamlet named Lewo Hajo.[9] Here they lived comfortably for a time, but once a woman from the clan Tana Kĕrofa was pounding maize when unexpectedly the pestle slipped from her grasp and the mortar tipped over, crushing a baby chick. Tana Kĕrofa, who until then had held the leading rank, was unable to pay the price demanded by the local owner of the chick. Another member of the refugee party, Korohama, then gave what was demanded, reported as a gold chain or a gold ring, whereupon they left. As a consequence of this payment Korohama assumed leadership from the Tana Kĕrofa clan. When they reached the shore and started to board their boat, the head of Tana Kĕrofa told Korohama to sit on the deck, 'we will sit on the thwarts and row—we will stand in the bow and all the way to the stern in order to push you forward'.

From there they sailed the short distance across the bay to Doni Nusa Léla (the village Nualela and today's market-place Wulan Doni).[10] At Doni Nusa Léla, they were well received and permitted to settle. Here there was a momentous exchange of crafts and functions. Lamalera's ancestors received iron harpoons in exchange for their own brazil-wood harpoons. They reciprocated by giving Nualela the skills to make earthen pots (and *fato faka*, the stone and the wooden paddle used for shaping the clay), which today remains their monopoly. The head of Nualela then gave his rank of *kebélen* (great person) of the earth to Korohama, who, announcing that he was now of the same standing as the leader of Nualela, assumed the name Korohama ('I with him am the same') for the first time. Through this act the office of *kakang*, district leader, passed into the hands of Lamalera. Korohama's original name is unrecorded.

The refugees dwelled comfortably at Wulan Doni for a long time. However, when they went to sea the winds and currents frequently carried them far to the west bringing them ashore in the land of Libu Lāma Mau[11] and Gési Raja, or Gési Guã Bala Bata Bala Mai.[12] Since they felt that this was a more convenient situation for their fishery, they requested permission to settle here. At first it seems this permission was refused (or at least that is what members of Lango Fujo, Gési Raja's clan and the principal lords of the land, say). However, agreement was eventually reached, and a site in the upper village was purchased from Lāma Mau clan with five brass bracelets and a chain. Because the chain always fled back to Korohama, they built a boat to replace it and gave it to Lāma Mau clan. According to Dasion [1979] this boat was named *Baka Fai*, although it is now called *Baka Ténã*.[13]

Once this transaction was completed, they moved up to the upper part of the present village. According to Dasion (1979), Korohama's eldest son remained in his father's house in the clan Lefo Hajo/Běliko Lolo.[14] He became the ancestor of Běliko Lolo ('top of the stone wall') clan. The second son was told to settle in the lower section of the village to guard the beach and assist passers-by. His descendants became Bata Onã clan and its various offshoots (Bata Fo, Sula Onã, Bedi Onã). The youngest son was ordered to the centre of the village to guard the peace. From him descends the clan Lefo Tukã ('centre of the village'), and through this line has passed the office of *kakang*.

This history tells us the following about the ancestors of present clans of Lamalera. All clans descended from Korohama have a comparable status as core clans, but in particular Běliko Lolo, Bata Onã, and Lefo Tukã are in a sense the aristocrats. Korohama and the ancestors of Tana Kěrofa clan and Lāma Nudek clan travelled together from Lapan Batan and shared a common history and fate, although Tana Kěrofa lost its original position of leadership to Korohama. The ancestor of Lāma Nudek clan was the master builder of the boat they travelled in, *Kebako Pukã*, and today members of this clan still claim the position of premier master builders.[15]

In the very earliest days then Korohama and his family, his dependants in Léla Onã, as well as Tana Kĕrofa and Lāma Nudek, lived closely together (as indicated by the locations of the various clan temples) and not far from the indigenous lord of the land in Lāma Mau clan (and possibly at that time the ancestors of Tufa Onã clan, who later supplanted members of Lāma Mau as lords of the land). When the ancestor of Bata Onã clan moved down to the beach, he established himself on land associated with a different lord of the land in the clan now called Lango Fujo. This second lord of the land is today the more significant of the two, at least in the sense that he has certain powers over success in the fishery.

There are certainly many inconsistencies, contradictions, and reversals in this tale. At the beginning a sterile old woman raises a creature of the sea as her own child, which then nearly annihilates the children of the village. When the adults destroy this creature, the land itself is inundated. On their journey they are rebuffed in various ways when they seek a place to settle. They are forced to display wealth and then destroy it or give it away in order first to secure their safety at sea (twice) and then on land (once). Twice they have to purchase a calm sea. At Lewo Hajo above Labala, the injury of an insignificant animal forces another large payment. There are two changes of rank, at Lewo Hajo and later at Nualela. At Nualela, this transfer of rank is accompanied by an exchange of primary subsistence skills, establishing the specialities which to this day remain basic to the economic contract between the villages. All of these important transformations occur before they move to their present village, where although powerful they remain virtually landless and dependent upon the indigenous clans, not only for such land as they managed to purchase, but also in important respects for the very success of their fishery upon which they depend for a living. The *tana alep* or lord of the land in Lango Fujo clan played and to some extent still does play a crucial role in the annual fisheries ceremony.

There are a variety of, if not proofs, then evidences of authenticity which villagers resort to in relation to this history. Important among them are the heirloom items that have come from Lapan Batan, which if they are positively disposed toward a visitor, they may bring out and show him. Both in the narratives and today these heirlooms demonstrated and demonstrate wealth and status, and in doing so follow a widespread South-East Asian pattern. Part of the test the ancestor of the 'Second' Raja of Larantuka was put through involved just this act of demonstrating the precious objects which he owned and had brought with him in his boat (Seegeler 1931: 80–2). Other material evidence of veracity includes the petrified standing woman and the other topographical features referring to known places in the local region. Then there is the comparative dimension. When scholars, such as Vatter, Dietrich, and myself, emphasize that the story of the disaster at Lapan Batan is widely shared and often associated with the name Lewo Hayong, we are doing no more than what locals do themselves. These points are also made by Dasion and Bataona (also Kumanireng 1990: 45). They lend authenticity to aspects of the story and demonstrate its power to take over even foreign narrators. Like Vatter I am convinced that there is a historical truth in the narrative, but the 'proofs' available to me are no sounder than or different from those of locals.

It should also be acknowledged that whatever historical validity these legends may or may not have, various of their features belong to stereotypical patterns of wide distribution. The theme of a sea creature found inland, representing a categorical confusion and leading to disaster and dispersal is one (Barnes 1974*a*: 35). McKinnon (1991: 55) notes than in the Tanimbar Archipelago the dispersion and migration of people is related most often to a catastrophe, such as a flood, plague of mice, or epidemic illness. Categorical oppositions of broad cultural importance, such as that between land and sea, land people and sea people, play a prominent part in the legends, just as they do in everyday life. Furthermore, the shores of eastern Indonesia are liberally dotted with petrified boats and people.

Genealogies

Unlike their neighbours in Kédang and some other Lamaholot-speaking groups, the people of Lamalera are not great genealogists. Certainly there is nothing now like the fifteen names from Raja Lorenzo Oesi Dias Vierra Godinho to his ancestor Patigolo, which Raja Oesi (Usi) wrote down in his account of his line (Dias Vieira Godinho n.d.), nor the twenty-three generations which the raja's agent in Riang Koli, Flores, was able to recite for Vatter (1932: 135). Petrus Bau Dasion's genealogy goes back only to his great-grandfather Atakebĕlaké Dasi, and this lack of depth is currently typical for the village, although it is possible that this situation is the result of Bode's suppression of the native priesthood, who may have been responsible for preserving the extended genealogies of at least the more prominent lineages. Be that as it may, there is no equivalent of the genealogical chronicals found elsewhere (Fox 1971: 70–1 see also 1979*b*) and no attempt to rework origin accounts into genealogical form (John R. Bowen 1989: 678–9).

3

Descent Groups

The sociological make-up of descent groups, both unilineal and non-unilineal, in Nusa Tenggara Timur is extraordinarily various, ranging from fairly straightforward patrilineal or matrilineal arrangements, through a combination of patrilineal and matrilineal clans and lineages in a configuration of so-called double descent, toward more complex mixtures of unilineal principles and cognatic practices in places on Timor and the islands to the east of Timor. Scattered here and there are communities lacking unilineal descent groups of any kind (for a survey see R. H. Barnes 1980a). Throughout most of the Lamaholot-speaking region, descent-group membership is patrilineal. However, the matrilineal customs of Tana ʿAi are said to be found also in the extreme west of the Lamaholot area on Flores, contiguous with Tana ʿAi (Kennedy 1955: 256).[1] In eastern Adonara, the division into clans seems to have disappeared or lost its meaning. There the basic feature of social organization is the patripotestal family (Vatter 1932: 166, 174–5). In the district of Horowura in west-central Adonara clans are missing in most places (Beckering 1911: 172–3).

In Lamalera, and indeed, Lembata generally, descent groups are in principle patrilineal, although there are significant exceptions in practice. At one end of the spectrum of such groups are large clans divided into further named second-order groupings. At the other end are families with distinct descent-group names, who otherwise are of no greater significance than individual families within the second-order descent groups, but who, because they stand apart, might appear in a list of clans. Under the circumstances, any figure given for the number of clans in the village is arbitrary. Fig. 1 lists the more significant, together with their divisions. Clans are generically referred to by the commonplace word *suku*, which in eastern Indonesia is often used in this sense, but which in western Indonesian languages is used to mean leg, ethnic group, tribe, or a quarter.[2] The fuller expression for a descent group is *suku-lāma*. The divisions of clans are generally called 'great houses', *lango bélã*. Clans and their divisions are supposed to be strictly exogamous.

Clans and the divisions of clans are associated with great houses, where rituals pertinent to the group are carried out. Today these houses are usually normal dwellings, although Lefo Tukã has a modern building for this purpose which is not normally inhabited. In the larger clans, one of the big houses of its constituent groups serves as well, at least potentially, for the whole clan.

Clan	Sub-Clan	Clan	Sub-Clan
Bĕliko Lolo		Tapo Onã	
	Téti Nama Papã		Musi Langu
	Lali Nama Papã		Guna Langu
Lefo Tukã			Mana Langu
	Dasi Langu		Sola Langu
	Kéda Langu	Bata Onã	
	Lima Langu		Kĕlaké Langu
	Béra Onã		Kifa Langu
Lãma Nudek			Jafa Langu
	Kĕlodo Onã		Ola Langu
Tana Kĕrofa			Baso Langu
	Haga Langu	Sula Onã	
	Laba Langu		Kebesa Langu
Ata Kéi			Kĕloré Langu
Léla Onã			Kiko Langu
	Sinu Langu	Bedi Onã	
	Bĕlaké Langu		Miku Langu
Tufa Onã			Muri Langu
Ebã Onã		Bata Fo	
	Daé Langu		Kéda Langu
	Guma Langu		Kaja Langu
	Sita Langu	Olé Onã	
Ata Folo		Lãma Nifa	
Lãma Kéra		Hari Onã	
	Badi Langu	Lefo Léin	
	Lafa Langu	Ata Gora	
	Sinu Langu	Lango Fujo	
	Pĕrafi Langu		

FIG. 1. Descent groups of Lamalera

The internal structure of clans, however, can be in some cases quite loose. Several descent groups have incorporated families which have come from outside and which, at least initially, had no genealogical links to the village. Kennedy (1955: 49, 74–5) found in Wailolong, East Flores, that there was a class division within descent groups between families from the great houses, the masses or *ata ribu* (the 'thousands'), and the slaves. Those in the clan who were in the great houses had more power. He found another expression, *lango kéni*, or small house, for the other sections. Although this expression would be perfectly acceptable in Lamalera, it was never specifically drawn to my attention as part of the stereotypical model of clan division. In Wailolong there was little outward sign of status, but, Kennedy wrote, 'the main thing seems to be a general knowledge of everything in the kampong [village] and also whether a person lives in a "big house" or not'. It is also of interest that in the oldest former site of Wailolong, houses were very large, large enough to accommodate as many as five families (Kennedy 1955: 73). In these democratic times, the people of Lamalera do not emphasize class divisions, but they are certainly implicitly present. Three great houses distinguish themselves from all others, these are Dasi Langu of Lefo Tukã, Balé Olé Mau of Bĕliko Lolo (the Téti Nama Papã section), and Kĕlaké Langu of Bata Onã. The last is also known by the name Lango Bélã.

Some clans and many sections of clans are named by a word followed either by *langu*, which means 'house', thus Kĕlaké Langu, 'the house of the leading elder', Badi Langu, 'Badi's house', or by *onã*, 'within'. In the latter case, the first word is usually interpreted as a personal name, and the whole phrase indicates within that person's house, but sometimes the first word is interpreted as a location, thus Olé Onã, 'within the field'.

Each clan or separately organized clan segment has a hereditary head. This leader will normally be the first-born male, unless that person is incapacitated or has taken up a modern occupation and left the village. According to Gregorius Keraf, the eldest male son in a descent line will always get more intensive and careful training than the other children. He is expected from his adolescence to follow customary ceremonies and is instructed in the kinds of knowledge and skill appropriate to his future position. This training prepares him to take responsibility for other families in the descent group, as well as his own. 'A candidate clan head who has shown himself to be wise and capable, loving and intelligent from his adolescence will become the pride of his whole clan. Respect of other clans for his clan, honor and estimation of other clans for his clan, are very much dependent on the maturity and bearing of the person chosen candidate or clan head' (Gregorius Keraf 1983).

The *lango bélã* is a temple as well as a dwelling and serves as the place for the members of the clan to assemble and deliberate descent-group issues. All arrangements concerning marriage, death, and other customary law matters must be discussed at the great house. There are at least two occasions when a member of the clan not normally resident in the great house is especially accommodated there; these are marriage and death. At marriage the couple must stay for some time in the great house, and when a person dies, his corpse should be displayed there, before being brought to the grave. Construction of a great house is the concern of all clan members, who should contribute labour and materials. The great house also serves as the ritual centre for at least one of the whaling boats of the clan and for its corporation.

It may be remembered that formerly each clan had a stone seat in the clearing in the upper village.[3] Kennedy (1955: 154–5) found in Wailolong and Leloba, East Flores, that all clan chiefs had 'anchor' stones (*sao-niwang*) in front of their houses. They held the power of the chiefs, war power, marriage power, descent-group power, and so on. They appeared long ago, coming down during a heavy rain. If any parallel to the anchor stones ever existed in Lamalera, I found no trace of it. However, it can be inferred that similar power invested the stone seats.

Clans

I will use the word clan merely to indicate the undivided descent group, without any intention to imply any sociological or demographic equivalence among the various groups so designated. This usage corresponds closely to local use of the word *suku*.

Except for the two 'lord of the land' clans Tufa Onã, some of whose families have land in Lamalera A, and Lango Fujo, which has land just above the historical village boundary on the mountain side of the village, all of the groups in Lamalera regard themselves as being descended from people who moved to the site from elsewhere. Central to legendary history, and until recently to the political structure and ritual life of the community, are the three principal clans which claim descent from the founding ancestor Korohama. Korohama's descent group was named, so it is thought, Lefo Hajo prior to his settling in Lamalera. But it seems to have given itself the name Běliko Lolo ('top of the stone wall or fortress') once Korohama and his party settled in the upper, more easily defensible part of the present village. Plausibly the location of their settlement explains the name, meaning that they lived in the fortress constituted by the upper village, although there are several quite unrelated clans in neighbouring villages bearing the same name. According to Arndt (1937: 7), in Witihama, Adonara, *beliko belolong* means the higher, more important segment of a clan. Tradition states that the present members (excluding those incorporated from outside) of Běliko Lolo descend from the eldest of Korohama's three sons, a figure known as Kělaké (or Ata Kělaké) Muda Ama. In his old age Korohama distributed his wealth and responsibilities among his sons. He instructed Kělaké Muda Ama to guard the village temple and to live in the clan big house, Korohama's dwelling.[4] The youngest of the three sons, Kělaké (or Ata Kělaké) Dasi was delegated to stay in the middle of the village and to keep the peace.[5] Only later was this modest responsibility transformed into leadership of the district. From Kělaké Dasi descend members of the clan Lefo Tukã ('middle of the village').

Korohama ordered the second son, Ata Kělaké to live at the beach, the lower half of the present Lamalera, and to assist people passing by at sea. He established himself at a location enjoying the extensive name Gési Guã Bala Bata Bala Mai. This name derives from the two members of the present Lango Fujo clan who gave Korohama permission to settle in Lamalera, Raja Bala Mai(k) and Gési Gua Fasa. Members of this clan who were in the habit of tapping palm trees at the shore set up a bench made of several layers of flat stones, which were arranged as seats for the elders and near which was erected a branching pole from which palm wine containers could be hung. This object, of which similar arrangements can still be found in nearby palm-tapping hamlets, was called Bata, or in the longer form Bata Bala Mai. The descent group which descended from Korohama's second son acquired its name Bata Onã ('within Bata') because they settled inland from it. The three clans Běliko Lolo, Lefo Tukã, and Bata Onã are said to be *lika*, that is like the three stones that make up the hearth.

A clear implication of this legend is that to the eldest son was delegated a superior religious authority, while to the youngest was accorded a subordinate secular authority. This relationship is analogous to that between the lord of the land (internal, religious, superior) and village head (external, secular, subordinate) in many Lamaholot and Kédang communities. Under the circumstances of course the two relationships cannot be identical. Nevertheless the second relationship is realized in the opposition between lord of the land (in this case doubled) and both *kakang* and village head. The second son was also delegated a subordinate responsibility to deal with outsiders.

In addition to the clans descended in the male line from Korohama are clans who travelled in his party on their way to Lamalera. These groups include Tana Kěrofa, who surrendered leadership to Korohama, during their brief stay at Lewo Hajo, near Labala, as well as Lāma Nudek ('Place of [or Below] the Fort'), who were boat builders for the boats in which they made their journey, and Léla Onã, who joined them on the last stage of their migration, when they moved from Nualela to the present site.

Léla is a personal name, but it can also mean to seize, confiscate, to place a mark of ownership on, or to put up a sign of prohibition (Gregorius Keraf 1978: 39, 258). Arakian Léré Géré was the ancestor of this group who accompanied Korohama to Lamalera. Léla Onã used to be a very rich clan. It is said that they once possessed *manu sili goko* (a corruption of the Malay Manuk Sering [Ber]Kokok, 'the bird that always crows'), the bird that always crows wealth. The design appropriate to this clan is a zigzag pattern, representing a cock's comb and referring to this bird; this they must use on the decorated stern pieces of their boats. They are said to have brought much gold with them. When they sold any of this and received payment, the objects would return to them of themselves. They lived east of the great house of Dasi Langu, Lefo Tukã in an area called *koker* (= *korké*), that is, village temple.

The wife of one man in Léla Onã was from Lāma Kéra. Her husband treated her badly, cursed her and beat her. One day he beat her nearly to death. She ran and reported to the elders of Lāma Kéra and Běliko Lolo. They decided then to kill everyone in Léla Onã, their wives and children. They went from house to house in the village looking for members of the clan, killing them. A boy named Boli Léla was the only survivor. He ran through a back way to the house of a family in Kělodo Onã descent group. The owner took a turtle shell and covered him, so when his house was searched Boli Léla was not spotted. Boli Léla was then raised by that man until he was grown. The man promised to help with bridewealth and so on, but Boli refused. He may have been, according to an interpretation, influenced by his ancestral spirits who told him not to enter another clan or become a slave of it by allowing them to assume responsibility. He arranged his own bridewealth and therefore became the ancestor of the present Léla Onã. When the villagers were killing the members of Léla Onã they took all of their valuables. The former site of the clan great house is now occupied by that of one of the branches of Lefo Tukã. A contributing cause of the attack on them was the fact that people, including the wife from Lãma Kéra clan, thought that they were witches and felt that they were being bothered by them at night. Another was the fact that the valuable objects they sold returned to them as described above. In the massacre a man named Pati Mangun disappeared in mid-air into the sacred grove, today called Duang Rego Pati Mangun, above the clan houses of the two halves of this clan. At full moon he still stalks the area with an iron walking-stick which shines and makes a sound like a bell when it strikes the ground. When people hear that sound they know that someone in the clan is going to die. It is prohibited to take wood from this grove. Today it is prohibited for members of Lefo Tukã and Léla Onã to intermarry, and various attempts to arrange a reconciliation and overcome this prohibition have been frustrated by the ancestors of Léla Onã.[6]

Korohama's second son Ata Kĕlaké had five sons of his own. From them descend three of the present sections of Bata Onã and two further clans. Their names, together with the associated descent groups are as follows:

1. Kĕlaké Ubas: Bata Onã, Kĕlaké Langu (or Lango Bélã)
2. Pajo Kifa Ama: Bata Onã, Kifa Langu
3. Pandai: Bata Onã, Jafa Langu
4. Sinu Kéfa Ama: Bedi Onã
5. Gélu Bala: Bata Fo

Legend records that when Ata Kĕlaké settled at the shore a member of Lãma Nudek clan named Ola Bélu Taran accompanied him. From Ola Bélu Teran descends the section named Ola Langu, which became joined, no longer to Lãma Nudek, but to Bata Onã. The separation of Bata Fo is accounted for by a legend that the villagers were holding a festival in which they were going to sacrifice a buffalo. Members of Bĕliko Lolo, Lefo Tukã, Bata Onã, and Bedi Onã arrived in time, while the ancestor of Bata Fo was late. By the time he arrived, the others had already killed the buffalo. His response was to draw a line and say 'you Bata Onã are inside, and we Bata Fo are in front'. Indeed Bata Fo means outside the stone platform described above, and the present houses of Kĕlaké Langu, Kifa Langu, and Bata Fo maintain the same positions relative to the former site of Bata. The occasion for the separation of Sula Onã is said to have been anger over the death of a child who had been bitten in the groin by a pig while excreting. *Bedi* may derive from Malay *bedil*, 'rifle', but I lack a convincing explanation for the name Bedi Onã or any explanation for their separation. They, however, have an especially close association with

Lango Fujo clan. In the past, members of Bedi Onã protected men of Lango
Fujo who were threatened with assault by members of Lefo Léin clan.

The only clans with claims to being autochthonous which are associated with
the two traditional sites of Lamalera are Tufa Onã and Lango Fujo. Lango
Fujo is the clan with the rights of 'lord of the land', *tana alep*, of Lamalera B.
It is the senior of the two 'lord of the land' groups and takes precedence, particularly in relation to affairs of the sea. Strictly speaking it does not count as
one of Lamalera's clans (except in terms of the new bureaucratic structure
of the village government), but is associated with the mountain hamlet
Lamamanu. Its dwellings and temples are situated on the mountain slope
just above the traditional boundary of Lamalera at a place called Fūka Léré.
Tufa Onã are lords of the land for Lamalera A, where some members have
their houses. Many members of this clan live in the neighbouring village of
Lewotala. Their rights devolved to them from another clan, now extinct,
named Lāma Mau (according to some Lāma Au), who held the position in
Korohama's day and sold the site of the upper village to him. Lāma Mau indicates that this group drifted in from elsewhere (*mau* means 'to float'). Tufa
Onã have a tradition of having found a woman inside a *tufa* tree.[7] The Lango
Fujo account is that this woman eventually produced a child, which should
have belonged to Lango Fujo, since the woman was found on their domain.
However, since Tufa Onã found the woman, they were allowed to care for the
child. Lango Fujo gave Tufa Onã a field to provide for the child. This field
became the basis for their claim to being lords of the land. This legend would
appear to situate Tufa Onã as in effect wife-takers to Lango Fujo.

When the missionary Bode came he charged Rp. 25 or Rp. 50 for a mass. At
that time there were very few fish. Lango Fujo told their 'sisters' Tufa Onã to
take care of paying for mass, while Lango Fujo would concern itself with ceremonies in the mountain and bring the fish down from the mountain. Later
there was a period in which they caught a great amount of 'fish', i.e. sperm
whale, sometimes ten or more per day. There were only about fifteen persons
in Lango Fujo clan to divide all the meat from the lord of the land's share in
the whale's head, but it was religiously prohibited not to accept it. Therefore
Lango Fujo called in Tufa Onã and allowed them to take some of the meat.
The share Tufa Onã was given was an upper portion which is the first share
given to an elder sister. Tufa Onã actually has no traditional right to the head
of whale. It is Lango Fujo's responsibility to *pau lefo*, 'feed the village', i.e. to
ceremonially guarantee the success of the fishery.

All other descent groups descend from outsiders who came to Lamalera at
one time or another after its founding, some quite recently. Lāma Kéra clan
came by boat from Soge Paga (or Songge Paga) in the vicinity of Ende and
Sika, Flores. One account has it that they came together with the ancestors of
Lāma Nifa. These clans descend from Nogo and Ema, Nogo being the ances-

tor of Lāma Nifa and Ema the ancestor of Lāma Kéra. Their journey began
on the north coast of Flores at what is now called Labuan Bajo (the harbour
of sea gypsies or Bajo Laut). From there they travelled to Ende in south-central
Flores, and then to the village of Lamakera on Solor. From Lamakera they
travelled to Lamalera. Related groups remained behind in Lamakera, the clans
Nogo and Ema Onã. There is also a clan called Nogo in the village of Boleng,
Adonara. Lāma Nifa travelled in the boat *Kefaka Futu* ('tip of the *kĕfaka* tree').[8]
The ancestors of Lāma Kéra travelled in *Bĕlida Ténã*, which later belonged to
Kema (Sinu) Langu section. On the way they met *Kora Kora*, the boat later
associated with Lafa Langu. I have no explanation for the name Lāma Nifa,
although *nifa* means 'anchor' and the whole name might mean the place (in a
boat) for the anchor. The name Lāma Kéra is said by some to refer to a lontar
palm-leaf water bailer (*kéra*). If these interpretations were acceptable, it could
be inferred that both names refer to locations in the boat in which the ancestors travelled, but I have uncovered *no* such legend. However, given Lāma
Kéra's connection to the village Lamakera, it is reasonable to refer the name
to that village's founding legend which involves a feast in which food was
served on lontar palm-leaf plates (*lāma kéra*), as still often happens in fact in
Lamalera. According to some, the tie-dye pattern appropriate for use in the
cloths of this clan is the baleen whale, *kelaru*.[9] Lāma Kéra is unrelated to the
clan of the same name in the mountain hamlet Lamamanu.

Ata Kéi is a small group. There are many unrelated descent groups of the
same name in neighbouring villages, including Lamamanu, and on other
islands. The name means People from the Kei Islands, and generally these
groups are thought to have come from that region in the past. However,
members of this clan in Lamalera think that they came more immediately from
Soge Paga on Flores and do not know if their ancestors ever lived in the Kei
Islands.

Ebã Onã came from the village Lamakera, Solor, but before that, as is the
case for so many people in Lamakera, their ancestors lived in Soge Paga, Flores.
Ebã is a dry ravine of the kind which is subject to violent floods when there is
a rain storm. The ancestors of this clan once lived in such a dangerous location. The springs at the shore, *Fai Belolo* and *Fai Léré*, which once were the
village's sole supply of drinking water, are linked by legend with this clan. An
ancestor of the clan went to the shore at his original home to look for a small
boat. There he saw a very large baleen whale. He asked the whale if it would
take him. The whale agreed, so the man got a bamboo pole, like those they tie
to lontar palms as ladders. He made a hole in the whale and stuck the ladder
in it. He also had a bamboo of the kind called *bélã* filled with water and another
bamboo of the kind they used to use to catch flying fish. These he hung on the
ladder. When the whale dived, he climbed the ladder to stay out of the water.
When they came to Lembata the whale said it would drop him off anywhere

he wished. They reached to the rock outcropping below the village and the ancestor said he would get off there. There he dropped the bamboo of water which shattered, leaving the spring behind.

Tapo Onã is said to derive its name (i.e. 'within the coconut [grove]') from the fact that they planted a coconut grove in Lamalera in which they lived. Their ancestors left Awé Lolo, an island in the sea near Lewoleba on the north coast of Lembata, which according to oral history sank under the waters.[10] Eventually they settled in Lamamanu, where they have ties of kinship with the clans Ata Kéi and Lāma Kéra (NB: *not* Ata Kéi and Lāma Kéra of Lamalera). Tapo Onã was told to guard the shore and fish, Ata Kéi the mountain and woods. Tapoona still gives fish to the *lango bélã* of Ata Kéi, which, however, now has very few members. There is a triangular-shaped, large stone in the wall behind the boat shed of the *Kebéla Ténã* called *fato fajo* which marks the boundary between the terrain of Lango Fujo and Tapo Onã. Apparently the ancestors of Tapo Onã should have been lord of the land of Lamalera A, but through misbehaviour involving a woman lost this right to Tufa Onã. Their ancestress was Peni Bélã Lolo ('Peni Bamboo Leaves'), who was found inside a bamboo by the ancestor Belafa. Two dogs, Kefakal ('loin cloth') Také ('does not have') and Bada Ilé Golé (*bada* means 'animal' and *ilé golé* means 'around the mountain'), barked at the stand of bamboo until Belafa took an interest in it. He cut a bamboo and a voice inside said 'cut lower so you do not cut my feet'. Then he cut above, and the voice said cut higher. He took the bamboo to his field hut where he split it open and found Peni Bélã Lolo inside. Bélã is a bamboo of the species *Schizostachyum brachycladum*. This event occurred in the mountain, and Tapo Onã later descended from Labalekang to the shore. The whaling boat *Soge Ténã*, which belongs to this clan, has a little flag which they hoist when they get fish. The flag is a small white rectangle, upon which is drawn a woman, a dog, a field knife, and a stand of bamboo. Also on the flag they have written Peni Bélã Lolo.

Olé Onã is said by some to be another of the clans which came from Soge Paga, Flores. However, others say that they descend from a young man who drifted in from Timor. The word *ōlé* means 'field'. Olé Onã and Lāma Kéra are by tradition historically related, in that Olé Onã lived in and kept the fields of Lāma Kéra. Both clans are still prohibited to inter-marry. Olé Onã is one of several small groupings which round out the list of Lamalera descent groups. The others are Hari Onã, Ata Folo, Lefo Léin, and Ata Gora. Hari Onã are recent arrivals in the village, who settled late in the nineteenth century. They left Lamakera, Solor, after some difficulty there and fled to the west coast of Lembata, where they were met by a man named Juang in the Kĕlodo Onã section of Lāma Nudek, who arranged to bring them to Lamalera. Like so many other groups in the village of Lamakera, their ultimate derivation is Soge Paga, Flores. Ata Folo, consisting of only one or two households, came in from one of the villages in the mountains in the interior of the island.

Lefo Léin is now a single household. There is no consensus in the village whether the name, 'Foot of the Village', is explained by their location just above the wall which separates the houses from the beach or the location this clan occupied in some other village before it came to Lamalera. Some argue that they came here from the village Lewolein, Solor. According to others they came to the village from Soge Paga, Flores, on the boat named *Lefoléin*. However, Korohama's second son is said to have married a woman of this clan named Benga, so their association with the village is an ancient one. At some time in the past, Lefo Léin had a falling out with the clan Lango Fujo because a man named Gési Guã Fasã of Lango Fujo committed adultery with a widow of Lefo Léin named Daté. The stories of both clans about these events confirm each other. Because of this infraction or about that time, Lefo Léin decided to attack men of Lango Fujo who were out fishing. According to Lango Fujo's memory, these two men were named Fasã and Labi Solé. They say that Lefo Léin wanted to seize their territory, which also seems to be confirmed by other accounts of these events. However, men of Bedi Onã protected them and saved their lives. The men had brought a fish to shore with them, which they wanted to give the men from Bedi Onã, but Bedi Onã divided its heart in two and shared it with them. Through these events Lango Fujo came to be regarded as like younger brothers to Bedi Onã. Today Lango Fujo still divides the head of whale with Bedi Onã. Perhaps as a consequence of these disruptions, Lango Fujo gave up the former site of its clan temple at the beach.

According to a written version of Lango Fujo's traditions, people of Lefo Léin apprehended Gési Guã Fasã and made arrangements to use the boat named *Jafa Ténã* to take him to Timor to sell him there. On the fateful day of departure, Gési Guã Fasã grabbed a handful of earth upon leaving his house which he said he would save for his descendants. At the beach, he grabbed another handful of sand for the same purpose before boarding the boat. When they were part-way to Timor, the crew wanted to turn back. Gési Guã Fasã refused and pointed them in the direction of Timor. He continued to stand in the boat and point the way to Timor, which they eventually reached and where he was sold into slavery. As legends go, this one has the unusual feature of confirmation in the person of a Catholic brother from Timor stationed in Lamalera in 1979, who belonged to a Lango Fujo clan in Timor and who had secured his posting to Lamalera because of a family tradition that they derived from a man from Lamalera who had been sold into slavery there. He actively tried to re-establish ties with both Lango Fujo and Lefo Léin, but, although he was cordially treated by them, he never achieved a ceremonial reconciliation. In the genealogies of Lango Fujo, Gési Guã Fasã appears as a great uncle of members of the clan in their late forties and early fifties at the time of the field research, suggesting that this episode may have taken place in the 1880s.

Some time after the events related above, Lefo Léin came to be in danger of extinction, so the Lango Fujo version goes. Therefore they bought a buffalo and a human being, whom they named Gési Guã Fasã. These they took to Lango Fujo. A man named Miku from Bedi Onã was brought in to kill the buffalo, but was unsuccessful in severing its head. Therefore only two males, father and son, remain of Lefo Léin.

Of all of the stories associated with descent groups, the most colourful belongs to the tiny clan of Ata Gora. The name suggests that they are people from the island of Goran in the Moluccas. However, their more recent source of origin is Lewokukun in the northern part of the island. When they came to the village they had to buy land from the lord of the land with precious clan possessions. Today only two brothers remain. It is said that they were once rich and envied, to the point that Bata Onã began to kill them off. Finally they were so reduced that they fled and asked protection from Béra Onã section of Lefo Tukã clan. They now have a quasi-membership in Béra Onã. The clan Golok in Lamamanu is essentially the same clan as Ata Gora. In the 1920s or thereabouts a man of Ata Gora moved up to Lamamanu and his group are now Golok. Ata Gora have a fish trap, *bĕlutu*, which stands to them in the same way that whaling boats stand to other descent groups. They are one of two lines in the village that traditionally used such devices.

Ata Gora are distinguished by being masters of mice and rats. In the distant and recent past, Ata Gora have been called on to use their extraordinary powers to assist others. They used to be called upon if the village were going to war. They would then send a plague of rats into the war area ahead of the troops. They have used their powers against the village Atawuwur. Also, if a house is bothered with mice, this clan can feed the mice bits of wood of some kind and the mice will disappear. They can call the mice and ask them to stop doing damage. But you must not fall out with or curse Ata Gora, because they can send a plague of mice, as they have done at Ata Déi. Members of Ata Gora have been invited in the past by a village near Bobu and also by one in Kédang to save them from a rat plague. They should be given something in return. The proper amount depends on the distance they need to travel, but an animal is appropriate. You must be sure they are satisfied, because if they are not they can turn the mice loose against you. Through their ability to control mice they can take revenge on you if you hit them.

Some said that at the request of the Raja of Larantuka Ata Gora once sent an infestation of mice against the raja's enemies at Kupang, Timor. Ata Gora carried mice from Lamalera to Kupang, where they let them loose. At Kupang the mice ate the eyes of the enemy. However, others contradict this report and claim that in the war at Kupang, it was not Ata Gora, but a man named Paung of Bata Onã who provided the assistance. He carved a mouse of wood and took it to Kupang, where he released it. The decoration which the boat *Nara Ténã* places on its stern includes a black and white flag, representing a black and white mouse and commemorating the time when *Nara Ténã* accompanied the

Kebako Pukã, belonging to Bata Onã, to Timor on this war expedition. It seems that the war in which Ata Gora helped was not at Kupang, but the Portuguese war at Occusi on the north coast of western Timor. According to some, they did not actually go to Timor, but achieved their aim by putting mice on wood at the beach and sending them off.

According to another story a special kind of bird once was digging at the entrails of Mandiri mountain at Larantuka, Flores, causing continuous rumblings. The Raja of Larantuka sent to Lamalera for men to come and kill the bird. In Lamalera the village elders decided to send animals instead of men. They turned to the clan Ata Gora, which prepared a bamboo container into which they put a male and a female mouse. These they took to Larantuka where the raja said he was turning proceedings over to them. They opened the bamboo and out came thousands of mice. These swarmed over the mountain and killed the bird, bringing an end to the rumbling. Villagers say that the raja kept the talons and beak of the bird as proof.

In recent years a prominent offspring of the village was involved in court action against a former government minister in Jakarta. Villagers have told me that he turned to Ata Gora, successfully, to get them to use their powers against his opponent. They concluded contentedly that, 'The powers of the village still exist!'

Members of Ata Gora were reluctant to speak to me about their background and specialities. However, I had a neighbour who had grown up in their household to which he stood as a wife-taking affine and who was more than willing to talk about them. The now deceased father of the brothers in Ata Gora could call the mice and rats, including the mouse king. If the mouse king comes, the rest come too. On one occasion my neighbour described the mouse king, whom he had seen in youth, as a black and white animal with red eyes. On another occasion he described the mouse king as red. The home base for the mice of the whole region is Lamalera. They go out to other places on the island (or other islands) like the men of the village (for example students) do, but their roots are here. Ata Gora always feed the mice before or after members of the group eat. My neighbour had seen wave after wave of mice come to eat, then go away to be replaced by another wave. He suggested that if I wished, I might be shown the mice dutifully trooping in to eat. Ata Gora have a whole set of equipment, including a plate and a metal gong, for dealing with the mice.

My neighbour's house was often overrun with mice, which scampered through it in broad daylight. These mice enjoyed a life free of human threat. He explained that you can get along with mice so long as you do not curse them or kill them. If you find them running through your things or up and down your arms, just shoo them out of the house like you do children. If they move into a box or basket in your house, put a plate with some food near it, so that they will go away. If you kill or curse them, the mice will 'arrange things with you' (take revenge on you). Once they start on humans, that is it (the end).

Clan Divisions

Some discussion of this topic has already taken place. Clan divisions are commonly associated with a house which serves as dwelling and ceremonial centre. In the case of small undivided clans, the same may be said of the clan as a whole. Besides the house and group name, other signs of corporate identity may include heirlooms, personal names, boats or other fishing gear, migration tales, family histories, ties to ceremonial locations, textile patterns, and long-standing patterns of marriage alliance. Typically these various features are intimately intertwined. Heirlooms may include elephant tusks, swords and knives, woven wire chains in the form of snakes, cloth, including valuable Indian patola, porcelain, ambergris, and so on. Personal names tend to be names of ancestors, male or female, which are passed from generation to generation. However, there is no monopoly of names, just that some are particularly meaningful to a given group and not to others.

Běliko Lolo divides itself into two great houses, Téti Nama Papã and Lali Nama Papã. These phrases literally translate the east and west sides of the *nama*, the ceremonial clearing and meeting-place in the centre of the upper village. The more important of the two is Téti Nama Papã, whose great house, a recently built structure of commercially produced planks with a roof ridge imitating buffalo horns, lies immediately to the east of the clearing, just below the road. The other is a commonplace brick- and tin-roof dwelling on the western side. Within Lali Nama Papã there is a significant, but unmarked, division between the descendants of an ancestor named Hidang and another named Solé.

Lefo Tukã currently consists of four recognized divisions: (1) Dasi Langu, (2) Kéda Langu, (3) Lima Langu, and (4) Béra Onã. Many families of this clan live elsewhere, including especially Lewoleba. Dasi Langu, of course, is named after the founding ancestor of the clan Ata Kĕlaké Dasi. The *kakang* derives from this house. The great house for this section is located unsurprisingly in the centre of the upper village just above the road which separates it from the central clearing. This is the only great house which does not normally serve as a residence. Important ceremonies, however, regularly take place there. Kéda Langu has separated only in the last three or four generations. Its great house should occupy the site which was formerly that of Léla Onã, in the higher part of the upper village. However, only one family remains in the village, and they live as it happens in the lower village. Yohanis Mura, who was officially *kakang* from 1917 to 1934, belonged to this section. Dasi Langu and Kéda Langu regard themselves as *lango bélã tou* or *deko tou*, that is of a single great house, or more strikingly two legs of the same set of shorts. Lima Langu is located west of the central clearing in the upper village. Béra Onã is another very small grouping, consisting at the time of research of an older woman, two young men, and their married sisters. Formerly, they were responsible for leadership in war and for slaughtering animals, distributing the meat, and so on at feasts of the clan. They are the *mélo huri*. Villagers interpret their name to mean 'quick to the centre'. They are the ones who should quickly get to the centre of a battle or ceremony. The oldest traceable ancestor in the genealogy of this small grouping unfortunately died in a battle at the village Lamabakan, where he went after only a month of marriage.

The site for the big house of Lāma Nudek is just below that for Téti Nama Papã of Běliko Lolo in the upper village. During most of my field research it consisted merely of a temporary hut. However, in 1982 they laid the foundations for a modern building. Lāma Nudek proper is a single family. However, it has incorporated a section called Kělodo Onã. It was a man from Kělodo Onã who sheltered the ancestor of the present members of Léla Onã, when people in Lefo Tukã clan were trying to exterminate Léla Onã. Kělodo Onã originally came from Soge Paga, Flores, but lived for some time in Lamakera, Solor, before coming to Lamalera. However, they died out, the last remembered direct descendant being a man named Juang and his daughter Uba, who married a man of Muri Langu in the clan Bedi Onã. Juang is the same man who brought the ancestors of the clan Hari Onã to the village. Juang's daughter was involved in bringing in Basa from suku Motong Onã, Nualela to join Kělodo Onã. Basa is the ancestor of the present members of Kělodo Onã. Today this group consists of a former schoolteacher in Maumere, Flores, and his brother, a carpenter who is usually resident in Larantuka, Flores, but who returns to the village from time to time and participates in the affairs of the clan.

Some say that the great houses of Tufa Onã, Běliko Lolo, Lefo Tukã , Lāma Nudek, and Tana Kěrofa are the principal ones for the upper village. The other clan houses are secondary because their owners came later. Tana Kěrofa had come to Lamalera with the group fleeing the catastrophe at Lapan Batan. Until the stop-over near Labala they were superior, but since they could not pay the fine incurred by the woman whose mortar crushed the chick, they told Korohama to take the superior political position. According to one tradition, Tana Kěrofa should be the lord of the land of the upper village, not Tufa Onã. Tana Kěrofa brought a coconut shell of dirt from Lapan Batang (they were the only ones to do so) and a large pot. The pot is still in their possession, but sometime during the 1970s the earth was used in a clan ceremony and left in a spot outside, where it disappeared. The great houses for the clan are just east of that for Téti Nama Papã of Běliko Lolo in the upper village. It is divided into two sections, Haga Langu and Laba Langu, the first of which is regarded as the elder.

Ata Kéi is an undivided, quite small, grouping whose great house is situated in the upper village just above that of Dasi Langu, Lefo Tukã. Léla Onã has two great houses: (1) Sinu Langu and (2) Bĕlaké Langu. The buildings are adjacent, Sinu Langu being above Bĕlaké Langu, and the lower Bĕlaké Langu being the cadet branch. They are situated on the ridge called Fung on the north-east boundary of the upper village, just below the sacred grove Duang Rego Pati Mangun. The land on which they were built used to belong to the clan Ebã Onã, whose houses are just below them. The clan's founding ancestor, Arakian Léré Géré, is associated with a large tree in this grove, Pati Mangun with a boulder above the tree. Once there was a stone altar, *nuba nara*, there as well, which, however, allegedly disappeared by itself. On special occasions the clan may hold ceremonies, involving the killing of a goat, on the location of either the tree or the boulder.

Tufa Onã is the lord of the land group for the upper village and its great house lies above that of Ata Kéi. Being small, it is undivided. According to one report they stand as eldest child of the other lord of the land clan, Lango Fujo, but I encountered no confirmation of this claim. As lord of the land they share with Bĕliko Lolo, Lefo Tukã, and Bata Onã the right to slaughter a sheep at their ceremonies. In the ranking of (former) sacrificial animals the sheep comes first, followed by buffalo, then cow, then goat, then pig. The sheep is the elder sibling, the buffalo the younger, but the elder is small and the younger is larger. For this reason, Lefo Tukã chose the younger species for their ceremonies to make sure there was enough meat to go around. There is an expression in use which goes *tité téi di Libu korok lolo*. Libu is a given name which is handed down through the clan, but it is also the name of the clan's founding ancestor. *Téi* means 'to stay', while *korok* means chest. The sentence means 'we stay on Libu's chest'. The metaphor is of the lord of the land lying down. The villagers from the rest of the clans stand upon his chest—that is their place.

Ebã Onã consists of three divisions: (1) Guma Langu, (2) Daé Langu, and (3) a small offshoot called Sita Langu. Their houses are just below those of Léla Onã at Fung in the eastern part of the upper village. There are three divisions of Lãma Kéra clan in the upper village: (1) Sinu (Kema) Langu, (2) Lafa Langu, and (3) Badi Langu. The great house of Badi Langu is just above that of Téti Nama Papã, Bĕliko Lolo, on the other side of the road in the upper village. It is in this house that I stayed during three of my visits to Lamalera. Near Badi Langu a little further up the mountain slope and opposite each other are the houses of Sinu Langu and Lafa Langu. Originally, according to one villager, the whole of Lãma Kéra gathered at Sinu Langu. A fourth division of the clan is Pĕrafi Langu, which is located near the shore in the centre of the lower village. I was never able to obtain any concrete and convincing evidence of any kinship or other link between this division and those of the upper village, although no one denied that there was a link. Indeed everyone claimed that there was one, without being able to give details or examples. Professor Gregorius Keraf, who is himself a member of the branch of Lãma Kéra located in the lower village lists the following houses of the clan in the lower village associated with boats: Laba Langu, Lango Bélã (general), and Suku Hama Langu ('Same Clan House') (Gregorius Keraf 1983). Another member of the lower branch of Lāma Kéra identified the following branches, Laba Langu, Ola Langu, and Kila Langu, but said that for large affairs they come together and chose to speak of the great house only as 'Lāma Kéra'.

The various divisions of Bata Onã have been described above. The great house of Kĕlaké Langu is on the landward side of the central village clearing in the lower village. That of Kifa Langu is on the seaward side of that clearing. The great house of Jafa Langu is above the east end of the beach. Sula Onã has two divisions: (1) Kebesa Langu and (2) Kĕloré Langu. It is associated with a snake spirit called *Bélé Gora*. Bedi Onã has two great houses, Muri Langu and Miku Langu. The large house of Miku Langu is adjacent to that of Kĕlaké Langu. Bata Fo had two divisions, Kaja Langu and Kéda Langu. Lāma Nifa is undivided and its houses are in the western part of the lower village, where the divisions of Tapo Onã are also located, as well as Olé Onã. The single house of Lefo Léin is next to the beach in the east adjacent to the houses of Sula Onã. Those of Ata Gora are near by on the eastern side of the lower village site. Houses of Ata Folo are in the upper village.

Non-Descent Means of Acquiring Clan Membership

The way in which a family of Lāma Nudek shifted their membership to Bata Onã at the time of the establishment of the lower village has already been described, as have the circumstances of the Kĕlodo Onã section of Lāma Nudek. The particular alliance between Lango Fujo and Bedi Onã as well as that between Ata Gora and the clan named Golok of Lamamanu have also been mentioned. There are in fact several other families who cannot trace lineal descent connections to the ancestors of the clans in which they are members, including a large and influential family in the Téti Nama Papã section of Bĕliko Lolo.

One of my neighbours was a member of Lāma Kéra clan, whose father came as a student to Lamalera from the village of Tapobali and was adopted into the great house of Badi Langu. His mother from Dasi Langu section of Lefo Tukã was adopted into that descent group as an infant and originally came from the region to the west called Ata Déi.

There was a family living in the village until World War II who were called Bernusa after the name of a region on the north coast of the island of Pantar. The boat *Sia Apu* found their ancestors at sea. There were three men in a small boat, named Ula, Sai, and Naga, who were fleeing Bernusa for some reason. Because *Sia Apu*'s boat builder came from the clan Léla Onã, Ula was given to that clan. Sai and Naga were given to Lāma Nifa clan. These men gave rise to the descent group Bernusa and were regarded as *ari-ana*, *léi-lima* (younger sibling-child, foot-hand), that is as slaves.[11] Their descendants, in particular two brothers named Asa and Kerak, came to be regarded as witches as well. Allegedly the brothers acknowledged that they were witches. According to report, people felt that they were being 'bothered' by the brothers at night. They would tell the brothers that they had seen them in the night and Asa and Kerak would say that they had not been able to sleep, therefore they must have been visited by an evil spirit. During the Japanese occupation of the island in World War II, the Japanese had a round-up of all of the reputed witches on the island and took them to Hadakewa on the north coast of Lembata, which was then the administrative centre for the island. From Lamalera they took the brothers Asa and Kerak. The Japanese made the 'witches' march into the sea up to their necks. They then made them confess. The Japanese asked them what tasted better, bananas and yams or human flesh. The 'witches' said human flesh. According to this version of events the Japanese did not punish the 'witches', who lived around Hadakewa until the war was over, when most eventually drifted home. Asa and Kerak, however, never returned to Lamalera.

Villagers have claimed that there used to be many slaves in Lamalera and that their descendants still live in the village although they are not now regarded as slaves. Members of Lamalera used to buy slaves from the interior during the hunger season for a small quantity of maize. This story has the ring of truth to it, but I never encountered anyone willing to openly speak of any member of the village as of slave descent or even to imply such. However, one man did carefully call me into this house one day to detail his family history because he had heard, falsely as it happened, that someone had told me that his ancestors had been slaves.

This history is interesting in its own right. The man's father originated in one of the mountain villages and was one of twelve children. One day the grandfather was visiting a friend in Lamalera, who despite having married three times had no living male offspring. This man asked to be given one of the male children, since the grandfather had too many children, and he had not enough. An agreement was reached and the child grew up in Lamalera, not knowing who his true parents were. When the family in Lamalera had too much fish, they would give some to their friends in the mountain village. When this family had too much palm wine, they would give some to the Lamalera family. The child was intended to serve as both younger sibling and as child (a potentially significant combination, given local idiom). When his parents visited, no one told him who they were. Eventually he learned. When the child grew up, he too eventually had twelve children. He also built the great house for his section of his present clan. He was a successful harpooner, who once harpooned a whale in which were found four pieces of ambergris, which became treasures of the clan segment, and about which there were later disputes with, at least what was interpreted as, lethal effects during the period of my research and earlier. The man who told me all of this said that he had gone to the knowledgeable elders of the lower village and asked them if his father had been a slave or servant, which they denied. Nevertheless, he feels to some extent aggrieved and marginalized by his lack of say in group affairs.

Groups which have Disappeared

Two tiny groups, Kiko Onã, originally from Lamakera, and Keto Pukã, have disappeared in this century. One man and his mother remain in the village from Keto Pukã. He has been taken in by Bedi Onã. Another, Beni Onã, was represented at the time of research by only one married woman. A more spectacular and distressing case concerns the formerly rich and powerful, but highly exclusive clan named Lefo Séfo. These people were so arrogant that, not only did they wear fine ceremonial clothing at all times (even when working in the kitchen), but when villagers went to the houses of Lefo Séfo to trade maize for fish, they would have to wear the same fine ceremonial clothing or be turned away. They had one boat named *Fao Pukã*, but they would not let members of other clans join its crew. With this boat they were able to get fish every day; smaller porpoise they could get in such numbers that they piled them up in the boat. If hunting pilot whale, they might get up to three in one day. They did not beach their catch at the shore in front of the lower village as the other boats did, but on a lava outcropping below the upper village called *Lodo Ikã* (drop [or unload] the fish), which is still occasionally used for this purpose. Their land was near by above this point. When the other boats would sail near in order to try to harpoon the companions of the slain porpoise, they would stick their harpooning pole in the water so the porpoise would disappear. When the other boats left, they would call the porpoise back. Or if another boat were about to harpoon a porpoise, they would strike their harpooning rope against the hull of their boat to drive it off.

Once the *Fao Pukã* turned over at sea, the harpoon rope being pulled to the centre of the boat, making it easy to tip the boat over. The harpooner of the nearest boat ordered his crew to leave them to their own devices. He also ordered the other boats to return to shore without helping them. The other boats told each other not to help and not to mention the accident when they reached shore. As a result most of the men of *Fao Pukã* boat died, although some survived and came ashore west of the village. By the time they got back to the village, the ceremony for their deaths had taken place and they had to call from outside the village, not being allowed to enter immediately. However, people regarded their voices as the voices of their dead spirits. Thereafter the remaining members of the clan began to die in large numbers, leaving only a brother, Sinu Kiko, and a sister Lo Kuku. When Sinu Kiko died sometime before 1920, he had no clothing, so Lo Kuku wept in front of the house of a man in the Lali Nama Papã section of Bĕliko Lolo clan who was his wife–giver. That man was out at sea at that time, so Lo Kuku begged a cloth of his wife in which to bury Sinu Kiko. She replied, 'Wait until my husband returns.' Lo Kuku, who then was a childless widow, did not wait, but went to the house of the Badi Langu section of the clan Lāma Kéra, who were Sino Kiku's wife-takers. They provided the needed cloth. As a result they inherited the land and what remained of Lefo Séfo's wealth, which included a golden chain, *loda mas*, and golden earrings, *bĕlaong mas*. Lo Kuku died sometime in the 1920s. Their land is said to be very restricted religiously; however, several members of Bĕliko Lolo now have built houses on it. This story is regarded as being true by the several people I have heard it from. The man whose wife was first approached for the burial cloth is the father's father of one of the people who told me about it, and I lived in the house owned by the son of the man who did provide the cloth.

4

Marriage Alliance

Marriage alliance is now recognized in anthropology to constitute not only a potentially coherent set of practices relating groupings of people in a series of mutual obligations lasting longer than a lifetime and occasioned by exogamous marriages, but also in some societies a principle of social organization on a scale comparable to that of unilineal descent. The literature on the subject is huge, and the topic has a long and varied history. Even to selectively mention such important contributions as those by van Ossenbruggen (1930), van Wouden (1935, 1968), Lévi-Strauss (1949, 1969), Leach (1951), and Needham (1962) is to seriously misrepresent the breadth and richness of that literature and the controversies it has provoked. The interested novice might best be advised to look first at Dumont (1968) and Needham (1986) and to read the works cited by them, before branching out.

Marriage alliance is a familiar topic in the literature on eastern Indonesia, particularly the asymmetric form or, as the Dutch called it, circulating connubium, which J. P. B. de Josselin de Jong (1935, 1977) and van Wouden (1935, 1968) thought to be one of the key features of social organization in the whole region. Subsequent ethnographic research has demonstrated a great deal more variety than de Josselin de Jong and van Wouden anticipated, although it has also confirmed the existence of asymmetric marriage alliance in some places (see for example R. H. Barnes 1974a; Forth 1981; Renard-Clamagirand 1982). Such information as we have from the Lamaholot region indicates that here patrilineal descent groups are linked by inherited ties of marriage alliance in which women pass from group to group, while substantial gifts, generally speaking elephant tusks, circulate in return (R. H. Barnes 1977a, Graham 1987). There are also indications, although never very fully documented ones, that there is substantial variation in how this theme is implemented in different communities. Such ethnographic variation is something which we have learned to expect. The impact of Catholicism and other influences of the modern world have also contributed their quota to the variation in the present workings of marriage alliances.

Alliances between Descent Groups

Gregorius Keraf (1978: 98 n. 1) writes that the people of Lamalera know precisely how each clan relates to all the other clans. There are three possible relationships, the first of which is that with clans which are 'brothers', ari-ãmã.

The second is with those who are wife-givers, the *opu-laké*. The third is with those who are *ana-opu* or wife-takers. 'Given these three kinds of relationship, everyone knows how to refer to everyone else in the village.' *Ari-ãmã* is compounded from words meaning 'younger brother' and 'his father' and stands in particular for a person's whole descent group. Other expressions which serve the same purpose include *inã-ãmã* (his mother-his father) and *kaka-ári* (elder brother-younger brother). Another expression for descent groups deemed like brothers to one's own is *kĕlé* or *kĕlé-kenapé*.

In his history of Lamalera the schoolteacher Yosef Bura Bataona (n.d.) characterizes the community as having divided itself into three groups, labelled A, B, and C, which are united in a closed cycle of marriage alliance, A giving women to B, B to C, and C to A. He then provides a list, giving the membership of each of these groupings, as in Fig. 2.

He writes that the set headed by Bĕliko Lolo was in the relationship of *opu-laké* (wife-givers) to that headed by Lefo Tukã, while that headed by Lefo Léin was *opu-laké* to Bĕliko Lolo's group. In time, he writes, slowly the nature of the alliance ties changed so that some wife-givers became wife-takers and marriages took place between descent groups within the same set. Quite unaware of Yosef Bura Bataona's history, I recorded a nearly identical, but longer list with the assistance of the former *kakang* Petrus Bau Dasion. A more comprehensive list completely compatible with the other two, indicating places for even the tiniest groups, is in Fig. 3.

The pattern described above has been given me in smaller or greater fragments by various people at various times and in various contexts during my visits to the village since 1970. It is remarkable that all of this information, once collated, is thoroughly consistent. People have emphasized that marriage must not be reversed. You must take wives from wife-givers and give sisters to wife-takers. In the past, so I have been told, the ancestors would insist on strict compliance with these regulations, but today in a more liberated climate, people can choose their partner from any descent group. In fact, the genealogies reveal that the pattern given in Fig. 3 is only a rough guide to practice and

Lefo Léin	←	Lefo Tukã	←	Bĕliko Lolo
Lãma Kéra A and B[a]		Tana Kĕrofa		Lãma Nudek
Lãma Nifa		etc.		Léla Onã
Tapo Onã				Bata Onã
Olé Onã				Ola Langu
Ebã Onã				Bedi Onã
				Bata Fo
				Sula Onã

FIG. 2. Marriage alliance ties among Lamalera descent groups
according to Yosef Bura Bataona

[a] See p. 98.

Lefo Léin	←	Lefo Tukā	←	Běliko Lolo
Lāma Kéra		Tana Kěrofa		Lāma Nudek
Lāma Nifa		Ata Kéi		Léla Onā
Tapo Onā		Tufa Onā		Bata Onā
Olé Onā		Ata Gora		Ola Langu
Ebā Onā		Lefo Séfo		Bedi Onā
Ata Folo				Bata Fo
Hari Onā				Sula Onā
				Keto Pukā
				Beni Onā

FIG. 3. An ideal pattern of marriage alliance among Lamalera
descent groups

that a good many marriages do not conform to it today. Tables 9 and 10 compare actual marriages with the favoured pattern set out in Fig. 3. Altogether, 951 individual marriages are involved, comprising 633 marriages between men and women of the village plus 216 marriages outside the village by males and 102 outside the village by females. In addition there are two marriages which breach clan exogamy. One occurred some generations ago, and no further information was forthcoming. The other was a liaison between members of different sub-clans of the same clan which had not yet been formalized at the time of research, although it had produced a child. Table 9 shows that among men some 39 per cent of marriages have been in accord with Fig. 3, while around 17 per cent have reversed the direction, nearly 19 per cent have been with women in descent groups in the same section, and 25 per cent have been with women from outside the village. For women, 44 per cent of marriages fit Fig. 3, 19½ per cent reversed the direction, nearly 22 per cent were with men in descent groups in the same section and 14 per cent were with men from outside the village. The differences in percentages for men and women result from the larger record of marriages by men outside the village, which itself is affected by a bias in social memory in favour of men. Taking only the 633 marriages within the village, 52 per cent (51.97) were as would be expected from Fig. 3, 23 per cent (22.75) reversed expectation, and 25 per cent (25.28) were between partners belonging to descent groups in the same set.[1] Not all of these marriages involved people who were currently resident in Lamalera at the time of research. Some were permanently resident in locations as far away as Jakarta and Bandung.

In principle, men and women should select a spouse from among persons who stand to them as *réu*, a word which otherwise means friend. At feasts men and women who regard themselves as *běréun*, that is *réu* to each other, sometimes sprinkle or pour water on each other, women on men, men on women. In the past, elders of the village strongly favoured marriage into this category. In general in Lamaholot culture, this category includes the genealogical mother's brother's daughter (MBD) for a man and the father's sister's son

Marriage Alliance

TABLE 9. *Marriages of Men in Lamalera Descent Groups*

Clan	Sub-Clan	Givers	Takers	Same	Outside	Total
Bĕliko Lolo						
	Téti Nama Papã	10	2	6	11	29
	Lali Nama Papã	19	3	5	13	40
	Unknown	2	1	1		4
Lāma Nudek		4	1	2	4	11
	Kĕlodo Onã	3			4	7
Lefo Tukã						
	Dasi Langu	13	1	1	6	21
	Kéda Langu	18	3		2	23
	Lima Langu	8			1	9
	Béra Onã	4			3	7
	Unknown				1	1
Tana Kĕrofa						
	Haga Langu	11	3		5	19
	Laba Langu	12	3		4	19
	Unknown	4	1			5
Ata Kéi		13	2	1	6	22
Léla Onã						
	Sinu Langu	16	2	11	14	43
	Bĕlaké Langu	7		2	4	13
	Unknown	1		1		2
Tufa Onã		15	2	1	15	33
Lāma Kéra						
	Badi Langu	8	4		12	24
	Lafa Langu	11	5	1	3	20
	Sinu Langu	1	4	2	8	15
	Pĕrafi Langu	4	21		3	28
	Unknown	1	2			3
Bata Onã						
	Kĕlaké Langu	18	4	3	9	34
	Kifa Langu	25	4	10	5	44
	Jafa Langu	3	1	7	4	15
	Ola Langu	19		2	3	24
	Baso Langu				1	1
	Unknown				1	1
Sula Onã						
	Kebesa Langu	5	1	6	2	14
	Kĕloré Langu	4		2		6
	Kiko Langu		1			1
	Unknown	1				1
Bedi Onã						
	Miku Langu	12	2	18	9	41
	Muri Langu	3	6	17	7	33
	Unknow		1	5		6
Bata Fo						
	Kéda Langu	1		12	5	18
	Kaja Langu	6		5	6	17
Olé Onã		9	5	6	7	27
Ebã Onã						
	Daé Langu	3	1	2	5	11
	Guma Langu	5	1	5	3	14
	Sita Langu		1			1
	Unknown	1			1	2

TABLE 9. (*Continued*)

Clan	Sub-Clan	Givers	Takers	Same	Outside	Total
Ata Folo		6	1		7	14
Lāma Nifa		1	11	3	1	16
Tapo Onā						
	Musi Langu	4	10	3	3	20
	Guna Langu	9	21	2	6	38
	Ado Langu		1			1
	Sola Langu		1			1
	Unknown	2	1	4	1	8
Hari Onā		3	8	11	2	24
Lefo Léin		1	2	1	3	7
Ata Gora		2				2
Lango Fujo		1		2	6	9
		329	144	160	216	849
		38.75%	16.96%	18.85%	25.44%	

(FZS) for a woman. Catholic regulations prohibit the marriage of genealogical first cousins of any kind, so first cross-cousin marriage is prohibited, although it may occasionally occur, but Church regulations do not interfere with marriage of more remote relatives of the appropriate terminological category.[2] By the same token, marriage in the opposite direction, that is for a man with his FZD and for a woman with her MBS, is forbidden not only by the Church, but also by cultural standards.

Of the handful of reversed marriages in my records involving traceable genealogical relatives on both sides, only one is between either first or second cousins of the prohibited kind. A man married his FZD and was thrown out of his clan for doing so. I have no record of anyone marrying his first cousin of the preferred type. Of the parallel cousins, FBC is a prohibited partner because of descent group exogamy. However, MZC, who in many cases will not belong to ego's descent group, is also prohibited on the grounds that he or she is like a brother or sister. I have no record of any marriages with first parallel cousins.

Lamalera conforms to Lamaholot convention, and the convention characteristic of asymmetric marriage alliance throughout Asia, in that wife-givers are superior to wife-takers and are owed deference and respect. An individual has a particular relationship to the people who have given his or her mother. They are singled out as *opu pukã*, or 'trunk wife-givers', in a metaphor commonplace in this part of Indonesia. The *opu pukã* are those who have primary ceremonial responsibilities to their sister's children and who have primary claim on marriage prestations resulting from the marriages of their sisters. In the past they were deemed to have the power to curse or to heal their sister's children, as is also true in Kédang (at the eastern end of the same island) and among the Toba Batak of Sumatra.

TABLE 10. *Marriages of Women in Lamalera Descent Groups*

Clan	Sub-Clan	Givers	Takers	Same	Outside	Total
Běliko Lolo						
	Téti Nama Papã	10	3	1	5	19
	Lali Nama Papã	11	4	13	6	34
	Unknown	4	4	8		16
Lāma Nudek		3		5	1	9
	Kělodo Onã		1	1	4	6
Lefo Tukã						
	Dasi Langu	6	5	1	3	15
	Kéda Langu	8	7	1	2	18
	Lima Langu	5	1			6
	Béra Onã	4	1		2	7
	Unknown	2				2
Tana Kěrofa						
	Haga Langu	2	3			5
	Laba Langu	7	8		3	18
	Unknown	19		1		20
Ata Kéi		8	1		4	13
Léla Onã						
	Sinu Langu	12	4	8	8	32
	Bělaké Langu	2	3	1	1	7
	Unknown	3	3			6
Tufa Onã		8	3		7	18
Lāma Kéra						
	Badi Langu	4	1	2	3	10
	Lafa Langu	9	1		2	12
	Sinu Langu	2		1		3
	Pěrafi Langu	12	2	7	1	22
	Unknown	11		3		14
Bata Onã						
	Kělaké Langu	9	7	8	4	28
	Kifa Langu	19	13	12	5	49
	Jafa Langu	1	4			5
	Ola Langu	4	8	11	1	24
	Unknown	1		5		6
Sula Onã	Kebesa Langu	3	2			5
	Kěloré Langu	1	2	2		5
	Kiko Langu		1			1
	Unknown	4	4	4		12
Bedi Onã	Miku Langu	1	13	13	5	32
	Muri Langu	1	7	8	2	18
	Unknown		3	2		5
Bata Fo	Kéda Langu	3	3	4	6	16
	Kaja Langu	7	6	7	2	22
	Unknown	1				1
Olé Onã		23	1	3		27
Ebã Onã						
	Daé Langu	7			2	9
	Guma Langu	10			2	12
	Sita Langu	2		1		3
	Unknown	9				9
Ata Folo		10			2	12
Lāma Nifa		9	1	4	4	18

TABLE 10. (*Continued*)

Clan	Sub-Clan	Givers	Takers	Same	Outside	Total
Tapo Onā						
	Musi Langu	12	1	2		15
	Guna Langu	12		8	8	28
	Unknown	15	3	3		21
Hari Onā		6	5	2	2	15
Lefo Léin		6		3		9
Ata Gora		1				1
Beni Onā			2	2		4
Keto Pukā			3			3
Lango Fujo				3	5	8
		329	144	160	102	735
		44.76%	19.59%	21.77%	13.88%	

Relationship Classification

Since ideally the social world is divided up, as indicated by Keraf, into three categories linked by marriage in a circle, that is *opu-laké, kaka-āri* (and synonyms), and *ana opu*, or wife givers, sibling groups, and wife-takers, it could be inferred that all relatives will fall into one of these three broad groupings. Essentially this picture is a correct one. As is shown in Appendix I, a person can infer his relationship to a third group by knowing its relations to a second group to which his own is also related. These inferences are based on the simple model of a three-part circle. Allowing for Church interference with first-cousin marriage, which is unlikely to have ever had a very high incidence in any case, Lamalera relationship terminology can be ordered for asymmetric marriage alliance and patrilineal descent with a categorical prescription for *réu*, including MBD and FZS. The terminology makes characteristic equations and distinctions indicative of these two rules. There are certain differences in the way a woman classifies relatives from the way a man does so, which are compatible with the fact that the woman is the moving element in the alliance relationship. The relationship terminology is presented and analysed in Appendix I.

Improper Unions

Not all marriages are proper ones. The genealogies reveal two cases of unexplained marriages or permanent liaisons which breach clan exogamy. Usually these are between lines whose genealogical connection cannot be traced. One marriage was expected in 1982 between a man and a woman of different great houses within a very large clan, with several substantial branches and offshoots. This arrangement was not liked, but was regarded as inevitable because the couple already had a child. There must have been similar cases in the past when the first marriages took place between Bata Onã and its offshoots Sula Onã, Bedi Onã, and Bata Fo.

The most blatant case of improper marriage was the occasion of attempts to bring about a reconciliation in 1982. In this instance, a young man married his genealogical father's sister's daughter, presumably first getting her pregnant. The nature of the genealogical connection was even more scandalous than the fact that this former Catholic lay brother had taken up with a woman who at the time was still a nun. When it was found out what had happened, villagers beat on the house of the man's father, where he had sought shelter, and there was much shouting. The young man was subsequently expelled from the clan and village. A man from Adonara who was wife-taker to the young man's descent group was brought in to attempt to negotiate a reconciliation with the man's father's brother, who was the guardian of the great house, so that the young man could be brought back into the clan. A reconciliation within the woman's descent group had up to that point not been possible.

One day in 1979 a man and his daughter arrived in Lamalera to negotiate with one of the clans. According to an acquaintance involved in the negotiations they concerned a young man who was then a high school student in Lewoleba, his potential wife being a Muslim woman from Lamahala, Adonara. It seems this boy was for some time working in Waiwerang, Adonara, where he met the girl and got her pregnant. Apparently things had been arranged to the point of engagement, when the boy returned to the school in Lewoleba. The relatives of the girl were extremely angry. At the time my acquaintance was working in Waiwerang. Because he was there he had to represent his clan in discussions with the angry relatives—a job usually reserved for a special person within the clan. The relatives were all for going to Lewoleba and cutting the boy up, but were talked out of it.

In any case the girl was taken to Lewoleba. After a while the boy asked her to return home so that she would not disturb his school work. In the event the young woman and her father went to Lamalera for discussions. The boy's clan came off rather badly. The Lamahala people said that according to their custom they must receive Rp. 250,000 in cash (US $595), plus a large elephant tusk and three goats and finally this is what was agreed. In Lamahala they claimed they might receive as many as ten tusks and up to thirty goats, for which there was no return, other than some food given the couple. One man in the boy's clan complained that under these circumstances the youth's group loses out entirely, while under Lamalera customary law both sides do well. In the end, the girl's father was seen off on the passenger boat with Rp. 5,000 (US $12) travel money and one goat. The girl stayed in Lamalera, while the boy became, at least nominally, a Muslim.

The source for this information was himself in trouble because of indiscretions on Adonara, where he got a woman pregnant, even though he was already married to a woman from Lamalera. The young woman came to Lamalera, where she lived with his parents, while he and his wife lived in a separate dwelling. His sister was handed over to the family of the woman from Adonara, which meant that when she married they would get the marriage prestations owed for her. In the meantime she was ordered to do all kinds of menial work. She travelled back and forth between Adonara and Lamalera, but spent most of her time on Adonara. The circumstances sounded like a traditional form of debt slavery in all but name.[3]

One prominent member of the village had been away from the village for six months, when he returned to discover his youngest daughter not only pregnant but about to get married. He not unsurprisingly became angry and tried to obstruct the marriage. He thought the young man in question would never be able to provide an elephant tusk. I have no further information about circumstance and motives, but it is clear that premature pregnancy may be the only option for a couple faced with the implacable opposition of their parents for whatever ground, including the husband's inability to meet his obligations concerning marriage prestations.

Marriage

To marry or to wed is called *kafé* or *kafé-gaté*. *Gaté* means to hook, but in this case is just an extension of the verb *kafé*, which in itself is in danger of being confused with its apparently unrelated near homonym meaning harpoon. Such is the explanation provided me by Professor Gregorius Keraf. When things go well today, weddings are conducted in the church at a proper interval after the reading of banns. Receptions following weddings often involve a feast under temporary bamboo awnings, perhaps using sails as a shade. During much of the festivities, bride and groom sit formally in chairs adjacent to each other nearly motionless and in what looks to be a state of acute embarrassment. The bride dresses in a white bridal dress, the groom in a dark suit. Both wear white lace gloves. Their European clothing is in strong contrast to normal village wear. Opposed to their subdued manner is the generally exuberant celebrating and mutual entertainment indulged in by friends and relatives of all kinds around them.

Before the wedding a considerable amount of formal negotiating and ceremony should already have taken place following the requirements of traditional culture. These steps are initiated once it has become clear that the pair have made their choice. Young people may well have known each other from childhood or have met at school. From time to time dances are arranged for the youths and maidens, usually by the village head, in the village clearing. For those living in houses near by but not participating, these events can make for an uncomfortable evening, as the young people circle dance and sing (repetitiously) into the early hours of the morning. Sometimes one village will invite another to a football match, which provides opportunities for socializing.

Other opportunities for meeting or assignations exist at markets or on the way there. Munro wrote that markets served the same purpose as balls among Europeans, where young women appeared in their finest attire. The role of chaperon was filled by the village head. People left their village in time so that they reached the market just as it was getting dark. The whole night would then be spent in singing (*solé*) and dancing, with much use of palm wine. The next morning the market itself finished very quickly. There most engagements took place, and during the period of engagement, when sexual relations were permitted, the young woman would dance alone with her fiancé (Munro 1915: 15).

Nowadays, with improved transportation, people travel by boat to other towns, where they may be relatively out of the eye of parents and relations. One way and another they seem to overcome social obstacles and inhibitions. A fair number of weddings take place once the bride is pregnant. Of course such weddings often have the sole purpose of satisfying the demands of the Church and simply formalize an established relationship. Since the Church insists that a couple build or have built for them a modern brick house with a tin roof, which can cost very substantial sums in building materials and in any case requires a great deal of preparation, they have a strong incentive to postpone the Church ceremony.

At times relatives inside or outside the descent group may put pressure on young people to initiate the customary law arrangements, when they appear to be delaying overly. These require that a relative of the man be chosen as spokesman, *ata marang*, who then notifies the family of the bride of the youth's intentions and sounds them out to see if they are favourable to the match. In many cases, these approaches are perfunctory formalities, since in effect the decision has already been taken. But in some cases they can be delicate or even unsuccessful. Today, love (in Bahasa Indonesia, *cinta*) is supposed to determine choice of partner. In the past, if a young man had made up his mind, he might wait at an appropriate hiding place and capture the woman. He would run the risk of great injury, and his friends would give him plenty of hard drink, so that he would come back to the house without feeling the damage. He would be chased all the way to the house, where the men of his group would come out and fight. After the woman had been in the house long enough—a few months or a year—things would quiet down and the appropriate negotiations could be taken care of. Bride capture is no longer an acceptable way to overcome resistance, but elopement is still an option. Becoming pregnant is usually an effective way for a woman to overcome parental opposition.

Seegeler (1931: 51–2) gives a classification of types of marriage in the territory under the Raja of Larantuka. It is extremely unfortunate that his companion report about the territory of the Raja of Adonara has been lost, for the essential details were in this report, to which he refers the reader. Nevertheless, it appears that bride capture was a common option, at least in some cases, however, only with the consent of the woman. Elopement seems also to be indicated, and it is plain that early pregnancy was also a strategy.[4]

Remarkably, Prior found that over 90 per cent of marriages in Wolofeo district of central Flores are by elopement, while they make up around 50 per cent in northern Lio and just under 50 per cent in southern Lio (Prior 1988: 99–100, 130). The minority of marriages which are arrived at by formal negotiations are made by, 'the children of families with land and status and therefore [who] still have the influence and wealth to insist upon a formally negotiated settlement for their offspring.' 'Elopement is the usual way for the poor to get married' (Prior 1988: 140).

In all the islands of the Solor Archipelago, there is a tradition that formerly women were often captured and taken as wives. This happened often enough in wars, and sometimes it led to wars, but as an institution it normally occurred in much more peaceful circumstances. If the parents of the girl did not take a favourable attitude to the advances of the young man, or if the girl herself refused to go, then he would gather together a number of friends and relatives and waylay the girl when she was going to market or going out to work in the fields. The more audacious youths would even steal into her house and take her there. Often the whole affair was carried off with considerable bravado. Once the girl was secured, part of the party would stay behind and, when the alarm was raised, exchange blows with her family (Arndt 1940: 185–7). The girl was taken to the home of the youth, where she was made to step over an elephant tusk to insure that she would not flee (Arndt 1940: 134), then she was kept locked in the house for several days until she accepted her condition. Her family may have entered the village of the thief to avenge itself by killing a few animals, but unless they were prepared to start a war this was the limit of their response; the girl, in any case, was never taken back. In a few days the parents of the young man would visit the girl's former home, where they would inquire of her parents how much bridewealth was to be demanded in order to close the affair. Bridewealth paid after a theft of this sort was always much higher than usual; often it was doubled and in Flores it may have amounted to as much as fifteen tusks (Arndt 1940: 12).

Bride theft was outlawed by the Dutch (Arndt 1940: 130). Most villages deny that they still practise it, but they are often ready to accuse their neighbours of doing so. Vatter found that in the Ilé Mandiri district of Flores people accuse the community of Bama of stealing women, while Bama accuses them of doing so (Vatter 1932: 80). The authors leave the impression that in their day it still occurred more frequently than was admitted; indeed, Vatter speaks of Lambunga in Adonara as still practising the custom openly. It may not always have been a matter of simple theft, but may at times have had the character of a traditional and stylized display of exuberance by the groom, often perhaps with the knowledge and complicity of the bride's parents. In Larantuka, after the Catholic wedding ceremony, a Christian bride returns to her father's house where she is removed forcibly by the husband and his companions.

However, it should be observed that bride capture in its rawer forms is related to slave raiding, which was formerly common practice in the region, not only by locals, but also by outsiders, in earlier centuries often acting as commercial agents of the Dutch East Indies Company. Beckering (1911: 181) says that on Adonara there was the practice of stealing children to settle old debts. It is remarkable, he wrote, that despite the fact that such children were given considerable freedom, they did not run away, nor were they retrieved by their relatives. Above all young girls were captured, in order to obtain their bridewealth. Theft of children to settle debts also occurred in south Lembata (Beckering 1911: 196–8).

Once agreement has been reached between the families of bride and groom, a ceremony is held at the great house of the bride-to-be's descent group. This ceremony is called *sigé*, a term which people of Lamalera believe to be Portuguese in origin, but Portuguese *signo* seems an unlikely source. In fact Arndt (1937: 12) translates it as 'to tie or lay something on as a sign'. It is also used in East Flores, where it is pronounced *sige*, and refers to formal reserving of infants for cross-cousin marriage between MBD and FZS (Graham 1991: 130, 292). In his dictionary of the dialect of Malay spoken in Larantuka, Flores, Monteiro, lists *sigi*, 'the day of the official announcement of the engagement of a couple exchanging binding love' (Monteiro 1975: 111–12). This ceremony is also known as *roi bala*, 'to look at the elephant tusks' (Gregorius Keraf 1978: 175).

The relatives of the groom-to-be provide large quantities of boiled pork or dog meat, palm wine, and lontar palm-leaf plates, *kéra*. The purpose of the meeting is to discuss the bridewealth values associated with the marriage, *tutu ina-biné féli*. The layout of such meetings depends upon local circumstances. However, in general the meeting is held in the open, with men sitting on benches or in chairs in one group and women doing so in another. Palm wine and cigarettes are served. Then formal, but usually brief, speeches are made. It may be announced when banns will be read in the church and when the marriage will take place. On one occasion the wife-takers announced that they had six elephant tusks in readiness. Since they did not in fact show them or measure them, one of the purposes of the meeting, there was no decision taken on what would be given in return, although on other occasions there would be. The return given by wife-givers to wife-takers is called *oé* or *oi* (obligations, debts), and would consist in ivory arm bands, *kala*, or resist-dyed cloths, *kefatek*. There is an official spokesman, *ata marang*, for the wife-takers, who may or may not be a member of the same descent group. None is required for the wife-givers, who are represented by the head of the descent group. Before these speeches, the wife-takers fill the palm-leaf containers with meat which they tie they up, before distributing them to the guests, everyone present including

PLATE 8. Lontar palm–leaf plates being distributed to
women during a festival

children being given one such plate (see Plates 8 and 9). Unlike Kédang, where
any festival involving food and drink would also include extended commensality, in Lamalera no one eats during the ceremony. Once the speeches are finished, the relatives of the bride immediately break off and return home. Soon
thereafter most of the rest of those present leave too. All present take their
plates of meat home for later consumption in private.

On one such occasion, a friend commented favourably on the brevity of such
ceremonies in Lamalera, contrasting them to those held in interior villages,
which the government has outlawed except on licence of the district head. He
commented, however, that the district head's office is far away, with the implication that this prohibition had little practical effect. He also mentioned an
article in the magazine *Dian* which in 1981 defended these ceremonies against
the government ban on the grounds that in cities there is plenty of entertainment, but ceremonies serve the purpose of entertainment in the villages as well
as uniting people. On the same occasion the women in the wife-giving clan
complained that they had been given too little meat. So there was another distribution to the women only, on the grounds that it was the women who had
worked to provide the thread which goes with the bride when she moves to her

PLATE 9. Women attending a discussion of marriage prestations

husband's house. The speeches given at the time centred on the fact that no arrangement had yet been made concerning the marriage prestations.

The next formal event takes place on the day before a wedding. This is called *mao/mau* a word which derives from *pao/pau*, which means variously to feed, to provide, to breed, to grow, to tend. This ceremony is in honour of the bride and during it they *pau kebarek*, that is feed or tend to the maiden. On this day all males of the bride's clan and those of her mother's clan come and offer her gifts, such as thread, plates, ivory bracelets, and cloth or clothing. The thread of course has been prepared not by the men, but by their wives, mothers, or sisters. If people want to make a big thing of the event, the gifts will be very large indeed. The thread alone for example might fill a very large basket called *bĕlifo*, which normally is intended for storing unhusked rice. These days, such gifts are usually moderate. Each person presents his gifts to the bride-to-be together with a plate of rice. If she is satisfied, she will take a spoon of rice and eat it. If not, she may ask for more, before eating her rice. Each male is treated in this way in turn. In the evening elders of the two descent groups may gather in the bride's great house for a serious discussion of marriage prestations. They will be accompanied by the *opu pukã* of the bride as well as that of the groom, if different from the bride's father. These two men simply go along to witness the negotiations and are not themselves principals. This meeting is called to undo or open the door, *hoi kenafé*.

Following the wedding, the couple go to the great houses of the source wife-givers, *opu pukã*, of the bride and that of the groom, where there are simple greetings, including coffee and hand-shaking. Then they slowly process in the company of the bride's *opu pukã* to the bride's great house. Those accompanying the couple help carry the gifts which the bride has received (see Plate 10). In Plate 10, the woman is carrying a box for betel quid, in eastern Indonesia a widely recognized symbol of the sexual relationship between a man and a woman. On one occasion the bride's *opu pukã* refused to participate because her descent group had failed to deliver bridewealth it owed for several marriages. When the procession reaches her great house, people present break into weeping. Awnings will have been set up and chairs placed outside. People in the background will be cooking meat, the women will be preparing cakes and so on. Then the couple will be taken to the husband's great house (see Plate 10). In such an affair, there may be as many as twelve families or more contributing to the festival, and each may agree to provide a large pot of palm wine. The principals may provide three.

For four days after the wedding, the husband and wife may not bathe. There is no special name for this period of restriction. The restriction is broken by a

PLATE 10. A bride entering her husband's great house

ceremony called *o rata*, which means to clean the hair, which is done by rubbing coconut oil into their hair. However the expression is merely figurative. The husband's sister sprinkles water on the couple, who then bathe themselves. All of the gifts offered at the *mao* ceremony on the day preceding the wedding are taken from the wife's great house to the husband's great house. The husband's descent group will return a great deal of cooked pork and a large pot of palm wine so that the wife-givers and their guests may have a meal. It is proper for marriage prestations to be exchanged at this time. At the very least, the wife-takers should present a tusk called *olung*, for which there is no specific return gift.

Residence

Residence is in principle patrilocal, although Church pressure leads to neo-local arrangements. Occasionally, especially in the absence of marriage presta-tions, a couple will take up temporary residence in the bride's parents' home. According to Munro (1915: 16), on Lembata when a young man could not pay his bridewealth, he would take up residence with his wife's parents until he could. However, this form of bride service, common enough in eastern Indonesia, is not the usual requirement in Lamalera, at least for any extended period. There are a variety of household arrangements, depending on demo-graphic circumstances, but the standard pattern, insisted upon by the Church, is now individual nuclear family residences. One of my friends claims that there were once houses in the village with several families living in them, and that he remembers one such. This report is compatible with information supplied by van Lynden for the 1850s. He wrote about the islands that both in the moun-tains and on the coasts each house consisted of four or five families, just as Kennedy had stated for Wailolong (van Lynden 1851*a*: 323; Kennedy 1955: 73). Multiple family houses in Lamalera were, however, broken up under pressure from the Raja of Larantuka, and no doubt the Church.

Speaking of the need to do away with extended family dwellings and to impose the rule that every new family must provide itself with a separate house *before* the Catholic wedding may take place, Bruno Pehl, who was the mis-sionary resident in Lamalera from 1951 until 1962, wrote,

For years I have pointed out before every marriage in an almost unmerciful way to both young and old that they are already Catholics in Lamalera and that therefore they must follow the 'Catholic' marriage regulations. That means in practice one pushes the old-fashioned, heathen marriage arrangements somewhat into the background and in the best of circumstances completely forgets them! I maintain the principle that at every suitable or unsuitable opportunity I hammer into their heads: bridewealth affairs must be changed into an affair of an orderly house for the young couple who are to marry. To express it more primitively: provision of bridewealth means Heathen Marriage, provision of a house means Catholic Marriage! (Pehl 1959: 88)

Though the character of the rhetoric has changed, this principle has been maintained, and, as I have witnessed, at least occasionally causes bitter anger among family members responsible for making the necessary arrangements. Marriage is always a collective matter with serious obligations on and implications for a wide range of relatives. It is precisely these collective implications that Pehl was not willing to tolerate.

Although there may be several houses belonging to a clan or clan segment, and some of these may be located at the new suburb of Futung Lolo, for ceremonial and customary law purposes membership is in the great house of the descent group. It is here that marriage and death ceremonies take place, especially those dealing with the entailments of marriage alliance. The woman ceremonially joins the household of her husband there following a hair-washing ritual. This change of membership, which perhaps is better described as joining the husband's household than as joining the husband's descent group, by no means implies that a married woman severs her relations with her natal descent group. Males will continue to take active interest in the welfare of married sisters and their offspring throughout their lifetimes. Furthermore, the mutual obligations of the alliance extend beyond the lifetimes of the parties involved.

Kefina Muko Pukã

Each descent group is associated with a single other descent group which stands to it as *kefina muko pukã*, banana trunk *kefina*. *Kefina* includes among other relatives women of one's own descent line who have married into another such line. *Kefina muko pukã* are traditional wife-takers, but are not necessarily the immediate wife-takers of the active members of the descent group. They play a significant role in customary affairs and ceremonies of a descent group. For example when a great house belonging to a descent group is erected or repaired the *kefina muko pukã* is required to initiate the building work by bringing, symbolically, the building materials and tools. On one occasion when such a house was being reroofed, a man with no immediate family connection to the owners performed this function and handed up the first sheet of tin on the morning when the roofing began, before going home and leaving the others to get on with the work. Other members of his group might well have taken on this role, but he was of an appropriate age and standing. On the day before, when the framework of the roof had been put in place, the workers put up as flags a resist-dyed cloth of two panels (*kefatek nai rua*), a sarong suitable for daily wear, and a commercial cloth. The custom is that such cloth may be taken away for keeping by wife-takers, but anyone who does so will either have provided animals for the associated feast or will be committing himself to do so in the future. Villagers were able to supply the descent group names of the *kefina muko pukã* of each of the clans. Unlike the ideal alliance patterns listed above, in this case they broke the older and larger clans into their constituent great houses. However, in keeping with a general vagueness about the internal organization of Lāma Kéra clan, they divided it simply into two, which they designated A and B, associated respectively with the upper and lower village (see Fig. 4).

The relationship which obtains between wife-givers and wife-takers is designated *opu-maki*. In this all-embracing phrase, *opu* indicates the wife-givers, while *maki* refers to the wife-takers. *Opu alep*, in which *opu* is qualified by the adjective indicating possession, *alep*, is another expression for wife-givers and is equivalent to *opu-laké*. Wives of wife-givers are designated female *opu*, that is *opu-faé*. A descent group's relationship with its women who have married into other descent groups is indicated by *ina-biné* (approximately 'mothers sisters'). This expression comes into use, for example, in sessions in which they *tutu ina-biné féli*, that is discuss the value of the marriage prestations.

Descent Group	*Kefina Muko Pukã*
Upper Village:	
Lefo Tukã	Lāma Kéra A
Lāma Kéra A	Lāma Nudek
Bĕliko Lolo,	Lefo Tukã,
Lali Nama Papã	Dasi Langu
Téti Nama Papã	Lima Langu
Lāma Nudek	Tufa Onã
Tana Kĕrofa	Ebã Onã
Ebã Onã	Léla Onã
Léla Onã	Tufa Onã
Tufa Onã	Lāma Kéra A
Ata Kéi	Lāma Kéra A
Lefo Séfo	Lāma Kéra A
Lower Village:	
Bata Onã,	
Kĕlaké Langu	Bata Fo
Jafa Langu	Bata Fo
Kifa Langu	Lāma Kéra B
Ola Langu	Lāma Kéra B
Bedi Onã	Lāma Kéra B
Sula Onã	Lāma Kéra B
Lāma Kéra B	Bĕliko Lolo
	Teti Nama Papã
Ata Folo	Léla Onã
Lāma Nifa	Olé Onã
Tapo Onã	Hari Onã
Hari Onã	Bĕliko Lolo
	Lali Nama Papã
Lefo Léin	Bata Onã
	Kifa Langu

Fig. 4. *Kefina muko pukã* of Lamalera descent groups

Marriage Prestations

Unlike Kédang on the eastern end of the island of Lembata (R. H. Barnes 1974*a*), where negotiations over marriage prestations is always a public matter in the presence of the assembled elders of all of the clans and under the supervision of the village head, in Lamalera the village head is not normally involved in such discussions unless his descent group is concerned. Only members of the descent groups directly involved in a given marriage, together with the *opu pukã* of the bride and groom, play a role. In Lamalera fewer people know precisely how marriage prestations are valued and measured, because only one or two people are responsible for talking.

Some say that the original marriage gifts were gongs and mortars for stamping rice. Later elephant tusks and *patola* cloth from India were substituted. These commodities villagers think were introduced by the Dutch and Portuguese. The Dutch and Portuguese did of course deal in these goods, although the evidence indicates that they figured in inter-island trade before either the Dutch or the Portuguese arrived in the east. Ivory and silk cloths were mentioned as trade items in the Moluccas by Tomé Pires in his Suma Oriental of 1512 to 1515 (Pires 1944: 198). Barbosa, writing in 1516, specifically mentions gongs, ivory, patola (Cambaya cloths), and porcelain as treasures stored up in Banda and acquired in exchange for nutmeg and mace. Such cloth was among the goods attracted to Timor in ships from Malacca and Java in exchange for the white sandalwood prized in India (Barbosa 1921: 2: 196–8).

Cambaya cloths are held in great value here [Ambon], and every man toils to hold so great a pile of them, that when they are folded and laid on the ground one on the other, they form a pile as high as himself. Whoso possesses this holds himself to be free and alive, for if he be taken captive he cannot be ransomed save for so great a pile of cloths (Barbosa 1921: 2: 199).

Lamaholot interest in patola and ivory was mentioned as early as 1643 (de Sá 1956: 480) (for a summary see Ruth Barnes 1989: 126–9). They continued to be mentioned from time to time in historical documents thereafter. In 1625 Portuguese ships were bringing cloth from the Coromandel Coast and Bengal (as well as raw silk, silk cloth, and Chinese porcelain from Macao) to Macassar in the months of November and December, returning to Malacca and India from May to July, loaded with, among other things, sandalwood, wax, and tortoiseshell from Ende (Flores), Solor, and Timor. Malays and Macassarese traded this cloth to other islands including Solor and Timor (Heeres 1896: 124). In 1653 Lamahala upset its Dutch allies by establishing a contract of neutrality with the Portuguese, in which Lamahala gave the Portuguese two slaves and nineteen patola, for which the Portuguese compensated them with a return of elephant tusks (Coolhaas 1964: 684). In 1663 the Queen of Solor wrote to the Governor-General of the Dutch East Indies Company requesting, among other items, an elephant tusk to use as a pillow in her grave (van der Chijs 1891:

499). In February 1681 the Company sent to her sister's daughter and successor two *patola* plus five patola handkerchiefs as well as other goods in payment for a slave (de Haan 1919: 134).

Beckering (1911: 178–81) found on Adonara that family treasures often contained silk double ikat *patola* (in Lamaholot *ketipa*) and elephant tusks, which were also used as marriage gifts. Much the same is still true on Lembata, except that *patola* are heirlooms which are no longer used in marriage exchanges. Instead, return gifts from the woman's group include fine dyed and decorated cloths of local cotton manufactured by village women. Some patterns used in local cloth derive from these patola.

Of interest is Radermacher's report (1786: 181) that at the end of the eighteenth century Macassar ships included elephant tusks in the goods they traded on Flores for, among other things, slaves, oil, and rope. Hogendorp (1780: 427) describes great trading in the same century on Solor of iron, elephant tusks, silk *patola*, and other cloths which the islanders obtained for slaves, wax, ambergris, bird nests, fish (i.e. whale) oil, and other products. Traders from Ende acquired elephant tusks in Singapore, often in exchange for slaves, many of whom came from Solor. Elephant tusks served in the Flores area as the principal means of payment. Endenese trade with Singapore was slowed first by the prohibition of slavery and secondly by competition from the Royal Packet Company (Koninklijk Pakeetvaart Maatshappij) (Freijss 1860: 527–8; Bouman 1916/17: 113). Brummund (1853: 127) mentioned that Macassarese *padukang*[5] brought elephant tusks, knives, gongs, copper wire, Chinese porcelain, and linen to trade on Flores for sandalwood, rubber, bird nests, coconut oil, wild cinnamon, sulphur, saltpetre, gold, bezoar, and ambergris.[6] In 1869 Veth wrote that annually in February and March boats came to Flores from Celebes (Sulawesi) loaded with gold, elephant tusks, cloth, coarse porcelain, native field knives (*parang*), and copper work, and returned in August and September laden with bird nests, rubber, wax and oil (Veth 1869: 323). Four years later Kluppel wrote that in the months of December, January, and February the Macassarese arrived, bringing gunpowder, arak, field knives, knives, elephant tusks, cloth, etc., which they sold to the population on credit. They then went on to Timor and elsewhere, returning in June, July, and August to pick up payment in the form of coconut oil, tortoiseshell, whale oil, shark fins, bird nests, etc. The Butonese traded cloth for cotton, maize, or unhusked rice (Kluppel 1873: 387).

Beckering (1911: 178) supposed that the elephant tusks brought into the islands in former centuries derived, like the *patola*, from India. According to Cornelis Speelman's 1670 report on Macassar trade, the Macassarese acquired the elephant tusks they brought in to Flores and Timor from Siam and Cambodia (Noorduyn 1983: 119).[7] According to Kluppel, when a Solorese had got together fifteen or twenty guilders, he used it to buy a small elephant tusk, which he traded later when his wealth had increased for a larger one. 'The tusks

however just lie around, thus a dead capital' (Kluppel 1873: 387). On Adonara
and Lembata the maize harvest normally exceeded consumption; so that in
1915, 398 *pikul* (or 27.26 short tons) of maize were exported (Hens 1916: 46).
Munro (1915: 17) observed that in some places on Lembata, such as Kédang,
Labala, and eastern Lewoleba district, where the maize and rice harvest could
be very rich, the surplus harvest was used to purchase elephant tusks and
gongs, which demonstrated the degree of prosperity of the mountain dwellers.
They would pay very high sums for them. Often the market value represented
no more than 10 per cent of the purchase price. Rifles and powder were also
sold for fancy prices. In 1884 the Resident of Timor reported that elephant
tusks and silk shawls (which he specified were *ketipa*, the Lamaholot name)
were the two foremost articles of trade in the Solor Islands. The tusks had
great value there although the import of both articles almost did not exist any
longer. He made a similar comment in 1887, when he remarked that silk shawls
of a singular pattern had a value between 35 guilders and 90 guilders (Greve
1884 and 1887).

The Minutes of the Batavian Society of Arts and Sciences for 1908 contain
a remarkable letter from First Class Medical Officer G. A. J. van der Sande
dated 4 May 1908 concerning around twenty-five old elephant tusks in the care
of the civil officer in Larantuka, First Lieutenant of the Infantry J. G. van den
Bossche, which he commented were from ancient times regarded by the population of Flores as valuable family possessions and held by them in great
esteem.

The great monetary value of these objects rests not at all in the market value of their
ivory—for that they are too discoloured and chipped or cracked—but in the circumstance that they derive from a period of trade by Chinese merchants, of which the
written history has only incompletely come to us and the oral history of which the
natives no longer remember.

These tusks have had and still have a very great role to play in the lives of these
people and constitute in fact a chapter in the history of these islands; those resting with
the Civil Officer were for the most part surrendered in settlement of fines.

These tusks were destined to be sold again to the local population to the benefit
of the district treasury.

With the speedy and deep-going changes in the political as well as the economic realms
which are taking place today on Flores as in the whole Timor Archipelago, the significance of these tusks for their present owners before long will disappear and for the
most part they will certainly be lost.

Observing that no examples of such tusks were to be found in Dutch
museums and that the high price of these 'by western standards worthless
pieces of ivory' had been an obstacle to their purchase with private funds by
scientific collectors, van der Sande proposed that the Batavian Society take
advantage of his good offices on the spot to acquire the tusks already in the

possession of the Netherlands-Indies government in order to send a large and a small tusk to each of the ethnographic museums in Batavia, Leiden, Rotterdam, and Amsterdam. The Batavian Society decided to purchase ten tusks, five large and five small, for this purpose (Liefrinck 1908: 63–4). Unfortunately for the project, the Resident of Timor wrote back that in the view of the civil officer at Larantuka, the tusks belonged to the district treasury and acquired no ethnographic interest by virtue of having earlier been imported via Singapore. They looked like other elephant tusks, and despite being discoloured on the outside they still retained value because the ivory on the inside had not deteriorated. Furthermore they still had value for the people of East Flores as a capital investment. They would readily pay between four hundred and six hundred guilders for large tusks. Hearing this, the Batavia Society changed its mind and decided not to purchase them (Pott 1908: 89).

Marriage prestations are referred to as 'goats-elephant tusks' (*fiti-bala*) (Gregorius Keraf 1978: 166). Bridewealth *per se* is known by the common Lamaholot term *féli*, elsewhere *wélin*, meaning broadly both price and marriage gift. Kruyt (1923) observed that for the Toraja of Sulawesi purchase is broadly associated with gift giving and has magical implications. Van Ossenbruggen (1930: 221–2; 1935: 13, 15) took up Kruyt's interpretation and emphasized what he regarded as the magical character of marriage gifts in Indonesia, as did Fischer (1932). Vroklage (1952: 137) commented that, 'Nowhere have I found even the vaguest indication that the bride herself represents a material value'. Marriage gifts ('brideprice' as he prefers to call them) he views as compensation for the loss of the bride, who becomes incorporated into another family group, and for the trouble and expense of raising her and the sorrow of parting. Finally it is a consolation for the ancestors. 'As they themselves say, a woman is "the source of life" and her children will belong to the family group of the husband.' Generally speaking, ethnographers have confirmed that marriage gifts from the husband's group to that of the wife do not express her material value, but do relate to the spiritual importance of what they are receiving in turn, above all life. As Prior observes concerning the wealth goods exchanged by the Lio, there is no clear distinction in them between the sacred and the secular, the material and the spiritual. 'Women, gold, land, fruit of the soil, are all forms of exchange. All have "sacred" aspects, all have material consequences, all have symbolic and cosmic dimensions' (Prior 1988: 109).

Vroklage (1952: 143) also commented on the regularity with which the goods used as standard marriage prestations in Indonesia, cannons, elephant tusks, Chinese plates, gold bracelets, bronze kettledrums, gongs, and so on are objects which have been brought in from outside. MacKnight (1973: 203) too has noted that certain imports acquire special non-utilitarian significance, becoming embedded in a web of social obligation. This is a comparative theme of considerable significance for understanding the workings of both social organization and economic life in eastern Indonesia, especially prior to monetization but still today. Barraud (1979: 205–46) showed for Tanebar-Evav in the Kei Islands that oriented and hierarchized cycles of wealth objects, including money, relate to the interior of Kei society and in a sense make it up, even though they have been brought in from the outside world and acquired by commercial exchanges. These systems have the ability to transform even currency into objects expressing primarily social rather than commercial values (cf. R. H. Barnes 1980*a*: 119; 1985: 214–15).[8] The objects used as marriage gifts are not items of utility but stores of wealth and prestige. Their acquisition originally took place in the same context as barter for utility goods. In this way they link the internal values of the community, in particular marriage alliance and its exchanges, with this foreign trade. Since one way they were obtained was in exchange for agricultural products and since in need they can be and are traded for food, they can represent stored up agricultural (or hunting and fishing) surplus. In the past, when they might also have been obtained in exchange for slaves, they could also represent a dubious demographic surplus product.

Van Lynden wrote (1851*a*: 323) that formerly elephant tusks were principally purchased with slaves, tusks of thirty to forty pounds being worth three or four good slaves. Meanwhile, on Solor a princely marriage entailed five elephant tusks worth fifty to sixty Dutch guilders (van der Hoeven 1867: 283). In the middle of the nineteenth century, coastal peoples of Solor, 'supported by a Prince of Timor', are said to have hunted mountain peoples, who were sold in Ende, Flores, along with other slaves from Flores, Sumba, and Timor, to Buginese, who in turn took them further to Sumbawa, Lombok, and Bali (Freijss 1860: 528). Moor wrote of the Solor region (1837: 11),

There are a great number of petty states (many of them not consisting of more than one village) who are constantly at war for the purpose of making slaves, for whom they always find a ready sale on the coast; they are much esteemed as slaves, and become very good artificers; they are also uncommonly faithful to their masters, and quietly behaved. Great numbers of them were imported annually at Macassar before the prohibition of the slave trade; numbers are however still introduced on those parts of Celebes not under the authority of the European government.[9]

The Dutch restricted trade in slaves in 1818 and made slavery illegal in 1860 (Reid 1983: 34). In 1902 on East Flores and Adonara, a young slave was worth around fifty guilders, paid mostly in trade goods because money even then was still not generally known or used. A young girl was sold on Lembata for two casks of arak and two pieces of linen (Timmers 1902: 44). It should be remembered that it was not just Asian traders who were involved in the slave trade. The Dutch East Indies Company jealously guarded its position in dealing for slaves from Solor and Timor.

Lamalera customary law requires that wife-takers eventually present six elephant tusks to their wife-givers. As we have seen, these six tusks must be men-

tioned in the public negotiations preceding marriage. What is eventually actually given may be no more than one or two, depending on ability to pay. Today
tusks are often difficult to acquire. They have gradually been sold off to people
in the interior or to merchants on Adonara to raise money to build solid houses
or to send children to school. In 1979 a small tusk might bring Rp. 80,000,
c. US $190, while a larger one might fetch Rp. 200,000, or *c.* US $480. In 1982
a large tusk might bring between Rp. 600,000 and Rp. 1,000,000 or between
US $900 and US $1,500.

The person who quoted the higher of these last two figures, who takes a
decidedly eccentric view of marriage prestations, argued that only two or three
people produced by the village were rich enough to afford tusks at these prices.
They were in fact people living elsewhere in Indonesia with good incomes. In
his view the consequence of the demand for elephant tusks was that the village
was now full of spinsters, naming persons with whom I was well acquainted
as examples. A couple would agree to get married, but the woman's parents
would demand so-and-so much bridewealth and the prospective husband
would then respond 'no thanks'. According to the same man, another reason
why there were several unmarried women in the village is that women would
hold out for schoolteacher husbands, but schoolteachers were in short supply.
In 1987 I overheard the same man explaining that he does not ask for marriage
prestations, just the tusk called *olung* (in Bahasa Indonesia, *air susu mama*, i.e.
'mother's milk'). One of his daughters married a man from the island of Alor,
where bronze drums called *moko* are used as marriage gifts. He rejected a *moko*,
telling the husband's family that he would be laughed at if he brought it to
Lamalera. In fact, he told them he did not want any payment. However, they
forced him, according to his account, to take Rp. 900,000, which he brought
home and put in a bank.[10] I have often overheard this man say that there is no
point in marriage prestations. What is important for him is that the couple are
acquainted with each other's parents. This same man, however, is delinquent
in providing bridewealth for his own wife. I know the wife's brother very well.
He maintains a friendly and constructive relationship with the person in question, but in important ceremonies in which their alliance would require him to
take part, he refuses to participate, citing the lack of payment as the cause.

Another man who has only a single son, commented that, although he had
supplied his wife's clan with two elephant tusks, and her *opu-laké* with one,
they would have to find another way to arrange marriage gifts for his son. Tusks
are rare now. People may have brick houses with tin roofs and furniture and
tape recorders inside, but be unable to provide a tusk because they did not
inherit any. Tusks are given now only when people are able to provide them.
While he said this a man who was about to marry off his daughter explicitly
agreed with him about the tusks, saying that he does not expect to get any
because they are a thing of the past. I once congratulated a man who had several
daughters, saying that he would surely get plenty of bridewealth. He replied

that he would be given only a tusk if people can provide it. The main thing is not to make trouble for the children. He also responded to my comment that in Kédang they like to arrange circles of obligations which can be cancelled out in a single ceremony, leaving no one the worse off, by saying that the same is sometimes done in Lamalera (although I have never witnessed it). He went on to compare Lamalera practice to that on Solor, where they agree on the amount to be given but do not actually pay it.[11]

Marriage obligations and the values of the objects given as prestations are measured in terms of an abstract unit of value called the *kesebõ* (Barnes and Barnes 1989: 408–9).[12] The *kesebõ* is spoken of as coming in two forms, that is large (*kesebõ bélõ*) and small (*kesebõ kẽni*) or high (*kesebõ bĕlolo*) and low (*kesebõ léré*), both of which are essential in estimating value. One large *kesebõ* is supposed to equal two small *kesebõ*. A large *kesebõ* is deemed to be worth ten twenty-litre tins of unhusked rice, a small one five such tins.[13] In 1982 a cloth worth one large *kesebõ* was worth *c.* Rp. 60,000 or US $90, while a set of five ivory bracelets worth a small *kesebõ*, could cost as much as Rp. 40,000 or US $60.

In measuring elephant tusks, the lowest number of *kesebõ* which they recognize is five (*léma*), which is a tusk in length from the finger tips of one arm to the centre of the chest, with a base wide enough to leave a gap between the thumb and index finger of three fingers' width in the encircling hand. Seven (*pito*) would be to the opposite breast, with a five-finger gap. Blossom (*bunga*) reaches to the inside of the elbow on the opposite arm or further with a base too wide to span with both hands and is ten *kesebõ* or more. 'To see' (*hulã*) is to the opposite forearm in various places and is counted in the teens. 'More' (*rai*) is to the opposite finger tips or farther and is counted as twenty *kesebõ* or more. There are no tusks counted as four, six, eight, nine, or eleven *kesebõ*. Any tusk which falls between the points indicating five and seven *kesebõ*, would be reckoned as five. A tusk which has the length of a seven-*kesebõ* tusk, but the breadth of one which is five *kesebõ*, would be referred to as *bala pito kelen léma*, that is a seven-unit tusk with a body of a five-unit tusk.

The tusks which at least ideally the husband's group should give the bride's relatives are as follows:

1. *olung* ('normal') worth seven to ten *kesebõ*.
2. *lango umã* ('the house's share') worth seven to ten *kesebõ*.
3. *meka* worth twenty *kesebõ*.
4. *ina umã* ('mother's share') worth twenty *kesebõ*.

The descent group of the bride's mother should receive

5. *lango umã* ('the house's share') worth seven to ten *kesebõ*.
6. *uma lima* ('house hand') worth twenty *kesebõ*.

The *olung* for the bride's descent group and the *lango umã* for her mother's descent group must be available or at least promised before the wedding, and they must be given before the year is out. Nowadays it is only these two tusks which are actually given.[14] *Meka*, *ina umã*, and *uma lima* have almost disappeared. If *olung* has not yet been given for the mother, then her descent group has the right to take the *olung* owed for the daughter. One man, who has five as yet unmarried daughters and no sons, told me that he stands to collect *olung* from all of them because the *olung* for his wife has been handed over. However, his wife is dead and he would like to marry her unmarried younger sister. He told me that he stands to get so much bridewealth, but since he has no sons, when he dies it will just go to someone for free. He also commented rather mournfully that since the daughters will all leave home when married, it is better for him to build a grave than a modern house.

It is common now for the *opu-laké* to refuse to participate in marriage ceremonies because they have not been given *lango umã*. Since tusks are now so hard to find, they commonly substitute cash. For *olung* that may be as much as Rp. 100,000 or $150 in 1982 (possibly considerably more). Although this might appear to be buying a bride, there is a return; so in local eyes the bride herself has no price. On one occasion a group which had no tusk available for the *lango umã* owed to the *opu pukã* of a woman from Lamalera brought a substitute called figuratively 'goat-earring' (*fiti-belãu*). This consisted in a goat, a pig, six large bowls of unhusked rice, and two large bowls of shelled maize. This food was divided evenly between the wife's descent group and that of her *opu pukã*, and each share was then evenly divided within each descent group. One man commented on this occasion that the people of the interior are even more fair. Not only do they divide the meat, bones, and skin evenly, giving equal shares to a man, his wife, and all his children, but they will give a share to his unborn child too if his wife is pregnant.

The size of the tusks used to meet these obligations depends on what the bride's relatives request. Except for the tusk called *olung*, all tusks which the wife's descent group ask for must be balanced by a return gift of cloth at the 'same level'. This rule serves as a brake upon requests. The return consists in cloths and associated ivory bracelets. These are said to 'redeem the tusk' (*poi bala*). The return of a tusk worth ten *kesebõ* is supposed to be five cloths plus fifty ivory bracelets. The return of a tusk worth twenty *kesebõ* would be double these amounts, i.e. ten cloths and 100 ivory bracelets. The ten cloths would be divided into five three-panel cloths (*kefatek nai telu*) representing five large *kesebõ* and five two-panel cloths (*kefatek nai rua*). The person who has the right to receive *olung* (either the father or as the case may be the father's brother) must give two *kesebõ* to his daughter. These two *kesebõ* are referred to as *mau*, the same term as the gifts presented to the bride at her marriage described above. The return of these units will be in the form of five bracelets plus a three-piece cloth considered worth a large *kesebõ* or two cloths of two sections worth a small *kesebõ* each and taken together worth a single large *kesebõ*. The return to the wife-takers for a tusk worth ten *kesebõ* (excluded the two *kesebõ* given to the woman) would be divided into four large *kesebõ* and four small *kesebõ*. Taken together they are counted as eight *kesebõ*, but since the small *kesebõ* are worth half the large *kesebõ*, the actual value is equivalent to six large *kesebõ*.

There are two principal types of bracelet used as return gifts. The more valuable of these are shaped with a raised centre all the way around and are called *kala ufung* ('ridged bracelets'). Bracelets are tied together in sets of five. The expression for a set of five *kala ufung* would be *kala ufung kulu léma*, or 'five seeds of ridged bracelets'. A set of five *kala ufung* is valued as a single large *kesebõ*. Five *kala ufung* may accompany a three-panel resist-dyed cloth, also worth a single *kesebõ*. Notice that this generalization does not match that given in the previous paragraph (which derives from a different authority) in which a ten-unit tusk was balanced against five cloths and fifty ivory bracelets. There may be an error of some sort, unless my source had in mind only bracelets of the second type which are worth exactly half the value of *kala ufung*. These are 'round bracelets' (*kala belopor*), in fact just ivory bracelets which are flat on the outer side. Five *kala belopor* equal a small *kesebõ*. A set of five *kala belopor* may accompany a resist-dyed cloth of two panels. Two sets of five *kala belopor* are equivalent to one set of five *kala ufung*. There is another rarely seen variety of bracelet made from sea shell called *kala flo* which derives from the island of Pantar. Were they to be used as marriage prestation, five of them would accompany a three-panel cloth. However, their value depends on size. One acquaintance showed me a set of five sea-shell bracelets in his possession which were large and which he reckoned was worth two sets of five *kala ufung*. In 1982 villagers offered some tourists a set of *kala ufung* at Rp 10,000 (*c.* $15) per bracelet and *kala belopor* at half that price.

Although wife-givers are superior to wife-takers, the returns made by the wife-givers are an important element in the alliance relationship between them. It is understood that marriage gifts from one group to another will be passed on by them to their own wife-givers and that these gifts entail reciprocal gifts of the appropriate kind. When marriage prestations have been given by one group to another, the receivers of these gifts become *senubang*[15] to those who have given them. As a result they must eventually make a return. More specifically, a woman should present cloth or thread to her husband's sister and that woman's husband. The expression for such a return is *moé hopé poé*, 'redemption goods buy redemption'. They also say *bĕlãu lengata ara fiti géré bãu*, 'earring dropped, but the goat rises and floats', that is an earring given without immediate return, so that one day it will be replaced by a goat.

I once overheard an elderly man ranting at his wife's brother's son, therefore his *opu-laké*, for his general unwillingness to pitch in and help others at work, claiming he never did anything but talk. The elder man then said that when the younger man's wife-takers brought him an animal, he was supposed to return a shirt or pair of pants, but that he had never done so. Furthermore, the younger man had never given his father's sister any clothing. He rounded off his tirade by saying that the younger man's parents had known how to value their wife-takers, but he did not. The return should be presented to the wife-takers sometime when that descent group is having a feast. They may in turn provide an animal to the wife-givers when that group is having a feast. One day when one of the great houses of Léla Onã was having a festival to mark the completion of rebuilding their house, a woman presented them with a cloth. The obligation to give it was independent of the festival, but she chose it as a proper opportunity. Any return gift, including those from wife-givers to wife-takers, is called *hoder* or *noder*.

The full cycle of marriage prestations may take generations to complete. The final payment is *ãé marã*, that is 'dry face', which is intended to wipe away the tears. If a couple has sons, this payment to the wife's descent group may be postponed until the death of the last living son, but there may be a series of smaller payments as each brother dies. If they have only daughters, there is no such payment. However, in some cases of sudden illness, the same gift must be made to insure recovery. One man who lost a young son and was troubled by other deaths in his descent group and by the illness of his mother, sought assistance from his brother to pay *ãé marã* for his son, even though he had other sons living and in good health. He said he was afraid that if the payment were not made, the deaths would continue. Such a gift may consist in a goat, pig, cash, or an elephant tusk which should be presented to the deceased person's *opu pukã*. The *opu pukã* in turn gives clothing called *létu lofat* ('to close'). This gift to the *opu pukã* is also called pillow (*bĕloné*). If the family of the dead man can afford an elephant tusk, they refer to it as *uk kajo*, that is the 'bones', i.e. cartilage, of the *uk* (rear torso) section of a manta ray. In marriage negotiations, if the wife-givers refer to *uk kajo*, they are asking for a tusk. The return in cloth for *bĕloné* or *ãé marã* is called *senia beléré*, or a low fence. If the wife-takers of the deceased are numerous and well enough off they would provide the animal which would then be transferred to the deceased's *opu pukã*. If not, the family of the deceased would have to be responsible for providing the animal. On one occasion, an elderly man provided a young pig as *ãé marã* to his mother's brother's son (the mother's brother was not living) for his recently deceased younger brother. Since the man was himself still living, the recipient commented that it would have been a serious religious breach to have demanded a larger animal.

In traditional Lamaholot culture, divorce was permitted, but not overly common, especially after substantial marriage gifts had been exchanged. Because the people of Lamalera are Catholic, there should be no divorce at all, except under the circumstances permitted by canon law. However, so I am told, there are some lines in some descent groups, where men have a reputation for divorcing their wives and taking on new spouses.

Life, Development, Spirits, Faults, and Retribution

Pregnancy and Birth

To be pregnant is *bĕlūtu*. Childbirth is *bua ana*, but it can also be referred to as *meti fulã*. In general, the expression *meti fulã* (in which *fulã* is the moon) indicates that the time for a change of some sort is imminent. This phrase refers to changes as diverse as shifting tides and the life changes a person experiences in maturing. It is also used to refer to menstruation. Of a woman whose pregnancy is reaching its term, people may say *meti fulã dãé*, 'the time is near'. A child not yet ready to crawl is *meti fulã nãé fati ka* 'his time has not yet come'. Many women in the village act as midwives in assisting at a birth, but only a few are especially expert in dealing with the difficult ones, especially breech births, *ufã nolo*, or those which are feet first, *léi nolo*. Today women may receive vitamin B and other assistance from the polyclinic. In the past, the common Indonesian practice of having the woman sit next to a fire during a period of restriction after birth was usual on Lembata (Barnes 1974a: 151–2). According to Reid (1987: 39), some authors saw in this procedure of 'roasting' mothers after childbirth the cause for what they deemed an early loss of fertility, but in many parts of South-East Asia the reason given for it was to restore the heat lost in childbirth.

Seegeler (1931: 51) wrote that in East Flores and on Solor and Lembata, unlike Adonara, people did *not* give a new-born boy weapons and a girl women's implements. Afterbirth was placed in a basket filled with ash and taken away by a man and a women, called *uri*, who later in life were regarded by the children in the same way as Christians regard godparents. Together with family members they took the afterbirth to a tree. Then, if the child was a boy, it was shot at with arrows by the men. If the child was a girl, nothing was done at this stage. Afterwards the *uri* were pelted with all sorts of fruits. They then fled back to the house where the child was born, followed by the family. The purpose was to harden the child against conflict, pain, and sickness. At the house, there was a feast at which the *uri* were also present.

Twins

Twins of any combination are spoken of as *gerédo*, a word which Arndt (1937: 60) renders, 'to quiver', 'to shake'.[1] Generally in Indonesia the birth of opposite sex twins is unpropitious, unless, as is the view on Bali, it occurs in the families of kings. Something of the same abhorrence of opposite sex twins occurs in Lamaholot culture as well (Arndt 1940: 144). I have encountered no express statement of this disliking in Lamalera, other than the cryptic comment that some people are good and some are not. One of our neighbours had opposite sex twins who were thriving during our stay. If the twins are two boys or two girls, nothing especially needs to be done. For opposite sex twins, however, they must immediately hold a ceremony after birth. Directly after birth they lay the babies side by side on a bed (which on which side does not matter), then change sides three times (*gefalet*). Next they put them down together again and put a banana in their hands so they can share it. Then they exchange their positions again three times. They do the same procedure with a shawl, so they can share it. In the changing around, the boy has to be given the breast on the girl's side, the left, the girl on his, the right. This custom has a serious purpose. If they do not carry it through, one of the children must die. My neighbour held this ceremony for his twins, and they were healthy. He said that twin births are characteristic of his descent group. More than one pair of twins appears in the line of his ancestors.

Babies

A new-born infant is a 'red child', *ana méã*. People make a paste from turmeric, which they place on the fontanelle to cover the opening between the skulls of the bone. The paste is supposed to help close it. They want it to close soon so the baby will not be so badly hurt if it falls. The fontanelle is called *kelefuk tukã*. Infants are always carried and kept clear of the ground, not to mention of the ever present pigs and dogs. However, after a certain stage of development, they are allowed to play freely on the ground. One morning I saw a baby sitting on the ground eating dirt. When I mentioned this to an acquaintance, he said that the older people used to order that children be placed on the ground so that they could do this. The male nurse in the village, however, was against the practice.

   Babies are particularly vulnerable to disturbance by the spirits of the recently dead. We had a son of only a few months with us in 1979, who occasionally suffered from colic, possibly from the antimalarial prophylactic we gave him. Friends were quite anxious that we not take it to a house close by where there had been a recent death. Once he started in his sleep and began screaming. The women in our household rushed into the house, poured some water in a small container and then passed it over his head, before pouring the water out the back door. They then quickly repeated this procedure, before pouring the water out the front door. At this point they explicitly said that a small baby is especially vulnerable at the time of a death in the village and that the 'satan', i.e. dead soul, can harm it. For this reason they sternly instructed us not to take him outside again until after the funeral. Once the corpse was brought to the great house and public mourning began, they closed the front door of our house to keep out all bad spiritual influences. Some days later, he was ill again and the women circled a cup of water over his head, together with a hair one of them took from her scalp. This was following the disaster at Waiteba when so many people died in the earthquake and tidal wave. The explanation given was that with so many dead souls around, they were causing small children to be unwell. In each case the circling was done counter-clockwise as seen from above. On a subsequent occasion, our son again became quite ill, again possibly in reaction to the antimalarial prophylactic. The women took some raw cotton and touched it against an earring. It had to be touched against something gold, be it an earring, bracelet, or ring. They circled the cotton around his head while asking the ancestor who was troubling him to go away, leave the house, and find another place to stay. They said that he was acting like he had been bothered, and in such cases it would be by the spirit of a dead person. We were particularly vulnerable in their eyes to such distur-bances, because we were staying in a great house in which both the living and dead members of the descent group come together to consider important descent group affairs.

One evening, when our daughter was suffering from a stomach ache, the overseer of our house came into the front room and spit a mixture of garlic and other herbs at all the doors, windows, and corners. Then he said a short spell, which ran as follows.

> *Ata lefo-tana doé*
> People of a distant land
> *Raé beso raé té tobo*
> They came here [toward the land] to sit with us
> *Raé ramé paté*
> They are paying [rent]
> *Suru raé sĕnarèng melang hénu*
> Give them only good fortune
> *Timu teka, fāra teka*
> East wind arrived, west wind arrived
> *Naé béra hogo tobolo*
> May she quickly sit up

One evening while I was away his wife had seen five persons sitting in our house. They were dressed in ancient styles and were descent group ancestors.

Birth Control

Some families manage to space their children approximately two years apart, with others the pattern is more irregular. Women who have children too close together often suffer physically from the strain of maintaining them while keeping up their other work. Birth control aids are available at the polyclinic, while traditional medicines may be used as abortives. These include a root which is pounded and diluted with water. Its purpose is supposed to cause the foetus to be reabsorbed, rather then expelled. Women count their periods with the days of the moon, and may become anxious when a period is overdue. Of course, modern birth control methods and traditional ones pose moral problems in a Catholic community. In general, it can be said that in any case large families are favoured. Nevertheless, women do feel that they would be better off if they could limit the size of their families or at least have control over the age gap between children.

Names

When young children are baptized, they receive a saint's name. A person's modern legal identity is made up of his or her saint's name, a village given name, and a surname derived from the descent group. Of these three types, the last is the most recent and has resulted from governmental requirements. With certain exceptions, surnames either are identical to the clan name in a simple spelling suitable for Bahasa Indonesia, or they are shorter forms of the clan name. Among exceptions may be mentioned a family in the clan Bĕliko Lolo who have taken the name of the village founder Korohama as their surname. Dasi Langu section of Lefo Tukã has adopted Dasion, which might be viewed as a truncated version of Dasi Onã. Exceptions apart, Table 11 displays the surnames for each of the clans of Lamalera.

In addition, all of the variously named small descent groups in the mountain hamlet Lamamanu have adopted the common surname Manuk.

Adults are universally addressed as *bapa*, father, or *ema*, mother, sometimes with the addition of the saint name in order to catch their attention. This practice, widespread in the area, which seems very rustic to Indonesians from other parts of the country, is considered good breeding, and allows for respectful, yet friendly address to everyone from the president of the nation or the governor of the province down to the youngest child without on the one hand causing offence or on the other hand stressing status differences. This is quite an achievement in a country whose cultures, especially those to the west, make it extremely difficult or impossible to communicate without signalling status inequalities. Aged persons and dignitaries may be addressed as *magu*. Otherwise, relatives elder than ego must be addressed by the appropriate relationship term of address. Those younger than ego, with the important exception of young children, are never addressed by a relationship term, but by name, whether the saint's name or the village name.

A person may be baptized with more than one Christian name, but generally only one is in common use. As a rule, they adopt the Latin form of the

TABLE 11. *Surnames of Lamalera Descent Groups*

Clan	Surname	Clan	Surname
Bĕliko Lolo	Belikololong	Bata Onā	Bataona
Lāma Nudek	Nudek	Sula Onā	Sulang
Lefo Tukā	Tukan	Bedi Onā	Beding
Tana Kĕrofa	Krofan	Bata Fo	Batafor
Ata Kéi	Kein	Ata Folo	Atafolo
Léla Onā	Lelang	Lāma Nifa	Nifak
Tufa Onā	Tufan	Tapo Onā	Tapon
Ebā Onā	Ebang	Hari Onā	Haring
Olé Onā	Oleona	Lefo Léin	Lein
Lāma Kéra	Keraf	Ata Gora	Gorang
		Lango Fujo	Fujon

name. In daily use, however, Christian names are routinely shortened, sometimes in a way which makes for difficult recognition. Linus, for example, is the short form of Marselinus, but then so too is Marsel. Ani might not be quickly recognized as Yohanis. Alo derives from Aloisius, Fredus from Alfredus, Gorys from Gregorius, Sisu from Fransiskus, Stanis from Stanislaus. Fina and Sinta are Yosefina and Yasinta. Yuli is short for Yuliana.

Concerning village given names, one of my acquaintances once commented that like European names, Lamalera names have meanings, giving as an example Nara Beto, which means the troops are coming. Some names reproduce those of legendary personages, and such names are most likely to be passed down within the descent group. An example of this kind is Pati Mangun, still in use in the clan Léla Onā, keeping alive the memory of the man who disappeared into thin air when members of the village were trying to exterminate the clan and whose ghost still stalks the sacred grove near the great houses of this clan's descent segments. Another is Somi Bola Deran, the name of the pregnant woman who gave birth in the boat near Ata Déi when the ancestors of Lamalera were trying to round the point, while fleeing from the natural catastrophe which forced them to leave their homeland. Others, such as Hopi Lefo, 'purchase [i.e. ransom] the village', refer to semi-historical events. Other names may have a private significance. Some names have comical or ridiculous meanings. Not all names necessarily have any implied extra significance. In Kédang, normally a person, male or female, bears two village names. The first is his or her given name, the second is the given name of his or her father. This pattern does not seem to be found in Lamalera today, but there is evidence to suggest that this is because it has been supplanted by the Christian given name plus the village given name. Munro, for example, referred to a former *kakang* of his day as Molan Dasi, rather than as Mikael Molan, the version of the name commonly used today. Dasi was the village name of his father.

It is quite common for a man to name a son after his father and for a woman to do so after her mother. Although this practice occurs frequently enough to be a recognizable pattern, it by no means always happens. Furthermore, names may be derived from more distant relatives, such as a father's brother or even a mother's father. Gregorius Keraf (1978: 102, 105–6) writes that people may not address or refer to people older than themselves by name, and that it is particularly prohibited for a person to do so to his parents. This regulation, he says, has led as a form of compensation to addressing all children, whether unrelated or closely related, by *ina* or *ama*. These words are no longer used in everyday speech in their normal sense, i.e. as 'mother' and 'father', except in compound expressions such as *inã-ãmã*, and have been replaced by *ema* and *bapa*, respectively. Since people are not supposed to use the name of an older person for any reason, they cannot use the name of a child when it has been taken from its parent's parents. For this reason, he says, they use *ina* and *ama* for all children too. The more recent terms *ema* and *bapa* are used in the same way. According to Gregorius Keraf, the prohibition also explains why children here and throughout the Lamaholot-speaking area are generally called by their Christian names rather than the village names.

Hair Cutting

When a child is born, there may be a little feast, but the real festivity is the cutting (shaving) of the hair, *géi ratã*. This ceremony takes place about two to six months after the birth of the first child. The act of shaving the hair is initiated by the child's mother's brother, who cuts just a little bit at first as a sign that he has participated and then leaves the rest to be done by someone else. They shave off all the hair, leaving no sign of sex. The whole of the mother's natal group should come, bringing some article of clothing, whatever they wish. In return the parents entertain them with a feast of rice and enough meat for the occasion, say one pig and one goat, which they should provide themselves. This ceremony is still the common practice in Lamalera, but only for the first child, whether male or female.

As a practical measure, parents will shave a child's hair several times during childhood, not because it is lice infected, as it is likely to be, but so that the body will grow strong. They think that if a child's hair is not cut, the child will not be healthy. Typically on Lembata a shock of hair may be left above the forehead for a boy cr at the back of the skull for a girl.

Baptism and First Communion

All children are baptized shortly after birth. First communion for children takes place when they are 11 or 12 and is the occasion for much tearful emotion during the ceremony and large bustling parties in all the houses of the children involved in the evening afterwards. Relatives come from Waiwerang, Adonara, Lewoleba, Lembata, and elsewhere in numbers. Palm wine flows endlessly and some houses keep festivities going until dawn.

Constituents of the Person

A person consists in body *feki* and soul *tuber*. The information collected on this subject further to the west by Arndt and Vatter indicates that some say that men have only one soul, while others say as many as five or even ten. Most often the report is that there are two souls, *tuber* and *manger*. While in some districts the representation is that the *tuber* can leave the body and move around, in Pamakayu, Solor, Arndt was told that it is the *manger* which leaves the body but not the *tuber*. When the soul leaves, a person may become ill. The soul also leaves the body during dreaming, but soon returns so that there is no occasion of illness. The souls of the dead are *kewokot* or in Lamalera *kefokot*. A person's shadow is thought to be the manifestation of the soul. Consequently, people should avoid standing on another man's shadow, for that might cause illness (Arndt 1951: 30–1, 51, 171–3; Vatter 1932: 88). Inner states may be indicated by the words *até* (liver) or *onã* (interior) modified by the appropriate adjective. There are also specific verbs, such as *pétã*, 'to remember', 'to think of', 'to love', for specific intellectual and affective acts or states.

Spirits and Witches

The spirit of any object is called *pung alep*. Normally, it cannot be seen. There is a *pung alep* of everything, including fish, boats, and great houses. These spirits are the object of various ceremonies and acts of propitiation. There are several types of evil spirits: *bopo lari* which come out at midday; *nitun* found in the sea near the beach; *tenebe* which come out in the evening; and *léfa haring* associated with the sea. A witch is *menaka*. The soul of a witch is *eor* (elsewhere *eo*). There are people in the village who are regarded as witches, and witchcraft accusations have been made, but not to my knowledge with any consequences in recent decades. One man, when he was serving as *pamong*, or assistant to the village head, was called to the home of a young women who said that she had been accused of being a witch. According to his account of the incident, he told her family to get some palm wine ready and he would go to their house to discuss the case. After she explained the accusation, he told her that she was not a witch. An evil spirit had borrowed her appearance. 'Let's have palm wine. End of case.' Until now there has been no further comment. On an occasion when women were expressing worry about witches and ghosts in our house another man and his wife said that there was no cause for concern, 'all the witches in the village are harmless as they are in our (the villagers') power, not we in theirs'.

This is an optimistic view for a village which according to legend indulged in the murder of suspected witches and for a region where such activity was repeatedly reported in the nineteenth and twentieth centuries. In 1870, during a smallpox epidemic, three 'witches' were slain in Lamahala, Adonara (Caspersz 1870). According to Hens (1916: 140), murder and manslaughter were common on Adonara and Lembata. Among the victims were many so-called witches. In 1936 a whole household in Lewuun, Solor, with six persons was murdered (Arndt 1951: 190); and Vatter reports that a leading figure in Leloba, Flores, had in the past slain fourteen witches, men, women, and children, in a single day (Vatter 1932: 89). The case of the two brothers Asa and Kerak, who with many others on the island were accused of being witches and taken to Hadakewa by the Japanese has been mentioned above. During the coup and counter-coup of 1965, the village head of a nearby village killed himself because there was a rumour that the government was going to kill not only all communists but also all witches. He regarded his wife as a witch and so expected to be taken to Lewoleba. Rather than being killed there, he did it himself at home.

One evening in 1982, a small boat turned over in the surf. Subsequent commentary was that the accident was caused by a sea spirit impersonating a human being on the beach and telling the boatmen where to go ashore, in the wrong place as it turned out.[2] Even more mysterious was the fact that after the boat turned over, it seem to go ashore by itself. Sometimes people waiting for a regularly scheduled passenger boat hear a noise suggesting it is approaching only to find after they have reached the beach that there is no boat at all. In this case what they have heard is a witch motor boat, *motor suangi*. The sound has hurried ahead of the boat, in the same way that the soul of someone who has died at sea may be encountered before news of his death reaches the village. Somewhat the same may happen when boats which have been away fishing at Lobetobi, Flores, for an extended period return to the village.

Once when we went to inspect the two small tide-covered springs at the shore which used to be the only source of fresh water in the village, on our return women told us that we must not leave any of our things there. A woman also took a bit of fresh water I had brought up and flicked some of it toward the spring with her fingers. This action is called *gĕlara* (the word itself means 'religiously prohibited', see Leemker 1893: 433). She said she had to do this because we were new people here. The problem was with the *nitun*, spirits which inhabit the place. People might go there and find goods, such as a prepared meal. But these things must not be taken, for they belong to the *nitun*.

If someone leaves things there, he may get sick. A woman related that she had a jerrycan there which she could not lift. She got others to help, but they could not move it. She was forced to leave it behind, then it disappeared. She became prostrated by illness. While she was ill, someone saw her at the spring carrying the jerrycan. It seems that when something disappears there people often see its owner with it there, although the person is somewhere else. In the middle of this explanation she murmured something about people having seen someone very white and with white hair there (i.e. my daughter) and about how thin my daughter was.

Healers

Illness is *bĕlarã*. To be healthy is *sĕnaré*, which also means good or pleasant. Illness is typically attributed to some fault or offence against spirits or ancestors. Of course the educational system has introduced them to modern explanations of disease and to the benefits of proper sanitation. Someone who knows how to help a person plagued by spirits is a *hupã alep* or *hupã tuber*, that is someone who is adept at greeting the soul of the troubled person. In the case just described the woman was helped by such a *hupã alep* who went to the spring and twirled, *tuser*, a candlenut, *kemié*. This cured her. Such a person may also be able to search for and find faults which have brought about misfortune, such as deaths at sea. Village healers are called *amu alep*, that is masters of medicine or roots. One such was called in and said to have been successful in curing a case of what seems to have been erysipelas or St Anthony's fire (intense inflammation of the skin) when the polyclinic and I proved unable or incompetent to help.[3] Satisfied patients will reciprocate with palm wine and a chicken. Healers are one variety of *ata molã*, who are skilled or adept craftsmen of one kind or another. Gregorius Keraf (1978: 169, 243) defines an *ata molã* as an expert, master craftsman, boat builder, weapons builder, house builder, shaman, healer, massager.

One village bone setter related to me a series of stories about people he had healed. One man harpooned a whale which bit him and severed all the ligaments in the forearm, so that he could not move his hand. The bone setter told him he would heal him and that he would be a harpooner again. A month later he took his boat out again and harpooned a whale and a shark. Another man fell on an arrow which went all the way through his chest. My acquaintance healed him. Yet another man went mad, cut himself in the stomach, then fell on wood which entered his stomach. My acquaintance healed him. A boy from Lewotala fell. A stone fell on top of his head, opening his skull. He too recovered. The missionary got angry with him about this case, accusing him of practising magic. My acquaintance said God's attitude is that He has given him medicines and does not want him to pray for additional help. A man from Lewuka had cuts about the throat including one which cut his wind pipe. My acquaintance told him to drink water; it all came out the cut. My acquaintance took tassels of a resist-dyed cloth, stuck them in the cut and wrapped a white cloth around the wound. When, subsequently, he took the cloth off, the wound had healed. A former *kakang* (named Blida) cut a man with a field knife on the back severing ribs along the spine. My acquaintance's ancestor cured him too.

Bode (1925: 115–16) described the practices of the last non-Catholic healers in the village, and I present his account below, not only for its useful ethnographic information, but also to show his combative and patronizing tone. I have left the Lamaholot terms as he spelled them and have kept his abrupt sentence breaks.

As much as successful fishing, health and life stood in the power of the many spirits. Often they cooled their anger or took revenge on the living through making them ill or striking them dead. What more natural medicine therefore than to ward off the spirits or to propitiate them. The molang [expert] was once again the mediator, the doctor. Karowe, Parason, and Haga, although baptized thirty or forty years ago, were the chief molangs of Lamalera. . . . From far in the mountains came people to consult them, and in all kinds of illness and vicissitudes villagers had recourse to them. Karowe was the principal hero. An illness for example would be taken to him. With words and great gestures he called the manaka, the evil or angry spirit, and it came. The molang's whole body trembled and all his limbs gave proof of it. Then the patient had first to bathe and thereafter to be sprayed with the holy spittle of the molang. Afterwards he massaged him and rubbed him with both hands for a while all over the body. Until finally the actual mischievous cause of the illness appeared. Triumphantly the 'doctor' let the bystanders see it: a pebble. It could just as well be a thorn, a piece of thread, a chicken or piglet bone or something of the sort. Thereby the invalid was absolutely healed, and palm wine, a chicken, small goat or piglet was the well-earned payment for the molang.

Nota Bene. It happened in Lerek, also on Lembata, not so far from Lamalera. About a year ago the mission established an elementary school there. Late one evening the village gathered under a great tree. Even the head of the school, Bernardu, was there. An invalid lay in their midst and a molang squatted near him. Naturally to ward off the illness and to suck out the pebble that caused the illness. Bernardu offered to go get his petroleum lamp, so that it would be easier to see. But, oh no, he should not do that, then it certainly would not work. But the teacher went anyway and lit up the situation. And he discovered that the pebble was already in the mouth of the molang before he had sucked it out. A loud laughter of amusement [came from] the believers in the molang. For the moment he had lost his prestige. But the unfortunates, as soon as they again needed help and knew not where to turn, they knocked again on his door.

A child was sick. That came from the ancestors, the *kewoko*. They had become angry with the child and naturally had to be warded off. The elders took a candlenut and took it to the temple of the skulls of the dead. The nut was laid at midday on one of the skulls and retrieved the following morning, then finely chewed and the chewed nut then smeared on the head of the child. That was their medicine.

Faults

A serious fault committed by members of a clan could cause, so it is thought, serious disasters to its members for *seven* generations, even if they did not know of the fault involved. A case in point was the disaster concerning the boat named *Téti Heri* in 1925, when it turned over and lost ten men (see the account of this event in Chapter 14). The cause was that members of the clan owning the boat, Bata Fo, had once taken a brother and sister who committed incest and tried to drown them by sinking them in the sea weighed down with stones. The members of the clan had kept very quiet about this, telling not even their own children, who did not know about it. However, the couple involved did not, it appears, drown, but reached Sikka in Flores, where they founded a clan. They too kept very quiet about their origins, but the personal names in their clan fit those of Bata Fo. The true cause of the disaster would have remained unknown, it seems, had not Bode miraculously known about it and told them so that they could arrange to clear up the matter with the proper ceremonies. How Bode knew of the cause is unexplained, except that they credit him with the powers to see into the past and find causes. If Bata Fo had not finally found its fault, it could in the end have been reduced to the point of disappearing.

Such serious faults must be corrected ceremonially, if an end is to be made to their consequences before the seven generations elapse. When the cause is no longer known, they have to go to someone who knows how to search for these causes, *hupã alep*. He determines a cause and they have a ceremony. If that brings an end to the problem, that means he was right. If the problem recurs, it means he was wrong and they look again. If they do not search or do not find it, disaster continues. The source of this information told me that this way of thought is hard to understand in rational terms.

The local expression for such infractions is *koda kiri*, elucidated in Bahasa Indonesia as *kesalahan*, mistake, error, blunder. A European would label some examples as mere missteps or social blunders, while regarding others as heinous crimes. In some cases a European would not be inclined to recognize any moral blame at all for the person or persons involved. For example, a clan which had suffered repeated deaths recalled that an ancestor had been injured in a trap and concluded that had led to the descent group continually shedding blood. Injury by a shark is always attributed to a fault of some sort. One man was bitten in the foot by a shark after harpooning it. This injury, from which he eventually recovered, was attributed to a problem of some sort within the clan.

The organized search for a cause of misfortune is called *méi nafa*. *Méi* means 'blood', and *nafa* derives from a proto-Austronesian root meaning 'soul' (Dempwolff 1938: 109; Fernandez 1988: 527). One person glossed the phrase as referring to the return of hot blood (in Bahasa Indonesia, *darah panas*) to a person or his clan, if he murders someone else and nothing is done to set it right. Retribution for murder would of course be only one of several exemplifications of *méi nafa*.

Some such procedures can be relatively modest and uncomplicated. How they are performed depends on the conventions of the experts called in to carry them out, and as is to be expected there is a good deal of variation in the requirements of individual ritual leaders. One acquaintance told me that he merely requires that a red pig be found. This animal he brings in through the front door of the ritual house of the descent group. Everyone in the family has to confess his faults. The pig is then led out the back door to be prepared for a feast. Everyone who has confessed must eat some of the pork. Understandably, people are often reluctant to hold such a ceremony or to make a candid confession during the ritual, which may at times degenerate into a struggle by the expert to force information from the participants. He is prone to blame failure of the ritual on the incompleteness of the confessions. In 1982 I participated in an extremely complex *méi nafa* ceremony, just above the upper village boundary, which lasted all night and involved fourteen separate cases from five different villages resulting in bad deaths (for details see R. H. Barnes 1989).

6

Death

Historical

According to the missionary Heslinga, in 1891, the people of Lamalera had the habit of burying their dead in the sand on the little square in the middle of their village. The shallow graves were covered with great stones. He is plainly speaking here of the lower village, where at that time the missionaries stayed on their visits to the village. He went on to write that when the corpse was so decomposed that the soft parts had disappeared, the family then dug it up, removed the skull from the skeleton and took it with great veneration to the family boat house, where they set it next to the heads of the ancestors. Remarkably, he said that these boat houses were usually built from whale jaw bones, shark bones (*sic!*), and other leftovers of the large fish that they had caught. At fixed times they paid reverence to the skulls which they had stored in a row in these sheds by means of a meal of rice or fish placed in front of them as an offering (Heslinga 1891: 74–5). During a visit in that year the missionary ten Brink lived in one such shed at the beach, watched over by the family skulls (Heslinga 1891: 73).

In 1894 Wintjes visited the village and described a funeral which he witnessed on 27 April. A woman died whose body they wrapped in what Wintjes described as old tatters and rags. She was carried to the grave on a sort of stretcher. As the people stood there and looked on, they laughed and giggled from amusement, while they mockingly pointed at the sad procession with their fingers. After the funeral, he found the grave covered with leaves, four pieces of wood (which would have been the stretcher), some stones, a betel basket, a water pot, and some rice and fish. The food was eaten by dogs and pigs. When the people had seen the food disappear in this way, they said, 'See there, she has eaten well and now can sustain herself excellently there.' Possibly there was some particular reason for the derision, having to do with the person who died. More likely no disrespect for the deceased was intended, but the ridicule and food both were intended to encourage the soul of the dead to travel on to the land of the dead and leave the living in peace. Such rowdiness while carrying a corpse to the grave and during burial is a widespread cultural theme in Indonesia (cf. R. H. Barnes 1974*a*: 188 and the sources cited there). Vatter witnessed a funeral in 1928 in Leloba, East Flores, in which, despite loud and regular displays of grief by female relatives sitting near the corpse prior to burial, the crowd behaved in an amused and festive manner during the actual burial (Vatter 1932: 85–6).

Wintjes went on to say that when a body had lain in the ground for a year and a half, or even less, then they would dig up the head and clean it in the sea, lay it on a board and bring it in this way to the family. These accepted it solemnly. Three shots would be fired, and the skull would then be set aside in one of the many ossuaries that were found there. When he asked where the soul of the dead went, he was told that it travelled to one of the great monsters which populate the sea. The soul leads the fish back to them and makes it possible to capture them easily (Wintjes 1894*a*: 33–4).

In 1911 Beckering wrote that in the district of Lamalera and in the rest of the western portion of Lembata, the remarkable practice occurred of digging up a corpse, which was buried shortly after death, when it had completely rotted in order to retrieve the head and place it in a specific shed. 'It is a striking sight to see such a building on entering a village in which several rows of skulls grin at passers-by.' However, he stated quite specifically that the members of the three most prominent clans, Lefo Tukã, Bata Onã, and Bĕliko Lolo, did not participate in this usage. These three clans buried their dead and placed more or less freely stacked monuments on them. He specified that the graves were located on the shore to the east of the village site and above on the cliffs. The other clans collected the skulls. One of these clans in the lower village had them laid out under the roof of one of the boat sheds. The grave of the former district head (*kakang*) Dasi (i.e. Yosef Raja Muda, also known as Dasi Dasi) was located on the eastern entrance to the upper village toward the sea. He mentions that in Mingar and Kawéla further to the west, the dead were buried a day or two after death, while the bodies of chiefs were buried after a week. After six months or more, depending on the wealth of the family, the skulls would be dug up, whereupon there would be festivities. Only in the case of very young children would this not happen. Although he does not say so, this last description could be taken to apply to at least some of the clans of Lamalera as well (Beckering 1911: 199–200).

Writing generally about Lembata in 1915, Munro stated that burial took place without any ceremony, which may be assumed to be an incomplete characterization of practices. In any case, he said that there would be a feast in honour of the deceased, whereby there would be much palm wine and all the relatives would be present. At the place of birth, a grave would be dug, in which the corpse would be buried or, when a family member died at a great distance and could not be returned, a piece of banana tree trunk would be placed there in its stead. No more sign was placed on the grave, and, although for a few months sacred and forbidden, afterwards it disappeared and was no longer remembered. He attributed scaffold burial to prominent men, such as rajas and *kapitans* (district chief), where the corpse would be left for years, until only the skeleton remained. Then the bones would be wrapped in cloth and returned to the house, when the proper festivities would take place. From all around relatives and acquaintances would be called. There would be much eating and drinking. Guns and rockets were fired in the air, and toward morning the bones would be carried through the village in a hollowed-out tree trunk in the form of a ship decorated with many flags. Thereafter it was buried for good. During this procession the men performed a sort of war dance, while the women howled and sang (Munro 1915: 16–7). Scaffold burial seems not to have been practised in Lamalera, but the theme of secondary burial, known from elsewhere in Indonesia (Hertz 1960) and still practised in Kédang (Barnes 1974a) comes out clearly in these reports.

Bernardus Bode mentioned that in a case of death, a priest (*molang*) would place a cup of palm oil on a holy stone. The next morning he would closely inspect the oil. Should it have turned reddish, that was a sign that some guilt in the family was the cause of the death. Another stain indicated a different sort of sin. A man of the same clan would then have to watch over the corpse for four days, neither bathing nor eating, but only drinking some coconut water. On the fourth day, he would be led to the beach by two women. One would carry a burning stick, the other a stone used to crush maize. Standing in the water, the man then had to take the fire and the stone and throw them into the water. The angry spirits were then placated, and the family would be protected from all forms of misfortune, such as sickness and death (Bode 1925: 116). Bode eventually persuaded people to remove their ancestral skulls from the sheds and to bury them, together with their sacred stones. Some brought him wooden bowls on which the sun was carved and in which they had earlier offered their sacrifices to their boats. Others delivered to him small stones which they had kept in their houses in order to obtain the protection and help of the spirits (Bode 1925: 130).

The ethnographer Vatter (1932: 206), who visited the villages a few years later, repeated the episode about the cup of oil.

If someone dies, then the witchdoctor must establish whether the death may have been caused by the fact that some unresolved guilt weighs on the clan. For this purpose he places a cup with coconut oil on a stone and leaves it overnight. If on the next morning he finds a red drop floating in the oil, it is proof of the guilt. In a dream he recognizes the guilty person, who must atone for his offence through the sacrifice of a pig or goat. The corpse is wrapped in cloths and a pair of silver *belaung* (earrings) are placed in the mouth.

Further to the east these earrings would have been placed on the eyelids, but were taken back before the burial. Large death feasts, such as those on Adonara, were unknown. Dead souls were called *kewoko* (properly, *kefokot*) in Lamalera as elsewhere in the Lamaholot language area, but the souls of people who had fallen in war were *mélung* (from *bélo/bélu*, to cut, kill, murder), while those who had fallen from trees were *mahol*. The *mélung* went to Lera-Wulan (God), while the *kewoko* and *mahol* settle near the village. As elsewhere, in Lamalera the skulls would be dug up after a time and set aside in greater numbers in a small house on posts. Before going out to sea fishing, the villagers would make offerings to them. By 1929 (the year of his visit) this account of things was purely retrospective, for, as Vatter acknowledged, 'Today these skull sheds no longer exist; some years ago Pater Bode delivered their contents ceremonially up to the earth'.

Memories

Villagers remember that Bode arranged to have the ancestral skulls buried behind the old church, where today's church graveyard is still located. However, it seems that when Bode ordered people no longer to keep the skulls of their ancestors, many hid them in the rocks at the shore. One man remembers many being there, but apparently by now most have disappeared. The male nurse serving the village was said to have retrieved two, which he kept in the polyclinic. The ancestors would rub the skulls with oil before going out to sea so that they would get fish. Formerly a platform or shelf was hung up in the back of a boat shed on which were kept the skulls of the ancestor. This ran the length of the back wall. On the first day of taking the large boats to sea each year this shelf was taken down, and placed on the ground behind the shed. The skulls were then washed with sea water, rubbed with coconut skin, and then anointed with coconut oil (*not* whale oil), in order to insure a good catch. In certain ceremonies they might also be given a bit of chicken and rice, or chicken blood. Although the shelf was set directly on the ground the skulls were placed on porcelain plates.

These porcelain plates, called *pīga*, had pictures of animals and dragons on them, and villagers think the plates were brought to the area by the Portuguese. Today they put a pillow under the head of a dead person when taking him to be buried, whereas in the old days they used a *pīga*. In recent years people digging the earth near the point just to the east of the beach, which was a former place of burial, have found numbers of these *pīga*, some broken, some still whole.

The former graveyards were often along the shore. The mission's storage shed is now located near one of the passages to the beach where two such plates were found which had been used to support the heads of people buried there. There are still prominent stone graves which may be seen east of the lower village close to the shore. These graves are those of closely related members of the Kĕlaké Langu section of Bata Onã clan who lived in the mid-nineteenth century. One of them, Kupa, was the grandfather of the oldest man living in the village during our visit of 1970, Adreanus Ubas, who was born in 1893. A retired schoolteacher recalls helping build the grave of Kupa, even though

Kupa died before he was born. Another man recalls a large festival held in connection with these graves, although they were there before his birth.

Once the group which own the boat named *Kopo Paker* were digging out the accumulated sand in the shed of that boat, so that it would be easier to get the boat in and out. After digging only a short way they found old, fragile human bones, without a skull. At one time dwellings used to be located where the sheds are, and the boats were further south. Later the boats and houses were moved inshore to get away from the waves. At this early time, before Bode, dead persons were buried near the houses or in them. Now of course they are buried in the church graveyard. On another occasion the boat master of the *Sili Ténã* was digging the hole for a post at the back of the boat shed, when he encountered human bones, which he took and buried near his house.

Another ossuary is said to be located on the hill just east of the lower village. It seems to consist of a stack of skulls and bones lying on boulders. Some skulls show signs of violence. One appears to have received a blow to the right side from a sword held by a left-handed person. Allegedly, these bones are the remains of people of the interior whom the ancestors of Lamalera killed secretly and brought to this spot. Apparently the people of Pesiwatu were especially vulnerable and never approached the village unless they were bearing weapons. The ossuary is supposedly guarded by a python, *punaj*, an animal of which there are said to be many on the island, described as capable of killing animals by wrapping itself around them and crushing them. It can, for example, wrap itself twice around a goat, once at either end, and then pull the animal, breaking all its bones. It swallows the animal whole. Later it hangs down from a tree and vomits the bones back out.

Funerary Rites and Observations

The moment of death in the case of someone who has died in the house, perhaps after an extended illness, will be signalled by the outbreak of loud lamenting and weeping. This public mourning, as well as quieter keening and singing of death songs, especially by women, may continue at intervals throughout the day until burial. It may trail off, but is likely to be taken up again by new parties of relatives as they arrive. Sometimes it sounds quite unspontaneous. Even though much the same behaviour occurs in parts of Europe, foreigners are sometimes prone to wonder whether stylized expressions of grief have any connection with true inner emotions. Such doubts miss the point that public expressions of emotion serve public purposes. In most cases the feeling of grief is genuine enough and is experienced independently of any occasion of expressing it. Cross-cultural misunderstandings of this kind can work both ways. One of my friends once asked with concern whether westerners really care about their dead relatives. He had heard from Father Bruno

Pehl that westerners regarded the dead as being finished once they had been put into the earth, a view Pehl certainly did not approve of and which of course runs counter to Lamalera preconceptions.

Today burials take place in the churchyard in the upper village just to the west of the church which Bode had erected in 1920.[1] Instead of using the older method of protecting the bones with a construction of stacked stones, villagers now build concrete and brick tombs which stand above ground, a practical solution for a site where there is only a limited layer of soil over a stony lava flow. Formerly it was the responsibility of the wife-givers to dig out the first dirt for the grave and to put the first dirt into the grave, but today this requirement is ignored. A small meal will be provided for the gravediggers. Funeral services are conducted at the graveyard, after last rites have been held in the house and the procession has brought the body to the yard in a rapidly constructed wooden coffin transported on a bamboo stretcher. Mass for the deceased may be held in the church. Despite the addition of Christian observations, much of the traditional Lamaholot custom is still very much in force.

Like other Indonesian peoples (Barnes 1974*a*: 175), the people of Lamalera especially prize a life which has been lived to the fullness of its allotted days. They also distinguish certain forms of death which are out of the ordinary and may be unpropitious. Among unpropitious deaths are those which come suddenly, unexpectedly, called *mélung* or *mélung beléong* (cf. *beléong*, 'shot from a bow' (Arndt 1937: 71)). However unfortunate they may be, deaths in childbirth or from illness are not normally included in this category. However, among those which are included are deaths at sea, death from falling from trees, murders, disasters, and even from snake bite. The corpses of people who have died such deaths are buried in the church graveyard, but must not be brought inside the descent group's great house; instead they are placed outside it. In such instances there are no large common feasts and only four nights of guarding and restriction are observed by only the closest relatives involved. I know of only two suicides in the village in a period going back about twenty years, one a young man, the other a woman. In neither case were the reasons for the deaths public knowledge.

In the case of ordinary deaths, relatives observe a period of restriction called *nebo* or *penebo*. A fuller phrase is *nebo ata matén*, 'death rites' (Arndt 1937: 12). *Nebo* occurs in Larantuka Malay with the meaning the prayers on the third or sixth night after burial (Monteiro 1975: 81). Those held on the third night, according to Monteiro, are the great *nebo* (*nebo besa*) and those on the sixth the lesser *nebo* (*nebo kecé*). In Lamalera the term great *nebo* (*nebo bélã*) applies to the first four days and nights after burial. Burial itself takes place if possible on the day of death, or the next day at the latest. The great *nebo* involves all the closely connected relatives and acquaintances. The rites are observed, even when the death and burial have occurred far from home. They are even observed when the deceased is a distant descendant of the clan who has spent his entire life living elsewhere. It is followed normally by the lesser *nebo* (*nebo kéni*), a further period of restriction involving only the immediate family. This second period also lasts four days and nights, though it may occasionally be shortened to two days and two nights. Gregorius Keraf (1983: 43) writes,

The period of mourning is three full days. The day of burial is not counted, even though in practice people are also in mourning on that day. On the fourth day there is a festival for the soul of the dead called *penebo*. Afterwards there follows a second stage of mourning of 3 days which closes with the festival called *helãdiké*. After *helãdiké* mourning is over.

Helã diké is the same as the lesser *nebo*. *Diké* means 'good', and *helã* means 'oil'. It may be that this expression is explained by reference to the inspection of oil mentioned above. That is to say this further period of restriction takes place in the cases of death which are not attributable to a fault within the descent group such as are revealed by stains in the oil. The ending of the lesser *nebo* in my experience is sometimes marked by inviting neighbours to coffee on the morning after this period has expired.

Gregorius Keraf writes that, as on other occasions concerning the use of the boat and harmony of its corporation, the boat master must loosen the *kemité léo*, the bindings which hold the loop at the end of the harpoon rope called the *léo fã* and that called the *léo bélã*. These two ropes must be taken to the great house to be left there overnight prior to taking the boat to sea again.

Friends and relatives mark the nights of the great *nebo* by sitting up in the yard of the great house and guarding, *tĩa*. Especially on the first night after death people should in principle stay awake all night. In fact, although the evening may begin with a large crowd, many or most will eventually drift off home. During this period people will sit and carry on conversations. Carpenters may build the coffin. There may be some joking or even humorous quarrelling. Toward daylight those who have decided to stay may well have fallen asleep on boulders, piles of wood, or whatever is available. At dawn those who are left will disperse, some going off to dig the grave. The obligation to stay up until dawn to watch, figuratively, the corpse falls especially on close family members and persons living close by. It is a common experience in the village, especially for men. I have done it two or three times myself and have found it fairly trying, but no more so than various overnight bus trips I have taken.

In some cases, a man in the descent group will observe very special restrictions and place himself in a state called *pĩ*, a word which Arndt (1937: 34)[2] renders 'prohibited'. During this period of restriction the person who is *pĩ* does not wash, comb his hair, or eat for four days. This is the period mentioned by Bode, who wrote that the person under this restriction took no nourishment other than coconut water. My information is that he must eat by himself in the great house and, of course, not bathe or comb his hair during the four days of his isolation. The end of the four-day period is marked by a feast. The person who is *pī* first *bomak* (eats first), that is eats a chicken specially provided for this purpose by the wife-takers (*ana-opu*). An explicit analogy was drawn by the source of this information with a similar practice in connection with the ceremonies for building a boat. I was once asked to join a group who were sitting up during great *nebo* with a prominent elder of the village who was *pī* in relation to a recently deceased estranged younger brother. It was a sad and rather uneventful session at the great house, except that it was punctuated on one evening by the elder's rather heart-rending claims that there had never been any occasion in his mind for his brother's sense of estrangement.

According to A. Sonny Keraf (1982), *pī* has two senses. In the first place, it refers to the period of mourning lasting three or ten days, in other words the greater and lesser *nebo* (the number ten does not correspond to either my infor-mation or my observation). The second meaning refers to the person who becomes the centre of attention during the mourning period. This person is a male member of the descent group of the deceased, who must observe certain prohibitions including not being permitted to bathe, to speak, to eat, and so on. During this period, he must stay in the great house, where he remains isolated night and day in a room in the great house. If these restrictions are broken, he will suffer consequences such as illness, accidents, poor luck, a troubled life, or disturbing dreams. Moreover, these misfortunes might strike not only the person who is *pī* , but may affect other members of his family or descent group. Obviously there are variations within the village in interpreta-tions of these restrictions, and I have never been aware of anyone who was subject to the complete set of rigours A. Sonny Keraf describes.

A. Sonny Keraf interprets the person bearing these restrictions as serving as a symbol of the presence of the deceased. Living members of the family and village are convinced that the deceased is still present among them. He becomes a mediator (or medium) between the deceased and the living. It is for this reason that he must observe restrictions. He must strip away and release himself from all his human weakness and limitations in order to become one with the deceased. At this point Keraf draws an analogy with Christian ascetic practices. Another aim of the restrictions is to lighten or redeem all sins and faults of the deceased. The first meaning of the ceremonial restriction of *pī* is concerned with safety of the deceased, that is with the effort to help the soul of the deceased to escape from the torments and fetters of evil spirits. It is also concerned with the well-being of the living members of the community, from whom it is hoped to keep all dangers and disturbances by evil spirits. The restrictions end with the ritual meal, *nebo*, and the man who has taken them on emerges in association with traditional ceremonies into an atmosphere of happiness because all will now be safe.

Commonly, during the period of the greater *nebo*, the family of the deceased may feel obliged to provide three communal meals on each of the four days following death, with people from different groups taking part on different days. Various people help, and those who are invited bring a plate of rice or other provisions with them. The principal wife-giver of the deceased should provide a cloth to be used for the burial. This cloth may actually take the form of a tubular cloth (*lipa*), thread, a shirt or some combination of these if the deceased is a man or a woman's cloth and blouse if a woman. This clothing bears the name *nōni lārā*, 'to show the way' (exactly the same sense and purpose as the *tubén lala* in Kédang (R. H. Barnes 1974*a*: 181)). It is also known as *létu lofat*, i.e. to close or shut up. After the feast, the deceased's family would return a small goat or pig to dry the face, *aé marā*. The trunk wife-giver, *opu pukã*, should also bring a plate of rice or maize kernels on the day that the person observing the restrictions of *pī* emerges. His function is to 'open the door', *pĕlédar kenafé*, and he also crushes the maize in preparation for the special meal or *bomak*. The chicken for this meal should be supplied by the deceased's wife-taker, particularly the 'banana trunk' wife-takers, *kefina muko pukã*, who traditionally provide ritual services to the descent group. The wife-taker should also bring the coconut oil to rub in the restricted person's hair as part of his grooming and his re-emergence. Another small gathering and festive meal may be put on by the family forty days after a person's death. This seems to be the time when the dead soul has finally completely left the environs of the village and of the living. This is also an appropriate time for a private mass.

The souls of the dead are *kefokot*. Whatever individual belief may be, Lamalera tradition is that the souls of the dead go to two small islands in the strait between Lembata and Pantar, identified as Deer Island (*Pulau Rusa*) and Goat Island (*Pulau Kambing*) on maps and called in Lamaholot the Great Island (*nua bélã*) and the small island (*nua kéni*) respectively. This attitude they share with Kédang (Barnes 1974*a*: 202; Vatter 1932: 214; A. Sonny Keraf 1982). A schoolteacher in the village described to me a visit he made to Deer Island in December 1947 with a missionary. According to him the people of Kédang and those of Lamalera had a tradition that there was a spring on the island and at the spring was a statue. If the statue faced the spring, people coming to it would be successful hunting deer there. If it faced the other way, they would not. The island is covered with high grass and a few trees. The missionary found a small cave with a human skull in it. Someone had put an areca nut in the mouth as an offering to the dead spirit to obtain help in hunting. The teacher located the spring up a ravine. There was no statue, but there was an ordinary clay pot on three stones. Bouman visited the island in the 1930s and found there an object lying like a great shell near the beach, a small bronze Hindu figure on a small knoll and a monolith erected near the beach. There were also many scattered potsherds and bronze rings. These antiquities were greatly venerated by the inhabitants of nearby islands, Pantar and Marisa (Bouman 1943: 498).

Deaths at Sea

Those who have died at sea are referred to as *haring*, from *hari* a word with connotations of the sea and which may among other things refer to sea spirits. If a person dies in a boat or is lost overboard, the boat will put up a piece of clothing, such as a cloth (*lipa*), on the mast to signal others for assistance or to alert those at shore to the misfortune. If someone disappears at sea and the boats searching for him find him, they will put up the cloth as a signal if he is dead or a hat if he is still alive. Boats searching for someone lost at sea may not harpoon fish, no matter how tempted, before they have found him. Generally, when someone disappears at sea and is not immediately found, they may take a nautilus shell, *sĕnili*, and drop it into the sea. If it disappears, that is a sign that the body will never be found. If it reappears, it means that they will find it. If the body proves unrecoverable, they will hold a funeral and bury a nautilus shell in place of the corpse. At the burial of such a person, villagers, especially those who go to sea, must bring a small piece of white cloth to the grave to place in the coffin, called *tīfa saboq*, 'to throw away white cloth'.

Should a person die at sea, his kinsmen must observe a complete prohibition on all contact with the sea, including fishing, salt making, and bathing for a period of four days, i.e. the period of the great *nebo*. This closing of the sea is called *tāi muru* (from *tāi*, 'sea water', and *muru*, from *puru*, prohibited). In the case of an ordinary death, that is one not at sea, crew members of the boat associated with the relevant great house, if they are not of the same descent group, may put out to sea the next day in another boat, but close relatives of course cannot go to sea because they are observing the restrictions of the great *nebo*. After this period is over, members of the descent group who belong to a different great house may go to sea. The boat of the dead person's great house and the head of the great house must remain at shore the full eight days. Sometimes a death in a boat may have the effect that the boat itself is rendered unseaworthy for organizational reasons for several years.

As I have witnessed, people may be quite frightened during the period immediately after someone has died at sea. The soul of such a person will come ashore and frighten people by appearing before them, or banging on the window or door. The soul usually does no worse than this. People do not like to go out at night during this period, but stay home and close the doors and windows. This danger lasts forty days. In the night of 17 July 1979 a combination of volcanic eruption and earthquake destroyed two villages on the south coast of Lembata, Waiteba and Sarapuka. In response to a request by the village head of Labala, Lamalera decided to send several boats to sea on the 20th to look for corpses. I went out in the *Notã Ténã*, which did not find any human corpses, although we did see a great deal of debris including dead animals, household implements, parts of houses, and boats, and a great many coconuts stretched in a long line running through the sea for miles. However, the *Muko Ténã* did find the partially dismembered corpse of a young woman from Waiteba, whom one of the villagers recognized. The boat took her back to the village, where the crew buried her. She was deemed to have entered the clan Ata Kéi, owners of the *Muko Ténã*, who therefore had to hold formal funeral observations for her and to submit to the restrictions on putting out to sea during the eight days of the greater and lesser *nebo*. However, when asking for boats to search for victims, the village head told them the situation was different from what it would be had the dead been from Lamalera and that it was permissible to harpoon fish if an opportunity arose. The crew of the *Muko Ténã* succeeded in harpooning a large manta ray on their way back to shore.

Although the disaster at Waiteba took place some twelve miles away on the far side of a peninsula which sheltered Lamalera from any direct damage, some fourteen persons from Lamalera and the nearby village of Lewotala who happened to be in the region at the time died. Most tragic was the fate of a businessman of Lewotala origin whose family were temporarily living in Sarapuka where he was acting as a business agent purchasing peanuts. He was taking a daughter to school on Adonara when the catastrophe occurred. He lost his wife and five children, aged 2 to 10, whom he left behind, as well as three other relatives who were staying with them at the time. None of these persons were found again. We had the very sad experience of attending the mass burial for them held at Lewotala. We met the man and his daughter the day before when we were visiting Lewotala; both were very distraught.

On the day of their funeral, it took some time for people to gather. When all were ready, they took eight sections of banana trunk to the sea, which were to serve as substitutes for the missing bodies. It had proved impossible to locate enough nautilus shells for this purpose. We went down a steep winding path through fields and down a rocky ravine. The path was narrow and rugged, and the air was full of dry plant smells until we were quite near the shore, when they were replaced by the smell of the sea. It led to a small cove, protected on either side by projecting points of lava rock—not large smooth boulders but sharp rugged conglomerate that was hard on the feet.

One elderly man was intended to enact the search for the bodies. He stood out on one point and threw the banana stalks into the water. Then he put on diving goggles and jumped in. Although the banana stalks were floating on the surface, the intention was that this man was diving to find them. Then he encountered bodies and brought them back to the opposite shore. Everyone else rushed around to the other point, while he handed the banana stalks up one by one. All the way down several of the women were wailing. These and others carried cloth which had been provided by the *opu-laké* and by the family, male cloths for men and female cloths for the women. The woman carrying this cloth took the banana trunk pieces as they were handed up and wrapped them in the cloth, then with additional wailing started back up the hill. One of the pieces of banana stalk shed a section while in the water, which was left floating in the sea.

The group then went up to the clear area in the centre of the village, where a small awning of coconut leaves had been set up. Next to it men were busily making small coffins, of various sizes. The largest of these were for the adults, the smaller ones for the children. Completing the coffins took a couple of hours. Meanwhile, a man showed up with another bundle. The man who had done the searching in the sea felt ill when he came back to the village. He decided to return with another man to get the piece of banana trunk left in the sea. When they were near, they heard a voice crying from that direction. They decided that the ninth victim (a woman, who was related and for whom they were responsible, since they had sent her with others to the area) was crying not to be left in the sea. Although her clan might carry out its own ceremony for this woman, they decided to include her. The remaining pieces were wrapped in a cloth and a ninth coffin was built.

When the coffins were ready, the banana stalks and cloth were put into the coffins. In fact, two coffins were so small that the cloth had to be left outside, but I was told that in the case of a death of this kind, they should not be. All of the cloth was eventually buried. Also placed in the coffin of the man's wife were strands of resist-dyed, but not yet woven, threads which had been brought for this purpose by her father. Her trunk wife-giver, *opu pukã*, in this case her mother's brother, brought two cloths for the ceremony. In a normal death this cloth might be claimed by the deceased's wife-takers, but not on this occasion.

Before the coffins were closed, we all went past them to put small pieces of white cloth, *saboq burã*, into each of the coffins (see plate 36 in Ruth Barnes 1989). My pieces had thoughtfully been provided for me, without my knowledge or knowing they were needed, by a companion. The point of this white cloth is that the souls of the dead will protect those persons who give them; and they should be provided by everyone in the case of a death at sea. After the white cloth had been given by every man present, the elders of the clan sat together and had a brief discussion of the cause of the misfortune. It seems that husband and father had brought the ill luck upon himself by refusing to attend functions of the clan on various occasions because of his business commitments.

The nine coffins were taken from their shelter and placed on stretchers, *kelata*, made of fresh bamboo. The stretchers were two large, long poles underneath for the two men to grab. Across this perpendicularly were three pieces of split bamboo. Above them, lengthwise were four pieces of split bamboo. They carried the coffins down to the great house, where they lined them up one next to the other, with the wife's coffin furthest east, the children next, then the two other people from the same clan, and the one from another clan furthest west. In the midst of arranging this, they spoke of the west end as being the tip and the east as the base. On each of the coffins they put candles, which I had been asked to give as my contribution to events. Candles are part of Catholic tradition and had never been used earlier.

From there the coffins were taken to the graveyard, where they were buried with Catholic ceremony. The Catholic side of events began just before the coffins were picked up to be carried away. In the graveyard, the stretchers were placed over the grave, with two stones at either end. On that to the east they placed one of the candles. One of my companions started to pile up stones over the grave he had helped cover, but people told him not to do so. Placing stones on the grave may be done by anyone when the dead person has died an ordinary death, but in a bad death, the stones must be piled up by a special person. This is a man in a specific clan in Lewotala, and it is a hereditary position. He and his ancestors are skilled at dealing with spirits, and only he fits with the spirits of these dead. When we returned from the grave, we had to go to the descent group's great house first, so that the spirits do not go to the wrong place.

Injury and Illness

Since the early 1960s the village has had a polyclinic staffed by a nurse. It is able to provide, at cost, a variety of medicaments and medical aid. There is no doubt that it represents an improvement in health care. In the past the missionary was the sole source of medical aid, a role which the government no longer permits him to assume. Lives have been saved in the past by these providers of modern medicines. Anti-dehydration packages of sugar and salt are now easily available to combat dysentery. High fevers can be lowered with aspirin. Pregnant women receive vitamin B supplements. Anti-malaria drugs can also be purchased. First aid and the treatment of wounds is provided for. Nevertheless the medical knowledge of the nurse, like his pharmacopoeia, is limited. More important is the lack of a reliable source of electricity, so that there is no refrigeration for essential vaccines such as that against tetanus. The nearest hospital may be reached after a five-hour boat trip on those days in which the passenger boat makes its scheduled runs. An emergency trip by foot would take a day and a night. In any case, many villagers either cannot or will not spend money for such medical care as is available. Too many women die in childbirth and children from fevers who if given access to full modern care could have been easily treated. Because of their reluctance to incur costs, villagers sometimes postpone seeking attention until it is too late for conditions that could be treated successfully locally. This behaviour is not a matter of misplaced faith in traditional healers. Although they do consult such persons, sometimes it seems successfully, they are generally anxious to receive any effective medical care they can obtain.

7

Cloth, Salt, and Markets

Apart from raising children, performing domestic chores, and finding employment in modern occupations such as schoolteaching, women contribute to economic life primarily by spinning thread for ropes and clothing; weaving and dyeing cloth; carrying loads, such as firewood, water, meat, and trade goods; manufacturing salt and lime; and trading.

Weaving

Weaving was the only industry which Beckering (1911: 196) recognized on Lembata, apart from crafts for local use, such as boat building in Lamalera (see also Munro 1915: 10). The women in most of the mountain villages knew how to weave except in Kédang, where it was prohibited. In fact, Mingar, in southwest Lembata, also did not weave. Today the three principal areas of weaving on Lembata are Lamalera, the Lerek peninsula to the east, and the Ilé Apé (Lewotolo) district on the north coast (Ruth Barnes 1989: 96–100). Of course weaving in all of these regions is affected by pronounced shifts toward commercially produced cloth from outside. There is some decline in weaving in Lamalera, but it is still done. In previous centuries cotton and silk cloth from India was traded into the area in considerable quantities, affecting both traditions of use and decorative patterns. Commercial cloth of types familiar today was certainly reaching the islands by the nineteenth century (van Lynden 1851a: 324), as were, by the end of the century probably, chemical dyes now in common use.[1]

  The differential distribution of weaving traditions on Lembata is part of a patchwork pattern of resist-dyed, *ikat*, industries throughout the Lamaholot-speaking area (Ruth Barnes 1987: 24). In some interior districts of central Flores, dyeing of cotton cloth is forbidden, although the district produces cotton and dye-stuffs. The raw materials are traded to the coast, where cloth is dyed and then traded back to the mountains. Burger (1975: 64–5) interprets these customary restrictions as guaranteeing that the coastal peoples have something to offer in trade for the food which is usually more abundant in the mountains. The fine cloths used in marriage transactions among the Lamaholot are typically red; those which are supplied by Lamaholot-speaking peoples for such use in Kédang must be black (actually dark blue). The opposition between red and black or blue cloths is also an ethnological theme for eastern Indonesia.[2] These oppositions and prohibitions are part of a general picture of craft and decorative specializations throughout the region, whereby peoples both establish economic interdependence and mark community and cultural differences.

Lamalera women produce a variety of kinds of cloth used for clothing. A tubular wrap made of local cotton thread for use in everyday wear by men is a *nōfi*. These cloths are of blue, black, and white plaid, occasionally with some red. Although Ruth Barnes (1989: 52) says that they are never used in marriage gift exchange, it may be inferred that their role as gifts has been assumed by the commercial cloths, *lipa*, which are presented by wife-givers to sister's children at various occasions, such as first hair-cutting or burial. These cloths contain no decorative designs, *mōfa*, and are therefore easier and quicker to make than the elaborate woman's cloths. Men's cloths are made either entirely from local cotton thread and dyes or from imported dyes and thread.

Large decorated import cloths, often from India, which would not be used for ordinary wear and which, despite a modest value on international markets, may become part of a family's heirloom cache, are called *nōfi bĕlaja* (Ruth Barnes 1989: plate 29). They nevertheless have neither the value nor the cultural importance of the Indian double ikat silk cloths which, like elephant tusks, were for long centuries sought-after imports and which had a profound impact on marriage exchanges and the decorative patterns of locally woven cloth (Ruth Barnes 1989: 73). The latter are *patola*, the Lamaholot name for which is *ketipa*. Gregorius Keraf (1978: 166) lists the paired phrase *bĕlaja-petola* as a general expression for heirlooms and inheritable goods. Silk *patola* are also called *kewatek suntera* on Adonara (from Indonesian *sutera*, silk). One man, who bought one for Rp. 100,000 (US $243) in 1978, wished to sell it in 1982 for Rp. 500,000 (US $750), an increase considerably in excess of inflation.

Women's cloths are *kefatek*. All such cloths contain decorative resist-dyed bands of greater or lesser elaboration, except sometimes those intended for daily wear and work. Cloths are made in panels, *nai*. Men's *nōfi* have two panels, *nai rua*, as do the more colourful *kefatek olung* (ordinary cloth), made for everyday wear for women, and the *kefatek menikil* made for festive wear. The highly decorated and carefully woven cloths used as return gifts to wife-takers are two-panel cloths, *kefatek nai rua*, or more valuable three-panel cloths, *kefatek nai telo*. Festive cloths today often contain commercial thread and typically employ commercial, aniline, dyes. Cloths expressly made for ceremonial exchange should use only local thread and natural dyes. Three-panel cloths are also called *tukã-hebã*, for the central panel, *tukã*, and the decorative bands of the outer parts, *hebã*. *Tukã-hebã* is also an expression in use for referring to the whole set of marriage gifts returned for bridewealth. Two-piece ceremonial cloths are worn in Lamalera only at very important festivals, but never for daily use. Shoulder cloths, *senai*, are decorated woven cloths appropriate for wear by men or women on festival or religious occasions (Ruth Barnes 1989: 51–3).

PLATE 11. Weaving with a back-strap loom

Women weave cloth on body-tension or back-strap looms (see Plate 11). An important item in this equipment is the weaving sword, *huri*. This sword should be made of fine wood, such as teak or heart of tamarind, by a man, who must not receive payment for it. The base of the sword should be carved in the design appropriate to the decorated stern piece of the boat belonging to the descent group of the woman for whom the sword is made. To weave is *tané*, the loom *tenané*. To spin thread is *tūlé bua*, while a spinning-wheel is *tenūlé*. *Tué* is to twist, turn, reverse, from which comes *menué*, the swift. For details of spinning, dyeing, resist-dyeing, and weaving see Ruth Barnes (1989: 24–48).

Trade in Cloth

When Beckering described weaving as an industry, he meant production for trade. Although Lamalera produces a good amount of cloth for local use, it also produces it for barter within the village and in mountain communities. Women regularly trade fish and meat in the interior and have good established contacts there, which serve them as well when it comes to providing cloth. Cloth making is an important additional source of income. Woven cloth made for sale is called *beragi*. Women also share out different tasks in producing a cloth, which is another potential source of income. To weave a cloth which has already been prepared to the point that the warp is set up and the weft provided, a woman might charge Rp. 2,000 (US $4.75) in 1979 or Rp. 2,500 (US $3.75) in 1982. This low commission assumes, as will probably be the case, that the transaction is carried out by close kin. Standard relative values of cloth in 1979 and 1982 may be found in Fig. 5.

Salt and Lime Production

Throughout the Lamaholot-speaking region salt and lime production are linked in local perception and are thought to be characteristic of coastal communities (for a survey of salt-making techniques in the vicinity of Flores see R. H. Barnes 1993*a*).[3] Lime is needed for use with betel quid and in dyeing. In Lamalera too the production of salt and the burning of lime are culturally linked forms of work. Both activities are low-prestige, emergency occupations of minor economic importance which supplement the principal crafts and subsistence pursuits. In periods when no fish or whale meat is available, women take salt or lime to the market at Wulan Doni or to mountain villages to trade for agricultural products. The small descent group Lāma Nifa changed the name of their whaling boat from *Téna Tapoona* to *Sia Apu*, as a reminder of their misery when their boat has no catch and their women must make salt and lime to sell in the mountains. *Sia* is salt, and *apu* is lime.

For the production of lime, blocks of uplifted coral are broken up and burned, and the resulting powder collected. The tongues of flat basaltic lava which reach into the sea at various places along the shore make useful evaporation pans for brine. These often have depressions which form pools, where salt water collects during calm periods in the dry season and where it dries leaving behind salt crystals. Where necessary, women build up the sides of such depressions with ridges of stones held together with clay. Men and women fill these pools with sea water, but this is especially a woman's task. When the water

Cloth Type	Value in Local Produce	Value in Currency			
		Rp.		US $	
		1979	1982	1979	1982
1. Men's cloth	1,000 ears of maize	7,500	10,000	17.80	14.99
2. Women's cloth, daily wear	five *bĕlék*[a] of unhusked rice	7,500	10,000	17.80	14.99
3. Women's cloth, festive wear	up to ten *bĕlék* of unhusked rice	15,000	20,000	35.63	29.98
4. Two-panel marriage exchange cloth	twenty *bĕlék* of unhusked rice	20,000	40,000	47.51	59.97
5. Three-panel marriage exchange cloth	thirty *bĕlék* of unhusked rice	30,000	60,000	71.26	89.96
6. Shoulder cloth		5,000	7,000	11.88	10.49

Fig. 5. Relative values of different types of woven cloth in Lamalera, Lembata, in 1979 and 1982[b]

[a] A 20-litre cookie (or biscuit) tin, used for storage and as a general standard of measure of volume.
[b] After Ruth Barnes (1989: 57).

has evaporated to a thick brine, they collect it to be boiled in pots (see plates 3 and 4 in R. H. Barnes 1993*a*). Use of the concentrated brine greatly reduces the amount of firewood needed to turn the sea water to salt. Men do help in carrying sea water and in preparing the limestone blocks for calcining lime, but collecting firewood and minding fires is generally women's work. Metzner calculates that one cubic metre of wood is required to produce about 120 to 150 kg. of salt (Metzner 1982: 234).

A handful of salt, called *monga* or *munga*, will bring twelve ears of maize at harvest time, six ears during the dry season, and only three ears in the hunger season. These ratios chart the relative abundance of these two products during the year. Maize grows during the rainy season from December to late February, when it is harvested. Salt may be made during the dry season, from April to November, but the hottest and most windless months and the best for making salt are October and November.[4] Therefore salt should be plentiful during the hunger months of late December and January just preceding the availability of young ears of maize in late January to early February. During the rainy season, salt cannot be easily made, so it is less abundant just as the maize is being harvested. Salt from some producers, particularly those on Solor, finds a very wide distribution, and today salt may be purchased for cash in regional market-places and towns. Its role in barter, however, remains important. In 1979 a small *sokal* (a cylindrical container of woven palm leaf containing about two kilos of salt) sold in Larantuka for between Rp. 750 and Rp. 1,000 (US $1.78 to 2.38). In Lamalera and elsewhere in the islands, salt is usually set out at feasts and meals in small bowls. Often salt is served mixed with chopped red peppers.[5]

Markets and the Absence of Markets

According to Burger (1975: 64–5) there was, at least until the 1950s, a great variety of trading arrangements on the island of Flores, ranging from the absence of markets, to isolated markets, to networks of markets with a limited turnover of goods centred on larger towns such as Ende and Maumere. In remote parts of Flores where there were no markets, incidental trade unlinked to kinship ties did take place and mostly involved exchanges between the coasts and the mountainous interior. People in the mountains provided mostly food-stuffs, while the coast returned fish, woven cloths, and earthen pots. In some places on Flores, Sumba (where incidentally trade followed marriage ties), and Timor, groups of men from the coast occasionally met groups from the interior on specific days in order to trade. These arrangements, according to Burger, usually occurred in regions where there were no markets and perhaps may be regarded as precursors to markets.

In contrast to Flores, on Timor, where there were many organized rajadoms, there may anciently have been many very tiny markets within the principal-ities of the interior, but, as a result of chronic war, there was no trade between rajadoms. Restrictions on weaving were unknown, and trade was not bound, as on Sumba, to marriage ties (for some comment on European influence on politics and trade on Timor see Forman 1977). Burger believes that the difference between Timor and Flores lies in the weaker development of rajas and the greater independence of villages, which on Flores were involved in more frequent wars. Peace, which the Dutch brought to Timor at the beginning of the twentieth century, encouraged links between the individual market networks of each of the rajadoms and the appearance of new, central markets.

On the basis of his visit to Adonara in 1949, Burger (1975: 66) describes the island as possessing a market network, despite the pattern of continuous feuding and small wars which earned it the unenviable reputation as the 'murder island'. During that visit, two villages were in a state of war, but because war is strictly regulated by customary rules, their women were able to pass unharmed through enemy territory on their way to market. Similar outbreaks of hostilities, uneasily suppressed by the police and army, occurred on Adonara during our visit in 1982. Adonara may be described, as Burger does, as the middle point of sea trade that is linked to the market net. Waiwerang on the south coast, originally established as a Dutch administration centre, has become a commercial town linking the island to national and international trade. As such it is comparable to nearby Larantuka, Flores; and both are directly important to Lamalera, whose villagers routinely visit them. Many people from Lamalera and other south Lembata villages have moved permanently to these towns, and others find intermittent employment there.

Lembata displays all or at least most of the variety so far mentioned. The principal town, Lewoleba, as well as to a lesser extent, Hadakewa and Balaurin (all three on the north coast), provide the centres for commercial trade in the modern sense. Labala, near Lamalera, does so to a much less significant degree on the south coast. By 1982 a government programme to promote small kiosks within villages through small loans had provided half a dozen Lamalera persons with opportunities to purchase goods such as plastic sandals, clothing, thread, dyes, matches, and small implements at these centres (Waiwerang, Adonara, was preferred as least expensive and most accessible) for sale for cash within the village. Turnover was still quite low, and most persons made their own purchases at these towns or arranged to have friends make them on their behalf.

Different from these arrangements is trade for necessities of various kinds produced on the island. Among these are trade in goods, mostly food, at weekly nearby markets, barter with individuals in inland villages, transactions with itinerant merchants visiting Lamalera, and arrangements between individuals for procuring materials and services needed in fishing, house building, weaving, and other village pursuits. The yearly total of all these exchanges is probably rather large and in any case beyond my present knowledge.

While fishing and hunting is the preserve of men, trade (Lamaholot *penétã*) is predominantly in the hands of women. There are two prominent patterns of trade. Women either go directly to villages of the interior, where they hope to find the goods they need, or they carry their goods to market. There is a weekly market at Wulan Doni near the border between the old districts of Lamalera and Labala (presently the boundary between the Kecamatan Naga Wutun and the Kecamatan Leworaja). This market meets on Saturday mornings. A weekly market takes place in Labala on Wednesdays, and villagers from Lamalera and nearby communities occasionally participate. The Wulan Doni market is a walk of about an hour and a half from Lamalera, while Labala is about three hours away by foot. These are the only markets near enough to be frequently visited, although the availability of regular transportation by passenger boat means that people now attend the market at Lewoleba and the commercial centres at Waiwerang and Larantuka. Although cash is readily accepted and normally used in these modern market centres, Wulan Doni is distinguished by the prevalence of the exchange of goods in kind and the relative difficulty in purchasing foodstuffs for cash.[6] Labala is an ancient Muslim trading community with some shops which sell for cash non-indigenous goods, such as kerosene, machine-woven sarongs and shirts, sugar, tea, yarn and thread. Trade at Labala market is in kind as well as cash. In addition to these two markets, there are several places where trade on a very small scale takes place on specified days. One such location is Lamalera itself, where people from the mountain hamlet Lamamanu come on Saturdays to sit by the road to trade betel pepper or areca nuts and a few ears of maize for fish or salt.

Two historically closely related south coast villages, Lamalera and Nualela, have developed economic specializations to supply regional needs. Lamalera men hunt and fish for the large sea animals, which provide dried meat or fish to be bartered by the women. Lamalera also produces salt and textiles, while Nualela makes earthenware pots. Lamalera women must trade for most of the cotton from which to weave indigenous textiles and to spin the thread needed to make the ropes and cords used in the fishery. If they choose to use natural dyes, rather than the commercially produced powders purchased in the towns, they may have to obtain the necessary plants from the interior. Natural dyes and local cotton are required for cloths intended for use in marriage exchanges.

The Market at Wulan Doni

Wulan Doni market takes place on a wide sandy space near the shore, comfortably shaded by many trees, contiguous to Nualela.[7] By 1982 the government had induced Nualela to move down from its more remote and higher-lying site; so that it now actually borders the market-place on the landward side. Until this happened, the market was isolated. To the east about ten minutes walk away is the site where the government has begun moving Labala,

after it suffered in 1979 some damage and loss of life from a volcanically gen-
erated tidal wave. In 1982 there were a small shop and a storage shed, containing little but rice, a polyclinic, the district head's (Camat's) office, and
several houses there.

It was near Nualela where, according to the legend of the founding of
Lamalera, their ancestors once anciently settled at the site of the present
market, where they exchanged skills and political position with Nualela, bringing to Lamalera the knowledge of forging iron, enabling them to replace their
wooden harpoons with iron ones, and to Nualela skills in making pots, which
became their monopoly. Implied in this legend is a picture of indigenous, pot-
making, hosts of the interior living amicably with landless, shore-based, fishing
newcomers, who exercise political functions, the authority for which was
derived from the hosts.

Traditions concerning the origin of the actual market are, however, somewhat different. One account has it that an ancestor named Dato took the
whaling boat *Dato Ténã* out to fish. They happened to harpoon a sperm whale
which pulled them to the island of Pantar, just east of Lembata. They were at
Pantar so long the village decided that they were dead and, using nautilus shells
as substitutes for their bodies, buried them. Subsequently, Dato and his crew
returned safely in the *Dato Ténã* as far as Doni Nusa Léla (Wulan Doni and
Nualela), where he heard what had been done in their absence. Thereupon he
cut up fish and meat and sent pieces to all of the villages in the mountains with
the message that he would be staying at Doni Nusa Léla. The mountain
dwellers were to bring their maize and other field products and trade for fish.
This exchange, according to the tradition, was the actual origin of the market
(*wulan*) at Wulan Doni, that is Doni Nusa Léla. Dato also sent fish to Lamalera
with a message that he and his companions were alive and waiting at Wulan
Doni. The elders subsequently conducted a ceremony to undo the funerals, so
that the fishermen could re-enter their village. Had they made any appearance
in Lamalera prior to this ceremony they would have been regarded as and
treated like the souls of the dead.

The ancient economic contract between mountain agriculturalists and
coastal fishermen was celebrated in the tradition of loading a newly built
whaling boat with meat, fish, and salt and sailing it to Wulan Doni, where
by pre-arrangement people from mountain villages would await them with
agricultural produce. These were exchanged without regard to cost.
Afterwards the fishermen would load their boat with the farmer's produce,
with which they sailed back to Lamalera (cf. Vatter 1932: 204; R. H. Barnes
1974*b*: 151).

In the morning, people gathering at Wulan Doni approach it generally from
three different directions, coming from Nualela, Lamalera, and other villages
in the west, Labala and the Lerek Peninsula to the east, and from villages in
the mountains to the north such as Lewuka, Kalikasa, and Boto. The three

groups do not generally mix in their seating arrangements. Each stays close to the place where they entered the market space. In a crowd of several hundred, women far outnumber the men, making up perhaps 90 per cent of those present.

Labala traders, who may be men or women, offer a wide variety of goods, often not indigenous. The few men, usually young, either are petty merchants or represent stores. They offer in particular machine-spun yarn, both dyed and undyed, commercial dyes, thread, sugar, packets of monosodium glutamate, and so on. There was in 1982 also a single kiosk set up at the seaward edge of the market by a Labala trader where cloths are sold, both locally woven and imported. These are the only textiles offered in the market, as Lamalera women never bring cloths there. Labala women, who are easily recognized by their white, powdered faces, their 'gold' earrings and their aggressive voices, sell fish, kerosene, coconut oil, and *krupuk*, shrimp wafers. For fish they offer only small anchovies, depending on size either split and dried whole or threaded on split bamboo sticks, three in a row, and sold in bundles of four (making twelve tiny fish in a bunch).

Women from the interior bring maize, bananas, sweet potatoes, coconuts, and seasonal green vegetables. They may also bring coffee, sugar cane, citrus fruit, pineapples, and mangoes in season. A few men from the mountains bring areca nuts and betel peppers, as well as palm wine. Lamalera women bring dried fish or meat, salt, and occasionally lime for chewing betel. Some women from Nualela may bring pots, although most of the trade in pots is carried on in the old site of Nualela early in the morning of the market day, well before the market begins.

Many mountain people go further down the road to Lamalera, some even into it, to exchange with people coming the other way before they reach the market. The latter can then return home early. Some people sit by the road on the Lamalera side of Wulan Doni and trade there without entering the market-place. There are two minor market-like sites between Wulan Doni and Lamalera. Twenty or so people may choose to trade with passers-by at a place named Duli Pukā for example, but people may stop anywhere along the road. Travellers to market are likely to encounter women returning to Lamalera and neighbouring communities balancing on their heads stacks of pots firmly bound together with palm leaves so that they can be lain horizontally for carrying. These women have risen early and completed their trading at the specialized Nualela pot market.

The market place does not start filling up until around 10.00 a.m. By about 10.30 or 10.45, the *Mandor Pasar*, or market official, goes through the seated groups of traders with a basket hanging from a pole. As he goes from person to person, everyone drops a small amount of goods into his basket. There seems to be no definite rate; he takes from each what he deems appropriate, never much. Before the start of the market proper, the Mandor goes up the road a way to collect from the people waiting there. What he collects, he turns over to the head of the hamlet of Nualela, who sells it for cash which he sends to the district officer.

As soon as the Mandor is through collecting, after about twenty minutes or so, trading can begin. Women from Lamalera who have brought fish and meat then all get up at the same time and start moving through the crowd. After a time they rush back to where they had been sitting in the shade while waiting, landward of the market, and unload their agricultural gains in heaps, before plunging back into the crowd. Small piles of maize, yam, bananas, areca nuts, coconuts, and so on rapidly build up on the edge of the market-place, while the women trade.

The Labala traders also get up and move through the crowd with their goods at the same time as the Lamalera contingent. Meanwhile the women from the farming villages squat or sit around on the ground in the centre. It is the people from Lamalera in general who walk about, the mountain people who sit, because fish is lighter than agricultural goods. People say that the load for a person from Lamalera is light on the way to the market, heavy on the way back, while that for a person from a mountain village is heavy on the way to the market, light on the way back. During our visit in July 1979 many of the mountain people got little or nothing in the market and had to go home with the goods they brought with them because Lamalera had not been very successful in catching whales and had little to offer. Local fishermen offering their small amounts of dried fish find that interest may shift quickly against them when whale meat is available in sufficient quantity.

Although Indonesian markets are often convivial, Wulan Doni market, though by no means an example of silent trade, is a fairly quiet and subdued place during trading. Not much is spoken, and such verbal exchanges as do occur are generally confined to the transaction of goods. Trading is done rather quickly, and as soon as a trader has all she wants or needs, she packs her goods and prepares to leave. By around noon, the market begins to thin out, as people make off in all directions, the women with goods piled high on their heads.

All goods are displayed in little piles, usually three, six, or twelve together, depending on size. In the established rates of exchange, the unit of twelve dominates. It is generally considered that one strip of dried fish or meat from Lamalera is equivalent to twelve ears of maize, twelve bananas, twelve pieces of dried sweet potatoes, twelve sections of sugar cane, or twelve betel peppers *plus* twelve areca nuts. One large handful of salt (approximately a tea-cup measurement) also brings the equivalent of twelve ears of maize. The cash value of twelve ears of maize or the equivalent in other goods was estimated in 1982 to be Rp. 100 (*c*.15 cents US). Larger or smaller goods are worth the appropriate fraction of twelve. The basic unit is three times four. This is made visually clear in the fish sticks sold by Labala women: three fish per stick (they are not sold separately), made up into a bundle of four sticks, i.e. twelve fish. It is possible to go down to the unit of three, but not below. Coconuts may be had three for a strip of meat or fish. A pot might bring 60 ears of maize, a smaller one 50 ears.

According to Gregorius Keraf (1978: 146–8), in trading women use various units of reckoning. Groups of six, such as bananas, limes, or ears of maize, are *munga*. Multiples of six are treated as multiples of *munga*. Thus eighteen limes would be *munga telo*, three *munga*. Remarkably, he attributes the practice of counting in groups of six to the influence of the English, without further explanation. If this apparently most unlikely interpretation were to be substantiated it might just be by reference to the importance of Singapore for trade goods brought to the region, especially in the early nineteenth century. *Munga* is also used for goods sold in undifferentiated heaps, such as tobacco, salt, and lime. In these cases, the size of the heaps is determined by the seller and the buyer in the process of bartering. According to Gregorius Keraf, *munga* derives from the verb *bongã*, meaning to measure things in heaps and it is this application to undifferentiated heaps which is the original sense of *munga*, while the application to groups of six is derivative and due to foreign influence. The word is used only for goods of local origin, never for commercially produced goods. Thus pencils or shirts are measured in terms of dozens, *lōsi* (from Malay *lusin*, which derives from English dozen),[8] but never *munga*. Another local phrase is *fēla*, or *fēlak*, a tied-up bunch or batch, which may be used for bunches of a hundred ears of maize or a hundred bananas or ten coconuts. In fact the word does not imply a specific number. The number involved for each type of good is determined by convention or circumstances.

These rates are established general expectations that facilitate the exchanges, but do not as such take into account seasonal variation in supply, immediate demand, or the quality of the actual items offered. In 1982, for example, an acquaintance traded in one transaction three strips of shark for 34, rather than the expected 36, ears of maize. One woman who was trading for fish thought that a double spine of in total 6 fish would bring 6 bananas or 6 yams, hence also 6 ears of maize. One man had several bamboos of palm wine, which he said would bring 4 or 5 strips of fish each. He offered us palm wine at Rp. 100 a bottle or 12 ears of maize, but we obtained three at Rp. 75 each. Kerosene was on offer at Rp. 100 per bottle or 5 coconuts. We found it impossible to obtain yams for cash. The values of the exchanges are said to fluctuate somewhat as the market goes on, scarce items bringing more toward the end if they are exchanged then.

Trading Journeys

The market at Wulan Doni is not the major supplier of food staples for Lamalera. The women routinely make journeys into the mountain villages and as far as Mingar to the west. Mingar is particularly sought out as a potential textile market, as the region has a prohibition on weaving. This form of trading is called *du hopé* (to sell and to buy). Typically a group of friends will gather around 2.00 a.m. before setting out on the long walk to the interior. Their destination is a village such as Boto where they have a few regular acquaintances and trading partners and where they are recognized as familiar visitors. Each woman may go from house to house, visiting her acquaintances on first arrival, offering each in turn a piece of meat or fish and receiving an equivalent amount of maize, coffee beans, bananas, or other goods. Then they continue trading with persons who have gathered along the road for that purpose. As is the case with the trip to Wulan Doni, local aphorism says that women travel light in the morning and return heavily laden in the evening because fish and meat are lighter than the farmer's goods. A very common sight is a group of exhausted women returning towards 5.00 p.m. carrying very sizeable loads (see Plate 12).

The same exchange rates prevail in the interior as those just described for the market-place. The question arises therefore why women sometimes subject themselves to these strenuous journeys at periods when the market may remain undersupplied with meat. Of course there may be social reasons such as the desire to have an outing or to see old friends, but the economic reasons seem to be that the main aim is to obtain maize, which is relatively undersupplied in the market where other consumables are more abundant. Although under government pressure the people of Lamalera are becoming increasingly involved in farming, even in 1982 there were few in the village who maintained large fields of their own. Some had sharing arrangements with persons in other villages, whereby they helped in working the land and received a share of the crop. Nevertheless, almost no one produces all the maize and rice needed to support a family through the year. A family of four or five needs four or five large storage baskets, *mata gapo*, of husked maize, each holding the equivalent of about 900 ears, or a total of about 3,000 to 4,000 ears, in order to survive the year. This estimate does not include their needs for feasts and other inessentials. By preference they keep most of a year's supplies stored away for at least a full year before using it.

There are a variety of strategies for amassing this quantity of staples. One of them is the sharing arrangement just mentioned. Another is the barter of sea products as described. During a period when there was a dearth of game from the sea, a neighbour of ours traded some maize for fish in the hope of taking 20 ears worth of fish to the mountains and trading it for 40 ears. When the boats come in empty, people may make up the gap by making salt, but they may also sell a pig or a goat. Widows often resort to salt making, but they may also *hodi kenaing*,[9] receive payment for weaving passed on to them or they may receive payment for helping people carry their goods from the interior of the island.

The standard for interrelating values of more important goods such as animals, cloth, ivory bracelets or tusks, and large quantities of maize is the

PLATE 12. Women returning from a day's trading in the mountains. In the background is the great house of Téti Nama Papã sub-clan of Běliko Lolo clan

twenty-litre can of unhusked rice, *bĕlĕk*. This means that the value of the abstract measure of marriage exchange obligations and valuables, the *kesebõ*, can also be expressed in terms of unhusked rice. Since the cash value of this quantity of rice in Chinese stores is always ascertainable, it provides a means for estimating the cash equivalent of goods not normally purchased with money.[10] Hence, as is also the case for the smaller values of market-place exchange, there is always a means of relating the non-cash economic sphere to the national cash economy. House building, taxes, school fees, or the desire to send children away for further education do in practice sometimes require the sale for cash of goods, such as elephant tusks or maize, otherwise not alienated in this way.

Beckering (1911: 193) wrote that at the time the Dutch moved into the island in force in 1910, the *kesebõ*, which he encountered in Labala, was then worth 5 Dutch guilders. Copra was exchanged for salt, ornaments, household goods, and clothing, and the *kesebõ* was used to determine the value of these objects, hence it was a medium for trade in objects of foreign manufacture. Coconuts and maize were given in exchange for sarongs, yarn, necklaces, bone or ivory armbands, earrings, elephant tusks, and silk cloths. These objects were often advanced to the traders by Chinese merchants in Larantuka, who required repayment mostly in copra.

For a discussion of early trade in the eastern part of the archipelago, see MacKnight (1973), especially his comments (p. 203) about the tendency of some imports to acquire special ceremonial or other non-economic significance. In 1851 van Lynden (1851*a*: 324) remarked that in the coastal markets of Solor and Adonara goods were traded because money was unknown. Earlier, Kruseman (1835: 40) reported that in the market-places of Adonara, in place of small change, people used square patches of linen. According to Semmelink in Larantuka in 1861 money was still little known. Almost no one would accept the new cents, and some would not accept silver coins, with which they were unfamiliar. They would, however, accept *duiten* (farthings), bottles, and pieces of coloured silk or cotton, which were very much desired (Semmelink 1864: 64).[11] Given the continuous presence of traders in these islands coming there from Macassar and Buton, this cloth currency in all probability was either the same as, or else was related in some way to, the *kampua* of Buton. *Kampua* were cloth money pieces first encountered in the seventeenth century and in use into the twentieth. 'Their colors and stripes were distinctive to the high official who issued and backed them with coin. Originally their manufacture and distribution were the prerogative of nobles, but in the course of time, lesser administrators also issued pieces' (Gittinger 1979: 201).[12] In Manggarai, Flores, in 1916, cloth (*lipa*) was the primary means of payment (Hens 1916: 61). In the early 1870s, trade both with overseas traders and in the local markets was still largely through the barter of goods. Among mountain people money could not be used, though coastal dwellers were familiar with it (Kluppel 1873: 388–9). The same was true in coastal markets of Adonara in 1911 (Beckering 1911: 180). Hens expressed the determination of the Dutch authorities to oppose barter exchange. One of their means to encourage the spread of money use was to demand payment of taxes in this medium. An obstacle to the spread of money was the scarcity of very small change, which today is still a serious problem that outsiders might not appreciate given that the denominations actually needed are so minute (Hens 1916: 59–60).

There are of course parallels with some of these trading relationships in other parts of the world.[13] Miksic discusses production and trade specialization in iron-smelting, metalwork, weaving, pot making, and wood working on Sumatra (Miksic 1985: 442, 444, 446, 461–2). Several similar examples are to be found in Gell's recent summary of Melanesian trade, including individual trade partnerships in the interior and trade-dependent coastal or riverine communities which relied on trade to obtain vegetable staples and valuable exchange goods. Gell sees in Melanesian prehistory a drive towards trade specialization responding to a cultural impetus 'to participate eagerly in commodity exchange even when local production could provide substitutes for commodities obtainable through trade' (Gell 1992: 147–8). The art of pot making or producing salt was gradually lost in some areas as others obtained a monopoly. Of Lamalera it can be said that they were, and to some extent still are, dependent, but not absolutely, on a single set of trade partners for subsistence, namely village communities of the interior, and on external trade for symbolically significant objects, such as elephant tusks and fine Indian cloths. Of course they could sometimes acquire these symbolic objects immediately from the first kind of partners in individual transactions. The opposition between the two sources of goods is over-rigid for south Lembata. Once the symbolically valued objects entered the region, they were exchanged along whatever lines were established by marriage links, and one type of symbolically valued good, locally woven cloth, was produced in Lamalera on a semi-monopoly basis. The situation in respect of trade in raw materials is even more complex. Raw materials come mostly from the interior and are essential both for subsistence production (ropes, boats, and so on) and for the production of symbolically important goods (cloth).

These goods are acquired both by barter and by a wide variety of individual arrangements and accommodations between controllers of the raw materials and men and women of Lamalera. Men and women take characteristically different positions in the various cycles of production. For example women take meat and fish acquired by men to trade for cotton, from which they make thread. Several different things may happen to this thread. Women may present bundles of thread to a young female relative as part of the prestations appropriate at marriage. Alternatively they may take the thread to use in cloth production. The cloth produced may either be used in marriage exchanges or traded for other goods for consumption or production purposes. Some thread is given to boat corporations as part of the obligations incumbent on membership in them. Men then weave ropes from this thread to use in hunting and fishing, to produce meat which is either consumed or traded by women in other consumption or production cycles. Weaving swords for the back-strap looms are made by men, which are used by women to make cloth. These examples of course are not exhaustive of the various production relationships engaged in by men and women.

Seasons, Winds, Tides, Currents, Celestial Objects, and Directions

Seasons

Local seasons are determined by the two great monsoons and the transition periods between them. A season is *mūsi*, from Malay *musim* and Arabic *mausin* (Wilkinson 1932: 2: 157), or *naung* (Arndt 1937: 93; Gregorius Keraf 1978: 242). The monsoons affect not only temperatures, rainfall, and the growth of vegetation, but also of course productive activities. As is characteristic of rural communities, the local calendar is comprised of a sequence of time marks referring both to recurring events in nature and to characteristic human activities. The two principal divisions of the year are the rainy season *kĕrōnã* and the dry season *lerã matã* or *lerã*. The transition periods between are *temaka takã* (harvesting) and *barafãi* (the hot months).

Of these names, only that of the dry season is easily and obviously analysable into its semantic elements. *Lerã* is the sun and *matã* means eye among other things.[1] *Lerã matã* is, at least etymologically, a longer phrase for the sun, which dominates this season. *Kĕrōnã* is probably best left as it is, but I would hazard a guess that it relates to the word *onã*, inside, and is explained by the fact that the heavy weather of the rainy season keeps the boats at shore and causes people to tend to stay inside their houses. *Temaka takã*, meaning to harvest the ripening crops, is not to be confused with *temaka taka* which, according to Arndt (1951: 13), means 'the thief steals', as in *temaka taka gohuk*, 'the thief stole everything'. In Lamalera *tāka* means to steal, while *takã* means ripe. *Barafãi* is unexplained. One interpretation in the village is that *barafãi* refers to the period when the lontar palm is giving the most palm wine. The full phrase is *ubã futu, bara fãi*. *Ubã futu* is the tip of the inflorescence of the lontar palm. During *barafãi* the environment becomes very hot, the ebb tides go far out exposing tide pools, in which small fish die causing a stench, the wind dies away and the sea is white (calm). During low tide it becomes impossible for the large boats to be brought ashore.

The dry season begins after *temaka takã* and continues until the hot months of *barafãi*, approximately September, October. The rainy season is also called *nuang urã*, literally the rainy season (Arndt 1937: 93). The beginning of the rainy season is in late November and early December when *urã sedã tana*, the rain strikes or drums on, i.e. wets, the earth. These rains are brief and very erratic showers, with little environmental impact. Then comes *tenika* in late December and early January, when the dry season is definitely over. This is the time when the rain storms become heavy and persistent. Gregorius Keraf (1978: 196) says of *tenika* (from *tika* to divide, to set aside) that it is an implement for dividing or setting aside, but also the period of change between the rainy season and the dry season and again between the dry season and the rainy season. This definition gives the impression that *tenika* coincides with the periods of *temaka takã* and *barafãi*, whereas the account being summarized here places it at the beginning of the rainy season. Frankly, I think these ambiguities are inherent in the weather patterns and probably local usage as well. Keraf (1978: 197) gives the example, *Kofa pé legur-legur bolo pi pé tenika lépé*, 'The clouds keep rumbling, perhaps now is the season of change'. From January to February is *nalé datã onã*, when the wind and rain are so bad that people cannot go outside. March is the time of *nalé saré*, when the weather is calm, followed by *temaka takã* and shifting winds. *Nalé* are seaworms (*Leodice viridis*). *Nalé datã* means the bad seaworms period, while *nalé saré* means the good seaworms period. The bad and good seaworms periods refer to the prevailing weather conditions, *not* to the worms. Coastal peoples in Nusa Tenggara Timur commonly include in their time systems two occasions when seaworms release their sexual parts, which can be gathered in large quantities and cooked (see Fox 1979a: 153–4). These events occur first during the height of the storms of the rainy season in February and second in the calm, sunny weather of March. According to Gregorius Keraf (1978: 242 n. 1) these worms appear for two nights when the tide goes out around 7. 00 or 8. 00 p.m. and at dawn. Precise reckoning is needed in order to determine when the worms will rise.

Gregorius Keraf (1978: 240–5) includes as appendix 2 in his grammar a description of the pursuit of livelihood as described by Gabriel Blido Keraf, master builder of the boat *Nara Ténã*. This description, which I here condense and paraphrase, includes an account of the working calendar.[2]

In a year, he says, there are several seasons: *lerã*, *barafãi*, *keronã*, and *temakataka*. *Lerã* lasts around five months, beginning in May and continuing until September. At that time the sun is very bright and rain never falls. *Barafãi* lasts one or two months during September and October. During *barafãi* the sun is extraordinarily hot, the trees all lose their leaves, palm wine flows abundantly, and there is no wind. Following *barafãi*, we pass to *keronã*, which begins with November and ends in February. In *keronã*, much rain comes down. We further divide *keronã* into the planting season, mid-*keronã*, and bad seaworms.[3] March is the beginning of *temakataka* which is also called good seaworms.[4] *Temakataka* ends with April. Thus they [*sic*] reckon the seasons in a year in relation to rain and sunshine.

Oleona (1989: 25) summarizes (in his own orthography) the seasons as follows:

a. *mussi kronã*: the wet monsoon, from November to February. During these months they prefer to stay at home because conditions at sea do not permit them to go out.
b. *mussi nalé dateng onã*: in January and February, rainy season and gales.
c. *mussi nalé snaréng onã*: in the months of March and April, when the sea becomes calm again, but people prefer to fish in the shallow sea.
d. *mussi léfa* or *léfa nuang* or *mussi lerrã*: the season to go to sea or the dry season. From May until and including September. In these months, whales are more frequently seen passing, therefore people go to sea, *léfa*. They also *plaé bã léo*, that is suddenly chase whales because whales are not visible every day.
e. *mussi barafãi* or *mussi léfa bogel*, that is in October. During that month the sun is very hot and the wind is dead. Therefore people do not want to go to sea. Therefore October is a month of rest for the fishermen.

The period from May to October is also known as *fãti léfa*, still the period of the sea. *Léfa* is the sea. Gregorius Keraf (1978: 171, 183, 244) says that *léfa-ari* is the sea and all that it contains as a source of livelihood for the fishermen. This pronunciation is surprising in so far as the second element might be expected to be *hari*, the other Lamaholot term carrying associations with the sea or the edge of the sea, as in sea spirits. During these months the boats go out every day looking for whale, porpoise, and manta ray. *Léfa nuang* means the season of open-sea hunting and fishing. Towards the end of September the impulse to put to sea in the large boats decreases and eventually disappears. Some boats may make an extended trip to the fishing ground at Lobetobi in this month, while others may take small boats to Bobu on the south coast of Lembata to the east of the Lerek Peninsula. *Léfa* does not stop on the dot come 1 October though. If the fish are still active people continue going to sea every day past the middle of October, even to the end of the month. But if the boats are getting no fish, the crews will stay in, turning to other things like cleaning their fields or building houses, and they will eventually just give up any interest. *Léfa* then just peters out, dying from lack of attention. In October the days are not only very hot, but the wind can be absolutely still. The boats row all day long. According to Gabriel Blido Keraf, for this reason people become lazy, and *barafãi* is also called the lazy *léfa* period, *léfa bogel* (Gregorius Keraf 1978: 245).

In November and December open-sea fishing is at an end, and the boats are stored in their sheds. These months may be referred to as *heri téna lépé*, the boats are put up. These two months are the favoured period for firing bricks, laying foundations, and other house-building activities. They are also the time to make major repairs on the boats and to begin rebuilding those which have been scheduled to be remade. House building and boat building continue into January and beyond if necessity requires and circumstances permit. Another activity associated with January and April, although in fact it may occur at any time of year, is the opportunistic chasing of whales that appear near shore, or *baléo*. From time to time a great cry of '*baléo!*' may go through the village, and men will rush to the beach to put the large boats out and give chase. Normally, the village gets no whales during November to April, but in unusual years they have taken quite a few whales in this fashion during January and February. From November, increasing numbers will take small boats *sapã*, to various locations along the south coast of the island to fish with lines or with modern nylon nets. Use of such boats to fish with lines continues through the rainy season, when sea conditions permit. When the new leaves of the *kalabai* tree, *Schleichera oleosa*, Merr., emerge, *gītã*, it is a sign of the time for whales to come, i.e. the period for open-sea fishing is nearing. This time mark is therefore called *kalabai gītã*.

The hunger period, which may be especially marked if there has been a crop failure in the mountains, generally occurs in February and March. In famines they eat a type of wild bean, *ūta kéda*, which is poisonous and has to be cooked and the water thrown out four times. They can eat it only when the water is no longer bitter. There is also a variety of wild yam which has to be cooked in the same way. Children have died from eating *ūta kéda* because their parents went out to get water or otherwise left the pot unguarded and the children ate the still poisonous beans in their absence. Ancestral wisdom says that in a period of hunger they should watch the goats and pick only the leaves the goats will eat.

People of Lamalera used to buy slaves from the interior during the hunger season for a large bowl of maize kernels. In those days cassava had not yet been introduced, and mountain villages grew only maize. If the crops failed there was nothing to fall back on, but in Lamalera people could take their boats to other islands that had maize and buy it there. They are protected from hunger by their practice of filling large baskets, *mata gapo*, with maize. A household may have 2, 3, even 4 of these. They put them above where they will be cooking, boiling water down to salt, or otherwise always have a fire. The smoke protects the maize from weevils. They may open these baskets only in February and March, the hunger season. If before then they have no food, they must hold on. Sometimes they may go as long as three years before opening a basket.

Winds

The prevailing wind direction from December to March is from the west, bringing the storm winds, *angi nadé*. Winds are *angi*. West winds are *fãra*. Boats face a constant wind from the shore during this period, which is one of the reasons why open-sea fishing ceases. The ideal wind for the large boats is the east wind *timu*, which blows from April to September. The prevailing direction of the east wind tends to be from the south-east, or, as they say, these are sea winds *angi léfã*. The winds shift back and forth from east to west in August and September, before dying out during *barafãi*. *Fura* is a west current, *olé* an

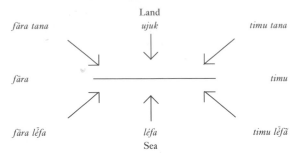

FIG. 6. Wind directions

east current. From these names come the combined expressions *fura-fāra* for the west current and wind and *timu-olé*, for the east wind and current.

From Lamalera, the wind rose appears as in Fig. 6. *Angi* may precede each of the specifications, as in *angi timu lẽfã*. A wind from the interior is *ujuk*, 'in the midst, middle of', or *angi tana*, i.e. a land wind. Gradations of *ujuk* may refer to specific places, such as *ujuk Fai Nãé* (from the source of the water, a spring above the village of Lewotala) or *ujuk Ilé Belopor* (from that mountain on Lerek).

An east wind from the direction of one of the peninsulas is called *angi Fato Méã nãé*, wind from the red stone. At Lobetobi when they have their sail on the left and a wind from the mountain, the wind is *angi Fāi Lula nãé* (the wind from Lula spring). When they have their sail on the right and a wind down the strait from Larantuka, the wind is *angi kota futu nãé*, wind from the point of the city. In February there is a week-long strong wind that blows down branches and buildings. This is *angi pānga*, i.e. storm winds. The old men say *fulã malu*, the wind continues until it has gone to market and bought betel peppers and areca nuts, then it goes, i.e. it is going past the village toward Wulan Doni to the east.

Near shore, land and sea breezes modify the prevailing wind patterns. Onshore winds in the afternoon and offshore winds in the early morning affect the height of the sea (US Navy Hydrographic Office 1962: 37).

Tides

The people of Lamalera know that the tides follow the moon. *Meti fulã* (*fulã* is the moon) indicates the time for a change has come, such as menstruation or the end of a pregnancy. If they see that the conditions at sea are too bad to put out, this is *meti fulã elã* (wrong). A rising tide is *meti ofã* or *meti géré*; high tide, *meti peno*, i.e. 'full'; an ebbing tide, *meti etã* or *meti lodo*; low tide, *meti mara* (*mara* means 'to dry out'). Low tide is also called *meti nefu*. A very low tide is *nefu bélã* (great). A very moderate low tide is *nefu kéni* (small). The lowest ebb tide of the month is *meti marak patak* (from *marak*, dry, and *patak*, far).

When the moon is full or new, the tides are highest and lowest (the spring tides), *meti bélã*, 'great tide'. The tides are smaller (neap), *meti pĕlerong*, during the intervals between new and full moon (the first and third quarters).

Tides in the Savu Sea are mixed, that is there are two tidal cycles of unequal height per day, as opposed to diurnal, a single cycle every twenty-four hours and fifty minutes, as in parts of the Java Sea and in the Gulf of Mexico, or semidiurnal, every twelve hours and twenty-five minutes, as in the North Atlantic. The lowest levels are reached in April and November. The tides in the straits from Flores to Lembata and Pantar are mixed, but predominantly semidiurnal. In the Flores Strait between Flores and Solor the current turns about the time of the moon's transit and six to eight hours later. In the strait between Solor and Lembata the north-east-heading current occurs between two to three hours before the moon's transit and two to three hours after transit. The opposite current occurs between three to four hours after transit to nine to ten hours after transit. In the strait between Lembata and Pantar there are powerful semidiurnal tidal currents. The south-west-heading current is stronger and lasts longer than the north-east current. The south-west current prevails from two to nine hours after transit, and the north-east the rest of the time. Spring tide occurs two to three days after the full moon and new moon, and neap tides two to three days after the quarter (Gross 1972: 270–7; US Navy Hydrographic Office 1962: 31, 247–9, 262).

Currents

During the wet monsoon, from November to March, the general surface current of the ocean in the Savu Sea and Timor Strait flows from the west to the east at from $\frac{1}{5}$ to $1\frac{2}{5}$ knots. During the transition periods between the monsoons the surface currents are weak and variable, but tend to be from the east to the west. During the dry season, from May to September the general surface current in the Savu Sea and Timor Strait flows from the east to the west at $\frac{7}{10}$ to 1 knot. Tidal currents, except in straits, are generally weak, in which case they simply strengthen or reduce the speed of the non-tidal currents (US Navy Hydrographic Office 1962: 31–6). Nevertheless, counter-currents do occur near the south Lembata coast and these are exploited by the fishermen.

The currents are *enã*. A current from the east *olé*, goes with the low tide. The west current, *fura*, goes with the high tide *meti ofã bélã*. However, *meti pĕlerong* can have either an east or a west current all day long. The east currents are calm, but the west currents bring large waves. Of course there are differences in direction between inshore and offshore currents. During low tide the inshore current is from the west and the offshore current from the east. Sometimes when the boats are returning from the sea, they will make land well to the west of Lamalera and, in order to take advantage of an inshore current from the west, will hug the rocky shoreline as close as the waves will permit, so close in fact as to appear dangerous to the inexperienced. If they are pulling a whale, they must be careful not to let the current take them past the beach, which does sometimes happen and which can cause long delays in getting to shore. A line from a song runs, *fura molo ko, fura molo, go kã doré*, 'west current lead the way, west current lead, I will follow'. People associate a strong east current with sperm whales. While a prevailing and persistent current from the west is said to mean that manta ray, *bĕlelã*, will be present and whales absent, a prevailing and persistent current from the east is said to bring sperm whales, but means that there will be no *bĕlelã*.

Enã odo means the current is going toward the sea. *Odo* is a verb meaning to push, such as pushing a boat toward the sea. The proper noun form of this phrase is *enã bodo*. *Enã taduk*, from *tadu*, to hit, is a current toward land. If this current is below the surface of the sea, there are large waves. If it is on the surface, there are only ordinary waves. *Enã onã* is an underwater current. *Enã fafé ferong* is the meeting of currents. *Fafé* means pig, *ferong* has an unknown meaning and the underlying meaning of the whole expression is not clear. *Enã bĕliku*, from *liku*, to protect or shelter, occurs when the east current is weakening and facing the west current, when it tends to be near the beach. *Ena lolong* is a surface current. *Ena benak*, like *ena taduk*, means a current flowing toward land. *Benak* derives from *enak*, to put into something. *Ena sĕmugur* (from *sugur*, to lift up) is a current moving from below upwards. The opposite rarely occurs except in cases of unusual below-surface conditions, caused perhaps by large rocks, or like the whirlpool near Pantar which in the 1970s sucked under a boat with a wedding party of which only one member survived. However, there is an expression *enã nabé dupa* meaning a current pulling down (under the water). *Enã ba* means the current flows. A fast-moving current is *ena kĕléa*. *Ena keperek* is a slow-moving current. Waves or breakers on the shoreline or at sea are *menoté*. *Fura nalu* is the breaking of waves in a west current. *Olé nalu* is the breaking of waves in an east current. *Keléla* are long sea swells which do not break.

Ojo, waves and breakers, is the movement of the sea, which must be distinguished from *tāi* which is the sea water. *Léfa* is the general, collective idea of the sea. Thus *ojo gefoket* is the swelling of a wave. *Ojo pĕrefa* is when a wave breaks (just once). *Ojo golo* is a rolling, breaking wave. *Ojo éfél* (wave tongues) refers to the meeting of shadows of waves recoiling from shore at different angles. *Tai lolo dataf* (ruined sea surface) or *Tai lolo kesafut* (confused sea surface) is a destructive sea. *Ojo bĕlino* or *tai bĕlino* is a calm sea. *Ojo bélak* means that the waves become large.

Moon and Stars

The moon is *fūlã*. The general term for stars is *funo*. The southern cross is part of a constellation called *nua tapo*, coconut island. It is the top of the tree,

1. *fūlā léi tou* (first step or time of the moon)
2. *fūlā léi rua* (second step of the moon)
3. *fūlā léi telo* (third step of the moon; the moon is not visible during these three stages)
4. *fūlā léi pa* (fourth step of the moon, it can be seen in the east about 6.00 p.m.)
5. *fūlā léi léma* (fifth step of the moon)
6. *fūlā léi nemu* (sixth step of the moon)
7. *fūlā léi pito* (seventh step of the moon)
8. *fūlā léi buto* (eighth step of the moon; during stages seven and eight the moon is in the centre of the sky at sunset and the moon is visible during the morning)
9. *fūlā léi hifa* (ninth step of the moon)
10. *fūlā léi pulo* (tenth step of the moon)
11. *fūlā léi pulok tou* (eleventh step of the moon)
12–15. *fūlā kukar nong* (full moon)
16. *fūlā bisak* (the moon breaks)
17. *fūlā bisak mu tou* (breaking of the moon plus one)
18. *fūlā bisak mu rua* (breaking of the moon plus two)
19. *fūlā bisak mu telo* (breaking of the moon plus three)
20. *fūlā bisak mu pa* (breaking of the moon plus four)
21. *fūlā bisak mu léma* (breaking of the moon plus five)
22. *fūlā bisak mu nemu* (breaking of the moon plus six)
23. *fūlā bisak mu pito* (breaking of the moon plus seven)
24. *fūlā bisak mu buto* (breaking of the moon plus eight)
25. *fūlā bisak mu hifa* (breaking of the moon plus nine)
26. *fūlā bisak mu pulo* (breaking of the moon plus ten)
27. *fūlā bisak mu pulok tou* (breaking of the moon plus eleven)
28–30. *fūlā mitang* (the new moon)

FIG. 7. The stages of the moon

tapo lolo, while the two stars to the east, Agena and Rigil Kentaurus, are the trunk, *tapo pukā*. At nights boats may use the southern cross as a guide. Antares is *nua bāko*, basket island. The morning star is *apa bélā*. When it rises early in the morning, then is the time to plant. Some say there are two morning stars close together: *apa bélā laké* and *apa bélā roné*, the male and female morning stars respectively. The evening star is *pari*. The Pleiades, *funo pito* (the seven stars), seems to be screened by the hills. Its evening rising is not seen; and it becomes visible only in late December, too late for it to serve as a sign for planting, as is so common in the world, including other districts of Lembata.

During an eclipse of the moon, *fūlā maté*, some people in Lamalera beat drums and others sing. A halo around the moon is called *kenolé*. It is a sign that turtles are about to lay eggs. They say *kenolé golé fulā*, the halo surrounds the moon. The dark of the moon is *fūlā mitang*. When the moon is small it is called *fūlā kenéka*, when full, *fūlā kukar nong*, the waning or broken moon is *fūlā bisak*. *Bisa(k)* means to break or shatter. The first four days after the full moon are counted as *bisak mu tou*, *bisak mu rua*, *mu telo*, and *mu pa*, that is, the breaking of the moon plus one, plus two, plus three, and plus four. These phrases therefore refer to the first, second, third, and fourth days after the full moon, or after it has 'broken'. During these four days it is expected the currents will be strong and the manta ray will not come to the surface. The moon goes through this cycle: (1) small moon, from the west *fūlā lali haka*; (2) the moon appears in the centre of the sky at sunset, *fūlā haka Lefotukā*; (3) the moon rises at sunset, *fūlā géré mau*; (4) the moon disappears, *fūlā hobing* (see Fig. 7).

The Sun

The stages of the sun are as follows. Night time is *remā*, midnight *remā tukā*. Day is *lero*. Dawn is *lera géré*, the sun rises, *éka* or *éka daé*. Noon is *lera tukā*, midday. Afternoon is *lera léré* (low sun), and sunset is *lera helut* or *lera lodo* (sun descends). An eclipse of the sun is *lera mata* (the sun dies) or *lera maté* (the sun is dead).

Generally, the sun is associated in Lamaholot culture with the idea of the Deity, especially in combination with the name for the moon, as in Lera Wulan. The Lamalera version is Lera Fūlā. Lera Fūlā, generally regarded as male, is both opposed to and associated with a female earth deity, Tana Ekan, in Lamelera, Tana-Ékā. Gregorius Keraf (1978: 168) gives examples of prayers addressed to Lera Fūlā.

Lera-Fūlā, Tana-Ékā, hito-hibaj lau nai doa, raé nai doa, haka nai doa, lali nai doa. Néi kamé saré-melang héna.

Sky God, Earth Goddess, chase away and distance [misfortune] to the sea, to the interior, to the east, to the west. Give us only good.

Ina-Ama, Lera-Fūlā, Tana-Ékā, mata tutu, mata māri, mata liko, mata lapak, mata līmu, mata tědā kamé

Ancestors, Sky God, Earth Goddess, may you speak, may you become spokesmen, may you protect us, may you guard us, may you place us on your lap [raise us], may you carry us in your palm [care for us].

Today, *Lera Fūlā* is commonly accepted as the Lamaholot name for God as understood by Catholics and Muslims. As Dietrich (1992: 117) observes, much missionary ethnography on Flores was directed towards the study of the Supreme Being (see Verheijen 1951 and Arndt 1936–7, 1951). 'Where it was found that it indeed reflected original monotheism, its name was adopted for the Christian God.' Speakers of Lamaholot of all faiths fairly spontaneously identify the local name Lera Wulan with God and indicate that it is a translation for the Indonesian 'Tuhan Allah' and the Arabic-derived 'Lahatala' (from *Allah ta'ala*). Vatter (1932: 90; see also Kohl 1986: 211), wrote that in the 1920s the mission wanted to find a suitable word for God for a Lamaholot translation of the catechism. They intended to use Lera Wulan, but priests stationed on Lembata objected on the grounds that there Lera Wulan was merely a sub-ordinate being.[5] They were also worried that the double name endangered the monotheistic conception of God. Such inhibitions seem now to have been long forgotten.

It is difficult or impossible today to explore pre-Christian conceptions of divinity directly in Lamalera, but a good deal of information was gathered by early ethnographers for other parts of the Lamaholot region. Lera Wulan lit-erally translates as 'Sun Moon' and fits a pattern which is commonplace over a wide range of eastern Indonesia. As Dietrich also notes, older missionaries like Arndt saw in these names remnants of a former sun cult and moon cult, although Arndt also recognized that these names were not generally taken to refer in fact to the sun and moon as a divinity. Arndt's collection of informa-tion about Lamaholot religion (Arndt 1951) demonstrates a good deal of vari-ation in representations of Lera Wulan. In general, however, Lera Wulan is associated with the sky. There are several other terms which are also names of God, for example Laga Doni and Doni Bélen (Arndt 1938: 7). Lera Wulan is male and is sometimes depicted as an old man with a long white beard. He is said to have power over everything. He is the highest and the mightiest, and he is said to have created the heavens and the earth, the lesser spirits, men and animals.

Any temptation to interpret Lamaholot understandings of God as being the actual sun or moon should be inhibited by the recognition that the name, which itself refers to a unity, is a compound of two distinct things. The name takes its form, not because of specific theological doctrines, but because of certain dualistic and pairing patterns which are common to Indonesian languages. Arndt (1951: 17) does say that while Lera Wulan is usually interpreted as a personal being, or human, some do understand it to mean the actual sun and moon, or rather the sky. Vatter (1932: 91), on the other hand, found that his informants uniformly denied that Lera Wulan was the sun and moon in the concrete sense. It may be noted in passing that the moon is said to be a witch, blood sucker, and corpse eater (Arndt 1951: 59).

Lera Wulan's female companion is Tana Ekan. *Tana* means the land, while *Ekan* refers to the region or environs. This compound has the general sense of earth and clearly designates the lower world in opposition to the upper world inhabited by Lera Wulan. Arndt often speaks of Lera Wulan/Tana Ekan as though it were a unitary godhead or total divinity. Traditional invocations occasionally begin, 'O, Lera Wulan, Tana Ekan', but no statement has been recorded equating them explicitly. Normally, Lera Wulan and Tana Ekan are addressed separately; but this is due, for the most part, to the dual structure of the chants through which they are invoked at ceremonial occasions. They are nevertheless addressed simultaneously and in a manner which indicates that they share the same functions. When addressed in the same ceremony, they unite a number of oppositions, among them the upper world and the lower, the heavens and the earth, male and female, creation and destruction, kindness and ferociousness. Taking an example from Arndt (1951: 100), Dietrich also speaks of Lera Wulan Tana Ekan as a double divinity (Dietrich 1985: 295). Despite the general association of Lera Wulan with the heavens and Tana Ekan with the earth, in the chants their relative positions are sometimes reversed, so that Tana Ekan is spoken of as being above, Lera Wulan below (Arndt 1951: 22).

Although Lera Wulan and Tana Ekan are explicitly recognized as male and female, they are frequently also addressed as 'Ema [Mother] Lera Wulan, Bapa [Father] Tana Ekan'. As Arndt (1951: 22, 157) noted, the sexual designations are commonly reversed in ceremonial chants and the custom is not confined to the Lamaholot-speaking communities, but is also found elsewhere in the vicinity. Arndt was told that the custom occurs because, 'Tana Ekan is ferocious, because she is a *menaka* [witch], that is a blood sucker and a corpse eater' (Arndt 1951: 247). Arndt also comments that Lera Wulan too has a ferocious aspect, both as a deity who accepts human victims as sacrificial offerings and as a wrathful God who punishes moral and ceremonial infractions. In any case the form 'Father Tana Ekan' often occurs in invocations in which Tana Ekan's character is entirely benevolent and is not in fact distinguished from Lera Wulan's. Sometimes, indeed, the pair are addressed by both gender designations. Arndt recorded the following mode of address from Pamakayu, Solor, '*Ema* [Mother] *Bapa* [Father] *Lera Wulan*' and '*Ema* [Mother] *Bapa* [Father] *Tana Ekan*'. This form of address represents Lera Wulan and Tana Ekan each as simultaneously male and female. An informant in Pamakayu, Solor, told Arndt (1951: 156) that Lera Wulan is called Mother-Father because he made us. Whatever the reason for this formulation, it suggests that the more common simple inversion requires another explanation than that given Arndt. Vatter (1932: 91–2) recorded the address '*Ema Ratu Lera-Wulan, Bapa Nini Tana Ekan*', which he translated 'Mother, Man Sun-Moon, Father, Woman Earth'. *Ratu* in fact means 'prince', while Arndt (1951: 16–17) interpreted *nini* as a title suitable for a noble woman.

In the texts published by Arndt, not only is Lera Wulan addressed as female and Tana Ekan as male in the great majority of instances, but many other figures are spoken of in a way that obscures their gender. Ilé Woka ('mountain, hill'), sometimes said to be the High God, is invoked as 'Mother Ilé, Father Woka'. Hari Botan, the God of the Sea, is spoken to as 'Ema [Mother] Hari, Bapa [Father] Botan'. An example from Lekluo begins 'Ema Demon, Bapa Pago'. Demon and Pago are synonyms and denote the ancestral father of the Demons, one part of the Demon/Paji opposition which divides the population in the Solor Islands east of Flores. Most chants which show this formulation are consistent throughout; when pairs of names are mentioned or addressed, the first is referred to as female, the second male. The practice is not dependent on the subject of or occasion for the chant, or indeed its structure. It does fit, however, other linguistic habits, as seen in the commonplace Lamaholot term for elders, ancestors, or elders and ancestors, *ina-ama*, consisting of the term *ina*, meaning 'mother', and *ama*, meaning 'father'. The female term always precedes the male.

The above material shows that Lamaholot concepts of divinity are rather complex. There is a form of what Fox (1989: 44–7) has called recursive complementarity. Lera Wulan, as sun and moon, is a dual unity in his own right. In conjunction with Tana Ekan he forms yet another dual unity. Dual unity is further emphasized in expressions such as 'Mother Father'. The resulting representation of divinity is marked by unions of further oppositions, such as those mentioned above. As Fox (1989: 46) remarks, in respect of recursive complementarity, 'nothing is exclusively of one category; anything that is categorized according to one component of a complementary pair can *potentially* contain elements of its complement'. This figurative folding in and enveloping and further enveloping of relationships in itself suggests that the overall representation of divinity is far more abstract than any of the concrete images used to express it. The pattern also has the effect of implying that the, to us, negative aspects of the Lamaholot divinity, such as witchcraft, head hunting, corpse eating—what, taken with His good-natured benevolence, Arndt (1938: 28) saw as Lera Wulan's double-sidedness—are intimately tied to the positive life-giving and fortifying aspects. Furthermore, examples of linguistic usage given above confirm evidence abundant in daily life and ritual practice that Lamaholot-speaking peoples assimilate the living elders to the ancestors and the ancestors to divinity.

The Candraditya Centre on Flores has published an extract by Frans Amanue from his MA thesis at the University of San Carlos, the Philippines, devoted to the Lamaholot conception of the Supreme Being Rera Wulan (as it is pronounced in some districts) (Amanue 1989). He states that the interpretation that Rera Wulan is a personification of the sun and moon must be rejected. Amanue reasonably relates the expression to the fact that by virtue of providing light during the day and night respectively, the sun and moon are images of great power. Furthermore height is a symbol of nobility, power, authority, and divinity in Lamaholot culture. The Lamaholot people also regard rain as coming from the sun and moon, or at least from their direction, and of course rain plays an essential role in their lives, in respect of agriculture for example. Rera Wulan is thought of as having powers far in excess of men and therefore as being full of nobility. Rera Wulan is also conceived of as the distributor of prosperity on earth. The sun and moon serve therefore as analogies of the perfection of the Supreme Being.

Amanue also takes up the question whether Tana Ekan is regarded as the wife of Rera Wulan, as reported by Arndt and Vatter for some places. He relates this issue to the parallelism and binary pairing characteristic of ritual language in order to argue that Tana Ekan is merely the ritual language parallel of Lera

Wulan. Thus Rera Wulan becomes Rera Wulan Tana Ekan, namely God, in the same way that an ordinary personal name like Sabon would become Sabon Suba Raya paralleled with Raya Lau Bera in ritual language, both of which phrases refer to the same person. In appearance polarized, in fact Rera Wulan and Tana Ekan are not in contradiction with one another, but are linked to each other and represent principal elements referring to a single unity. Possibly, he says, Rera Wulan represents the transcendental aspect, while Tana Ekan is the immanent aspect. Addressing Lera Wulan and Tana Ekan as mother and father does not mean that they are actually mother and father; rather these terms merely express an appropriate affective attitude of high honour and full hope of protection and help.

In general, I think Amanue's interpretations are correct, if somewhat sanitized, and in keeping with those reached by others in so far as they go. An overly concrete interpretation of Lamaholot ritual texts and statements about Lera Wulan will certainly lead to misunderstandings. Nevertheless it is characteristic of eastern Indonesian cultures and linguistic usages that they combine opposed qualities in their representations of divinity which outsiders are certainly not prepared for.

The question may be raised what happens to these unexpected features and characteristics when Christians accept Lera Wulan as simply the Lamaholot name for God? Do they get left behind, so that 'Lera Wulan' is indeed merely a name (in Malay, *nama saja*), as his informants in Leloba, Flores, told Vatter in 1928 (Vatter 1932: 91), or do they remain to enrich the Christian conception of divinity? Will the Christian God be seen as having a dual aspect, one part male, the other female? Although Amanue seems to deny that Tana Ekan is Lera Wulan's wife, Arndt's and Vatter's information from the places where they have reported it is explicit (Arndt 1951: 20; Vatter 1932: 92). Furthermore, Muda (1989: 62–3) accepts that there is an understanding of a divine marriage between heaven and earth among the Ngada and many other ethnic groups of Flores. Vatter remarks also that people occasionally refer to male genitalia as Lera Wulan. Oddly he says that he never saw a phallic representation in the Lamaholot area. Kohl (1986: 210), however, says that in the village temple in Belogili, East Flores, Lera Wulan is represented by a great phallic-shaped stone and Tana Ekan by an associated vulva-shaped flat stone. People who retain the older religion and maintain the temples told Kohl (p. 211) that Lera Wulan is the Christian God the Father and Tana Ekan is the Mother of God, Mary.

This identification represents much more than a more or less spontaneous justification of the old religion to a Western visitor who it was assumed shared the prejudices of the Javanese governmental representatives or also of some missionaries about the backwardness and paganism of this religion. This equation rather fits with the fact that today in popular belief the darker aspects of both gods increasingly retreat to the background and they are increasingly conceived more abstractly and transcendentally.

The idea that Lera Wulan eats humans and demands the taking of human heads and that Tana Ekan is a witch and blood sucker is not often expressed by Catholics, if at all. Interestingly, these features did not inhibit an earlier generation of missionaries from recommending the identification of Lera Wulan with God; so presumably they thought that they had the matter in hand, or could get it in hand. It is also noticeable that Amanue found no occasion to refer to the negative features of Divinity, either as part of present attitudes or of past tradition.

Directions

Although there are many references in the literature to the peculiarities of Indonesian orientation terms, virtually all coverage of these parts of daily vocabulary by outsiders is inadequate. The extreme linguistic complexity of direction terms in the neighbouring Kédang language can be traced in Samely (1991), while some of their symbolic implications may be found in R. H. Barnes (1974*a*: 78–88). The discovery that such terms are misinterpreted when translated directly by European ideas about the cardinal points is an old one, but modern writers do not consistently acknowledge the cogency of this insight. Comparative implications of issues about spatial orientation in Indonesia has been addressed in R. H. Barnes (1988*b* and 1993*d*).

When at sea, directions toward something are indicated by the terms displayed in Fig. 8. *Tai* in these expressions means we (inclusive) go and changes as the pronoun changes. I go to sea, *lau kai*; we (exclusive), *lau maikem*; we (inclusive), *lau tai*; you (singular), *lau mai*; you (plural), *lau mai*; he, she, it, *lau nai*; they, *lau rai*. The same paradigm works for the other directions. When it is a matter of something coming from a specific direction the phrases in Fig. 9 are in order.

The intermediate points may be added as in Figs. 10 and 11.

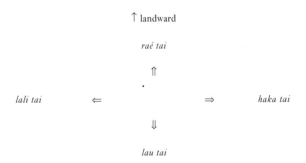

FIG. 8. Directions away from speaker

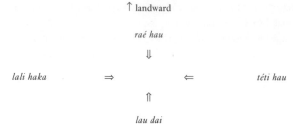

FIG. 9. Directions toward speaker

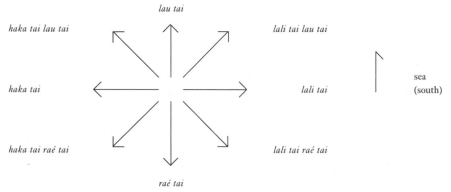

FIG. 10. Directions away from speaker showing intermediate directions

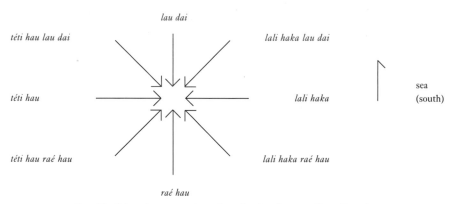

FIG. 11. Directions toward speaker showing intermediate directions

Fig. 11 may be supplemented as follows (*lodo* = descend; *géré* = to go up):

> from above, *téti lodo*
> from the east, *téti hau*
> from below, *lali géré*
> from the west, *lali haka*.

If *téti lodo* is from above down, toward above is *téti géré*. If *lali géré* is from below up, toward below is *lali lodo*.

It is plain that *téti* and *lali* do not always or primarily mean east and west, as is shown by the relative positions of the two halves of the village. The upper village, called *Téti Lefo*, lies to the west, while the lower village, called *Lali Fata*, down at the shore, lies to the east. The east is *téti* because they think of the east as being higher, while the west is *lali* because they think of the west as being lower. The true names for east and west are incorporated as names for the east wind, *timu*, and the west wind, *fāra* (compare Indonesian and Malay *timur* and *barat*). All faraway places are *lau*, or from there, *lau dai*. Thus: *lau Kupang dai* (from Kupang), *lau Makasar dai* (from Macassar), *lau Belanda dai* (from the Netherlands). Closer places, however, depend on the position relative to the village, thus from Larantuka is *lali Serani haka* (because of its association with Christianity, Serani).[6] From Waiwerang, Adonara is *lali Fera haka*, but occasionally some people say instead *raé Fera hau*. *Fera* is the local pronunciation of *merang*. From Lewoleba is *raé Lefoleba hau*. Although the north/south orientation changes, if a boat were to sail to the bay in front of Lewoleba, they would still say *rae Lefoléba hau*. The terms depend on the distinction between land and sea. From the south-east is *téti hau lau dai*. From the south-west is *lali haka lau dai*.

A Lamalera boat in the sea in front of Lewoleba on the north coast of Lembata would use the terms in the way set out in Fig. 12. Particular applications of these terms in specific locations, which can be so difficult for Europeans to comprehend, can be doubtful for native speakers too when they

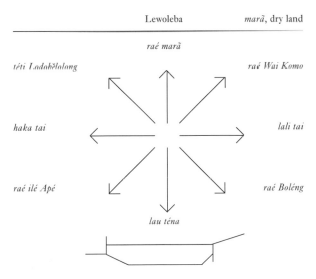

FIG. 12. Direction terms as used by a Lamalera boat in the bay in front of Lewoleba, Lembata

go to unfamiliar locations (Arndt 1937: 106).[7] In such a situation, they have to wait and listen to what the locals say.

Sailing Directions

Sailing with the wind is *soro*, which also means to be carried by the current. Sailing against the wind is *āpulolo*.[8] *Āpulolo* is also used, for example, when they see a fish on the right, while the sail is on the left; or when they see a fish on the left, while the sail is on the right.

The boats can sail into the wind at only a very shallow angle. In tacking they always turn away from the wind. This means that when going against the wind the crew must rely on rowing and the aid of favourable currents. Horridge says rotating the sail so that it lies fore and aft turns the boat into the wind. The boat of course is steered by both sail and stern oar, but when they are trying to face directly into the wind, the sail is useless. Only the steering oar can bring the boat into the wind, but it can do so only when the crew row to give the boat momentum. In such circumstances, the paddle of the man sitting in front of the helmsman may have to be used by him as a supplementary steering oar.

When the boats set out in the morning sailing out into the open sea south of the village, the following steering directions obtain.

> An east wind with a strong west current, causing the crew to place the sail on the right and the helmsman to put the steering oar on the right, leads the boat to sail *legã*, to the south-west.
> An east wind with a strong current from the east, causing the crew to place the sail on the right and the helmsman to put the steering oar on the left, leads the boat to sail to the south-east, *léa*.
> A west wind with a current from the west, causing the crew to place the sail on the left and the helmsman to put the steering oar on the right, leads the boat to sail south-west, *léa*.
> A west wind with a current from the east, causing the crew to place the sail on the left and the helmsman to put the steering oar on the left, leads the boat to sail to the south-east, *legã*.

On returning, assuming that the winds and currents remain constant, the pattern is as follows.

> If they go out with an east wind and west current with sail and steering oar on the right, direction south-west, *legã*, they return with sail on the left, steering oar on the right, direction north-east, *léa*.
> If they go out with both an east wind and current and the sail on the right, steering oar on the left, direction south-east, *léa*, they return sail on the left, steering oar on the left, direction north-west, *legã déké*.
> If they go out with a west wind and current, sail on the left, steering oar

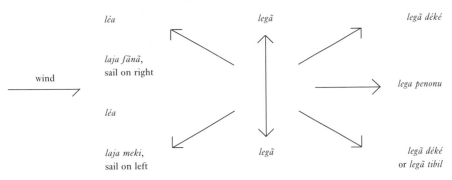

FIG. 13. Sailing directions

on the right, direction south-west, *léa*, they come back, sail on the right, steering oar on the right, direction north-east, *legã déké*.

If they go out with a west wind and east current, sail on the left, steering oar on the left, direction south-east, *legã déké*, they come back sail on the right, steering oar on the right, direction north-west, *léa*.

The sail, of course, is always on the opposite side of the boat from the direction from which the wind is blowing.

Léa indicates sailing against the wind, *legã* with it. Fig. 13 demonstrates the terms appropriate for a boat sailing on various bearings in respect to a prevailing wind. There is no reference with these terms to compass directions.

As is to be expected, since the boats do not sail directly into the wind, there is no standard expression for doing so. Instead, a boat may tack off the wind with the sail on the right or left, as is appropriate, *léa laja fãnã* (against the wind, sail on the right) or *léa laja meki* (against the wind, sail on the left). A boat sailing with the wind, may do so at an angle to it, *legã déké* or *legã tibil*. *Déké* means a diagonal cut. *Tibil* means slightly askew or slanting slightly. Sailing with the wind direction is *legã penonu*. When they row with the wind behind them they may say *bai tabé soro*, we row together with the wind. To row against the wind is *bai huba menoté-angi*, to row against the waves and wind.

9

Fishing

Hellmuth (1853: 233) wrote that the straits of Solor and Flores are very rich in fish, the manifold distinct and splendid species of which are almost uncountable. As Medical Officer Second Class stationed at the small Dutch outpost at Lohayong, Solor (then called by the Dutch Lawaijong, etc.), he made a collection of some sixty-six types of fish which together with the contributions of other naval medical officers became the basis of several scientific articles by Bleeker (see Hellmuth 1853: 234; Bleeker 1851, 1852, 1853, 1854). Unfortunately neither author recorded any of the Lamaholot names for fish. A start was made by Wintjes (1894*b*), but without identifications in any other language, and his list has had no effect so far, in part because it was until recently unpublished and inaccessible.[1] More information about local fish, together with some certain and some possible identifications, may be found in Appendix II.

Shellfish Gathering, Traps, and Spearguns

According to Gregorius Keraf (1983), in the local classification, fish are distinguished as *ikã fato feki*, fish near stones, i.e. near the shore, and *ikã lemé*, fish in the depth of the sea, pelagic fish. Fishing with a line and bamboo pole is *bĩtu*, the pole and line itself *mĩtu* (Gregorius Keraf 1978: 24, 190).[2] To fish in a dugout or skiff near the shore during the day is *feda*, and a fisherman is *befedã* (Gregorius Keraf 1978: 194, 203). To do so at night is *nuang*. In both cases the line takes stone weights, *fato bĕlang*. Rowing the boat while trolling unweighted lines is *bai*, while fishing from a stationary boat fairly far out to sea with an unweighted line is *sĕlaba*. Fishing along the shore takes place throughout the year, conditions permitting. In addition, the shoreline is a rich source of limpets (*kenima*), oysters, sea urchins, and similar marine life, which people, particularly women, collect from time to time in buckets for home use, *penimafa* or *penimari* (see Plate 13). A tool, resembling a screwdriver, *õla meting* (i.e. shellfish iron), with a wooden handle and a blunt blade is ideal for prising shellfish from the rocks. They also collect edible seaweed, a short variety which grows on the same rocks and which they like to mix with salt, tamarind fruit, and red peppers. The season for collecting seaweed is from August to October. Thereafter the winds change and the waves get too high.[3] Delicious giant barnacles called *kĕlõki* grow on boulders at a distance under the surface of the sea,

PLATE 13. Collecting shellfish and edible seaweed

where they are available for collection by skilled divers in the months from October to early December.

In the months of the rainy season, when fishing is severely restricted, some who own them may place fish traps on the sea floor. There are not many of these, however, and those that I had an opportunity to inspect closely were in Lamakera, Solor, where they are called *nama*. These were flat boxes of woven bamboo. Some are quite small, less than a yard in length, for small fish. For large fish, they can be quite large, thus there are large *nama*, *nama bélã*, and small *nama*, *nama kéni*. All are built according to the same plan, a cylindrical tube, running into the interior, with an opening at the end which admits the fish to the main part of the trap, but prevents their exit. The trap itself is the casing surrounding the tube. Once inside the fish swims around and around without being able to spot the way out because of the way its eyes are positioned in its head. Large traps in Lamakera are dropped out at sea in 100 metres of water. They are not marked with floats, because of the danger of the many people passing by in the Solor Strait, some of whom might cut the lines and take the gear. Instead the fishermen drop out lengthwise in front of the trap the rope by which it is let down and pulled up. The owner takes his bearings on a hill behind the village or on a hill on Adonara. In this way, only he knows where the trap is and which way it is facing.

They weigh the *nama* down with four stones, two tied to either side, and leave it for about a week. They then take it up and empty it. There is no way to tell before hand whether it is full or empty or to estimate how many fish may be in it until they have brought it up and looked. Since the trap cannot be seen and there is no sign, everything depends on the owner's memory. To bring it up they use a special device consisting of a flat round stone like a curling stone. Around it they weave a rattan frame with a long rattan hook. They drag this object on the ground by means of a rope until it crosses and hooks the rope in front of the trap. Once they have secured this second rope, they have control of the trap.

This device is called *wato lita* in Lamakera and *fato lité* in Lamalera. The rope for it is *beka*. It is used in exactly the same way in Lamalera. The traps are put out in the rainy season, in front of the beach or further to the east. In Lamalera these traps are also called *bĕlutu* and *bĕlika*.[4] *Nama* is used in Lamalera for a large trap, *fufo* for a smaller trap, and *bĕlika* for the smallest. *Nama* may be used to take fish called *banko*, *kombo*, and *kemara* (*Acanthurus* spp.). The latter two may be taken in the other traps too. Some traps may have two mouths. The rope in front of the trap is called *lapa*. The stone at the end of the rope is *keli*. In Lamalera, fish traps were traditionally the preserve of the small descent group called Ata Gora and of a line in Bedi Onã.

When the tide is very low leaving pools, villagers may rub roots of a plant called *nufa* (a *Derris*, possibly *Derris elliptica*) under rocks to poison fish (see Gregorius Keraf 1978: 45; to poison fish is *tuba*). The fish then swim out, trying to escape, but they die. The roots of *nufa* are very small and thin. For poisoning fish they take enough to make a large bundle. The plants grows far from Lamalera in the mountains of Bobu and Lobetobi, Flores. People from Lamalera must trade for it. At Lobetobi they obtain it by trading fish or pots from Nualela. For a summary of the literature on fish poisoning see Burkill (1935: vol. 1: 783–9; see also Gimlette 1923: 208–22.).[5] Among other poisons known, the seed of the tree called *keluraj* and the leaf of *kĕlua* may make a person dizzy or quickly drunk if it is rubbed on a glass.

Working from shore or in the surf, men may fish with home-made spear-guns, *bedi*, consisting in a wooden rifle stock, a long stiff metal wire and a rubber sling. Normally, these are used for smaller fish, but when opportunity arises they may go after larger animals. One man spotted a large ray which came in close to shore to feed. He shot it once in the brain and killed it immediately, but it took eight men to lift it out of the water. Commercially available trot-lines, called *longlin* (i.e. 'long line' in current international usage), are now used with some regularity. Whenever there is a whale carcass lying in the surf, they are sure to put out at least one trotline to catch sharks attracted by the blood. I have even seen them wade into the surf and grab a shark by the tail in order to pull it up the beach where they dispatched it. Apparently they are even pre-pared sometimes to grab a shark swimming next to the boat by the tail and pull it into the boat. In fact, I have been told that sometimes people here can ride on a shark. It is easier to get a cash return from using trotlines than other forms of fishing because they regularly catch sharks and shark fins and tails are easily sold to merchants. Bombing fish, which is illegal, used to be commonplace, but the authorities have finally eliminated it along the south coast of Lembata.

Two men have died while fishing with a speargun. In December 1974 a man speared a turtle. When he tried to turn it on its back so that it could not move, he caught his foot in the rope between the speargun and the turtle. He was dragged under and drowned. The gun was later found on the shore and placed in his great house. In January 1979 a man spear fishing by himself failed to return home. The next day people searching for him found him lying on the sea floor. The cause of his death was never discovered. It has also happened that young children swimming in the breakers have been carried away by currents and lost.

Floats and Small Boats

In September, October, and November, when the larger boats are no longer in much or any use, people may be seen in great numbers fishing along the shore in small boats or floating astraddle logs. Hornell distinguishes between swimming floats and riding floats. He describes a Tamil fisherman of South India floating with a log float under his arms. The image is close to what can be seen in Lamalera, except that they do actually ride their logs, bobbing up and down in the sea like so many mermen. These floats belong to Hornell's second category, riding floats, but he deems tree-trunk floats to be so unstable as to be usable only in quiet waters (Hornell 1946: 1–17). Those used in Lamalera are more likely to be large trimmed branches than small trees, and they are brought out only when the sea is calm, but they are used in the sea at a distance from shore. The verb *bao*, to float, specifies this form of fishing.

Lamalera employs three types of small boats, the first two of which have almost disappeared in favour of the third. The first is a dugout, *kĕlaba* (from *laba*, chisel) or *béro kĕlaba*, carved from a seasoned trunk of a mango, silk-cotton (kapok), *rita*,[6] or other tree. The sides are extended upwards with a woven palm-leaf screen, *senirã*.[7] Bamboo outriggers either side maintain balance. These boats were used for fishing in shallow water. One day in August 1982 two *béro kĕlaba* from Mulan Doro on the Lerek Peninsula beached at Lamalera. Each was made of a single dugout hull from a large tree trunk and had wide bamboo outriggers about six feet from the sides. Their sides were built up with splash screens made from lontar palm-leaf strips folded over a bamboo runner and sewn down with *pelepah* (bindings made from the skin of a lontar palm branch) through the whole length of the hull. They had broader sterns than bows, and one carried a triangular sail.[8] Nooteboom (1932: 7–13) offers an extended description of the construction of dugouts, particularly near

Palembang, Sumatra, and in Borneo, including the method of stretching out the sides by means of simultaneous wetting and burning (see also Doran 1981).

The second boat type, once the most common type, is the *béro* or *béro baololo* (the *béro* which floats on the surface), a high-sided planked boat with outriggers used for fishing in deep water. These boats were extremely narrow at the keel, very high-sided, and only wide enough at the top for a man to sit. They carried two men, and balance critically depended on the extended outriggers. They tended to be longer and higher than *kĕlaba* or indeed than the newer *sapã* (cf. Oleona 1989: 10). More recently these types have been supplanted by wider two-manned, planked boats without outriggers called *sapã*.[9]

The difference between a *béro* and a *sapã* is that the *béro* has high sides, outrigger booms, *gĕlefé*, attached to outriggers, *ĕlé*, and sticks, *bako*, attached to the ends of the outrigger booms to extend them and put the outriggers in the right position (see Nooteboom 1932: illus. 25 for a demonstration of this arrangement). *Sapã* are wider and have only outrigger booms, which are useful in pulling the boat up and down the beach, without outriggers. People now prefer *sapã* because they are lighter and therefore easier for two persons to handle if they are pulling the boat up a strange beach after a long journey or when they return to Lamalera late at night.

The *sapã* are attractive little boats, but still fairly heavy. By a rough count in 1979 there were some thirty-four *sapã* and five *béro*, plus an unknown number in Futung Lolo. By 1982, there were sixty-two *sapã* at the beach, plus a few which were unserviceable. They were parked in and around the boat sheds, sometimes as many as three or four crowded around a large boat. Perhaps it is significant, given the decline in use of larger boats by groups from the upper village, that forty-one of these *sapã* were on the side of the beach associated with the upper village, while twenty-one were on the side associated with the lower village. In addition there were twenty-seven *sapã*, three dugouts, and two high *béro*, both unserviceable, at Futung Lolo. The heavy, high-sided *béro* held vertical by outriggers had completely disappeared. All had been replaced by *sapã*. The only *béro* was a light dugout with wide-spaced outriggers, but although it was unusual in design, people regarded it as a type of *sapã*.

One *sapã* on the beach in 1982 had a device at the stern intended to assist in holding the steering oar when taken out by only one man, essentially a stout wooden cross which could provide leverage to the oar when placed on either side.[10] Because the sampan are pulled up the beach bow foremost, they have the drain hole in the stern. The sail for *sapã* is a very simple triangular affair fixed to a boom and a single mast which comes out of the boat along with the sail and the boom. Some sails are quite crude, being made of patches of all sorts of bits of cloth, some coloured sections of clothing, some white. Unlike the large boats, *sapã* do not have names. Some do have decorated bows, however; for example one had a striking imitation of a shark's head painted on its bow. Another had eyes painted on either side and on the right '*Anak*', on the left '*nelayan*', i.e. fisherman, and on the stern on the right *bora*, on the left *ora et la*, the whole in Latin '*ora et labora*', 'pray and work'.

In the past not many people actually had *béro*. They knew about *sapã*, but did not build or use them. There were not many people who owned small boats because nylon lines were not yet available and cotton fishing lines were difficult to use. When nylon fishing lines became easily obtainable, it became easy to fish for flying fish. Many started doing so and therefore many acquired boats. Some owners built the *sapã* themselves. Others used the services of a master builder with the resulting obligation to share the proceeds. Whenever such a boat is used to catch fish, the master builder must receive a prescribed portion.

The *sapã* are suitable for line fishing, but they are ideal for use with modern gill nets and they are commonly used for catching flying fish, which are especially plentiful between March and May, when a single *sapã* may bring in as many as a hundred or more in a single day's fishing. *Sapã* are planked boats built by the same methods of construction as the larger boats, i.e. the lashed lug technique, with internal dowelling, edge to edge planking, ribs placed in last, and the whole compressed by lashings between planks, ribs, and thwarts. They are two-man boats, approximately three metres in length, although they can be handled by one man. Lacking outriggers, they require ballast. Because they are wider than *béro*, they can carry loads, like the bulky fishing nets. They can also transport the quite large manta rays and porpoises which sometimes blunder into the nets. Two rowers can make fair time in a *sapã*, but these boats normally are provided with a small triangular sail and mast like those used in *béro*.

Nets

One of the reasons for the expanding numbers of *sapã* is the recent availability of nylon gill nets.[11] These have the attraction of being able to supply increased numbers of fish of various sizes, including especially shark and devil ray, *moku*. My net in 1982 once caught a very large devil ray of the variety called *bōu*, while another net captured a goosebeak whale, *ikã méã*. These catches were of course exceptional. Normally they bring in smaller fish, devil ray, and an occasional shark. The fact that nets often catch several *moku* at a time makes them especially valuable. However, the initial cost and the expenses of upkeep make them doubtful economic investments. In 1979 a stripped-down net, lacking floats and other gear cost Rp. 50,000 or US $119 at Waiwerang, Adonara. In 1982 I bought a complete, good-quality net, with all its gear in Kupang, Timor, for Rp. 95,000 or US $142; smaller nets were then available in Waiwerang for Rp. 75,000 or US $112. By 1987 the same net could be obtained in Waiwerang, complete with ropes and floats, for Rp. 80,000 or US $49. Seven nets were introduced into the village by the Food and Agricultural Organization project in 1973–5, but nets were already slowly spreading in the province at that time. Subsequently they became much more common. In 1979 there were eighteen nets in private hands. By 1982 there were said to be some sixty to seventy nets in the village. Of these thirty-four were given in that year by the Food and Agricultural Organization, seventeen going to Lamalera A and eighteen to Lamalera B. The FAO also gave each of the two official villages two outboard motors, only one of which was still useable in 1987.

These nets were handed out by representatives of the Fisheries Service just before the national election, and the officials tried to persuade people into believing that they had been provided by Golkar, the government's political party. The true facts, however, were known. The village governments distributed them to the ward associations, *rukun tetangga*. In Lamalera A, the three wards of the mountain hamlet Lamamanu received no nets. All the other wards except for one received three each. One small ward received two. In most, but not all, wards each net was assigned to a specific group, which cared for it and used it. As a sign of things to come, within a few months of receiving its nets, one ward was using only two, having cannibalized the third for floats and other gear. Two inexperienced youths took another net out and caught it on coral on the sea floor. Instead of waiting until daylight and diving to free it, they cut it loose, thus losing half of the net and ruining it. For reasons never clear to me, the wards of Lamalera B received only one net each. One explanation I received is that there were too many wards for any one of them to have more than one net in Lamalera B, but this was not true.

The wards shared among themselves the rights and responsibilities of ownership. The nets were made available for use by anyone in the ward who asked, on a share basis. In general the owner of a net gets the torso section called *ūk* of a devil ray or manta ray or the tail of a shark. The rest of the animal is divided evenly between the net, the boat, and a share each for each crew member.[12] Since there are usually two crew members, there are usually four such shares. The net owner thus gets *ūk* or tail, plus a share. Other larger fish or porpoises are treated like shark. If the net gets one or two small fish, these are usually left to the people doing the actual work. Thus a ward will divide among themselves the shares owing to the net owner. However, since the nets were actually given by the village government to the wards, the wards must take the other net share, or fins, bones, etc. for sale to raise money (small amounts) for various purposes, such as buying palm wine for the man they ask to fix holes in the net. There was, so far as I could discover, no effort made to save sums large enough to make it possible eventually to replace the net with another, which presumably had been the ambition of the FAO. It must be said, however, that one of the more responsible groups had taken eleven devil ray and two marlin with their net by September 1982, from which they obtained Rp. 30,000 or US $45.

One of the village heads in 1979 denied that people could borrow money to buy nets. The main problem is not in getting the fish, but in turning the fish into money to pay off the debt. He could not manage to do so himself. He is skilled in repairing nets, and was often called in to do so, for which he was paid off in fish. Most nets, he explained, were bought for the people by their children or other relatives who have wage-paying jobs elsewhere in Indonesia. Even in the semi-monetized economy of the early 1980s, fish remained a commodity which almost without exception was traded only in kind. A further hindrance to covering the costs of nets and their use through their product lies in the share system, in itself fair enough, which breaks up and distributes the catch. I totally failed in my own attempt to operate my net on an economically realistic basis, even had I charged myself a bookkeeping sum for the fish which my household consumed. The purpose of the net was not to supply myself with fish, which was a welcome consequence, but to serve as an experiment to see if nets were economically rational additions to the local economy. Certain exceptional individuals may well have succeeded in paying for them from the catch, but on the whole I think that my results were typical and a confirmation of what villagers themselves said. This conclusion may seem paradoxical, given that the nets seem now to be a permanent part of village economy. However, I take it that the vast majority are still purchased by relatives with secure incomes living outside the village. My own net was generally successful in catching fish, although it had some bad days, but it all too frequently came back heavily damaged from being caught in the coral on the sea floor. Perhaps those using it were unlucky or incompetent, but other nets had similar difficulties.

Like boats, nets require a small feast and ceremony, *toto*, when they are new or they will never catch any fish. For this feast a small pig or dog should be supplied. For my net, I secured palm wine, a dog, and two chickens, which was my responsibility as net owner. Also if the net is to be successful the number of floats has to be an uneven number. This condition resembles certain requirements in the gear of the large boats, to be described later. When they fish with a line, they must use an uneven number of feathers on their lure, for the same reason. Also the bindings, *kemité*, should have ginger tied to them, like those of the harpooning ropes used in the large boats, so that the net will be successful.

Although many nets may be seen hanging in the boat sheds, people prefer to bring their nets to the house for a similar reason to that for storing the principal harpooning rope, *léo fã*, in the great house. They claim that it is common practice for people who see that a net has been too successful to urinate near by or to put pig or goat excrement on it in order to keep it from getting fish, in the same way they may do to a boat. Once the man who was managing my net asked me to purchase some liquid soap so that we could use it to wash the net, which in due course we did. The purpose was not a routine cleaning of the net, but remedial action required by poor luck. It had been taken out one evening, but had caught no fish. This poor result he interpreted as a sign that

someone had urinated on it at the beach. Afterwards he brought a little piece
of garlic, *bafã burã*, and another of ginger, *lia*, to the net where he chewed these
roots. He stood silently near the net for a few seconds, then spat on the ropes,
in no particular pattern. That was the extent of his preparations, and he did
not bother to tie any medicine to the net. There are several varieties of ginger.
One, which is not planted and must be acquired in the mountain, is red and is
especially effective—suited for use on the large boats. Once this type of ginger
has been put on the equipment the fish cannot get away. If it is put on the net,
the fish must enter. Among other varieties are a yellow type and an orange one.
These two are effective when used with garlic. There is also a white variety.

The best places for using nets are fairly far from Lamalera. They are Peni
Kéni and Wai Léi about a day's trip to the west and Bobu even further away
to the east, beyond the Lerek Peninsula. Mulan Doro on the west coast of the
Lerek Peninsula is supposed to be a very good fishing area for nets, but villagers say that the people of Mulan Doro try to make trouble for Lamalera
people who go there. I once went with a group to Peni Kéni, where we had
several days of successful fishing, while sleeping on the beach and enjoying the
lavish hospitality of the lord of the land. Nets require checking and emptying
two or three times a night, which can become tricky work if the *éto lata ria*
(*Brachirus brachypterus*) with its many poisonous spines or a large and potentially dangerous animal like a manta ray, shark, or porpoise is in the net. The
phosphorescent plankton is remarkably bright at night when the men work on
the nets. Every dip of the paddle leaves a bright streak of blue-green light, and
light drips off the paddle and falls into the water when the paddle is lifted out.
Tiny bits of light get on their hands and stay there. The net in the waters is
full enough of light so that it is possible to see where it is on a dark night. Some
fish are so full of plankton that their stomachs shine as they lie on the bottom
of the boat.[13]

Other Forms of Fishing

Currently the village uses hooks with chicken feathers to catch flying fish,
kemãnu, having converted to this method when a youth returned from
Maumere where he had seen it and tried it out with success in Lamalera. They
all quickly followed because this method produces more fish than the old one.
Before that only one or two would fish for flying fish with small floating lures.
The old method is as follows. A stick with a rectangular cross-section and of
about 40 cm. length made of wood of the *Hibiscus tiliaceus*, *fao*, has a cord tied
to it in the middle. One end of the stick is split a little and the rope is passed
through the split which fastens it. From this point the line with a hook on the
end is suspended from the floating stick. The length of the suspended line can
be adjusted between ¹/₂ and 2 fathoms. The end opposite the split is narrowed
down. This whole device is called *sopé utã* or *utã*. A *béro* would have about

seven of these devices, which would be left floating free in the sea. If a flying fish gets caught with one, it will be capable of flying with the device so long as the line remains caught in the split at the end. As soon as the line slips out, the drag of the stick is enough to stop it. While the *utã* is set up waiting for the fish to bite, it follows the wind like a weather vane. No one uses the *utã* any longer.

Bobu

Until the disaster at Waiteba and Sarapuka in 1979, it was common for men to go to Bobu at the east end of the Waiteba bay each October to hunt fish. By 1982 a few had begun to go again even though the village government had forbidden them to do so, but only for short stays of a few days or at most a week or two because of fear of further disasters. Because the area had become sacred, they stopped and had a little ceremony for the victims when they came to Waiteba before going on. More people, however, went to Mingar, Loang, or even as far as Lewoleba, especially those who had acquired a net. The season for Bobu is October and November, but some also go in April and March.[14] They may take a line and a speargun. If they are going to spear fish, they walk, but if they were going to fish with a line, they may take a *supã*. At Bobu during October they could get a great amount of fish and could end up with many large tins of maize acquired by trading the fish there. Sometimes they do well enough there to bring a large boat up from the village to carry the maize back. In 1978 they used three boats for this purpose. A man must take with him a wife, sister, or wife's sister, who will be able to trade his fish for him. At times there might be as many as fifty women from Lamalera at Bobu. Two or three groups may get together and build a lean-to on the beach to live in for the time being. They either take their cooking things with them, or they go across the island to Hadakewa on the north coast of Lembata to buy them. Hadakewa is very close. It was also easy to get money in Bobu. A Chinese merchant from Hadakewa travelled across to buy fish there. Some people go from Bobu to the market in Balaurin, Kédang.

Early in September 1982 two sampan set out for Bobu and were successful in harpooning porpoise, among other animals. At the end of November, four heavily laden sampan returned to the village, and two of the *téna* set off to transport the results of six sampan which had been in use there for two months, returning also heavily laden with, among other things, several large storage baskets, *mata gapo*, of maize.

The return trip around the Ata Déi Peninsula can be treacherous because of the currents. Once men fishing at sea in the large boats saw a signal fire in the afternoon indicating disaster. They said nothing, according to custom, but came in. It turned out that *Demo Sapã* had disappeared while being used to bring fish back from Bobu. Three of the crew reached shore, crossed the peninsula, and brought the news to the village, where they sent up a smoke signal. Eventually they found the boat at Sarapuka. The six people who were in it sat on a bamboo pole and were carried to near Pulau Rusa at the eastern tip of Lembata where in the evening a boat from Lamahala picked them up. They lost all their goods, but no one died. The *Léla Sapâ* also sank once bringing goods back from Bobu.

10

Boat-Owning Groups

The larger fishing and whaling vessels, called *téna* in Lamaholot and *pělédang* in the local version of Bahasa Indonesia, which are used for chasing whales, porpoise, manta ray, and other large game, are owned and maintained by corporations centred on a hereditary core, which are augmented by other ties, typically those based on marriages of women from the descent group.[1] Each boat (with one exception) is associated with either a patrilineal descent group or with a named segment of such a descent group. Most of the clans in the village own at least one boat. Just as some clans are larger than others and internally more complexly organized, so too are there more boats in some clans and the pattern of ownership is more complex. Table 12 lists the boats and the groupings to which they belong.

Corporations

Each boat is associated with a dwelling or 'great house', *lango bélā*. Usually this house is either the ritual centre for the clan or that for one of its segments. Boats of secondary importance, including several of those called *sapā* (not to be confused with the small skiffs called *sapā* which were described in the previous chapter), with the implication that they are shorter by a section than the others, are associated with a residence with no ritual implications for the descent group as a whole. Among the reasons why the connection between the boat and the house is important are the following. The highly flexible lead rope for the harpoon called the *léo*, which is usually the rope kept at ready when at sea, is stored in this house during periods when the boat is inactive. Formerly, it is said, the harpooner would bring this rope to the house every evening after returning from the sea, but it is no longer common to do so. When there is any meeting concerning the conduct of the boat, its crew, or its corporation, especially when there is a question of clearing up the consequences of dissension, this rope is brought to the house for the occasion. All ceremonies connected with the boat except those conducted at the beach are held at this house, as are all discussions concerning the affairs of the boat-owning corporation, such as those concerned with the building and repairing of the boat or with the distribution of rights and responsibilities within the corporation.

The head of the corporation is the boat master, *téna alep*. The Lamaholot could be translated in other ways, for example as 'boat owner' or 'lord of the boat'. One person described him as 'chairman of the co-operative'. None of

TABLE 12. *Boats and Descent Groups*

Boat	Clan	Great House
1. Muko Ténã	Ata Kéi	Ata Kéi
2. Demo Sapã	Běliko Lolo	Lali Nama Papã
3. Baka Ténã	Tufa Onã	Tufa Onã
4. Pěraso Sapã	Léla Onã	Sinu Langu
5. Léla Sapã	Léla Onã	Sinu Langu
6. Notã Ténã	Lãma Nudek	Lãma Nudek
7. Menula Belolong	Lãma Kéra	Badi Langu
8. Dato Ténã	Lãma Nudek	Lãma Nudek
9. Kebéla Ténã	Lefo Tukã	Dasi Langu
10. Boli Sapã	Hari Onã	Hari Onã
11. Gěléko Ténã	Tapo Onã	Guna Langu
12. Boko Lolo	Běliko Lolo	Lali Nama Papã
13. Sika Ténã	Sula Onã	Kěloré Langu
14. Bui Pukã	Běliko Lolo	Téti Nama Papã
15. Sia Apu	Lãma Nifa	Lãma Nifa
16. Nara Ténã	Lãma Kéra	Pěrafi Langu
17. Kopo Paker	Olé Onã	Olé Onã
18. Téti Heri	Bata Fo	Kaja Langu
19. Holo Sapã	Bata Onã	Kifa Langu
20. Soge Ténã	Tapo Onã	Musi Langu
21. Horo Ténã	Bata Onã	Kifa Langu
22. Dolu Ténã	Sula Onã	Kebesa Langu
23. Sili Ténã	Bata Onã	Kifa Langu
24. Kéna Pukã	Bedi Onã	Miku Langu
25. Kelulus	Bedi Onã	Muri Langu
26. Kebako Pukã	Bata Onã	Ola Langu
27. Téna Ãnã	Bata Onã	Kělaké Langu
28. Sinu Sapã	Bata Onã	Kifa Langu
29. Jafa Ténã	Bata Onã	Jafa Langu

these terms conveys all of the nuances of this position.[2] Ownership is not vested in the boat master alone, but in the corporation, and the corporation includes other people than the boat master's immediate family. Elsewhere (R. H. Barnes 1980*b*: 22) I have compared him to a managing director. If this analogy leaves out the hereditary implications of the position, it does highlight other aspects, especially the extent to which the welfare of the boat and its corporation depends on his ability to get corporation members to co-operate. Although his position may have come to him by heredity, if he wishes to derive the income which is his traditional right, he must see to it that his boat is in good order and has a crew willing to take it out. He, above all, bears the onus of reconciling conflicting opinions and containing disputes.

The corporations are not always harmonious, and bad luck at sea often gives rise to bickering. So too does the division of the fish. Although the crew shares are in principle equal, the division of the fish depends on the skill of the man who does the cutting. For ray, the crew often relies on a man who is known for his abilities and whom they ask to take over. Typically this person would be either the boat owner or the boat's master builder, or someone working under his direction. Nevertheless, sometimes a crew member may complain. Villagers say that if anyone complains about his share, the boat will get no fish until they have had a ceremony to remove the fault. These ceremonies take place with moderate frequency.

Corporation members are not necessarily crew members. But normally the physically active members of the corporation form the core of the crew. They then try to draw in others through various familial and other ties to ensure that enough men (usually at least nine, but up to fourteen) are available, so that the boat can go out on most days during the season of fishing and hunting on the open sea. There is steady fluctuation in the crew from week to week, as other demands on individuals' time wax and wane. Schooling keeps the boys out of the boats, except during periods when the schools are out. Occupations, such as carpentry and construction work on government sponsored projects, disrupt the natural pool of labour. Some potential recruits work on the passenger boats, which have been a prominent part of local transportation since the early 1970s. The fact that many of the offspring of the village have found success through education and have secured wage-paying employment, become schoolteachers, or have moved into the professions and business places the fishery under duress. Often, when conditions are right and the large boats are not being successful, people will prefer to take the small boats out fishing or netting, making it difficult or impossible for the large boats to muster a crew. Several boats have fallen into disuse, simply because they have been unable to find reliable crews, while other seaworthy boats are unable to put out for long periods even during the height of the season. The fact that a boat lies unused and unrepaired in its shed is sometimes a sad consequence of the relative success of the descent group which owns it in other, usually modern, walks of life.

In the best of times, the boat master must try to keep his crew satisfied enough to take his boat out. He must rely on his personal qualities, but he must also see to it that wood and other materials are available for rapid repairs. When the boat is rebuilt he must turn an eye to seeing to it that the corporation includes enough potential crew members to keep the boat working. The constraints on his doing so are the facts that decisions must be taken collectively and that the shares in the corporation are hereditary rights. Anyone who has a specific right cannot be told to give it up, if he is ineffective in meeting his responsibilities. At best the corporation can endeavour to persuade him to transfer it to someone else, usually a close kinsman. It is quite usual for an ageing person to do so readily, perhaps even initiating the transfer. Nevertheless, it does not always happen that shifts occur to everyone's liking. A boat I was closely associated with went unrepaired for some years and finally spent a year unable to put to sea, even though its corporation was active and its crew guaranteed, simply because the man who held the hereditary right to be its master builder wanted to concentrate his attentions elsewhere. Finally, an arrangement was reached whereby one of his kinsmen stepped in to oversee the actual building and the two of them split the master builder's share in the boat's catch. Nevertheless, it was he who had to strike the first blow with a mallet on the day that the boat was disassembled in order to prepare it for reconstruction—to signal his approval of the undertaking and to publicly assert his right. Had the boat been rebuilt without his approval and participation, then the corporation feared that it would be unlucky.

Not only is the system of co-operation intricate, the corporations, so I have been assured, are full of problems and disagreements. What holds groups of persons together is that a disgruntled member usually has nowhere else to go. Other boats will not quickly accept him into membership. In order to earn a livelihood, most men must accommodate themselves to the group where they have inherited a place. This economic constraint is the boat master's principal ally. It also explains why this traditional form of co-operation may not automatically carry directly over into new undertakings, such as the two fishing co-operatives which have at different times been organized and which have both failed (R. H. Barnes 1984: 18–20).

Included in the corporation are shares for three craftsmen, who need not belong to the boat's descent group. These men are the carpenter, *ata mõlã*, the sail maker, and the smith. The carpenter does not do all of the carpentry by himself. Rather, he measures, marks out, and supervises the cutting and fitting of the planks. A given *ata mõlã* may serve in this capacity for several boats, and his office cannot be taken from him by another man without his consent. Much the same can be said of the smith, who prepares the harpoons. So long as he wishes to keep his attachment, he may. The metal he uses, however, must be provided by the boat owner. The sail maker, however, is responsible for providing all the materials needed in his sail: the bamboo for the booms and the gebang palm leaves (*ketebu, Corypha utan*, Lam.) and bark of the *fao* tree (*Hibiscus tiliaceus*, Linn.) used in the sail and ropes.[3] Every three years or so the members of the association which owns the boat (rather than its crew) will take it to Ata Nila on the south coast of Kédang, where there is a stand of gebang palm. They cut a sufficient supply of gebang palm leaf to meet the needs of rope making until their next trip. The sail maker can join the expedition and cut what he will need for his sails. If kept indoors, the leaves store very well.

A critical contribution to the working of the boats is the provision of the thread from which men of the corporation weave the ropes. The making of cotton thread from locally grown cotton (usually obtained from mountain villages) is entirely done by women, either wives of the men of the corporation or their sisters and sisters' daughters.

Rights and Distribution

Although there is variation in detail from one corporation to another in how it distributes rights to game animals and in the rights it recognizes, there is nevertheless a common general pattern. There are also important variations depending on the species of animal which has been killed. There are also specific rights which inhere in a single species. The first division in any animal is that between the section which goes to members of the corporation which owns and maintains the boat and those parts which go to the members of the crew on the day it was caught.

There are traditional names for the shares in the corporation. Despite variations, these names are standard from corporation to corporation. The following are common names.

1. Chisel and peg (*laba ketilo*). This portion belongs to the man who is responsible for supervising, as master boat builder (*ata mōlā*), the actual construction and major repairs of the boat. In several boats, this section is shared between two men. In some cases this occurs because the person who inherited the right to be the master builder of a given boat is inexperienced and still learning his craft. In such cases, agreement may be reached to bring in an older and more experienced craftsman, who is the effective master builder for the time being. As Malinowski (1922: 114) noted for the Trobriands, the master builder has a distinct sociological role from the boat master, and, as in the Trobriands, in the past might have held responsibility for the boat ritual as well. Typically, but not always, the master builder is a different person from the boat master. Often, but not necessarily, the master builder will be in the same descent group as the boat master. Sometimes he is a wife-giver, but never a wife-taker, which is probably significant, given the authority relationships between wife-givers and wife-takers.

2. Lower jaw (*mimã*). One or two corporation members have the right by inheritance to this section and are called *mimã alep*.

3. *Tenarap* (no translation available). One or two members inherit the right to this share. In one boat it is divided equally by all members who received shares.

4. Ring (*kīlã*). One or two members inherit the right to this share. In two boats this section is divided into half, one half going to a single person and the other half being shared by two people. *Kīlã* meaning simply ring applies in this generic sense to the other sections, that is the torso of the animal is sectioned completely through at either end of the 'ring'. Nevertheless, it is also common to speak of *kīlã* as being the name of a specific section. Gregorius Keraf (1983) also lists a section by this name, which, however, he identifies with number 8 below. *Kīlã* is treated as equivalent to *bĕfãnã*

bélã by Sika Ténã, Téna Ãnã, and Nara Ténã. It is not recognized as a separate share by Gĕléko Ténã, Notã Ténã, and Horo Ténã.

5. Shares (*umã*) or *kefoko seba* (no translation available; possibly 'the dead souls
   [i.e. ancestors] search for'). Many shares, between six and fifteen, of this
   kind are held in each corporation, with ten or eleven being most common
   and nine being the average. A substantial number of these shares are held
   by widows with family connections to the boat-owning group.
6. Sail (*laja*). This share belongs to the man who makes and maintains the sail.
   About half of the sail makers belong to the boat-owning group. All the rest
   or nearly all the rest have family connections of various kinds.
7. Chest (*korok*) for a section called *nupã* (which in other contexts means
   'greeting' or 'reception'). This share is specially reserved for the smith who
   makes the harpoons.
8. Large *bĕfãnã* (*bĕfãnã bélã*). Smaller shares which go to the handful of relatives of corporation members, typically but not invariably the husbands of
   children or sisters of corporation members or these sisters themselves.
   Bĕfãnã comes from *fãnã*, 'right (side)'. Gregorius Keraf (1983) defines
   bĕfãnã bélã as being *ãnã-opu ina-biné*, that is sisters and daughters of the
   descent group who are still close. Oleona (1989: 44–5) defines *bĕfãnã* as a
   gift to *ãnã-opu biné-maki*, while specifying that the latter are the males who
   have taken wives from ego's own group.
9. Some corporations recognized the small *bĕfãnã* (*bĕfãnã kéni*), smaller parts
   of flesh which may be given to crew members to supplement their crew
   shares, to relatives of corporation members, or to persons who help in small
   ways or are otherwise thought deserving. Recipients may or may not be
   specified.

Fig. 14 displays the distribution of shares held in corporations by relationship. A summary of the distribution of the various rights in the different boat
corporations may be found in Appendix III.

According to Gregorius Keraf, near the tail of a whale or porpoise is located
a section called *fadar*, which is divided into four sections, two on the left and
two on the right sides. These are (1) for *bĕfãnã kéni*, that is more distant sisters,
(2) for those men who often help pull and push the boat across the beach
(*belãku*, from *laku*, 'to give' or 'gift' (Gregorius Keraf 1978: 31, 247)), (3) for
wife-taking allies who may bring animals when there is a festival associated
with the boat, and (4) for people who may be working on another boat or
making harpoons for another boat while the whale is being cut up. Another
man spoke of (2) as being called *belãku* and as being intended for the *ēlé alep*,
figuratively those who grab the outriggers to help in pushing the boat up or down
the beach, but the purpose is the same. Oleona has it that *belãku* goes to old
men who sit in the boat sheds and watch men cut up the animal. He also speaks
of *nãké* as being gifts of meat to women who have been asked to carry meat

Share Type	Same Great House	Same Clan	Different Clan	Wife-Giver	Wife-Taker	No Relation	Other	Widows	Total
Chisel and Peg	15	0	13	3	0	10	0	0	28
Lower Jaw	35	3	9	0	3	0	3	3	47
Tenarap	26 (1 widow)	6	7	0	7	0	0	0	39
Ring	11 (1 widow)	5	17	0	15	1	0	1	33
Shares	129 (3 widows)	37 (2 widows)	84	5	47	4	15	13	250
Sail	14	1	13	2	6	3	2	0	28
Chest	9	0	19	5	4	10	0	0	28
Large *Béǰānā*	20 (6 widows)	13 (1 widow)	66	0	60	3	0	3	99
Totals	259	65	228	15	142	31	20	20	552
Percentages	47%	12%	41%	2.7%	25.7%	5.6%	3.6%	3.6%	

Women who received shares: 34 widows, plus two others, totalling 36 or 6.5%.

Armpit *lango bélā nūé*	22 boat master	7 (1 woman) close relative	29 total

FIG. 14. Distribution of shares held in boat-owning corporations according to type of relationship

from the beach to the drying rack and of *bẽti* as a gift to a close friend, from the results of going to sea. The *fadar* is given to the *téna alep*, who is responsible for dividing it among those who help in pulling the boat. Such a person might get a palm's length piece of meat. People associated with boats which have caught nothing may barter for meat from corporation or crew members of a successful boat by *pafã lama*, that is putting out plates filled with maize kernels in the hope of having them returned filled with meat. Children may beg or barter for scraps to cook and eat on the beach, *du sũsu*, 'sell [mother's] milk'. *Fadar* means tip. It is the back part of the tail and is reasonably large.

The harpooner gets another section called *kélik* or 'armpit' which is owed to the man who provides the harpoon poles. In most cases, the harpooner provides his own poles and gets this section. An exception would be when a trainee harpooner uses the poles of an experienced harpooner. The trainee harpooner would have no right to this section. *Kélik* refers to the circle around the chest fins in a whale or porpoise. Half of the circle goes to the provider of harpooning and steering poles. The harpooner's *kélik* must never be consumed by the harpooner or his children. Many different kinds of misfortune may result from breaking this prohibition. Instead it should be given over to his parents or elder brother, if they are living. Only when there are no living relatives of the right kind, may he use this section himself. Another part of the *kélik* ring, referred to as *kélik lango bélã nãé* ('the great house's ring') goes to keeper of the boat's great house who is not invariably the same as the boat master. The great house owner receives this share because he supplies the lighting and the tobacco, palm-leaf wrappings for self-rolled cigarettes, and the makings of betel quid for festivals associated with the boat which are held in his house. This share is to help him 'buy fire and torches, palm leaf and tobacco, areca nuts and betel peppers', *hopé apé-padu, kolé-tebaka, fua-malu*. Of twenty-nine people who received or potentially received this section for the great house, some seven were relatives of the owner of the great house, rather than the owner himself, always close relatives, such as a brother or father. Only one woman received such a share, the elder sister of a boat master.

The individual rights of corporation members bring responsibilities. Anyone who possesses one of them must contribute a corresponding part of the expense of building and maintaining the boat. There is some sentiment in the village that the larger shares such as *mimã* (lower jaw) and *tenarap* (untranslatable) should be pooled, for a more equitable division within the corporation, and indeed a few boats have done so. Such a step, however, cannot be taken without the agreement of those who hold these hereditary rights. Their ancestors got the rights in the first place by taking a greater part in organizing the building of the boat. They also had to sustain more of the expense, and today those who have inherited these rights must still contribute more. For any change in procedure which runs against traditional rights agreement must be unanimous. If the person affected objects to the change, his word outweighs a majority.

In 1979 one boat group was consulting about redistributing corporation rights in conjunction with their plan to rebuild their boat, which they achieved only in 1982. One of their aims was to reduce the number of people who received shares, *umã*. When there are too many such shares, individual shares become inadequate. The number of *umã* in individual boat corporations ranges between about six to as many as fifteen. The boat in question then had eleven such shares. The harpooner, who was well placed because of his other rights in the catch, planned to surrender a share to his wife's brother. This gesture had a special meaning in terms of Lamaholot marriage alliance, but it also was intended to be a means of binding the second man more closely to the boat and thus encouraging him to continue to serve in the crew. The harpooner exercised by default an absolute control over the section called *tenarap*, which is commonly divided between the harpooner (to be transmitted by him to his parents) and the owner of the boat's great house. They were discussing again dividing this section between two persons. This is one of the boats which in the past had made the 'lower jaw' available to all members of the corporation; but they were contemplating reverting to the more common practice of dividing it between two persons. All of these suggestions were aimed at finding ways of expanding the corporation. For the most part, the beneficiaries would be members of the crew, but they also considered offering a share to a man in another village who helps supply wood for the boat.

Not all members of the corporation necessarily come from the same clan. When personnel is lacking, then individuals may be brought in from outside. As a result, some of the larger shares may pass down through lines in other clans. More commonly, however, outsiders hold rights in the sections called *bĕfãnã bélã* (large *bĕfãnã*) and *bĕfãnã kéni* (small *bĕfãnã*). Persons receiving shares from these sections do not derive from them a voice in the organization of the boat and the quantity of the meat is relatively small. However, these rights are generally distributed according to a characteristic and socially significant pattern, although there are exceptions. Recipients may include widows of former members of the corporation, or men who are related to the corporation through their wives, mothers, or sometimes father's mothers. It should be noted that it is the women to whom they are married who qualify the men for these shares, and these shares may be interpreted as a means of provisioning mature women born into the boat-owning descent group and the families of these women. The men are all categorically wife-takers. Because they are, as wife-takers, subordinate in standing, their participation involves no conflict of authority and they may also easily be asked to assist. Nevertheless, their participation secures them a right to receive the relevant portions of the boat's catch.

Small *bĕfãnã* (*bĕfãnã kéni*) is not recognized by all boats, and for some it seems an undifferentiated section for those who provide casual assistance on the beach. Some boats accord crew members, among others, this right to supplement their crew shares and as an inducement to continue work in the boat.

The previous description is limited in general terms to the shares held by members of the boat's corporation. Crew members get portions from a completely different part of the animal. In general the harpooner receives a distinct portion, and the man who provides the sail and the boat master also get a share of the same size as the harpooner. The boat master's share may be referred to as *téna-kajo umã*, that is 'the share for the provider of the boat's wood'.[4] These shares are vested in the sail maker and the boat master independently of whether they go to sea in the boat. It is quite usual for a sail maker not to go to sea, or to make up part of the crew of a different boat. Boat masters do not always go to sea either, especially if they are elderly. It should be clearly understood that what is in question here is the sail maker's and boat master's rights to participate in the crew section of the animal, independently of their rights in the corporation's section. For those who do go to sea in the boat for which they are master or sail maker, they earn an additional share as an ordinary crew member. Regardless of all other considerations, the remaining part of the section which goes to the crew is divided evenly among those men working in the boat, to the exclusion, as said, of only the harpooner, who has a special share.

A precise account of the distribution of the meat produced by the animals taken at sea requires treatment of the separate varieties of game.

Whale and Porpoise

The division of the various kinds of whale and porpoise differs primarily in the treatment of the head. In every case, the villagers make three primary divisions of the animal: (1) the head, (2) the fore part of the torso, and (3) the back part of the torso including the tail. The crew take their shares from the second section, while the corporation does so primarily from section (3). As for the head, that of the sperm whale is differently divided from that of the killer whale, primarily because of the presence of the spermaceti cask in the sperm whale's head, which is available to everyone in the village (see Plates 14–21).

The master builder for the boat which captured the animal, or for the first boat to harpoon it when several boats share in the capture, carefully marks each section, before the men who have the relevant rights begin to cut into the animal. They sever the whale head from the body between the atlas and axis vertebrae. Gregorius Keraf (1983) writes that the head of a sperm whale is divided into the following sections:

1. boat master (*bĕlāda alep*, i.e. 'lance owner')
2. crew member, or sailor (*mĕ̆ng*)
3. lord of the land (*lefo alep*), and
4. village (*lefo*), open to everyone.

PLATE 14. Killer Whale

PLATE 15. Sperm Whale

PLATE 16. Removing blubber from the torso of a Sperm Whale

PLATE 17. Cutting up Sperm Whale in the surf

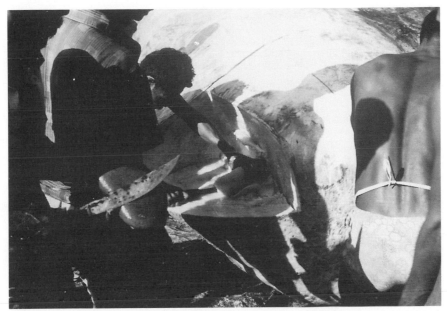

PLATE 18. Cutting into the spermaceti reserve in head of a Sperm Whale

PLATE 19. Slices taken from the tail of a Sperm Whale

PLATE 20. Women preparing to carry meat from the beach

PLATE 21. Whale and Manta Ray meat in a drying rack

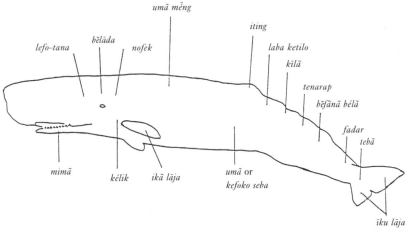

FIG. 15. Share locations in Sperm Whale

My information is somewhat different from this list (see Fig. 15). According to what I was told, the harpooner receives the flesh and blubber of the section called *nofek*, from the base of the skull towards the eyes by about one hand span. Elsewhere Gregorius Keraf (1983) mentions this section and describes it as being in the neck. This share compensates the harpooner for providing the bamboo poles for the harpoons, and he may use some of this meat to repay the man from whom he in turn gets the bamboo to make the poles. Above the eyes, the flesh and meat, called *bĕlāda* (lance), belong to the smith, who takes this piece from the side of the head, and the crew, who add the other side to their shares. The meat around the eyes on either side, as well as the brain, the skull, and the part of the *lefo-tana* ('village-land') section adjacent the eyes, go to the lord of the land. This is the same as section (3) above. The tip, which Gregorius Keraf indicates is *lefo* ('village'), belongs to the crew, but the rest of the *lefo-tana* section and the spermaceti reserve are free for anyone who wishes to take portions. Oleona divides the snout of the whale into crew (*mĕng*), and village (*lefo*), which is essentially in conformity with what I was told. Just behind that he places *lefo-tana alep*, for the lord of the land, again in essential agreement with Gregorius Keraf and myself. However, the lance section (*bĕlāda*) he moves just forward of the eyes, while he places *nofek* where I had indicated *bĕlāda*. He agrees with neither Keraf, nor myself, as to who gets *bĕlāda*. For Oleona it goes to the person who succeeded in finishing off the whale by stabbing it with the lance. Since few boats carry lances or make use of them in recent years, it seems reasonable to interpret these disagreements as representing divergent practices among the different boats. He does confirm that *nofek* goes to the harpooner.

Parts of the head of the sperm whale go to the lord of the land, so that he can store the soul of the animal in his temple. The expression for this is *lango ikã bĕlifu* ('the house contains the fish'). Mans Bataona (1974: 2) writes that the lord of the land may distribute portions of meat from this section to people who are too old to go to sea. Since there are two lords of the land, which one receives the relevant portions depends upon where the boat shed is located that belongs to the boat that first harpooned the whale, although Lango Fujo clan says that Tufa Onã has no traditional claim to the head of the whale and was only granted a concession by them in a period when whale were abundant. Boats located on the west half of the beach give the whale head to the lord of the land in Tufa Onã clan. Those with sheds on the east half of the beach do so to the lord of the land in Lango Fujo. In my first visit to the village in 1970, I was told that should a boat which has harpooned a whale get into danger, the boats of Bedi Onã should come to its aid. If it does so, it shares the relevant parts of the head with the clan that is lord of the land for the lower village, namely Lango Fujo. If no such case occurs, neither clan gets a share. They also said that Tufa Onã rarely receives the portion owing to the lord of the land from the boats on the part of the beach associated with the upper village. In fact it is often a boat of a different descent group which renders assistance, since everyone realizes that they have a mutual stake in standing by each other at sea, not to mention the fact that there are likely to be kinship ties of various kinds between the crew of any two boats. This reference to Bedi Onã is to be explained by the legend of its saving men of Lango Fujo from the wrath of Lefo Léin.

Gregorius Keraf remarks that the general pattern for dividing sperm whale is followed for all forms of whale, porpoise, shark, and marlin, but of course there are differences in these other species. In particular, the description just given of the division of the head of the sperm whale is peculiar to that type of animal. Neither lord of the land receives anything from the head of any animal except sperm whale. As Keraf remarks, for killer whale, pilot whale, *temu bĕlã*, and goosebeaked whales there is a different pattern in shares held in the head of the animal. The lower jaw is retained by those who have the general right to the share of this name. In the killer whale, etc., *nofek* again falls where it did in the sperm whale. The section around the eyes is *roi*, 'to see'. This part belongs to the person who first saw the animal at sea (*ñaé noi*, 'he sees'). The snout is divided into right and left halves. One side is 'lance' (*bĕlãda*) and goes to the man who provided iron for the harpoons, i.e. usually the boat master. He also gets teeth from the upper jaw, skull and skin about the eyes. The other half of the snout is called 'forehead' (*kenito*), and it belongs to the crew.

In porpoise, the head and brain go to the crew member who first spotted the animal. If one boat first spots the porpoise and another boat harpoons it, then the brain goes to the smith who forged the lance for the latter boat. In both kinds of whale and in porpoise, the smith's share, *nupã*, is located under the chest between the two pectoral fins, and stretches back to the tail division, which begins after the last rib. Gregorius Keraf, however, draws it as terminating just after the pectoral fins.

The torso, including the ribs, above this pectoral region, called the 'crews' share' (*umã mẽng*), is divided evenly among the crew on the principle given above. The corporation takes its shares from the rear part of the torso in the following order, 'shares' (*umã* or *kefoko seba*), 'chisel and peg' (*laba ketilo*), ring (*kīlã*), *tenarap*, and the large *bĕfãnã*. In keeping with his equating *kīlã* with *bĕfãnã*, Gregorius Keraf places *tenarap* immediately behind 'chisel and peg' and *kīlã* behind *tenarap*. The portion of the tail from which small *bĕfãnã* pieces are taken is called *fadar* ('tip'), nominally for those who help about the beach in pulling the boat up and down the shore. Of the tail fins, *īku lãja*, one goes to the boat, i.e. to the corporation. The other goes to the crew. Keraf writes that the fins *ikã lãja* go to members of the crew who cut the whale, while it was still alive. As Mans Bataona (1974: 3) writes, not every member of the crew is entitled to share in this section. The dorsal fin, *iting*, is divided among all of the crew of the boat. Between the tail fins is a section called *tebã* which belongs to the boat master. However, my information is that this section goes to whoever succeeded in finally dispatching the animal (which would not necessarily be the harpooner). One pectoral fin goes to the descent group great house, to pay for refreshments used in ceremonies and meetings connected with the boat. The other pectoral fin is the prerogative of the harpooner for providing the bamboo poles.

Oleona (1989: 45) writes that the tail fins, *faij*, are divided in the following way. The tip of the right fin goes to the crew member who held the harpoon rope taut while the boat was being towed by the whale. The tip of the left fin is used to finance repairs. The base of the tail fin is for the crew member who [may have] jumped on the back of the whale when it began to weaken in order to finish it off. In my experience, the fins are used for other purposes as well. Once when several boats landed a killer whale, the boat owner cut off the tail fins and divided them, so that the crew could eat them that night, instead of waiting until the next day, when the cutting up of the animal began in earnest. On another occasion, when men were cutting up a pilot whale, they cut off the dorsal and tail fins and divided them into slices, which they gave to small children who were playing on the beach.

The heart (*puo*) belongs to the corporation. The kidney, *kepa*, stomach contents, *onã-furã*, liver, *onã*, and lungs, *furã*, are divided in half with one half going to the corporation and the other to the crew. The penis (*folar*) may be taken by anyone who wants it. It is generally reckoned part of *fadar*, the whole being spoken of as *fadar-folar*. Blubber (fat) is *forã*, while oil is called *lala*. Spermaceti is 'oil in the head', *lala di kotã*, while the oil from blubber is 'oil in the skin', *lala di kãmã*.

Ray

In ray, the person who first saw the animal receives in addition to his normal crew share, the lower jaw, including the lower half of each of the ten gills. This person may be referred to as *roi* ('to see') *alep* (a possessive), as may the section he receives for this achievement. The two bailers (*fai matã alep*) divide the upper part of the head and upper part of the gills, *ikã ãng*. If on the same day, the crew catch more than one ray of the same species, such as *bĕlelã*, the bailers take this portion from only the first fish harpooned. Other crew members get the head from the second animal and still others from the third. In this way this right circulates among the crew. If the first ray is small and subsequent ones large, the bailers still received only the head from the first fish. However, if the crew captures ray of two or three different species, the bailers take the head from the first fish of each species. It is only from ray that bailers receive a special section, but it is a valued right. The meat of five gill sections from *bĕlelã* may be traded for one large tin of unhusked rice. The gills themselves may be exchanged for a quantity of palm wine. Gregorius Keraf (1983) writes rather differently that the bailers receive the projections extending in front of a ray's head (head fins), called by the villagers 'ears', *tilu*, less a certain portion called 'the interior of the ears', *tilu onã*, which goes to the person, often the boat master or the boat's master builder, who divides up the ray. He also writes that,

There are two sets of ray gills, one above, one below. Each set consists of two sections, right and left, each consisting of five pieces of vertebrae. Of gills of large manta ray, *bĕlelã* and *bõu*, the top, numbering ten parts, are given to the person who first saw the ray. If two people see it at the same time, both will get five parts. If more people see it simultaneously, or if the fish has already been seen and pursued by another boat, then all gills of the ray will be divided among all of the crew, including the ten parts of the lowers gills. The gills of all other species of ray are all divided among the crew. The first to see the fish does not get a specific share.

He continues to the effect that the cartilage, *tebõngã*, between the two 'ears' belongs to the bailers. The 'ears' themselves are cut off behind the eyes of the ray.

I take it that Keraf's description applies in particular to the boat belonging to his descent group, the *Nara Ténã*, and that the discrepancies here and elsewhere between his information and my own result from different arrangements in detail in different boats (see Fig. 16).

Mans Bataona (1974: 4) only writes that of the ten pairs of gills, five pairs are given to the first person to sight the ray. In smaller ray, the gills are divided evenly among the crew, including the sail maker and boat master. The cartilage in the head is divided evenly by the two boat bailers. Oleona (1989: 43) says, in agreement with my report, that the person who first sees the ray gets

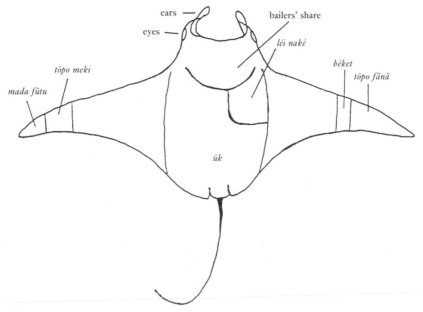

Fig. 16. Share locations in Manta Ray

the lower gills. However, the upper gills, *ang kotã lõlong*, he writes, are divided evenly among the crew.

The body of the ray may be separated into the fins, locally called 'sails' (*lãja*), and the trunk or *īku ūk*. The person in charge of dividing the ray carefully slices steaks, locally compared to planks but called 'tips' (*fūtu*). The smallest of these is called *sĕgépot*. The largest, that adjacent to the larger *tõpo*, is *béket*. These slices or steaks are stretched upon crossed bamboo sticks, which hold them open while they hang to dry. One such slice is quite valuable. Each crew member receives an equal share in these slices taken from the fins, with the following exceptions. The number of equal shares is the number of the crew who participated, plus one for the sail and one for the boat master, minus, however, a share for the harpooner and one for one of the crew. The last two are subtracted, because these two men receive larger than average shares (see below). The very tip of the left fin, called *mada fūtu* or 'tip of *mada*', the name for this part of the fin, is severed from the fish and then stored in the boat shed. The next time the boat goes out, the harpooner will sprinkle the tip with holy water in a brief ceremony before putting out to sea. The rest of the left wing tip, *tõpo meki*, goes to a different crew member with each fish caught, so that this privilege circulates among the crew. The man who receives it gets none of the usual slices, but the *tõpo* is just a larger slice. The tip of the right fin, *tõpo fãnã*, is the special prerogative of the harpooner. The right *tõpo* of the first *bĕlelã* (*Mantis birostris*) taken by a boat each year belongs to the church. Once one of the boats went for a period without catching anything and finally had to have a ceremony to patch things up with the church, because the boat master had embezzled this share. Each *tōpo* may be worth from three to five large tins of unhusked rice at, in 1979, *c.* Rp. 1,500 (or US $3.56) per tin. A small slice may bring no more than Rp. 1,000 (US $2.38) worth of rice. The harpooner also receives the slice adjacent to his tip (called *béket*), which is the right attached to the man who provides the bamboo harpoon poles and corresponds to *nofek* in whale.

Finally the harpooner receives a section from the upper portion of the body on the right side of the spine. This is called *léi naké*, wages for the feet. Figuratively, this section is payment for his ability to stand and balance on the harpooning platform, an essential skill for the success of the boat and its crew. It is noteworthy that he derives this payment from the part of the animal which belongs to the corporation.

The *ūk* or body of the ray belongs to all those who have a share in the corporation. The boat master and his group strip the meat from the cartilage, cut it and the large intestine up (*fāré*) and take it to the great house, where they dry and store it. The cartilage and liver are immediately divided among the corporation members for consumption. Gregorius Keraf (1983) says that the liver is in fact divided in two, one half for the crew to further divide among themselves, and the other half for the corporation members. The boat master saves the accumulated meat over a season and distributes it only in October or thereabouts when the season is at an end. Mans Bataona (1974: 5) has it that a quarter of the backbone goes to the person who has a right to the lower jaw in whale. The boat master dries the rest of the spine for later use in purchasing materials for maintaining the boat, such as caulking and wood for dowels. Ray is the only species in which the corporation's section is dried and stored for later distribution. In all other animals, the relevant shares are distributed immediately. Sometimes ray are captured which have unborn young. If the animal is large enough to be on the point of birth, it belongs to the crew, who divide it. A smaller foetus, however, belongs to the boat master, who divides it among the shareholders of the boat. The stinger, *kenaté*, goes in turns to members of the crew.

Ray meat is highly prized. It is especially good when thoroughly dried in the sun, and a large ray may provide a ton of meat. Unlike the villagers of Lamakera who do not utilize the cartilage and gills, the people of Lamalera employ every part of the ray, even the lungs, which Keraf writes become liquid, so that they are immediately taken by anyone who wants them. The meat on the chest is whiter than that on the back. It is much finer and it brings a better price, if sold. Therefore in the final division each corporation member is given equal shares of red back meat and white breast meat. Both, however, are excellent when dried.

Turtle

The large leatherback turtle (*Dermochelys Coriacea*), called *mobo*, and several varieties of smaller sea turtle called *kéa*, including the 'white turtle' (*kéa burã*), which is the loggerhead turtle (*Caretta Caretta*), and the 'red turtle' (*kéa méã*), which is the hawksbill turtle (*Eretmochelys Embricata*), are taken by harpoon. I have seen men bring in a turtle, cook it whole and eat it together at the beach. But I also acquired this description of the proper division of turtle.

The head and neck go to the crew member who first spotted the turtle. The boat master gets the shell and one front and one back flipper. Some say that corporation members who have the right to *tenarap* receive the very back, but there is sentiment to change this regulation in turtle because many feel *tenarap* holders get too much. Evidently for some boats this change has been made. The rest of the animal is shared equally by the crew, including the sail maker and the harpooner. One report said that master builder also receives a share. Mans Bataona (1974: 5) denies that members of the boat corporation get anything of the turtle, all meat going to the crew, including of course the sail maker and the boat master. Turtle, however, he claims are rarely caught at sea.

Turtles of all kinds sometimes lay eggs on the beach during the night. The urge to lay overcomes fear of humans. If a turtle is taken when laying eggs, the section for the boat-owning corporation goes to the lord of the land, that for the crew goes to the man who finds it. The latter will simply turn the turtle over to keep it from getting away. Leatherback turtles put up a big fight. Loggerhead turtles are easier to capture. Sometimes they do the job themselves by falling off a rock and turning over, which leatherback turtles never do.

Marlin and Shark

Marlin (*fẽta*) and shark (*io*) are divided somewhat differently from whale, although they generally do conform to the same model. The head of shark and marlin goes to the persons who bail out the boat. In marlin, the person who sees the fish first gets the fore underpart or pectoral section (*korok*), split along the line at which the skin changes colour from light to dark. The rear portion of the torso goes to the corporation, and the crew receive the top fore part of the animal. The corporation divides the tail as in the case of whale, that is, shares go to all the named rights, chisel and peg, lower jaw, *tenarap*, *umã*, and so on. According to Mans Bataona (1974: 3), the lower jaw section owed to a member or members of the boat-maintaining corporation is dispensed with and for it is substituted a section similar to that of other shareholders.

In the case of the hammerhead shark (*io naka*) and the white shark,[5] the person who sights it gets his special share from around the dorsal fin. According to Mans Bataona (1974: 4), for whale shark (*Rhinchodon typus* Smith), the person who first spots the animal receives gills, as is the case with ray. The division is as in marlin. For other kinds of shark there is no section for the person who first spots it. The crew cut up their parts of these animals while still at sea. The animal is not divided into right and left sides, but into top and bottom. If ten men get *umã*, five pieces are taken from the top, five from below.

The harpooner and the owner of the house with which the boat is associated get the right and left pectoral fins, respectively. This regulation is true for marlin, hammerhead shark, and white shark. Otherwise the fins belong exclusively to the boat master. Shark fins are valuable and may be sold on the island to itinerant merchants. In 1979 they sold locally at Rp. 2,500/kilo (US $5.94). Merchants disposed of them at Ujung Pandang (Macassar) to Chinese, who bought them there for Rp. 4,500–5,000/kilo (US $10.69–$11.88) for use as medicine.

Division is different when marlin or shark are taken on a line instead of harpooned. In this case, the owner of the fishing line gets the fins, the tail, and intestines. The rest of the fish goes to the crew of the boat, and the corporation gets nothing.

Sunfish

Sunfish (*Mola Mola* [Lin.]) are called *kebeku*. Sunfish receive yet different treatment. Sailors find the moist, white raw flesh a refreshing delicacy, especially on a hot and windless day. They are very large, and when a boat catches one, men cut off portions and share them around the boat. Nearby boats converge and demand portions too. If the crew are in the mood to do so, and they frequently are, they may take the good fortune of catching a sunfish as an occasion to buy palm wine at one of the coastal palm-tapping hamlets or groves, which they consume along with the fish either in the boat or at shore. There seems to be no special rights or system of division of sunfish. If a boat harpoons a whale and then a sunfish, the crew feel especially satisfied, no matter how far from home they may be.

11

Large Boats

The large boats used in Lamalera for deep-sea fishing and hunting are hand-made, planked double outrigger vessels of over ten metres length and just over two metres at their widest point (see Plates 22 and 23). These boats comfortably accommodate fourteen men. A bamboo platform extends a further 1.5 metres in front of the boat upon which the harpooner stands when throwing his harpoon. These boats are propelled either by a rectangular woven palm-leaf sail or by oars and paddles and are designated locally as *téna lama faij* (boats with places for rowers). In local eyes, they are to be distinguished from the *kora kora* common in the Muslim villages of the Solor Strait, a variation of the widespread *leteh leteh* (compare Gibson-Hill 1950: 128), relying exclusively on sail, or, nowadays, outboard motors.

Background

The name *kora kora* is usually associated with the great thin, but very long raiding boats of the Moluccas, of which Valentyn (1724: facing 184) gives a fine etching (Hornell 1946: 259, 267; MacKnight 1980: 124–5; Horridge 1978: 9–10; 1981: 4–7; 1986: 6–9). There is also an instructive etching of the structure of a *kora kora* observed at Kupang, Timor, in 1801 and another giving an external view and showing the position of the boat's occupants in Freycinet (1825: plates 24 and 37). Like the names *sampan* and *junk*, this term shows how readily boat names can be used to designate completely different boat types in different regions. The *kora kora* of the Solor Strait are wide-bodied, outriggerless, open boats of perhaps twelve metres length suitable for carrying passengers and freight. True *kora kora* of the Moluccan type, now extinct even there, were built according to the same technique as the whaling boats of Lamalera. In some respects, however, with their multiple rows, up to five, of paddlers they resembled the differently constructed trireme of the ancient Greeks (Casson 1991: 88). If Horridge is correct, the *kora kora* evolved away from the great war and raiding vessels with outriggers upon which rows of paddlers sat and became eventually cargo vessels lacking outriggers. This development could explain the present use of the term in the Solor region. True *kora kora* designed for warfare did reach Solor in the past. In fact the Butonese belatedly sent a fleet of *kora kora* to help the Dutch when they captured the Portuguese fort at Lohayong, Solor, in 1613, and the Dutch troops used for the attack were accompanied by a *kora kora* from Ternate (Heeres

PLATE 22. *Téna* searching for game

PLATE 23. *Holo Sapã* shifting its sail

1907: 104–8; Tiele and Heeres 1886: 14; R. H. Barnes 1987: 223). In Kluppel's time the boats of Lamahala, Terong, and Lamakera were also called *kora kora*, while Lamakera used a special type, called *perahu ayam* (chicken boat), to hunt whales. These boats were distinguished by having a bamboo tail about a fathom in length attached to the stern, which the harpooner could grab if he fell overboard (Kluppel 1873: 385). In the closely related Alor language spoken in a few coastal villages of Pantar and Alor, large canoes with a capacity of between four and fifteen cubic metres are called *téna kora kora*. These are very slender and fast and are to be distinguished from their double outrigger canoes, *bérog*, and fishing canoes, *kalaba* (Meulemans 1983: 300 n. 67).[1]

An indication of past Moluccan contact or influence is given by the name of one of the boats in the possession of Bedi Onã. This boat, rebuilt in 1987 after long years of inactivity, is named *Kelulus*. I was never able to obtain any explanation of this word. The answer surely lies in the fact that *kalulus* represents a type of boat in the Moluccas without outriggers, with twenty to fifty rowers and capable of carrying ten to twenty warriors (Jacobs 1971: 161, 163; Horridge 1978: 10). Of course this description does not apply to the present *Kelulus*.[2]

According to the people of Lamalera, Lamakera learned how to build their present whaling boats in the Lamalera style when they captured the *Sili Ténã*. The local version has it that Lamakera attacked *Sili Ténã* and the *Kebako Pukã* in the Solor Strait while they were on their way back from delivering tribute to Larantuka. The attack was provoked by deaths inflicted on them by Lamalera when they were fishing or trading at Bobu, Lembata. Lamakera captured everyone in the *Sili Ténã* and took them to Lamakera, where they killed them. They also killed one man of *Kebako Pukã*, but this boat came to shore in Tana Boléng, Adonara, and the rest of the crew was saved. Although the effect on Lamakera boat-building technique cannot be confirmed, the incident is independently documented in the report of the Resident of Timor for 1883. At the end of October in that year, according to this report, Lamakera killed eleven men of Lamalera in a ferocious manner. In order to prevent bloody revenge, the Dutch arrested the Raja of Lamakera and the village head (Hagestein 1883). Raja Bai Palembang of Lamakera and his Temukung (lieutenant and village head) Melang were deposed from office in January 1884 and exiled to Kediri and Malang, Java, respectively (Greve 1884).[3]

Construction Principles

The boat and all its gear as well as everything to do with it are indicated in Lamalera by a compound term made up from the word for boat and that for sail, *téna-laja*. Gregorius Keraf (1983) writes about the building of boats,

According to hallowed tradition, boats of the kind *téna lamafaij*, must consist in several important and indispensable divisions. If a part is missing the boat will only have bad

luck; there will be not enough fish for the clan members. The boat forms a world possessed of 'life', it is considered to have a soul when all conditions are completely fulfilled. Improper behaviour toward the boat, or behaviour towards others which does
not match the appropriate behaviour among the community, will have fatal consequences for the boat.

Conditions to be fulfilled in making a boat are not just concerned with the parts
which each boat must have, but also involve measurements, procedures for building,
and ceremonies before and after making each section. Also during construction the
thoughts and attention of all family members must be completely devoted to the boat.
There should be no quarrels (*uno narã*), nor should grumbling and disappointment
(*punek edã*) develop among clan members or among clans. Unanimity in discussion,
submission to the leadership and influence of the clan head, forms the principal condition for success in building the boat.

According to Oleona (1989: 11), the ancestors prescribed solidary behaviour
for members of the boat's corporation with the following expression.

> *onã tou, mata tou, kemui tou, kã tou*
> one mind, one eye, one cord, I eat one
> one attitude, one point of view, one family unity, one action

The strength of their feelings about their boats is indicated by a comment
a village head made to Bode. 'For us the *pledangs* [boats] are precious, like a
child to its mother; and therefore we give its parts names of parts of the human
body' (Bode 1925: 114). The Bugis use the same metaphor, according to Pelly.
'The Ara people create a ship as a mother creates a baby in her womb.'
Launching of a new ship represents birth, and the parts of the boat include
muscles and a navel (Pelly 1975: 60; 1977: 93, 102). At the keel ceremony, the
Bugis even require the presence of one or two pregnant young women (Pelly
1975: 25).

Horridge (1982: 53) asserts that the Lamalera boat is one of the few
surviving examples of a system, called the lashed-lug (cleat) method, which
was developed during the Bronze Age by Indo-Europeans. Hornell (1946:
199–213) has shown that the same method can be traced to pre-Viking and
early Viking boats (see also Horridge 1981: 52–3; Scott 1981: 7). The same
method was encountered and actually employed in the Philippines by Fr.
Alcisco Alcina, SJ, who described it in a Spanish manuscript of 1668, as yet
only incompletely published in English translation ('Historia de las Islas e
Indios de Bisayas'), from which Scott (1981) and Horridge (1982: 6–18) quote.
As demonstrated by Hornell, lashed-lug and dowel methods developed from
sewn planked boats with internal lugs and thwarts (cf. Horridge 1982: 1, 62).
While the Scandinavian vessels were clinker built (overlapping planks), the
planking of the Indonesian boats was flush-laid, fastened edge-to-edge.
The design, according to Horridge's summary (1982: 1) consists of the
following:

1. a shell constructed on the keel prior to the internal framework,
2. planks dowelled internally along their edges,
3. lugs carved on the planks to be lashed to ribs and thwarts,
4. flexible frames pressing the planks into position,
5. transverse thwarts lashed to the lugs and ribs, squeezing the hull together.

Horridge (1982: 51) describes this structure in the following terms:

The lugs on the planks are lashed to curved 'ribs' which are really tension bars, because each of their ends is drawn up by a twisted rotan [*sic*] lashing to the corresponding thwart that runs right across the sides of the boat.

Hornell (1920a: 59), who described this method for Ternate, commented that each strake or plank had projecting perforated lugs at intervals, coinciding with those above and below. The planks were first fitted together by vertical internal pegs, before the ribs were fastened over the projecting cleats, upon which they rested, separated from the hull by the thickness of the cleats (see Plate 24). 'By this device no metal fastenings are required; such a hull possesses great elasticity and stands bumping in the surf in a way that no metal-fastened boat would long survive.' The thwarts and ribs compress the planks, pulling them together from above and below The dowels prevent the planks from slipping and take shearing loads from torsional and bending stresses on the boat (Horridge 1982: 2). Horridge (1982: 59) says of this structure:

PLATE 24. Internal compression structure of a hull, including ribs, thwarts, stringers, and bindings

The shear forces between the planks are thereby not transmitted to the ends where they would burst the joint with the stem and sternpost. Compressing the edges of the planks against each other increases the friction. The whole hull becomes one rigid pre-stressed structure, like the moulded shell of a modern reinforced plastic hull.

Lamalera Boat Construction Sequence

Construction of a boat begins with shaping the keel, *gofal ié* (to turn or turn back the keel), in which the keel, *ié*, the stempost, *menula*, and the stern post, *kōlé*, are made ready. Once these are shaped, it is appropriate to hold a feast for all the traditional expert boat builders of the village or their descendants. Afterwards full-scale construction gets under way, beginning with fitting the sections of the keel, *hūba ié*. The 'mother' keel (*ié īnā*) is to be distinguished from the false keel, *ié māé*, of soft wood later fitted under it to protect it from wear when the boat is pulled up or down the beach. The false keel pieces may last from three to six months, depending on the strength of the wood, the frequency of use of the boat, and whether they are knocked off by game animals. The false keel is not fitted to a new boat until the mother keel has worn down some. Gregorius Keraf writes that an additional function of the false keel is to aid the boat in resisting the action of the wind. In principle the keel consists in three sections, *ié tūkā* (middle), *ié fā* (fore), and *ié uring* (aft). The sections are joined to one another by tenoned joints. The central section has a tenon on either end, the aft section only on the end toward the sternpost, while the fore section does so only on the end nearest the stem (Fig. 17 and Plate 25).

While the stem and sternposts are made of *Cordia subcordata*, Linn., *kena*, the true keel is made of *Vitex*, Linn., *kepapa*, and the false keel of *Schleichera oleosa*, *kalabai*.[4] The keel has a roughly hexagonal cross-section, and like the planks, the keel has lugs for the ribs (see Fig. 18a).

The middle section of the keel has a ridge running between the lugs at either end of the well which keeps the bailers from wearing the keel thin. When adjacent sections of the keel are finally fitted, they may be drawn tight by a strong binding made from a strip from the outer skin of the stalk of the lontar palm

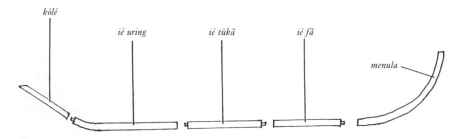

FIG. 17. Sections of the keel with stem and stern posts

PLATE 25. Preparing the keel

leaf (*pelepah* in Indonesian, *kelepa* in Lamaholot). This binding runs through
the hole of the lug adjacent to the connection on one section and around a peg
temporarily fixed upright in the other section. A stick is then inserted in the
loop and the loop twisted, forcing the sections together (Fig. 18). Sometimes
when a long piece of wood is available, they use only two in the keel, but false
ends must be carved to mark where the ends of the three sections are supposed
to be. The same must be done if more than three sections are used.

Extending backwards from the keel and free of the hull is a curved continuation called the *kōlé*. The word *kōlé* means the stem of a fruit. According to
Gregorius Keraf this expression is a metaphor suggesting that the boat is a
fruit which will provide food to its owners. It also has practical functions, such
as providing a place to grasp the boat to keep it straight in the surf. It also
serves as the toilet for the crew, when the boat is at sea. The *kōlé* tapers to the
end and is roughly triangular in cross-section, with the apex pointing down-
ward. On the *kōlé* rests the intricately carved *mādi* which terminates the highest
strakes in the stern of the boat, and on or against which the helmsman leans
while steering the boat (see Figs. 18, 20, and 21 in Ruth Barnes 1991). The
various parts of the *mādi* are distinguished as *kotã*, 'head'; *nafak*, body; *fẽu*,

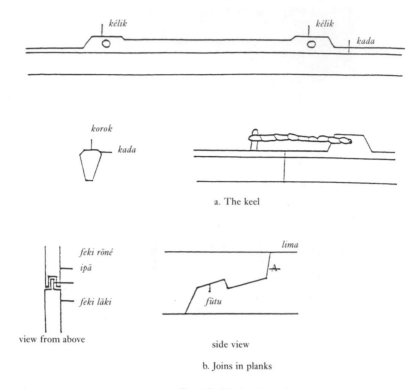

a. The keel

b. Joins in planks

FIG. 18. Keel and planks

the swirl; and *fŭlo*, the 'mast' which stands below *fĕu* (See Fig. 19 and Plate 26).

The bowsprit is called *menula*, from the *mula*, to erect, to plant. It terminates the bow extensions of the hull's planking and also provides a place for the harpooner or his assistant to lean when they need support. Some boats bore a hole diagonally from the right rear face of the *menula* to the right side. This hole represents the boat's ears, *tilu*.[5] Also a fingernail-shaped groove may be placed in the centre at the top of the *menula*, on the side nearest the boat. This groove is the boat's mouth, *fefã*. The elbow-shaped angle toward the base of the bowsprit is the *sarong*. The small area in the bow just behind the *menula* is the *ikã rã*, that is the fish's place, because this is the locus of activities to do with killing fish. A boat master showed me specifically a flattened-out boundary at the base of the *menula*, where the *bĕlobos* rests, which he said is *ikã rã*, marking the boundary of the boat. While the boats are in their sheds at shore, the *menula* is always covered with a sheath woven from lontar palm leaf, called *bĕlobos*. When the boat is about to be put out to sea, the harpooner removes the *bĕlobos* and usually hangs it in the shed to await their return. When the boats

PLATE 26. The *mādi* or decorated stern piece of a *téna*

are taken to Lobetobi, Flores, for extended periods of fishing there, they take the *bĕlobos* along.

Once the keel has been laid, work begins on the planks. Each plank (*ārã*) is named, though this generalization needs explanation. The planks on the port side of the keel have the same names as those to starboard. Work begins in the middle of the hull, so the names apply essentially to the planks there, most of which have extensions in the stern and bow. Horridge (1982: 60) therefore creates a misleading impression when he emphasizes the names of the planks in the bow, which are all merely extensions (*tenépa*) of the others. The plank on the starboard side is worked before the corresponding plank to port and both ends of the starboard plank are placed one palm breadth forward of the corresponding ends of the port plank.

With the foregoing understood, the pattern of planking is as follows (Fig. 20). That nearest the keel (the garboard strake) is the:

1. *ārã belikãng*, followed in order by, 2. *ārã kenãti*,
3. *ārã tūkã* (middle), 4. *nulu fūtu*,
5. *ārã bélã* (large plank), and 6. *néfi* and *nélu* (expands *néfi*).

On rare occasions, such as when bringing accumulated catch home after an extended stay at Lobetobi, Flores, they add a temporary strake of soft wood

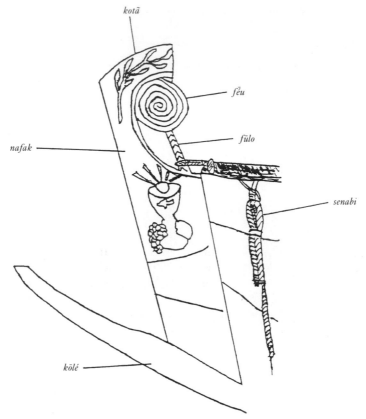

FIG. 19. Decorated stern piece

called *sasalāpi* (see Plate 47). There are extensions for 3, 4, 5, and 6. Bow planks are fore extensions, *tenépa fã*, of the corresponding strakes, while the stern planks are their aft extensions, *tenépa uring*.

The name of the *ārã belikãng* is explained as the plank which is continually submerged in water, in this case by water inside the boat from seepage (Gregorius Keraf 1983). It is the only plank which has a thickened shoulder or angle running its length. *Kenāti* is an adjective from the verb *gaté*, to hook, referring to its function in holding together the keel, a service, however, to which the other planks also contribute. *Ārã tūkã* means simply the middle plank. *Nulu fūtu* means the ends of the ribs. In fact the ends of the boat ribs correspond with the bottom of the top plank, not this one, and are tied to lugs of the second highest or fifth plank. The anomaly results from the fact that the boats anciently had only five strakes, but a sixth was subsequently added, thus distorting the pattern. According to Gregorius Keraf, the extra strake is the

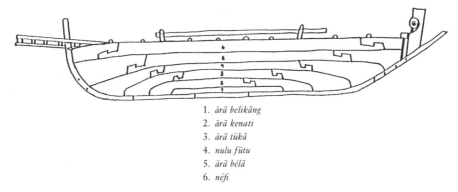

1. *ārā belikāng*
2. *ārā kenati*
3. *ārā tūkā*
4. *nulu fūtu*
5. *ārā bélā*
6. *néfi*

Fɪɢ. 20. The plank pattern

ārā bélā, the large plank and the last of those submerged when at sea. The last strake, and the one which is normally out of the water, is the *néfi*, or supplement. Where this plank or some part of it is not wide enough, it, as is also true of other strakes, may be supplemented with *nélu*, running the length of the boat or only as far as required. The top strake is made of softer wood of *Ceiba pentandra*, *fūka*,[6] while the others are made from water-resistant *Pterocarpus indicus*, Willd. When on returning from Lobetobi, Flores, they add yet another strake, *sasalāpi*, the outrigger booms, the upper thwart, and the harpooning platform must also be raised. The *sasalāpi* is made from a tree called *puo*, perhaps *Zanthoxylum myriacanthum*, Wall., the *kabu kabu hutan* or woodland Ceiba (Burkill 1935, vol. 2: 2284–5; Ridley 1922–5, vol. 1: 347). Neither *néfi* nor *sasalāpi* possess lugs. Both planks are held in place by means of the upper thwarts, *baut*.

For strength the ends of the top strake should encompass all the planks below. They correspond with the thwart between the first and second compartments in the bow of the boat and the thwart between the tenth and eleventh compartments in the stern. The ends of the *ārā bélā* are at the thwart between the second and third compartments and at the thwart between the ninth and tenth. The ends of both the *nulu fūtu* and the *ārā kenāti*, the fourth and second strakes, correspond with the fore outrigger boom and with the ninth compartment. The fore and aft extensions of *nulu fūtu* end, respectively, in the first and last compartments. The ends of both the *ārā tūkā* and the *ārā belikāng*, the third and first planks, are at the fourth and eighth compartments. The fore and aft extensions of *ārā tūkā* end in the second and tenth compartments. The second strake, *ārā kenāti*, is the only plank which must be divided (disregarding the extensions), at a point corresponding to the thwart between the sixth and seventh compartments. Keraf describes this arrangement by simply saying that this strake has an aft extension.

The effect of this pattern of planking is that the joints in each strake are overlapped by a solid piece of plank above it and that the top strake encompasses those below, a plan approximately followed by each plank below down to the keel. The structure therefore resists forces which might cause the sections of the keel and strakes to separate. The Lamalera pattern is rather different from that given by Pelly (1975: 91; 1977: 93), Horridge (1981: 78; 1979: 13), and Liebner (1993: 42) for south Sulawesi, and it is not strictly in accord with the Sulawesi prohibition on planks joining along a rib line.

The actual pieces of wood in the hull routinely vary from the ideal pattern. As is the case with the keel, the wood available may be too long or short to fit precisely as expected, and occasionally a large piece of wood can serve as an extension for two adjacent planks. The master boat builder in such cases carefully carves false ends on the hull, inside and out, where the ends of the planks should have fallen. These marks on the hull, and also those on the keel, are called *guã gaté*, or substitute marks, and are among several such marks in the boat (see Plate 27). There are also circular marks called *befajek* (betel basket) inside the boat on the keel, corresponding to *guã gaté* outside and showing where the keel piece should end. A line called *ūmã* runs up the sides inside the third compartment, marking the location of the drain hole (*ūmã*), which is bored through the keel and exits on the bottom side of the keel to the right.

PLATE 27. *Guã gaté*, substitute marks on the hull of the *téna* intended to deceive Sperm Whale into thinking the hull has been built according to the proper pattern

The *téna kepur*, boat's centre, is a line inside the hull in the well intended to mark the centre of the boat. Dowels may not coincide with either of these lines. The various marks are all essential to the boat. Tradition says that if a whale spots an imperfection in the construction of the boat, he will strike it at precisely that spot. The substitute marks are intended to prevent the whale from seeing where the nature of the wood available has forced the builders to deviate from the proper design.

Each section of the keel is made from a separate log, cut and brought to the village specifically for this purpose. Trees used in boat building must be traded for with people living in other hamlets well away from Lamalera. The trees are felled, branches lopped off, and then a groove is chopped lengthwise through the trunk with axes or large adzes. By working wedges into the groove, they eventually drive the halves apart. Splitting trunks in this way is *gīli kajo*. This job takes place on the site where the tree is found, which can be on the rocky sides of a hill or mountain, and it is very rough and exhausting work, involving much manhandling of heavy trunks wedged at awkward angles among the boulders. It is carried out by large parties of men and women who may be away from the village for two or three days.

Oleone (1989: 12) gives the following work song used when pulling the heavy tree trunks.

> *doro, sama doro*
> *kesuluro sama ula doro*
>
> crawl like crawling
> slide like a snake crawls

In the same place he also writes that while using rattan bindings to pull a trunk down to the shore they may sing

> *Kamé kéné-kéné sama kéi lēra matã*
> *Lēra feli géré kamé sokoto kaé*
> *Rié tobi ta kamé patalo kaé*
> *Tubu uaj o, uaj silaka-laka, oooooo . . .*
>
> We are very small like a dwarf
> The sun rising there we already prod it
> Post of asam wood pith we already try it
> Pull rattan o, rattan disaster
>
> We are as small as a dwarf
> Nevertheless we can prod the rising sun
> We try to split the asam pith posts
> We pull this rattan, but it brings us disaster, ooooo . . .

Before bringing the planks back to the village, they shape them roughly, leaving them nearly twice as thick as required. Planks are cut from large trunks, and because of the way the wood is roughed out and the need to leave wood for lugs, a single tree trunk can be used to provide only two planks. The centre of the trunk becomes the outer hull, while they adze down the curved outer trunk, leaving protrusions at specific places for the lugs, called the plank's armpits, *arã kélik*. Using a lontar-leaf measure, *tenutu*, they estimate where the lugs should be located and leave projecting blanks for them which are much thicker and longer than the eventual lug. Such roughed out planks are often stored for years awaiting the next occasion of rebuilding. Naturally, the seasoned wood is better, but nowadays much of the wood used is freshly cut.

When boat building begins in earnest, the planks are carefully cut and shaped to fit the need. This process requires much lifting the plank in and out of position, and many hands help. The master builder takes a blackened cord to mark the line for the bottom edge of the plank, where it is to fit against the keel or top of the plank below it. This cord, much like a bricklayer's chalk line, is the *kedolu*. At this stage he merely estimates by eye the position of the line. Excess wood is then removed with an adze. This roughing in the shape of the edge is called *bokil ãrã*. Once the fit is approximately correct, the final shaping begins, called *pili ãrã*. For this stage they bore holes in the two adjacent edges. Into the edges of the keel or lower plank they insert temporary dowels made of a soft wood called *kũgu*, *Schoutenia ovata* (*kayu kukun* in Indonesian; see Verheijen 1984: 66), which are called *ketilo bĕropong*. The plank being worked is then positioned on the dowels. The edge will not yet be flush; in places the planks touch, elsewhere there are gaps.

The master builder now uses a two-pronged device (known in English as a marking or mortise gauge) looking rather like a narrow tuning fork in which one prong is shorter than the other. This tool, called *naga* (dragon), has the same purpose as those depicted by Horridge (1981: 78; see also Scott 1981: 13) for Madura and Sulawesi, but a different form. The builder inserts the lower, longer prong of this device into the space between the planks, while the shorter end presses against the outside of the upper plank. By moving the *naga* along the edges of the adjacent planks, the builder can estimate by eye where further wood needs cutting away or by blackening the shorter prong he can mark the excess. A smaller version of the *naga*, for finer work, where the upper prong is a pencil tied loosely to a sliver of bamboo is called *ruki*. They repeat the process of comparing and shaping the edges, progressively improving the fit. They also blacken the top edge of the keel or, as the case may be, lower plank, which leaves precise marks on the edge of the plank being shaped, where the two touch. Careful application of the *naga*, blacking, and so on, as well as removing the plank two or three times, allow them to refine the fit further until it is sufficient. When the edges are reasonably flush, they again blacken the edge of the lower plank and force the planks tightly together by means of a twisted (*pelepah*) lashing from the skin of the lontar palm leaf stalk. This fastening, *fajo*, is looped tightly under the boat and bound to either end of a

PLATE 28. *Fajo*, fastenings from palm branch skin being used to force planks tightly together

branch laid across the boat over the top of the planks. As can be seen from Plate 28, the two ends of the fastening are restrained from slipping off the branch by another binding looped around them and running across the boat under the stick, into the ends of which are driven wedges, *pĕrĕka*, which expand the branch and tighten the bindings. The bindings can be further tightened by inserting a stick into them on either side of the boat and twisting them (*guté tenulaj*). Alcina describes precisely the same technique in the Philippines (Scott 1981: 14). Showing long carpenter's clamps borrowed from the mission workshop, a master builder commented that this device was the traditional equivalent of metal clamps. Indeed, by this means they can exert tremendous force on the planks, and when these are removed the soft temporary dowels are often crushed. The technique is also generally better suited to the awkward shapes in boat building than rigid steel clamps. The same technique is repeated when the planks are fitted over the permanent dowels.[7]

After this compression, any remaining pressure points are clearly marked in black on the edge being shaped and can be trimmed away. By this process the planks are formed not so much to some ideal shape (the substitute marks largely account for that), but are carefully made to fit adjoining planks. The seam between planks is not perfectly straight or level, but can be quite irregular, yet the fit is perfect. The substance used for marking and blacking formerly was burnt coconut husks or charcoal mixed in water. Today they use the carbon core of flashlight batteries. Planks and their extensions are fitted to each other by a tongue and groove arrangement (see Fig. 18b). The tongue is called *ipã* (tooth).

The side with the tongue is the male or *feki lāki*, the other with the slot is the female, *feki rōné*. Seen from the side, strakes and extensions do not join in a straight line, but are interlocked. The arrangement is a form of lock scarf, a technique employed in early Egyptian and Phoenician ships (Kemp 1976). From the point of view of plank A in Fig. 18b, the extended tip is *fūtu* and the recessed end *lima* (hand). The whole pattern, *fūtu-lima*, helps prevent the boards from pulling apart horizontally.

The eventual permanent bindings holding the frame of the boats to the planks are also made of *pelepah*, not rattan which is used in other parts of Indonesia and which Horridge attributed incorrectly to Lamalera. Rattan, *uaj*, like bamboo, has joints and internodes, while *pelepah* is smooth.[8] In preparing *pelepah*, they strip the skin off of the lontar branch. The strips are a centimetre or two wide. They use the resulting skinned branches for making fences to protect plants from pigs. The strips still have some of the inner wood attached when taken from the branch, and they scrape them down to remove this wood. Only the thick outer skin therefore serves as bindings. These *pelepah* bindings will be strong for a couple of months before needing replacing. Replacement goes on all the time, as soon as anything loosens, rather like the constant repair of sails; so there rarely is need to make a complete overhaul. It is only the lontar palm which provides these *pelepah* bindings. The coconut, they say, is not strong.

The tops of planks are essentially flat, though slightly slanted. The bottom of planks, however, are slightly grooved in recess to accommodate and hold fibre, *rapo* (in Indonesian called *ijuk*), of the sugar or areng palm, *Arenga pinnata*, Merr. or *Arenga saccharifera*, Labill., used as caulking. The areng grows only in the mountains, and the black fibre must be obtained from people living in inland villages. It naturally has a dusty look and feel, like black lint, and derives from the trunks and branches of the areng palm branches. Alcina describes exactly the same use of this fibre as caulking in the Philippines (Scott 1981: 13). The fibre is placed along the edge of the plank, which is wetted with water or greased with sap of *Aloe Vera*, Linn., just before it is finally placed over the permanent dowels.[9] In newly built boats, they commonly insert between the planks decorative strips of cloth, which eventually disappear with wear and age.

Normally they work and fit the starboard strake before the port, thus the starboard *ārã belikãng* before the port *ārã belikãng* and so on. The permanent dowels, *ketilo ama*, are made of water-resistant sappan or brazil wood (*Caesalpinia Sappan*, Linn.), called *hēpa* locally.[10] In locating the holes for the dowels along the keel, they begin by marking the position for the dowel on either side of the mark, *kepur*, for the centre of the boat, moving out from there. By tradition the first two dowels must be very loose in the boats built by the Běliko Lolo clan. Since the dowels are internal, their location must be marked by small vertical lines, *kéni*, on the outside of the hull.

Such lines, and the dowels that they mark, may not be directly above or below each other, but must be offset. If they are wrongly arranged, whales will strike the boat at that point and stave it in. In fact some dowels are fixed by pins, *běrã*, also of sappan wood, stuck into them perpendicularly through the hull. At each end of a plank there are three or more pinned dowels. Those without pins are *ketilo olung* (ordinary dowels), those with pins *ketilo běrã* (assisted dowels). The planks in principle are staggered, and *ketilo běrã* of one board should be above *ketilo olung* of the board below. The lower pins are fixed into the dowels before the upper plank is placed over the dowels, but they wait until the planks have been forced together with the *pelepah* clamp before inserting the upper pins. There are also very large dowels called *madil* which go through the keel and stem into the hull. Dowels may not coincide with *kepur* and *ūmã* lines.

The decorative stern piece, *mãdi*, may be put in after the aft extension of the *nulu fūtu* or fourth strake. The decorations are usually done before the big final festival. When all the strakes have been put in place, then the internal ribs and thwarts, and so on, are lashed into position. Next they provide palm wine and a small meal to attract labour for smoothing off the final excess wood on the outside of the hull.

At this stage they also burn the knots in the wood of the hull, *kajo matã*, with a red hot iron. This is done, they say, to fix them and keep them from falling out, but there is also a tradition that the purpose is to prevent whale from seeing them, *ikã aké nãé noi*. I have no evidence that they are specifically concerned to avoid joins in planks coinciding with knots, as are the Bugis (Pelly 1975: 30; MacKnight and Mukhlis 1979: 276–8; Horridge 1979: 15), although it would be reasonable to assume so.

Internal structure is provided by a set of thwarts and thick inflexible ribs. The ribs, *nulu*, are cut from wood naturally growing in the appropriate shape and are bound to the lugs in the strakes between the boat's compartments. According to Gregorius Keraf (1983), the ribs are made of *Vitex*, Linn., *Grewia*,[11] or a third, unidentified wood called *kelika*. The lower thwart, *tekã*, abuts the upper strake, *néfi*, on either side and lies adjacent to and just in front of the rib. Its ends are fastened with large dowels to the lugs in the *ãrã bélã*, the fifth strake, made extra long to accommodate both rib and thwart. The lower thwarts, according to Gregorius Keraf, are made from *Vitex*, Linn. or *Cordia subcordata*, Linn. The upper thwarts, *baut*, rest on the top of the uppermost plank of the hull, but are bound to the ribs. They are made from *Schoutenia ovata*. The two outrigger booms function also as thwarts in their positions, and the bases of the mast slip over the ends of the thwart, *puang uli* (place of the mast), next behind the front outrigger boom. The combination of thick inflexible rib, lower thwart, and upper thwart or boom occurs ten times in the boat, dividing it into its eleven compartments.

The outriggers, *ēlé*, are spaced close to the hull (varying between a third and a half-metre from it), where they do not provide much lift, except when the boat is canted strongly over while the crew heaves an animal into the boat. According to Gregorius Keraf (1983), their function is not to provide equilibrium, but to shield the side of the boat from a blow by a whale's tail, to provide a support while pulling animals into the boat, and to provide a hand hold when the boat is being brought up or down the beach. A wooden pin, *gélo*, is inserted in the stern end of either outrigger, transfixing it from left to right, to enable the outrigger to be strongly lashed to the boom. The outrigger may be made from a type of unidentified wood called *geru* or from *Schoutenia ovata*.

There are five bamboo poles or stringers, *lada*, running the length of the boat and resting on the ribs, to which they are lashed. These distribute the force of a blow to the hull throughout the length of the boat. The lowest stringer, just above the keel, is interrupted at the well, so as not to interfere with bailing. In addition to the inflexible ribs, there are flexible ribs, called *téna kenafang* (boat ribs), made of naturally curved branches cut from a suitable tree of no specific species and tied only to the stringers. They are much thinner than the inflexible ribs.

Underneath the upper thwart between the well and the seventh compartment, on the starboard side there is a curved, thick piece of wood called *kūmi* (beard) tied at either end to the rib. The end of the backstay for the mast is permanently tied around the *kūmi*. On either side of the boat under both outrigger booms are short boards bound at either end to the rib or the boom. This arrangement is called *oi laké*, male bindings. The purpose of this arrangement is to strengthen pieces which have to be stronger than the hull.

Inside the bow, at the very front on either side are two lugs, bound to each other. In the stern, just before the *mādi*, over the top strake, is a plank or stick. Holes in either end accommodate a thick *pelepah* or rope binding that runs around the hull and through a hole in the sternpost. This arrangement, called *senabi*, compresses the stern, keeping the planks from separating. The *mādi* is also bound to this stick (see Fig. 19). The seat for the helmsman rests on a raised wooden frame carved out of the planks in the stern section.

On either side of the compartment from the bow above the top strake is a frame of branches, *kada-fali*, to which are tied the large oars, *befaja*, and for which they provide support on operation. The lower, horizontal branch, *kūgu* (named after the wood from which it is made), extends through the first section along the top edge of the top strake, where it serves also as a runner for harpoon ropes, when an animal has been harpooned.

Projecting over the bow of the boat is a harpooning platform, *hãmã*, consisting of four bamboo poles, two on each side, bound together by short planks. The poles, about four and a half metres in length, extend through the first three compartments and abut the forward outrigger boom, the ends fitting into slots carved in the front side of this boom. The greater length of these poles, roughly three metres, lies therefore in the boat, and they extend only about one and a half metres ahead of it (see Fig. 24). The stem extends through the plat-form. The platform rests on a crosspiece just behind the stem called the *bĕlīna*, a word which means quiet or calm. Just in front of the stem is a crosspiece where the harpooner sits, *lama fa tobo*. Two further crosspieces are *kĕrāki*, and fourth as well as furthest forward is *rauk fūtu*.

As the harpooner regularly rests the base of his harpoon pole on the *rauk fūtu* in certain stages of the chase, this board is commonly provided with fea-tures designed to keep the end from slipping. There is much variation, some boats using an exposed peg, a raised ridge, a circular hole, or some combina-tion of these. Some are simply decorated with various patterns. The *rauk fūtu* slots into the bamboo poles on either side, while the *kerāki* and *lama fa tobo* are bound to the poles by *pelepah* lashings. The poles of the platform rest on the *bĕlīna* and on the two upper thwarts in front of the outrigger boom, to which they are bound with the same material.

The Mast

Lamalera employs a movable bipod mast, consisting of two bamboo poles joined at the top by a single, forked piece of wood. The mast poles are *puã méki* (port) and *puã fãnã* (starboard). The poles themselves are about seven metres long. Into their bases are inserted large wooden fixtures called *puang (uli) léi* (see Fig. 21). These act as pivots and are perforated with holes, permitting them to slip over the ends of the thwart called the *baut puang uli*, where they are lashed into place. These wooden extensions also serve to prevent the ends of the bamboo from splitting. The ends, top and bottom, of the bamboo are further strengthened with a woven ring made of *pelepah* or rattan. They are made of *Pterocarpus indicus* Willd. or *Vitex*, Linn. The pivots are inserted about fifteen to twenty-five centimetres into the poles. On the side which faces the interior of the boat there is an arrow which helps them to erect the mast without turning it around. When the mast is up, each arrow should be toward the inside of the boat. One or two dowels, *ketilo*, are driven through the bamboo into the wood to prevent the poles from twisting around. A small rope on either side called *kabi* is fixed to the upper thwart and used to lash the base of the mast poles to the ends of the thwart.

The forked, wooden termination to the mast poles, the *ōrã*, slips inside the top of the poles (see Fig. 21). From the base of the pivots to the very top of the *ōrã* measures over seven and a half metres. Just under the *ōrã* is a cross-piece of wood which holds the mast poles together and which is called *ida*. Loops in the ends of the forestay, *beléu fã*, and backstay, *beléu uring*, slip over the top of the *ōrã*. The two *beléu* are woven from gebang palm leaf and the

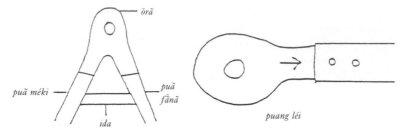

FIG. 21. Top and base of the bipod mast

bark of *Hibiscus tiliaceus* and have a circumference of 7.7 cm. Next a rope called *menāmi* passes through the hole in the *ōrā*. This rope, which is tied to the yard and is used for lifting the entire sail, including yard and boom, once the mast is erect, is properly called a jeer in English (Kemp 1976: 428, 711). It is made of gebang palm leaf and the bark of *Hibiscus tiliaceus* and has a circumference of 6.7 cm. On the front of the *ōrā* a thin vertical lug, *ōrā kélik* (arm pit of the *ōrā*), is left which is pierced laterally with a hole. In order to prevent the *ōrā* from pulling out of the mast poles, they run a cord through the hole in the *ōrā kélik* and tie it around the *ida*. If the mast is too upright, the boat will sail more slowly. The next time they raise the mast, they may correct this problem by leaning the mast more forward, helping the lift. When they take the masts down, they leave the *menāmi*, although tied to nothing, looped around the *ōrā* and store the *menāmi* with the masts and stays.

The Sail

The sail, *laja*, is made of twenty to twenty-four square sections across and eleven to thirteen up. Each section, *laja mātā*, is woven on a special frame, *selaga*, from gebang palm-leaf strips (see Plate 29).[12] The sails are easy to repair. By dividing the sail thus, the sail maker can unroll it on the beach each day after the boat has returned and make repairs section by section. By repairing a few sections every day, he can keep the sail in working order without ever having to engage in major repairs. The structure of the sail also prevents major damage, since a small tear will be confined to a single square and will never rend the entire sail. The sail therefore retains its strength even when damaged. According to Oleona (1989: 17), the cords framing each square automatically adjust the sail to the force of the wind. A strong wind billows the sail out, opening space between the squares through which pressure is released. With a weak wind these holes close and the sail holds the force of the wind better. The boat can sail in a strong wind with the sail completely unfurled without risk of turning over. Of course the networks of cords within the sail provide essential strength. Although the ancient sailors of the Mediterranean usually

PLATE 29. Weaving a section of the sail

used linen in their sails, the structure of the sail itself was very similar to those of Lamalera. It consisted in square or rectangular pieces of cloth sewn together and protected along the edges by boltropes (Casson 1991: 193–4, plates 42 and 45; see also the reconstructed sail in plate 30).

The sections of the Lamalera sail are approximately 28 to 30 cm. on each side. As the sail ages, the size of the square increases. I measured one long disused sail which was serving as an awning and found that it had stretched to the point that its squares measured 35 cm. by 40 cm. One sail maker reduced the size of his *selaga* by cutting off the base and then readjusting the rest. When I asked why, he said that he had decided to use smaller squares in the sail. With the larger squares he had been able to replace only about ten in a day. With the smaller ones he could get through as many as nineteen. I once casually timed a sail maker working at the beach and concluded that it took him about half an hour to weave a single section. The overall shape of the sail is rectangular. The largest sails are about 7 metres wide and nearly 4 metres from top to bottom edge. The sail is suspended from a yard, *kelatã lõlo*, and supports a boom, *kelatã lẽi.*[13] The yard and boom measure *c*.7.9 metres in length. The jeer is tied to the centre of the yard, and a mark called *kelara* on the yard shows where the best balance is attained. If this rope is not tied to the *kelara*, the boat will not get its best speed. Because the sail is suspended from the centre of the yard, the sail swivels when moved from side to side, the left being down when the sail is on the starboard side and vice versa. The cord around which the edges of each square of the sail are wrapped is *kelura*. The rope which frames the sail is the *peré* (corresponding to the bolt rope in canvas sails), which is bound to the yard and boom by a cord called *senégat* which loosely loops around the yard or boom and the knots where *kelura* are tied to the *peré*.

At either end of the boom are wooden extensions made of *Schoutenia ovata*, to which are attached two ropes, *menuli*, with loops at either end. One loop attaches to the boom; the other is available for slipping over the end of a stick, *nubit*, which runs fore and aft through the third compartment, emerging in the fourth under the front outrigger boom to which it is loosely bound. There are two *nubit*, one on either side. When the sail is on the left side, the *menuli* on the right end of the boom is looped over the left *nubit*, while the *menuli* on the left end of the boom hangs free in the air. When the sail is on the right, the ropes are reversed, with the *menuli* from the left end of the boom looped over the right *nubit*. This procedure holds down what is in effect the bottom corner of the sail. Pressure from the sail pulls the *nubit* tight against the fore outrigger boom. Some boats vary this arrangement by tying a short rope to the thwart, the other end of which has a wooden hook, which they then hook into the loop of the *menuli*. There are four sheets, *ĩfi*, suspended from the ends of the yard and boom (distinguished as *ĩfi lōlo* and *ĩfi léi*, depending upon whether they are attached, respectively, to the yard or the boom). When the sail is on the left, and the left side of the sail is highest, the sheet from the left end of the yard is run down and bound to the aft outrigger boom on the right side, while the sheet from the left side of the boom is run down to the left side of the aft outrigger boom. The two sheets from the right side of the sail are coiled and hung over a wooden hook, *tenigi*, fixed half-way down the forestay. The position of the sheets shifts correspondingly when the sail is on the right and the right side of the sail is uppermost. When tacking they untie the upper sheet from the aft outrigger boom and release the lower sheet and *menuli*. The upper and lower sheet then have to be handed around the masts, while the sail swings around and the boat turns away from the wind. The harpooner's assistant usually handles the sheets in the bows, but the harpooner or another may also do so too. The two men sitting in the section in front of the rear outrigger boom tie and untie the sheets there. They can sail into the wind at only a very shallow angle. This means that when going against the wind they must rely on rowing and the aid of favourable currents. Only the steering oar can bring the boat into the wind, but it can do so only when the crew row to give the boat momentum, which they will do while hunting. They let the sheets loose, and the sail swings around fore and aft where it flaps. If it causes too much trouble, for example when chasing a large animal, they take it down.

The forestay, *beléu fã*, is tied to the lower thwart between the second and third compartments and then bound over the upper thwart and harpooning platform poles at this point. The jeer sustaining the sail is brought down the mast on the port side and looped over the end of the upper thwart at the base of the mast. The backstay, *beléu uring*, runs back to the upper thwart just aft of the well where it is permanently tied to the thwart and the *kūmi* under it.

When the sail is taken down the harpooner or other crew member in the bow inserts a marlin spike, *menūla*, into the ropes at the lower corner of the boom and twists to roll the sail while someone loosens the jeer and lowers the sail. The sheets and both *menuli* are rolled up inside the sail, which when fully rolled is bound by short cords suspended from the yard about a metre or so in length and called *kemui*. These correspond to gaskets for the sails of square-rigged ships (Kemp 1976: 332, 339). The jeer is untied and the sail temporarily placed on the two *nodé*, which comprise the rack for the harpoon poles. The forestay is loosened and then the mast lowered into the boat until it is horizontal, when the bases are removed from their pivots. The mast and sail are stored in the centre of the boat and rest on a fork called *nagat* inserted upright in the centre of the upper thwart between the ninth and tenth compartments. The *nada* and the *nodé* may be used to rest the sail when it is taken down on the left or right side, respectively. Once the sail is rolled up, it is rested in one or the other of these, to free their hands so they can get the mast down. Once it is down and laid in place in the centre of the boat, they then move the sail to its place in the centre of the boat where it rests on the *nagat*.

Weaving the Sail

The mature leaf of the gebang palm is a fan composed of several segments symmetrically arranged on spines extending from the centre of the leaf. Each section of the leaf, *ketebu lolo*, is attached to the adjacent section for a distance outwards from the centre until a point where they grow apart. Such a leaf can be pulled apart first by separating each of the sections, then splitting each section along the spine, leaving two long strips and a useful thin spine, *ketebu riuk*. A bundle of spines may be used as a broom. The young gebang leaf shoots used for sail making, *ketebu nubu* (shoot) *menuré* (young), are compressed bundles of as yet unexpanded leaf when they emerge from the trunk of the palm. The shoots are chosen for their suppleness, but a coincidental advantage is that they are compact and therefore much better suited for transport and storage.

The sail maker will prepare his supplies of this material by first splitting the leaves apart, then carefully scraping them, *leli*, so that they become thin and flexible and then cutting them into strips, *kenema*. Each of the strips eventually used is about a third the width of the strip taken from one side or other of a spine, just under a centimetre. It is cut so thin to keep it from curling up. The sail maker rolls the prepared strips by means of a marlin spike, *menūla*, in a flat spool, *gaol*. The roll gives the impression of one continuous length of material, like tape; but of course it consists of many strips, each about the

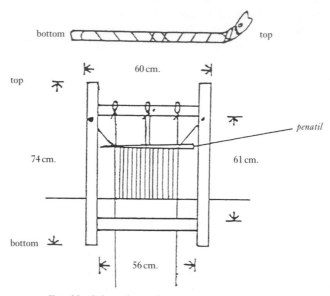

FIG. 22. *Selaga*, frame for weaving sections of a sail

length of the leaf from which it was cut, something like a fathom. The purpose of winding the strips on the roll is to flatten them so that they will be even.

Before the sail maker begins weaving a section of the sail, he cuts out the old pieces of matting. One sail maker whom I was watching work gave his young granddaughter some discarded sail squares and a roll of gebang strips for the black sections he was working on. She took them down to the sea, threw away the scraps, and soaked the roll before bringing it back. The soaking made the gebang more flexible and easier to work. Typically the sail maker leaves the scraps lying on the sail, where they stay when he rolls up the sail again. It is a common and picturesque sight to see the remains of the repairs on the sail flutter out of the sail into the sea when it is unrolled as the boat first puts out the next morning.

The frame used in weaving the sail is somewhat larger in outline than the squares it is designed to produce and is called the *selaga* (see Fig. 22). This name is also used for the frame which holds the threads which are being tie-dyed for a sarong. The sword used to guide the strips through the square and to tighten the weft is called *nefã* (it catches). The sail maker uses two of these, a larger one, of 46 cm. length, for the main work and a thin one for when the going is tight at the ends. The *selaga* overlaps the adjacent squares on either side as well as top and bottom by several centimetres. The top of the frame curves up, presenting a convenient slant to the weaver. In setting up to weave a new square, the sail maker moves the *selaga* into position, then loops the two cords on either side of the *selaga* through the upper corners of the square formed by the *kelura* (frame cords of the sail) and around the *penatil*, a loose stick of 46 cm. length, before tying them to the top of the *selaga*. The bases of these cords are fixed through a hole on the sides of the frame. The holes for these cords open on the top of the frame. Here the cords are knotted. But each hole emerges on the inner face, through which the cord passes. A third cord fixed in a similar fashion in the centre of the top of the frame is looped around the centre of the *penatil* and fastened at the top of the frame. The *penatil* is a round, thin stick—larger for a *téna* sail, thinner for a *béro* sail, although these days the latter are almost always made of cloth. These three cords are said to have no special name. The warp strands, *nekat* (from *neka*, to store) are wrapped around the side of a good square at one end. At the other end the warp strands are warped around the stick tied into the frame, *penatil*. The *penatil* must go to the right. That means its base is on the right, tip on left. Warp strands run in the direction from top to bottom of the frame (see Plate 29).

The frame is held tight, but not too tight. The aim is to get a reasonable square. The warp strands loop twice around the *kelura* at either end on each pass. The last pass then goes through the side *kelura*, so that warp and weft are continuous. There are no regulations about the number of strands in the warp or the weft; they may be an odd or even number. Setting up the warp strands is *pano*. The bamboo guide for the strips is called *nefã*. The weft strands are *tanã*, from *tané*, to weave. This name contrasts with the expression for the weft strands in cloth, *beloé* from *loi*, to strip off, to loosen, to free (Ruth Barnes 1989: 36; Gregorius Keraf 1978: 78). The weaving is done from the bottom of the square. The sail maker pushes the *nefã* carefully through the warp, beginning by going over the first warp strand and then under the next, and so on. When it is in place, he turns it around once. This pushes the last weft strand tightly into its place against the others. Then he slips the tip of the weft into a slice in the *nefã* and pulls the *nefã*, guiding the weft through the warp. He then wraps the weft strand once around the frame string (*kelura*) in the next free place, and again in the following free space. Then he passes the *nefã* through from left to right. This is easier this time. The stick is just put in through at the top of the warp strands. Then the procedure is repeated on the other side. When he completes weaving the weft, he weaves the last strand half-way through, bends it over and weaves it back into the warp.

Since the strips of gebang leaf are around a fathom in length, after a strip has passed through three or four times, the next one must be added. This is done by folding and wrapping. Adding one piece to another is called *bokel ketebu* (literally, to extend the gebang). The procedure is as follows. The new strip B is placed perpendicularly under the end of the old one A. Then B is folded under three times (see Fig. 23*a*). This folding produces a compact little bundle around B. B2 is then folded over in a perfect loop, without twisting, so that it continues in the same direction as A. B1 is now bent over B2 and stuck

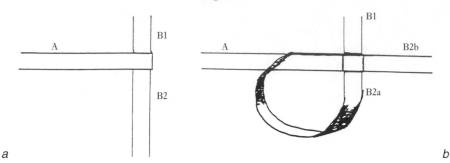

FIG. 23*a*, *b*. Extending a gebang palm-leaf strip while weaving a sail section

through the bundle underneath B2 (see Fig. 23*b*). The bundle is now held firm with the thumb, while B2a is pulled to tighten. Then B2b is pulled tight to complete the operation.

Sail Decorations

The sails of several of the boats are individually decorated to distinguish them, and this individuality often makes it possible to identify a boat at a distance (see Appendix V). The sail of the *Soge Ténã* carried a distinctive pattern in 1979 consisting of two upended rectangles opposite each other in the centre. These were made up of indigo-dyed squares, but were very faded and hardly visible from a distance. There were also two black cloth banners hanging from the boom. They were not very long, about a metre, and they were very faded too. These pendants are called *kenelep*.

The *Soge Ténã* also has a little flag which they hoist when they get fish. The flag is a small white rectangle, upon which someone has drawn a woman, a dog, a field knife, and a stand of bamboo. This depicts part of the history of the clan Tapo Onã, which owns the boat. Also written on the flag is Peni Belan Lodo referring to the legend in this clan of the woman who was found in a bamboo of the type named *bélã*. *Menula Belolong* used to sport a large black cross on its sail, by far the easiest to distinguish at a distance. Although these decorations are normally made of squares woven with indigo-dyed gebang, in one or two cases boats substituted black cloth in these sections. The indigo-dyed gebang-leaf strips for weaving the sail squares are dyed only by women.

Sections

The hull of the *téna lama faij* is divided by thwarts into from ten to eleven sections, *uak*, each named either for the gear kept there or for the other purposes connected with the composition or use of the boat (Fig. 24). Villagers occa-

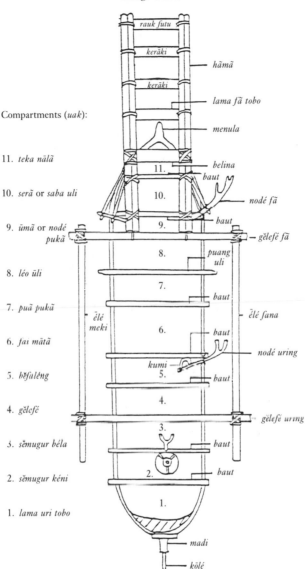

Compartments (*uak*):

11. *teka nālā*

10. *serā* or *saba uli*

9. *ūmā* or *nodé pukā*

8. *léo ūli*

7. *puā pukā*

6. *faɪ mātā*

5. *bᵉfaléng*

4. *gᵉlefé*

3. *sĕmugur béla*

2. *sĕmugur kéni*

1. *lama uri tobo*

rauk futu

kerāki

kerāki

hāmā

lama fā tobo

menula

11.

belina

baut

10.

nodé fā

baut

9.

gĕlefé fā

8.

puang uli

7.

baut

ēlé meki

ēlé fana

6.

baut

baut

nodé uring

kumi

5.

baut

4.

gĕlefé urɪng

3.

baut

2.

baut

1.

madi

kōlé

Fig. 24. The Lamalera *téna*

sionally distinguish the whaling boats as *téna* or *sapã*, a distinction which carries over into the names of the boats. *Téna* presumably are larger, containing eleven rather than ten compartments, specifically two sections near the stern are called the large and small *sĕmugur*, rather than only a single *sĕmugur*. Not all boats named *téna* or *sapã* today bear out this explanation. But the fishermen claim that the terms described the first boat of a given name, which may later, when rebuilt, have been made larger or smaller by adding or removing a compartment.

Boats which are *uak kenetang* (all sections) must possess the complete total of compartments. *Kenetang* derives from *getang*, all, everything (Arndt 1937: 10). Smaller boats, lacking one of the two *sĕmugur* sections are *uak nãlã*. *Nãlã* means a mistake or fault (Leemker 1893: 448; Gregorius Keraf 1978: 247). The number of sections must be uneven, namely eleven. The sections are counted from the stern to the bow. The eleventh or foremost section is the *teka nalã* which means 'to contain a mistake', 'to contain an oddity'. According to Leemker (1893: 457), *teka* means to touch or hit the mark, and Keraf records the interesting expression *teka-elã*, true-false (Gregorius Keraf 1978: 178, 184). This compartment, he says, functions to make the number of compartments odd.

Odd numbers express a way of life, a continuous dynamic. This case represents something important in the life view of the people of Lamalera. Even numbers indicate that everything is finished, complete. Hence there is no living dynamic, no life.

For this reason he says that boats which are *uak nãlã*, lacking in fact an odd number of compartments, are still regarded as possessing an odd number. This interpretation seems to depend on one of two possible interpretations of the phrase *téna uak nãlã*. The first is 'a boat with an incomplete number of sections', while the second is 'a boat with an odd-numbered set of sections'. This ambiguity arises because languages in Indonesia commonly speak of even numbers as being complete numbers and odd numbers as being incomplete numbers. At least in Keraf's interpretation, the two senses are used in a form of verbal casuistry to claim that there has been no violation of the prevailing norm.[14]

The first, stern, section means the helmsman's seat. Next in order come the smaller *sĕmugur* and the larger *sĕmugur*. According to Keraf *sĕmugur* derives from *sugur* meaning to lift or pull up. This expression he attributes to the fact that they regard the bow as being higher, the stern lower.[15] Crew members sitting in these sections push the boat up, figuratively, while rowing.

The next section, the *gĕlefĕ* takes its name from the outrigger boom which crosses the boat just behind it. The section called *bĕfaléng* is distinguished by the fact that the rear rack, *nodé uring*, for the harpoon poles is located here as is the *kūmi* to which the backstay is attached. The name of the section derives from *falé*, which means to tie something with the middle of a rope, so that something can be pulled with the two ends of the rope. The rope called *bĕfalé*, which is used for *falé*, is kept in this section, hence the name of the compartment. The two largest hawsers, the *talé gĕlefĕ* and the slightly smaller *talé bĕfaléng*, are kept respectively in the *gĕlefĕ* and *bĕfaléng* sections.

The well of the boat is *fai mātā*, which translates as spring, well, or water hole. It is important to the boat because it is central. The centre line of the boat is marked here. It is also capacious and therefore the place where captured animals are stored if they are small enough to bring inboard. As the name implies, it is in this section where water collects from seepage or splashing waves. The two bailers sit here, who from time to time scoop up water and pour it out over the sides of the boat, or on hot windless days sometimes pour water into the boat to keep the planks from drying out. The keel in this section is especially raised to keep the scraping of the bailing pots from wearing it thin.

The next section forward of the well is the *puā pukā*, the base of the mast. The thwart between it and the next section is especially constructed so that the ends of the two mast poles can fit onto and be attached to it. The important ropes called fore *léo* and great *léo*, the *léo fā* and *léo bélā*, are coiled up and stored in the next section, which accordingly is called the *léo*'s place, *léo ūli*. The practical and religious importance of the *léo* adds a certain significance to this compartment. The fore outrigger boom separates the *léo ūli* from the section called *ūmā*, hole, or *nodé pukā*, base of the harpoon rack. These terms are also descriptive of structural features. The *nodé fā*, the fore harpoon pole rack, is fastened to the thwart in the fore side of this section. This section is also distinguished by the fact that the hull is pierced by a drain hole. This hole permits the hull to drain as it is being moved up the beach at the end of the day of work or on those occasions when it is necessary to fill the hull with water to check it for seepage. It can be startling to watch its location being demonstrated at sea by a crewman who pulls its stopper out. A strong stream of water shoots straight up into the air.

In front of the *ūmā* section is the section called *serā*. This is a term for which no one was able to offer an explanation. The section is also called sometimes the *saba uli*, or the place for the *saba*, a cord attached to the hull with one end, which the harpooner's assistant can loop over the harpoon rope after a whale or other large animal has been harpooned, in order to keep the rope from being pulled back along the hull, i.e. to keep the bow in the direction in which the animal is pulling, to prevent the boat from capsizing. The meaning of the name given the foremost section has been explained above. For measurements of the various sections and parts of the boat see Appendix VI.

Bow Decorations

Each boat has an individual name, which, until quite recently, was never painted on the boat. Most boat names are narrowly descriptive, although one or two, such as *Sia Apu* or *Kebéla Ténā*, convey an explicit or implicit message. Boat names in which the second element is *ténā* or *sapā* are to be understood as meaning 'so-and-so's boat', the personal name involved being that of the first boat master, thus 'Muko's boat', 'Demo's sampan', etc. The boat master of *Menula Belolong* mentioned the interpretation of that name as 'elevated (or prominent) bowsprit', in order to deny that that was its significance, without being able to offer an alternative interpretation; but the interpretation he rejected is indeed a literal translation of the Lamaholot. Others have told me that *Menula Belolong* was once built with a high *menula*, whence its name. *Kebéla Ténã* is to be understood as meaning the *kakan*'s boat. Its original or 'true' name is *Téna Bĕlã*, which means the long boat. At one time it was unusually long. *Kéna Pukã*, *Kebako Pukã*, *Bui Pukã*, *Fuka Pukã*, and *Fao Pukã* are named after tree types, *pukã* meaning trunk. *Sia Apu* means salt and lime, while its other name, *Téna Tapo Onã*, means the boat of Tapo Onã's descent group, a confusion arising from the fact that a member of that descent group participated in its first construction. *Téna Ãnã* means a small boat. *Téti Heri*'s boat house was once at the outside edge (east side) of the row of boat houses, and its name means stored or placed to the east. It has since moved toward the centre but retained its name. *Kopo Paker* refers to a youth named Paker—or at least that is the current interpretation, but further information is lacking. Villagers are unaware of the meaning of *Kelulus* or of the fact that it implies a connection with the Moluccas.

All of the large boats and many of the smaller ones nowadays have highly decorated bows. An important feature of these decorations is the representation of eyes, in some cases little more than circles or other abstractions, in others quite explicit and graphic paintings of eyes.[16] The use of eyes, or oculi, on the bows of boats is a world-wide and ancient habit, about which a good deal has been written. It was common in Europe, the Mediterranean, the Indian Ocean, South-East Asia, and China in the ancient past, and survives everywhere where Islam has not forced its abandonment. There is a fairly large literature on boat oculi, in which the lead was taken by Hornell (see Hornell 1920*b*, 1923, 1934, 1938, 1943, 1946; Kerchove 1954; Gilliland 1955; Romula U. Anderson 1955; Richard LeBaron Bowen 1955, 1957; R. C. Anderson 1956; Quigley 1955, 1958; Prins 1970; R. H. Barnes 1977*b*: 311). I have heard no specific interpretation of these oculi in Lamalera, such as that they may ward off evil spirits or that they are necessary to bring the boat to life, as elsewhere; but given the insistence on completeness of construction and the other references to the anatomical aspects of the boat, the eyes fit in well with the general pattern.

In addition to the eyes, there are paintings and slogans of various kinds. These slogans are in several different languages, including English, Latin, Bahasa Indonesia, and Lamaholot. Oleona (1989: 18) writes,

Formerly people used to carve words from the Bible on the bow of the boats as a special motto, like 'In Verbo Tuo, Domine!' (By Thy Word, Lord!) or 'In manibus Tuis, tempora mea' (My destiny is in Thy hands). Nowadays, this is hardly done any more.

The present generation is more comfortable using poetical words from the region, such as *Āsa téti Lepā hau, ūsu lau Batā dai* (Derived from Lepan, Came from Batang).

Whatever popularity or unpopularity biblical slogans may enjoy today, both kinds of slogan were commonplace in the 1970s and early 1980s. The decorations current in 1979 are as follows (the spelling of Lamaholot words is as on the boats, i.e. not that of Gregorius Keraf).[17]

1. *Muko Ténā*: The bow was painted on either side with a yellow field, in which was found an irregular red strip and a small red triangle with a dot in the centre (the oculus). On the right front behind the field was a yellow parallelogram within which was painted *Cinta* in brown. *Pusaka* was painted in brown on a similar field on the left side. Otherwise the hull was bare. *Cinta pusaka* is Indonesian and means love of inheritance. On the left rear was painted in Indonesian, *Lupa Budi*, a contraction of *Jangan Lupa Hutang Budi*, do not forget your indebtedness. In 1982 the field was painted red with a light wash of yellow over the red and the eye outlined in black. By 1987 *Muko Ténā* had a simple design of eyes placed in a blue field on either side of the bow.

2. *Demo Sapā*: A plain hull except for the bow. The bow field on either side was beige with a red frame. The oculus was an eye within a triangle, behind which were drawn a steering oar and a harpoon, harpoon pole and rope. The eye was in black with a touch of red in each corner. The slogans were red with black shadowing for relief on a silver field. On the right side was written *Quietus Deus*, Latin for Serene Deity, on the left *Bintang Laut*, Indonesian for star of the sea. In this case, it is not the starfish which is intended, although this is a possible translation of *bintang laut*, but Mary. According to Hornell (1946: 286), with the spread of Christianity in Europe pagan goddesses were replaced by the Madonna, who also assumed their protective role toward fishermen while she became their *Stella Maris*. In 1987 *Demo Sapā* retained the same slogan, but had a simple eye within a triangle on either side of the bow.

3. *Baka Ténā*: The hull of this boat was so faded that it was almost bare. There was a small yellow bow field with red strip at the rear edge, finished with curling flourishes. A long curling strip ran backwards from the field. In the centre of the field was an eye with red lids and white ball. On the right front was discernible *Kehendak Allah*, Indonesian for God's will. On the left front less visible was *Terserah*, Indonesian for as you will.

4. *Pěraso Sapā*: The hull was so faded that the bow field could not be seen. The slogans were in red letters on a yellow field with a red frame. On the right front could be read *Janda Gembira*, Indonesian for cheerful widow, on the right rear, *Janda Setia*, Indonesian for loyal widow, on the left front, *Pusaka Mahal*, Indonesian for treasured inheritance.

5. *Léla Sapā*: The plain hull was distinguished with a black bow field, with

a white eye in the centre, a red bowsprit and red stripe below. The slogans were in red letters on black field. On the right front was in Latin *Dei Genitrix Intersede Pro Nobis*, Mother of God intercede for us, on the left front *Ja Bunda Allah Doa Kami*, Indonesian for Mother of God pray for us.

6. *Notã Ténã*: The decoration was very faded. The boat field contained a solid, large red circle, surrounded by a triangle of green, then a border of red and another of yellow. Behind this was a two-pronged wave rolled away, made up of a red outline and yellow centre. The writing was in red script on yellow field, speckled in green and framed in green. On the right of the bow was written in Latin *Duc In Altum et Laxate Retia Vestra in Capturam*, 'Launch out into the deep and let down your nets for a draft', Luke, 5: 4b. On the right stern was *Bulan Pernama*, Indonesian for the full moon. On the left bow was in Indonesian *Saya Pertjaja Kepada Allah*, I believe in God.

7. *Menula Belolong*: The hull was plain, the bow field yellow. In the field was an eye with a red outline and dot. The field was outlined in red. Two adjacent stripes to the rear of the field were yellow and then red. On the right bow was to be found *Sinar Soge*, ray of Songge. This phrase refers to the tradition that the ancestors of Lāma Kéra, which owns the boat, came from this part of Flores. On the right rear was *sedia maju*, prepare progress, on the left front *Bintang Laut*, star of the sea, i.e. Mary, on the left stern *Capricorn*. In 1987 *Menula Belolong* was very faded; it had once had standing animals holding harpoons. On the right of the bow was painted in Lamaholot *Bao lau key dai*, 'floated here from the direction of the Key Islands', presumably referring to the movements of ancestors before they settled in Songge, Flores, and before they left there to settle in Lamakera and Lamalera.

8. *Dato Ténã*: This hull, soon to be dismantled for good, was completely bare, except the carved slogan, *In Nomine Iesu*, in Jesus's name, on either side in red. The bow field could no longer be seen.

9. *Kebéla Ténã or Téna Bĕlã*: The rich yellow field contained a crudely drawn eagle, outlined in red, with green and yellow feathers. The bird on the left bow was the same except its head looked more like a pigeon or dove. The eyes of the birds served as eyes of the boat. The slogan was painted in bold red letters, black shaded, on a yellow field, framed in silver. On the right bow it read *Tempora Mea*, on the left *In Manibus Tuis*, in other words, *In manibus Tuis, tempora mea* (My destiny is in Thy hands). On the right rear was *Di Abad '20*, in the twentieth century. On the left, *Karna Nanggis Ibu*, because of mother's tears. This phrase is a reference to the elderly widows of men in the descent group.

10. *Boli Sapã*: The hull was very faded. A white eye, outlined in red, was located in a green field, surrounded by yellow, red, and green stripes, and

a back-running two-pronged wave outlined in red with yellow interior. The letters were green on a yellow field. On the right front was written in Indonesian *Bintang Pari*, the evening star. On the left in English, 'God's Will Be Done'.

11. *Gĕléko Ténã*: The hull was faded. The green and yellow bow field contained an eagle catching fish in the sea. The field was surrounded by yellow stripes and a red border. Colour contrasts were used in the bird and field, neither of which was a single solid colour: the beak was red, the bird over all yellow, except where green contrast was used to set off the back of the head from the wings. The field behind the bird was green, in front white. On the left front in red letters on a yellow relief was painted *Deus est Caritas*, God is merciful, on the left *Solatium Nostrum Maria*, Mary is our consolation.

12. *Boko Lolo*: The bow field was yellow with a red border and an adjacent red stripe to the rear. Within the field was an eye with red outline and dot. The slogan consisted in simple red letters on a yellow field. On the right front it stated in Indonesian *Dasar Hidup*, basis of life, and on the left *Harapan Keluarga*, the family's hope.

13. *Sika Ténã*: This boat was newly built and very freshly painted with blue side boards with a yellow stripe on top and red stripe at bottom. On either side of the bow was a black snake with yellow bottom. The boat had a pale white eye in front of the snake. There were still strips of cloth hanging from the bow. On the right of the bow in red letters was written in Indonesian *Pusaka*, heirloom, on the left, *Sederhana*, simple, i.e. *pusaka sederhana*, a modest inheritance.

14. *Bui Pukã*: Almost nothing could be seen of its letters and bow decoration. On the right bow was written *Usu teti lepan hau*, Lamaholot for derived from Lapan; on the left *Asa lau batan dai*, descended from Batan. The slogan of this boat, belonging to the Bĕliko Lolo decent group, refers to the fact that the boat was one of two which according to tradition came with the group fleeing the disaster between Lembata and Pantar at Lapan-Batan.

15. *Sia Apu* or *Téna Tapo Onã*: the hull was completely faded. Nothing was to be seen, but once on both sides of the bow had been painted in Lamaholot *Sia Apu*, salt and lime, i.e. the goods which must be sold to get by when the boat has no result.

16. *Nara Ténã*: The bow was graced with a stylized red eye in sweeping strokes. Behind the bow field was a red, silver, yellow, and green rose (see Plate 30). The slogan was painted in silver letters, with black relief, red field, yellow stripe above and below. On the right bow in Latin was *Deo Yuvante* (i.e. *Deo Iuvante*), with God towards youth, on the left *San Rosa*. In 1987 the newly painted *Nara Ténã* retained its slogan, but had grape bunches painted on either side of the bow.

PLATE 30. Bow of the *Nara Ténã*

17. *Kopo Paker*: Being newly built this boat was very freshly painted, with strips of cloth along bow and sides. On both sides of the bow in a yellow field outlined in red was a naturalistic white eye with black outline and a large green crocodile with black outlines, white teeth, and red eye (see Plate 31). On the right bow was written in Latin *Carpediem*, from Horace, *Carpe diem quam minime credula postero*, 'Enjoy the present day, trusting as little as possible to what the morrow may bring'. On the left front in Indonesian was *Harapan Jaya*, glorious hope, on the right stern *Tunas Muda*, young shoot, on the left stern in what seems to be a mix of Indonesian and Lamaholot, *Timur Toto*, perhaps spray from the east wind.

18. *Téti Heri*: The hull was plain, the bow freshly painted and decorated with reddish purple drawings on either side of a dove and a bunch of grapes on a white field bordered in red. The slogan was written in silver letters on a red scroll, on the right bow in Latin, *Fiat*, let it be done, on the left in Indonesian *Harapanku*, my hope.

19. *Holo Sapã*: The bow of this boat was freshly painted, on both sides of the bow in a black line beneath a green field in which was positioned a naturalistic representation of a sperm whale in black (see Plate 32). There were no eyes to be seen because the eyes of the whale were hardly visible. The slogan was represented in red letters on a yellow field. On the right front it stated in Indonesian *Putra Bata*, son of Batan, and on the left *Putra*

PLATE 31. Bow of the *Kopo Paker*

PLATE 32. Bow of the *Holo Sapā*

Nelayan, son of fishermen. In 1988 the newly built *Holo Sapã* had a smaller yellow bow field, outlined in black, with a much smaller black sperm whale in the field. For the first time its name was painted on the bow in black on a white scroll.

20. *Soge Ténã*: This boat had a bare hull with no slogan visible. The bow field was obscured on either side by a replaced plank. The slogan had been on the right front in Indonesian, *Asal Dari Gunung*, descended from the mountain; on the left in Lamaholot, *Gogo Nere Asa Lau Batan*, 'I took [borrowed] descent from Batan'. These phrases refer to the fact that the descent group which owns *Soge Ténã* claim descent from the interior of the island, but have settled in this village of refugees. In August 1979 they repainted the bow with a yellow field, on the right they painted in Lamaholot *Ile Lodo*, descended from the mountain, on the left, *Gogo Nere*, I took.

21. *Horo Ténã*: The boat had a bare hull and freshly painted bow field on either side of cream colour, with a naturalistic eye in black outline and a large grey anchor with black outline and shading, all surrounded by black and red outline (see Plate 33). The slogan was in red letters with black relief, on the right bow Sint Piter, on the left in Indonesian *Samudra Jaya*, glorious ocean.

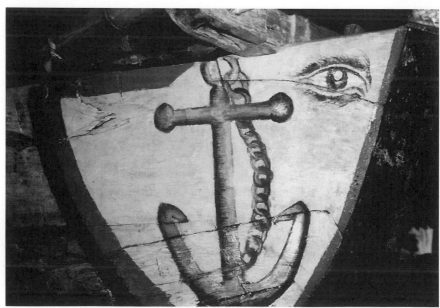

PLATE 33. Bow of the *Horo Ténã*

22. *Dolu Ténã*: The bow field showed the fantastic head of a snake, with red tongue, black muzzle, red eye dot in a white circle, red dot in a white nostril, gray teeth, and a red, gray, and white fringe of hair. The slogan was done in red letters on a yellow field with a red stripe above and below. On the right bow was painted in Latin *Amor Patriae*, love of our country, on the left in mixed Latin and Indonesian, *Amor Laut*, love of the sea. *Dolu Ténã* and *Sika Ténã* both use a snake image because the ancestor Bélé Gora of the descent group Sula Onã which owns both boats was both a human and a snake. By 1982 the *Dolu Ténã* had a chalice on the right side of the bow.

23. *Sili Ténã*: The hull was very bare. The bow field was yellow, with a red floral design and border. The slogan was mostly obscured, on the right bow in Latin *Matrix Magistra*, our lives are ruled by our origins, on the left, *Unitatis*, of unity. The whole phrase was *Matrix Magistra Unitatis*, our origins are the basis of our unity. On the right rear was painted *Djakwa*, a contraction of Indonesian *Jangan Kewatir*, do not fear (from Arabic: Wehr 1966: 247; Wilkinson 1932: 1: 594). In 1991 the newly built *Sili Ténã* had a completely painted hull, light green under the water line, blue above. A red outline formed the triangle of the bow field, within which was a large graphic eye, eyelids and eyebrow in black on an indistinctly outlined patch of purple and gray. A single red pepper was placed in the blue field. The boat's name was painted on the left side of the hull in large black letters, outlined in white. Festive strips of cloth were wedged between the planks of the hull. On the right side was painted in Lamaholot *Kopo Gere*. The whole phrase thus is *Kopo Gere Sili Téne*, that is youth get into [or ride in] *Sili Ténã*. This phrase is included in a work song reproduced by Gregorius Keraf (1978: 247). On the right stern was *Kepite Paun*, Captain Paun, and on the left, *Inak Dulo Amak Nange*, Mother Dulo, Father Nange. These phrases refer to the time when *Sili Ténã*'s harpooner was called before the Raja of Adonara at Kalikur, Kédang, to defend the boat's crew after they had taken a wild goat at Pulau Kambing (Goat Island, between Pantar and Lembata) around 1890.[18]

24. *Kéna Pukã*: The hull was very bare, and the slogans and bow field were obscure. The bow field was white, bordered in red. Within the field was a green triangle, within which was a yellow eye. Behind the field were various stripes in red, green, and yellow. On the right bow in Latin was painted *Immaculata*, Purity, and on the left in Indonesian *Engkau Maria*, Thee Mary. In 1982 the bow field contained a floral design, and on either side was painted in Indonesian, *San Mery Damai*, St Mary Full of Peace. In 1987 *Kéna Pukã* had jumping marlin painted on either side of its bow.

25. *Kelulus*: The bow was freshly painted in a complex pattern of yellow, blue-green, green, and white. Within this pattern on the right was depicted a yellow bunch of bananas, on the left a coconut. The slogan in black letters

with white relief on a green field on the right was in Indonesian *Ratu Damai*, Princess of Peace, and on the left in Lamaholot *Muko Te* [i.e. *tã*], *Tapo Ari*, ripe banana, young coconut. The implication of the latter phrase is that if they are successful at sea they feel like someone eating ripe bananas and drinking fresh coconut water.

26. *Kebako Pukã*: The hull was bare and the slogans invisible. The bow field was obscured by a replaced board, but contained the remnants of a snake's head. The appropriate slogans were, on the right bow in Lamaholot, *Tena Asa Lau Batan*, boat derives from Batan, and on the left *Laja Asa Teti Lepan*, sail descends from Lepan. These slogans refer to the fact that Kebako Pukã is the boat which brought the refugees from the disaster in Lapan-Batan.

27. *Téna Ãnã*: The hull was bare and the slogans obscured. The bow field consisted of alternating yellow and red stripes running up from the bowsprit, finished off with a flourish at the bottom. The slogans were in yellow letters on a red field, on the right bow *San Yosef*, on the left *Ave Maria*.

28. *Sinu Sapã*: This boat was just an abandoned hulk at the time with a bare hull. Nevertheless the bow field was visible. It was yellow and contained a white eye with red outline. The border was red. At the bottom was a red flourish with yellow shadowing. The slogan was in red lettering, on the right bow in Indonesian, *Tenaga Noe*, Noah's workers, on the left in Latin *Bone Pastor*, Good Shepherd.

29. *Jafa Ténã*: This boat had a bare hull with slogans and bow field obscured. On the right bow had been painted in Latin *Suaviter*, gently, on the left in Indonesian *Sandar*, to lean or depend on.

None of the boats had their names painted on the hull until 1986 and 1987, when *Téti Heri* and *Kelulus* took up the practice with an eye to the tourist trade. Since then, it has become common to do so.

Stern Decorations

Among the ethnographic objects collected in Lamakera, Solor, by ten Kate (1894: 239) was a white and red flag and pendant, decorated with two bunches of cock's feathers, designed to be fastened to the stern post of a boat and called *tamóto*. In general, decorations are called *temóto* in Lamaholot. Each boat in Lamalera is fitted out with an eleborate decoration of individual design to be lashed to the *kõlé* on any sort of festive occasion, of which boat launching, trips to Wulan Doni, the beginning of the season, and any trip to other islands are typical. Some boats may go for a period using the *temóto* every day as they work, but most boats will dispense with them for everyday fishing and hunting.

A typical *temoto* is that of the *Nara Ténã* (scc Plate 34) which consists of a flattened beam decorated in red, yellow, and white, a small *mãdi* in its centre,

PLATE 34. *Temōto of the Nara Téna*

behind which is a small upright bamboo stick to hold a flag, an upright-standing bunch of young lontar palm leaves at the end, called *nedek*, and two pendants also made of bunches of young lontar palm leaves and called *bĕlĕréng* or *bĕlélã*. Of the two pendants that farthest astern is the tail, *īku* (Gregorius Keraf 1983). In general *bĕlĕréng* are signs of ownership, such as those which they put on coconut trees, often enough just a young coconut leaf tied around the trunk. The *temōto* of *Notã Ténã* is similar to that of *Nara Ténã*, except that it has a cloth pendant hanging down behind the small *madi*.

According to a member of the Bĕliko Lolo descent group, the following boats have *bĕlĕréng* hanging from their *temōto*: *Bui Pukã, Demo Sapã, Boko Lolo, Notã Ténã, Kebéla Ténã, Muko Ténã*. The first three boats belong to Bĕliko Lolo, and these signs of ownership seem to have a relationship to their claims to preeminence. *Notã Ténã* belongs to Lāma Nudek, and, so I was told, has these signs because they have such a close relationship with Bĕliko Lolo. *Kebéla Ténã* and *Muko Ténã* do so because they were once built by the same master builder, a prominent man from Bĕliko Lolo.

Some deny that the decorations on these devices have any meaning, other than providing individuation, but others claim that each design, called *keriki kĕlada*, is an identifying sign which has its own meaning. That for the boats of Bĕliko Lolo indicates 'we will protect'. The *temōto* of the *Nara Ténã* has a black and white flag. This flag comes from the time when *Nara Ténã* accompanied

Kebako Pukã to Timor on a war expedition. They seem to have taken the apparatus of the descent group Ata Gora, because the flag represents a black and a white mouse. The *Notã Ténã* uses a flag of repeated red and white stripes. The *mādi* on the *temōto* of the *Menula Belolong* was expertly carved with keys representing those of St Peter, whose name was once written on the bow. Below the keys in the centre was a cherry. No further meaning was forthcoming. The *temōto* of *Léla Sapã* is called *temōto lako īku*, the civet cat's tail *temōto*. The *temōto* of *Boko Lolo* contains a decoration which represents the fact that in going out the boat is always in the van and when returning always in the rear. This object is mounted at the very end of the *temōto*, and consists of a crosspiece with a bit of cloth at either end. Only *Boko Lolo* has such an arrangement.

12

Boat Construction Ceremonies

Before construction begins, or at least ideally so, a ceremony must be performed at the ritual house associated with the boat, called *pau laba ketilo alep* ('feeding the masters of the chisel and dowels')[1] in which all of the master builders of the village (*ata mōlã*, essentially 'craftsmen' or *laba ketilo alep*, 'masters of the chisel and dowels') are called together and feasted. In the past the Kĕlakĕ Langu section of Bata Onã kept in its great house at the right house post, *rié fanã*, a large stone, *fato kener*, lying on the ground and another, *fato bani*, lying on a platform. The *fato kener* was the stone upon which they had to kindle fire with bamboo fire sticks whenever they had a ceremonial feast. When they planned to rebuild their boat, they summoned the men of Lāma Nudek clan[2] to bring their tools (chisels, dowels, and adzes) and place them on the *fato bani*. They cut the mouth of a chicken used for sacrificial occasions, *bomak*, and put blood on the tools, the stone, and the right house post.

Master builders are distinguished figuratively as *kĕlepé* or *kĕlapa*, and may be referred to collectively as *kĕlepé-kĕlapa*. Traditionally there are two kinds of *ata mōlã*. Those of higher standing were *kĕlapa*. *Kĕlapa* are wooden tool boxes. The meaning is that the higher standing craftsmen keep their tools in such boxes. To my knowledge, however, there was only one such box, and that disused, in the village during my visits, if we overlook packing crates and other such *ad hoc* arrangements (see Plate 35). The lower status *kĕlepé* are woven baskets.

One man explained to me that although he is not a boat builder, his ancestor was. Therefore, when another master builder builds a boat and invites the master builders to a feast, he must also be invited, because he continues the line of his ancestor. He went on to say that another master in his clan tells all the other builders where to sit and divides chicken meat among them. Great master builders (*ata mōlã bélã*) get chicken legs, small master builders (*ata mōlã kéni*) get wings. Then this builder takes a flat wooden mallet (*meningo*) and hits each master builder on the elbows hard enough to hurt and tells them to eat and drink and tomorrow to work the way he does. This information was recounted with evident pleasure and with laughter.

At a version of this ceremony I attended in 1982, all of the master builders of both villages, a total of fifteen, were collected together and fed. The point of this ceremony is that although only a single master builder is in charge of a given boat who receives the rights in game attendant on building it, the boat owners hope that the other experts will drop by and lend a hand from time to

PLATE 35. A boat builder with a wooden tool box, *kĕlapa*

time, when free of other responsibilities. Although those who were *kĕlepé* were to be given chicken wings, while *kĕlapa* were to receive legs, in fact all fifteen were given both. Two distinguished master builders, who were not themselves responsible for the boat in question, told the other master builders that they had eaten, therefore they must help building the boat, if they had time free from other jobs. The master builder mentioned above did not play his game of striking the rival builders on the elbows with a mallet, perhaps because he was not himself directly associated with the boat or otherwise judged that it would be unsuitable to do so in the situation. This ceremony began with a prayer led by the other master builder, after which they sprinkled a few tools with holy water.

Although today boat building is accompanied by provision of food and drink and its stages are marked in various ways, the previous pattern is usually simplified and concentrated on the feast at completion. Formerly after the three sections of the keel were ready, on the night before they were to be joined, there would be a feast in which about ten chickens would be used. This feast is called *todã menula kolé* ('to fit the stem and stern posts') or *todã ié* ('to fit the keel'). According to Oleona (1989: 13), the purpose of this ceremony was to obtain God's (*Lera-Fūla*'s) blessing, so that work on building the boat would go flawlessly. The master builder would circle a chicken head over the boat's keel, then rub blood on the bowsprit, keel, and stern piece. He would pour palm wine on the same parts, while praying. Then the boat corporation members would roast the chicken and participants would consume it with palm wine.

Next when the lowest plank of the hull (the *ārā belikãng*, the 'submerged plank') was fitted there would be a feast of one or two goats. This is the *toto ārā belikãng*. *Toto* means to splash, sprinkle, to stain something (with chicken blood) and has come to mean a festival celebrating the completion of some form of construction, etc. (Gregorius Keraf 1978: 56; 1983). Oleona says that this ceremony is more of a consecration, than the previous one. The same number of animals would be used for the ceremony following the fitting of the next lowest plank, the *ārā kenati*, then again once the *ārā tukã*, the *nulu futu*, and their various extensions had been put in place. A similar feast took place after fitting the 'large plank' (*ārā bélã*), that is the second highest, and again once the highest plank (*néfi*) was added. All of these rites preceded the final feast, *odo mãdi* ('to shove the stern piece'), when the decorated stern piece, *mãdi*, was attached. Complementary to the *pau laba ketilo alep* was a similar episode after the boat was finished called *pau soru-naka* ('to feed the *soru*[3] and the adze').

When a new boat is ready to be taken out fishing for the first time, and also each year separately for each boat when it is to be taken out for the first time, a ceremony is required in its clan house, comparable, when it coincides with the beginning of *leja*, with the new maize ceremonies of the mountain peoples. The fire for this feast in the past had to be started by rubbing two pieces of bamboo together. Steel could not be used. The bamboo would be passed around so that everybody could touch it. Then the pieces would be rubbed together. If the fire started immediately, that was a sign of good luck. Some chicken would be cooked on the fire and eaten with palm wine.

During this ceremony it was forbidden to sneeze, *dapu*. On another occasion, I was told that if anyone sneezed during my arrival or departure, it would be a bad sign for me. It is also a bad sign if it happens during the launching of a new boat.

The next morning the harpooner, *lama fã*, would take the harpooning rope, *léo*, down to the boat. There they would hold another small ceremony. Here a baby chick would be killed, or an egg substituted for it, and fed to the boat. They would cut the mouth of a living chicken and drip its blood on the boat. The same would be done when a *léo* rope was changed. Today, of course, they use holy water. Then they could go to sea. Blood would be put on the boat beginning with the prow, then the stern, and then along the right and left sides. They would either take a chicken egg or cut a chicken's head and rub blood on the bow post, *menula*, and all the joints in the bamboo harpooning poles, *lada*.

Furthermore, before Father Bernardus Bode forced those clans which kept their ancestors' skulls on a shelf in the back of their boat houses to bury them, they would take a skull and rub it on the bowsprit. Then they could not fail to get fish. Holy water seems less effective today, although everyone uses it. On the first day of the fishing season each year, the boat owner would take the shelf of ancestral skulls from the back of the boat house and place it on the ground in front of the shed. Although the shelf was placed on the ground, the skulls themselves were set on porcelain plates. Members of the descent group which built and maintained the boat would wash the skulls with sea water, rub them with coconut skin, and then anoint them with coconut oil (*not* fish or whale oil). This activity assured a good catch. In various ceremonies, the skulls might be fed a bit of chicken, rice, or blood.

According to Bode (1925: 114), when a boat went for several days without catching anything, they would take a large piece of cloth, some cooked rice, fire in a coconut shell, and go to the grave of an ancestor. They would spread the cloth on the ground at the head end of the grave, place the shell with the fire and some fragrant wood in it on the grave, and put some grains of rice in it. They then spoke to the deceased as follows, 'Tomorrow we are going fishing; come with us and help us.' They then took these materials to the straw-covered stone construction where they stored the skulls of the ancestors and repeated the ceremony. After the incense had spread about in the air, they carefully removed the cloth, which was then filled with the *kefokot*, that is the dead souls, and took it back to the house, where betel quid had been prepared, one for each type of animal they wished to catch. They slaughtered a chicken and sprinkled blood on the betel and on the door posts. They then roasted the chicken and ate it. Afterwards they took the betel preparations to the boat, where they chewed them and then laid them on the sacred parts of the boat.

Today when boats have a long period without luck at sea, the owners may arrange a private ceremony at the beach to correct the problem. Other than the harpooner, the crew may not necessarily be involved. In addition to having a prayer and splashing holy water around on the special parts of the boats, they may give some fish to certain of the large stones near the beach. These are sacred and may need being presented with their 'share' of the catch. The ceremony is held at night, and no one other than the participants may know precisely when it will take place. Such a ceremony is called *upa ikã pung alep*, wages for the spirit of the fish. They may also take a candlenut, *kemié*, or an areca nut, *fua*, and go to the edge of the sea. The nut represents the spirit of the fish, *ikã pung alep*. Formerly they would act as if they were pulling the nut up the beach and sing '*Yo he, yo he*', etc. Today they just carry it to the front of the boat after sprinkling holy water on the boat and the participants. They also use another nut representing the spirit of the boat, *téna pung alep*. They would sprinkle more holy water around in connection with this nut. Then they take the nuts to the great house, where they would again sprinkle holy water on participants. The great house also has a spirit, *lango bêlã pung alep*. Indeed everything has a *pung alep*. *Pung alep* is the spirit, which cannot be seen, of any object.

Bode also wrote that before going out to sea, they would make an offering to the spirit of the boat. They would cut the head from a chicken and smear blood on the head, shoulders, and breast of the boat. Afterwards they would roast the chicken and place a piece in the boat's mouth. It was forbidden to touch the holy parts of the boat with a knife or other sharp object. Whoever did so would die a sudden death.

The places where chicken blood might be put on the boat include the following:

1. the mouth, *fefã*, of the bowsprit, *menula* (at the very top),
2. the base of the bowsprit,
3. the fore outrigger boom, right and then left,
4. the well, right and then left,
5. the aft outrigger boom, right and then left,
6. the triangular apex, *ōrã*, joining the two mast poles at the top,
7. the base of the decorated stern piece, *mãdi*, on the inside,
8. the fork of the blade of the harpoon, *kãfê léo*, used for ray and porpoise,
9. the bindings which hold the loop at the end of the *léo* rope through which the looped leader rope, *kêlīfa*, attached to the harpoon is passed before the harpoon is then drawn through it so that the harpoon leader and the rope are fastened to each other,
10. the hole at the base of the harpoon poles where the harpoons are inserted, specifically those poles used for ray, the *kenāda*, and for pilot and killer whales, the *nũba*, also, but perhaps not last in the sequence,
11. the harpoon platform.

To this list may be added that the diagonal hole sometimes bored through the *menula* and representing ears, *tilu*, and the *ténu kepur*, the central line drawn down both sides of the boat inside the well, would be fed.

Today this ceremony is not held in this form. Instead they just gather and pray together, requesting help from God. However, if a boat is struck with a great wind, today the harpooner will grab the bow sprit and say *fefã* (mouth) *bélã* (large), *alang* (voice, call) *meloan* (clear), 'Great mouth, call clearly'. Formerly the brain (*kelura*) of ray of various varieties would be taken and rubbed on the various parts of the boat, including the *menula*. At this point in the conversation, there was disagreement whether this step would be done with ray or pilot whales, apparently indicating a difference in practice among villagers. Those who feel like doing so, so they said, still do.

On the first day that a new boat goes out, it may not be put to sea first. It is last to leave and must be the first to return, unless the boat is held up by game. Every time it gets a fish, some of the fish is cut up and cooked in the clan house and divided up in very small sections of about three inches. This is done for the first ten fish taken, then the practice is dropped. During this period the boat bailer who sits on the right side of the well, *fai matã alep fãnã*, may not get out of the boat upon returning from sea until it has been pulled far enough up the beach to keep him from getting wet. After ten fish are taken, the regulation is dropped. If large game like a pilot or sperm whale were taken, the regulation would also be dropped. However, supposedly this custom is no longer observed.

Gregorius Keraf (1983) has written as follows,

The life of the people of Lamalera depends on the produce of the fishery. Therefore all patterns of life and belief are coloured by the sea. The boat represents a special device for uniting members of the clan. Boats which are diligently taken to sea show that the members of a clan or sub-clan are united in word and deed. They show that the members within the clan are in harmony.

Because the boat represents a special device which guarantees the livelihood of the clan, it is given special care. The boat is regarded as being alive. That it is alive is not because it became a boat, but because it was built with complete specifications. To leave these out is like not giving a soul to the boat. A boat without a soul implies that the whole clan will experience disaster, either famine or an accident at sea, which will kill the souls of the people who take it out.

The boat symbolizes a large fruit, which will give [a rich] harvest to the clan members. The fruit will not just have its contents eaten, but also possesses life, which in turn will give life to the clan members and the whole of the village of Lamalera.

My predecessor Ernst Vatter, also not an eyewitness, recorded a description of boat launching in 1929 when memories were considerably fresher than they were some fifty years later.

At the launching of a pledang [boat], a large festival lasting three days takes place. Early in the morning, it is pulled out of the boat house and once more carefully examined in all its parts, each mortise, each binding is tested. Then goats or pigs are sacrificed; their blood is smeared on specific parts of the boat, especially the bow extension and the harpooning platform, as well as the tools used in the construction. Moreover, they give the pledang itself, in which they see a sort of living being, meat and rice 'to eat'. Only then is it ready and seaworthy; however, it is not yet allowed into the water on this first day, but is brought back into its shed. After sundown, the whole village comes together for a feast; throughout the night there is singing and dancing (Vatter 1932: 203).

In 1970 Adreanus Ubas Bataona, then the oldest man in the village,[4] told me that in the past when the boat was finished, they sacrificed some animal (goat, pig, dog, or chicken) and put the blood on the boat beginning with the prow, then the stern, then along the sides from prow to stern on the right side first and then the left. Before taking the boat down the beach to the sea, they held a baby pig to the prow and squeezed its throat to make it squeal. This was done so that they would get whale; if they did not do so, they would not get any. In 1970 the custom, according to villagers, was still followed. Subsequently the pig was struggled over or plundered by those present and went to the strongest.

Children were told to climb into the boat, where they were to eat the chicken killed at this time, while the other animals were eaten outside. After the feast in the evening, a large tray of rice was taken to the 'gates' (*bafalofë*) of the village, including the various paths leading from the beach to the houses. A portion of the rice was dropped on the ground at each such entrance, and some of it was strewn along the ground as the celebrants walked from door to door. Following the feast, the craftsmen who built the boat and others guarded it from evil spirits.

Vatter says that when the sun came up the next day some men took the boat out into the water and rowed it a distance out to sea. They then lay down in the bottom of the boat and pretended to sleep for about a quarter of an hour, while the whole village waited on the beach. After a while someone shouted, 'Hey, you out there, where do you come from?' The crew jumped up and shouted back that they came from Lapan-Batan (between Lembata and Pantar) or Soge Paga (Sikka on Flores), that is the supposed place of origin of the clan which owned the boat. Afterwards the men practised throwing harpoons and in the evening there was another feast and dance.

Early on the third day, they sail with the new pledang to market at the village Nualela [*actually the adjacent market site at Wulan Doni*], some eight kilometres north-east of Lama Leràp, and load it there with maize, sweet potatoes, bananas, tobacco, sirih [peppers of *Piper betle*, Linn.], and pinang [nuts of *Areca catechu*, Linn.] and decorate it with fresh branches. On the return to Lama Leràp, it is shot at from the beach with arrows and finally stormed and robbed. The sham battle continues on shore, until at nightfall all the villagers unite again for a feast and dancing (Vatter 1932: 204).

Adreanus Ubas Bataona said that prior to this trip to the traditional market, the villagers would arrange to meet people from the mountain village of Lewuka at the market. They would then fill their boat as full as possible with fish, salt, and so on and take it to Wulan Doni. The people of Lewuka would bring an abundance of vegetables, rice, maize, cassava, etc. This would all be exchanged against what was brought in the boat without regard to relative value. When they returned to Lamalera, there would be a great scramble for the goods, presumably as part of the mock fight described by Vatter. This trip is known as *gĕroi téna*. Both at the market and when returning, everyone splashed and sprinkled each other with water—a common practice in this area at festivals and which I have experienced when returning from an expedition to cut planks for rebuilding a *téna*. After they returned, they had to offer an animal to the adzes, chisels, and gouges to eat, before the boat could be taken out on a hunt.

The goods brought back from Wulan Doni go to the children on the beach. During the *gĕroi téna* ceremony, the boat, bearing a symbol of a small child, is taken to market carrying balls of cooked rice (*ketupat*) made by all the members of the group that built and owns the boat. These are divided among the mountain people, who give in return maize, banana, a pig, and a goat. According to Oleona (1989: 21), the goods brought from the mountain are called *kĕru-baki*, after a fruit which grows in the ravines and a wild banana. The animals are eaten, but the maize and bananas are thrown out on the beach when they return for the young children to grab. Then there is a great *demonstrasi*. The grown men fight each other with swords made of lontar palm branches. Oleona (1989: 22) says that the returning boat can expect to be ambushed when they reach the point just to the east of the beach, where people will pelt them with stones, to be answered with fruit from the boat. While attempting to get the boat safely to shore, the crew are subjected to even more intense hostilities, because when the boat touches shore the people waiting on the beach will invade it to plunder the fruit and other goods in it. Full-bodied youths in the boat are delegated to jump from the boat and run with the goods the length of the beach scattering them on the way. People on the beach will then scramble to pick them up. If there is a goat, the men will struggle over it. A day or so after the ceremony for a new boat, they may put it out in the sea and let children practise harpooning from it.

The sham battle, *sādo*, occasioned by taking a boat to sea for the first time has come up as a topic of conversation several times in the course of my research. The struggle took place between men of the two halves of the village, the upper (western) and lower (eastern) halves of historical Lamalera. The men fought with simulated swords, *bélo fika* (my notes have these variously described as made of wood, palm branches, and bamboo, the latter offered as the translation of *fika*) and shields, *dopi* or *sĕnudem*, made of buffalo hide. More recently they just fought, 'several mornings in a row'; Oleona says up to a week. If anyone were injured there was no fine, no return, and no ceremony, according to one report. Oleona says that apologies would be extended for injuries after the combat finally came to an end. According to another report, the ancestors used wooden swords and shields. The younger people fought with their fists, after they had had plenty of palm wine. They would line up and face each other at the site of the St Peter Chapel. Then they would fight until there were injuries. This account, dating from 1982, had it that the practice was discontinued some ten or more (in Indonesian, *belasan*) years before. The source, who himself is a man of Lamalera B, said that Lamalera A always lost. His group would chase the others up the rocks as far as the Catholic church. The men of Lamalera A would claim that the church was theirs and would threaten them, but the men of Lamalera B would chase them even further behind the village. Since, however, this rowdiness was carried on with sufficient energy to cause injuries, the village governments forbade them to do it any more.[5]

My only opportunity to witness the ceremony connected with boat launching came on 30 May 1987, when I was in the village to make a television film. In that year, *Kelulus*, which had been awaiting rebuilding for nearly a decade, was at long last built afresh, this time, however, from commercial planks and with all-nylon rigging. The boat master, who was the master builder as well and had been a seminarist and village head, intentionally modernized it with an eye to giving simulated harpooning exhibitions at sea just in front of the beach to package tourists.

I arrived a few days after the feast before the launching. However, the *gĕroi téna* did take place. I was not specifically invited; nevertheless, I made sure that I arrived at the market, Wulan Doni, by 9.00 a.m., where I remained until it was ready to disband. On the return walk, I found that *Kelulus* had gone no farther than Ongaona, about half the distance to market. The boat master called me down to join their modest, but jovial festive meal. He had made no effort to alert the mountain villages to meet them at market, and there was no ceremonial exchange with them. In due course, time came to return to the village. Just as we were about to leave Ongaona, everyone started pouring water on everyone else. I escaped, although I got wet later. All of this took place in a spirit of good fun. We then rowed the boat very slowly home. On shore, one man threw stones at us, taking care not to hit us. This incident was the only sign of sham hostilities. Instead of being fought over, a young pig provided for the occasion was carried off by a crippled man. Altogether, everything took place in a good atmosphere, without too much ado.

Market day, 30 May, was a Saturday. On Sunday, according to local commentary, had they chosen, they could have had the mock battle between the two villages. This did not happen because people were afraid of the government. It may be noted that both Indonesian government officials and Catholic authorities oppose and propagandize against both ceremonial waste and ritual violence. Certainly this boat master and former village head agrees with them.

Harpoons, Ropes, and Other Gear in the Boats

In addition to the paddles, sail, and rigging used to propel the boats, each boat carries an extensive kit of poles, harpoons, ropes, fishing lines, and so on used in fishing and hunting. A boat is not ready for use until it has all the harpoons and ropes needed for the many specialized purposes. Ropes, *talé*, are woven either from cotton thread or from a mixture of gebang leaf and the bark of *Hibiscus tiliaceus*, Linn. The harpoons, *kāfé*, are made of iron and are forged in the village. A description of the moderately sized *kāfé léo fã* and its associated leader and rope will serve in general for all the other harpoons.

The Principal Harpoon and its Attachment to its Rope

When a boat first puts to sea, it is this harpoon which is put at readiness, by being attached to its pole and rope and propped up on the harpooning platform and the fore part of the harpoon pole rack on the right side of the boat. The harpoon is suitable for moderate- and small-sized game, and it can quickly be replaced by a heavier harpoon and rope if large game looms into sight. Because it is always at the ready, its rope is coiled in the first unobstructed section of the boat behind the bow, namely the fourth section, which is called the place of the *léo* rope. In general the ropes increase in weight and thickness moving from the bow to the stern; and they are arranged so that they can be fastened to each other in that order. As a consequence the thickest and strongest ropes are either attached to the boat or close to it, while the weakest are closest to the harpoon. If a rope breaks, the loss is likely to be confined to only a shorter section of thinner rope. Of course, the larger the game the fewer the sections are that are used, because the thinner sections are left off. This arrangement makes physical and economic sense. Some may be surprised, therefore, to be told that it is the thinnest rope and the rope which is normally kept at the ready which has the greatest religious significance.

The harpoon head consists of a piece of iron which has been pounded and flattened by the smith to give it a particular shape and length. During the process of pounding, the smith takes a chisel and splits an ear away from the shaft. This ear he bends out to make the barb, leaving the rest of the shaft to make a pointed staff around which the rope leader is tied and the end of which fits into the base of the harpoon pole. He further flattens and shapes the tip of the shaft and the ear to make a continuous blade. The smith varies the angle between the shaft and the barb to fit the purpose of the harpoon; thus the large

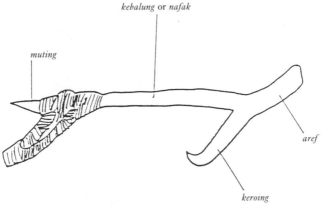

FIG. 25. Harpoon, *kāfĕ*

kāfĕ suka bélã, designed for manta ray, cannot be used for whale because the angle is too large and the harpoon cannot be pushed through the tough hide (see Fig. 25).

The smith uses a bellows, *rokã*, of a commonplace South-East Asian type made from two large bamboo tubes, about 80 cm. high (see Plate 36). The air pipes are of a thin bamboo with long internodes, *Schizostachyum brachycladum*, Kurz., and are called by the name of this bamboo, *fūlo*. These run from the base of the large tubes to a small charcoal fire between two bricks, *mini*. Charcoal is *arã*. Air is pumped by means of pistons made of sticks with rags tied to the end. The rags are called *kōlo loti*, or bird feathers. Formerly they would have used feathers, most likely those of chicken, *mãnu*. If the air pipes are too short, the cloth will begin to smoulder, requiring that they be doused with water.

Wrapped around the shaft of each harpoon are the ends of a loop of rope, *kĕlīfa*, which acts as a leader and is about three or four metres of effective length. They pass this loop through a much shorter loop on the ends of one of the main ropes and then over the harpoon. They pull the harpoon through and tighten the leader, attaching it to the rope. This process of attaching the leader to a rope is called *hangak* (see Fig. 26).

Both ends of the leader are fastened to the base of the harpoon with wrappings of a cord called *pĕrãnã*, made from two-stranded thread. Visitors have suggested that the attachment would be stronger if there were a hole in the iron, so that the leader could be tied to it, but based on experience the fishermen think that their manner of attaching the leader is stronger. According to Gregorius Keraf (1983), the two ends of the leader must first be unwoven thread by thread, *buna*. Threads from *pĕrãnã* are wrapped around the base of the harpoon; this procedure is called *gĕlōto*. They spread sap from *Sesbania grandiflora*, *teluma*, on this thread to act as a glue. They tie the unwoven ends

PLATE 36. Bellows, *rokã*, used in manufacturing harpoons

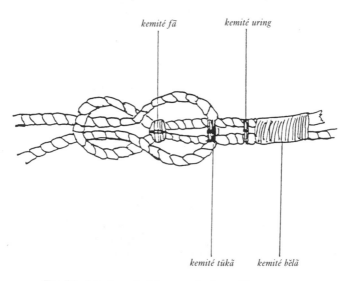

FIG. 26. Attachment of harpoon leader and harpoon rope

of the leader on this thread, and repeat the procedure several times building up several layers. A good tie will not easily come loose, *sĕlorut*. If this were to happen it would show that the person who made the attachment did not summon his whole strength while tying the ends, and it might also be a sign of a problem within the descent group of the boat. The whole process of attaching the leader to the harpoon head is *gĕlīfa*.

Keraf says that the leader for the *léo bélã* harpoon and that for the *léo fã* harpoon must be woven, *pāno*, to specific requirements. That for the *kāfé léo fã* must be woven with a basis of thirty strands to which an additional odd number of strands, 1, 3, 5, 7, or 9, may be added as needed. The leader for the *kāfé léo bélã* must have a basis of fifty strands with an additional odd number of strands. The leader for *nodé pukã* harpoon is made like that for the *kāfé léo fã*, while that for the *suka fã* harpoon is made like that for the *kāfé léo bélã*. For the two largest harpoons, the *kāfé suka bélã* and the *kāfé kotekĕlema*, they would make the leader from discarded *léo fã* and *léo bélã* ropes, because these must in any case be woven from odd-numbered strands. In order to prevent the leader for the *kāfé suka bélã* and that for the *kāfé suka fã* from being frayed by being rubbed against the rough skin of the largest manta ray, *bĕlelã, Mantis birostris*, they wrap them with the skin of the lontar palm branch. The *pelepah* is wrapped once around the rope, then pulled under itself, then wrapped around again, and so on down the length of the leader. The procedure is quite simple, although it looks neat and the projecting folds spiral around the rope. The wrapping is called *kĕfatã*.

Harpoons

The boats differ somewhat in the equipment with which they are outfitted, but each will carry seven to nine harpoons and one or two gaffs, *kĕnaté*. Some boats also carry lances *bĕlãda*, the blade of which is stored by being secured to the lower thwart between the large and small *sĕmugur* sections of the boat, though lances have generally fallen into disuse. Crew members bring along their own flensing knives, *duri*, and sharpening stones, *ēlu*. Individuals also bring privately owned shark lines and nylon lines for flying fish.

The list in Table 13 gives the names and measurements of the harpoons in the *Menula Belolong* in 1979 (see Plate 37).

In comparison, the complete set of harpoons in the *Soge Ténã* in that year was as follows.

1. *kāfé suka uring* (stern *suka* harpoon)
2. *kāfé léo fã* (fore *léo* harpoon)
3. *kāfé léo bélã* (great *léo* harpoon)
4. *kāfé nodé pukã fãnã* (right harpoon pole rack base harpoon)
5. *kāfé nodé pukã mĕki* (left harpoon pole rack base harpoon)
6. *kāfé suka bélã* (great *suka* harpoon)

7. *kāfé munung* (the first harpoon for whale)
8. *kāfé nomang* (the second harpoon for whale)

On the day that I made the latter list, the *Soge Ténã* happened to be missing its *kāfé kubi*, which it normally would have in the bow.

Munung normally just means the first harpoon used on any occasion, while *nomang*, to assist, refers to any subsequent harpoon used on that animal. The small *kubi* is designed for harpooning shark or turtles. Commonly a boat would

TABLE 13. *Harpoon Head Measurements in* Menula Belolong *in 1979*

Harpoon	Length of shaft	Outer edge of blade to tip of barb	Gap between tip of barb and shaft	Inner edge of barb to shaft
1. *kāfé kubi* (*kubi* harpoon)	22 cm.	8 cm.	3 cm.	4 cm.
2. *kāfé léo fã* (fore *léo* harpoon)	33 cm.	17 cm.	7 cm.	8 cm.
3. *kāfé léo bélã* (great *léo* harpoon)	27 cm.	13 cm.	5 cm.	6 cm.
4. *kāfé nodé pukã* (harpoon pole rack base harpoon)	36 cm.	13 cm.	6 cm.	5 cm.
5. *kāfé suka fã* (fore *suka* harpoon)	37 cm.	19 cm.	8 cm.	8 cm.
6. *kāfé suka bélã* (great *suka* harpoon)	45 cm.	21 cm.	9 cm.	11 cm.
7. *kāfé kotekĕlema* (sperm whale harpoon)	48 cm.	20 cm.	7 cm.	8 cm.

PLATE 37. A set of harpoons appropriate for a *téna*

keep one such harpoon in the bow and another in the stern. It might be used to dispatch a shark or marlin which has been caught on a line. The *kāfé léo fā*, which is normally kept at the ready, may be used for harpooning smaller and fleeter animals, such as whiptail devil ray, *moku*, shortfin devil ray, *bōu*, small porpoise of various types, *temu bĕlurā*, marlin of all varieties, and most kinds of shark, excluding in particular the whale shark. The *kāfé léo bélā* may be used as a second harpoon for almost any kind of animal. It is also used to harpoon killer whale, *Orcinus Orca*, called *seguni*, short-finned pilot whale, *Globicephala macrohyncus*, called *temu bélā* (large porpoise), and the false killer whale, *Pseudora Crassidens*, called *temu bĕlā* (long porpoise). The *kāfé nodé pukā* may be used as a third or fourth harpoon on a sperm whale.

If the harpooner spots a manta ray, *bĕlelā*, near by, he will quickly change to the harpoon and rope called *suka fā*. If, however, the harpooner has time he will use instead the *suka bélā*, which is a larger harpoon and therefore is stronger. This harpoon is specifically designed for harpooning manta ray. It is also called *kāfé bélā*, the big harpoon, and *kafé bĕlelang*, the harpoon for manta ray. It can also be used for harpooning whale shark.

The first harpoon used on sperm whale is the large *kāfé kotekĕlema*, which is specifically designed for this purpose, with a longer shaft and a flange closer to the shaft, so that the harpoon will go more easily and deeper into the blubber. It has a double leader, each half of which is separately bound to the harpoon. This harpoon and its leader are stored when not in use by being tied to the stringer on the right side of the *bĕfaléng* and *gĕlefé* boat sections. The second harpoon used on a sperm whale in the *Soge Ténā* is the one they identified as *kāfé nomang*, that is additional harpoon, or *kafé mafang*, reserve harpoon. This would normally be the *suka fā*. The third harpoon used would be the *kāfé nodé pukā*. When there are two *nodé pukā*, on either side of the section called *nodé pukā*, either may be taken first. If a fourth harpoon were used, it would be the remaining *nodé pukā*. Some boats would try to weaken the whale by lancing it with the *bĕlāda*. As soon as possible, they would hook gaffs into the animal.

Harpoon Poles

In order to insure that the harpoon is held securely in the pole, *lekā*, the harpooner places an insert, *unaj*, about eight or nine centimetres long and made of thin bamboo inside the end of the harpoon pole. The bamboo used for this purpose is called *au*, *Gigantochloa scortechinii*. Because the harpoon pole is often quite wide, it may be stepped down by an extension, *noloj* (more specifically, *noloj kenāda nãé*, the *kenāda*'s extension), a narrower bamboo, into which the *unaj* is inserted. The harpooner tightens the outer bamboo, and prevents its end from splitting, with a woven rattan ring (*sĕluku*), which continues up the pole as a spiral wrapping. When the harpooner attaches a harpoon to the pole, he inserts the point at the end of the shaft into the *unaj*, and then he, or someone else, pounds the other end of the pole with a mallet, driving the point home. When through use the *unaj* no longer grips the harpoon, it must be replaced. With the *lekã kenãda puã gãda* which is the pole used with the *kãfé léo fã*, this must be done very frequently, at least once a week, and of course it must also be done for any pole which has actually been used in harpooning a large animal. This pole is the soul of all the other poles and must be given special care. When a harpooner changes its *unaj*, he will sprinkle it with holy water. The purpose of this arrangement is that while the harpoon must be firmly enough held to the pole to allow the harpooner to strike it into the animal, the pole must be able to come loose after the blow and float away. Since the poles are made of bamboo, they not infrequently shatter under heavy use and must be replaced from time to time.

The poles and their extensions are made of the bamboo called *teri*, *Gigantochloa verticillata*. Gregorius Keraf says that they may also be made of bamboo called *petung*, *Dendrocalamus asper*. This bamboo and another called *au*, *Gigantochloa scortechinii*, may also be used for the extensions. The harpooner must obtain the bamboo from the interior. For this purpose, he will ask someone living in one of the mountain hamlets to cut the bamboo for him. In return, after the boat has harpooned several animals, the harpooner gives him two are three sections of meat from the share especially reserved for the bamboo poles. The harpooner must shave the nodes of the bamboo smooth and straighten any bends by heating the pole in a fire and bending it in the opposite direction. The poles used in a boat should be ten in number and are as follows, with measurements of those used by Marsel Kalang Keraf in the *Menula Belolong*:

1. *lekã kenãda puã gãda* (pole put up at readiness on rests) (5.8 m.): this pole is attached to the *kãfé léo fã* and then put up, *pũa*, on the harpooning platform, to rest at readiness (*gãda*) on the harpoon platform. Keraf says that a pole with short internodes is selected for this purpose so that it will be heavier. One harpooner said that this pole must be exactly three and a half arm spans long for proper balance. The harpoon is inserted in the end of the bamboo which was the upper tip when it was growing.
2. *lekã kenãda mafang* (reserve pole on rests) (5.8 m.): this is the reserve pole for the previous one. It too takes the *kãfé léo fã*.
3. *lekã nubã* (*nubã* pole) (6.2 m.): this pole may take the *kãfé léo fã*, but more particularly it takes the *kãfé léo bélã*. It is especially used for pilot whale, false killer whale, killer whale, and Goosebeak Whale (Cuvier's). This pole must be longer than the others because the animals it is used for can turn quickly and more easily evade the boat. Although it is longer, it must be lighter than the previous poles, because the rope and harpoon it is used with

are larger and heavier. The harpoon is inserted in the upper end of the bamboo.

4. three *lekã tĕlākā nomang* (stretching out pole for second harpooning) (4.1 m., 4.65 m., and 5 m.): these are used for placing the second harpoon in a whale or ray and can take the *kāfé suka fã* and the *kāfé nodé pukã*. *Tĕlākā* means to be stretched out. The harpoon is inserted in the lower end of the bamboo, because of the added strength it gives there.

5. two *lekã tĕlākā bĕlelã* (stretching out pole for manta ray) (4.4 m. and 4.55 m.): this pole takes the *kāfé léo bélã* which is designed for the giant manta ray *bĕlelã*. It is also used for harpoon whale shark and sperm whale. It has a wooden extension on the end opposite to the harpoon, which is pounded, especially when the harpoon for sperm whale is inserted. Because it is wood it absorbs the blows better than the bamboo would. The harpoon is inserted in the lower end of the bamboo.

6. *lekã tĕlākā kotekĕlema* (stretching out pole for sperm whale) (4.55 m.): this pole is used with the harpoon for sperm whale. The harpoon is inserted in the lower end of the bamboo.

7. *lekã tĕlākā ōjo bélã* (stretching out pole for large waves) (5.75 m.): this pole is used only for manoeuvring the boat in the surf. The name means the pole to be stretched out in large breakers. It has a wooden extension on the end used to push against the ocean floor for protection which is made of *Schoutenia ovata*, or *kũgu*.

Ropes

There are nine separate harpooning ropes, not counting their extensions. The circumferences given below were measured on the ropes of the *Muko Ténã* in 1982.

1. *talé suka fã*: this is a rope with a circumference of 8 cm., made of gebang leaf and bark of *Hibiscus tiliaceus*, which is kept in the second section in the bow of the boat, *serã*. It lies on a wide plank (*ida*, which otherwise means ladder) running crosswise to the boat and situated about the height of the lower thwart.[1] Thus it is handy, but well out of the way of the crew when not needed. This rope and its harpoon may be used, when rushed, for harpooning giant manta ray and for follow-up harpooning for whales and large porpoise. The name means the fore *suka*. I have been given no explanation of the word *suka*. It is not the homonym which means 'to like'. There may be no connection, but I will simply draw attention to Verheijen's reconstruction of a Proto–Malayo-Polynesian root **suka* for *Gnetum gnemon*, Linn., the bark of which produces an excellent fibre useful for making thread and cords (Verheijen 1984: 58). This rope has an extension, *bĕloi*, because it is sometimes employed for first harpooning.

2. *talé léo fã*: this is the thinnest and therefore easiest handled, as well as the ritually most significant rope. It has a circumference of 3.1 cm. It is the rope kept in immediate readiness and is stored in the boat section called place of the *léo*, *uak léo ūli*. The word *léo* means to throw, catapult (Arndt 1937: 7). This is called the fore throwing rope because it is attached to the harpoon and pole placed on the harpooning platform. In 1982 the *léo fã* of the *Sika Ténã* was 68.63 metres in length. When this rope breaks, the boat owners must make it anew or if possible borrow a replacement before the boat can go to sea again. The rope is made entirely of cotton thread. The extension of this rope is about 7.2 cm. in circumference and is woven of gebang palm leaf and hibiscus bark. According to Gregorius Keraf, its tip is attached to the *léo fã*, while its base is attached to the rope called *puã pukã* (base of the masts). Keraf, also writes that like the other ropes the base, *udép*, of the extension is wrapped with gebang leaves or hibiscus fibre so that it is stiff and pointed, easing attachment to other ropes. To add one rope to another is *hangak*, to separate them is *legã*.

3. *talé léo bélã* (great throwing rope): a similar but somewhat thicker rope, stored underneath the *nodé pukã* rope in the boat section of that name, i.e. the section where the base of the fore harpoon rack post is located. The circumference is 3.7 cm. This rope in *Sika Ténã* in 1982 was 75.85 metres long. Generally speaking it should be the same length as the *léo fã*. Its name means the large or great throwing rope.

4. *talé nodé pukã fãnã* and *talé nodé pukã mẽki*: these are the right and left harpoon pole rack base ropes, respectively, stored in the section which is called by that name or *ūmã* after the drain hole located there. These take harpoons of the same name. According to Gregorius Keraf, they have a circumference of 6 to 7 cm. and are attached to extension ropes of 8 cm. The rope I measured was mixed with plastic wool and had a circumference of 4.7 cm. The *léo bélã* and both *nodé pukã* rest on a wide plank arranged like that in the *serã*.

5. *talé suka bélã* or *suka bělelã*: this is the large *suka* (for the name see number 1 above), stored, on a wide plank, on the right side of the section named after the base of the mast poles, *uak puã pukã*, and used, if there is time to change, with the harpoon of the same name for giant manta ray or whale shark. Normally its base is tied to the upper thwart at the back of the section it is found in, but if it is about to be used to harpoon an animal for the first time, it is untied and attached to the large hawser called *bĕfaléng* in the centre of the boat, after this rope has been released from the rope to which it in turn is normally attached. It has a circumference of 8 cm. and is made of gebang and hibiscus.

6. *talé puã pukã*: this rope is placed on the left of the same compartment as the previous rope. My information is that it provides extra length to the previous rope, but that it may be switched for the same purpose to other

ropes. In some boats it may also have its own harpoon, *kāfé mafang* (reserve harpoon). However, Gregorius Keraf writes that its tip is connected to the extension of the *léo fā*, while its base is attached to the *talé běfaléng*. It is 8.5 cm. in circumference and is made of gebang and hibiscus.

7. *talé běfaléng*: this is a very thick rope, the first section of the rope used for sperm whale. While in most cases it is remotely connected to the harpoon via the *puã pukã* rope, it will be detached from the *puã pukã* and attached directly to the *kāfé kotěkema* when a sperm whale becomes a target. It is kept coiled in the compartment of the same name. The *běfaléng* is 9.5 cm. in circumference and is made of gebang and hibiscus.

8. *talé gělefé*: this is the last in the main sequence of the harpooning ropes and the thickest. Its tip is permanently attached to the *talé běfaléng*, while its base is permanently tied to the rear outrigger boom. The *gělefé* is 10 cm. in circumference and is made of gebang leaf and hibiscus bark.

In addition to the ropes listed here, some boats keep in the bow section called *serã* a thin rope called *kubi* for the harpoon of that name used for shark. The *kubi* rope I measured was 3.1 cm. in circumference and made of plastic wool. The *kāfé suka uring*, kept in the sternmost section and used for shark and fish caught on a line, has a thin rope of the same name. I measured one made of plastic wool as 3.7 cm. The gaffs, *kenaté*, have their *talé kenuté*, as well, with a circumference of 8.5 cm. and made from gebang and hibiscus. They are located on either side of the boat section called the large *sěmugur*, *sěmugur bélã*. A substantial rope, not used for harpooning, and stored beneath the *běfuléng* and *gělefé*, is the *talé mãda*. Its uses are multiple: whales may be tied to the boat with it; whales or boats may be pulled with it, and a fish or porpoise may be pulled into the boat with it.

Rope Making

According to Svensson (1971: 21), 'Almost all rope is right handed, hawser laid and usually three-stranded'. This description fits Lamalera rope very closely. All Lamalera ropes are three-stranded. Hawser-laid rope is rope which has been twisted three times. First the fibres are twisted to make rope yarn, then the yarn is twisted into strands, which are then twisted into the final rope, exactly as in Lamalera. The strands of Lamalera rope are individually twisted left-handed. They are then twisted into right-handed rope (see Svensson 1971: 22–3 for an explanation of these terms). According to Svensson (1971: 26), right-handed rope is coiled clockwise, and the ropes in the Lamalera boats are always coiled clockwise. To coil rope is *galu*.

The smaller ropes, like the *léo*, are woven from cotton thread. The large ropes are manufactured with a mixture of gebang palm leaf and hibiscus tree bark. They obtain the hibiscus bark from the interior. Gebang leaf they must collect a considerable distance away at Ata Nila, in Kédang, near the eastern end of the island, which is the source too for the gebang leaf used in weaving the sail. Cotton is either locally grown, a minority, or traded for in the interior. The thread is all or almost all locally spun by the wives and sisters of the men in the boat-owning corporation. That this is far from an insignificant economic contribution made by women to the fishery can be seen by the ritual and economic importance of the two *léo*. Without their cotton thread the boats would not put to sea, for they would have no way of catching animals. The use of substances other than cotton in the larger ropes by no means weakens this point, for cotton thread is required in attaching the leaders of all the harpoons to their harpoons. If, as may have been the case to some degree in the distant past, a fibre other than cotton was used to make thread, in all probability it was still women who spun it.

By one estimate 111 spindles of thread make up a ball *mōrã*. Each member of the boat-owning corporation must provide two such balls for the manufacture of a *léo* rope. These balls are in fact prepared by his wife or other female relatives. Assuming eleven members, these figures would mean that twenty-two balls or 2,442 spindles of thread were needed for the manufacture of the rope. To weave a rope is *hodi talé*, thus *hodi léo*, *hodi kĕlīfa*, and so on. According to Gregorius Keraf, the number of threads used in a rope must be odd too, so that the *léo fã* would require 90 threads, plus an additional odd number, bringing it to 93, 95, 97, or 99. For the somewhat thicker *léo bélã*, the basis would be 130, and the total, 131, 133, 135, 137, or 139 threads.[2] When a boat group wishes to spin a new rope, they assemble very early in the morning, around 4.00 a.m., or as Oleona (1989: 26) colourfully puts it, when the *kokila* bird begins to quarrel or the *murai* bird begins to warble, well before anyone else is about. Women bring down large pans full of thread, if it is a cotton rope. Men situate themselves all down the beach in order to wind the thread around posts very widely spaced apart, perhaps 100 to 150 metres. The spacing should approximate the length of the eventual rope, allowing for the fact that the eventual rope will be shortened by the process of weaving in comparison to the length of the original strands. Therefore most of the beach is needed, free of other activity and obstruction. This process is important in estimating the thread required and is called *pano léo*, if that is the rope in question. Thread is taken back and forth three times, to establish a rotation. Each corporation member makes enough rotations to contribute his share to the total number of threads. Thus if there are 15 members, each contributing 6 rotations, there would be the 90 threads of the eventual rope. Once this number were achieved, another rotation would be contributed by only 1, 3, 5, 7, or 9 members to make up the final number of threads. A rope of 99 threads would therefore represent 297 individual passes of thread up and down the beach. Three passes are kept distinct from each other on each revolution, but are cumulative over the whole process. They are then cut, so that there are three bunches of 99 threads each.[3] Each bunch is rolled up on a large spindle, *bōpa*.

The next stage is to unwind each *bōpa* at the beach, where the coils are stretched out again and each coil is twisted to tighten it, called *puper léo*. Then the three lengths are matched and each given a mark, before being wound again on its spindle. The *bōpa* is a polished and strong piece of *Schoutenia ovata* wood about 75 cm. long with a hook at one end. According to Gregorius Keraf, before the rope is finally woven, the crown or centre of the rope, the *léo kepur*, must be made, which is the loop at the base (not tip) of the *léo*. This item of manufacture they mark with a ceremony called *toto léo kepur*, in which they formerly would asperse the loop with chicken blood, but today do so with holy water. Then they can commence the final weaving of the rope, *hodi léo*. One man sits in a convenient spot in a boat in a boat shed and holds the developing rope taut. The three *bōpa* are suspended over a crosspiece. Three men then grab a spindle each and, while holding them as taut as possible, pass them to each other in unison from right to left. They do this in short spurts, further twisting the individual strands each time before passing the spindles. By constantly keeping tension on the strands they considerably reduce the circumference of each strand. Enthusiasm to keep up a long and boring job is supplied by palm wine and work songs. The men make big heaves in unison, stretching the strands, and lots of noise (see Plates 38 and 39). Gregorius Keraf writes,

PLATE 38. Rolling the strands on to spindles, *bōpa*, prior to weaving the rope

PLATE 39. Pulling the strands taut in rope weaving

When weaving the *léo*, they sing songs which are in the appropriate rhythm and breathing for the movement of weaving which requires strength, accompanying and stimulating the movement of transferring *bopa* to *bopa*. This division [of the labour] is a division full of ceremony regarded as the most important, noble and exalted. The theme from morning to midday is full of glory and nobility, while the theme from midday to evening has the character of mourning and wistfulness. The text of the songs narrates the history of the clan involved or expresses hopes that the ancestors will give a generous livelihood to the clan and village by means of an abundant harvest from the sea. There are also songs that allude to members of the clan and so on.

He goes on to say that it is impermissible to have a section of the rope which feels soft, *léo menōlã*, the *léo* breaks. When such an imperfection is found, they must unwind the rope to that point and retwist it. To prevent this from happening, they roll the rope as it is being woven onto a large piece of bamboo or wood, called *molã*. During weaving, they rub the strands and finished rope with the sap of *Sesbania grandiflora* to glue the strands together. They prepare this substance by taking a branch from the tree and scraping its bark down to the wood. These scrapings they then take in their hands and rub on the rope. Once the rope is finished, they asperse the tip, *léo fūtu*, with holy water, formerly chicken blood, and also asperse the rope itself and each of the spindles. Finally they anchor the new rope in the sea, *pepal léo*, so that by soaking, the rope straightens out the kinks acquired from being rolled on the *molã*. Once the rope has been brought ashore and dried at the beach by being stretched from long poles, they stain it again with sap. The sap oxidizes in sea water, turning the rope reddish and eventually shiny black.

Keraf writes that particularly with the *léo*, there is a ceremony and festival called *toto léo* marking the completion of rope making, which takes place before the rope is placed in the boat. In the past, the chicken used to stain the rope had to be brought by a woman, *kefīna*, of the descent group married into another descent group. More significantly, this woman should also bring a pig or goat for the festival, which takes place at the beach next to the boat. This woman will be compensated with a return, called *hoder*, of fish subsequently caught. For a large goat or pig, the return would be one torso, *ūk*, of giant manta ray. For a moderate-sized goat or pig, the return would be half of the section called *fadar* near the centre of the tail of a pilot whale or sperm whale.

The boat owner periodically checks, *lafã*, the rope. When part of it becomes weakened, he wraps it, *bité*, with thread and stains it with the sap of *Sesbania grandiflora*. A rope with uncorrected weak spots, according to Keraf, will bring bad luck. The boat will not encounter fish for days, or if any are seen, they will not be harpooned. A rope with too many repairs, therefore, should be newly woven.[4]

Rope made from gebang leaf and hibiscus fibre, such as the two largest, is woven in much the same way as that woven from cotton thread, once the individual strands have been prepared. The job of twisting a strand can be done by one man. He attaches the newly started strand to a post in the boat shed and then pulls it around a second post. By pulling against the rope with his body weight he maintains tension on it. They place a hollow wooden cylinder, called *kenalat* (from *galat*, to produce, create), around the finished part of the rope to serve as a constant guide for the diameter of the rope as it is produced, so that the rope will be uniform throughout. This device for the strands of the *běfaléng* or *gělefé* ropes is 7 cm. long, with an outside diameter of 4.5 cm. and a diameter of the hole of 2 cm. It is made of *Pterocarpus indicus*. Much more gebang leaf than hibiscus bark is worked into these ropes, and the hibiscus fibre is kept to the outside, because it is slippery and the diameter guide pulls more easily over it. Keraf writes that if the boat master is diligent, he will make the *talé běfaléng* and the *talé gělefé* entirely of hibiscus bark. However, because such ropes are very slippery when wet, they will receive an outer wrapping, *bōlé*, of gebang palm leaf. When the gebang leaf wears out, they will unwind the rope, rewrap the strands, and then reweave the rope.

The harpoon leaders are made of cotton thread. The circumferences of the various leaders are as follows:

1. *kělīfa kāfé kubi* 2.7 cm.
2. *kělīfa kāfé suka fã* 3.7 cm.

3. *kĕlīfa kāfé léo fã* 2 cm.
4. *kĕlīfa kāfé léo bélã* 2.2 cm.
5. *kĕlīfa kāfé nodé pukã* 3.5 cm.
6. *kĕlīfa kāfé suka bélã* 5 cm. (including *pelepah* bindings)
7. *kĕlīfa kāfé kotekĕlema* (4 separated strands) 3.3 cm.
8. *kĕlīfa kāfé suka uring* 2.2 cm.
9. *kĕlīfa kĕnaté* (the gaff's): 3.3 cm.

In order to weave a harpoon leader, they must first twist the individual strands. Two men take two large spindles and hook them through loops at either end of the thread to be twisted. They then face each other and twist the thread clockwise, giving the strands a left-handed twist. Once this strand has been completed, they cut it into the three equal strands from which the final leader will be woven in the normal way. Each of the three sections is wound onto its own spindle for this purpose.

A single man can weave the cord, *pĕrãnã*, used to attach the leader to the harpoon. A weight, such as an old iron cannon shot (*c*.4 cm. in diameter), fixed in a *pelepah* frame with a stick on top and called *pĕloru*, is attached to either end of the strands to be twisted, making a long loop. The loop is hung over some convenient projection, and twisting the cord is then easy.

Kemité

The loop at the end of the main rope, through which the leader passes is *nangak onã*. The loop is the mouth of this rope, *léo fefã*. This loop is not tied, but fixed by bending the rope back and wrapping either cotton cord or lontar palm-branch bindings around the end and the adjacent part of the rope. Again villagers argue that these wrappings are much stronger than a knot would be. These bindings, *kemité*, are very important and those on the *léo fã* must be wrapped according to quite specific regulations (see Plate 40).

Kemité derives from *bité*, bindings. While the rope called the forward *léo*, the *léo fã*, is the most important of all the harpooning ropes in the boat, the bindings of that rope are the most important part of the rope. This rope is said to be like the body of the whole boat. It must be made correctly first; the rest may follow. If it is wrong, everything else will be wrong. If its bindings are not correct, the crew will never get a chance to harpoon a fish, for the fish will stay away. According to Gregorius Keraf, the *kemité* of the *léo fã* is the power of the rope to attract (*geféã*) the fish. For this reason the bindings are among the spots which will be aspersed with holy water in rituals connected with the boat. Some boat owners will feed ginger, possibly mixed with edible swallows' nest, *kolo kafak*, to the bindings. The ginger must be sharp *lia méã*, red ginger, to give energy to the rope. Others would rub the bindings of this rope with sandalwood, *kajo kayana*, or wood of *Canarium commune*, if available. The regulation concerning the uneven loops may be expressed as *toro nalã* (we

PLATE 40. *Kemité*, bindings securing the loop at the end of the main rope

it uneven). A binding with an even, *kenetang*, number of loops is already a mistake guaranteeing lack of success. The bindings of the *léo fã* must be checked every week or so, or whenever the boat fails to get any fish. The loop suffers wear and tear, and must be carefully inspected and repaired as soon as it is damaged.

There are quite distinct rules and procedures for the boats which use *pelepah*, on the one hand, and those who use thread. The following applies for those who use *hua* (thread). The tying is always done by the boat master. He begins with the centre of the loop, counting 13 (some use 11) twists of the strands (*bōpa*), that is the raised ridges as the strands spiral through the rope, taking one in the middle, then six on each side (see Fig. 26). There he ties the two sides of the loops together. This first wrapping is the *fã* (front). Five more *bōpa* on there is the second wrapping, made in the same way and called *uak tukã* (central section). Three more *bōpa* along is the third wrapping, called the *uring* (stern). The *fã*, *uak tukã*, and *uring*, all being done in the same way, consist of 5 *bité* (wrappings, or *pĕruang*), 5 *tékél* (wrappings encircling and crossing the first wrappings), and 5 *hofil* (wrappings encircling the second wrappings). Some call *hofil* continuations (*holoj*). The *bité* consists in threads wrapped each side of the loop. The *tékél* are threads then wrapped around the *bité*, between the two sections of rope being held together. *Hofil* are then wrapped around the *tékél* in the centre. The loose end of the *léo* may not be trimmed off. Instead a finger length extends beyond the *uring*. The final wrapping is the long wrapping, *kemité bĕlã*, which is one *bōpa* further down and which makes sure that the unravelling end of the rope is completely covered.

This wrapping of about a finger's length is called *bité lorak* or *bĕlorak*. At the very tip, it is tied to the other side of the *léo* with 5 *hofil*. The ends of the thread at the *fã* and *uak tukã* are twisted under the strands and pulled out toward the loop. That at the *uring* goes under and is pulled out toward the wrapping of the tip of the *léo* which fastens the loop closed. The end of this string is brought back and twisted under three strands from the end. Only the *léo fã* and the *léo bélã* are treated in this way, the other ropes being given no such attention. To change the *kemité* is *heka kemité*. This must always be done for both *léo fã* and *léo bélã* at the same time, about every week or so or whenever they find that they are getting no fish. The following boats make their *kemité* of thread: *Demo Sapã, Baka Ténã, Pĕraso Sapã, Léla Sapã, Dato Ténã, Gĕléko Ténã, Boko Lolo, Sika Ténã, Téti Heri, Holo Sapã, Soge Ténã, Horo Ténã, Dolu Ténã, Sili Ténã, Kéna Pukã, Kelulus, Kebako Pukã, Jafa Ténã.*

For those boats which wrap with *pelepah* (*kelepa*) rather than thread, the quite different procedure is as follows. They start from the tip of the rope as it lies in the loop, thus the stern end of the loop in their eyes. *Bōpa* they do not bother to count, the measurement being taken with the angle formed by the thumb and forefinger. The tip of the rope corresponds to the tip of the index finger, and the loop follows around passing the thumb. The *uring* this time corresponds with the end of the rope. Corresponding to the joint in the finger comes the *uak tukã*, beyond that at the next finger joint is the *fã*. There is no *kemité bĕlã* when this method is employed.

There are differences too in the prescribed number of threads in the ties, *bité*, *tékél*, and *hofil*. *Nara Ténã* uses four for each, but no explanation why was forthcoming other than that they had always done so. The *Kopo Paker* and *Boli Sapã* use three strands in each case. For them, there is an explanation. The first version of these two boats was built by an *ata mōlã* in Lāma Kéra clan who was the *ata mōlã* too for *Nara Ténã*. He insisted on making the boats smaller than *Nara Ténã* and also insisted that they use fewer threads. The following boats use *kemité* made of *pelepah*: *Muko Ténã, Notã Ténã, Menula Belolong, Kebéla Ténã, Boli Sapã, Bui Pukã, Sia Apu, Kopo Paker, Nara Ténã, Téna Ãnã, Sinu Sapã.*

Other Tools and Gear in the Boat

Additional items in the gear of the boat include small wooden blocks, shaped in fact like very tiny benches without backs, about 30 cm. broad and 12 cm. wide, called *nōbé*, which are tied to the boat by cords and which may be placed on the lower thwarts by rowers who sit on them, so that they will be more comfortable. In the *sĕmugur kéni* section of the boat in the stern is a large water pot, containing around 25 litres of water and firmly tied to the boat with *pelepah* bindings. A small shaved bamboo bailer or cup, *kenãjo*, around 20 cm. in length is used to dip water from this pot. In the well of the boat are two large bamboo bailers, called *bō*. Another form of bailer used when the boat is swamped is a large basket woven from lontar palm leaf called *sidu*. A further type of bailer sometimes encountered is the *kéra*, made from an unsplit lontar leaf and similar in design to the containers used on the island of Roti for carrying palm wine. It is stiffened by being woven from several layers and by having a piece of lontar palm branch inserted around the mouth. There may be as many as four of these bailing baskets in the boat. Each section of the boat from the *puã pukã* to the *sěmugur kéni* in the stern is supplied with a pair of paddles, *fāi*. Although it is not unknown to place oars in the stern of the boat, most boats confine themselves to two oars, *faja*, fixed to supports in the *nodé pukã* section in the bow, which are rowed by crew members facing backward when giving chase or when there is otherwise a need to move the boat rapidly or when it is needed to move it with greater power, such as when towing animals or boats. In addition to the normal sharpening stones, each boat keeps a coarse-grained sharpening stone for removing rust from harpoons, such as the little-used *kāfě kotekělema*, as well as the lance blade. A short wooden crutch with a rope which is used to keep the sail half furled when sailing with a strong wind is the *tenuda*.

14

Open-Sea Fishing and Hunting

Once the transition has taken place to the calmer south-east monsoon winds of the dry season, the time has come for daily use of the *téna* for open-sea fishing and hunting. In the past, the beginning of this season was marked by a large ceremony in the centre of the beach attended by residents of both the upper and the lower villages. Today the ceremony continues to be held in a mixture of Christian and traditional forms.

Annual Fishing Ceremony

The open sea is *léfa*, and this word is understandably associated with this activity and the ceremony which precedes it as well as the period of the year in which this form of fishing and hunting is routinely carried out. The ceremony is intended to insure that there will be fish in the sea. In the past the clans of Lamalera would ask the head of Lamamanu hamlet to approach the lord of the land of the lower village, *lefo-tana alep*, in Lango Fujo clan to hold the ceremony. Nowadays, the missionary takes a leading role.

There are several places of importance in the mountain. The highest of these is (1) Rangafak, followed by (2) Itok Kefélong Fata, (3) Pau Léré (Low Mango), and (4) Fato Kotekĕlema (Sperm Whale Stone). The lord of the land used to go to Rangafak, where he would bake a chicken and rice in a bamboo container. After eating this, those involved in the ceremony would call all the varieties of fish in the sea.

From Rangafak, the lord of the land and entourage descend to Itok Kefélong Fata, a boulder with a hole in it and shaped like the nose and blow hole of a whale. He puts a grass leaf in the hole and pulls the whale to sea. He must not pull it toward the land. At Pau Léré there is another stone, like a gravestone, called *nuba*. If this stone has fallen over, the village will get no fish; so the lord of the land must check it. If it has toppled, he must give it an egg and put it back in place. There is no ceremony at Fato Kotekĕlema, but this boulder gets its name from the fact that it looks like a whale. It is said to have been a whale from the mountain that was trying to get to sea when it was caught by daylight and turned into stone.

From Pau Léré, the lord of the land descends to his own ritual temple, now situated just above the upper border of Lamalera. Actually Lango Fujo clan has two next to each other. One of these is the clan temple, *lango bélã*, and is called *Fūka Léré* (Low Kapok), which is also the name of the location where the lord of the land lives. The other temple is especially for fish and is called *Korké Ikã*, that is 'fish temple' (see Plate 41). Both structures are kept small and unobtrusive so as not to offend the mission. All clans used to have such *korké*, but they have all disappeared, 'now that religion has entered'. The *Korké Ikã* of Lango Fujo consists of a raised floor on four house posts, covered by a coconut-leaf roof. It is forbidden to use grass or lontar leaf for this roof.

From here, the party descends to the beach, where at the request of the clans of Bata Onã and Bĕliko Lolo, the head of Lamalera A orders all the clans to gather at the beach in front of the St Peter Chapel. At the chapel, they now have a Catholic ceremony. The two groups sit together and exchange holy water, *fai lera fulã* (sun-moon water),[1] that is they hand it back and forth. This exchange is supposed to increase their sense of unity. If eventually the fish fail to appear, they may return to the mountain and repeat the ceremony. In 1979 the ceremony, including the trip to the mountain by the lord of the land, had been held just before the beginning of May.

Appendix II of Gregorius Keraf's grammar of the dialect of Lamaholot spoken in Lamalera reproduces a description of the village's mode of livelihood dictated by the master builder and former harpooner Gabriel Blido Keraf. That description contains the following account of the ceremony beginning large-scale fishing.

PLATE 41. *Korké Ikã* (Fish Temple) at *Fūka Léré*, just above Lamalera

When the *temakataka* season [*c*. March and April] begins to change into the *lerã* season [the first part of the dry season, May to September], all the elders of the village assemble the population [*ribu-ratu* (literally, thousand-hundred)] of the two villages together with the lords of the land in order to discuss the question of fishing [i.e. to hold the annual village ceremony at the start of main fishing season, now conventionally assigned to 1 May]. Half of the beach belongs to Libu [Tufaonã clan], the other half to Gésiraja [Lango Fujo clan]. People call the boundary of the land owners *ikã-kotã* (fish heads). The whole populace gathers at *ikã-kotã*. All those who live to the west of *ikã-kotã* sit facing east, and those who live to the east of *ikã-kotã* sit facing west. When everyone has gathered, the two groups offer each other baskets of betel nuts and sirih peppers. After chewing betel, an expert or a village elder from one side begins to speak, discussing the question of fishing, so that in the coming year the two villages will face only favourable conditions at sea, many fish will also show up at sea, and all boats will harpoon game until they are fully laden, so that they can feed all of the people in the village, including the small children, the adults, the orphans, and the widows, as well as all the people around the mountain (in the interior). Of all the fish encountered, not excluding a single one, the tails, fins, and bones are gathered at *ikã-kotã*. After discussing the question of fishing, they call for a market—not a market like the one on shore, but a market at sea. They appoint one or two boats located at either the eastern or western end of the beach to go to announce a market, that is they are the first to go to sea. The next day one or two boats go to sea by themselves. The day after that for the first time all the boats go to sea together (Gregorius Keraf 1978: 242–5).

Gregorius Keraf explains the idiom 'fish heads' for the border through the centre of the beach by the fact that boats are obliged to give heads of sperm whale (actually only specific portions) as tribute to the lords of the land. Which lord of the land receives this tribute depends on where the boat is located on the beach, and that in general by where its descent group and clan house is located in the village. According to Keraf, the lords of the land store the bones of sperm whale heads at this border (Gregorius Keraf 1978: 243 n. 2). These days, the bones are not so gathered. Instead, generally they are gathered together and burned when they have become an obstruction to work on the beach.

It used to be that during this annual ceremony, all of the sacred stones in the village would have to be fed. One such was an upright, flat boulder near the clan house of Běliko Lolo in Lamalera A, called *lefo nubã*, 'the village sacred stone'. Formerly if the fleet could get no fish, the head of Lefo Tukã clan would have to rub oil on this stone. On the day when the boats first go out, and also at other times if there were any serious trouble in the village, two pieces of white cloth would be sewn together at the temple at the centre of the beach where the St Peter Chapel now stands.

In 1982 the resident missionary attempted to organize the *léfa* ceremony, not only to strengthen its Christian elements, but to emphasize traditional custom and traditional ritual language. He seemed unsatisfied with the result, feeling that too many people did not enter into the spirit and complaining that he had been left to shape things more than he wanted. They gathered in front of the descent group great house of Kĕlaké Langu section of Bata Onã clan), with great displays of the principal ropes, *léo fã*, of each of the boats. They then moved to the chapel at the beach. All was fancy, but too many did not do the right things. The language used for speeches by the village leadership was unimpressive, whereas the missionary had wanted real ancient language, such as that in Gregorius Keraf's grammar (Gregorius Keraf 1978).

Independently of this conversation, and actually on the previous July day, a villager complained that in May the fleet had caught nothing, because the lord of the land had held the ceremony as a Christian service in the yard in front of a clan house of Bata Onã (Kĕlaké Langu), without inviting various leaders of the principal clans.[2] Because there were no fish, the lord of the land quietly redid the ceremony properly (that is, by calling the spirit, *pung alep*, of the fish) at the chapel in the centre of the beach in June. This event took place on a Sunday (when the large boats are not permitted to work). On Monday, one boat got a whale. Soon thereafter, six other boats caught one each.

Launching the Fleet

On those days when the *téna* are in use, the boats generally sail as a fleet, putting out one at a time as the crews collect at the beach, but usually by about 6.00 a.m. Some days, when crew members are distracted by other obligations or lacking in enthusiasm, the full complement may fail to assemble around a given boat, preventing its launching for the day, while others with more active and committed crews nevertheless do put out. There is therefore not only a fluctuating composition in the crew make-up of a given boat, but also in the number of boats at sea from day to day, even at the height of *léfa*.

Before launching their boats, crew members gather in the boat shed, while the harpooner removes the cover from the bowsprit and hangs it on a post of the shed, and then sprinkles holy water about the boat and on the crew, before they collectively recite a prayer. Then they place their shoulders to the outriggers and upper thwarts and move the boat quickly down the beach over wooden runners into the surf, each sailor scrambling rapidly into the boat as he reaches the water's edge (see Plate 42). Then they paddle the boat well out beyond the breakers, where they stop to say a *Pater Noster* before raising the masts and sail and getting under way. Sometimes they say the prayer after the sail is up.

Gregorius Keraf (1983) writes that if the boat has not been taken to sea several days in a row, they fill a bailer with sea water and splash water on the keel in the bow on the right and left sides. If they do not do this, the boat will not shift from its spot, when pulled toward the sea. If it proves difficult to move the boat at any other time, they will quickly fetch sea water and splash it. Afterwards the boat is easily moved. Keraf explicitly compares this procedure

PLATE 42. Launching of a *téna*

to a person taking a bath who wets parts of his body first before freely bathing. Even in the tropics, sudden application of unheated water to the unprepared skin causes an unpleasant shock of coldness, which quickly disappears, especially if the surface of the skin has been prepared a leg or an arm or so at a time.

The light in the early morning is often very unusual. In a characteristic sight, the beach may be in the sun, while the boat sheds and a bit of space in front of them are in the shade. In the right conditions, smoke from the houses drifts straight out to sea along the beach, and in the shade, this smoke becomes clearly visible. In the shadows, indistinct groups of men stand in front of each of the sheds—the disappointed crews of boats which will not be launched on that day. Eventually these men begin to get up and drift back to their homes.

Hunting and Fishing

The decision as to where to sail depends in part on the wind and currents. An east wind and the prospect of a strong west current give reason for the boats to sail west in hopes of returning on the west current. An east wind and a strong east current should send them toward the south-west. Other combinations and directions are possible, depending on the balance of factors and the shifting currents and winds. The boats which are slower putting out follow those ahead of them. If there is no wind, most of the day may be spent in rowing. But if there is any wind at all, the men give up this tiring occupation, except when actively chasing an animal. There are many rowing songs, generally selected for their appropriateness. Here is a commonplace one:

> *Bapa Laga Doni, Bapa Kelaga Doni é*
> Father Laga Doni, Father Laga Doni é
> *Doni Peten Kamé Usi*
> Doni think of us a little.

Laga Doni is one of many Lamaholot names for God.

While sailing, crew members stand or sit in the boat and scan the sea in various directions hoping to spy game. Since the boats return empty more than 70 per cent of the time, by far the most common experience on the sea is this silent sailing and watching. Commonly, they will run out fishing lines, *talé ura*, for catching flying fish, *kemãnu*, which may then be used to bait lines for shark and marlin. Both types of line are held away from the boat on forked sticks, *tenigi*, the bases of which slot into square holes through the stern ends of the outriggers on either side of the boat. Especially on the return voyage, when there is no other activity, individuals may spend some time pushing areng palm fibre between the edges of planking to renew the caulking or replacing frayed *pelepah* bindings.

Today, sailors dress in all sorts of gear, including plastic hats of various styles. Nevertheless, once at sea they usually take off their tubular cloths, *lipa*, and wrap them around a thwart and wear just tee-shirt and shorts, or indeed just shorts. Nevertheless, several still wear conical hats woven from lontar palm leaves with a decorated crown, called *beletu*, from *letu*, to close, to cover up. After the rainy season, the crews regularly suffer from sunburn, to the point of vomiting and eventually peeling of skin. Crew members never suffer from seasickness, except for beginners, who may be violently ill.

While waiting the crew also keeps an eye on other boats both before and behind. They can easily tell by the nature of their movements and activities such as taking down sails what kind of animals other boats may have encountered; and some men can return from a day at sea with an astonishingly accurate estimation of what success the other *téna* have had. If sperm whale are spotted, the fleet generally turn to give chase. But their best hope is if the animals surface near by and are heading downwind. On many occasions during our visits, the boats gave chase to whales without luck, because the animals were moving against the east wind. When attacking sperm whale, the boats drop their sails and mast for safety as soon as they are in the vicinity of the whale, but even so the drag of the wind on the boats slows them, and the men cannot sustain for long the needed speed.

Some boats, as is always the case, are swifter than others, but all boats are relatively heavy and somewhat cumbrous to handle when it comes to quick turns and reversals of direction. For this reason, although the sea may be full of hundreds of dolphins, it is quite common for the boats to sail past them without making any attempt on them. I have seen boat crews attempt to harpoon porpoise only when it seemed the movement of a shoal was going to bring the animals directly under the harpooning platform. Even on those occasions, as it happened, the animals proved too agile, and although we continued to pass close to them our boat made no further effort. Their equipment makes it difficult for the harpooner to get into position for a proper try at dolphin or porpoise, and for this reason the village takes relatively few of them during a year.

Other than sperm whale, *kotekĕlema*, and killer whale, *seguni*, Lamalera hunts the goosebeak whale (Cuvier's), called *ikã méã* (red fish). Among smaller animals taken are the short-finned pilot whale, *temu bélã* (large porpoise); false killer whale, *temu bĕlã* (long porpoise); various other types of small porpoise, *temu bĕluã* (slender porpoise); grey (Risso's) dolphin, *temu bũrã* (white porpoise); many toothed blackfish, *temu kebong* (stupid porpoise); pygmy killer whale, *temu kebung* (stupid porpoise); spinner dolphin, *temu kirã*; Fraser's dolphin or Sarawak dolphin, *temu notong*; and an unidentified, small soft-skinned dolphin called *fefakumu* (moustache mouth). For the scientific identifications of these animals, see Appendix VII.

Lamalera touches none of the baleen whales by traditional prohibition. However, in 1976 the *Kebako Pukã* came across one which was weak and just going around in circles and which it harpooned. But none have been harpooned subsequently. The boats will sail right through a pod of baleen whales without making the slightest effort to hunt them, although some varieties are hunted in the Solor Strait by the village of Lamakera. All baleen whales are called *kelaru*, except for the blue whale, which is *lélangaji*. One interpretation of this name given me is that it comes from *lélang* which means ancestor and *aji* implying that its size is too great to estimate.

On 26 July 1979 I was a guest of the *Soge Ténã*, which was about second from the front of the fleet. We sailed out some way to the south-east when one of the boats turned east. The men in our boat said that they had spotted whale. Soon the other boats also turned in that direction and the chase was on. We were looking into the sun, and I never saw a sign of a whale, but before long the boats began to put their sails down one by one in order to row. About this time, the *Sika Ténã* put out from shore to join us. People later said they had seen we were after whale and decided to *baléo*, that is to put out at a moment's notice with a scratch crew. When we put our sail down we were still very far from where the whale must have been. Nevertheless, we immediately began to prepare for whale, and this was the most interesting part of this incident, because we never got near a whale.

Once the sail was down, the men began a variety of hasty activities. Some collected the cloths and tied them together around the upper thwart in front of the section where the helmsman sits. Other loose things were tied down. The *léo fã* and its harpoon and pole were taken down from the harpooning platform. Then the *bĕfaléng*, which was already tied to the *gĕlefĕ*, was passed forward and tied to the *suka fã*. The relevant harpoon was fished out of the *sĕmugur* and given to the harpooner who attached it to the rope and to its pole.

Once the boat was ready, we began rowing across the sea. Sitting in the back where I would interfere least with the others, I felt I could try my hand too. Eventually I fell into their rhythm. It was fast and followed two patterns. One was a firm bite followed by a weak one allowing a bit of a rest, and so on in alternation. Every once in a while, they took four firm bites in a row. We carried on like this until we covered quite a distance. In the end rowing slowed and followed a simpler, more leisurely rhythm. Then we just stopped, drifted a while, and eventually gave up on this group of whales. About this time, the *Sika Ténã* put up its sail and returned to shore. People in *Soge Ténã*, and later those in the *Menula Belolong*, said they returned because their crew had not yet had breakfast.

The rest of us put up our sails and headed south. On one of our cuts back to the north-east, we passed just in front of a large school of small, sharp-nosed porpoise. They were heading west, in our direction, and we were very close, but no one paid them any attention. Nor did we make any effort for them when we passed them a second time. Shortly after our first sighting of porpoise, we saw a whale blowing off behind us to the south. It blew about four times, and we sailed for it, but although this was the closest we came to catching whale all day, we never got near enough to see the animal itself. Late in the day, I spotted a fish near us which turned out to be *bōu*, shortfin devil ray, *Mobula kuhlii*. We were close enough to try, but the harpooner missed. As we were returning in the afternoon, we caught a flying fish on a line, and this was the sum total of the day's product for the entire fleet.

The crew said that if a man fishing with the shark line catches a shark, he gets the tail. The man using the flying fish line gets nothing, if he catches a fish, because the flying fish is intended as bait for shark. If he gets several, they may be divided among the crew. They told me that sometimes if a flying fish is caught, someone may take it home to save for the next morning. Then he may cook and eat it. When they ask the next morning what happened to it, he says the cat ate it. This seems a widely appreciated joke, but one of the crew followed it up by commenting about how badly the rest of them feel the next morning if they see shark near the boat and there is no bait.

On 30 July 1979 the fleet had an early start. The sky and air was very hazy and hot. For a time I thought hazy yellow clouds would turn into squalls, but they never did. We had a fair east breeze until later in the day when we turned for home. It died down then, and we rowed in. I went again on that day in the

Soge Ténã. We sailed due south until we were quite far out. About this time *bĕlelã*, the giant manta ray, *Mantis birostris*, began to surface. *Menula Belolong* was the first to spot and chase one, but the manta ray was too far below the surface and the harpoon did not stick. Before long several boats were chasing them, including ourselves. Like the *Menula Belolong*, the *Soge Ténã* had bad luck most of the day. Usually we could not get close enough to try to harpoon. The animals would turn and swim another direction too quickly for us to do anything. Other times we tried but were not really in the right position, and did not touch the animal. While we sailed back and forth without success, the rest of the boats began to harpoon and kill rays one after another. If the animals were large enough to require it, the boats would take their sails down, while they worked on them. This involved placing the sail in the harpoon rack and hefting the manta ray up over the outrigger on the left side of the boat and cutting the animal into four sections (head, wings, tail), which could be put entirely into the *ũak puã pukã*. There were as many as four boats at a time rolling in the sea with bare masts. It looked from a distance as though the boats themselves were stricken and not the fish.

Soge Ténã's luck held bad into the afternoon. Once a ray we were after turned and dived under us, an awesome sight. Finally the *Menula Belolong* caught a ray. We then saw one, which turned just as the harpooner was about to pounce, presenting a bad angle. This ray got away, and this was too much for the crew. We immediately had a prayer. It seems some crew member had said the wrong thing—as I gathered at the time, someone had asked a member of the crew why he had not gone to mass on Sunday and had been called stupid for his pains. This fault was keeping the boat from getting any fish, and none would be caught until it was set right by a prayer. The prayer over, the harpooner sprinkled the harpoon platform and *kãfé léo* with holy water and flicked some at the crew.

We immediately spotted another giant manta ray and this one we did harpoon. It appeared as a big black shadow in the sea. We got it at first try and soon had a second harpoon in it. It was smaller than several others caught that day and did not force us to take our sail down, but it was still a large animal. We had it on the right side and had to work it around under the boat to the left. There we forced its head over the outrigger and heaved it up into the boat until the head was fairly far in above the boat's well and the tail hung out into the sea. Then we took the stout wooden pole called *nada ikã*, which is kept in the boat to support the outrigger in just such circumstance, and tied it to the upper thwart just behind the well. We then cut the head off in two sections. The rest of the body was secured with ropes and hooks while we did this. Then we heaved the animal farther into the boat and disposed of the two wings. Finally we lifted the tail aboard. All sections were pulled up and stored in the *ũak puã pukã*. Afterwards, the crew had another prayer.

The centre sections of the boat were by then smeared with slime and gore from the fish. As we got under way again, the bailers gradually bailed out the blood and sea water we shipped when pulling the animal aboard and then washed down the insides of the boat. It occurred to me to ask again at this time why it was that the two bailers get the gill sections of ray. The well in fact is not only the well of the ship, but also the operating theatre when there are fish the size of large ray and porpoise to cut up. These activities leave quite a house-cleaning job behind them, which is more or less done by the time the boat gets back to shore. The answer to my question was not the one I anticipated, but the one I had always been given. The bailers get this share of ray because they always bail out the boat. I suppose the accumulated labour of bailing is the greater after all.

On our way into shore the wind died down entirely. After a while the *Menula Belolong* which was near us began to paddle. After some hesitation we did so too, quickly overtaking the *Menula Belolong*. Shortly after we started paddling, a school of large porpoise sailed right in front of us. Since they were in the right spot and we were paddling anyhow we made an attempt at them. The harpooner missed a try off the side of the harpooning platform. But no one now seemed especially disappointed.

We kept up our pace, eventually overtaking the heavily loaded *Téti Heri* rowing ahead of us. When we got to shore the fish from the first boats were already on shore. Others, like ourselves, were throwing the fish overboard and towing it to shore and up the beach with lines. Once the boats were ashore the division of the fish began. I received a small share too for my day at sea. That afternoon we left the *Soge Téná* half out of its shed, because the men wanted a fast start the next morning. I helped bring the *Téti Heri* up the beach too, and they also decided to leave it poised for the jump. The men expected that many boats would want to go out the next morning and that they would all want an early start.

Subsequently the crew of the *Soge Téná* told me that the problem which caused us to miss the fish earlier in the day was that an elder had asked the missionary to give a mass for the dead at sea, that is for a man who had died the previous year. The missionary replied that they just wanted the mass so there would be fish. The elder retorted that they would get fish regardless of deaths at sea. It was this comment that was at fault and that the ancestors were avenging.

The following morning I again went out with the *Soge Téná*. A whole flotilla left with us. It was a most impressive display. Despite our showing up early for the early start, the *Soge Téná* got away slowly. When we started, we first had to turn the boat around on the beach. On the previous day, the ray had knocked off the forward part of the false keel. They did not want to run the boat over the rocks in this condition; so we swung it around by brute force and backed it into the water. We took the decoration on the stern post, *temōto*, off so the boat would clear the post of the shed during the operation of turning the boat around.

We had no wind on a hazy hot day. So we rowed all the way out to sea. We rowed SSE, almost due south. It was a long hard row, and we were nearly as far out as we would go when we stopped. But we did put the sail up before we finished rowing, and we had a break about then. Eventually we went off further west until we were about SSW of the village. Like the day before, Timor was invisible and Pantar and Roti became visible only slightly on the second half of the day.

It was a frustrating day for the fleet as many boats chased ray which eventually got away from them. The *Holo Sapã* started things off. From the distance I thought that they had got theirs, but they eventually came home empty-handed. Soon though other boats got ray, and several stood about with bare masts while their crews worked.

Soge Ténã caught a ray about 10.00 a.m. It succumbed after a brief chase; and we had no trouble with it, although it was much bigger than the one we had harpooned the day before. It thrashed about both sides of the boat quite a bit, but they kept it on a short line, and eventually got it tight to the left side of the bow. There it flapped and pounded against the hull and the man who was bending over it, trying to kill it. He was hit several times, but without injury. These animals are killed by cutting a slice in the head, through which they put a bamboo stick or iron rod which they poke into the brain. This stops the animal, which they then pull around to the side and start to haul in.

Our ray was so large that when we got it to the side and started heaving, a great deal of sea rushed into the boat. The harpooner and I placed ourselves on the right outrigger, from which I pulled on one rope. The other men pulled on ropes attached to grappling hooks fixed in the animal. Mine was a loose rope tied to a slit cut into the flesh of the wing. The men were in the boat, but backed up against the right side as the ray came further into the boat. This combination of shifting weights helped right the balance. While I was standing on the outrigger, some feet out of the water, the men spotted a large shark, plainly visible in the clear water about three metres under the surface. This animal was swimming around back and forth under our stern looking for a chance to get a meal. The presence of the shark did not prevent one of the crew from jumping into the bloody water to work on putting hooks into the ray, which for most of the cutting was half in and half out of the water.

Some men got the shark harpoon in the back of the boat ready, and it looked as if they were about to harpoon the shark, but they were stopped. Instead they baited a shark line and put it out. Within a minute the shark had taken the hook. This was the end of the shark, for he was now in the control of the men. He fought for some time, usually staying on the wrong side of the boat.

Eventually, they pulled it up close and a young man had a go at him with the shark harpoon, but the harpoon just bounced off its tough skin. His father, a more experienced harpooner took the harpoon away from him and gave it a great heave into the shark and it bounced off again. The young man had a second try with the same result. Then a stronger man took a turn. He sank the harpoon, and before long the shark was finished. That was all they caught for the day, but it kept their spirits up while they lost the rest of the fish. Although it is easier to bring a ray in over the left side, because the harpoon poles are in the way on the right, I saw one boat working on its fish on the right side.

The rest of the day's story was about the fish that got away. None of these were much bigger than the one we had already caught, but they were large. The first was one we came close enough to get a fair shot at. The harpoon struck but did not take. We chased the fish trying to get another harpoon in it, but we were rowing and it outran us. It was heading toward *Kéna Pukã* so we called to them, and they then chased it a long way without success. I asked what would happen if they got it. The answer is that it would be entirely theirs. There is no division of the animal between the two boats. Usually boats do not bother an animal another boat is chasing, but on that day *Jafa Ténã* and *Menula Belolong* were racing for the giant manta ray that ended up being the first one taken by the *Menula Belolong*. *Jafa Ténã* was ahead in the race, but the ray took a fortunate swerve toward the *Menula Belolong*. On the previous day the *Menula Belolong* lost a ray to another boat. The *Menula Belolong* had been chasing it first and thought they had a right to it. The other boat crew did not agree and took it, but hot words were exchanged.

After we missed our first ray, we went on to miss two more. The second ray surfaced near us and swam such tight circles around us that we turned circles on our stern trying to put the harpooner close enough to try. It dived before we had a chance. The third swam away from us before we came close enough to do anything with it. All of the boats seemed to have been having the same experiences for two or three hours at midday. We also missed a small turtle. It floated past us looking like a dead fish. No one took any interest in it until it was behind us. Then someone noticed that it was a turtle. We gave chase and it woke up and led us in spirals. We finally gave up, laughing.

We were paddling most of the day, and chased the fish paddling. The sail was up, but not in use. The *menuli* was cast loose from its usual position (with the sail on the right, the *menuli* is on the left) and moved to the other side (the right). This helps keep the sail out of the way of the men who man the forward oars. With no wind, the sail hangs limp, and almost vertically, while the boat charges across the calm sea in pursuit of a great underwater sail of an animal.

On 11 August 1979 fifteen boats went out expecting good luck because it was just after the full moon. We had little luck, but they were expecting much of the next Monday, the first fishing day after four days following the full moon. *Téna Ãnã* harpooned a *bōu* and caught a shark on a line. The rest of the boats came back empty, if one overlooks one or two flying fish. We had a strong east current and strong east wind for most of the day. There were not many fish to be seen, though we chased and missed two *bōu*. In the morning we saw a spout near us. This was a Goosebeak Whale, *ikã méã*, but we did not try for it. During the day, depending on shifting angles and conditions of atmosphere, we saw Ilé Boleng, Ilé Mandiri, and Lobetobi volcanoes and Pantar, but never Timor. Because the wind was strong in the morning, we went very far out, drifting to the west with the east current. Toward the middle of the day we sailed against the wind far to the east. From there we came in with a dying wind behind us. The day of fishing was almost without event.

Hunting Ray

The marine biology of the large rays is relatively underdeveloped in relation, for example, to sharks and cetaceans. The rays which the *téna* harpoon are the giant manta ray, *Mantis birostris*, the shortfin devil ray, *Mobula kuhlii*, and the smaller whiptail devil ray, *Mobula diabolus*. These rays are known in Lamaholot respectively as *bělelã*, *bōu*, and *mōku* (see Appendix II). The first of these animals can exceed 7 metres in width and reach a weight of 2 tons (Grzimek 1973: 125). They feed on plankton and small fish, and are viviparous, giving birth by forcefully ejecting the young into the air as the mother spins out of the water (Compagno, Ebert, and Smale 1989: 117). They follow the plankton to the surface and sweep through the water or leap high into the air, falling back with loud slaps. Lamalera boats frequently find large and well-developed foetuses in the animals they harpoon. Some writers call them harmless giants which may allow humans to touch and ride them (Coleman 1991: 281). They are less gentle to fishermen of Lamalera trying to subdue them after harpooning them. Their great wings pounding against the side of the boats and men may crack ribs, and they have been known to wrap their wings behind them around a man and carry him under the surface. According to Gregorius Keraf (1983), the people of Lamalera distinguish *bělelã* according to whether they inhabit the open sea, *bělelã lemé*, or shore waters, *bělelã haring*. The first of these has a stinger (*kenaté*) near the base of the tail, the second does not. Compagno *et al.* say that *Manta birostris* is usually without stingers, which confirms that there are varieties with and those without stingers. Both varieties are further divided as *fulolepã*, *kang*, and *kã*. The first of these has skin which is white both top and bottom. The second is dark blue-black on top and white on the bottom, while the last is black on top and bottom. Compagno *et al.* write of the giant manta ray as ' "flying" bird-like through the water and into the air in spectacular leaps'. Lamaholot distinguishes the three character-istic motions of this animal as travelling about under the surface, *pana*, staying in place with its wings raised and joined above its back, *segao*, and jumping, *dopã*.

There is only one locally recognized variety of *bōu*. *Mobula kuhlii* is smaller than *Manta birostris*. Compagno *et al.* give its wing tip to wing tip width as 1.1 metre, but those taken in Lamalera are typically a good deal larger than this. This species lacks a stinger. The colour on top is a dark, reddish brown; on the bottom it is white. Under the water, the top appears yellowish. For this reason, in songs addressed to a harpooned *bōu*, the fishermen refer to the animal as *kuma*, yellow. Compagno *et al.* say of *Mobula kuhlii* that its biology is virtually unknown. Although considerably smaller than giant manta ray, it is a highly valued food source. It requires greater skill to harpoon, and surprisingly, given its smaller size, it is capable of pulling a boat rapidly when harpooned, which the giant manta ray cannot do.

Boats frequently take the smaller whiptail devil ray, *Mobula diabolus*, and these rays are often caught in nets as well. The identification is from Hembree (1980: 42). Given that several varieties of *mōku* are recognized locally, more than one scientifically named species may be involved, and its identification at the moment is probably best regarded as *Mobula*, spp. Marshall gives their overall wing width as about 8 feet, 2.4 metres (Marshall 1966: 168), which is considerably larger than the great majority, if not all, *mōku* taken by Lamalera. It should be borne in mind that *bou* is definitely a larger type of animal than *mōku*, whatever measurements may be given in books; and the discrepancies here have two possible sources, one being uncertainties in identification, the other being the poor state of scientific knowledge about these animals in general.

Mōku have a smoother skin and grain of meat. According to Gregorius Keraf, the meat is regarded as not causing side-effects if eaten by someone who is ill, implying that the meat of other types of ray is thought to cause these effects. These varieties, following Keraf, are known. *Mōku éak* (possibly the singular or only *mōku*) is dark blue on top, and completely white on the bottom. Its gills are white and black. *Mōku anamīté* (presumably 'black child' *mōku*, implying a description of the new-born animal) is smaller than the preceding type and is black on top, with a white chest. Near the tips of the wings, the underside becomes black. *Mōku pilifato* (the *mōku* which selects or picks over the rocks) is smaller yet, black on top, white on the bottom. Its mouth is to the bottom. In all the others just mentioned, the mouth is more toward the front. *Belébã* or *mōku belébã* (the 'carrier *mōku*') is the smallest of all and has a completely white body. *Mōku pilifato* are found close to the shore, *mōku anamīté* further out, and *mōku éak* at sea. The last two are large. *Mōku* jump in great numbers near the shore in January. It is an interesting, if unexplained fact, that *moku* in the neighbouring Kédang language means porpoise and not a variety of ray.

Among other rays is the Blue-spotted Sting Ray, *Urolophus Armatus*, known as *pāé* from Malay *pari*. There are two varieties, *pāé bĕlelang*, with a larger body and rougher skin, and *pāé bōu*, with a smaller body and yellowish skin like *bōu*, so the difference is one they compare to that between *bĕlelā* and *bōu*. A smaller ray with smoother skin is *belepa*, Ribbontail Ray, *Taenyura Lymma*. This is a disc-shaped animal with a mouth underneath, which is frequently seen adhering to the sand at the bottom of the sea. Comparable to *mōku* in size and colour is *kajo lōlo* ('tree leaves'), except that the skin on top is speckled white. The head is bumpier, looking like a pig's head. It has a stinger at the base of the tail, but the number of stingers increases with age. This has been identified as *Aetobatus Narinari*, Spotted Eagle Ray. It stays near shore, where it has been speared, but never as yet caught in a net. Burkill (1935, vol. 1: 60) writes that *Aetobatus Narinari* is caught from time to time in Malaysia in fish-traps, in small driftnets set for Spanish Mackerel, or on long lines baited with fish. *Kérakotā* is a yellowish-brown ray like *bōu*, which has teeth described as being like coral and which lives near the mouth of rivers, perhaps *Rhinoptera Javanica*.

Fishermen regard the best times for catching giant manta ray to be just after the full moon and just after the new moon. The passing of baleen whales is also regarded as a sign that manta ray will come to the surface, because their food is the same. There is an expression for this relationship which runs *kelaru tegel ané*, baleen whales eye the bait. When manta ray are feeding on the surface is also a time when they expect to see blue whale. When the sea is 'dirty', that is opaque because it is full of plankton, it is easier to harpoon manta ray, not only because of the obvious point that it is then that they rise to the surface, but also because the ray cannot see the boats so well.

The rope and harpoon called *léo fā* are used for harpooning small and fleet game, and even larger animals such as killer whales, because they are light and the harpooner can throw them far—something which is necessary for those animals, such as *bōu* and dolphin, which do not allow the boats to close up on them. Once the first harpoon is in place, they can try to get a heavier harpoon into the animal and then finish it off. The harpooner will grasp the pole farther down the shaft so that he can put his weight behind the harpoon when he jumps with it to harpoon a sperm whale. For killer whale, porpoise, ray and shark, and so on, he holds the pole at the far end so that he can throw it. For animals such as dolphin and *bōu*, the harpooner will usually have to jump while throwing the harpoon. He will never jump while harpooning the dangerous species of shark. If a man falls in when such a shark has been harpooned, they will immediately throw a piece of wood into the water to distract it. The harpooner's assistant must, in any case, pull the harpoon rope tight as quickly as possible to keep the shark from biting through it (Plates 43 and 44).

If an animal is stationary or moving only very slowly, the harpooner aims for where he sees it. If it is moving rapidly, he aims ahead of it. It is not difficult to show a novice how to harpoon a whale, *bĕlelā* or whale shark, but he

PLATE 43. Preparing to harpoon

must be shown a special approach for porpoise and the smaller fish. He needs to be taught what to do when the porpoise is moving slowly and what to do when it is moving fast. In either case, he must harpoon in front of the animal. A novice has to wait until the man who is training him retires. Meanwhile he serves as an ordinary crew member. He needs above all to be able to stand strongly and firmly on the harpooning platform, not just in everyday weather, but in high winds and waves. *Déi mega gé mo tūba ikã*, stand firmly and you will harpoon fish. That is, if a learner can develop the skill to balance all day under all circumstances on the platform, then he has achieved the prerequisite for learning to harpoon. Especially the harpooner must feel that his body is light and his feet must constantly move. His mind must think not only of the fish, but of his body and its movements as well. A man who cannot fulfil these requirements must be an ordinary crew member, even if his father was a harpooner. Three things therefore are required to become a harpooner, (1) hereditary right, (2) ability to take responsibility, and (3) the skill to harpoon. In practice, and especially in present circumstances, these criteria have been stated in an order of increasing importance. A harpooner whose boat is not currently in use is likely to be borrowed by another boat which is having trouble locating a youthful harpooner. At best inherited right means that a competent harpooner can expect to replace his father, but if he is not competent, someone who is must be found to take over.

PLATE 44. Harpooning

The boat crews cannot always tell the difference between the species of ray at a distance. One day several boats saw large *bōu* which they mistook for *bĕlelã*. This mistake caused them to miss harpooning the animals, because they had set up the short harpoon poles and big rope and harpoon they use for giant manta ray. The harpooner stands and holds the pole perpendicularly until the boat is very close to *bĕlelã*, before lowering it until it is horizontal and holding it there before driving it into the back of the animal. It is very important that the harpooner holds his left hand very still, while the right hand moves about aiming. In the case of *bōu*, he uses instead a long pole and the *léo fã*, which he catapults at the animal while still at a distance from it. As soon as *bĕlelã* have been spotted, members of the crew may shout *gélu, gélu* (change, change). That is to say, the harpooner and his assistant must take down the *léo fã*, and if rushed rig up the lighter *suka fã* rope and harpoon, or if there is time the heavier *suka bélã*. Whale shark are harpooned in the same way as *bĕlelã*, but receive none of the special treatment accorded the two large varieties of ray.

When there are many giant manta ray near the surface of the sea and the boats are rowing after them they may sing a rowing song like the following.

Peni Péti Lera, Péti Kofa Sudi Lera
Peni in the sun, in the clouds longing for the sun
Peni Muko Lolo, Olé lolo lali nai
Peni Banana Leaf, On the east current travel west
Butu lau tena dai, lodo koro koi fulé
Call the boat from Buton here, descend, I and he will see the market
Fulé lali Boné Raté, lodo hopé ake uré
Market at Bonerate, descend and buy, do not refuse.
Ari nei dai é, féka téna gaja laja
Younger brother give here, divide for the boat, share for the sail
Ema soro dai é, soro dai go ka hodé
Mother give here, give here I will take
Faja koli méa é, soro-nõto léré léré
Betel basket of red koli leaf, give low

In Lamaholot myth, Peni Banana Leaf often represents the daughter of God, the sun.

A giant manta ray which has been harpooned may flounder about on the surface of the sea or dive. In either case, the crew must hold the line taut or the harpoon may well pull out. In general with ray, the fishermen do not feel that they have the animal securely in their control until they have placed at least two harpoons in it or until they have killed it and hooked gaffs into it. A boat with a large ray which has dived with a single harpoon in it is in for a long and uncertain struggle. Unless they eventually succeed in bringing the animal to the surface and gaining control over it, there are two unfortunate outcomes which are possible. One is for the harpoon to pull loose. The other is for the diving ray to overcome the strength of the crew and pull the rope down until all that remains is the end tied to the boat, which might well result in capsizing the boat. In the case of both *bělelã* and *bõu* the crew must sing as long as the animal is under the surface of the sea, although the songs appropriate to each species are quite different. A song which might be sung for *bělelã* is as follows.

> *Kidé ajaka tani-tena*
> Many widows cry
> *Lié doré angin*
> Request follow the wind
> *Hari hélu bo kanato*
> Fish replace something sent for us

The idea is that there are many widows in the village who cry for a favourable wind that may send fish.

Gregorius Keraf (1983) gives a different song appropriate for *bělelã*.

> *Āri maku héluro, héluro bo kanato*
> Younger brother replace it, replace that which was sent

For which the solo would be something like this.

> *Ié tāfanga, lāgā di palité*
> The keel of the boat has sprouted, the supports are also growing
> (because we have been hunting so long)
> *Kéra īnā, tau matāmā sao ata māté*
> Mother Kera, place your eyes (harpoons) like the anchor of the dead
> (so they will not easily get loose)
> *Tobolo féli tukā-tukā*
> Sit there in the middle
> *Lodo-lodo, lōlo gouka kala hodi lōlo*
> Descend-descend, the leaves are gone, I will gather leaves
> *Kākā Samo lau Bolé*
> Elder Brother Samo at Boleng

The last line, by the way, is an allusion to the legend of the founding of the realm of the Raja of Larantuka, in which Kakang Samo submitted his region of Adonara around the Boleng mountain to Larantuka.

For *bōu* they would sing words of which the following are a representative example.

> *Kuma hukoko doang gara lélaja, bai toi ãé pipé*
> Yellow sad so far so very long, we will meet today
> *Paja mété baliko, o ari hélu bo kanato, o ari hélu di kanato*
> Troubles are returning, o younger brother replace that which was sent,
> Oh younger brother replace that which was also sent
> *O Bapa Kosan botiro lali géré*
> Oh Father Kosan lift him up
> *O Bapa boti roro, o ata héku lodo ni moko modé géré*
> Oh Father lift him up, oh who will descend? You yourself must come up.

These songs go on until the animal has been brought above the water, which can mean that the men threaten to become exhausted not only from the strain of pulling on the rope, but from the need to sing and to keep coming up with new words. The pattern is to vary the text between repeated refrains. The text is solo, and members of the crew take turns providing it.[3] Usually a pair of men at a time hold the rope, but they quickly lose their strength and must be replaced by another pair. Since a ray does not need to return to the surface to breathe, the whole procedure is a straightforward contest of strength. Eventually, after many minutes, the crew may sense a weakening in the animal and will collectively pull on the rope to force it to the surface. When it is near enough, a member of the crew may dive into the water with a gaff to hook into the animal's mouth. Gregorius Keraf (1983) says that if a ray sees him, it will try to twist away, so that he must approach from the head side.

The diver will place his foot on the head of the ray and pull the gaff until it pierces the flesh. At once those in the boat will start pulling the fish. One thing that must not be done is to stand on the back of the ray in order to gaff it. The *bělelã* would join its two wings and wrap the diver up so that he could not get away.

Once they have gained control of the ray and have killed it by inserting a bamboo or metal rod into its brain, then the process begins of hoisting it over the edge of the boat and cutting it into pieces small enough to pull into the *uak puã pukã*. The wings are severed first, and then the head is cut from the torso. The head fins, which the fishermen call ears (*tilu*), must be properly stored, so that no one touches or covers up the eyes which are attached to them. Bode (1925: 114) mentions the prohibition on touching the eyes of a fish, as well as a prohibition on disembowelling it before the morning after it was caught. In my experience, the fishermen are still quite anxious to see to it that no one touches the eyes. Gregorius Keraf explains that the consequence is that the boat will become drunk, *téna kebuénga*, and will catch no more fish. The result of any infraction in respect of giant manta ray is that no fish of any kind will be caught until the fault has been found out. Then a ceremony to clean the mouth, *hapus nu*, must take place, involving the confession and sprinkling everyone with holy water.

The Téti Heri *Disaster*

The worst misfortune with the boats which the village recalls happened to the *Téti Heri* in July 1925. The boats were out when the manta ray (*bělelã*) were rising in such numbers that all the boats got several, some as many as four or five. But there was a strong east wind, and most of the boats eventually decided it was time to head for home. Only the *Téti Heri* stayed out, carried away by enthusiasm, until they had caught seven (the number usually cited). By this time they were by themselves, and the sun was setting while the wind and waves were becoming strong enough to be dangerous. Eventually in the night they had to throw out all the fish and struggle for home. Wind and waves picked up and turned the boat over. The men clung to the boat that night and the next day. The wind and waves continued extremely strong. During the night though, they saw something white rise in the sea and thought they were near land. According to survivors it eventually proved to be a giant octopus, but some villagers now interpret it as having been floating coral forced up from the bottom of the sea by the currents. Thinking that they were approaching the shore, the harpooner stuck a pole into it to keep the boat from being swept onto the rocks. When his pole penetrated the floating coral, it broke up and released a terrible smell which crazed several of the men, overcoming them.

Nine swam from the boat thinking they were nearly ashore. These disappeared. Because the boat was partially submerged it was difficult to see, and the boat which went searching for it did not find it until the third day. Eventually the *Soge Ténã* found the survivors in a state of extreme exhaustion and thirst. They were in such a reduced state that they did not speak or seem to hear. The *Téti Heri* turned over on a Thursday and was not found until Sunday.

The last survivor of the accident, Fransiskus Sinu Keraf, was in his eighties in 1982. As he remembered the event, on the first day they got five manta ray. Because the boat was too full that night they wanted to throw some pieces out, but others objected. After a while the *koba ĩna*, giant octopus, appeared, with the result that the boat turned over. Several died that night. When the boat first turned over, the sail was floating near it. They sent two boys to swim to it and paddle it back. However, they found that they could make no headway with it in the seas, so one boy swam back to the boat, the other being too frightened to attempt to. The boy who swam back to the boat was among the five survivors, while the other boy died. The sail showed up on the beach at Lamalera before the boat was found. They had a strong southeast wind all night. In the morning they wanted to turn the boat over, but there were already too few crewmen left. They were at Tanjung Suba (the southwest tip of Lembata opposite Witch Island, *Pulau Suangi*) when *Soge Ténã* found them. They had put up a sign that there was trouble. *Soge Ténã* asked how many there were. They answered five and one dead tied up. A young boy named Kaja Kĕrofã who had died of exposure was floating in the boat until one of the men tied him to it with a rope so that his body would not disappear. The first food *Soge Ténã* gave them was ripe bananas, because their throats were so dry they could not eat. Fransiskus Sinu, who died during the 1980s, became withdrawn after this disaster, but remarkably continued to go out on the *Téti Heri*.[4]

15

Hunting Whales and Other Cetaceans

The Hunt

An example of how normal mediocre luck can suddenly turn favourable for some may be taken from three days in September 1979. On the 13th all boats came in empty except the *Kéna Pukã*, which caught a spinner dolphin. There were many whales, but none of the boats managed to harpoon one. On the 14th ten boats went out, of which eight got at least a share in a whale. The *Sika Ténã* harpooned a large whale which then pulled it under for a quarter of an hour to a half-hour. The crew was picked up by other boats. When the whale came up, it was already weak. Four boats finally helped, one way or another, to subdue it—and five shared in dividing it. The *Kopo Paker* harpooned another whale and was helped by the *Soge Ténã*. The *Ténã Ânã* harpooned the child of the second whale and got it back to shore by itself. On that day, I was with a group who had gone to the top of the Labalekang volcano. As we began our descent we saw a line consisting of one boat to the east, two further to the west, and five yet further west—all close to the village. The whales were taken early in the morning, and we saw them about 9.30 or 10.00 a.m. In the group of five, one sail was noticeably darker brown than the others, and one of my companions immediately commented that it had sunk. The *Muko Ténã* and the *Kéna Pukã* remained at sea all day. The *Muko Ténã* got only a shark on a line, and the *Kéna Pukã* came in empty. On the 15th only the *Muko Ténã* and the *Kéna Pukã* went out. The *Muko Ténã* quickly harpooned a sunfish, but otherwise both boats spent a fruitless day at sea. The eight boats which had been involved in harpooning the whales were kept in so that their crews could cut the animals up.

Another example of the vagaries of luck occurred in June 1982. In that year *Soge Ténã* went out the first day of the season and immediately got a fish. Their results continued good until early in July. Then one day *Téti Heri* harpooned a large male sperm whale, but the rope broke. They chased it again and lost another harpoon. *Kéna Pukã* then lost their harpoon. *Soge Ténã* harpooned it and the line wrapped around the whale until none was left and *Soge Ténã* was firmly fixed on top of it. People who jumped into the water to cut it came back to their boats instead frightened. The whale kept beating *Soge Ténã* with its tail. Other boats just waited near by, afraid to harpoon it. Finally they cut the rope; the fleet lost four harpoons in one day. The *Soge Ténã* returned needing repairs that kept it out of action for many days. Its good luck shifted then to *Muko Ténã*.

On 21 August 1982 the *Kebako Pukã* harpooned a whale around 1.00 p.m., and the *Kéna Pukã* harpooned it second. *Soge Ténã* refused to help, because of its bad experience earlier in the year. *Sili Ténã*, *Demo Sapã*, and then the *Téti Heri* joined in. The whale broke in a large plank on the left side of the bow of the *Kebako Pukã*, as well as shattering a board on the right side of the stern, but the *Kebako Pukã* did not sink. The animal hit the *Kebako Pukã* once with its tail, from the left in the bow, doing the damage in both places. Apparently shock forces carried to the opposite point in the back. A man showed me where he had torn his shirt and stuck it into the break in the stern where they were shipping water, but there was no water coming through the bow. He then went on to say that they felt there was enough meat for the five boats. The whale dived once after first being harpooned taking the *gĕlefé* rope, *bĕfaléng* rope, and the additional rope for the *bĕfaléng*. After that it came to the surface where it remained, swimming slowly in circles. The animal died around 3.00 p.m. While finishing it, some dived under and some got on its back trying to kill it. The boats had a west wind coming back so they did not paddle until they were close to the shore, where the west current a little way off helped them.

When a boat is sunk at sea, they empty it of water by pulling it up on one of the other boats. They either bring it in over the outrigger into the well, or over the stern outrigger boom up through the second boat. This boat of course ships water too, as they do when bringing in giant manta ray, but they try to judge things so the right balance is reached. After a quantity of water has drained from the stricken boat, they shove it very quickly back away, so that not much water comes into it during the process. Then they bail both boats out. When they bring the boat in over the outrigger, they support the outrigger with the stout wooden pole, *nada*, provided for this purpose, so the outrigger does not break.

When the sea is dirty, i.e. opaque because it is full of plankton, pilot whales are extremely tame. When the *téna* are at sea at night, dolphin will play around the sides, which they do not do during the day—although they will do so with the motor boats. The fishermen will try to harpoon dolphin at night, and despite the difficulty of seeing what they are doing, do occasionally get them.

They regard the killer whale as a very fierce animal which will kill and eat anything else in the sea, including shark. Sometimes they run across killer whales that are eating other fish. If the killer whales are full, they are not so fast or difficult to harpoon, but they must be killed quickly after they are harpooned or they will vomit up their meal. When their stomachs are emptied, then they become quick and difficult. The fishermen do not regard killer whales as a variety of whale, but a kind of porpoise. Killer whales hunt porpoises in packs. The killer whales will ram a porpoise, throw it into the air and then hit it with its tail to kill it. Then the killer whale will bite the porpoise in two and divide the pieces among the other killer whales. The fishermen say that the meat of the killer whale cannot be eaten while it is warm, but must be allowed to cool. Otherwise, it causes headaches and vomiting. The oil of the killer whale is said to be very strong. Just a little put on a tree will kill the tree. A ring made from the tooth of a killer whale will protect from the effects of black magic.

Cuvier's goosebeak whale is called *ikã méã*, or the red fish. It is similar to the pilot whale in size and general shape, except that its snout is long, like the pygmy killer whale. The flesh is supposed to be excellent. Cuvier's goosebeak whales and killer whales have a thin skin and therefore more flesh in proportion than sperm whales or pilot whales. We were told in Lamakera, Solor, that although *méã* means red, this is not the import of the name. A person can be called *méã* if he is aggressive and fearless. The *ikã méã* earns its name by its behaviour. It will bite and break up a boat. If someone breaks whatever the mystical restriction is connected with it, the *ikã méã* will approach and attack the boat. It is rarely, if ever, taken in Lamakera. However, the men of Lamalera, who do harpoon this species, say that it does *not* attack boats. It is like a large porpoise, but can pull a boat very strongly. The people of Lamalera attribute its name solely to the fact that it is reddish brown in colour. It is very fast, but dies quickly. Unlike killer whales, it does not pull in a straight line when harpooned, but goes very rapidly around in a circle once and then collapses.

Dugong or sea cows, *Dugong dugon*, are a genus of mammals to themselves, and are unrelated to cetaceans. Called *juru* in Lamaholot, they are rarely encountered or caught near Lamalera. They are, however, commonplace along the shores of the sheltered Solor Strait and the northern coasts from Flores to Lembata, where they are frequently caught, mostly by Bajo Laut. People from Lamakera, Solor, do take them as well. The dugong is never encountered at sea, but only along the coast. People from Lamalera say that its ribs are very close together so it cannot be harpooned there. It has hair, but it is otherwise like porpoise, and it tastes like porpoise. One harpooner, who had never harpooned one, had seen one and had eaten the meat. The place to harpoon it, he said, is in the tail.

Fishermen recognize sperm whales at a distance by their behaviour and can distinguish its spout from that of other species. The spout of baleen whales is long and straight up. That of sperm whales is lower and toward the front, and it quickly breaks into a spray. The spout of a whale is *nãi*. This word means breath and is the same in a human. 'To spout' is *fisar*; so the full phrase is *nãi fisar*. Slijper (1979: 119) says that while it is difficult even for experts to distinguish the spouts of various Rorquals (baleen whales) from each other, particularly on windy days, identification is easier with sperm whales. The pear-shaped spouts of sperm whales emerge forward at an angle of about 45° from the left side of the tip of the head. Because it does not go straight up, it is a good deal longer than it looks, up to five metres. *Physeter* in its scientific name is from the Greek for whirlpool. The first explosive exhalation after a dive can be heard from a kilometre away.

Each following breath lasts about 3 seconds on the exhalation and 1 second for the next intake of air. The whale usually spends about 10 minutes at the surface, breathing deeply every 10–15 seconds before diving. There is an old whalers' rule of thumb which predicts that for every foot of a Great Sperm Whale's length, it will breathe once at the surface and spend one minute submerged during the subsequent dive. In our experience, this works remarkably well. A 50-ft (15-m) male does blow about 50 times and then disappears for roughly 50 minutes; while a 30-ft (10-m) female can be expected to reappear again about 30 minutes after the last of her 30 breaths.

After the final blow of a series at the surface, the whale draws its head under and a cloud of spray persists as the long back bends down to expose the hump and the knuckles along the spine. The dive is almost vertical and the broad tail flukes are always thrown well up into the air (Watson 1981: 172).

When boats spot signs of sperm whale in a position and direction relative to currents and wind where they can reasonably hope to harpoon one, they will immediately turn and give chase, unless they are already attached to another large animal, such as a giant manta ray. Depending on the distance and conditions, they will either leave the sail up and sail, while paddling and rowing, or they will move it out of the way and rely on main strength alone. When the game changes from porpoise or ray to whale, the nature of the hunt drastically alters, and the crew mark this transformation by pausing just before entering the fray for preparation. They lower the sail, which otherwise would be just an encumbrance. This process of taking down the sails in order to attack whales is called *belulung* from *lūlu*, to wind up, roll up. Those who need to relieve themselves over the side of the boat, before they hold another collective prayer.

Other boats, even at a great distance, can tell by the lowering of the sail what is afoot, and if there are no whales near them will turn towards the boat which is attempting to harpoon a whale. If the whale under attack is a single male, it may be strong and wild enough that the first boat will request the assistance of other boats, so that there will be a chance for later comers to share in the catch. Gregorius Keraf writes that if an animal is too fierce to permit the boat to approach after it has been harpooned, it is usual to invite other boats to place additional harpoons in it, *hōmã*. In this situation, the harpooner or helmsman will say *Ika lefo, ka tetiro tã raé tai; téna nã téna, mĕng nã mĕng*, 'this fish belongs to the village, therefore let us together carry it ashore; boat with boat, crew member with crew member'. This statement carries with it the implicit promise that all boats so invited will share equally in the division of the animal.

If it is a pod of females with their young, then there is a chance that the late-comers will be able to harpoon their own whales. When one of their fellows is wounded, whales draw around it, and the best opportunity to strike another is offered by sailing into this milling group.[1] In Chapter 88 of *Moby Dick*, Melville (1851: 504) writes, 'Say you strike a Forty-barrel-bull—poor devil! all his comrades quit him. But strike a member of the harem school, and her companions swim around her with every token of concern, sometimes lingering so near her and so long, as themselves to fall a prey.' On 17 April 1831 the *Elisabeth* set sail from London and a whaling voyage to New Zealand. Dakin (1938: 77) quotes the following from its log.

One meets cow whales in schools with perhaps one large bull in attendance, if by any means you fasten to him the cows will all take off and leave him to do the best he can, if on the contrary you get fast to a cow or calf the rest will immediately heave to, and if at a great distance off will all flock down to the wounded whale, it is then an easy matter for the other boats to get fast but great care must be taken not to get foul lines as in that case you are obliged to cut from your whale which will then take off and is mostly followed by the other loose whales at too rapid a rate to be overtaken.

Watson (1981: 174) also writes that a herd will gather around an injured animal, all facing inward, with their tails hanging out and down, until the animal dies or they too are picked off. Such a pod or herd of whales is known in Lamaholot as *ikã mobok*. An isolated porpoise or whale is *ikã kenéã*.

While chasing a whale or any other animal, *pera ikã*, the harpooner stands unsupported at the tip of his harpooning platform. If they are still at a distance, he leaves the harpoon and pole at rest on the platform and will drop both arms to his side and rock them forwards and backwards in unison urgently while balancing on the platform. The purpose of this signal is to encourage the crew to row faster, so that he can get close enough to harpoon it. While doing so, he calls *nuro menaluf*, hunger spoon. The implication is that the crew should row fast like someone spoons his food while he is still hungry. It is forbidden for him to utter the normal encouragement to *bai béra muri*, row faster, in the presence of whales. If he breaks this prohibition, the whale will surely strike the boat. They approach the whale from the side, in order to avoid being rammed or struck by its tail.

Once the boat is close enough, the harpooner will jump with his full weight behind the harpoon, trying to thrust the harpoon as deeply as possible into the *iting lango*, the house of the dorsal fin, that is the area around this fin, while twisting the harpoon head to fix the flange in the blubber so that it will not pull out. Once the harpoon has struck home, the whale starts and either dives or pulls the boat at great speed, usually in circles. Having been in such a ride in July 1970, in which the *Menula Belolong* was pulled through a group of thrashing whales and in front of charging boats, I can attest that it is an exciting experience. On that occasion, we eventually suffered a collision with another boat, which cost it a harpooning platform and the *Menula Belolong* an upper strake, but we suffered no other injury and never lost control of the whale. Once the harpooner has sunk his harpoon home, he rolls off the back of the animal, and if he has a chance grabs an outrigger and pulls himself back into the boat, as the boat shoots past. Meanwhile the harpoon pole floats free, to be picked up later, often by some other boat.

It is extremely important on such occasions that the harpooner's assistant, *bĕréun alep*, keep the small rope called *saba* in the bow firmly around the harpoon rope as the crew pays it out, so that the bow of the boat stays pointed in the direction of movement. If the *saba* breaks or he loses control, the harpoon rope will pull to the side of the boat, which will inevitably capsize. Gregorius Keraf writes that when the join between lengths of hawser, *kefokel*, is about to pass through the *saba*, the crew shout *kefokel*, so the harpooner's assistant can loosen the *saba* sufficiently to allow the join through. If the whale dives, all the crew can do is pay out the rope and wait until the whale returns to the surface, hoping that in the meantime the boat will not be pulled under. If the boat capsizes or is sunk, then they have to swim in place until the boat returns to the surface or until they are picked up by other boats. Usually at least the sail will be floating free, giving them something to hold on to.

If there is an opportunity to put another harpoon in the whale, they will try to do so nearer the head, so that they can pull the animal closer to the boat. If possible they try to get several harpoons into a whale. As soon as the whale weakens sufficiently, they pull the whale to the side of the boat and begin to cut on it with their flensing knives, hoping to cut an artery or some other vital point. If they cannot get it so close, men may swim to the whale and even climb on its back to try to cut on it. Those boats which carry lances, *bĕlāda*, may try to lance the animal from a distance, the range being determined by the length of the pole to which the blade is fixed. They will lance the animal anywhere they can reach, but the preferred spot is under the pectoral fins. In any case, men are likely to dive into the blood-clouded water in order to cut from underneath, disregarding sharks which may be attracted by the smell. It is not uncommon for men to be in the water, while their companions cut flesh off the whale to bait shark hooks which they throw in next to them. As soon as possible, they try to place the gaff in the blow hole. A whale which is not easily subdued may pound the boat with its tail, threatening life and limb. For this reason, the crew try to keep as low in the boat as possible during the critical moments. I have listened to more than one account of hapless crew members cringing in the boat or scrambling to safety into another boat, while the boat was at the mercy of a lashing tail; and of course people have lost their lives or suffered serious injury in such circumstances. A whale may be lost because the rope breaks, *ikã gōkala*, the fish falls. Furthermore, they may cut themselves free of a whale which they feel is too fierce for them to control. In this case, they will *pĕratã ikã*, say farewell to the fish.

Prohibitions

When hunting at sea, especially when attacking a whale, the crew must be quite careful about their actions and speech. Once they have struck a whale they may not smoke, drink, relieve themselves, or carry on conversation until the whale is dead. They are not prohibited to speak about the matter at hand, and there is a great deal of rather subdued shouting and talking while working on the animals. It is noteworthy that this is hardly done in a boisterous manner and that even the shouting is in a more restrained tone than is normal. These prohibitions are sacred religious restrictions. They may not use the names of places and persons, or curse, even after the animal is dead. When striking whale, as opposed to other game, they may address each other only as *bapa*, 'father' (the common term for addressing a male in Lamaholot). To use a crewman's name would invite disaster. In the television film *Whale Hunters of Lamalera*, Petrus Hidang mentions these prohibitions and gives the example of an elder named Bélo. As he explains, *bélo* means to cut or kill. To use that name unguardedly at sea would certainly invite the whale to strike the boat, with lethal results. One may not use the word for the sperm whale, *kotekĕlema*, but must always refer to it as 'the fish', *īkã*. There are also special terms for the parts, tools, and operations in the boat which must be employed instead of the more common expressions. Gregorius Keraf (1983) writes that the terms which are replaced are especially those which suggest distant places, spearing or pounding, weapons, and so on. These restrictions apply after the animal is dead and indeed until they have returned with it safely to shore. Even though it is dead the whale can still strike the boat, if they make a mistake. If they speak wrongly while the whale is still alive it will hit the boat, but even after it is dead there is still danger. For example, the boat may already be near the harbour when the mistake is made. The sea conditions will immediately change and the boat will be pulled far out again. The names of ropes remain the same. A schoolteacher was once in a boat that harpooned a whale. Afterwards he told the crew to head toward Mingar and pick up some palm wine. He said he did not believe in superstitions such as that against using the name of places. They were kept out two days as a result of this indiscretion. When another boat eventually found them, one of his kinsmen greeted him with an indelicate comment. He responded, 'Do not say that, we already have enough trouble.' Boats have been known to be in front of the beach and then pulled away by the current because someone spoke wrong. The people of Lamalera think that the fishermen of Lamakera do not hunt sperm whale because they always curse and use bad language at sea. 'You can't do that around sperm whale.'

The custom of using special terms during the hunt (on land) is found in other societies in Indonesia. For discussion of special vocabularies of this type see Gonda (1948, esp. 337 ff.). Snouck Hurgronje (1893, 1906) reports a special vocabulary for fishermen in Aceh and refers to similar customs during hunting or at sea on Java. He notes that in Aceh, there are a number of words which cannot be uttered without danger at sea. This restriction holds good for all seafaring men, including users of fish nets and other fishermen.

Among the fishermen on the North coast of Java whole lists of words can be collected which are prohibited at sea and have to be replaced by others. This is also the case to some extent among the seafaring folk of Acheh. For instance, those at sea must not call a mountain by its proper name, *gunòng*, lest waves as high as mountains should overwhelm their vessel; the euphemism employed is *tanòh manyang* = high ground. *Gajah*, the elephant, is called by his nickname *pò meurah*. If the fisherman wishes to say that something is 'ready', he must not use the ordinary word '*lheuëh*', because this has also the meaning of 'free' or 'loose', and its use might give the imprisoned fish a chance of escaping; accordingly the less dangerous synonym *leungka* is employed. If he wants to speak of a rope being cast off, he uses in place of *lheuëh* its synonym *leupaih*; so too *lōb* 'to pass under something by stooping', and several other words have to be replaced by synonyms or paraphrases by those who are fishing or on a voyage (Hurgronje 1906: 281).

Van Gennep (1908: 333) relates the use of special languages to his analysis of rites of passage and remarks, 'special language is a commonplace phenomenon'. Bulmer describes a special vocabulary called 'pandanus language' used by the Karam of the highlands of New Guinea when hunting cassowary or harvesting pandanus nuts (Bulmer 1967: 12, 15).

In Lamalera too a fairly extensive set of terms is used exclusively at sea in place of ordinary phrases. In Table 14 some of these are listed.

The proper expression at sea for harpooning a whale with a second harpoon is *fãja*, 'to offer betel quid', or *fãjako*, 'to offer him betel'. Gregorius Keraf (1983) explains that in this special context *huro* has two separate applications, meaning either 'row fast' or 'cut fast'. He also mentions *nuro menaluf*, 'hunger spoon'.

This expression means, 'Row fast like someone spoons food when he is hungry'. As with *huro* which has two meanings, so *nuro menaluf* also has two meanings, that is 'cut quickly like someone spooning up rice quickly when he is hungry'. The word *nuro* is also used for *bĕlãda* and *duri*, two tools provided for catching fish. There is a prohibition against uttering the everyday names of these two tools. If people use those words, the whale will certainly get angry and strike the boat so that it shatters.

When the whale is pulling the boat rapidly (*titi*), there is a large possibility that a great deal of sea water will come into the boat. In these circumstances people may not order the bailer '*Ẽma fai!*'—'bail water!', but must say '*Onã mara!* or *Onã néro mara héna!*' which means 'Thirsty!' or 'Always give thirst!', which metaphorically means 'Dry inside' or 'Inside always dry'. On the other hand, if someone is thirsty, he may not call out and ask for 'Fai!', 'water', but must say '*Gĕleteng tou!*' 'cold one (water dipper)'. If a crew member carelessly says *fai*, the fish will strike the boat so that

TABLE 14. *Word Substitutes Used in the Presence of Whales*

	Everyday speech	Special speech
sperm whale	*kotekĕlema*	*ikã*, fish
harpoon	*kãfĕ*	*nuro*, spoon, or *sudu*, submission, or *kerung mega*, hard short one
flensing knife	*duri*	*nuro*, spoon
paddle	*fãi*	*nuro*, spoon, or *kĕnaer*, wooden maize roaster or spatula
sharpening stone	*ĕlu*	*nã*, with
drinking water	*fai*	*gĕletã*, cold
to row	*bai*	*huro*, to ladle
row fast!	*bai béra!*	*huro menaluf héna!*, ladle, already hungry!
to bail	*ĕma fai*	*onã marã* interior dry, i.e. thirsty
harpoon it carefully!	*bapa, pĕleba*	*kelabo*, young coconut; for manta ray, *robek*, to bury, to dig
provisions	*keniki*	*kĕloma*, maize husk

water comes in, either because the boat shatters or because it is turned over. So long as they are pursuing the whale or while working on a fish which is not yet dead, thirsty crew members must go to the stern themselves in order to dip water. They may not ask help from others, because everyone is busy. If a boat is struck or butted by *kotekĕlema* so that a plank breaks or separates, then the crew member who sees that will quickly ask for '*rapo bélã*', which means 'big fibre'. This expression refers to a sarong or shirt which will be used to stop up the broken area so that the boat will not become shipwrecked.

Once a boat has been successful in harpooning, other boats will come and watch for '*kéa*' which literally means 'watch for turtle'. This expression is used to refer to other companion whales which have not yet been harpooned. Before harpooning, the *lamafa* will always ask the crew of the other boat 'where is the target'. To do this he is going to ask *Ina ama tité nala di ga?*, 'where are our ancestors?' Before that he will also ask *Ina ama tité beribu ilé teratu?*, 'are our ancestors thousands or hundreds?' The meaning is are we going to harpoon in order to give food to thousands or hundreds of people. An estimation of the strength of the boat crew will determine where there will be a target.

While catching whale and afterwards, the names which have an association with destructive actions for the boat or crew may not be uttered. Personal names like: *Bélo* (cut), *Bĕlida* (long cutlass), *Kupã* (Kupang), *Serani* (Larantuka), *Nuo* (war), *Besi* or *Ōla* (iron) may not be mentioned, because the words may produce a negative result. The words *Nuo, Besi, Bélo, Bĕlida* will produce misfortunes like breaking up of the boat or death of crew members, while names of places like *Kupã, Serani*, means that the boat will be pulled in the direction of Kupang or Larantuka. It is said that the Nara Ténã which once succeeded in harpooning a *kotekĕlema* was already around 3 miles from shore at the end of the afternoon, but because a member said '*aké goé tutu nuã Felãdã ka moé taku mengerti ha*', 'am I speaking Dutch, so that you do not understand?', the boat was unable to advance to shore. The whole night they were left at sea, and in the morning saw that they were fairly far from shore. The word *Felãdã* means *Belanda* [the Netherlands] which implies a place very far away.

Therefore the prohibitions hold not just while harpooning fish, but also afterwards so long as the boat has not yet reached shore. While pulling a whale, the crew hope that the wind will be strong. An east or west wind will always be called *lamaléfa* which means 'wind from the sea'. Boats which are late returning to shore hope for help from shore in the form of food and water. Family ashore will send other boats to take provisions to those returning. Boats pulling *kotekĕlema* will always hope for boats bringing these provisions. If a boat becomes visible from afar, they must say *'kĕloma bao pau!'* which means 'corn husk float toward us'.[2] The provisions in the boat must be divided equally. Should there be any fraud, then all members of the crew will suffer misfortune. This misfortune will take different shapes: the current will shift and become a current from the front, or the wind will change and become an opposing wind. Therefore everything must take place honestly and equally, there may be no dissatisfaction or unhappiness by anyone.

While pulling *kotekĕlema*, also *seguni*, *temu bélã*, and *temu bĕlã*, there is a custom of singing songs called *Gata poli ga*, which contain worship of the ancestors of the clan of the boat for catching the large fish. For example for the Nara Ténã this song is sung: *Béi pi mo uri ratu, Ratu ata Lamakéra, O Kabi, Kabi Daté Ãmã. Sogé haka puké jaji, jaji laba lali limak, O Éro, Éro Usé Inã*. 'Suddenly now you belittle the King, the King of the clan of Lamakera, O Kabi, Kabi father of Daté. Deriving from Sogé, given birth by the mother of skilled craftsmen, O Éro, Mother Usé' (see Gregorius Keraf, 1978: 259).

At sea, if they see or hear a whale to the west, especially after they have harpooned it, they say *Libu hir kaé*, if to the east, *Nara Guan hir kaé* or *Gési Raja hir kaé*. These expressions are fairly difficult to interpret, even for native speakers of the language. Libu, Nara Guan, and Gési Raja are personal names and at first sight this custom appears to be a violation of the prohibition on calling a person by name while whaling. However, the Libu in question is the lord of the land for the upper village at the time when the ancestors first settled in Lamalera, a member of the now extinct Lama Mau clan. Gési Raja was the lord of the land then for what is now the lower village, a member of the descent group now called Lango Fujo. Nara Guan was his son. The intention is to call on them to keep the whale from damaging their boat and to make it submit. *Kaé* is an imperative, meaning something like 'do it now', easily translated into Bahasa Indonesia by the appropriate usage of the word *sudah*. Professor Gregorius Keraf explained *hir* to me as possibly deriving from *hi*, to humiliate, to insult, to disparage, and *ro*, an enclitic particle meaning him or it. The underlying meaning seems to be a request to the ancestral lord of the land to make the whale submit itself to the crew of the boat. However, the same phrase may be used for similar purposes in connection with the name of master boat builder, that is indicating the direction of their houses, such as *Bĕlido hir kaé*, and the Catholic church, *Gereja hir kaé*. Another aspect of these usages is that there are ways of avoiding place-names, such as Lamalera. To use Lamalera in times of such commotion would almost guarantee that the boat would not soon return to the village, while to use the name of Larantuka,

Pantar, or Kupang would invite being pulled by the whale a long way in those directions.

Although in recent decades some female tourists have been permitted in the whaling boats, local women have never gone to sea in them when they were in use for hunting or fishing. They have, however, travelled in the boats when they were used as transport or when parties have taken them to cut timber for boat building. One or two women are actually accomplished seamen, but a great many of them cannot stomach even a slight sea swell.

Luck

Fishermen's luck is largely a question of getting into the right place at the right time. The people of Lamalera have in their control only the power of their arms and to some extent their ability to estimate the whims of the wind and currents. Not surprisingly they constantly talk about their luck or good fortune and that of their guests, for which they use the Indonesian expression *nasib* (from Arabic: Wehr 1966: 969; Wilkinson 1932: 2: 166), the Lamaholot equivalent of which is *lerong senaréng*, propitious day. Even when they have no '*nasib*' they say, they must go out. That is their work. When things go well, they also comment on their good fortune. Such was the case one day when a boat harpooned a whale. While they were struggling to get control of it a current from the south brought them toward shore. When it was finally dead they looked up and found the shore closer than it had been when they started. Also the whale went limp when harpooned and therefore did not cause much damage.

If they have a period in which they can get nothing they then sit together and try to think of what they may have done wrong—perhaps someone has not been fair to someone else in dividing the fish. Whoever thinks he might be the cause, then washes his mouth. Formerly, this was apparently done with blood; now they use holy water. If a boat turns over and part of its contents, such as a *lipa* or sharpening stone, falls into the water and disappears, then the next day the fish will not rise and the boats will get nothing. One day when all of the boats came in empty, the explanation given was that one of the boats had lost a harpoon the previous day. It is said that if anyone complains about the size of his share, the boat will get nothing until there has been a special ceremony to make up the fault. The expression for removing the fault is *hapus nuté*, to sweep away the words, or *hapus nu*, to clean the mouth. On 5 September 1979 the *Demo Sapā* did not go out to sea because the results of the previous two days showed that it had a fault, and they had not yet searched to find what it was. The *Jafa Ténā*, with exactly the same luck, nevertheless went out that day. They knew what their fault was: when dividing a recently caught killer whale, a porpoise, and a ray, they had given the smith's share to the old man who had the normal right to it. However, the work on the harpoons had actually been done by another man, who felt he had a right to payment. Therefore the fish disappeared for them. Until mercy is asked of the man who complains, the fish will stay away. In this case they had done so. The very tip of the right wing of giant manta ray may be stored in the right side of the boat's well. If there is a fault, they pour holy water on it as part of the ceremony and later store it in the boat shed.

If the children are rowdy in the great house to which the boat belongs or if the old people fight while the boats are out, the boat will get nothing no matter how many fish there are. For example, a long line of bad luck for one of the boats began the day it caught two porpoise. The harpoon maker was not satisfied with his share of the smaller animal, so he left it. Thereafter they caught no fish and a porpoise and two giant manta ray even got away after being harpooned. Then someone said when they were standing at the boat that the boat master should take holy water to the harpoon maker. He did this and the next day they got a small ray.

Bode (1925: 114) wrote that during the period when the boat is at sea fishing, the owner must keep the door of his house closed, barred with thorny branches, so that no one can go in or out. One day he saw Demon squatting on a high platform, busy cutting up a magnificent shark. 'I wished him good luck with his wonderful catch. But Demon just turned his head toward me indignantly and said nothing.' He quietly went on with his work, his whole attention on the cutting and flaying the fish, without giving Bode another look. Bode's assistant, however, told him that, 'If Demon had greeted you and spoken to you, while he was busy with the fish, the spirits, according to his belief, would not let him catch any more fish.'

I never encountered any overt indication that it was prohibited to speak to someone cutting up an animal either at the beach or on a drying rack near the house. The custom, however, would be comparable to the widespread prohibition on speaking to anyone in a field harvesting rice. As to the question of the doors to the great house, we were told precisely the opposite, namely that while the boat is at sea hunting fish, the doors must be kept open, so that the fish may enter the great house.

Returning Home

Once they have killed the whale, all that remains is to secure it with a hawser and start the long journey home. The other boats involved, if any, will pass out hawsers, until all are tied in a line, and then they begin sailing homeward. Usually, no matter what luck they have had at sea, the boats manage to get back to shore by nightfall, but this is not always what happens.

While paddling and pulling a whale to shore, they may sing the following song.

Sora taran bala tala lefo rai tai
Buffalo with horns of elephant tusks we must return to the village
Tuba béra rai nai ribu lefo golé
Pull quickly to the populace of the whole village
Kidé ina-fai tuba béra rai nai
Widows pull quickly to the shore

These words carry the implication that a whale contains enough flesh to feed a whole village, including especially its widows and orphans.

When the *Kebako Pukā* and four other boats harpooned the whale on 21 August 1982 described above, they were kept out well into the night. They sent word ahead by other boats to have provisions sent out. At around 5.00 p.m. four *sapā* headed out to sea with food. By 8.00 p.m. the *sapā* had returned to shore, having delivered the food. People lighted whale-oil lamps and pressure gas lanterns in the boat sheds. Children gathered on the beach in numbers and started many small fires. The tide at the time was far out, exposing the coral in front of the beach. The children moved through the exposed coral, catching crabs and finding shellfish which they roasted in their fires, causing a stench. A few old men, some young men, women, and many children made up the party waiting on the beach.

By 9.00 p.m. the tide was very far out and the boats had come close enough to be heard from the polyclinic on the point overlooking the beach, and it was possible to see the crew lighting cigarettes, but they had not yet arrived at the beach. By 9.30 p.m. the west current set and the boats were swept past the beach. Just after 10.00 p.m. they appeared around the point at the east of the beach, their sails looking like five very tall and very pale ghosts on a very dark night. The boats soon took down their sails and were floating within easy shouting distance of the people on the shore while the crew enjoyed a smoke. However, a strong east current this time threatened to carry them quickly west around the point on the west side. At that point the rope holding the whale got tangled in the anchor of the motor boat *Urfal*, which was anchored there, causing a great deal of consternation on the beach. No doubt in the daylight or in strong moonlight it would all have appeared much less dramatic, but in the dark the atmosphere became electric at times. One of the men dived down and freed the rope, and after a time the boats rowed back up to the beach. Suddenly a figure dashed out of the surf and ran up the beach, while someone shouted *Atadiké!*, human being! He grabbed a rope from a shed and streaked back into the water. Before long we were pulling a long rope up the beach. For some reason some of the boys decided to snake it all the way down the beach to the east end. Although the tide was still low, occasionally there were some very great breakers, carrying very far up the slope of the sand. This all added to the general sense of urgency. Soon we were pulling the whale ashore in the centre of the beach. This sperm whale turned out to be 15.4 metres long, one of the largest the village has ever caught. The only way to get it, or indeed any whale, onto the beach was to wait for high tide to bring it in and take in slack in the rope to which it was tied. As it was, during the next several days it took to cut it up, the animal spent as much time rolling in the surf as it did lying high and dry.

Sometimes in the afternoon the boats appear from around the point on the east or west of the harbour, as the crew drop the sails and begin rowing rapidly. They sing while they row and they row in unison, four or five men on a side facing forward. With each thrust of the paddle and in time to their song, they hit their paddles against the side of the boat before taking the next bite. The singing and the hollow, rhythmic beating of the paddles can be heard all over the village. The beach is a noisy place as the boats return and the men pull them to their sheds.

One August day in 1982 fast winds and choppy waves, as well as the absence of fish, brought the boats in early. The boats angled toward the east of the village coming from the west, to get the west wind behind them as they approached the beach. Then they turned back from the east and came booming down the short distance along the coast, probably sailing nearly as fast as they are capable, their sails puffed out festively in front of them (see for example Plate 45).

PLATE 45. Boats returning to shore while towing a Sperm Whale

Every day when the boats come home, they are pulled one by one up the shore to the sheds, one of the characteristic scenes of the village life. The boats usually wait offshore just beyond the surf until men have gathered on the beach for them. Meanwhile some men or children start taking the wooden logs which serve as runners out of the shed and laying them in a row along the beach where the boat will land. These logs, which might be described as rollers except they rarely roll, are slightly curved and the keel of the boat slides over their centre from one log to the next.

The helmsman turns the boat stern toward the beach. Then when a favourable opportunity presents itself, the crew catch a wave and start rowing in. The harpooner, and sometimes his assistant too, grabs a pole and stands in the boat ready to hold the boat steady in the surf. The action of the waves often causes the impression that just when they are rowing most furiously, they are standing still. Then the wave catches the boat in passing it, and the boat rushes forward more swiftly than the oarsmen alone could make it go. As soon as the boat gets to the shallow water, most of the crew begin piling out, leaving the harpooner to steady the boat against the pull of the receding wave. As quickly as they can, they shove the boat beyond the waves, other men who happen to be near by on shore rushing to grab the boat, and others placing logs under the keel while it is still in the water. As soon as the boat is high enough to give secure footing, men line up on either side and some place their shoulders under

PLATE 46. Pulling a returned *téna* up the beach

the outrigger beams and outriggers. Most pull with their arms, but others virtually lift the boat with their shoulders. Other men grab a rope and stretch it out up the beach and tow (see Plate 46).

The boat then moves up the beach in stages. On land it is heavy and difficult to get moving. The men shout and chant in unison, rocking the boat back and forth until the combination of efforts breaks the inertia and the boat begins to move. This is a critical moment, and the men shout more urgently and struggle to keep the boat moving as fast as possible. The beach is shaped differently in places and the angle of approach also differs depending on where the sheds are located. Raised coral rocks prevent a direct approach for some boats. Unless the slope is very steep the momentum can usually be kept up until they run beyond the log runners. Then those that have become free behind are brought to the front, and the pulling and shouting begin again. When the boat comes in from the side, much effort goes into swinging it around at the right time while it is moving. Once the stern has entered the shed, the going is usually easier, but the effort all the more urgent. The men seem not to want to stop so close to the goal, and during the last foot or so their shouts are loudest and their efforts most pressing. Through this whole process, they shout, count, chant, and sing work songs.

Boats Towed by Sperm Whales

Occasionally boats are not so lucky and may be towed a considerable distance away from the village, in which case fires are kept on the beach all night and signal fires are built on the points on either side of the beach. These signal fires would also be built if they needed to signal the boats of a disaster in the village, such as an attack. Just west of the polyclinic and below the upper village is a place called *bata nama pota apé*, the name of which means the clearing in front of the stone platform where fires are started. The other place for a signal fire is on the rocks projecting into the sea at the east end of the beach, the *pota apé* at *Emu Sia*, where salt pans lie.

According to Seegeler (1931: 69), a boat from Lamalera was allegedly once pulled four times around the island of Lembata, before being pulled to Timor. Vatter (1932: 204) wrote that once a boat was pulled by a sperm whale to Timor and that some Lamalera boys were named Kupang to commemorate the event after the main town on Timor. I have been unable to substantiate or confirm this particular story or indeed to find evidence for it in genealogies, although *Kupa* does occur as a given name in a generation which would have been too early for this incident. Nevertheless, since Vatter's day boats have been pulled quite far, including nearly as far as Timor.

In 1942 a whale towed the *Dato Ténã* and the *Menula Belolong* close to Timor. One man who had been in the *Dato Ténã* was able to date the event from the fact that when they were near Timor they could see shells being fired into the sky and exploding in the air. This would have been during the Japanese attack on Kupang early in 1942.[3] In order to get back they observed the southern cross and the morning star, although in fact they never lost sight of the Labalekang volcano during the day. On the return, before found, they did not row, but simply slept. One crew member had brought some food, which he divided—a handful to a man. They also divided the water they had with them, a sip per person. Afterwards when they were thirsty, they cut off pieces of the tail of the whale and sucked them. They were so weak that the whale had to be killed by shark. The current carried them first to Mingar, then on the evening of the third day back to Lamalera. The *Kebéla Ténã* found them on the third morning and gave them food. No one was injured or ill, although the *Menula Belolong* had suffered some slight damage to planks. The *Kebéla Ténã* carried in addition to the large water pot, several bamboos of water. It also brought plenty of food; so they were able to eat and drink to satisfaction immediately. After the *Kebéla Ténã* found them, the *Kopo Paker* showed up. The men then ordered it to take two boys in the boats, including the narrator of this incident, back to the village ahead of the rest. The villagers were afraid the children would not be strong enough to survive and were afraid for their lives. Therefore, the children spent only three days and two nights at sea, instead of the three days and three nights the other crew members had to put up with. When they came back to shore, a large section of the whale had been eaten by shark. The meat was also turning bad. There were so many sharks around the dead whale that one man reached into the water, grabbed a shark by the tail and pulled it into the boat. *Menula Belolong* got 18 sharks, *Dato Ténã* 24, and *Kebéla Ténã* got 6. *Baka Ténã*, which went looking for them carrying provisions but did not find them, caught one *bōu*. The *kakang* ordered all the people to sleep on the beach while the boats were gone. They took lamps with them so the boats could see the harbour.

On one occasion around 1951 or 1952, the *Nara Ténã* harpooned a whale, and afterwards the whale was harpooned in addition by the *Menula Belolong*, the *Sika Ténã* and the *Kéna Pukã*. All four boats were towed to Pantar. When they came back to the village four days later the meat of the whale was rotten and the flesh was already breaking off. No other animal they hunt can pull the boats for days—not even killer whales or giant manta ray.

The *Kebéla Ténã* went out by itself on 1 May 1976. They had a crew of nine, but one was a child, so in effect it was only eight. The other boats were not going out, so the boat master went to the beach and worked up a scratch crew. They ran into a mother whale and child not far from the beach. The mother pushed the infant down, so they harpooned the mother. This whale rocked the boat so that it filled with water, even though it was not turned over or damaged. Then the companions of the injured whale gathered round. The men were sitting in the sea although they were in the boat, and the whales were so close around them that they could have stepped out and walked on them. Several *béro* had gone out fishing. One of these was near by and came up to them. The man in it wanted to borrow a harpoon and go after another whale, but the boat master would not let him do so in a mere *béro*.

They had put up a sign before harpooning so the other boats would put out. The *Nara Ténã* had arrived before the *Kebéla Ténã* harpooned its whale. The boat master of *Kebéla Ténã* asked them to help them by harpooning their whale a second time as it was still alive. The *Nara Ténã* told them to wait until they had harpooned their own first, which they promptly did. Then the *Téti Heri* showed up. The *Kebéla Ténã* boat master asked them to help and received the same answer. The *Téti Heri* then harpooned and killed two whales. The *Nara Ténã* and the *Téti Heri* pulled their whales to shore leaving the *Kebéla Ténã* being pulled around submerged by a live whale, but promising to come back. The *Téti Heri* came close to shore and gave the lines on their whales to several *sapã* which were near by fishing, telling the *sapã* to take the whale in. They then returned to help, but by then the *Soge Ténã* had arrived. The two boats harpooned the whale of the *Kebéla Ténã*, which by this time had been towed near Ata Déi. Here they killed the whale. The boat master let the dead animal loose near the shore so that it would be carried by the waves up to the land, but the lord of the land of the area came down and spoke to the whale telling it that this was not the whale's resting-place and that it should go back to Lamalera. The waves then brought the animal back out to sea. The boat master was surprised. In any case it took them three nights before they came back with the dead whale. By then the meat was already breaking up. It was no longer good to eat fresh, but was usable once dried. The sharks had also been numerous and the *Kebéla Ténã* caught five. The *Kebéla Ténã* was not submerged for three days, even though it had been too full of water to be bailed out. They had pulled the *Kebéla Ténã* up on one of the other boats to empty it.

On another occasion the *Kebéla Ténã* harpooned a whale that flipped the boat all the way over. It then wrapped itself in the sail, so they had to choose between killing the whale and ruining the sail or hope to get the sail free and lose the whale. The boat master ordered them to kill the whale, which they did, ripping the sail to shreds in the process. He then asked one of the other boats to help pull them home.

On occasions in the past the *Soge Ténã* has been pulled under by whales for a long time. While floating in the water the crew could see the boat below them. Sometimes a single boat may be at sea, and spot whale. In that case it would put up a sign, namely a cloth, *lipa*. People on the shore would bring out boats, and as soon as they were close the first boat could harpoon the whale. It would not do so before because of the danger of being turned over, unless it were close to the village.

Baléo

If at any time during the year when the boats are not at sea, whales are spotted close to the shore, the shout of *Baléo! Baléo! Baléo!* is apt to go up in the village. The same may happen if only a few boats are out, but appear to be harpooning sperm whales or other large cetaceans or giant manta ray. Once this call is heard, fishermen will rush to the beach and try to get their boats out as rapidly as possible to join in pursuit of the game. To show how profitable this activity can be in an exceptional year, in 1969 by means of *baléo*, the boats captured 22 sperm whales, one pilot whale, 42 giant manta ray, 12 *mōku*, and 33 sharks among other animals. This year was, of course, exceptional in every other respect too, as well as coinciding with the threshold of the long slow decline the fishery has suffered ever since. Nevertheless, irregular launching of the big boats and hunting animals opportunistically remains an important part of Lamalera's subsistence life. In 1991 they again caught five whales in January.

The word *baléo* is to some degree problematic. It is somewhat similar in sound to the Portuguese word for whales, *baleia*, which of course is related to the English word baleen. This similarity seems, however, to be a mere coincidence.[4] The majority view in the village, which Gregorius Keraf (1983) shares, is that the word derives from the fact that when the big boats are not in use, the ropes called *léo fũ* and *léo bélā*, are kept in the boat owners' great house. Hence, when the cry goes up to launch the boats at a moment's notice, the harpooner must *bã léo*, that is, carry the *léo* rope to the beach. There is no question that this task must in fact be carried out, but the phrase has become conventional and now refers to the whole process of getting crews and boats to sea in the shortest time possible. There are dissenting views in the village to the interpretation given here. Some see no connection between the word *baléo* and the rope, but there is little doubt that there is a connection of some kind. Arndt (1937: 7) reports that *léo* means to hurl or toss a piece of wood, charcoal, and so on, which immediately explains why this name is given to the harpoon and rope it applies to. *Baléo* he says is a sling-shot or catapult. This meaning must at least be recognized as an alternative explanation, whatever relative force or cogency may be attributed to it.[5]

Dangers at Sea

Boats can be very roughly handled by whales. On occasion they have been pulled under and kept down for a very long time. In 1965 a crewman was covered by an overturned boat which the whale then pulled under drowning him. In 1972 another man in the *Gĕléko Ténã* was struck and killed by the tail of a whale. Around 1973 or 1974 the *Dolu Ténã* was broken in two by a whale.

The other boats pulled the halves to shore and the owners rebuilt the boat immediately. With whale the principal danger is a slashing side blow of the tail, directly striking a person or breaking the planking and killing him with flying pieces. One active boat master had been a skilled harpooner until the day when he landed in the sea beside a harpooned whale which struck him with its tail. The whale crushed his right shoulder, so that he can no longer work with it. Another man had his face slashed by such a blow. The tail went through the harpoon pole rack and harpoon poles, losing its force on them before hitting him. He was brought in and sewed up in the polyclinic.

Unfortunately, these misfortunes continue to happen. In 1991 a harpooner was injured after harpooning a whale and had to be taken for treatment in the hospital at Larantuka. In March 1994 four boats (*Kelulus*, *Kebako Pukã*, *Kéna Pukã*, and *Téti Heri*) were pulled a great distance by a whale, which eventually escaped when the rope broke when they were near Pantar. *Téti Heri* was the first to return, with seventeen men, after two nights at sea. The others, with thirty-four men, were carried to near the little island of Semau, off the west coast of Timor, where the men were rescued by a tourist ship which had been alerted and went looking for them. This ship took them into Kupang harbour. For four or five days the people of Lamalera dropped their work and spent all day and all night waiting and watching at the beach. Fortunately everyone involved returned safely, but both *Kelulus* and *Kebako Pukã* disappeared.[6]

One young boat master gave a vivid account of the dangers in the boat from a whale. Once he was in *Kelulus* when it harpooned a whale. He jumped into the well of the boat and was almost crushed by the rest of the crew jumping on top of him. More recently he was sitting in the stern of *Téna Ãnã* when a whale began knocking it about with its tail. He jumped out and swam over to the *Sika Téna* and found safety in that boat. On another occasion he was in *Kelulus* when it was being knocked about with no other boats around. There was nowhere else to go and nothing to do but stick it out.

With manta ray, the main danger is to the harpooner, who is at risk of getting caught in the rope and pulled under. A harpooner must by nature be aggressive, and his assistant, the *běréun alep*, must be quick to pull the rope taut so that it does not entangle the harpooner and drown him. This occurred to a harpooner in the *Kopo Paker* around 1949, which boat remained unseaworthy for years thereafter. The same misfortune struck a harpooner in June 1963. Another harpooner, aged 26 years, died in June 1976. He was the younger brother of the regular harpooner and was training for the job. That day the regular harpooner could not go out; so the younger man had to take his place. He harpooned a ray and simply disappeared. He was not, however, caught in the rope. Although he disappeared, the ray was captured. A friend commented on this event, that in his view there are women in the sea who have pulled men under. Once another senior figure in the village was hanging on to the side of the boat and called others to help him, women were pulling at his *lipa*, cloth, trying to drag him down. One man who survived getting caught in the rope was carried down its full length. He later stated that he had the sensation at that level that he could breathe and that the water was extremely cold. When they pulled him up, they emptied him of water, gave him artificial respiration and after a few minutes he began to breathe again. The harpooner of the *Téti Heri* suffered an amputated arm in 1986 after it became tangled in the rope when he harpooned a manta ray. The largest manta ray, *bĕlelā* , may wrap their fins around a person and take him under water. They can also easily knock a person unconscious. After a week in which a large number of these animals were landed, several men in the village had wounds to the legs and rib cage from struggling to control the animals and kill them while they held them to the edge of the boats. One man had cracked ribs.

As opposed to their wariness of whales and manta ray, the men of Lamalera are remarkably unconcerned about sharks. I have twice seen men wade into the surf at the beach, grab a tiger shark in a breaker by its tail and pull it up the beach to kill it. I have also seen men dive into bloody sea water to cut up a manta ray in order to get it into the boat quite unconcerned by a large shark visibly waiting near by. Some men, so I have been told, have even ridden sharks. Only the *io temu*, the Mako, or the *io temu i burā*, the White Shark, are thought to be especially dangerous. The harpooner must not jump or fall into the water when harpooning these sharks. In general, they think that only a shark injured by a harpoon is likely to be dangerous. If a man falls in when a shark has been harpooned, they throw in a piece of wood to distract it, while the *bĕrĕun alep* must pull the rope tight as quickly as possible to control the shark and to keep it from severing the rope. Only two men could be remembered who had been killed by a shark, both while fishing near the shore. Another man who was quite active in the boats had been bitten in the foot by a tiger shark after harpooning it. The injury did not permanently slow him down, although it took a long time to heal.

The Results of Fishing and Hunting in Large Boats over Time

Little or nothing in the carcasses of the larger fish and cetaceans caught by the sailors of Lamalera is wasted. Flesh, including intestines, organs, etc. is either cooked fresh or sun dried for later use and for trade. Fish and cetacean intestines may be fermented in bamboos to make a delicacy called *bĕromé*. Oil collected from sun-dried blubber may be used in lamps or sold for the same purpose. Spermaceti will be used for the same purpose, although recently a market has reappeared for it after a lapse around a century and a half. Large skulls and vertebrae may eventually be burned on the beach to get them out of the way, but mountain peoples may acquire bones to burn in their fields for the purpose of breaking up boulders. Smaller bones may be disposed of in the interior and on other islands to be cooked with papaya leaves to remove their bitterness. Whale teeth may be sold or cut into sections to make finger rings.

A nine-metre sperm whale may yield approximately 3.5 tons of edible products (Hembree 1980: 41; Lockyer 1976). Nine metres can be taken to be a typical length for the sperm whales and killer whales taken in Lamalera. By the same token, nearly a ton of fresh flesh and cartilage may not be far off the typical weight of the larger rays captured by the boats. These figures then suggest the relative economic worth of a large ray and a typical whale. Roughly speaking, therefore, between three and four large rays may have the same economic value as a single whale. This is a remarkable conclusion, considering that a boat can usually accommodate four giant manta ray without too much trouble, but would sink under the weight of even a small sperm whale.[7] A great part of the difference, of course, is represented by the weight of the whale's skeleton, for which there is no counterpart in a ray, which is nearly all muscle.

In trying to form an idea of the total value of Lamalera's hunting and fishing it should be borne in mind that the records available for Lamalera's fishery are haphazard and intermittent. Most are due simply to the chance that a retired schoolteacher in the village took an interest in keeping them. They generally account only for larger items of game, and therefore give no indication of the catch for the mass of smaller fish and crustaceans taken in various ways throughout the year and bear uncertainly on the total annual capture of protein from the sea. The records begin in 1959 and continue with interruptions until 1995 (see Table 15).[8] They show a substantial fluctuation. For example the combined catch of two large species of ray ranged from a mere 29 in 1960 to an overwhelming 360 in 1969. The late 1960s and the early 1970s seem to have been a generally favourable period for the fishery with high takes of both ray and whale. Between 1965 and 1971 they averaged 36 sperm whales per year, and in 1969 they captured no fewer than 56. Since 1971 there has been a steady decline in whales taken. An average of only 24 whales per year was caught between 1972 and 1979. For ray the record does not exist after 1970, apart from ethnographic observations in 1979 and 1982 (and the figures for 1983 to 1993 given in Table 15). What is plain, however, is that 1982 represented a disastrously bad year, with only 8 whales and 79 large ray; 1983 and 1989 were even worse. How it is to be explained is not obvious. However, there are several factors which suggest consideration.

As some villagers remark, the catch can hardly be good unless the boats are actually taken to sea. There is a clear decline in the use of the large boats over the period of available records. In 1969, the best year on record, twenty-five boats were in use, of which eight made the supplementary trip at the end of the principal season to the fishing ground at Lobetobi, Flores. Seventeen of these boats caught whale and all caught ray. In 1982 fourteen boats were in use,

TABLE 15. *Running Record of Annual Catch of Sperm Whale and Large Ray, 1959–1995*

	1959	1960	1961	//	1965	1966	1967	1968	1969	1970	1971	1972	1973	1974
Sperm whale	34	26	31		34	15	25	43	56	37	43	36	23	26
Ray (*bĕlelā + bōu*)	249	29	87		97	195	269	186	360	188	*	*	*	*
	1975	//	1977	1978	1979	//	1982	1983	1984	1985	1986	1987	1988	1989
Sperm whale	21		21	15	15		8	2	7	11	9	7	7	4
Ray (*bĕlelā + bōu*)	*		*	*	148[a]		79	99	62	10	138[a]	225	*	*
	1990	1991	1992	1993	1994	1995								
Sperm whale	12	14	7	10	27	38								
Ray (*bĕlelā + bōu*)	*	*	40	*	*	*								

* No record. [a] Record incomplete.

only two of which went to Lobetobi. Eight got whale. One boat caught absolutely nothing for the year. Figures for the number of days each boat put out to sea are available only for part of the 1979 and 1982 seasons. From 23 July until 19 September 1979 nineteen boats mounted up 446 days at sea, while for the same period in 1982 fourteen boats totalled 238 days; 73 per cent of the days fishing in 1979 were fruitless, while 80 per cent of those spent fishing off Lamalera were without result in 1982.[9]

These considerations refer only to the large corporately organized boats, which even in the best years are employed for a fraction of the season. In bad years they are used less, and their season is shorter. More people turn more often to alternative means of fishing which involve at most two or three people working together. The recent introduction of modern gill nets, partly through a gift of thirty four nets by the Food and Agriculture Organization in 1982, has increased the pressures for the work-force to desert the large vessels. A corresponding change has been the recent rapid increase in small *sapã* built and owned in the village.

Another possible cause of the declining numbers of animals taken is that the game has moved away from the general area. The sharp decline of the sea-bed permits whales to come very close to the south shore of Lembata. Though little is known about the migration routes of the animals through Indonesia, the deep seas and narrow channels of eastern Indonesia attracted and concentrated the animals sufficiently to have made them favoured whaling grounds in the nineteenth century in preference to the broad but shallow Java Sea where sperm whales were rarely encountered (van Musschenbroek 1877: 509).

Twice in the nineteenth century seamen told Kupang authorities that the whales had been overhunted and had moved on. It would be fair to conclude from this evidence that the numbers of whales visiting the strait changed from year to year. What is most uncertain is the extent to which their changing numbers responded to natural factors, such as the presence of food, and how much they were affected by the activities of human hunters. The same uncertainty obtains in the present. So little is known for the area that we have no idea what the normal fluctuations are over a period of years.

Even less is known from a local perspective of the frequency of smaller cetaceans and other game. Villagers are aware that manta ray follow plankton upon which they feed and that ray are accessible on the surface only when plankton rises to that level. Plankton depend on nutrients leached from the volcanic soils and washed into the sea by rains; so there are unresearched issues concerning soil content and the effects of variations in meteorological patterns still to be explored. Hembree (1980: 6) concludes that the sea off Lamalera is low to moderate in features related to biological production. The experience of Lamalera is that plankton and consequently ray are found during the dry season in greater quantity and more persistently at the end of the narrow Flores Strait between southern Flores and southern Solor, overlooked by the continuously active twin peaks of the Lobetobi volcano. Another factor whose effects the people of Lamalera speculate about is the new volcano which appeared in the sea to the east of Lamalera in 1974, and which was possibly related to the multiple disaster which struck the eastern side of the Lerek Peninsula in 1979.

16

Fishing near Lobetobi and Pantar

Lobetobi

Toward the end of the period of deep-sea fishing in the middle of August it is common for some boats, six to nine in the best years, to load themselves with provisions and sail away from the village to other locations for up to a month or so of intensive fishing. In the 1960s as many as twenty boats would go to Lobetobi, Flores, to the point where the village was nearly empty of men. They would stay several months, sometimes coming back to Lamalera to unload and then going back to fish some more. The most popular of these fishing grounds is near the villages of Lewotobi and Lewourang on the shore underneath the Lobetobi volcano in south-eastern Flores. Around the middle of August manta ray come to the surface in numbers there. Lobetobi is a good area for fish because the east current coming past Solor meets the west current coming up through the Flores Strait forcing the plankton to the top. Near Lamalera the sea is too deep, so that sometimes the plankton is nearer the bottom, only occasionally on the surface. The fish follow the plankton. The people of Lewotobi fish only in *béro* for porpoise and *mōku* near the shore. Occasionally they get a *bĕlelã* that comes too close.

However, not all boats go to Lobetobi. Some stay in the village and continue fishing there. In order to go a boat must have provisions. For the month's stay normal in recent decades, each man must provide himself with a 20-litre tin of roasted and crushed maize, *fata biti*, the standard way of preparing this staple food on the island, and four or five kilos of maize kernels. The boats will go with a full crew of as many as fifteen, but not less than twelve. Of this complement, one, usually the boat master, stays ashore procuring wood and water. With the wind and current behind them they can make the trip to Lobetobi in half a day, sailing south of Solor past Lewolein, although more commonly the journey takes about a day. They build themselves a small lean-to on the beach at Wai Otan to store their possessions, but access to the shore where they camp is restricted by offshore reefs and affected by tides and currents so that there are only certain times of day when the boats can get out. For this reason they must put out to sea as early as 2.00 a.m., which means that they sleep at sea. Their shelter includes a little altar for a cross or holy picture. This is where they put the rope called *léo* and this is where the harpooner should sleep. No one may sleep near him for fear of disturbing him while he is dreaming. He is supposed to dream and receive the help of the ancestors, who have contacted

the spirits of the place and brought fish for them. If members of the crew frequently become ill at Lobetobi, the helmsman will never be able to go there
again in that capacity. It means his spirit is not strong enough to deal with the
spirits there and he cannot take responsibility for the welfare of the crew.
At Lobetobi the harpooner and the helmsman are regarded as the *ina-ama*,
elders.

While they are there they do not hunt sperm whale because of the danger
of damage to the boat. Some repairs can be made there, but they will prolong
the stay and waste the chance of getting other fish as well as increasing the risk
of running out of provisions. Although they will hunt any other kind of fish
or sea mammal, including killer whales, the purpose of the trip is to get manta
ray. A successful boat may come back with ten or more such ray. The first taken
is always given to the church in Lamalera.

Local records show, for example, that in 1969 eight boats made the trip to
Lobetobi. While they were there, *Kelulus* caught eleven *bĕlelã*, two *bōu*, two
mōku, and one shark. *Kéna Pukã* returned with eight *bĕlelã*, three *bōu*, two *mōku*,
and one turtle, while *Soge Ténã* was fortunate to have harpooned one killer
whale, fifteen *bĕlelã*, one *bōu*, four *mōku*, and two sunfish. *Holo Sapã* had eleven
bĕlelã, four *bōu*, four *mōku*, six sharks, and one sunfish; and *Nara Ténã*
took fifteen *bĕlelã*, three *mōku*, one small porpoise, and a sunfish. *Boli Sapã*
brought back a whale shark, twelve *bĕlelã*, one *bōu*, seven *mōku*, two sharks, and
a sunfish. *Menula Belolong* harpooned fifteen *bĕlelã*, three *mōku*, one shark,
and one sunfish; and *Notã Ténã* took home eleven *bĕlelã*, two *bōu*, two *mōku*,
and one small porpoise. These returns compared very favourably with their
results during the rest of what was one of their most successful years. In 1978,
by which time the fishery was much less productive than it had been in
the 1960s, another eight boats went to Lobetobi for nearly four weeks before
they returned, when *Téna Ãnã*, which caught absolutely nothing during
that entire period, decided to go back. The catch for the other boats was as
follows:

> *Jafa Ténã*: six *bĕlelã* and one spinner dolphin
> *Horo Ténã*: five *bĕlelã* and one shark
> *Dolu Ténã*: seven *bĕlelã*, one spinner dolphin, and one tiger shark
> *Holo Sapã*: four *bĕlelã*
> *Soge Ténã*: six *bĕlelã*
> *Menula Belolong*: six *bĕlelã* and one spinner dolphin
> *Muko Ténã*: five *bĕlelã*.

Lobetobi's potential was demonstrated again in 1982, when only two boats
made the trip. *Muko Ténã* captured thirteen *bĕlelã*, one *bōu*, one loggerhead
turtle, four sharks of various kinds, and a sunfish. Two of the *bĕlelã* were pregnant with small foetuses. *Dolu Ténã*, which turned over at sea while it was there
and had to be rescued by boats from Lamakera, came back to Lamalera with

seventeen *bĕlelã*, one *mōku*, a sword fish, two sunfish, and four hammerhead sharks. What is more two of the *bĕlelã* were pregnant with foetuses that were larger than *mōku*. These results considerably improved on what otherwise was a poor year.

While in Lobetobi they may sell ray for food for use while there, but they do not dispose of the final catch there. The reasons are that (1) selling it for money is not desirable because they want it so they can barter for food, and mountain people on Lembata will give food only in return for fish; (2) if they bartered it there for large quantities of food, they would have a much heavier load to bring home. They may also trade pots which they have brought from Nualela. All in all, though, the crews which returned from Lobetobi in 1982 had a considerable quantity of maize and other agricultural products stashed about the boats.

The routine in Lobetobi can be strenuous. In the morning, a man may have only a piece of cassava for breakfast, for lunch only a handful or so of crushed maize, at night for the first time boiled rice. Food and meals are always shared by a group. Each boat crew divides itself into three separate messes. Each is a cooking group. No one may eat separately, or go off on a walk and eat by himself on the walk, and no one of them may eat before the others. An individual may not eat, even if invited, with any boat other than his own. This prohibition lasts four weeks. After that, everything is free. During the period of prohibition, a crew member may eat in someone's house, if invited. No one takes anyone else's tobacco without asking permission first. Nevertheless, while there a person's tobacco is common property. It is not permissible to roll a cigarette secretly.

The three mess groupings are called *lama fa* (bow), *lama lukã* (middle), *lama uring* (stern)—each consisting of approximately five men. Each person should provide about three bowls of husked rice and ten litres of crushed maize which should be eaten before the tins of maize are opened. Also they may take bananas, yams, coffee, and sugar. All is pooled within the group. During the trip only one person takes out and distributes food of a particular type. When they return to Lamalera whatever is left over is divided equally.

They may not curse, nor may they touch the local women. The women there are prohibited, although they come down in numbers to visit them. It is all right to touch their breasts, but not to open their blouses. If you begin to think of them, if they enter your heart, you will get no fish. Lobetobi is like a sacred place, and if they violate any of these restrictions they will get no fish until they have said a prayer to make it good. If someone breaks the restrictions by eating in secret, the consequence would be that the harpoon would pull out or not go in far enough when they harpoon an animal. While they are there they add a prayer during the middle of the day. Anyone who violated these prohibitions would have to confess, either there or later in Lamalera. Afterwards the boat group would hold a ceremony, involving among other things splashing everyone with holy water. They take a quantity of holy water with them to Lobetobi, which can be replenished there. The hardships are felt to be light because they are shared. If they were not shared, they would be regarded as being heavy.

One person stays ashore all day getting water and wood ready. It is the same person all the time, normally the boat master. They do not take turns, unless in case of illness. The water is very near the camp, a public well sunk in 1969. Formerly the source was a tidal spring called Wai Otan. Wood they gather in the forest; there is no need to buy it. The site is between the villages of Lewotobi and Lewourang. People from Lewourang have their fields near by and the boat crews can trade fish for palm wine with them. The youngest person from each mess usually acts as cook, although the others help him. The idea is to get things cooked quickly so they can eat and sleep soon, since they may need to be at sea again by 2.00 a.m. to get through the entrance through the reef.

They have good relations with the lord of the land at Lobetobi. They normally meet him when they go there. If a boat gets seven ray, they will give him one. It used to be the custom at Lobetobi that the lord of the land received one *ūk* section from each boat. They would search out the largest and mark it. When the boats were ready to return, the people at Lobetobi would give them a big feast and also prepare provisions for their return journey. Now they do not give them this food. The lord of the land would still like to get his *ūk*, but the boats now give him only some long strips of meat in return for the wood they cut. The Lamalera position is that they have maintained the customary arrangements, but the Lobetobi group have not. However, the village head there is understanding and there has been no trouble. Nevertheless in 1982 each of the two boats did steal a dog to eat while there. Misfortunes, however, can cause the seamen to reassess their relationship with the lord of the land at Lobetobi. Once there was an accident there which caused a man to have his leg amputated. The boats did not return to Lobetobi for about a decade because of fear. In 1978 a man died of a heart attack in the *Demo Sapã* when it was on the way to Lobetobi. Some attributed his death to his careless treatment of the lord of the land, expressing the view that more boats would make the trip, if *Demo Sapã* would make peace with him.

Boats from Lamakera, Solor, work the same waters off Lobetobi, but whereas the Lamalera boats are pulled up on shore every evening, the Lamakera boats anchor at sea. In Lamalera, if one boat is chasing a fish, the others must leave the fish alone. According to the men of Lamalera, the Lamakera boats, on the other hand, will not hold back and will take a fish away from a Lamalera boat. If the men from Lamalera object, those from Lamakera say the fish belong to God, not to you. 'What can you answer to that?' By 1979 the Lamalera boats were fitted with outboard motors bought on credit through a government programme, which meant that they were able to come and go between the fishing ground and Lamakera, thus shortening their stay on the ground. The Lamakera boats can take the torso of manta ray to the market at Waiwerang, Adonara, where in 1979 they could get Rp. 20,000 (US $48) for it. The crews of Lamalera boats come straight home and do not want to exchange fish for money because they would then have no means for getting food. In the early years of this century, however, the boats used to go to Waibalung, Flores, to trade for a little arak, and to Larantuka, before going on to Waiwerang where, as in Larantuka, they might trade for some thread and a bit of money. Whereas Lamalera boats always dry their fish before bringing it back, those from Lamakera bring their fish back fresh.[1]

In 1982 the *Dolu Ténã* turned over while the crew were trying to subdue their first manta ray, because the sail was in the wrong position. Furthermore, it had been in the process of boarding one ray when it spotted and harpooned another. *Dolu Ténã* rides high in the sea and is therefore less stable than other boats. When I returned to Lamalera from a trip to Waiwerang, Adonara, with the news I had picked up there that one of the boats had capsized, people in Lamalera immediately knew that it was the *Dolu Ténã*. The *Muko Ténã* did not help or was not in the position to help (stories vary). However, three Lamakera boats came to their assistance. One killed their manta ray for them and gave it back to them. The other two helped them right their boat. That day *Dolu Ténã* went on to get four *bĕlelã*, while *Muko Ténã* got three. The sea was so full of *bĕlelã* that it was like children swimming in the surf. The *Dolu Ténã* was not damaged by the accident and eventually gave one of their ray to the Lamakera boats in gratitude for their help.

When one boat decides to return from Lobetobi, all the others must return at the same time. If one boat goes back and the rest stay, the rest will get no fish the rest of the time they are there. By the same token all the boats must depart from Lamalera at the same time. If the boats have already left for Lobetobi, others may not follow or the boats will get no fish until they return. This restriction lasts for three weeks, or until those which went first have begun to prepare their return. In 1982 one of the boats was planning to do precisely this. Its crew argued that it was permissible for them to go and to go ashore if they remained until the others returned. They could return early, however, if they do not go ashore. They recognized, however, that if they went ashore and returned before the other boats, the others would get no fish. However, in the event, this boat's crew did not follow through with their plan and remained in the village, where instead they rebuilt their boat. In 1980 the village male nurse and a prominent person who originated in the village took a small boat with an outboard motor to Lobetobi to visit the boats there. When they returned they related how much each of the boats there had caught by then. Later when the fishing boats returned to the village, it emerged that none had caught any more fish, a result which villagers attributed to the early return of the nurse and his companion and to the fact that they had prematurely revealed the size of the catch.

While they are at Lobetobi, they must regularly dry their catch. They are in or quickly approaching the hottest and driest part of the year while they are there and the fish dries very quickly. A boat can take as many as twenty-one large manta ray back from Lobetobi, but the fish must be dry. It is not possible to carry so many if the meat is still fresh. Occasionally a successful boat will have to make two trips to bring its catch to Lamalera. The crew of a boat with a large load to transport will remove its top thwarts and add an additional plank, called *sasalāpi*, of soft wood above the hull before replacing the thwarts. This extra strake on the side of a boat returning from Lobetobi is a sign that it has more than seven large manta ray, or seven with other kinds of fish. Occasionally a boat will harpoon more fish on the return trip, which of course they would have no opportunity to dry.

The extra strake, the crew paints with lively decorations. For this purpose, they use either charcoal or battery carbon and red earth which they get on Solor. On the return voyage they fly the Indonesian flag and attach the decorative *temōto* to the stern of the boat. In 1982 the *Dolu Ténã* and the *Muko Ténã* sailed back from Lobetobi in a day, with a good west wind pushing them against an east setting current, but instead of coming all the way to the village, they stopped around 6.00 p.m. and spent the night in a small harbour called Peda just east of Wolo Wutun, where bird nests are harvested by the locals. This location is a walk of over an hour from Lamalera, but it is close enough so that the boats could easily have reached Lamalera had they wished to. The locals brought them palm wine in substantial quantities and received dried fish in exchange. By seven the next morning the crews had had quite a bit of palm wine and were relaxed but very tired. They had slept during the night and off and on during the previous day in the boats, which were full of dried fish, baskets, bags, and equipment.

About this time they rowed out in a desultory fashion and then stopped for breakfast and palm wine. Every once in a while someone stroked an oar, but there was no concerted effort to make any progress. A passenger boat on the way to Waiwerang, Adonara, with crew from Lamalera stopped at the two boats and received fish and palm wine. The boats then passed a point of lava rocks which look like they have just cooled after splashing into the sea. All around this point were people with bamboos of palm wine which they were hoping to exchange for fish, but the boats refused the palm wine on the grounds that there was no room for more. Finally the current and a bit of rowing brought the boats near the shore below the upper village and the crews made a more concentrated effort at rowing, soon arriving at the beach. There the boats were unloaded and brought up on the beach, but not yet into their sheds, for they needed to be washed clean so that termites and ants would not be attracted by the smell and make holes in the fibre caulking.

Villagers gathered around and helped unload the boats through a calm surf. The goods included a certain number of bundled ears of maize picked up either in Lobetobi or Wolo Wutun. Soon the beach was the site of impressive

PLATE 47. *Téna*, fully laden on its return from Lobetobi

PLATE 48. Dried fish and bamboos of fermented fish intestines brought back from Lobetobi

stacks of dried fish, large bamboos of fermented fish intestines, and other para-phernalia (see Plates 47 and 48). Women placed the larger sheets, *topo*, of dried manta ray on their heads, while others helped them by loading dried strips of meat onto these sheets so that they could carry them up to the great house for storage.

The meat had all been divided before they left Lobetobi. Each of the *tōpo* had its owner's name written on it. Members of the *Dolu Ténã* estimated that every crew member earned himself around 250 kilos of dried meat. Another estimate was that a simple crew share from the two boats was the equivalent of 30 to 40 twenty-litre tins of unhusked rice. An important difference between the division of fish in Lamalera and in Lobetobi is that at Lobetobi the har-pooner does not receive the right to *tōpo*, which is his prerogative in Lamalera. Other than the special share for his skill in standing on the platform, *léi naké*, at Lobetobi the harpooner gets no more than the other crew members.[2]

Pantar

Some boats sometimes go also to Pantar. The last to do so seems to have made the trip around 1973 or 1974. They go to a village on the south coast called Duli, not quite as far as Bean. The trip to Pantar is more difficult than that to Lobetobi. For Lobetobi they can leave any time and come back any time they want. For Pantar they must leave at a specific time and come back at a specific time. The currents in the strait between Lembata and Pantar are very strong, so strong that they once sucked under a motor boat carrying a wedding party. Motor boats going to Alor have to stay very close to the shore of Lembata. The currents are stronger than a boat sailing against it with the wind behind. Thus they have to catch the right current there and the right current back. There is a greater danger of losing an entire boat and crew. When sailing to Duli they have to calculate the moon and currents accurately in order to get past Pulau Kambing, there being only certain days that will do. Also, it is likely that if a man dies there he will have to be buried there, since they are not free to return immediately with the body as they can do at Lobetobi.

Bennett wrote that when the English whaler *Tuscan* passed through these straits in 1836, they found the current ripples as numerous and forcible as any they had experienced in the archipelago. At one point an eddy of waves turned the *Tuscan* completely around (Bennett 1840: 73). On 23 December 1687 strong tidal currents carried William Dampier and the *Cygnet* south through the strait, but nearly drove them against one of the small islands in the south end of it, by his description apparently Deer Island (Pulau Rusa). They tried to row against the current without success and finally had to push the ship off by thrusting against the steep sides with their oars. On 17 May 1700 in the *Roebuck* Dampier was again carried south through this strait, this time against a brisk gale. Dampier observed that there are two tidal currents, north and south, and that the northward current is weak and sets only three hours in twelve, while the southward current is of great violence (Dampier 1906: vol. 1: 448; vol. 2: 556–7). In 1687 he thought he went between Alor and Pantar, but in 1700 he corrected that mistake and realized he had been further west, i.e. between Pantar and Lembata. Currents during spring tides may average five to six knots, with eight knots having been recorded in the southern part of the strait, where the strength of the current is stronger than in the north (US Navy Hydrographic Office 1962: 262).

Only three boats or fewer go to Pantar, because there is room at the beach there for no more than three boats. The middle of August when the boats go to Lobetobi is the time when the *bĕlelã* come to the surface in numbers there, and the boats go there in preference to Duli. The time for Duli, however, is in October, after the boats have come back from Lobetobi. When the boats return from Flores, some may feel they have enough provisions left to make the trip to Pantar. In October, *temu bélã* and *bĕlelã* enter the bays there. Some suggested that they do so because the sea is hot in this hottest month of the year. Boats sailing to Duli may reach Pulau Rusa (Deer Island) on the first day, but they never put ashore there; it would be difficult. However, if they see *bĕlelã* near Rusa, they may harpoon them and put into Pulau Kambing (Goat Island) to cook the fish. From there they go on to Duli for a month of fishing. When they return from Duli, they still go ashore at Pulau Kambing and kill goats. They may take two or three, which they kill and cook as provisions for the return journey. They may also take a live goat or two, which they carry back as far as Ongaona. At Ongaona they buy palm wine, kill the goats, cook them and have a comfortable meal. No goat meat is stored up to bring into the village. The right to take goats at Pulau Kambing was given them in the eighteenth century by the Raja of Larantuka. There was a case in the 1890s involving a boat from Lamalera and a man who claimed to be lord of the land of the island, which was tried at Kalikur by the Raja of Adonara, who happened just by chance to be there. The result confirmed their right to take the goats.

They take fishing lines with them to Pantar and catch many fish with them. Duli seems a fisherman's paradise. Duli is also said to be a whale graveyard, since whales go there to die. The people there speak a language they cannot understand; it is 'like English'; furthermore their Indonesian is very bad. Some people in Lamalera seemed impressed with their Protestant ways. They invited the Lamalera people into their church and gave each man a chair. They also provided chairs for them at the beach. Of maize they eat only roasting ears; the rest of their maize they sell, because they raise red rice in such quantity that it is their staple. The area is extremely flat and broad. They are very careful in preparing their palm wine, which is delicious, much better than in Lamalera. The fishing area is a small bay, which is dead quiet, no matter what the waves are like outside. Crew members from Lamalera only anchor their boats in the bay, except Sunday, when they pull them ashore to dry them out and to provide shade from the sun. Whales and porpoise are numerous, but the Lamalera boats harpoon only porpoise. Fish are many and very quick to take the bait. At Duli it is easy to fill the boat after a month. If they were to take nets, they could do it in a week. People fishing with a line at Bernusa have caught as many as fifty big fish in a day. At Duli there is a large continuously running stream of sulphur water. This water is white, but it stains all the rocks red and white. The boats after a time are red, as if painted. They cannot drink the water, which is hot and sharp, but a few metres away they dig little holes and get drinkable water.

The little lagoon or bay in which they fish is very calm. The work is easy. They do not need to get up in the middle of the night, as at Lobetobi. The boats do not need pulling up the beach, since they can be anchored. At Duli the people there prepare cooked rice which they trade for fish. The land is flat, and they plant rice over a large area. They have several strains (red, black, and so on). They like to trade for woven cloth from Lamalera. The area is cold so they prefer the thicker cloth. They will trade two *lipa*, commercial cloth, for a *nofi*, man's cloth, or a batik cloth for it, or twelve plates. Some people in Lamalera possess bracelets made from sea shells, *kala flo*, which were acquired in Duli in exchange for woven belts or fishing lines made of locally spun thread. They got them as complete shells and finished them off when they returned to Lamalera. The people there fish only on the coral reefs. They will eat *segara* (moray eel) which are sacredly prohibited in Lamalera because of their poison and because people lost at sea may take this form. Some at Duli know how to cook them to counteract the poison, but this knowledge is unknown in Lamalera. For some years the boats from Lamalera did not go to Duli because one man, whose son told me of the incident, had been drunk at Duli and had sung while they were circling a porpoise. Thereafter they got no fish until the son subsequently went there and had a ceremony to make things good.

Shortly after the Dutch pacified the island, one of the boats went to Duli. The Dutch had collected all the guns, but a couple of men took gunpowder to sell at Duli, assuming there would be a need for it there. The Dutch police found the powder in the boat and arrested two of the men, whom they sent to jail in Kupang. After a year or so they returned home having enjoyed Kupang, where they had been allowed to run loose pretty much at will.

17

Early Whaling and Contacts with Timor

Early Records

In his *D'Amboinsche Rariteitkamer*, the Dutch naturalist Georg Everhard Rumf or Georgius Everhardus Rumphius (1705) discusses at length the theories of the origin of ambergris and records a good deal of original information about strandings of whales in the eastern islands, but makes *no* mention of indigenous whaling.[1] Hunting of whales by the islanders of Lewoleba, that is, Lembata was mentioned as early as 1643 in an anonymous Portuguese document (Anonymous 1956: 487).[2] The whales were hunted with harpoons for their oil, and the author implies that the islanders collected and sold ambergris at Larantuka, Flores. This early report (which was repeated verbatim by Santa Catharina 1733: 793) confirms that indigenous whaling in Lamalera is ancient and that it antedates the appearance of American and British whalers in these waters by at least a century and a half.

Most of our information about whaling and the trade in the Solor Archipelago up to the last decades of the nineteenth century refers to the village of Lamakera, Solor, and only implicitly, if at all, to Lamalera. The reason for the lack of knowledge about Lamalera among the Dutch is the fact that it was part of the realm of Larantuka, which until 1859 belonged to the Portuguese sphere of influence.

Sixty Solorese troops were among the auxiliaries who were led by the Dutch when they inflicted a decisive defeat on the Topasses (so-called Black Portuguese, mestizos) at Penfui, Timor, on 9 November 1749 (Anonymous 1853*b*: 333). Schulte Nordholt considers that had the Topasses won, Timor and the Solor Archipelago would still have been Portuguese at the time of his writing (Boxer 1947: 14–15; Schulte Nordholt 1971: 177–81). Following this war, the Dutch kept 2,000 Rotinese, Savunese, and Solorese troops in Kupang, and in 1756 they concluded a treaty whereby the Solorese were obligated to supply Kupang with troops. According to Hogendorp (1780: 427–8), Lamakera had to keep 150 of its subordinates in Kupang to serve the Dutch East Indies Company. By 1771 the Head (*Opperhoofd*) of Kupang warned his replacement that the *sengajis* of Lamakera and Lohayong came to Kupang yearly, but that those of Lamahala, Terong, and Adonara had not taken the trouble to do so for years (Cornabé 1771). On 13 March 1781 the Dutch East Indies Company even decided to ask its servants in Timor to attempt to arrange for fifty to a hundred Solorese, or as many as they could manage, to be sent, the earlier the better, to Batavia to serve as sailors in the service of the Company at a wage of from four to five rix–dollars per month as well as the usual ship's rations (van der Chijs 1892: 480). Müller wrote that during his visit to Timor in 1829, there were 100 Solorese, mostly from Lamakera and Lohayong, at Kupang, who were used as rowers because they were the only natives who freely chose to be sea-farers (Müller 1857: 98). They were replaced annually or every other year. As a consequence of treaty provisions, there were in 1835, 100 Solorese house-holds in Kupang, who were useful in fishing, boat building, and constructing houses (Kruseman 1835: 10, 37; Stapel 1955: 96–7). Trade along the coasts and between the islands was carried out by thirty boats of 2 to 12 tons kept at Kupang for this purpose. These boats were manned with slaves and Solorese. These were sent on voyages during the transitions between the monsoons. They returned in a month to six weeks. Trade was usually carried out with the chiefs, who often took goods on credit, to be repaid in six months with their own products (Kruseman 1835: 7).

Through these contacts, the Dutch learned a good deal about economic and cultural circumstances in the Lamaholot cultural area, and their various reports contain some occasionally quite vivid descriptions of these people (Spanoghe 1834, 1849*a*: 309–11). For a period there was a ward of Kupang called the Solor beach inhabited by Lamaholot-speaking peoples and their descendants. In the 1860s the Solorese in Kupang had their own mosque there (Wijnen 1863). The Dutch Resident in 1834 wrote that it is possible that there is no island in the world which produces such bad seamen as Timor. The Timorese did not dare to put to sea, even in canoes along the coast. Without the Solorese, there would have been no fish to be had in Kupang. The Solorese depended on fishing for their livelihood, and when they caught so many fish that they needed to pre-serve them, they did not use salt, but just dried them in the sun (Spanoghe 1834). According to Kruseman (1835: 39), the Solorese children were all trained at an early age to fish, just as soon as they had the strength to do so. Solorese would tie a cord around a child's waist, place a line in each hand, and set it on a bamboo. Then they would shove it off from shore and not let it return until the cord was pulled out full length.

Heijmering (1847: 46–8) reports a legend current in Kupang, which accounts for the coming of the Dutch to Timor. Two Solorese fishermen har-pooned a shark, which they were fast to but which they did not kill. The shark pulled their boat all the way to the bay in front of Kupang, where they landed on the island of Samao. The King of Kupang, who had a residence on that island, entertained them. They in turn told him about the Dutch, who had driven away the Portuguese on Solor. Eventually the King of Kupang used the good offices of his Solorese visitors to invite the Dutch to Timor. In histor-ical fact, Dutch interest shifted decisively from Solor to Kupang after 1653, when the Dutch took over the Portuguese fort at Kupang and renamed it Concordia.

Earl (1853: 178) wrote of these Solorese as follows,

The coast tribes of Solor are remarkable for their skill in managing their prahus and canoes, and are the most expert fishermen in these seas, frequently capturing the black-fish, a small variety of the cachelot, or sperm-whale, which no other fishermen in these seas will venture to attack. The blubber or fat obtained from them is used as food, and also as an article of barter with the inland inhabitants; and the oil and spermaceti is sometimes disposed of to the Bughis and Macassar traders, who prefer it to cocoa-nut-oil for burning in their prahus. Several of these Solor fishermen are always to be found at Coepang, the Dutch settlement on Timor, chiefly in the service of the government, from whom they obtain a fixed allowance of rice and maize. These men, who are relieved by others every year, are sent in compliance with an old treaty, by which the coast natives of Solor agreed to furnish an annual quota of men for the public service. As all the youths have to take their turn, the system makes them accustomed to inter-course with Europeans, and is attended with very beneficial results.

Whale Oil and Ambergris

Ambergris is very occasionally found today by the people of Lamalera, and a few pieces are kept among descent group heirlooms in the great houses. Its value is known, but it is not currently a significant economic product. Until about 1986, whale oil and spermaceti had a limited local market, but was mostly consumed within the village.[3] By 1987 a new market had appeared for whale oil, so they began to be careful in collecting it. Merchants from Lamahala began coming to the village to buy whale oil, and people from Lamalera found that they could sell it in stores in Waiwerang and Lewoleba. Presumably this development resulted from a shift in international markets. Prior to the mid-nineteenth century there was a market outside the local region for both whale oil and spermaceti, and of course also for ambergris.

Whale oil and ambergris are frequently mentioned in earlier centuries as items of trade in the Solor Archipelago. In 1563 Orta listed ambergris as being found in Timor, but infrequently and only in small quantity (Orta 1908: 25). About ambergris, Rumphius wrote that the common understanding in the islands was that ambergris came from a specific whale, which the Arabs called *Azel*. The Malay name for it is *Ambar* (in Lamaholot *abar*), but the peoples of the Southeast Islands and Timor called it *ikan tahi*, fish excrement.[4] The Javanese supposedly deemed it to be vomited or excreted by the *Garuda* bird (Rumphius 1705: 255, 257). Both interpretations were common along the shores of the Indian Ocean. We also hear of ambergris springs in the bottom of the ocean; for a summary of theories see Dannenfeldt (1982). Among other remarkable stories is al-Mas'udi's description of ambergris-hunting camels of the East African coast, who were trained to kneel down when they come across the substance on a beach so that their riders could pick it up (Sprenger 1841: 349; Reinaud 1845: 144). Although we now know that the whale origin theory

is the correct one, there is still a mystery about the circumstances that cause
its production.

Ambergris is a rare wax-like pathological growth found in the stomach and intestines
of the sperm whale (*Physeter catodon*). Its origin is still uncertain, but the condition
may be due to the irritation caused by certain indigestible food, especially when the
whale has been feeding on cuttlefish (*Sepia officinalis*), a favorite food. The horny beaks
or mandibles of the cuttlefish, almost invariably found in ambergris, are indigestible
and cause irritation. The unnatural growth is usually gotten rid of in the ordinary
processes of elimination, but frequently the sperm whale sickens and dies before the
apparently morbid condition is remedied. Ambergris is thus found on the coasts of all
seas frequented by sperm whales and in the carcasses of dead sperm whales. When
fresh, ambergris is black and mixed with blood and fecal matter, and it has an unpleasant odor. When the mass is exposed to air and sun, ambergris becomes light grey (*gris*)
and hard, and it has a sweet, musky odor. Ambergris consists largely (80%) of ambrein
(a cholesterin), fatty oil, and benzoic acid. Its odor may be derived from the cuttlefish
which the whale eats (Dannenfeldt 1982: 383).

A Portuguese text of 1643 mentions that on Lembata 'fish oil', i.e. whale oil,
was sold at a jar of two or three *almudes* for an iron axe or four old nails.[5] The
exiled King of Ade Manduta (Manatutu) on the eastern point of Timor, Raja
Solomon Speelman, told Rumphius that around 1665, a whale stranded in his
land and that they called it *iyu ambar*, ambergris shark. In this animal they
found ambergris, which the Timorese were unfamiliar with. They used it to
tar their boats, until some Macassarese put them wise, scraped it off, bought
it and took it with them (Rumphius 1705: 257).[6] Only a few years later, in 1670,
Cornelis Speelman mentioned ambergris as among goods Macassar merchants
obtained in Tanembar and Alor (Noorduyn 1983: 104). In all likelihood the
Macassarese learned of the market value of ambergris from the Arabs, who
were long familiar with its uses in their homeland. In the late eighteenth
century, Hogendorp (1779: 214) reported that the inhabitants of the Solor and
Alor Islands took oil from the *Noordkaper* (north Atlantic right whale (*sic!*))) to
Kupang, Timor, for sale. He also mentioned ambergris and oil as among the
products involved in an extensive traffic on Solor. Iron, elephant tusks, silk
patola from India and other cloth were traded in from outside in exchange for
slaves, wax, ambergris, bird nests, coconut oil, 'fish' oil, and other products.
On the coasts of Solor 'and other nearby islands', whaling took place in almost
the same way as in the European whale fishery. Not only did these seamen
derive oil from this activity, but they were also sometimes fortunate enough to
find ambergris in the intestines of the whales, which then commanded a high
price. Some years before the Solorese had learned of its value. Formerly, they
had boiled it down and used it to rub on their boats. Some, however, threw
it back into the sea in compliance with their superstitions. The reports of
Rumphius and Hogendorp leave open the possibility that in the island world
of South-East Asia there was a more ancient practice of applying ambergris to

the planks of boats in order to protect them, perhaps from spiritual influences. Interestingly, Hogendorp mentioned Lembata as among the nearby islands which were not under the government of the Resident of Timor and which were therefore not visited, except by a very few traders (Hogendorp 1780: 427–8).

The American traveller Delano wrote concerning Timor that,

On the beach immense quantities of ambergris are found. It was confidently asserted, that masses of this had been picked up weighing eighty or ninety pounds. I have since read a history of ambergris, which asserts that a piece was thrown ashore on the island of Timor, weighing a hundred and eighty two pounds, and measuring five feet two inches in length (Delano 1817: 106).

Delano frequently quotes the 'Edinburgh Encyclopedia', by which he means the *Encyclopædia Britannica*; so in all probability the history of ambergris to which he refers was in one of the early editions of that encyclopaedia. The third edition contains an article on ambergris in which the following comment is found. The island in question, however, is given as Tydor, which could as easily be interpreted as meaning Tidore as Timor. 'The piece which the Dutch East India Company bought from the king of Tydor, weighed 182 pounds' (*Encyclopædia Britannica* 1797: 526). It contains, however, no reference to the length. Perhaps Delano and the encyclopaedia simply shared a common source.

On 4 May 1812 in 'Sketches Relating to the Range of Islands Connected with the East Coast of Java' Callbrooke wrote,

the Floreans are said to be the most athletic, intelligent and manly race. Of this their spirit and dexterity in whale fishing is one proof and as singular an employment for Asiatics as it is worthy of notice. A Prow with thirty men is fully a match for the most formidable whale but the peculiar mode of attacking them though said to be attended with great hazard and characterized by much boldness, I have never heard described.

Callbrooke (1812) discovered that on 'Flores', i.e. Solor, 'The whale oil is a considerable article of trade from this island and though not imported to Java is in use at Timor & the Islands to the eastwards.' Francis found in 1831 that the Solorese were selling whale oil and dried whale meat. The people of Solor, who collected oil as it dripped from the drying blubber, also collected the spermaceti, but since they were not familiar with the proper means of dressing and preserving it, the spermaceti had little more value than the oil, a comment which would hold good today in Lamalera too. They sometimes found ambergris in the intestines of the whale, which they sold at a very high price (Francis 1838: vol. 1: 388; vol. 2: 46). This is one of the few unambiguous references to activities of Lamalera, since only they hunted sperm whales and therefore only they could derive spermaceti and ambergris from the carcasses of animals they had killed (unless perhaps the animals involved were bottlenose dolphins). What is less clear is whether Francis was dealing directly with people from Lamalera, or whether these goods were brought to Timor by Lamaholot middlemen from the Muslim communities. The second possibility may well have taken place, but as will be seen below the first possibility is also likely.

According to Kruseman (1835: 38–9), the Solorese bought food and other necessities with their oil, for which they got around 8 guilders per half *aam* (aum, a liquid measure, especially for wine and oil, equivalent to about 1.5 hl.). Rienzi (1836–7: vol. 1: 205) described the Solorese as enriching themselves by trade in whale oil and ambergris. Moor wrote in 1837 that the Solorese carried on a considerable trade with Kupang (Moor 1837: 10). They also traded wax and 'fish' oil to boats from Macassar and Sumbawa (Bima). According to van Eysinga (1841: 56–7), the Solorese derived ambergris and oil from *noordkapers*, which they traded for iron, silk, and other cloth, and especially for elephant tusks which they held in such high regard that they had them carried before them on ceremonial occasions. Spanoghe (1849*b*: 67; 1850: 766–7) said that the Solorese found much ambergris floating in the sea and that they sold ambergris, bird nests, and shark fins to the Bugis for the Chinese market. In his annual report for 1850, van Lynden (1850) explicitly mentions Lamalera, along with Lamakera, and, erroneously, Lohayong, as hunting whales. This is the first document to mention Lamalera by name in this respect. In the following year, he wrote that they sold the oil to the Buginese. He writes very circumstantially that in Lamalera the oil was allowed to drip out in order to collect it, rather than cooking it out and was used everywhere for caulking ships. No oil was collected in Lamakera! In both villages the dried flesh, and blubber was regarded as a delicacy and also sold in dried form to the mountain dwellers. Shark fins, whale teeth, and ambergris, which formerly had been found in greater quantity, were sold to Bugis, Butonese, and Kupang traders (van Lynden 1851*a*: 321–2). Van Lynden describes the animals taken as the *kotta kalemah* (i.e. *kotekĕlema*) and a large, edible, non-oily fish called *kraroe* (i.e. *keraru*, or *kelaru*), as well as a porpoise, *temoe* (*temu*). This highly accurate report suggests that early references to collecting and selling of whale oil and ambergris by the Solorese are exclusively or almost exclusively about products from Lamalera. If this is the case, a further implication would be that traders from Lamakera often acted as intermediaries for trade in these products, which is quite possible. Today, traders from Lamakera visit Lamalera to purchase shark fins and deer antlers for sale in Macassar. In 1853 Hellmuth identified *Physeter macrocephalus*, an older scientific name for sperm whale, as being the source of oil and ambergris, which again points to Lamalera. Some dolphins also produced oil (Hellmuth 1853: 232). As late as 1873, Kluppel said that the people of Lamakera were selling whale oil to the Macassarese (Kluppel 1873: 385, 387). The Solorese also took their oil and cloths to Kupang, Alor, and Atapupu on the north coast of Timor (Kluppel 1873: 388).[7]

Trips to Kupang

From the above evidence, we can safely conclude that Lamalera was providing whale oil, spermaceti, and occasionally perhaps ambergris to traders from outside and indirectly to the international market during the seventeenth, eighteenth, and nineteenth centuries. In 1853 Larantuka came under direct Dutch control as part of an agreement in which the Dutch East Indies loaned a substantial sum of money to Portugal (Kniphorst 1885: 321–2). This was the beginning of diplomacy that eventually led to the Dutch purchase of Portuguese claims in the Solor Archipelago, including Larantuka and the island of Lembata. It was also the beginning of expanded Dutch knowledge of this new territory, as represented in Baron van Lynden's compendious report (Lynden 1851*a*). This report represents a substantial movement beyond the Solor-centric perspective on the archipelago common in early Dutch commentary, and it is not surprising that van Lynden specifically mentions Lamalera.

While it may be unlikely that any of the Solorese trading with Kupang prior to about 1851 were from Lamalera, it would seem that the village did have a brief period of such contact about this time. Adreanus Ubas, whose birth year appears in the village records as 1904, but who told me that he was born in 1893, was able to confirm that none of the Lamalera boats ever took whale oil to sell in Kupang during his lifetime or that of his father, although he thought that they had done so during his grandfather's lifetime. In fact the village remembers a trip about the middle of the nineteenth century taken by the *Kebako Pukã* to Kupang for precisely this purpose. While they were there, the government staged a festival of some kind and invited the *Kebako Pukã* to race a horse from one end of Kupang bay to the other, the boat sailing from point to point, while the horse raced along the shore. *Kebako Pukã* won this race and received as a prize a flag, since disappeared, and a porcelain bowl of European manufacture which is still in the possession of the *Kebako Pukã*'s great house. Although people of Lamalera have relatives in Kupang, and some travel back and forth on public transportation, no Lamalera boats are known to have travelled as far as Kupang since the time of *Kebako Pukã*'s race (but see Chapter 15, n. 6).

European and American Whaling in the Timor Strait

It is little known that the Savu Sea and the Ombai or Timor Strait between Timor and Lembata were one of the very earliest whaling grounds for American and English ships in the Pacific. American and English whaling ships first sailed across the equator into the southern Atlantic in 1775 (Jenkins 1921: 207). Hembree has discovered evidence in whaling logs at the Western Australian Museum of American Whalers in Batavia (Jakarta) in 1797 and sailing through the Timor Strait in 1804.[8] The whalers first worked on the Molucca ground in 1803 (Beale 1839: 149), and Timor must have followed shortly thereafter. On 28 May 1813 Joseph Brown, then the British Resident on Timor, wrote from Kupang that the Chinese merchants were returning, following the hostilities between the British and the Dutch, during which,

they suffered by the fate of War by having their Prows and Trading Vessels captured, chiefly by the Whalers, who were long in the habit of frequenting the Coast as being the best fishing ground for the Spermaceti whale, at one time these ships collected in such numbers in the Straits of Timor, that the fish for a length of time actually left the coast and straits, they then turned their exertions as they had letters of Marque to seizing and plundering whatever they could, and actually took or destroyed, almost every vessel from Coupang, many of them of great value, which deprived Coupang of Trade for nearly two years; since the fall of Java, the People who quitted the place are again returning.

On 30 June 1813 Raffles, the British Governor-General of the Dutch East Indies, reacted to 'the observations of the Resident [of Timor] with regard to the Whale Fishery in the straights of Timor'.

There is too much proof that this system of Plunder of Vessels employed in the Whale Fishery is neither uncommon nor limited, and it has been carried to a height of later years in the eastern seas which has been attended with the injurious effects to the British name and the most serious injustice and injury to the inhabitants of these Islands.

There is no doubt that the practice of Piracy among the Native Inhabitants has been increased by the practice not only from being reduced to poverty by the plunder of their Prows but also from a spirit of revenge for the injuries suffered, and I apprehend that the establishment of some efficient Regulations to prevent the occurrence of these disgraceful Proceedings will be found during the early attention of your Honourable Committee (Raffles 1813: 83).

By 1820 whaling ships had established whaling grounds throughout the Pacific, and Scoresby (1820: vol. 2: 533) mentioned in this regard for the Indian Ocean, 'particularly about the island of Timor'. The Timor ground then preceded that off the Japanese coast which was first visited in 1820. After the British returned the Indies to the Dutch, Crawfurd wrote,

In speaking of the fisheries of the Indian Islands, one great subject has not yet been alluded to—the *whale fishery*. In the seas which surround the Spice Islands, and particularly towards Timur, and that portion of the Pacific Ocean which lies between the Archipelago and New Holland, the *Cachelot*, or Spermaceti whale abounds. While the Spice Islands were in our possession, our whalers were in the habit of refreshing in Amboyna, which they found a convenient station for this purpose alone, though perhaps to carry on no species of trade with it. Ten or twelve of them annually put in for refreshments at the port of Dili in Timur. It is evident, that any nation in possession of the Spice Islands, that has the wisdom to destroy the absurd monopoly of spices, and restore the industry of those countries to their natural state, may see them necessarily become a convenient station of the whale-fishery. If industry and capital were suffered to take their natural course, the spice trade and whale fishery would be naturally combined, each mutually aiding the other (Crawfurd 1820: vol. 3: 447–8).

In 1834 there were from forty-five to fifty square-rigged whaling vessels of various tonnage working out of Sydney, Australia. Their whaling grounds extended all over the western Pacific from Port Jackson to the Sea of Japan. London sperm-whalers were large ships, taking four months to reach the whaling ground and spending two, three, or four years on a voyage. Sydney whalers were smaller in size and were on the whaling ground as soon as they left port, so that they filled faster. Their voyages were shorter, lasting from ten to fifteen months. The numbers of Sydney-based whaling ships expanded rapidly from two in 1823. In 1826 there were five or six such ships, by August 1830, twenty-six. In 1832 Sydney exported £146,018 worth of oil and whale-bone (Lang 1834: 1: 299–300, 305–6). Proof that Sydney vessels were reaching Timor waters is given by Jukes. In 1843 a Sydney whaler, which had previously refreshed in Kupang, returned to land a sailor with smallpox. He was lodged in the small hospital in the fort (Jukes 1847: 381).

According to Jackson, for the British the southern fishery contracted violently in the 1830s and was a mere shadow of itself by 1840. The cause of this decline in his interpretation was American and Australian competition. British participation in the southern fishery finally ended with the establishment of a whaling station at Auckland by Charles Enderby in 1849 (Jackson 1978: 136–9, 142). Deep-sea whaling in New Zealand began in 1791–2, when the whaler *William and Ann* hunted whales there off its coasts. It was firmly established there by 1802. In 1839 there were an estimated eighty American whalers in New Zealand waters. In 1840 there were between six and seven hundred American whalers around the coasts of the two islands of New Zealand, about half the total of all whaling ships there. The numbers of British and Australian whalers working there declined in the late 1830s, and foreign whaling ceased after 1840 (Oliver and Williams 1981: 31–2; McNab 1913; Ommanney 1933: 243).

Reports of Dutch Residents of Timor show that British and American whalers continued to frequent the region after the restoration of the Dutch East Indies to the Dutch, with forty to fifty per year calling at Kupang in the late 1830s and early 1840s. In 1836 D. van den Dungen Gronovius, the Resident of Timor at Kupang, wrote back to his superiors at Batavia a glowing account of the possibilities of whaling, noting that each year the English and Americans took from the sea a treasure worth millions of pounds without encountering any competition from his compatriots. Indeed, he proposed that the authorities in Batavia set up a whaling establishment in Timor. No place in the world, he thought, was better suited. From the Sunda Straits between Sumatra and

Java as far as Timor, the Ombai Strait between Timor and Alor, the Banda Sea, the Tomini Bay of northern Sulawesi, and north of Sulawesi as far as the Sulu Sea all locations were good whaling grounds. Gronovius wrote that the average quantity of 'sperm' taken from these seas was ten shiploads, each containing 300 tons of oil, for which the price in England was £32 per ton; the total value thus would have been £96,000.

Although Batavia did not respond to this request, Gronovius was not the first to suggest that the Dutch should involve themselves in commercial whaling in the Dutch East Indies. An anonymous comment published in 1827 noted that some 200 British and American ships were involved in hunting whales in the Pacific Ocean, the China Sea, the Indian Ocean, and around Timor, and asked why the Dutch whalers could not join in with profit (Anonymous 1827*a*). The same anonymous author in the same year noted that in 1733 two ships of the Dutch East Indian Company had returned to Holland with baleen plates, but the author was unable to discover if they had been taken from whale captured by the Dutch or whether they had been purchased. He commented how desirable it would be for any Dutch whaling in the Indies to be continued, if it proved to have existed (Anonymous 1827*b*). Again in 1829 the same author contrasted the courage of Netherlanders who formerly whaled in the ice fields of the North Atlantic with Dutch inactivity in the Dutch East Indies, where whaling was left to the English and North Americans (Anonymous 1829).

Generally the Dutch considered choosing ports in the Indies as either the starting point or the end point of whaling voyages in the South Pacific. Around 1824 or 1825 the minister of economic affairs in the Dutch government sent a letter to the chamber of commerce recommending whaling both around Greenland and in the southern oceans. King Willem I felt that whaling could benefit Dutch settlements on Java, the Moluccas, and New Guinea, as well as providing employment to fishermen in declining coastal communities in Holland. He also wanted to involve the Nederlandsche Handel-Maatschappij in this activity. The act which established this organization contained in article 81 a requirement that it encourage fishing in seas of the East Indies, including whaling. The King suggested that they consider either imitating the British and Americans by undertaking whaling voyages lasting years or settling Dutch fishermen in Java and the Moluccas. At first nothing happened. Then once the organization had established its trading links in the Indies, South America, and the Levant, the King once again asked it to consider establishing a society for fishing in the south seas, which would be supported by shipments of soldiers and goods to the Dutch East Indies. The directors then decided to engage a whaling ship and captain from the United States and to hire a crew and to purchase a double fitting-out, so that a second ship could be prepared in the Netherlands. The American crew was to be shared between the two boats and complemented with Dutch sailors.

The American captain declined to be responsible for two ships, however, so only the *Logan* sailed from Rotterdam in 1827 with a partially Dutch crew. It had an unsuccessful voyage of two years and lost the society 22,000 guilders. The merchant house E. & S. & C. St Martin, N. J. de Cock and C. A. Vlierboom sent the *Eersteling* on two whaling voyages to the south in 1832 and 1834 and the *Proserpina* in 1836. The second and possibly third of these voyages was commanded by American officers. The second voyage made a profit because of high prices in the market when it returned, but the other two produced losses. In 1844 the barque *Anna & Louisa* under British officers but with a Dutch crew set out on a whaling voyage to the Indies. Its first port of call was Kupang, where it arrived in October 1844. It worked the Molucca Passage with some success. However, a British traveller who encountered it again in Kupang in October of the following year described constant dissension among the crew and predicted the certain failing of Dutch whaling. Subsequently the ship lost its first mate and some crew and Captain George Gray died in Kema, Celebes. The Resident of Menado appointed the second mate captain and converted the ship to carrying cargo and soldiers. It dragged its anchors and ran aground in Ternate. Once it reached Batavia, it was found to be seriously damaged. Therefore, the owners sold it and its small quantity of oil at public auction in Batavia, and that was the end of Dutch whaling in the East Indies, although the *Proserpina* sailed once again in 1845 and reached Sydney, Samoa, Hawaii, and Valparaiso. However, it leaked so badly that it could not round the Horn and had to finish its voyage in San Francisco. It seems to have made a loss too (C. de Jong 1978: 463–9; Broeze 1977: 72–106).

Müller, who was on Timor in 1829, observed that seafarers were aware that there is not a single harbour on Timor's coasts which is safe all year long. Timor has larger or smaller inlets here and there, but nowhere a truly inclosed harbour. It is difficult for ships to anchor on the south coast during the east monsoon or on the north coast during the west monsoon. Of all the bays around Timor, that of Kupang is the most prominent and the best during the east monsoon (Müller 1857: 99).

In 1838, 42 English and 9 American ships entered Kupang harbour; in 1839, 32 English and 15 American; in 1840, 43 English and only 3 American; in 1842, 40 English and 11 American ships. In 1843, however, Gronovius reported, 'There have been in comparison with the previous year, few whaling ships in these waters', only 20 English and no American ships. From 1844 to 1847, just over 20 English and a handful of American ships put into Kupang each year. Until 1843, we are told, most of these ships were whaling vessels, but thereafter whalers seem to have been a smaller proportion of the total. The seamen told the Kupang authorities that their numbers had fallen because the whale had been overhunted and had moved on (Gronovius 1838, 1839, 1840, 1842, 1843, 1845, 1846, 1847). A contributory reason may have been the reduction in 1843 of Britain's protective duty on spermaceti and whale oil, which marked the beginning of the end of British south sea whaling. In 1849 the duties were entirely repealed (Stackpole 1972: 382).

By 1849 the Resident of Timor, Baron van Lynden, wrote that the whale-boats usually sailed straight through to Japan. From 1848 to 1857 the Residents' reports list separately the number of whalers putting in annually at Kupang, never more than five.[9]

1848	3	1854	4
1849	5	1855	2
1850	4	1856	1
1851	4	1857	1
1852	3		

As late as 1857 the Resident S. G. F. Fraenkel wrote that, 'the results of this fishery are unknown to the government, but it cannot be significant, since whales are rarely encountered here, as a result of the hunting of them for years by English, American and French whalers, which now however very seldom visit these waters'.[10]

Commercial exploitation of the Timor ground extended from the beginning of the nineteenth century until 1843 and dwindled then until it had practically ceased in 1857. A fine whalebone plaque in the possession of the National Library of Australia contains a coloured engraving by William Lewis Roderick of the English barque *Adventure* whaling off Pulau Komba near the north coast of Lembata in 1858 (West and Barnes 1990). Townsend's charts of whaling grounds taken from American log-books show catches along the north coasts of Flores and Alor in September, but none at all anywhere else in the vicinity of Timor (Townsend 1935). This omission is in part due to happenstance in the selection of logs available to him and in part to the fact that he did not consult logs of English ships.

We have a published account of an English whaler in Timor waters in 1836. Bennett aboard the *Tuscan* speaks of English south-seamen putting in during the 'Timor-season' (Bennett 1840: vol. 2: 98).

Sperm whales frequent the abrupt coast of this, in common with other of the Malay Islands, probably attracted by the animated currents that prevail in their vicinity. Many English South-Seamen cruise, during the winter months, in the Straits of Ombai and adjacent seas, and usually with success.

He also claims wrongly that the Americans had not yet ventured into these waters. The *Nautical Magazine* for 1858 describes the whaling season in the Sulu Sea and west of the Sangihe Islands as being from March to July, while the best months to be in the Molucca Passage were January, February, and March, although there was good sperm whaling all year round. From November to March there was good sperm whaling south of Java and Lombok

(Anonymous 1858: 604–5). The *Tuscan* was near Timor in July. Bennett makes it clear that Kupang was not their only possible place of reprovisioning—a factor which must be kept in mind when considering the figures derived from the Residents' reports. Whalers liked to stop at various villages along the north coast of Timor, including Sutrana, Occusi, Atapupu, Dili, and Bacau (Bennett 1840: vol. 2: 78).

The *Tuscan* stopped at Sutrana in the Portuguese-owned district of Occusi, then temporarily in the hands of the Dutch. A large proportion of Sutrana's commerce derived from visits of the English ships. 'No pilotage or harbour-dues are demanded, permission to take wood and water is freely bestowed, and every essential supply may be readily obtained.' Persons from Sutrana eagerly purchased sperm whale teeth for local use in manufacturing ornaments or for export to other Malay islands and to China. 'The teeth of the largest male Cachelots bear an average value of two dollars each, those of adult females, three dollars the dozen' (Bennett 1840: vol. 2: 91). These ships carried trade goods intended explicitly to facilitate reprovisioning in remote locations. The twenty-five to thirty such ships stopping in Kupang in the mid-1830s carried hats, stockings, linen, axes, knives, and provisions. At that time no anchor tax was required at Kupang or Dili, or indeed any of the other stopping places, and the cost of food was less in Kupang than Dili (Kruseman 1835: 9). In 1840, however, Wilson of the *Gypsy* found Kupang to provide only water and a place for the crew to walk around. There was no wood to be had, and refreshments were scarce and expensive. Besides, 'the manners of the Dutch are offensive to English visitors'.[11] Dili, on the other hand, supplied cheaply every desirable refreshment, but its unhealthiness was its main drawback. However, he contradicted himself about Kupang, perhaps after better experience, and said that Kupang was the best place to ship water, refreshments were abundant, but dollars were in much request.[12] It was the healthiest port. At Sutrana, one musket would fetch two fine buffalo; one bottle of gunpowder would bring one dozen fowls; for five bottles of powder one large pig could be obtained. Oranges, limes, shaddocks (*Citrus maxima*), melons, pumpkins, bananas, plantains, and coconuts were also available—no doubt all were most welcome to scurvy-plagued crews (Wilson in Forster 1991: 54–5). In 1843 Kupang was still a free port and much used by whalers and other vessels for procuring refreshments, according to Jukes (1847: 377).

Fevers, ague and death are familiar to foreigners residing on the island. Ships have lost as many as eight or ten men in Port. Many and many is the Englishman who has fallen a victim to the proverbial 'Timor fever' and lies buried in the fatal soil (Wilson in Forster 1991: 55).

Bik (1864: 137–8) went on board a whaler which was working near Alor and Timor and which carried guns, swords, powder, and finished clothing which it traded for provisions. By 1869 Kupang was being avoided by native and Chinese traders and by American Whalers, even though it was the only port which the Dutch made open to international trade, because the authorities were demanding payment of duties. Instead, they went to the parts of Timor not under Dutch control, where there were no charges (Veth 1869: vol. 3: 965).

Possible Influence of Commercial Whalers on Indigenous Whaling

The evidence shows the coexistence of two quite separate whaling industries, the local and the European, in the Ombai Strait in the first half of the nineteenth century. Nowhere is there any explicit mention of contact. It is true that the ships put into ports along the coast, but they generally gave the islands of the northern arc a wide berth. Very typical of the attitudes toward these islands among the whalers is the following comment from Wilson,

Ombay [Alor], Pantar and Lomblen [Lembata] are inhabited by unhuman savages, which in person resemble the natives of Timor but in nothing else. In disposition as far as is known, they are bloodthirsty and cruel. They speak a language peculiar to themselves, and they go destitute of clothing. I believe they have not even canoes. Ships dare not venture to trade with them (Wilson in Forster 1991: 59).

Although the whalers occasionally filled out a crew by taking islanders, they appear rarely to have shipped any of the seafaring peoples near Flores and Timor.[13] According to van Musschenbroek (1877: 507), whalers, mother-of-pearl fishers, and China-bound merchantmen hired make-up crews in the Talaud, Sangihe, Siau, Tahulandang, and adjacent islands between Sulawesi and the Philippines. It is true, as mentioned above, that the ships put into ports along the coasts. Ten Kate (1894: 243) even attributed the troubles he had in Lamahala and Terong, Adonara, to unpleasant memories left there by English whalers. But there is no reason to think they stopped at Lamalera or for that matter at Lamakera either. In the event, these villages were hunting whales long before the English and American whalers entered the Indian Ocean, indeed long before the first American whaler captured a sperm whale (1712) and before the first American whaler crossed the equator (1774) (Jenkins 1921: 207). In the light of this evidence, the suggestions by Weber (1902a: 35; 1902b: 93; see Anonymous 1910: 158) and Vatter (1932: 202) that the villagers of Lamalera and Lamakera learned to whale from American and British whaling ships can be seen to be incorrect.

Although the villagers of Lamalera know that in the previous century their boats occasionally went to Kupang to sell oil, they are also certain that their whaling techniques have been handed down to them from their ancestors. They have no knowledge of contact with nineteenth-century whalers or of having boarded them, although British and American ships did frequent the Timor Strait. There is also no memory of such contact in this century, although they

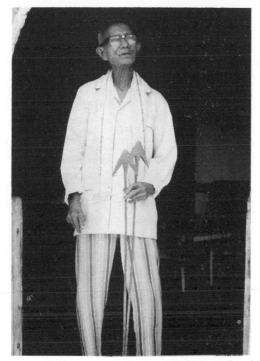

PLATE 49. Harpoons of Western manufacture found by *Kéna Pukã* in a dead whale in the nineteenth century

have gone on board the illegal Japanese factory fishing ships in these waters in recent years. The only indirect contact with European whalers occurred in the nineteenth century when the *Kéna Pukã* found a very large whale dead at sea, which had two western harpoons in it, one in each side (see Plate 49). These harpoons, which are quite rusty and bear no trace of a ship's name or marking on them, are in the possession of *Kéna Pukã*'s great house, and are of a type that went out of date around 1850.

Indigenous Whaling in the Indian and Western Pacific Oceans

Although passive whaling (the utilization of stranded animals) has been known on the many coasts of the Indian and western Pacific oceans from ancient times, the pursuit of whales on the open sea is extremely rare. When Alexander the Great's admiral Nearchus led a fleet to explore the seas between the mouth of the Indus and the Persian Gulf from November 326 BC until February 325 BC, he found that on many parts of the coast people used the bones of stranded whales in the construction of their houses (McCrindle 1879: 197). Strabo added the information that they used the vertebral bones of whales as mortars for pounding sun-dried fish (Jones 1930: 131). Later Arab voyagers of the ninth century described fishermen of Siraf in the Persian Gulf as cutting up whale blubber and taking oil from it in order to rub the joints of their ships' planking (Yule 1903: vol. 1: 108). In his *Cosmography*, El-Kazwîni wrote that whales became stranded in the river channels near Basra at the head of the Persian Gulf during low tide, where people harpooned them and pulled them to shore and took oil from the head for their lamps and to rub on their ships (El-Kazwîni 1868: 268). The Chinese author Chao Ju-kua wrote in 1225 that whales stranded annually on the Somali coast and were exploited by the natives for their oil (Pelliot 1959: 160).

More active forms of whaling were described by Marco Polo on the island of Socotra. The inhabitants of that island at the time (late thirteenth century) were Christians who allegedly used tunny as bait for the 'whale fish' (perhaps Killer Whale). They also tied flagged bottles to the harpoon rope to make it difficult for the whale to dive (Moule and Pelliot 1938: 189).[14] The second Dutch voyage to the Indies under Jacob van Neck and Wybrant Warwijck in 1598 encountered the Betsimasaraka actively hunting whales with harpoons in the Bay of Antongil in Madagascar (de Bry and de Bry 1600: plate IV; Lloyd 1851: 56). Additional original information about their whaling practices may be found in Flacourt (1661: 108, 167), Le Gentil (1781: 561–7), and Leguével de Lacombe (1840: 90). Owen describes Betsimasaraka whaling as follows:

The canoes are small, of the common form, and delicately made; but, slight as they appear, the natives venture far from the land, and will sometimes attack with success the largest whales, that sport in great numbers between the island and the main. They cautiously approach the monster, and, with their neatly-formed iron harpoons, which have a long line and buoy attached to them, strike him deeply in the side. Writhing in agony, he dives to seek relief in the depths below, but short is his respite: he finds but little space in this shallow sea, and rises again but to meet his watchful foe, who, guided by the tell-tale buoy, is prepared to repeat the deep and exhausting wound. He struggles, but it is in vain; the conflict is soon at an end, and terminates in towing the huge body in triumph to the shore. It did not appear that the people of this island had any particular form when attacking whales, like those on the main, who never pursue an old one, but always the young, when they humbly beg the mother's pardon, stating the necessity that drives them to kill her progeny, and requesting that she will be pleased to go below while the deed is doing, that her maternal feelings may not be outraged by witnessing what must occasion her so much uneasiness (Owen 1833: 168–70).

It seems that the Betsimasaraka no longer hunt whales (Valmy 1956: 29).

There is no reason to think that there is any direct connection between these forms of hunting whales in the western Indian Ocean and those found in eastern Indonesia, unless the practice among Betsimasaraka represents skills brought by their ancestors from Indonesian waters when they colonized Madagascar. Any such connection would of course be of great antiquity and would perhaps be even more surprising than the astonishing fact that Madagascar is populated by speakers of Austronesian languages.

A drawing on a sandstone wall in Ulchu County, Korea, of possibly neolithic date depicts men in a boat which is in the act of harpooning a whale (Ellis 1991: 90–1). Nieuhof describes the seamen of Hainan island south of China as hunting whales in boats (Nieuhof 1670: 158–60). A lengthy description of groups of boats hunting whales around Hainan and neighbouring islands during the months of January and February was published in the September 1844 issue of the *Friend*, a newspaper especially intended for whalemen and printed in Honolulu. Ellis (1991: 91–2) reproduces this difficult to locate article in its entirety.

Japanese whaling is a complex subject, especially in the nineteenth and twentieth centuries. A useful English language summary of the history of whaling in Japan may be found in Kalland and Moeran (1992: 65–94). Japanese scholars estimate that active whaling began in the sixteenth century. By the end of that century, whalers using several boats in a hunt pursued the animals with harpoons. By the end of the seventeenth century nets were being used to trap whales in narrow bays. The whales were driven into the nets and then killed with harpoons. The American and British discovery of the Japanese ground in the 1820s led to a drastic reduction in the number of whales caught by Japanese. Subsequently the Japanese attempted to adopt American methods using bomb lances and then Norwegian methods using harpoon guns on steamships operating from shore. Japanese participation in open-sea or pelagic whaling is a development of the 1920s and 1930s. By 1938 they were sending six fleets, consisting of 49 catcher ships and 8 refrigeration ships to the Antarctic. In 1940 the first Japanese fleet went to the North Pacific. Exploitation of stranded whales or drifting carcasses occurred anciently and still takes place. Apparently anciently whales were also occasionally hunted with bows and arrows or with nets. For centuries, Japanese fishermen have driven schools of porpoises, pilot whales, and killer whales into bays to trap them. These were cases of opportunistic whaling. When schools were spotted fishermen would surround them, lower their nets, shout and beat the sides of the boats, and herd the animals towards sandy shores in order to beach them. Harpoons found in prehistoric shell mounds may have been used to catch small cetaceans. There is no reason to think that Japanese coastal whaling had any influence on such activities outside of Japan or that there was any link with whaling in eastern Indonesia. It is a historical curiosity that the Dutch naturalist on Ambon Rumphius corresponded with a Dutchman in Japan whose Japanese translator had for many years been a whaler (Rumphius 1705: 262).[15]

According to Barraud, on Tanebar-Evav in the Kei Islands, the whale is a symbol of society (Barraud 1979: 37). 'Famous local tales have as their theme the death of whales which have run aground, celebrated events in these islands' (Barraud 1985: 121). Geurtjens (1921: 194) mentions communal hunting of large game including dugong, manta ray, turtle, and sperm whale by the inhabitants of the Kei Islands, but also implies that they prefer to leave sperm whale alone. Almeida (1945: 54–5) mentions in passing that the inhabitants of formerly Portuguese Timor would not hunt small whale without first carrying out propitiatory ceremonies to the spirits, although these rites were not required for porpoise. These are both fairly ambiguous pieces of evidence for whale hunting in Indonesia by communities other than Lamalera and Lamakera, and so far I have found no others. Neither source suggests that such hunting is anything more than occasional. The active pursuit of whales on the open sea as part of a routine subsistence strategy seems to be exclusive to Lamalera and Lamakera, and since each village pursues distinct types of whales, each is therefore unique in South-East Asia. It would seem too that their form of whaling is also extremely unusual in the Indian Ocean and western Pacific. The only known parallels are apparently ancient Socotra, the Betsimasaraka of Madagascar, Hainan, and perhaps some early Korean and Japanese communities. Harpooning or netting of individual porpoises, although the recorded evidence for it is scant, is probably more common.

18

Lamalera Past, Present, and Future

Lamalera is a community which straddles several dichotomies. As such it does not differ from its neighbours, except in the particular combination of dichotomies involved and its position in them. In the past it was landless or virtually landless. Today, this is less true, but still relatively so. Nevertheless, until recently the community and its leaders were politically potent in the region. It is a poor and remote community in an impoverished province, yet it has long served as a window of trade and communications to the outer world for much of south Lembata, and in recent decades it has achieved a degree of international fame drawing increasing numbers of tourists to it. In the past it was a magnet attracting population from elsewhere, and today still retains an essentially alien definition within its own cultural region, but today it has become demographically stagnant for reasons which are better attributed to its successes in accepting the challenges and opportunities of the modern nation and economy than to its failures.

An increasingly prosperous national economy has meant that the government has been increasingly able to put resources into a province too poor to be able to meet by itself the costs of developing infrastructural resources such as roads, shipping, schools, and public markets. This investment, and the growth that has followed on it, has meant that there are increased opportunities in the wider region for wage-paying employment. Other sources of cash income are payments sent into the region by relatives living elsewhere and of course tourism. These opportunities are still very restricted, but the increased access to money and the increased availability of consumer goods to spend it on, mean that local-level economic life is undergoing transformations that produce their own dichotomies. 'The possibility that the Indonesian economy as a whole has been experiencing strong growth while the majority of indigenous Indonesians have been experiencing declining, static or at best weakly growing living standards has reminded some observers of the theories of "dualism" which were much in vogue in colonial and early post-colonial times' (Garnaut and McCawley 1980: 289). It is not my intention to engage in the debates occasioned by the Dutch economist J. H. Boeke's concept of economic dualism (see for example Mackie 1980: 306, although he is in some particulars unfair; Boeke 1953), or indeed in those within social anthropology concerning spheres of exchange. I am more interested in the fact that economic and social change is forcing dichotomies in production activities and consumption patterns on individuals living in the community.

One side of community life, which is increasingly weakened by its inability to attract better educated youth in a normal pattern of generational replacement and renewal, involves dependence on very old traditions of land-based craft production and sea-based fishing and hunting which totally bypass a money-regulated, market-guided economy. In the past most clothing and almost all of the equipment used in fishing and hunting were produced within the community. What was not produced within the community, except to a very limited extent, was non-animal food. This production specialization linked the community to interior peoples who did produce vegetable foods, as well as many of the resources needed in cloth making and the manufacture of ships and gear. This description is still largely valid. Sherman (1990: 304 n. 1) quotes Godelier to the effect that the idea of a subsistence economy is inadequate because simple economies do not limit themselves to producing subsistence goods, but also produce a surplus used in the functioning of social structures (Godelier 1977: 110). Perhaps Sherman is right that, 'there is no clear-cut way to distinguish subsistence from surplus production' (Sherman 1990: 304). Godelier is drawing a very sharp line between subsistence and surplus, while it might be argued that the costs of the social structural functions he mentions are part of subsistence costs. For present purposes, I will continue to use 'subsistence' to refer to those economic activities not mediated by the exchange of cash. It has already been shown, however, how easily non-monetary values can be related to price. Clearly, the island economy did, and does, produce surpluses expendable on valuable goods which could be kept as heirlooms signifying wealth and importance and on marriage-related exchanges involved in social and physical reproduction. But these surpluses were, and are, produced in a fragile environment marked by unpredictable but periodic crop and fishing failures and resulting famines, economic dislocations, and loss of life. Surpluses can be replaced by deficits, with consequent catastrophe. Except for some cloth, most of the valuables used in the marriage exchanges derived from the outside and therefore represented returns on exports of the island's productive surpluses. Willingly or unwillingly, until the twentieth century, the island was also an exporter of human beings in the form of slaves. Whether human beings can be regarded a surplus product in an underpopulated island is debatable at best. Certainly slaves were not signs of a safe and secure economic environment.

Money in the form of specie or currency has been a factor in that environment since long before Europeans became such. However, despite Dutch determination to monetize the regional economy, money was not until quite recently a predominant factor in pricing and regulating production and consumption activities. There were abstract (verbal and conceptual) standards (such as the *kesebō*) which provided similar services and which are of a kind which usually fail to appear in the evidence available to historians. It may be supposed that they were and are more widespread than currently recognized. Also there were and are commodities, such as rice and elephant tusks, which fulfilled some of the roles of money, including commodities whose destined use was as gifts in ceremonial exchange. I would therefore agree with Parry and Bloch that the distinction between gifts and commodities can be overdrawn (Parry and Bloch 1989: 10; Parry 1989: 86; Stirrat 1989: 94). Conversions are made between all types of what might, in a now challenged convention, be called spheres of exchange; there is no other way that gongs and elephant tusks could have become part of the marriage exchange cycles (see Sherman 1990: 291–2). These conversions are not all one way either. Unloading an elephant tusk for maize at an unfavourable price is a way, under duress, to survive famine. In the past, accepting debt bondage for oneself or selling off a relative was another means to the same or similar end.

Bloch has argued that for the Merina of Madagascar money is morally neutral, while contrary to what the economists say, it is not neutral for Europeans. 'It is in European culture that money is far from morally neutral and its moral charge hinders conversion from one sphere of activity to another' (Bloch 1989: 167). What he means is that money is acceptable as a gift among the Merina, while for Europeans with their long history of Christian polemic against usury, money often brings with it negative connotations (Parry and Bloch 1989: 3; Parry 1989: 82; Le Goff 1980: 29, 61). This point is worth bearing in mind when witnessing the recent trend in Lamaholot communities toward substituting cash for bridewealth objects in marriage exchanges. There *is* something very ancient going on in such exchanges, but there is also a sig nificant change, which people are aware of and comment on. Moreover, cash is a potent attractor of meaning, especially in contexts where people are forced to seek wage-paying jobs in other areas in order to raise cash for taxes and school fees, with the concomitant dislocations in place of residence and work as well as in production patterns. It is important to realize that for many villagers, wage-paying jobs, if available at all, are not dependable. The monetary economy is also a fragile source of economic security at best, and if it competes with the subsistence economy and weakens it, the monetary economy also threatens to throw workers back into subsistence occupations with little or no warning. The phenomenon of underemployment also drives a number of educated young men and women back into the village.

Resist-dyed cloth production is especially characteristic of societies of eastern Indonesia, but each region's patterns are distinctive, as are the restrictions and meanings that may be imposed on such production. Salt making and lime burning are activities characteristic of coastal communities, as are fishing and seaborne trade. During the year both men and women of Lamalera may travel quite widely through the interior, along the coasts, and (especially now with better modern transportation) to other islands. The more successful are likely to go to other parts of Indonesia for further education and employment, and once they are established their parents and other relatives will travel after them later on visits. Lamalera, like other south Lembata villages, has, there-fore, its own established networks and avenues into the modern national, and international, economy, despite a degree of geographical remoteness which outsiders have sometimes underestimated in the past.

Its pattern of patrilineal descent and asymmetric marriage alliance, which has clearly been adaptable in the past, appears to retain resilience, but can hardly be said to be unchanged. Its religious life has been utterly transformed in this century, and yet much of the older ritual survives in a recognizable form. Just as the local economy is affected by the growth of national prosper-ity, so the local religious life is bound to be influenced by important trans-formations within the Indonesian Catholic Church, including especially the locally active Divine Word Society. An important change here is the now nearly completed replacement of expatriate priests and other personnel by Indonesians. What this transformation will mean for local ritual patterns remains to be seen.

Indonesia is moving towards becoming a more urban society. As it does so, rural areas may eventually experience real, and not just relative, population decline. There is a threat that more houses will stand empty in Lamalera and eventually be pulled down, as the village becomes less and less populous, and as its remaining inhabitants spend more and more time in the growing towns and cities. Except for cultural tourism, the south coast of Lembata today has little to attract economic resources and seems doomed to be bypassed by the growth which will take place elsewhere. Although its inhabitants have shown themselves to be good at acquiring modern skills when given the chance, there is little opportunity for them to use such skills at home. Villagers continue to express concern about their ability to attract crews for the boats and to keep the boats in repair and in use. Nevertheless, boats are being rebuilt, and fishing and cetacean hunting continues to be an important part of their economic life and a central aspect of the community's sense of its identity. However, the fate of the fishery is not the only, or perhaps even the most important, measure of the community's well-being. To the extent that its inhabitants share in national economic progress, their futures may increasingly be in more urban environ-ments and non-subsistence forms of occupation. If so, then a unique way of life may after all disappear.

Postscript (30 September 1995)

Inevitably, my visit to Lamalera of five days in July 1995 revealed further changes. Fourteen boats were seaworthy, of which thirteen were in regular use. Yet another would have been in use were it not for fear over the consequences of an alleged murder which had not yet been fully resolved. In addition, three boats especially built to non-traditional specifications and powered by outboard engines were used to hunt large game up to and including killer whale, but not sperm whale. Most boats were liberally supplied with plastic ropes. More of the boats without any hope of finding crews or being rebuilt had been dismantled. On the other hand, most of the traditional boats in use had been rebuilt within the last three years and there were plans to rebuild more, for which the provincial government was providing a substantial subsidy for each boat. It is now possible for motorized traffic to reach as far as Lamalera B, and one small vehicle provided regular transportation between Lewoleba and Lamalera for a period before becoming unusable. Tourism had become an established part of the village economy, there being three lodging houses for them. A constant stream of backpackers arrived and left again while I was there. Pigs having finally been tethered all year round, there was much more greenery, at least in Lamalera A, and correspondingly more variety to the diet. Population had stabilized without, however, showing signs of growth. Members of Lamalera were said not to be participating in the transmigration schemes and migrant labour which contribute to the depopulation of other parts of the island and regency. Such movement away for purposes of employment or education as occurs appears mostly to be toward more rewarding opportunities. Persons who have succeeded in acquiring higher education within or outside Indonesia continue to return and renew family ties. The drain of talented people away from the village, however, has led to more of the important great houses standing virtually empty. The traditional subsistence side of Lamalera economy has by no means disappeared, but its position has been further eroded by the necessity to secure a livelihood by exploiting the diverse means now available.

APPENDIX I

Relationship Terminology

Gregorius Keraf (1978: 99–100) lists a fairly extensive set of relationship terms, which I have reordered slightly in Table 16.

Keraf (pp. 151, 166) also gives the expression *opu-maki*, which he translates as 'wife-giving clan–wife-taking clan' and 'wife-giving clan and wife-taking clan'. In other words it includes persons of both groups, as when they are addressed in formal speech, following the example he gives in the appropriate place.

Some of the Malay words Keraf uses to gloss these terms, such as *paman* (uncle) and *bibi* (aunt) suffer from the same ambiguities as do their English equivalents, but his more extended glosses generally permit us to interpret him as he intends. Despite distinguishing generally between usage in address and in reference, he shows somewhat less care than might be desired. I think, however, that there is a reason for this lack of attention, namely a conviction that in general these terms are all employed for both purposes, with the explicit exception of *ari* and *ana*.

In respect of this issue, Keraf (pp. 102–6) tells us that in day-to-day life persons who are older than a speaker may not be referred to or addressed by name. It is forbidden to address mother or father by name. Younger people must therefore address their elders by use of a relationship term. Keraf lists the following terms available for this purpose: *bapa*, *ema*, *tata*, *kaka*, *nana*, *faé*, and *bĕlé*. Essentially therefore terms 1–7 may be used both for address and reference. *Tata* and *kaka* partially overlap for both purposes. On the other hand, an older person may simply address a younger person by name. Thus, *ari* is never used for address and therefore never appears in speech except in contexts where it refers to a specific relationship and therefore must possess a suffix indicating whose younger siblings are in question. Even should *ari* exceptionally be used in address jocularly, it would require a possessive suffix, whereas the other terms never require such a marker in the vocative form.

The same may be said of *ana*, except that there are reasons why a mother, father, or other elder persons might wish to avoid addressing the child by name after all. When the word means just a young person or children in general without respect to kinship relation, it requires no suffix of possession. Otherwise it behaves in speech as does *ari*. However, generally adults will address or refer to female children, whether related to them or not and whether known to them or not, as *ina* and male children similarly as *ama*. These terms in other dialects of Lamaholot (including nearby villages) and in related languages of the region have generally the same meaning as do *ema* and *bapa* in Lamalera. Keraf says that they still do in Lamalera as well in 'older language'. For example in customary ceremonies concerning marriage, the elders of the bride may be addressed either as *kebarafaé īnã-ãmã* or as *kebarafaé ema-bãpã*. Furthermore, when special emphasis is required, these two words may be selected to replace *ema* and *bapa*.

Keraf suggests that the reason these words are now used for children lies in the custom of giving names to children derived from those of their grandparents. Since grandparents and grandchildren often have the same given name, parents are constrained by the prohibition on uttering their own parents' names when addressing their

TABLE 16. *Lamalera Relationship Terminology after Gregorius Keraf (1978)*

1. *bēlé:*	grandmother, grandfather; refers to grandmother or grandfather on either the mother's or the father's side and everyone of the same generation as them or higher generations.
2. *bapa:*	father; *bapa* is used to refer to or to address genealogical father (*ayah kandung*), his brothers, and all males on the same level as father in ego's clan.
3. *ema:*	mother; *ema* is used to refer to or to address the genealogical mother (*ibu kandung*), and all wives of those who are referred to as *bapa*.
4. *nana:*	uncle; this word is used to name or to refer to all males of the wife-giving clan (*opu-laké*) whether of the same generation as mother or of subsequent generations.
5. *faé:*	aunt; used to refer to the wives of all of those called *nana*, uncle.
6. *tata:*	elder sibling (whether male or female); those who may be referred to with the word *tata* are: (1) genealogical elder siblings, whether male or female (2) all [classificatory] elder siblings, whether male or female, within the clan (3) all females in ego's clan of father's generation (4) husbands of those mentioned in number 3, the wife-taking clan (*ana-opu*) (5) children of the wife-taking clan (*ana-opu*), but older than ego (6) to address wives of genealogical or classificatory brothers within the clan older than *ego*.
7. *kaka:*	elder sibling, used to refer to elder genealogical brothers and all classificatory elder brothers within the clan.
8. *ari:*	younger sibling; this word is used to refer to (1) a genealogical or classificatory younger brother within ego's clan; (2) a genealogical or classificatory brother without regard to age (whether older or younger) by all classificatory sisters.
9. *biné:*	sister; *biné* is used to name or refer to all [classificatory] sisters, whether older or younger.
10. *anaq:*	child.
11. *opu-faé:*	to address generally those called *faé* [p. 166: mother or all wives of those called *opu-laké*].
12. *opu-laké:*	refers generally to those addressed as *nana*, also the clan [p. 166: father or all (classificatory) brothers of wife or wife's family; p. 183: uncle, male of the wife-giving clan].
13. *ana-opu:*	refers generally to the wife-taking clan [p. 166: wife-taking clans].
14. *ari-āmā:*	this word literally means [his] brother-father. It is used for ego's clan. In addition to the expression *ari-āmā*, the expressions *inā-āmā* ([his] mother-father) and *kaka-ari* (elder sibling younger sibling) refer to ego's clan [p. 167: younger brother-father, male sibling, and father; this expression is used for the parents and brothers of a woman who is about to wed].

children. To avoid doing so, they use *ina* and *ama*, words which once villagers used to address parents. Since there is also a prohibition on using the names of any older person, the custom spread, in Keraf's interpretation, for addressing all children, whether related or not, with *ina* and *ama*. Now this practice has been taken a further step, in so far as *ema* and *bapa* have also become appropriate for addressing children who bear the names of their grandparents. Keraf also concludes that the prohibition reviewed here is a reason why children are generally addressed by their Christian names rather than their village names.

As an example of how compounds such as *ina-ama* and *kaka-ari* may be used in address, Keraf (1978: 151) gives the following opening in a speech to villagers at a reception for an offical visitor from Jakarta.

Ina-ama, kaka-ari, opu-maki fakahae!
Mothers-fathers, brothers and sisters, wife-givers and wife-takers all!
Elders, brothers and sisters, allies!

Pi lero tité beso dipi mi
This day we come here so that
Today we have come to

tã hupã kebélek lau Jakarta dai.
we together meet important personage sea Jakarta come.
meet this official from Jakarta.

From various discussions on different trips with Petrus Bau Dasion, I acquired the
following information about terminology. The expression *opu-laké* stands for the males
in the wife-giving clan, while *opu-faé* are the wives of this clan. *Opu-maki* stands for
the relationship between wife-givers and wife-takers. *Maki* is eqivalent to the *ana-opu*
and applies to the same relatives. It would seem, however, from the genealogical specifications given me that *maki* is appropriate especially for the more senior males within
the group of *ana-opu*, which otherwise also includes females. *Ana-opu* may not be
married unless they are 'very distant'. Whereas *opu-laké* is a more formal and respectful phrase, all op*u-laké* may be addressed or referred to somewhat more familiarly by
nana. *Belaké* is sometimes heard for the same category of relatives, but it is regarded
as crude and as Larantuka usage, not properly included in Lamalera terminology. *Opu
alep* is a phrase of especial honour and applies to the closest member of the category,
such as the genealogical MB. The wives of *nana* (*opu-laké*) are all *faé* or also *opu-faé*.
The oldest generations are *bělé-magu* or *bělé* for short. *Bělé* may be distinguished as
male *bělé kebelaké* and female *bělé kebarafaé*. Although I recorded *ama*, Petrus Bau told
me that *bapa* was more common, thus confirming Keraf. He also said that *ema* may be
called *ina*. In view of Keraf's explanation of these usages, I take *bapa* and *ema* to be
the current category names (see Table 17). There is no special term for persons of the
generation of grandchildren.

These terms display the following equations compatible with patrilineal descent:

$$MF = MB = MBS = MBSS$$
$$WFF = WF = WB = WBS$$
$$SWF = SWB$$
$$MM = MBW = MBSW = MBSSW$$
$$WFM = WM = MBW = WMSW$$
$$SWM = SWBW$$
$$FZS = FZSS$$
$$FZD = FZSD$$
$$ZH = ZS$$
$$ZHZ = ZD$$

They show the following equations and distinctions characteristic of an asymmetric
marriage prescription between MBD and FZS.

$$MB = WF \neq F \neq FZH$$
$$MBS = WB \neq B \neq FZS$$
$$MBSS = WBS \neq S \neq FZSS$$
$$MBW = WM \neq M \neq FZ$$

$$\text{MBSW} = \text{WBW} \neq \text{Z} \neq \text{FZD}$$
$$\text{MBSSW} = \text{WBSW} \neq \text{D} \neq \text{FZSD}$$
$$\text{MBD} = [\text{W}] = \text{BWZ} \neq \text{Z} \neq \text{FZD}$$

The FZD may not be married, while the MBD may not now be married because of restrictions placed on near-cousin marriage by the Catholic Church. However, they like to keep the connections close, 'so that the bridewealth will return'. Petrus Bau later confirmed that '*réu* may be married, they are the proper people', except of course as currently restricted by the Catholic Church. *Réu*, which is related to the word *běréun* used in eastern Flores, actually has two kinds of application. One is to indicate the pre-scribed marriage category. The other indicates a close friend. A same-age clan mate may be addressed as *réu* in this latter sense.

If we compare this information with that from Keraf, we may see that there is mutual confirmation and even elucidation for terms 1 to 5, except that Keraf's wording would suggest that MF, WFF and MM, WFM are not referred to as *opu-laké* and *opu-faé* other than when the terms are applied comprehensively to the whole group. *Tata* possesses difficulties if we attempt to interpret it as an exclusively defined category, for in

---

TABLE 17. *Lamalera Relationship Terminology Used by a Male, after Petrus Bau Dasion*

---

1. *bělé-magu, bělé*
   FF, FM, MF, MM, FMB, FMBW, WFF, WFM, MMZ, MMB, FFB, FFBW, FMZ, MFZ, MFB, FFZ, FFZH, FZHF, FFZHZ, FZHFZ, etc. (all persons of this genealogical level and above).
2. *bapa (ama)*
   F, FB, MZH
3. *ema (ina)*
   M, MZ, FBW, WFZ (if old enough), BW.
4. *opu-laké, nana*
   MF, WFF, MB, WF, MBS, WB, SWF, MBSS, WBS, SWB, all males of the wife-giving clan.
5. *opu-faé, faé*
   MM, WFM, MBW, WM, MBSW, WBW, SWM, MBSSW, WBSW, SWBW.
6. *tata*
   MZ, FBW, FZ, ZHM, FZH, ZHF, FZHZ, FZHZH, eB, FBSe, MZSe, eZ, FBDe, MZDe, WZe, WZHe.
7. *kaka*
   eB, FBSe, MZSe, eZ, FBDe, MZDe, WZe, WZHe.
8. *ari-murin, ari*
   yB, FBSy, MZSy, yZ, FBDy, MZDy, WZy, WZHy.
9. *biné*
   Z, FBD, MZD.
10. *réu*
    MBD, MBSD, WBD, BWZ, WFZ (if my age, 'because I can marry her').
11. *kafaé*
    W.
12. *maki*
    ZHF, ZH, FZS.
13. *ana-opu*
    FZS, ZH, ZS, FZSS, FZD, ZHZ, ZD, FZSD, DH, DHB, BDH, FBDC, MZDC, DHZ.
14. *ana*
    C, BC, FBSC, MZSC, FZSSW, MBDC, WZC, SW, SWZ, BSW, ZSW, FZDH, ZHZH, ZDH, FZSDH, FZDC.

---

fact it overlaps with several others. *Tata*'s distribution would seem to be explained by the fact that it is a term of respect which nevertheless implies less distance than do *bélé*, *nana*, *faé*, *bapa*, and *ema*. Perhaps there are occasions when MZ or FBW, if for example they are relatively young, might be appropriately addressed as *tata*, unless these specifications are simply mistaken. I have no specific evidence to confirm that, as Keraf tells us, *tata* may be applied to children of the wife-taking clan elder than ego (such as FZCe) or wives of elder brothers, but I am bound to accept his statement.

Keraf does not confirm that *kaka* and *ari* may be applied to women by a male ego. Keraf offers no information relevant to *réu*, *kafaé*, and *maki* other than that *maki* refers to the wife-takers. Our data on *ana-opu* and *ana* are compatible. The two lists there-fore appear generally to confirm each other and we may bring them together in the revised version of the terminology appropriate to a male ego (see Table 18).

Ama fĕrui is a very refined way to speak of the older brother. The oldest child is *ana*

TABLE 18. *Relationship Terminology, Male Ego (Reference and Address)*

1. *bĕlé-magu*, *bĕlé*
   all persons two generations older than ego or more, regardless of the nature of the relationship.
2. *bapa*
   all males of the same generation as the father in ego's clan.
3. *ema*
   the wives of all *bapa*, BW, WFZ if old enough.
4. *nana*, *opu-laké*
   all males of the wife-giving clan.
5. *faé*, *opu-faé*
   the wives of all *nana*.
6. *tata*
   all women in ego's clan of his father's generation; all husbands of these women; children of the wife-taking clan who are older than ego; men of ZH's clan of his father's generation; women of that clan of the same generation; FZHZH; wives of males of ego's clan of his generation as long as they are older than ego; all persons of ego's generation whether male or female if they are older than ego.
7. *kaka*
   all persons of ego's generation whether male or female if they are older than ego (Keraf does not confirm the application of this term to female relatives).
8. *ari*, *ari-murin*
   all persons of ego's generation whether male or female if they are younger than ego (Keraf does not confirm the application of this term to female relatives).
9. *biné*
   all female relatives of ego's generation in his own clan regardless of whether older or younger than ego.
10. *réu*
    all women of marriageable age in wife-giving clans.
11. *kafaé*
    wife.
12. *ana-opu*, *maki*
    all persons of wife-taking lines (*maki* is equivalent to *ana-opu*, but there is some indication that in some usages it applies most appropriately to elder males in this group).
13. *ana*
    members of ego's clan one generation younger than ego; women of the same generation as SW in her clan; the equivalent relatives of the BSW, persons in the wife-taking line of the wife-takers.

TABLE 19. *Lamalera Relationship Terminology Used by a Female, after Maria Korohama, Maria Sura Belikololong, and Yosefina Sefai Keraf*

---

1. *bĕlé-magu*
   bĕlé
   FF, FFB, MF, MFB, FMB, FFZ, FM, FMZ, MM, MMZ, MMB, HMF, HMM, FFZ, HFM, FFZH, HFF, FFZHZ.
   bĕlé kebalaké (all males)
   bĕlé kebarafaé (all females)
2. *bapa*
   F, FB, MZH, HMB, SWF.
   bapa tata FBe
   bapa ari FBy
3. *ema*
   M, MZ, FBW, MBD, SWM, BWBD, MBSD, ZHM.
   ema tata MZe
   ema ari MZy
4. *nana, opu-laké*
   MB, MBS, MBSS (and the rest below in this line), BWFF, BWF, BWB, BWBS (and the rest below in this line), HFZH.
5. *opu-faé*
   MBW, MBSW, MBSSW (and the wives of the other males below in this line), BWFM, BWM, BWBW, BWBSW (and the wives of the other males below in this line).
6. *tata*
   FZ, FZH, FZHB (if sufficiently old), eZ, FBDe, MZDe, HF, HFB, HM, HMZ (if older than ego), ZHF, ZHM.
7. *ari*
   yZ, FBDy, MZDy, B, FBS, MZS, HMBS, HB, ZH, BC, FBSC, MZSC, MBDC, SW, SWB, SWZ, BDH, BDHZ, HMZ (if younger than ego), HMBD (if younger), HMBSD.
8. *reu*
   FZS (classificatory), FZHB (if young enough).
9. *kelaké*
   H.
10. *ana-opu, maki*
    HZ, ZHZ (all of the husband's *ana-opu (maki)* are also *ana-opu (maki)*, thus HZH, HFZC, HZC, HFZSC, HZHZ, HFZDC, HFBDC, HMZDC, DHF, DHM, DH, DHB, DHZ.
11. *kafinaj*
    BW, BWZ, BSW, HMBW, HMBSW, HFZ, FZHZ.
12. *ana*
    C, ZC, FZD, FZS (genealogical), FZSC, FZDC, FBDC, MZDC, HBC.
    ana kebalaké (male *ana*).
    ana kebarafaé (female *ana*).

---

fĕrui, the youngest *tuo-fūtu* (tip of the breast) or *dasi*. The term *opu alep* is an especial honour and it applies to the closest *opu-laké*, such as MB. Another term for the wife-giver, through one's mother, to whom one stands in a relationship of special signifi-cance is '*trunk opu*', that is *opu pukã*. *Belaké* is recognized as an equivalent of *opu-laké*, but it is deemed coarse and thought to be characteristic of speech in Larantuka. In other contexts, *laké* means a man, while *faé* means a woman. Husband and wife together are *laké-faé*. Siblings are *kaka-āri* (elder brother-younger brother), a term which also serves for the descent group as a whole and for other descent groups which stand in a sibling-like relationship to it. Given the circular model of alliance relationships among descent groups, I would have expected *ana-opu* of *ana-opu* (wife-takers of one's wife-

TABLE 20. *Relationship Terminology, Female Ego (Reference and Address)*

1. *bělé-magu, bělé*
   all persons of the second ascending generation and above, no matter what the nature of the relationship may be.
2. *bapa*
   all males of ego's natal clan one generation older than ego; SWF.
3. *ema*
   wives of all *bapa*; women of M's clan; ZHM.
4. *nana, opu-laké*
   all males of the wife-giving clans to ego's natal clan; HFZH.
5. *faé, opu-faé*
   wives of all those called *nana*.
6. *tata*
   all women in ego's clan of father's generation; all husbands of these women; all males of the husband's clan of his father's generation; the corresponding relatives of the husbands of women in ego's natal clan of her generation; all women in ego's natal clan of her generation older than ego.
7. *ari*
   all women in ego's natal clan of her generation younger than ego.
8. *réu*
   males of the wife-taking clans of appropriate age for marriage, now excluding the genealogical FZS.
9. *kelaké*
   husband.
10. *ana-opu (maki)*
    men and women of the wife-taking clans, as well as those of the wife-taking clans of wife-taking clans; HFZDC.
11. *kafinaj*
    wives of men in ego's natal clan, women in husband's clan of his father's generation.
12. *ana*
    all members of ego's husband's clan one generation younger than ego; the equivalent relatives of ego's sister; now the genealogical FZS, FZD, and FZDC.

| CC | | C | | B | | A | | AA |
f	m	← f	m	← f	m	← f	m	← f
		bělé-magu, bělé	*bělé-magu, bělé*	*bělé-magu, bělé*	*bělé-magu, bělé*	*bělé-magu, bělé*	*bělé-magu, bělé, opu-laké, nana*	*bělé-magu, bělé, opu-faé, faé*
	tata	*tata*	*maki, tata*	*tata*	*bapa*	*ema, tata*	*opu-laké, nana*	*opu-faé, faé*
	ana	*ana-opu*	*maki, ana-opu, tata*	*tata, kaka, biné, ari*	*tata, kaka, ego, ari-murin, ari*	*réu, kafaé, tata, kaka, ari-murin, ari*	*opu-laké, nana*	*opu-faé, faé*
ana	*ana*	*ana-opu*	*ana*	*ana*	*ana*	*réu, ana*	*opu-laké, nana*	*opu-faé, faé*

Fig. 27. Lamalera relationship terminology for a male Ego ordered for patrilineal descent and asymmetric marriage prescription

| CCC | CC | | C | | B | | A | | AA | |
f	f	m	f	m	f	m	f	m	f	m
			bẽlé-magu, bẽlé	bẽlé-magu, bẽlé	bẽlé-magu, bẽlé	bẽlé-magu, bẽlé	bẽlé-magu, bẽlé	bẽlé-magu, bẽlé, opu-laké, nana	bẽlé-magu, bẽlé, opu-faé, faé	bẽlé-magu, bẽlé
			kafmaj	tata	tata (ZHM) ari (HMZy)	bapa	ema, kafmaj	opu-laké, nana	opu-faé, faé	
		ana-opu	ana-opu, ana (FZD)	réa, kelaké ari, ana (FZS)	tata, ego, ari	bapa (SWF), ari	ema, kafmaj	opu-laké, nana	opu-faé, faé	
ana-opu	ana-opu, ana	ana-opu, ana	ari, ana	ari, ana	ari	ari	ema, kafmaj	opu-laké, nana	opu-faé, faé	

Fig. 28. Lamalera relationship terminology for a female Ego ordered for patrilineal descent and asymmetric marriage prescription

takers) to be classed as wife-givers, *opu-laké*. To my surprise, Petrus Bau classed them as *ana* (children). Other combinations do reflect the circular alliance pattern. *Opu-laké* of *opu-laké* (wife-givers of one's wife-givers) are *ana-opu* (wife-takers). The *ana-opu* of *opu-laké* (wife-takers of one's wife-givers) are *kaka-āri* (siblings). The *opu-laké* of *ana-opu* (wife-givers of one's wife-takers) are *kaka-āri* (siblings).

Maria Korohoma, Maria Sura Belikololong, and Yosefina Sefai Keraf assisted me in recording the terminology appropriate for use by a woman (see Table 19).

The following equations are indicative of a rule of patrilineal descent:

$$MB = MBS = MBSS$$
$$BWFF = BWF = BWB = BWBS$$

The marriage prescription is indicated by these equations and distinctions:

$$FZH = HF \neq F \neq MB$$
$$FZ = HM \neq M \neq MBW$$
$$FZS = [H] \neq B \neq MBS$$

The removal of the genealogical FZS from the category *réu* is to be attributed to the Catholic prohibition on marrying this relative. Placing FZD and FZDC in the category *ana* along with the genealogical FZS would seem to derive from the same influence. The distinction between elder and younger siblings of *bapa* and of *ema*, may be explained, I think, by the influence of Bahasa Indonesia. Petrus Bau indicated this distinction by reference to *bapa bélã* (large *bapa*) and *bapa kéni* (small *bapa*). The use of *ari* for all male siblings and equivalent members of ego's line of birth without regard to age confirms Keraf's statement to this effect. We may now compare this list with Keraf's information in order to arrive at the result in Table 20.

The evidence available is sufficient to permit the conclusion that the Lamalera relationship system is one which is compatible with asymmetric prescriptive alliance and patrilineal descent, that is, it is of the 'Kachin type', with differences in usages between male and female egos appropriate to their different positions within the system. It is thus of a kind which has been reported from other Lamaholot communities (R. H. Barnes 1977*a*; Graham 1987) and from the Kédang on the same island as Lamalera (R. H. Barnes 1974*a*). It may be represented as in Figs. 27 and 28. The difference in structural position of men and women is indicated by the different distribution of the categories *réu*, *ema*, *ari*, *tata*, *ana*, and *ana-opu* and by the category *kafinaj* used by a woman.

APPENDIX II

Fish, Molluscs, and Turtles Known in Lamalera

Bleeker (1851, 1852, 1853, 1854) published a series of short notes on fish species from the Solor Islands, sent to him by health officers of the Dutch Royal Navy, but in no case did he provide their Malay or Lamaholot names. This information passed over into his *Atlas Ichthyologique des Indes-Orientales Néerlandes* (Bleeker 1877), and from there into other works. With the aid of the drawings and plates in Carcasson's *A Field Guide to the Coral Reef Fishes of the Indian and West Pacific Oceans* (1977), I obtained a set of identifications from Marsel Kalang Keraf on 31 July 1982. These identifications were later amended and supplemented by Gabriel Blido Keraf and Prof. Gregorius Prafi Keraf.

In the following the local name appears first, followed by the Latin designation and, where available in Carcasson, an English gloss. Only a portion of the fish mentioned by Carcasson are depicted by him, which introduces a bias in the identifications. However, no such book is really exhaustive, and Carcasson's is fairly representative, as well as being lighter and therefore easier to travel with than most. The following may give an expert a starting-point, although it can be anticipated that he would augment and amend the identifications. Except for very common fish, no attempt was made to identify them from actual specimens. In some cases Marsel Kalang Keraf indicated several fish by a given name, such as 'fish on plate 19' (various clownfish) as *béto kefatek*, to quote my notes. Amplifications appearing in the notes are reproduced without quotation marks. Pertinent comments from Carcasson are reproduced in quotation marks.

bafo burã: *Caesio coerulaureus* (Lacépède) 1802; gold-banded fusilier [the Lamaholot reads 'white *bafo*'].

bafo iku kuma: *Caesio cuning* (Bloch) 1791; red-bellied fusilier [the Lamaholot reads 'yellow tailed *bafo*'].

bafo iku mẽa: probably a fusilier [the Lamaholot reads 'red tailed *bafo*'].

bafo pelã: *Caesio lunaris* (Cuvier and Valenciennes) 1830.

barafinã: *Trachinotus bailloni* (Lacépède) 1802; Baillons dart.

bedafa: *Thalassoma fuscum* (Lacépède) 1802; green-backed wrasse.

bedéo: *Fistularia petimba* (Lacépède) 1803; smooth flutemouth.

befajã: *Platax pinnatus* (Linnaeus) 1758; angel-fish.

belalo: *Sphyraena jello* (Cuvier and Valenciennes) 1829; slender sea pike.

bĕlelã: the largest species of manta ray; *Mantis birostris* (Walbaum) 1792.

belepa: *Taenyura lymma* (Forskål) 1775; ribbontail ray.

beripa: *Siganus virgatus* (Cuvier and Valenciennes) 1835.

beto kefatek: various *Amphiprion*; clownfish, i.e. those on plate 19 of Carcasson; [Beto is a name; so *beto kefatek* means 'Beto's sarong'].

borot: *Diodon hystrix* (Linnaeus) 1758; spotted porcupinefish; *Gastrophysus Sceleratus* (Gmelin) 1788; giant toadfish; *Amblyrhynchotes Hypselogeneion* (Bleeker) 1852; bar-cheaked toadfish ('poisonous').

bõu: a golden-brown ray, *Mobula kuhlii*, shortfin devil ray [identification from Compagno, Ebert, and Smale (1989: 117); 'Biology: virtually unknown'].

epo: *Echidna zebra* (Shaw and Nodder) 1797; zebra moray; *Echidna Nebulosa* (Ahl) 1789; starry moray.

éto lata ria: *Brachirus brachypterus* (Cuvier and Valenciennes) 1829; [covered with stingers; if they get one, they may not touch it until they kill it; then they take a stone and break all the spines; translation unknown]; *Torpedo fuscomaculata* (Peters) 1853; electric ray.

fai muat: *Variola louti* (Forskål) 1775; fairy cod.

fara: identification uncertain, family of *Scombridae*.

feletik: *Cephalopholis miniatus* (Forskål) 1775; coral trout.

fĕta: family *Istiophoridae* (*Makaira*); marlin of various kinds.

folo maga: *Ulua mandibualris* (Macleay) 1883; cale cale trevally.

fulo kerak: *Zebrasoma scopas* (Cuvier) 1829; brown sailfin-tang.

gué: family *Katsuwonidae*; skipjack.

ikã fai: family *Parastromateidae*; black pomfret [B. Ind., *ikan layang-layang*] or *Alectis Indicus* (Rüppell) 1828; plumed trevally; [the Lamaholot translates 'water fish'].

io ãrã: *Stegostoma fasciatum* (Pennant) 1769; zebra shark; [skin thick like a board].

io balu: *Galeocerda cuvieri* (Le Sueur); tiger shark.

io belepa: *Rhinobatos armatus* (Gray) 1834; shovel-nose ray.

io irumata: *Scyliorhinus capensis*; lazy sharks, skaamoogs; [the Lamaholot indicates a shark with nose near eyes].

io kiko: *Rhinchodon typus* (Smith) 1829; whale shark [Bahasa Indonesia, *hiyu bodoh*, a shark which they harpoon].

io lado: *Alopias vulpinus* (Bonnaterre); thresher shark [so named because its tail is shaped like *lado*, war decorations formerly made of chicken feathers].

io naka: family *Sphyrnidae*; hammerhead shark [named after the chopping adze, *naka*].

io oté: epauletted shark, *Hemiscyllium ocellatum* (Bonnaterre) 1788; [so named because its skin is like the iguana, *oté*].

io sajang: *Galeocerda cuvieri* (Le Sueur); tiger shark.[1]

io temu or *io temu ūk*: *Isurus glaucus* (Müller and Henle); the blue and black 'blue pointer' or mako; [the Lamaholot means 'porpoise shark' or 'porpoise shark trunk'].

io temu io būra: *Carchardon carcharius* (Linnaeus); white shark or white pointer [the Lamaholot literally reads 'porpoise shark white shark'; some say that the name of this animal is *io temu i būra*, where *i* is short for *ihik*, meat; thus 'porpoise shark (with) white meat'].

irupuna: *Liza oligolepis* (Bleeker) 1859; mullet.

kajo lōlo: *Aetobatus narinari* (Euphrasen) 1790; spotted eagle ray; [stays near shore, has been speared, never as yet caught in a net; the Lamaholot translates 'tree leaves'].

kaket: *Tylorsurus indicus* (Le Suer) 1821; giant long tom.

kebeku: *Mola mola* (Linneaus) 1758; ocean sunfish; ('attains 3 m in length and half a ton in weight', Carcasson 1977: 278); comes in two types *kebeku bĕlelã* (manta ray *kebeku*) and *kebeku ufã reket* (sharp bottom *kebeku*).

kebeku dota: *Pseudoblalistes flavim marginatus* (Rüppell) 1828.

kebeku funo: *Abalistes stellaris* (Bloch and Schneider) 1801; starred triggerfish; *Blalistoides Niger* (Bannaterre) 1788; white-blotched triggerfish; [the Lamaholot means 'starred *kebeku*'].

kebeku iku burã: *Balistapus undulatus* (Mungo Park) 1797; red-lined triggerfish;

Sufflamen capistratus (Shaw) 1804; masked triggerfish; *Melichthys vidua* (Richardson) 1844; white-tailed triggerfish; [the Lamaholot means the 'white-tailed *kebeku*'].

kebeku kepaung: *Hemibalistes chrysopterus* (Bloch and Schneider) 1801.

kebili bêlã: *Iniistius pavo* (Cuvier and Valenciennes) 1839.

kebuka lélé: *Heniochus varius* (Cuvier and Valenciennes) 1829; hunchbacked coralfish; *Heniochus acuminatus* (Linnaeus) 1758; pennant coralfish; *Heniochus permutatus* (Cuvier and Valenciennes) 1831; horned coralfish; *Zanclus canescens* (Linnaeus) 1758; moorish idol.

kefato pelati: *Parascorpaena picta* (Cuvier and Valenciennes) 1829; painted stingfish; [has a stinger but is easier to handle than *éto lata ria*; however, if people with teeth eat it, their teeth will fall out; so it is only for old people who have no teeth; it sits on the bottom like a rock, not moving, but its sting is very painful, hence its name 'hot rock fish'].

kefīna: *Cephalopholis aurantius* (Cuvier and Valenciennes) 1828; orange rock cod.

kĕlebu: *Scarus gibbus* (Rüppell) 1828.

kĕlefo: *Scarops rubroviolaceus* (Bleeker) 1849.

kĕlĕpa: *Forcipiger longirostris* (Broussonet) 1782; long-snouted coral fish; *Chelmon rostratus* (Linnaeus) 1758; beaked coralfish; *Gonochaetondon larvatus* (Ehrenberg); *Hemitaurichtys zoster* (Bennet) 1831; *Parachaetodon ocellatus* (Cuvier and Valenciennes) 1831; six-spined butterfish; *Gonochaetodon triangulum* (Cuvier and Valenciennes) 1831; triangular coralfish; *Chaetodon rainfordi* (McCulloch) 1923; Rainford's coral fish; *Chaetodon octofasciatus* (Bloch) 1787; eight-banded coralfish; *Chaetodon lineolatus* (Cuvier and Valenciennes) 1831; new moon coralfish; *Chaetodon vagabundus* (Linnaeus) 1758; vagabond coralfish; *Chaetodon aureofasciatus* (Macleay) 1870; golden-striped coralfish; *Chaetodon meyeri* (Bloch and Schneider) 1801; Meyer's coralfish; *Chaetodon ornatissimus* (Cuvier and Valenciennes) 1831; ornate coralfish; *Chaetodon melanotus* (Bloch and Schneider) 1801; black-backed coralfish; *Chaetodon xanthurus* (Bleeker) 1857.

kĕlĕpa king: *Taeniopsetta ocellata* (Günther) 1880; ocellated flounder, sole.

kĕlu: *Thalassoma hardwicki* (Bennett) 1830; six-barred wrasse.

kĕludem: *Cephalopholis argus* (Bloch and Schneider) 1801; peacock rock cod.

kemã·: *Uropterygius tigrinus* (Lesson) 1829; [in Bahasa Indonesia called *belut*], eel.

kemãnu: *Exocoetus volitans* (Linnaeus) 1758; flying fish.

kemara iku burã: *Acanthurus aliala* (Lesson) 1830; white-cheeked surgeon-fish; [the Lamaholot means 'white tailed *kemara*'].

kemara kedera: *Zebrasoma veliferum* (Bloch) 1795; sailfin-tang.

kemara keli méa: *Acanthurus olivaceus* (Bloch and Schneider) 1801; [the Lamaholot means 'red finned or red armpit *kemara*'].

kemara kopo léré: *Acanthurus theuthis* (Lacépède) 1802; widge-tailed blue tang; [the Lamaholot means 'firefly *kemara*'].

kemara tebã burã: *Acanthurus mata* (Cuvier) 1829 ('blue colour of fins only apparent in certain lights; in the water, especially at some depth it appears blackish with a whitish ring at the base of the tail', Carcasson 1977: 235); [the Lamaholot means 'white tail base *kemara*'].

kepake feki: *Pervagor melanocephalus* (Bleeker) 1853; lace-finned leatherjacket.

kepōi: *Lophalticus kirki* (Günther) 1868; *Istiblennius andamanensis* (Day) 1859; *Salarias fasciatus* (Bloch) 1786; banded blenny.

kéra kotã: perhaps *Rhinoptera javanica*; flapnose ray.

kĕro kīdé: *Kutaflammeo sammara* (Forskål) 1775; bloodspot squirrelfish; *Holocentrus ruber* (Forskål) 1775; red squirrelfish; *Holocentrus diadema* (Lacépède) 1803; crowned squirrelfish; *Holocentrus cornutus* (Bleeker) 1853; horned squirrelfish; *Holocentrus ensifer* (Jordan and Everman) 1903; [the Lamaholot translates 'fatherless *kĕro*'].

kĕro mata betek inap bélã: *Myripristis adustus* (Bleeker) 1853; blue squirrelfish; [the Lamaholot translates '*kĕro* with large eyes with large scales'].

kĕro mata betek inap bĕlura: *Myripristis murdjan* (Forskål) 1775; crimson squirrelfish; [the Lamaholot translates '*kĕro* with large eyes with fine scales'].

keroko pu: *Scolopsis bilineatus* (Bloch) 1793; two-lined monocle bream.

kĕro papa kafi: *Holocentrus spinifer* (Forskål) 1775; spiny squirrelfish; larger than the others.

kĕro temoki: *Holocentrus violaceus* (Bleeker) 1853; violet squirrelfish.

kesōjo: *Acanthurus lineatus* (Linnaeus) 1758; blue-lined surgeon-fish.

ketefa: *Thalassoma duperreyi* (Quoy and Gaimard) 1824.

ketoto: *Lactoria cornuta* (Linnaeus) 1758; long-horned cowfish.

ketuko kenaka: *Abudefduf sordidus* (Forskål) 1775; grey-banded sargeant-major; *Abudefduf septemfasciatus* (Cuvier and Valenciennes) 1830; seven-banded sargeant-major; *Abudefduf saxatilis* (Linnaeus) 1758; five-banded sargeant-major; *Dascyllus aruanus* (Linnaeus) 1758; white-tailed humbug; *Dascyllus trimaculatus* (Rüppell) 1828; white-spot humbug; *Dascyllus reticulatus* (Richardson) 1846; grey humbug; *Chromis caeruleus* (Cuvier and Valenciennes) 1830; blue puller; *Chromis ovalis* (Steindachner) 1900; *Pomacentrus taeniurus* (Bleeker) 1856; *Dascyllus melanurus* (Bleeker) 1854; black-tailed humbug; *Dascyllus marginatus* (Rüppel) 1828; red sea humbug [confined to Red Sea]; *Chromis opercularis* (Günther) 1866; *Chromis dimidiatus* (Klunzenger) 1871; *Eupomacentrus nigricans* (Lacépède) 1803; dusky demoiselle.

kofa kafa: *Histrio histrio* (Linnaeus) 1758; sargassum fish.

kokar: *Palinurus*; rock lobster.

komé: *Melichthys buniva* (Lacépède) 1803; black triggerfish; *Xanthichthys ringens* (Linneaus) 1758; brown-lined triggerfish; *Odonus niger* (Rüppell) 1840; red-toothed triggerfish.

komo: *Naso brevirostris* (Cuvier and Valenciennes); short-snouted unicorn.

koté hōlé: *Lutjanus sebae* (Cuvier and Valenciennes) 1828; red emperor.

kukak: *Gomphosus varius* (Lacépède) 1802; bird wrasse.

laba tīlu: *Muraenesox cinereus* (Forskål) 177; Arabian piked-eel; *Conger cinereus* (Rüppell) 1828; [the Lamaholot translates 'chisel and dowel'].

lapé: *Cheilinus undulatus* (Rüppell) 1840; giant wrasse.

liliata: family *Coryphaenidae*; dorade [B. Ind. *ikan tingiri*; the Lamaholot name means 'to watch someone', namely the fishermen].

lōra: *Lutjanus kasmira* (Forskål) 1775; yellow and blue sea perch.

lui: *Plectorhynchinae* [all those shown on plate 8 of Carcasson 1977].

māna: the small *hemirhamphidae*.

mata belãu: *Priacanthus hamrur* (Forskål) 1775; lunar-tailed bullseye; [the Lamaholot translates 'carring'].

mata kao: *Lepidaplois bilunulatus* (Lacépède) 1802; *Lepidaplois anthioides* (Bennett) 1830; *Lepidaplois axillaris* (Bennet) 1831.

menana: *Canthigaster bennetti* (Bleeker) 1854; Bennett's puffer; *Canthigaster margarita-tus* (Rüppell) 1828; ocellated puffer; *Canthigaster jactator* (Jenkins) 1901.

meneli: *Remora remora* (Linnaeus) 1758; brown Remora; short suckerfish; ('associated with large sharks, marlin or turtles', Carcasson 1977: 260); [the sucker *faja* of the sucker fish *meneli* is used on Pantar to put on trees where bees have nests, so that they will not change nests; in Lamalera the sucker is supposed to be useful food for dogs so that they will always come home].

menolar: *Leiuranus semicinctus* (Lay and Bennett) 1839; Culverin, large sea snakes, found far out at sea.

menufur: *Cyphomycter vlamingi* (Cuvier and Valenciennes) 1835; *Callicanthus lituratus* (Bloch and Schneider) 1801; green unicorn.

merã: *Gronovichthys cyanosoma* (Bleeker) 1853; pale-lined cardinalfish; *Grammistes sex-lineatus* (Thunberg) 1792; six-lined perch.

mõku: *Mobula diabolus*, whiptail devil ray.

moto lolo: identification uncertain, family of *Scombridae*; [the Lamaholot translates 'leaves of the *merunggai* tree' (*Moringa oleifera*)].

pada: *Siganus fuscescens* (Houttuyn) 1782; *Siganus spinus* (Linnaeus) 1758.

pãé: *Urolophus armatus* (Müller and Henle) 1841; blue-spotted sting ray.

paja ūpu: *Doryrhamphus melanopleura* (Bleeker) 1858; blue-banded pipefish; *Hippocampus histrix* (Kaup) 1856.

pelodek: *Chaetoderma penicilligera* (Cuvier) 1817; prickley leatherjacket; *Monacanthrus mylii* (Bory de Saint Vincent) 1822; centreboard leatherjacket; *Amanses pardalis* (Rüppell) 1835; *Cantherines sandwichiensis* (Quoy and Gaimard) 1824; *Cantherines howensis* (Ogilby) 1889; *Oxymonacanthus longirostris* (Bloch and Schneider) 1801; boaked leatherjacket.

segãrã: *Myrichthys maculosus* (Cuvier) 1817; spotted snake-eel; *Myrichthys colubrinus* (Boddaert) 1781.

senili nata: *Scomber japonicus* (Houttuyn); large-scaled tuna.

seréa: family *Thunnidae*; tuna, albacore.

temõto: *Halichoeres centriquadrus* (Lacépède) 1802; [the Lamaholot translates 'stern decoration'].

tenié: *Acanthocybium solandri* (Cuvier and Valenciennes); wahoo.

tenilo: *Scomberomorus commersoni* (Lacépède); Spanish mackerel.

tiaf: *Mullidae, Parupeneus*; mullets and goatfish; [all fish on plate 9 of Carcasson].

tobi lolo: *Thalassoma purpureum* (Forskål); 'sometimes found asleep among wet weeds at night' Carcasson 1977: 93; [the Lamaholot translates 'tamarinde leaves'].

tuna: family *Muraenidae*; moray eel.

ulu babu: *Echeneis naucrates* (Linnaeus) 1758; slender suckerfish; ('usually associated with big sharks', Carcasson 1977: 260); the suckerfish on whales; long and black.

uradfua: a bonito of some sort, family *Thunnidae*.

In addition both Wintjes (1894*b*; 1983: 280) and Gregorius Keraf (1983) list the following, as yet unidentified, fish:

bĕlida (sword)	*io tebéla feni* (a shark)
burak	*kujo* (a small crab)
ikã fafĕ (pig fish)	*mata méa* (red eyes)

io botanãta (a shark)

io itibura (a shark) [named after its white dorsal fin, *iti burã*;
    has the toughest skin of all sharks]

Only two additional names given by Wintjes are not found in the above list: *fato raki*
and *ikan fatun*.

Additional fish names from Gregorius Keraf (1983), not otherwise identified are as
follows:

baofua

bĕlida ina (deep sea)

bĕlida ina (at shore)

bokor

bota nata

burugãi

étem

ferãnatã

fẽta ãmã

fẽta bélã

fẽta bĕlopor

fẽta keder

foler

io bĕléring (a shark)

io bengkari (a shark) [a shark which they
    harpoon]

io ikãfafé (a shark) [like *ikãfafé* which
    they catch on a line]

io kebengu (a shark) [like *io kiko*, except
    that it can jump. It jumps at sea, but
    it is very rarely harpooned. It is so
    rarely harpooned that generations
    may go between occasions, the last
    remembered case being one taken by
    Holo Sapã in 1972. It resembles in
    shape the fish called *kebengu*]

kanga

kebeku atameri

kebeku lemé

kebengu [a small fish which swims
    around the coral in numbers]

kebetu

kelu

kénar [sold as a dried fish in the market]

kenoba

kepaké feki

keputu

ketengo

ketoto

ketuko (several varieties)

ketutu (sea porcupine)

koba ina (a sea monster, the largest
        possible octopus)

kopo bélã

kujo basãleuk

kujo botang

kujo faja

kujo kebetu

kujo kele

kujo keraka

kujo kolong

kujo lara

kujo matamea

langi

mai

mela

menafé

mukofaka

néba

nubo

seréa mafang

seréa repang

tébã [sold on spits of six at the market,
        probably a type of anchovy]

Some Additional Lamalera Fish Names

These names remain unidentified.

banko

io aténg: in June 1973 several men from Lamalera were poisoned at Peni Keni by eating
    something black in colour, which is normally yellow, along the insides of the spine

of a shark of this kind caught on a 'longlin', i.e. a trotline or long line. They lost consciousness. One of them died, and the rest recovered after being given injections to strengthen the heart. They lost skin and hair, which grew back as they recovered. This incident may have been a case of ciguatera, a form of poisoning caused by toxic fish. 'The toxic condition of the fishes causing ciguatera is usually temporary and quite localized, rather than general over large areas' (US Navy Hydrographic Office 1962: 57).

io bagajo: a type of shark never seen before it was harpooned by *Holo Sapã* in 1974. Similar in size to *io kiko*, the whale shark, but the shape of the head is different.

kombo

The fish specimens described, and in some cases named, by Bleeker (1851, 1852, 1853) contributed by Th. Reiche, van Stockum, and J. C. J. Hellmuth and deriving from Lohayong, Solor, are listed below together with the few Lamaholot names that it has been possible to supply with greater or lesser tentativeness.

Acanthurus scopas CV: probably a *kemara*

Alutarius laevis Cuv.

Amphiprion chrysargurus Richards: *beto kefatek*

Antennarius horridus Blkr.

Antennarius nesogallieus CV

Antennarius rainus Cant.

Apogon cyanosoma Blkr.

Apogon cyanotaenia Blkr.

Apogon roseipinnis CV

Balistes aculeatus Bl. Schn.

Balistes chrysospilos Blkr.

Balistes conspicillum Bl. Schn.

Balistes praslinus Lacép.

Balistes senticosus Richards

Belone cylindrica Blkr.

Caesio coerulaureus (Lacépede): *bafo burã*

Chaetodon selene Blkr.

Chaetodon unimaculaatus Bl.: probably a *kelẽpa*

Chaetodon virescens CV: probably a *kelẽpa*

Chaetodon vittatus Bl. Schn.: probably a *kelẽpa*

Cheilinus ceramensis Blkr.

Cheilodipterus quinquelineatus CV

Cirrhilabrus solorensis Blkr.

Dascyllus aruanus CV: a *ketuko kenaka*

Diagramma polytaenia Blkr.

Diodon orbicularis Bl.: possibly a *borot*

Glyphisodon melas K. v. H.

Gobius nox Blkr.

Gobius quinquestrigaus CV

Holocentrum orientale CV

Julis (Halichoeres) elegans K. v. H.

Julis (Halichoeres) Hoevenii Blkr.

Julis (Halichoeres) interrukptus Blkr.

Julis (Halichoeres) melanurus Blkr.

Julis (Halichoeres) miniatus K. v. H.

Julis (Halichoeres) solorensis Blkr.

Julis (Julis) lunaris CV

Monacanthus melanocephalus Blkr.

Opistognathus solorensis Blkr.

Ostracion cornutus L.

Ostracion rhinorhynchos Blkr.

Ostracion solorensis Blkr.

Ostracion tesserula Cant.

Petroskirtes solorensis Blkr.

Pimelepterus altipinnis CV

Platax blochii CV: possibly a *befajã*

Plesiops coeruleolineatus Rüpp.

Pomacentrus littoralis K. v. H.: possibly a *ketuko kenaka*

Pomacentrus moluccensis Blkr.

Pomacentrus pravoninus Blkr.

Premnas trifasciatus CV

Pteoïs antennata CV

Pteroïs brachypterus CV

Saurida nebulosa CV

Scolopsides lineatus QG?

Seriola tapeinometopon Blkr.

Serranus alboguttatus CV?

Serranus cyanostigmatoïdes Blkr.

Serranus marginalis CV

Solegnathus blochii Blkr.

Hemiramphus fasciatus Blkr.

Heniochus macrolepidotus CV: probably a
  kebuka lélé

Heterognathodon Hellmuthii Blkr.

Holacanthus bicolor Bl.

Holacanthus leucopleura Blkr.

Holacanthus melanosoma Blkr.

Synaptura marmorata Blkr.

Tetraodon laterna Richards

Tetraodon margaritatus Rüpp.

Tetraodon meleagris Soland

Tetraodon papua Blkr.

Tetraodon Valentini Blkr.

Therapon theraps CV

Turtles

kéa burã: *Caretta caretta*; loggerhead turtle; [the Lamaholot means 'white turtle'].

kéa méã: *Eretmochelys embricata*; hawksbill turtle; [the Lamaholot means 'red turtle'];
  hunted for its shell, which is carved into rings and bracelets. Burkill (1935: vol. 1:
  935–6) remarks that the shell of this turtle has gone steadily to China for two thousand years and that Java drew its supplies from Sulawesi and further east.

mõbo: *Dermochelys Coriacea*; leatherback turtle.

Gregorius Keraf (1983) lists two further types of turtle, which I have not identified,
kéa keduo and *kéa labé*.

Squid and Octopi

fafétãli (perhaps *fafétãlé*, i.e. pig's tether), the smallest form of octopus.

kepau lõlo: squid.

kĕrétu: a small octopus.

kĕrubi: a small octopus.

koba: octopus.

Some Shells and Shellfish

beraka: *Hippopus hoppopus*, *Tridacna squamose*.

buri: *Thais lamellosa*.

éba: *Oliva* in its varieties.

ingafuã: many shells of the general shape of *Pterynotus*.

kaloka: a large shell, called *batu laga* in Bahasa Indonesia, which goes to Australia
  where it is used to make paint. Chinese traders bought it in Labala and Lamalera
  for Rp. 1,000 per kilo, or US $2.38. Remarkably the same shell was known under
  the same name in Lamakera, whose members were able to obtain Rp. 5,000 per
  kilo, or US $11.88, perhaps because of their direct access to the Macassar
  market.

kĕloki: giant barnacles.

kenui: *Cardium costatum*, *Meiocardia moltiana*, *Cerastoderma edule*.

kepoi lifu: oysters.

sala bako: *Chiton*.

segomé: hermit crab.

sĕnili: *Nautilus pompilius* also *Spirula spirula*.

In Lamakera, Solor, the golden-lipped oyster is called *mutiara kama*, literally pearl skin. The black-lipped oyster is *lepit*. The turban shell is called *kĕlugé*. A shell of the general shape of *Oliva*, about five inches long, with a rich brown polished mouth, but rough back of no distinct colour is *sumburi*.

Summary of Share Distribution in Boat Corporations in 1979

1. Chisel and peg (*laba ketilo*). For six boats the boat master and the master builder were one and the same person. In an additional nine boats they came from the same great house. For thirteen boats, the master builder belonged to a different clan from the boat master. For ten of these there was at the time no direct relationship between the master builder and the boat master, although in some cases there may have been in previous generations. One man stood as mother's brother's son to the boat masters of two of the boats for which he was master builder. Another was the wife's brother of the boat master. No master builder was directly related as wife-taker or descendant of the sister of members of the boat-owning corporation. Apparently the responsibilities of a master builder are best exercised from a position of relatively equal standing with the boat master or from the superiority which goes with being a wife-giving affine.

2. Lower jaw (*mimã*). The great majority of boats divide this section between two people. However in four boats, *Kebako Pukã*, *Boli Sapã*, *Menula Belolong*, and *Demo Sapã*, the lower jaw was divided equally among those who held shares in the boat. In twenty-three boats there were forty-seven such shares, of which thirty-five went to members of the boat's great house and three more to members of other great houses of the same clan. Three were widows of men from the boat's great house. One was a man whose mother came from the boat's great house. One man was married to a woman from the boat's great house. One was a distinguished person who had long provided regional leadership and whose father's father's mother came from the great house in question, and two belonged to groups which had a nominal sibling relationship to it because of assistance they had received in the past (in one case legendary past). One was a man whose relationship I am unable to trace.

3. *Tenarap* (no translation available). Of thirty-nine separately held shares or half-shares in boats, twenty-five were in the hands of members of the boat's great house. Six were assigned to members of the same clan, but of different great houses. Four were held by husbands of women from the boat's great house, and another by the husband of a woman from the same clan but different great house. Two were held by men whose mothers came from the boat's great house, and one (the only woman) was a widow from the great house.

4. Ring (*kîlã*). Of thirty-three such shares held in twenty-three boats, ten were held by people of the same great house and a further five by people of a different great house of the same clan. Another was given to a widow born in the great house. Three went to men whose wives came from the great house and four more to men whose mothers did so. Another went to a man whose stepmother was from the great house. One man received a share whose father's mother came from the great house in question. One widow received a share via her husband's mother of the boat's great house. The most exceptional case was that of a man of a different descent group who held a share in

recognition of the fact that his great house had lent the location of a boat shed to the great house who gave him the share. Finally there were six men for whom for one reason or another I could not trace the reason for their participation. Only two women, both widows, were ñamed as having rights to the 'ring' share. 45 per cent of the thirty-three were members of the same descent group. Exactly a third were for women born in the great house or their husbands or descendants. Those percentages rise to 56 and 41 per cent if the doubtful cases are ignored.

5.   Shares (*umã*) or *kefoko seba*. Of 250 such shares held in twenty-eight boats, twenty were currently assigned to women, of whom eighteen were widows. Thirteen of these widows (65 per cent) were wives of men from the boat's great house. Three widows derive from the boat's great house and two more were from the same descent group. I was unable to obtain the reason why one woman, married but not a widow, received the share she held. The remaining woman was a spinster whose brother was the boat master.

Of the 230 men who held these shares, 125 (or 50 per cent) belonged to the boat's great house. Another thirty-five (14 per cent) belonged to the same descent group, thirty-two of them, however, to a different great house, with the great house of three uncertain in my records. For fourteen men, I was unable to establish the reason why they received the shares they did. Four men stood as wife-giving affines of varying degrees of remoteness. One man held a share because his sister's husband belonged to the boat's descent group, although to a different great house. The father's mother of four men came from the relevant great house, while the mother of nineteen men did so. Two men held shares by virtue of the fact that their mother's sister's husbands belonged to the great house. Two more did so through their mother's mothers. Twenty men were married to women from the great house. One man who received such a share was the boat's harpooner, but had no other claim, while three were not directly related, but given a share to keep their labour available to crew the boat.

6.   Sail (*laja*). Of twenty-eight sail makers, exactly half (fourteen) were from the boat's great house, while another was from the same descent group, but different great house. Two were *opu-laké*. One sail maker's father was from the great house, while another was from a different great house in the same descent group. Two had mothers from the boat's great house. Three sail makers were married to women in the great house, while another was the brother of a man who was. In three cases, I could trace no direct relationship.

7.   Chest (*korok*). Of twenty-eight such rights or potential rights, five were held by men who stood as *opu-laké* to members of the boat's great house. Nine were in the hands of members of the great house. Two were held by men whose mothers came from the great house, and two by men whose wives did so. In ten cases, there was no close relationship between the smith and the great house of the boat he served.

8.   Large *bĕfãnã* (*bĕfãnã bélã*). Of the twenty-one boats which distributed large *bĕfãnã* shares, fifteen were in use in 1979. Out of the ninety-nine persons who held rights to such shares, twelve were women. Nine of these women were widows. Six of the widows were born into the boat-owning descent group. One widow retained her share from her husband, who belonged to a different great house of the boat's clan. Another widow acquired her share from her husband, whose mother was from the boat-owning group. The third widow held her share from her husband who was a wife-giver to the boat-

owning group. Of the other three women, one was the daughter of the boat master, another had a right from her father's mother, and the third, who was not yet married, had her right through her mother of the boat-owning descent group.

Concerning the eighty-seven men with such rights, the majority held their rights either through their mothers (twenty-four) or their wives (twenty-eight). In one of these cases the mother and wife were of the same great house, and in two the mother was of the same great house as the father's mother. Another man held a share via his stepmother. Four more had rights through their father's mothers. One man held a right in virtue of his wife who was from a descent group which regarded itself as *kakang-ari*, siblings, to the boat's great house. Another eleven men were members of different great houses in the same clan as the boat owners. Twelve belonged to the same great house. One man belonged to a virtually extinct descent group and had been adopted into the great house which owned the boat. One belonged to a descent group which regarded itself as *kakang-ari*, siblings, to the boat's great house. Three had no particular kinship relation, but were said to always help in various ways. Of a single man, it was said that he was 'just an acquaintance'. These figures break down into three broad categories, wife-taking affines or offspring of women from the descent group (58), own group or sibling groups (25), and those with whom no particular relationship was recognized (4). Those whose rights depended on relationship through women made up exactly two-thirds of the total, while those from the boat's descent group or equivalent made up 29 per cent. Broadly speaking, it can be said that large *běfãnã* goes to dependants within the boat's clan, dependants who are the offspring of women from the descent group, and widows of men in the descent group or of men who are offspring of women from the descent group. Several of the men who received it are regular members of the boat's crew. Except for the four men to whom no relationship was traced, none of the men and women receiving this share fell outside of these categories.

9.   Small *běfãnã* (*běfãnã kéni*). See discussion in Chapter 10.

APPENDIX IV

Wood and Other Plants Used in Boat Construction and for Other Purposes

Allium sativum, Linn., garlic, *bafã burã*: may be put on fishing gear to insure a catch.

Alstonia scholaris, *rita*: used in constructing the hulls of dugout canoes.

Areca catechu, Linn., betel nut, *fua*: used to make betel quid, both the quid and the nut used in boat ceremonies.

Arenga pinnata, Merr. or *Arenga saccharifera*, Labill., the enau, areng, or sugar palm, *kebo*: the fibre, *rapo*, of the branches and trunk of this palm are used for caulking.

Borassus Flabellifera, Linn., palmyra or lontar Palm, *koli*: leaves used in stern decoration, skin of the branch, *pelepah* (Lamaholot, *kelepa*), used in bindings for various purposes.

Caesalpinia sappan, Linn., sappan or brazil wood, *hēpa*: used for making permanent dowels.

Calamus, Linn., spp., rattan, *uaj*: used as a wrapping to strengthen the ends of the mast poles and harpoon poles, and as ropes and bindings for rough work, such as hauling tree trunks, and for other purposes.

Canarium commune, Linn., kenari: the wood may be rubbed in order to attract fish on the bindings, *kemité*, holding the loop at the tip of harpooning rope called *léo fã* which connects this rope to the harpoon leader.

Ceiba pentandra, the kapok tree, *fũka*: used in making the top strake.

Cocus nucifera, Linn., coconut palm, *tapo*: skin of the nut used, burnt, for marking plank edges while shaping the planks.

Cordia subcordata, Linn., *kena*: used in constructing stern and stem posts and lower thwarts.

Corypha utan, Lam., gebang palm, *ketebu*: leaves used to weave the sections of the sail and to weave large ropes.

Dendrocalamus asper, Backer, a large variety of bamboo, *petung*: used for the yard of the sail.

Gigantochloa scortechinii, bamboo, *au*: used in constructing the boom of the sail.

Gigantochloa verticillata, bamboo, known in the Flores area as *pering*, *teri*: used, among other things, for making weaving swords for weaving sails.

Gossypium, Linn., cotton, *kapok lōlo* or *lélu*: used in making cords and ropes.

Grewia, spp., *kenīla*: used for making boat ribs.

Hibiscus tiliaceus, Linn., known as *baru* in Malay and locally as *waru*, *fao*: bark used in manufacturing large ropes.

Indigo fera tinctoria, Linn., indigo, *taõ*: used in dyeing gebang leaf strips for use in making decorative or identifying squares in sails.

Mangifera indica, Linn., mango, *pao*: used in constructing the hulls of dugout canoes. Among varieties of *Mangifera* are *pao belopor* (round mango) which is round and tastes bitter when young, *pao serani* (Christian mango) which is big and long, *pao pelã* which is small, and *pao dodo*.

Pterocarpus indicus, Willd., called *angsana* or *kayu merah* in Malay, *kĕnā*: used in constructing the main planks.

Santalum, Linn., sandalwood, called *chandana* in Malay, *kajo kayana*: rare locally, used as incense; if available it may be rubbed in order to attract fish on the bindings, *kemité*, holding the loop at the tip of harpooning rope called *léo fā* which connects this rope to the harpoon leader.

Schizosrtachyum brachycladum, Kurz., a bamboo, *fūlo*: used for, among other things, the air pipes of a bellows.

Schleichera oleosa, Merr., *kalabai*: used in constructing the false keel.

Schoutenia ovata, Korth., *kayu kukun* in Indonesian, *kūgu*: used to make temporary dowels useful in shaping the planks; used for making upper thwarts and outriggers, used for various smaller and supplementary structures in the boat; used to make the end of one of the harpoon poles where it is hit by the mallet; used to make the extension to the pole for controlling the boat in the surf; used for making the spindles on which strands for rope making are wound.

Sesbania grandiflora, Pers., in Malay *turi*, *teluma*: the sap is rubbed on new ropes to strengthen them, turning them black when they are immersed in sea water.

Tectona grandis, Linn., teak, *jati*: only recently used locally in boat construction for planks, from commercially obtained wood.

Vitex, Linn., *kepapa*: used in constructing the true keel and making boat ribs and lower thwarts.

Zanthoxylum myriacanthum, Wall., woodland Ceiba, *puo*: used for making an auxilliary top strake when returning heavily loaded from Lobetobi, Flores.

Zingiber officiale, Rosc., ginger, *lia*: may be put on fishing gear to insure a catch; in particular it will be put on the bindings, *kemité*, holding the loop at the tip of harpooning rope called *léo fā* which connects this rope to the harpoon leader.

Other Useful Plants

Aegle marmelos, Correa., the bel-fruit tree, *kedila*: the (edible) fruit provides glue used locally for trapping birds.

Aleurites moluccana, Willd., candlenut, *kemié*: torches can be made from the nut, which is used in boat ceremonies.

Allium ascalonicum, Linn., shallot, *bafā méã*: shallot, used as food.

Allium cepa, Linn., onion, *bafā*: used as food.

Annona squamosa, Linn., sweet sop, *dolima*: fruit eaten, used to make a green dye.

Arachis hypogaea, Linn., peanut, *ūtā tana*: common food.

Artocarpus communis, Forst., breadfruit, *kunu*: may be cooked.

Artocarpus integra, Merr., jack-fruit, *keferak*: flesh and seeds eaten.

Cajanus indicus, Spreng., tree bean, *ura*: source of food.

Calotropis gigantea, R. Brown, *keroko*.

Capsicum annuum, Linn., chilli plant, *sili*.

Carica papaya, Linn., papaya, *paja*.

Citrus aurantifolia, Swingle, lime, *mūda*: a common and important source of vitamins.

Coffea, Linn., coffee, *kopi*: occasionally available.

Coix lacryma-jobi, Linn., Job's tears, *dela*: planted in the mountains, but not eaten in Lamalera, can be used for dysentery.

Cucumis sativus, Linn., cucumber, *dīmu*: a common food.

Curcubita pepo, DC, pumpkin, *bési*: a common food.

Curcuma domestica, Velton, turmeric, *kumã*: used both to season food and as a yellow dye. In Lamaholot, this name otherwise means yellow.

Cycas circinalis, Linn., *ūtā kéda*: a poisonous wild bean, which is eaten during famines. The beans have to be cooked and the water thrown away four times, before they are safe. The beans can be eaten only when the water is no longer bitter.

Cymbopogon citratus, Stapf., lemon grass, *luo ketaka*.

Derris, spp., *nufa*: used as a fish poison.

Dioscorea esculenta, Burkill, the lesser Asiatic yam, *hura*: common food.

Dioscorea hispida, Dennst., poisonous wild tuber, Lamaholot name unrecorded: a famine food, must be cooked with many changes of water.

Eugenia cumini, Druce, jambu, *kai jafa*.

Ficus bengalensis, Linn., the banyan, *bau*: once the sacred shade tree of the village clearing.

Imperata cylindrica, Beauv., called *alang-alang*, a big grass, *luo*: used in thatching roofs.

Ipomoea batatas, Lam., sweet potato, *kastela, hura jafa*: food source.[1]

Lagenaria leucantha, Rusby, bottle gourd, *kelata*: food source, useful for manufacturing containers.

Lycopersicum, Mill., tomato, *tagalasi*: used as food.

Manihot utilissima, Pohl, cassava, *hura kajo*: used as food.

Metroxylon, Rottb., sago palm, *sagu*: exists only on Adonara in single individuals brought in from the Moluccas and planted by the Raja of Adonara.

Momordica, Linn., bitter cucumber, *pĕria*: used as food.

Morinda citrifolia, Linn., called in Malay *mengkudu, kelore*: used for red dye.

Moringa oleifera, Lam., called in Malay *merunggai, moton*: the leaves may be eaten as a vegetable.

Musa, Linn., banana, several varieties, *muko*: used for food, wrappings, place mats, etc.

Musa acuminata, wild banana, *baki*: edible.

Nicotiana, Linn., tobacco, *tebako*: used for smoking, generally part of the provision for festivals and conviviality.

Oryza sativa, Linn., rice, *kĕringi*: food, especially for feasts. *Kĕringi* is unhusked rice. Husked rice is *kĕringi laéng* (cleaned rice). Cooked rice is *kĕluo*. Rice steamed in a package woven from lontar palm leaves is *ketupat*. Rice fried in oil and then steamed in a package woven from coconut leaves is *keléso*.

Pachyrrhizus erosus, Urban, in Indonesian *bengkuwang* from a Mexican language, introduced via the Philippines, *képa*: an edible tuber.

Phaseolus, spp., beans of various kinds, *ūtā*: used as food.

Phaseolus aureus, Roxb., green gram, *féfé*: common food.

Piper betle, Linn., betel pepper, *malu*: the pepper, rather than the leaf as on Java, is used in preparing betel quid, used in ceremonies.

Piper nigrum, Linn., black pepper, *lada*.

Saccharum officinarum, Linn., sugar cane, *tefo*: sweet food source.

Saccharum spontaneum, *bĕlatā*: a grass.

Sapium baccatum, Roxb., *budi*: used as a shade tree in the village clearing.

Schizostachyum brachycladum, bamboo with long joints and relative thin walls, *bélā*: used for carrying water.

Setaria italica, Beauv., Italian millet or foxtail millet, *fětã*: used as food, but not commonly.

Solanum melongena, Linn., eggplant, *kelupu*.

Sonneratia acida, Linn. or *Sonneratia caseolaris*, Engl., *kayu gabus* in Malay, *bui*: one of the two most ancient boats, *Bui Pukã* is named after this tree.

Sorghum vulgare, Pers., sorghum, *fata holot*: an occasional food source. According to Vatter (1932: 106), sorghum is known as *wata belolong*, i.e. tall maize.

Tamarindus indica, Linn., tamarind, called *asam* in Malay, *tobi*: the fruit is used as a flavouring in foods; the hard red pith of the wood is valued for making weaving swords, the seed may be fried (for children or during the hunger season), pounded, soaked, and then mixed with coconut.

Uncaria gambir, Roxb., gambir, *gabé*: not much used.

Vigna sinensis, Savi, long beans, *ūtã kenoing*.

Zea mays, Linn., maize, *fata*: this is the staple food, eaten at almost every meal. The standard Lamaholot manner of preparing it is to make *fata biti*, which is maize kernels roasted in a pot until they split and which are then crushed by putting them on a stone and pounding them with another stone. This method is known only on Adonara, Lembata, Solor, and eastern Flores (Wignyanta 1979: 10). The variety which makes popcorn is called *fata pu* (flowering maize).

Unidentified Plants

gemoli: a tree which provides red dye.

geru: used in making outriggers.

kelua: the leaf of this tree may make a person dizzy or quickly drunk if it is rubbed on a glass.

keluraj: seeds of this tree serve as a poison.

kēru: a plant growing in ravines, the fruit of which is juicy.

padé: the leaves are used to make a green dye.

APPENDIX V

Identifying Characteristics of the Sails of Lamalera Boats

The following features of the sails help villagers recognize the boats from a distance. This record is from 1979. Of course not all of these sails existed in 1979.

1. Muko Ténã: white. Along with that of Kebako Pukã its sail is the largest of all. Unlike the Kebako Pukã, its *kelatã lõlo* is somewhat short.
2. Demo Sapã: when the sail is on the right, the black square near the centre is below.
3. Baka Ténã: only white.
4. Pĕraso Sapã: if the sail is on right, a black square on the bottom, left side.
5. Léla Sapã: only white
6. Notã Ténã: only white.
7. Menula Belolong: black cross.
8. Dato Ténã: only white.
9. Kebéla Ténã: streamers on top.
10. Boli Sapã: black squares in the centre on the right and left sides.
11. Gĕléko Ténã: white, one streamer at the bottom.
12. Boko Lolo: white sail on the right, black square on the side above.
13. Sika Ténã: only white.
14. Bui Pukã: black squares above, right and left
15. Sia Apu: white sail, streamers below.
16. Nara Ténã: much like the Téti Heri.
17. Kopo Paker: white, rather short.
18. Téti Heri: white, sail large, but torn, boat now uses *temoto*.
19. Holo Sapã: black squares above and below (in the middle).
20. Soge Ténã: black square in centre, 2 streamers at bottom.
21. Horo Ténã: white, a new sail which is a clean white.
22. Dolu Ténã: black square in the middle.
23. Sili Ténã: white, right side wide, left narrow.
24. Kéna Pukã: black square above.
25. Kelulus: black square below.
26. Kebako Pukã: white, sail largest of all peledang (see Muko Ténã).
27. Ténã Ãnã: black square below.
28. Sinu Sapã: none.
29. Jafa Ténã: white, small sail.

APPENDIX VI
Boat Measurements

In 1979 I took the following measurements from *Menula Belolong*. From stem to stern (from *menula* to *urin*) the boat was 10.3 metres in length. This measurement was taken from the *menula* to the back of the *mādi*. If measured to the end of the *kōlé*, the boat was 10.6 metres long. The left, outrigger, *ēlé*, was 5.4 metres, the right 5.3. The harpoon platform from the tip to the very end of the posts inside the boat was 4.5 metres, of which 2.95 metres was inside the boat and 1.55 extended in front of it. The *gělefé fā* was 3.4 metres, the *gělefé uring* 3.2 metres. The greatest width, at the *fai mātā*, was 2.2 metres. The internal depth here was 0.84 metres. The outside displacement from keel to water line here was .75 metres. The mast to end of bamboo was 7.1 metres, to the tip of the wooden fork 7.7 metres. The helm oar, *fai uring*, was 1.75 metres. One harpoon pole was 6.1 metres. The harpoon for whale .48 metres. In comparison, *Notā Ténā* was 10.1 metres from the *menula* to the back of the *mādi*, 10.5 to the tip of the *kōlé*. The harpoon platform, *hãmā* was 4.5 metres to the end of the poles, with 2.8 metres inside the boat and 1.7 metres extending in front of it. The right outrigger was 5.2 metres.

Further measurents of the *Menula Belolong* in 1979 are as follows.

	Length	Width front	Width back
teka nalā	122 cm.	35 cm.	111 cm.
serā	78	132	161
nodé pukā	75	164	186
léo ūli	83	187	193
puā pukā	89	204	204
fai mātā	100	204	204
běfaléng	93	204	204
gělefé	91	195	182
sěmugur bélā	78	178	164
sěmugur kéni	77	153	121
lamauri tobo			
to seat	61	116	66
to *mādi*	106		

Freeboard on the right side 27 cm., on the left 33 cm.

The following measurements were made on the right side of the hull of the *Menula Belolong*.

mādi	84 cm. high
ié tūkā	180 cm. from front to false line
	276 cm. to end.
ié uring	170 cm.
extension	113 cm.
kōlé	118 cm.

ié fã	233 cm.
extension	122 cm.
menula	119 cm.
tip of *menula*	48 cm.
ārã belikãng	310 cm. The *ārã belikãng* did not really overlap *ié tūkã* but did overlap false end.

Tenépa or continuing pieces for the *ārã belikãng* in front 60 cm. to false line, 103 cm. to end of board, 53 to another false line, 77 cm. to end of board; back 39 to false end, 85 to end. From there, overlapping by boards above.

arã kenãti	320 cm.
arã tūkã	290 cm.
nulu fũtu	350 cm.

At this point, I stopped measuring, not trying to get measurements for the *arã bélã* and the *néfi* for example. There were so many short pieces of wood in the hull that it was a mess from the point of view of a plan.

The *Notã Ténã* would make a better example, but its left hull is closer to the abstract pattern than the right. It has in any case much cleaner lines and smoother hull than the *Menula Belolong*, even if its wood is more bleached.

The following measurements for the *Menula Belolong*, the same version of the boat, were taken in 1982. Inside:

from the *menula* to the front of the *baut* (*serã*) 132 cm.
from the top of the *baut* to the top of the *tekã* 41 cm.
from the top of the *baut* to the hull just below the lug on either side 52 cm.
from the top of the *baut* to the keel in the bilge 76 cm.
baut, length 158 cm., diameter 7 cm.
tekã, length 79 cm., with about 2-cm. gap between the ends and the hull on either side.
inside hull breadth at *baut* 122 cm.

from the front of *baut* (*serã*) to the front *baut* (*umã nodé pukã*) 86 cm.
from the top of *baut* (*serã*) to top of *tekã* 32 cm.
from the top of *baut* (*serã*) to hull (either side) 45 cm.
from the top of *baut* (*serã*) to keel 95 cm.
baut length 178 cm./diameter 7 cm.
tekã length 125 cm., *c*.8-cm. gap on either side.
inside hull breadth at *baut* 169 cm.

from front of *baut* (*umã nodé pukã*) to front of *gĕlefé fã* 78 cm.
from top of *gĕlefé fã* to top of *tekã* 37 cm.
from top of *gĕlefé fã* to hull (either side) 47 cm.
from top of *gĕlefé fã* to keel 101 cm.
gĕlefé fã 348 cm./diameter irregular *c*.9 cm. at tips
tekã 150 cm./6 cm. gap, either end.
inside hull breadth at *gĕlefé fã* 198 cm.

from front of *gĕlefé fã* to front of *baut* (*puã pukã*) *c*.89 cm.
from top of *baut* to top of *tekã* 32 cm.

from top of *baut* to hull (either side) 42 cm.
from top of *baut* to keel 91 cm.
baut length 250 cm./diameter 7 cm.
tekã length 176 cm./8-cm. gap, either end.
inside hull length at *baut* 207 cm.
from front of *baut* (*puã pukã*) to front of *baut* (*fai mãtã*) 78 cm.
from top of *baut* to top of *tekã* 28 cm.
from top of *baut* to hull (either side) 51 cm.
from top of *baut* to keel 78 cm.
baut length 238 cm./diameter 8 cm.

from front of *baut* (*fai mãtã*) to front of *baut* (*bĕfaléng*) *c*.98 cm.
from top of *baut* to top of *tekã* 23 cm.
from top of *baut* to hull (either side) 47 cm.
from top of *baut* to keel 82 cm.
baut length 238 cm./diameter 8 cm.
tekã length 185 cm., gap *c*.4 cm., either end
inside hull breadth at *baut* 214 cm.

from front of *baut* (*bĕfaléng*) to front of *baut* (*gĕlefĕ*) *c*.96 cm.
from top of *baut* to top of *tekã* 26 cm.
from top of *baut* to hull (either side) 47 cm.
from top of *baut* to keel 87 cm.
baut length 133 cm./diameter 6 cm.
tekã length *c*.181 cm./gap in either side *c*.3 cm.
inside hull breadth at *baut* 200 cm.

from front of *baut* (*gĕlefĕ*) to front of *gĕlefĕ uring* 96 cm.
from top of *gĕlefĕ uring* to top of *tekã* 20 cm.
from top of *gĕlefĕ uring* to hull (either side) 42 cm.
from top of *gĕlefĕ uring* to keel 86 cm.
gĕlefĕ uring length 325 cm./diameter. 12 cm.
tekã length 167, no gap.
inside hull breadth at *gĕlefĕ uring* 180 cm.

from front of *gĕlefĕ uring* to front of *baut* (*sĕmugur kéni*) 63 cm.
from top of *baut* to top of *tekã* 19 cm.
from top of *baut* to hull (either side) 33 cm.
from top of *baut* to keel 80 cm.
baut length 167 cm./diameter 6 cm.
tekã length 135 cm., no gap.
inside hull breadth at *baut* 152 cm.

from front of *baut* (*sĕmugur kéni*) to front of *baut* (*lama uring tobo*) 88 cm.
from top of *baut* to top of *tekã* 26 cm.
from top of *baut* to hull (either side) 40 cm.
from top of *baut* to keel 70 cm.
baut length 138 cm./diameter 5 cm.
tekã length 95 cm., *c*.2 cm.-gap either end.
inside hull breadth at *baut* 110 cm.

from front of *baut* to front of *mādi* 113 cm.

steering oar, length 179 cm.; length of blade 88 cm.; width of blade 22 cm.

outrigger (*ēlé*) 514 cm.

The distance between the hull and the outriggers (*ēlé*) on each side:

	at *gĕlefĕ fã*	centre	*gĕlefĕ uring*
rt.	46 cm.	36 cm.	48 cm.
left	55 cm.	35 cm.	36 cm.

Outside:

from *menula* to line of keel 140 cm.

from *baut* (*serã*) to keel line outside *c*.105 cm.

From *gĕlefĕ fã* to *gĕlefĕ uring* the outside hull measurement to keel was rather regular, about 97 cm. on left side, 90 cm. on right. The difference on each side was due probably to the slope of the sand and the impossibility of getting a good angle for measurement in the cramped quarters. There was also some irregularity in the hull shape too. The curve of the hull on the right side was closer to a flat S than the rounder left. The corresponding measurements at the *baut* in front of *sĕmugur kéni* is 89 cm., *baut* in front of *lamauring tobo* is 79 cm., at *mādi* is 60 cm. The upward slope of the sand at the back of the *naja* shortened the last three measurements somewhat, but the keel itself curved, actually slanted, upward toward the back.

APPENDIX VII
Whales and Porpoises

fefakumu: a variety of small porpoise with a soft skin; the name means 'mustache mouth'. A porpoise, black in colour, of roughly the size of Spinner Dolphin, but with a very small mouth and very sharp teeth which can bite through a harpoon rope. Although I have no identification, among candidates might be included the Bridled Dolphin, *Stenella attenuata*; see the description of *Stenella malayana*, Lesson 1826 in Watson (1981: 266). However, fishermen told Hembree that an example harpooned 30 August 1979 was another example of *temu kirã* (see Hembree 1980: 13).

ikã méã: *Ziphius cavirostris*, Goosebeak Whale (Cuvier's); the name means 'red fish'.

kelaru: a general term for large and small rorquals, *Balaenoptera edeni*, Bryde's Whale; *Balaenoptera actorostrata*, Minke Whale; *Balaenoptera borealis*, Sei Whale; and other baleen whales, generally without further specification of species differences.

kelaru ãmã: a small baleen whale caught by Lamakera, Solor.

kotekĕlema: *Physeter catadon*, Sperm Whale.

lélangaji: *Balaenoptera musculus*, Blue Whale.

temu bélã: *Globicephala macrohyncus*, Short-finned Pilot Whale.

temu bĕlã: *Pseudora crassidens*, False Killer Whale.

temu bĕluã: various types of small porpoise.

temu bũrã: *Grampus griseus*, Grey (Risso's) Dolphin.

temu kebong: *Peponocephala electra*, Many Toothed Blackfish. According to Gregorius Keraf (1983), there are actually several varieties, *kebong lemé*, deep sea, *kebong mãrã*, shore, and *kebong nu burã* , white muzzled.

temu kebung: *Feresa attenuata*, Pygmy Killer Whale. According to Gregorius Keraf (1983), it lives near the shore and hunts small fish and eats coral. Its muzzle is like a pig's because it uses it to break up coral.

temu kirã: *Stenella longirostris*, Spinner Dolphin.

temu notong: *Lagenodelphis fraserii* = *Lagenodelphis hosei*, Fraser's Dolphin or Sarawak Dolphin.

NOTES

Introduction

1. According to Poerwadarminta (1966: 2: 70) *pesisir* is a Javanese loanword. The only grounds for preferring the Malay is the former widespread use of Malay as a trading language and its role as the foundation of the present national language. Recognition of a variety of coastal communities in the former Dutch East Indies and adjacent regions derives from Pigeaud (1938: 347–9, 477–8; 1967: 6–7), who applied the Javanese *pasisir*, meaning coastal areas, to the Javanese literature rejuvenated under the influence of Islam in the geographical range from Surabaya and Gresik in the east to Cerbon and Banten in the west from about 1500 and into the eighteenth century (thus 'Pasisir Literature'). He also spoke of the spread of 'Pasisir culture' to other islands. The 'Pasisir period of Javanese history' began with the introduction of Islam and the fall of the ancient Hindu kingdom of Majapahit, and was marked by wars among young Muslim states and against European traders (Pigeaud 1967: 134). Geertz (1963: 58) took up this generalization and claimed that coastal Malays and a long series of other maritime peoples, including some in the Lesser Sunda Islands, 'all have much in common culturally'. 'These scattered peoples can be considered to have a single but rather heterogeneous culture.' She did, however, concede that it remained to be seen how much they had in common culturally, since coastal peoples 'have been slighted in research and reporting'. For Pigeaud and Geertz 'Pasisir culture' was closely associated with Islam. This exclusive association with Islam has recently been challenged by Vickers (1987: 57; 1993: 56). Vickers (1993: 72) came to the conclusion that, 'The term "Pasisir" cannot be used as a definition of a uniform type of society or culture. It is rather a framework or matrix in which certain elements are constant, and others change according to locality. Pasisir culture is thus inherently pluralistic.'

   Rodney Needham has communicated to me his dissatisfaction with the use of the word *pesisir* (or *pasisir*) to designate a variety of society, mostly on semantic grounds, and suggested that any such variety would best be designated 'littoral societies' (personal communications 15 and 16 June 1995). In my opinion, what is common to such peoples is less culture than structural position in relation to the sea and to peoples of the interior. To the extent that they may share, or may have shared, common commercial or seafaring culture, such similarities must be set against cultural differences resulting from their assimilation to regional cultures and languages. Although Islam came to play a very important role in very many coastal communities, including several in the Lamaholot language area, in my interpretation the structural position was there before the coming of Islam, and it is plain that not all *pesisir* communities took up Islam. Essentially the same view is represented by Glover, commenting that perhaps by the second millennium BC a distinction can be recognized between inland and coastal communities. While agriculture supported the populations of the interior, 'Elsewhere, and especially in coastal districts and on the smaller islands, only the sea provided opportunities for expansion, and outward-looking, highly mobile communities developed, spreading common items of material culture, ideology, and artistic design throughout the region; the forerunner of the "Pasisir cultures" of recent Indonesian history' (Glover 1979: 183–4). The only point in which I disagree with him is his reluctance to see the same pattern on smaller islands, such as Solor and Lembata.

2. Lembata is the official name of the island, and the name which is current in the region. However, all national and international maps name it Lomblen. Indonesian authorities selected the name Lembata in the 1960s, taking the view that this was the old and proper name. That this view is justified may be seen from comments such as that of P. P. Roorda

van Eysinga (1841: 59) in his geographical handbook of the Netherlands Indies, where he commented that Lomblen was also known as 'Lombatta'. Beckering (1921: 136) wrote that the name Lomblem (Lomblen) was unknown to traders and to the population of the island. They only knew the names of the region where they lived or where they were going to trade.

3. Aernsbergen (1909: 262) wrote that the distinction between the coastal people and the mountain dwellers was so strongly fixed in local imaginations that when new missionaries arrived people tried to find out whether they were from the mountains or from the shore. Once that question was answered their curiosity was pretty well satisfied. A missionary from the flat interior of the Netherlands, such as North Brabant, counted as a mountain dweller (Aernsbergen 1909: 262). Of course the same opposition can be expressed in Indonesian languages as that between people of the shore and those of the interior, without inappropriate references to elevation.

   Smith and Watson (1979: 13) date the appearance of the evolving contrast between upland and lowland societies (or perhaps between interior and coastal) in South-East Asia from the first millennium BC.

4. Typical is a comment in the general review of the political state of the Netherlands Indies for 1839–48 (Algemeen Oversicht 1848). It simply remarked that during this period thare had been no contact between Lembata and the government in Kupang. 'The same is not included in the territory of Netherlands India by virtue of special treaties, but ranged thereunder as a dependency of Solor.' Of course only certain portions of the island, those subordinate to or allied with Lamakera, Lamahala, and the Raja of Adonara could be so regarded. The lack of direct European contact with Lembata was foreshadowed by a comment made by Pires in the very earliest days of Portuguese presence in South-East Asia, 'the other islands along by Solor [including of course Lembata] are not much good for trade because they are out of reach, I do not deal with them. They are all lands of heathen robbers' (Pires 1944: 205).

5. In April 1889 on the south-east corner of the island of Lembata at the entrance to the strait between Pantar and Lembata in a crater at a place named Pagoran there was an eruption immediately preceded by an underground rumble. Thirty years previously, that is *c*.1859, a village on the spot named Pagoran sank because of an earthquake (Villeneuve 1889). Villeneuve's description of the location is very circumstantial. If, as is possible, his report of the location is mistaken, then in all probability this incident refers to the village of Paugora on the Lerek Peninsula, further to the west along Lembata's south coast.

6. Hellmuth, who was stationed at Lohayong, Solor, experienced a day of complete darkness on 5 Oct. 1852. During the night there was a rain of ash at Larantuka. Eventually he learned that there had been a volcanic eruption on Lembata, in which a part of the mountain on the sea side had fallen in, greatly increasing the size of the crater (Hellmuth 1853: 220–1). Hellmuth does not specify which volcano it was, and Hartmann (1935: 824) assumes it must have been Lewotolo on the north coast, which had been active in those years. For some reason, he does not consider the possibility that it might have been this complex on the south coast of the island.

7. A news report in the national newspaper *Sinar Harapan* for Monday, 23 July 1979, has it that these names derive from Petrus or Peter Hobalt, a vulcanologist who predicted their appearance. I suspect, however, that this report is apocryphal because I have been unable to trace a volcanologist or geologist with such a name. I have no authority either, other than this newspaper report, for the statement that the volcano near the shore has been named Ilé Petrus.

8. The same news report mentioned in the previous note relates that earthquakes and volcanic eruptions in the Lerek Peninsula are interpreted as a fight between the spirit of the interior and the spirit of the sea. The spirit of the sea orders crabs to build a tunnel in the land. He then attacks with fire, which is the eruption.

Ilé Hobal, the undersea volcano, erupted on 25 Jan. 1980, and there was a landslide near the village of Paugora on 27 Jan. In neither case was there any injury to the population in the area (Dian 1980*b*).

9. During the 1970s and early 1980s Indonesian agriculture was transformed by the spreading use of a plant called lamatoro gung (*Leucaena leucocephala*). It is a plant with many uses. It grows rapidly, improves the soil, can be planted first on soil intended for other plants later, provides fire wood and animal fodder, can be used as a shade plant for coffee and chocolate plantations, and its seeds can even be used as food by humans. One of the principal attractions of this variety of lamatoro is that its roots grow thickly and deeply, but do not spread out from the base of the plant so that it can be planted at the edges of terraces on hillsides where it retains the soil, preventing erosion, without interfering with other crops in terrace fields. Lamatoro was promoted by the government and was widely planted in the Flores area, including Lembata (*Dian* 1980*a*; Metzner 1976*a*, 1976*b*, 1982: 52, 199; Webb 1986: 169–70). Then in 1986 a pest, *Heteropcylla sp.* (known as the jumping louse, *kutu loncat*, in Indonesian), of Caribbean origin spread through Indonesia destroying this plant (Webb 1989: 219–22). Like Flores, Lembata was also heavily affected.

10. These figures are from the capital of the District at Loang on the west coast of Lembata, a considerable distance from Lamalera. The total of 1,405 mm. is considerably higher than 800 to 900 mm. which Corner (1991*b*: 181) writes is the annual average of rainfall in the regencies of East Flores, Alor, and East Sumba. Between 1989 and 1994 (for which period the figures are available) the number of days of rain at Loang varied from a low of 41 and the total rainfall from a low of 783 mm. in 1991 to a high of 108 days and a high of 1,751 mm. in 1993. The average over that period was 68 days of rain and a total rainfall of 1,156.33 mm. (*Kecamatan Nagawutung Dalam Angka* 1989–1994). The province as a whole is supposed to have the lowest rainfall of any in Indonesia. According to Barlow and Gondowarsito (1991: 20–1), the rainfall in the province varies between 700 and 1,500 mm. per year. However, as they note, rain shadows created by the varying terrain cause large disparities in rainfall in closely adjacent sites.

11. Hairun was the third sultan of Ternate and Babulah the fourth. The first sultan was Djaialabidin, who received instruction in Islam in Giri, Java, in 1486 (de Clercq 1890: 152).

12. Significantly the places on Pantar (Bernusa, Blagar, and Pandai) and Alor (Malua and Alor) included those which have today the closest linguistic ties with Lamaholot.

13. The Government of Netherlands India concluded a treaty with the leaders of Lohayong, Lamakera, Lamahala, Terong, Adonara, and Larantuka on 28 June 1861, in which among other things, they agreed to act with all their power against piracy, to assist ships in distress and their occupants, to protect the goods of stranded ships, to repress kidnapping, slavery, and the import and export of slaves, and to protect the rights of debt slaves (Gouvernement van Nederlandsch Indië 1864–65: 184–6). Of the Lamaholot participants in this treaty, by the way, only the Raja of Larantuka was able to sign his own name.

14. 'That the people should have heaped themselves up on the highest mountain tops and [that] the plains are uninhabited, should not surprise us too much. That is the result of the continuing wars among themselves and also the result of the numerous kidnappings by the earlier so notorious pirates who made our Eastern Archipelago unsafe from the Sulu to the Lesser Sunda Islands' (Java-Post 1910: 729).

15. In 1980 with a total population of 2,737,166, Nusa Tenggara Timur had the 21st fastest growth rate of the 27 provinces of Indonesia (1.95) and the 16th greatest density (57/km. sq.) with 1.86% of the nation's population on 2.49% of its area (Biro Pusat Statistik 1981*a*). By comparison, the figures for the Republic as a whole were a total population of 147,490,000, with an average density of 77/km. sq., and a national growth rate of 2.32. By 1990, with a population of 3,267,919, the province had the 20th fastest growth rate (1.79), 17th greatest density (68/km. sq.), and 1.82% of the nation's population.

In 1990 the total population of the Republic of Indonesia was 179,379,000. Its average density was 91 per square kilometre, and the national population growth rate was 1.98 (Biro Pusat Statistik 1991). The general trends indicated for the period up to 1980 continued in more extreme form in the decade up to 1990. As can be seen from Table 5, the population of the Regency virtually stopped growing during the period and that of the island declined slightly. By 1994 it had reached 270,654 (*Flores Timur Dalam Angka* 1994). Table 3 shows that the Kecamatan Nagawutung actually lost population between 1980 and 1990, as did three other districts on the island. Lebatukan, which includes the north coast town of Lewoleba, continued to be a strong attractor of population from elsewhere on the island, but the island as a whole nevertheless became a net exporter of population. Although it had recovered its loss by 1994, the overall growth remained flat. Nagawutung in 1990 had a population density of 37.4 per square kilometre, by far the lowest in the Regency, the average for which was 86.3 per square kilometre. The district also suffered a poor balance between the number of males and females, with 75 males per 100 females, as opposed to 72 males per 100 females for the whole island. The fact that there are 68.6 adult males in the district per 100 adult females, shows that it is above all the active males who were leaving the district and the island. There was an average of 4.5 persons per household in the district, as compared with the Regency average of 5 (*Flores Timur Dalam Angka* 1994, Kantor Statistik 1992, *Kecamatan Nagawutung Dalam Angka* 1990, Biro Pusat Statistik 1992).

16. For what it is worth, in 1982 the male nurse estimated the population size of Lamalera A as 800, Lamalera B as 900, Lamalera A excluding Lamamanu as 500, Lamalera B excluding Ongaona and Nualela as 600. These figures are very comparable to those given above. In 1981 Lamalera A had a total population of 854, in 1982 of 866.

In a letter dated 12 May 1994, Father Dupont informs me that, working with church statistics, he arrives at a figure of 2,013 persons in Lamalera A and B, of which *c*.100 are in the distant hamlet of Nualela. The figure of 2,013 results from subtracting 479 from a total of 2,483 for Lamalera A and B, plus the nearby villages of Tapobali, Wolowutung, Lamabaka, and Lewotala. This larger figures comprises 1,138 males and 1,345 females, producing a ratio of 85 males per 100 females. As can be seen from Table 7, this ratio is slightly less favourable for males than that for Lamalera alone in 1979, but it essentially suggests that there has been little change over the decade in this respect. Statistics available from the Regency statistics office show a total for the two official villages (Lamalera A and Lamalera B) ranging from 2,522 in 1984 to 1,841 in 1994 (*Kecamatan Nagawutung Dalam Angka* 1985–1994), representing an annual growth rate over that period of −3.09%. The combined ratio in 1984 was 95 males per 100 females. In 1994 it was reported as 84 males per 100 females.

17. In 1780 there were 'many' on Solor, where the Dutch had treaty relations with Muslim villages, who could read and write Arabic (Hogendorp 1780: 428).

Earl (1853: 177) wrote that several people from the neighbourhood of Larantuka had been educated at the Roman Catholic College of Goa on the Indian west coast and had been ordained priests so that they could perform Christian religious services. Castro found in Portuguese Timor, which of course until 1859 had to provide for Larantuka as well, only two missionaries, who never left the capital, Dili. 'The mission is almost abandoned' (de Castro 1862: 476). However, the Raja of Larantuka, Don Gaspar, and his father the elder Don Lorenzo had been educated as children in Dili by Roman Catholic priests (H[umme] 1877: 90).

18. Semmelink, a naval health officer stationed at Larantuka, estimated that there were only thirty or forty Christians in the region in 1863 who could read and write, excepting the few children who received instruction in these skills from the end of 1861. Perhaps this teaching was a preliminary trial prior to the later establishment of more formal schooling. He was of the opinion that there was no one on Solor who could read or write (Semmelink 1864: 61).

19. Things did not always go easily with mission plans to take boys and girls from Lamalera for training in Larantuka. In April and May 1894, when P. A. Wintjes spend forty days there, he met resistance. 'It was my aim above all to get children for the school in Larantuka, and when I asked for four girls for the nuns, general muttering of disapproval broke out. The upshot was that they were not willing to do so. I was welcome to come, build schools and churches, dig graves and give out gifts, the more the better, but give up their children, never' (Wintjes 1894a: 31).

20. Letter from Father Arnoldus Dupont dated 28 Nov. 1984.

21. By 1984 the Bupati (Head) of Larantuka outlawed migration to Malaysia and Tawau and placed a watch on vessels plying this trade (see Habir 1984).

22. For what it is worth, in 1979 Lamalera A reported 185 fishermen, 253 housewives, 83 farmers (53 males, 30 females, mostly in the mountain hamlet Lamamanu), one foreign missionary, one lay brother, and eight schoolteachers. It claimed 349 coconut trees, 50 coffee trees, 880 candlenut trees, 50 kapok trees, 200 tamarind trees, 3,000 banana trees, 150 papaya trees, and 30 citrus trees. Except for a few kapok, banana, and papaya trees, none of these were actually within the historical Lamalera. It also admitted to 96 pigs, 68 goats, 61 chickens, and 47 dogs.

23. *Kakang* is a Malay word which is a form of address for an older brother or older man. Its use to indicate key figures in the realm of the Raja of Larantuka is in keeping with the Malay-speaking culture of Larantuka.

24. Hagenaar (1934) gives detailed accounts of such actions in the nineteenth and early twentieth centuries. Further information may be found in Kniphorst (1885), Wichmann (1891), B. and W. O[ort] (1905), Lulofs (1911), and Dietrich (1983, 1989: 8–11, 62–96). Individual events can be tracked in the pages of the annual volumes of the *Koloniaal Verslag*.

   Lulofs complained that under this policy, the *posthouders* (post-holders) placed on the islands were merely living armorial shields, the higher officers, including the Resident, not much more. In 1894 the government even considered abolishing the province and making it a district of the province of Celebes and Dependencies. The poor communications and the presence of a Portuguese governor on the north coast of Timor prevented this step being taken (Lulofs 1911: 281). 'Under this régime the archipelago remained what it was: a tangle of numerous little states living with each other in periodic discord' (Lulofs 1911: 282).

25. Government steamships began to visit Larantuka regularly from 1876. The *Afdeeling Larantoeka en onderhoorigheden* (District of Larantuka and Dependencies), the ancestor of the present *Kabupaten Flores Timur* (East Flores Regency), was created by the Dutch in 1879. In 1914 Adonara and Lembata became a separate subdistrict with a *gezaghebber* (district commissioner) at Waiwerang, Adonara, and a *bestuursassistent* (governmental assistant) at Waikomo, Lembata. Solor was placed under the *civilgezaghebber* (civil commissioner) at Larantuka. This arrangement cross-cut all traditional alliances and divisions (Hagenaar 1934: 106, 108). Waiwerang originated as a market set up in the early 1870s by Kluppel (1873: 393).

26. While J. J. Hangelbroek was Controleur in Larantuka (1937–8), a hollow, bronze dance ankle ring was found at Hadakewa, which Hangelbroek sent to the ethnographic museum in Batavia. It was recognized by the museum as a significant and unique find (Hangelbroek 1977: 136–7). It is still on display in the Museum Negara in Jakarta with the accession number 3745 and date 26 Sept. 1938.

Chapter 1

1. Beckering (1911: 192) also encountered the perfectly acceptable expressions Lefo Bělolo, the High Village, and Lefo Léré, the Low Village.

2. In Malay, *budi* is usually applied to *Ficus religosa*, which does have air roots. The tree in question here is probably *Ficus benjamina*. It is probable that Lamaholot *bau* applies to all three trees. Keraf (1978: 134, 169) indicates that the Lamaholot for *budi* is *gudi*. Another possible identification of *budi* is *Sapium baccatum*, Roxb.

3. This is only a partially accurate translation of these names, as will be explained below. Nevertheless they are essentially correct so far as they go.

4. I have no further information about the origin of these cannons, but they may well come from Manuel Tavares Bocarro's gun-foundry at Macao which supplied Portuguese settlements on Solor, Flores, and Timor and functioned between 1627 and 1680 (Boxer 1965b: 165, 167).

5. An analysis of a sand sample from this beach picked up by the Siboga expedition showed that it is made up of fresh plagioclase, pyroxene, and numerous blue-black grains from an ore which is a mixture of titanium and iron (possibly ilmenite). The sand also contains tiny fragments of black andesite (Wichmann 1925: 11).

6. In 1907 two heads of mountain villages bordering on the district of Lamalera complained to Couvreur through the Raja of Adonara about their treatment by the Kakang of Lamalera and the Raja of Labala, with whom oddly the *kakang* was in league. Women from Lamalera district had walked through a field in the mountain district where people were harvesting, violating a prohibition on people not involved in a harvest going through such a field. The harvesters had been angered, and, according to the Kakang of Lamalera, had stripped the women naked. Some days later a war party from Lamalera attacked the mountain hamlets and people were killed on both sides. The breast of one of the dead from Lamalera was cut open. The *kakang* turned to the Raja of Labala with the request that he go to the region and take three heads and deliver them to the *kakang* in compensation for the lost men. The raja and two companions then went to the area where they called on a young man to bring the raja sweet palm juice. When he did so, the raja killed him and cut off his head which he later gave to the *kakang*. Couvreur imposed fines of 1,000 guilders on the *kakang*, 500 guilders on the raja, and in addition 250 guilders each for lying, as well as giving stern warnings of what he would do if the offence was repeated and ordering Lamalera to rebuild the villages they had burnt down (Couvreur 1907). The Kakang of Lamalera at the time was Yosef Raja Muda, the Raja of Labala was Baha.

7. In January 1621 two Dominicans, João Bautista de la Fortalezza and Simão da Madre de Deos were driven by storm to Lembata and landed at Lamalera. The Muslims of Lamakera hearing of this event demanded that the priests be handed over to them. When Lamalera refused, Lamakera managed to capture three *kora kora* containing ninety people from Lamalera, including its leader. When Lamakera threatened to kill these people, the priests freely gave themselves up and were taken to Lamakera, where they were killed on the 18th. On the 20th they were taken to the fort at Lohayong, Solor, then in Dutch hands, where they were beheaded in the presence of the commander of the fort, who was a reluctant witness, but powerless to stop the beheading. He did, however, give the priests a decent burial. Three years before this event the priest Augustinho da Magdalena had been killed at Lamakera. After whipping him, the villagers of Lamakera launched a *kora kora* across him (Cácegas and de Sousa 1678: 388–9, 391; Biermann 1924: 31). Scott (1981: 22) noted that the Visaya of the Philippines in early centuries had a word for launching a ship over a prostrate slave as a form of human sacrifice, but this single incident is the only evidence we have of this practice among the Lamaholot.

Around 1627 or 1628 the Dominicans sent seven missionaries to Roti and Lamalera. As Biermann comments, this is the only time when a mission on Lembata was mentioned, but there was no report of its success (Biermann 1924: 38 n. 87). In a letter of 5 Dec. 1670 written in Macao to his General Fr. Giampaollo Oliva in Rome, Fr. António Francisco, SJ, states that the King of Lamalera visited him by night soliciting him to send Jesuit missionaries. For eighty years they had invited the Dominicans in Larantuka to baptize them, always in vain. Francisco claims that he comforted the king with promises for the future, but continued that only a measure of the King of Portugal approved by the Pope could change the situation (Jacobs 1988: 236–46).

8. Weber-van Bosse writes that in 1889 the pearl fishing in the strait between Lembata and Adonara was then in the hands of a firm called Parelvisscherij Maatschappij Djoempandang, apparently based in Macassar, today's Ujungpandang (Weber-van Bosse 1904: 55).

9. The circumstances surrounding the establishment of the Jesuit mission in Larantuka after the Dutch acquired the area from the Portuguese and their later replacement by the Divine Word Society (Societas Verbi Divini) are best followed in Dietrich (1989).

Chapter 2

1 Lamalera's central legend is related to the stranger-king theme widespread in the Austronesian language world (see the references cited in John R. Bowen 1989 and R. H. Barnes n.d.). For the Gayo of Sumatra, John R. Bowen (1989: 676) writes that in the stories of origin, 'Many of [the] subsequent founding events are ascribed to an outsider who is superior to an older ruler and in some cases displaced him'. These stories are the converse of Negri Sembilan legend in which, 'the legitimate claimant to the throne [is] supplanted by a usurper (and a foreigner's puppet at that) [but] who, after a year of humiliation, wins through and gains his heritage' (P. E. de Josselin de Jong 1975: 298). There are both interesting and, in my view, historically significant parallels between the situation in Lamalera (and indeed in Larantuka and parts of Timor) and the crucially shifting position of the emerging sultans of Ternate in the fifteenth and sixteenth centuries and the lords of the land (cf. Andaya 1990: 9–10, 14).

2. There are several sources for this history. The fullest was compiled by a schoolteacher (Yosef Bura Bataona n.d.). More concise, but also more complete, is an account written out for me by Dasion [1979]. A useful, but fragmentary, version may be found in appendix I in Gregorius Keraf (1978: 227–37). Another very good source is a report written by Petronela Ema Keraf, aged 13, in Sept. 1982, for her class in the local junior high school (for a discussion of these and other examples of Lamalera representation of time and history see R. H. Barnes 1995). According to the US Navy Hydrographic Office (1962: 262),

> Pulau Lapan, in the north entrance of the strait [between Lembata and Pantar], is very low. There is a high tree on the west coast of the island, affording a conspicuous mark. A drying reef extends about $2\frac{1}{2}$ miles from the north side, with a sandbank, always above water, on the northwest edge.
>
> Pulau Batang is covered with grass and is 846 feet high. The island has the shape of a cone when seen from north to south. A narrow coastal reef extends from the northeast point of the island; elsewhere the coast is steep-to.

Horsburgh describes them thus, 'Flat Islands, about 2 or 3 miles westward of it [Pantar], are two low isles, with some straggling bushes on them; they lie North and South near each other, and seem connected by a spit of sand or rocks' (Horsburgh 1852: 720).

3. Dasion [1979] gives the name of this boat as *Bui Pukã / Keroko Pukã*. *Pukã* means the trunk of a tree. *Bui* is a form of cork tree, *Sonneratia acida*, Linn. or *Sonneratia caseolaris*, Engl. I have had no other indication that this boat bears two names. *Kebako Pukã* takes its name from a coconut palm young enough still to have the base of the branches on its trunk. Such a trunk allegedly was taken to build the first *Kebako Pukã*. This boat belonged to Lāma Nudek clan. However, when a member of this clan went down to settle in the lower village accompanying the ancestor of Bata Onã, he took his right to this boat with him. His descendants form the Ola Langu section of Bata Onã, and in this way the *Kebako Pukã* came to be associated

with this section of Bata Onã. A reference to this trip in *Kebako Pukã* is contained in the phrase *téna kamé horo, laja kamé bua*, boat carried us, sail conveyed us.

4. From Lapan Batan they went to Riang-Roma, Tobi Lã Déké-Fato Bélã Bako, to the Nor Peninsula and the shore of Ham Bobu. Riang refers to the important market-place at Wairiang on the east coast of Kédang, opposite Lapan and Batang, but I know of no place called Roma there. Gregorius Keraf (1978: 227) implies that it is the island called Romang just to the east of Wetar. If so, this would again indicate the linking of remotely situated locations and possibly a temporary move back to the east, although this interpretation might not be necessary or accurate. The various sources all indicate that the north or east coast of Kédang is to be understood by Riang-Roma.

   Bataona situates Tobi Lã Déké and Fato Bélã Bako on the south coast of Lembata. In Keraf's account (1978: 236), his interlocutor places Tobi Lã Déké and Fato Bélã Bako to the south of Kalikur (which itself is on the north coast of Kédang). The tamarind tree he says still stands, and Fato Bélã Bako people describe it as very black, straight, and smooth. *Tobi* means tamarind tree. I have no translation for *lã déké*. *Fato bélã*, means large stone, presumably a boulder. *Bako may* mean either 'to erect' or a round basket, but I am not sure which is relevant here.

   The general location of the Nor Peninsula is easily found, although none of the toponyms associated with it in these accounts appears on any maps, where it is variously identified as Wato Manu Peninsula (Beckering 1911) (this is apparently a mislocation, Wato Manu being further east), Gelu Gala Wutun (Reconnaissance Map: East Flores and Solor Islands, East Sheet, US Army Corps of Engineers, 1943), and Komi Wutun (Straits Between Flores and Lomblen, London, Admiralty, 1962). Ham Bobu is a marketing location just beyond this point to the west in a sheltered part of the Wai Teba bay on the south coast (identified on Beckering's map and on the Reconnaissance Map of 1943 as Itambubu).

5. According to Petrus Hidang Belikololong, this bench was a buffalo in the form of gold with a place to sit (in Indonesian, 'karbau bentuk emas dengan tempat duduk'). *Bělaung* is usually an earring, but it has been translated variously as silver (Vatter 1932: 51), bronze (Gregorius Keraf 1978: 237), and gold (Müller 1857: 310). Petrus Hidang specified gold, as opposed to Keraf's bronze.

6. The currents at Ata Déi continue to be a danger to overloaded boats. In recent years both the *Demo Sapã* and *Léla Sapã* have sunk there for this reason.

7. Two people have told me that the Standing Person is rather Somi Bola Deran. Ata Déi (standing person) is clearly located on maps as a standing rock at the edge of the southern coast of the Lerek Peninsula.

8. The rajadom of Labala also has the tradition of coming from Lapan Batan (which in the Labala version was connected to Lembata until it was partly destroyed). The mountain people then fled overland to the beach at Wato Téna, where they then went into the mountains. The coastal people fled by boat to Luki Point, where their boats turned to stone. Wato Téna are some rocks just offshore to the west of Luki. The name means 'boat stones', althouth they do not much look like boats (*Wato/Fato*, stone, *Téna*, boat). They built the village Lewo Raja, which they had to flee because of a war with Nualela. The walls of this village were still visible in 1910. Warfare between Nualela and Labala used to break out from time to time whenever there was a drought. The blood of the fallen was needed to asperse the sacred stones, *nuba nara*, in order to bring rain (Beckering 1911: 187–8; 1921: 136).

9. Keraf describes Lewohajo as lying on a high slope above Labala, with room for around two houses. Bataona places it above Labala near the crossroads of the paths to the villages Waiwejak and Atawolo.

10. Doni market (Wulan Doni) is adjacent to Nualela on the west side of Labala Bay, and the two are combined in formal speech as Doni Nusa Léla. Nusa Léla, by the way, means the ancient island.

11. Petrus Bau Dasion renders this clan name as Lamaau, but everyone else has it as Lāma Mau. Lāma Mau was the clan of the lords of the land of the upper village of Lamalera (*Téti Lefo*, 'up at the village'). The clan has died out and this function has passed on to Tufa Onā clan.

12. Gési Raja was the lord of the land of the lower site of Lamalera, where there was a structure of layered stone which served as a place for the elders to sit and was called Bata Bala Mai.

13. *Baka Ténā*, which has long been disused (although rebuilt again and in use by 1994), belongs to Tufa Onā clan. I have been told that its former name was actually 'Baka Walang'. In this respect, it is interesting that the clan Lewo Hajon of Pamakayu, Solor, relates that when in Kěroko Pukan, they lived on an island named Nusa Toné Tobo Baka Walang Pai (the Island where the coral reef sits Baka Walang comes). *Baka Walang* is said to be a morass (Arndt 1940: 216). *Baka* is a wild banana.

14. This tradition contrasts with the practice in Termanu, Roti, where the youngest son inherits his father's house, the oldest has the right to replace his father in the ceremonies of former affines, while in the succession to political office all sons are considered equal (Fox 1971: 53).

15. What this story does not explicitly state is that at some point in their travels the ancestors acquired a new language, form of social structure, and local culture, that in Lamalera the population eventually grew as more clans came in or split off, and that the fleet expanded over the centuries. It also fails to mention that another industry which may have been introduced by the refugees from Lapan Batan is weaving and dyeing of cloth, although when Vatter was in Lamalera, he was told that it was groups of Lapan Batan origin who introduced cloth making (Vatter 1932: 205).

Chapter 3

1. Tana ʿAi social structure has recently been described (Lewis 1988), but no studies have yet been made among the matrilineal Lamaholot, so that we do not know how much they may resemble or diverge from Tana ʿAi.

2. Vatter (1932: 205) renders this word as *huku*, but I have never come across any confirmation of this pronunciation. Gregorius Keraf (1978: 31, 242, 256, 258–9) consistently writes *suku*.

3. For a photograph of such an arrangement in Riang Kamié, East Flores, see Vatter (1932: 128, plate 15.1).

4. Dasion [1979] writes that Korohama gave Kĕlaké Muda Ama the slogan *Luki Lokā Bua Fatu*, this is 'leave Luki behind, sail stones'. Luki Point lies in the Labala bay, near the present site of Labala (i.e. Lewobala). In the language in which traditions are expressed the two locations are joined in the phrase Luki Lefo Bala. Presumably the slogan refers to the time when Korohama and his companions left Labala and moved to Nualéla before coming further west to Lamalera. The reference to sailing stones possibly refers to the tradition that the ancestors of the present inhabitants of Labala sailed to Luki, where they came ashore and their boats turned to stone (Beckering 1911: 187–8; 1921: 136). Kĕlaké is a title for an important personage.

5. According to Petrus Bau Dasion, *dasi* means the youngest child.

6. A member of Léla Onā told me that Bode had taken steps to reconcile the two clans and both clans attempted to go along, but the intention, namely peace, had not been achieved because blood had appeared. When asked to explain this comment, he said that when two persons sit across a table and try to make up a split, blood may suddenly appear on the table. This blood is from the ancestors. Members of Lefo Tukā are still afraid to enter the *lango bélā* of Léla Onā.

7. Or *nufa*, *Derris* spp. (see Gregorius Keraf 1978: 45).

8. According to Teysmann (1874: 493), *kĕfaka* (*kawakka*) is *Aegialitis annulata*. According to Leemker (1893: 439), it is a kind of tree which grows in sea water near the shore. Burkill (1935: 54) writes that *Aegialitis annulata* is found in eastern Malaysia and northern Australia. A very similar species *Aegialitis rotundifolia* occurs on muddy coasts from the Bay of Bengal to Megui in Tenasserim and in Malacca.

9. However, we have never seen this pattern, nor was the information confirmed by women who were experts on ikat patterns.

10. See Vatter (1932: 9–10) and his reference to Tuakwutu, an island or land bridge between Adonara and the north-west peninsula of Lembata which sank under the sea after Lapan and Batan.

11. There is a similar group in Bata Onã, whose ancestors were fleeing Lewotobi when they were found near Naga Wutun by the *Kebako Pukã*.

Chapter 4

1. Strictly speaking Lango Fujo is not a clan of Lamalera and does not figure in the ideal set of alliance patterns. I have arbitrarily assigned it to the same section as Lefo Léin. However, only six marriages are involved, which do not much affect the overall results.

2. Writing about the Lio of central Flores, Prior (1988: 100) comments, 'The matrilateral cross-cousin [with MBD], arranged marriage has most symbolic importance. It has also caused most trouble for the Catholic Church.' He also comments, 'The Lionese think in relationship categories rather than in biological relationships. And so most of these cross-cousin marriages were not with first cousins' (Prior 1988: 101).

3. Arndt (1940: 9, 19, 126) and Vatter (1932: 78) say that the expense of marriage exchanges and the inconvenience of a tenure of bride service (common practice in some parts of the Lamaholot region) are often avoided by the exchange of a sister for the bride. This custom is an exception to the principle of asymmetric marriages. Unfortunately, neither Vatter nor Arndt discusses the matter further. Some clarification may be derived from Kennedy (1955: 198). He writes that in Wailolong, East Flores, if a man cannot provide the needed elephant tusks, he may pay with a daughter.

   It may be any daughter, the first, the second, or later daughter. If the man has no daughters, the debt remains and must be paid someday. But, she does not become a member of her mother's sib. That is, all that happens is that when she marries, her price goes to her mother's sib.

4. A recent classification of forms of marriage among Lamaholot-speaking peoples divides marriages into *rabe daha* (they ask), following proper procedures, *rabe rewan* (they get), bride abducted from her house without following proper procedures, *rabe loa* (they release), forced marriage because the couple have already had an intimate relation, *rabe pelae* (elopement), the man carries off the woman because of opposition among their relatives in order to bring the matter to a head, *isak biat deraran wutun kaane kolene* (untranslated), marriage resulting from rape (Tukan and Tukan 1995: 37).

5. *Paduwakang*, standard trading vessels (MacKnight 1980: 119).

6. Solor was known both as a harbour for ships plying the sandalwood trade with Timor and as a source of sandalwood (Rouffaer 1923–4; Boxer 1947). Sometime in the period of 1563 to 1581 the Venetian merchant Caesar Ferdericke wrote,

   I spake with a Persian that was three yeeres in that citie of Lanchin, and he told me that it was a great citie and of great importance. The voiages of Malacca which are in the jurisdiction of the Captaine of the Castle, are these: Every yeere he sendeth a small shippe to Timor to lade white Sandals, for all the best commeth from this Island: there commeth some also from Solor, but that is not so good (Hakluyt 1904: 407).

In the second decade of the sixteenth century, Pires wrote:

At the head of the merchandise appreciated in Cochin China is sulphur, and [they would take] twenty junks of this if they would send them as many as these; and sulphur from China is greatly valued. A very great deal comes to Malacca from the islands of Solor [i.e. Flores, etc.] beyond Java . . . and from here it goes to Cochin China (Pires 1944: 115).

Later he wrote:

The island of Solor [i.e. Flores] is very large. It has a heathen king. It has many ports and many foodstuffs in great plenty. It has countless tamarinds; it has a great deal of sulphur, and it is better known for this product than for any other. They take a large quantity of foodstuffs from this island to Malacca, and they take tamarind and sulphur. There is so much sulphur that they take it as merchandise from Malacca to Cochin China, because it is the chief merchandise that goes there from Malacca (Pires 1944: 203).

Early Portuguese visitors to Solor found an Indian Muslim from Calicut manufacturing gunpowder there in 1559 (Jacobs 1974: 302). According to Hogendorp (1780: 429), the people of Solor used the saltpetre and sulphur found on the island to make gunpowder, but since they did not know how to purify it and to mix it, the powder did not have the power of European powder and invariably became damp when exposed to bad air. Saltpetre, nitrate of potash, is found in bats' guano in caves. A gunpowder factory on Solor was destroyed in 1761 and the Chinese powder-makers forced to move (van Alderwerelt 1904: 207).

Burkill (1935: vol. 1: 321–3) provides an interesting article on bezoar. The original bezoar was a concretion from the stomach of a wild goat in Persia. In South-East Asia the product is derived from various animals, including especially deer, as well as cattle, porcupines, and monkeys. The substance forms balls from the size of a pea to that of a fist. A ball is scraped and the resulting powder taken as a medicine, but it has no real therapeutic value. Bezoar fell from favour in Europe around the beginning of the eighteenth century.

7. Elephants are native to mainland South East Asia and to Sumatra. Elephants were also reported by the inhabitants of Borneo to be in the north-east, supplying tusks for trade. Crawford assumed that these elephants were descendants of domesticated animals, since elephants are not otherwise known to be native to Borneo. Domesticated animals were used elsewhere in the archipelago, such as Java, where they were not indigenous and may occasionally have supplied some ivory upon their deaths (Crawfurd 1856: 135–6; see also Noorduyn 1983: 105 n. 52, concerning wild elephants descended from tame ones on Sulu). It is possible that African ivory was shipped via India to Indonesia at various times and by agents of various nationalities. Sung dynasty writings of the twelfth and thirteenth centuries appear to mention ivory as a product of Sumatra (Wheatley 1961: 67–8). Ivory was among the trade items obtainable at Palembang on the east coast of Sumatra (Tiele and Heeres 1890: xxiv). Elephant tusks were among items of tribute from the Malay Peninsula (Pahang) arriving at the Chinese imperial court in the fourteenth and fifteenth centuries (Wheatley 1961: 90). An Arabic text by Abū Said of AD 915 mentions Arabs trading in ivory in Kalāh, identified by Tibbetts with the west coast of Malaysia (Tibbetts 1979: 33, 121). The Malays did not themselves much use ivory (Burkill 1935: 1: 907–9).

8. Vergouwen (1964: 294–5) noted that in the pre-colonial Toba Batak economy in the highlands of Sumatra, 'In the main, money had other functions and served other purposes than just as a medium with which to buy goods'. Specie was minted in the outside world and 'was thus an imported valuable' (Sherman 1990: 46).

9. In his *Descriptive Dictionary of the Indian Islands*, John Crawfurd (1856: 433) makes plain by implication that he is the author of the contribution on Timor, Solor, etc., in Moor's Notices of the Indian Archipelago. There he refers in a description of Timor to 'the well-informed but anonymous author of an account of the islands contained in a compilation called Moor's

Indian Archipelago, being a collection of articles from the first newspaper published in Singapore, a considerable number of which were contributed by myself'.

Earl (1853: 180), however, surmised that the author was the former Assistant-Resident of Timor, E. Francis. 'I have been unable to discover who was the author of this essay, which occupies seven closely-printed quarto pages; but I suspect it must have been Mr. Francis, a native of Madras, who entered the service of the Dutch Government on the restoration of Java, and was at one time Assistant-Resident of Coepang. I have never had occasion to refer to the essay without experiencing a feeling of admiration at the extent, as well as accuracy, of the information which is given in so small a space.'

10. Representatives of the bank come around to the village, and he can put money into his account or take it out in Lamalera.

11. Munro wrote, with what justice I cannot fully judge, that while a woman was an object of great importance before her marriage, once married she was regarded as a kind of slave, who had to do all the work both in the fields and in the house (Munro 1915: 16). No doubt anecdotal evidence might have been available to support this interpretation, but I have never encountered any in Lamalera and much against it.

12. I have never been able to trace the origin or meaning of *kesebõ*. However, Beckering (1911: 193, 197) encountered its use in south Lembata in determining the value of trade objects. In 1910 it was equivalent to approximately five guilders.

13. Among the Toba Batak of Sumatra, who coincidentally have a form of social organization directly comparable to that of the Lamaholot peoples, unhusked (or husked) rice also served and serves as the primary standard of value and as a common means of payment in both ceremonial and secular exchanges (Sherman 1990: 45–7).

14. Beckering (1911: 198) commented that as soon as a couple has decided to marry, the parents of the youth go to those of the maiden to establish the amount of bridewealth required. Marriage took place as soon as it was paid. In some parts of Lembata, it might occur that the youth's parents were not wealthy enough to make an immediate payment, but often the marriage would nevertheless take place. In some places, however, such as Lamalera, the youth would remain in the house of the bride's parents until the bridewealth was paid.

15. I have no direct translation of this word. In most cases in Lamaholot, a word beginning with *sen* relates to a root beginning with *s*. The semantic relationship between the two forms can be various, unemphasized/emphasized, noun/verb, adjective/verb, and so on. I have no record of a *suba*. However, Arndt (1937) indicates that at least one such word, *senuré*, 'distaff' or 'spindle', derives from a word, *turé*, 'to spin', beginning with *t*. Possibly *senubang* relates to *tuba*, 'to support'. See *hũba*, 'to close up, to cork, plug (of two parts, one of which goes in the other)' (Gregorius Keraf 1978: 192).

Chapter 5

1. An earthquake is *tana gerédo*. *Gerédo* comes from *rédong*, 'to stir', 'to shake'.

2. According to Arndt (1951: 34), in East Flores a misfortune at sea, such as a boat turning over, is deemed to be caused by a Hari Botan, a sea spirit.

3. According to Leemker (1893: 428), erysipelas is called in Lamaholot *bĕlarã kalipĩn baa*, i.e. sickness of swollen cheeks, which is indeed the form it took in the case mentioned here. Sometimes it affects the private parts. The outer symptom is a localized painful and bright red inflammation of the skin. The disease, which is encouraged by poor sanitation and used to be familiar in Europe, is common in Lamalera, striking young children, adults, and very old people too.

Chapter 6

1. This building was damaged in a typhoon in 1931. It was replaced the following year by a stronger building which stood until 1975, the year in which the much larger church in present

use was consecrated (Beding 1986a: 42–3). The new church lies inland from the site of the older one. Interestingly, while the old church was oriented on the east/west axis, with the entrance to the east and the altar to the west (perhaps appropriately since this is the direction of the Christian homeland and of the local source of Christian influence in Larantuka, Flores), today's church is situated on the seaward/landward axis with the altar physically located toward the interior, coincidentally the orientation expectable in Lamaholot tradition.

2. *Pī* also occurs as *pīn*, *mīn*, and *pemīn* in East Flores dialect (Arndt 1937: 34).

Chapter 7

1. Writing principally about Sumba but with similar implications elsewhere, the Resident of Timor, P. F. J. Karthaus, complained about the effects of imported thread and dyes on the local weaving industries in 1931.

> Imported thread, often of the most vivid and garish colours, strongly and unfavourably contrasting with the softer self-prepared dyes, is applied hand over fist, very much to the detriment of the woven product.
>
> The originally typically attractive colour combinations characteristic of the fabric are in danger of disappearing.
>
> Besides imported yarn does damage to the quality of the heavy cloths woven from native cotton. Imported dyes do not give the pleasing effect of the native dyes.
>
> Through using self-prepared dyes the cloths exhibit a much to be appreciated colour combination. One colour thereby flows into another strikingly well, whereas with the use of imported dyes one gets as a rule sharply bordered figures on the cloth (Sumba) (Karthaus 1931: 37).

2. See Fox (1979c: 43, 48) where he discusses the use of either black or white bands in men's cloths in Roti and Timor as a mark of ethnic identity and the right to wear red decorations as a prerogative of certain ritually powerful clans on Ndao. Freijss (1860: 526) wrote that in Ende women wove with reddish brown thread, but elsewhere on Flores with blue. See also Maxwell (1985: 148–53) for a survey of the distribution of blue and of red cloths in the islands.

3. Konga on the east coast of Flores, a village whose ancestors came to the region from Macassar, formerly subsisted exclusively from making salt, firing pots, and fishing, which goods they exchanged with inland people for rice, maize, and other products (Kleian 1891: 499). The villagers of Wureh, Adonara, like those of Konga, are descendants of refugees from Macassar and before that of Malacca, which they were forced to leave when it fell to the Dutch (Boxer 1947: 7). Stefan Dietrich tells me that the head of one of Wureh's seven divisions related that their tradition is that they were granted the right to settle on the coast by the lord of the land who lived in the interior. Part of the arrangement was that they were to calcine lime and make salt to exchange in the interior for bananas and vegetables.

4. Ormeling (1956: 25) says that the dry season is the time for salt making on Timor, where it is carried out in a primitive fashion at many places along the coast. He remarks that salt was undoubtedly traded in ancient times. 'As in many other places throughout the world, salt was the means of barter of the coastal inhabitants when trading with mountain dwellers. Possibilities for salt-making are particularly favorable on the north coast with its long dry season. Old travel accounts by Roman Catholic missionaries show that this salt-making even gave rise to certain seasonal migration. Father van Swieten (1898) states that Belu women and children left the mountains in the dry season for the beaches, to lay in salt stocks for the wet period. Even today salt made on the north coast, around Atapupu and Kupang, mainly by Rotinese, finds its way to the interior' (Ormeling 1956: 116).

5. Stefan Dietrich has told me that in Larantuka, Flores, salt and peppers must be put first on the table and taken away last. To do otherwise would offend the guests.

6. Munro (1915: 10) thought it remarkable that at the beginning of the century most markets were held on the driest and least populated part of the coast. The Dutch forbade trade in kind in the coastal markets, but such trade continued to be carried out in markets in the mountains, where typically salt, dried fish, thread, and so on were exchanged for maize and coconuts. Wulan Doni was apparently unaffected by the Dutch insistence on the use of cash.

7. Scenes from this market shot in June 1987 are shown in the film, 'The Whale Hunters of Lamalera, Indonesia', Granada Television.

8. In his Malay dictionary Wilkinson gives several different pronunciations for this word, *lusin, losen, losin, longsen, longsin, dosen* (Wilkinson 1932: 1: 286, 2: 70, 71, 80). Of these *losin* comes closest to Lamalera pronunciation. Dutch *dozijn* was probably also a contributing influence on Malay.

9. From *hodi*, to receive, and *kenaing*, from *nai*, section of cloth, meaning having to do with cloth, thus 'to receive weaving and cloth making chores'.

10. Parallels with the Toba Batak of Sumatra have already been noted. As among the Toba Batak (Sherman 1990: 171–3), on Lembata rice serves as a medium of exchange, a standard of value, a unit of account, a means of payment, and, of course, is a commodity. Rice was a means of payment, medium of exchange, and rarely a measure of value in thirteenth-century Pagan; it was a means of payment for land in eighth-century Cambodia and a means of payment in early Java (Wicks 1992: 308).

11. The *duit* was so ubiquitous in the Dutch East Indies that it has become a name for money in Bahasa Indonesia and other Indonesian languages. According to Jukes, in 1843, the silver rupee contained 120 *duiten*, the copper rupee 100 *duiten*. Since silver was scarce, there was a premium on the silver rupee. The *duit* was a little copper coin, the value of which he reckoned at one-sixth of a penny sterling, the silver rupee of 120 *duiten* being valued at 1*s*. 8*d*. (one shilling eight pence, i.e. 20 (old) pennies) English. 'An English shilling, however, would only go for half a rupee, but a Spanish or Mexican dollar for 2½ rupees'. The arithmetic is somewhat complicated, because there were 12 pennies (12*d*.) in the shilling and 20 shillings in the pound sterling (i.e. 240 pennies). Since according to Jukes one penny was equal to six *duiten*, a shilling could be expected to equal seventy-two *duiten*. It was therefore attracting an unfavourable rate at half a (silver) rupee or sixty *duiten*. 'We afterward learnt that the rupee, instead of 20*d*., was not at present worth more than 15 and ½*d*. [15.5 pennies] sterling.' Later he found that in Java, in 1844, the pound sterling was worth 15.40 rupees silver. These comparisons work out as follows. In 1843 in Kupang (at 1*s*. 8*d*. per silver rupee), the pound was worth 12 silver rupee or 1,440 *duiten*. Later, at 15.5 pennies per silver rupee, the pound would have been worth 15.48 silver rupee, or 1,858 *duiten*. Finally in 1844 on Java at a rate of 15.40 rupees in the pound, the pound was worth a little less at 1,800 *duiten* (Jukes 1847: 369, 377).

12. In eighth-century Cambodia, rice fields were valued in terms of silver and double cloth. In ninth-century Nanzhao, precious valuables such as gold, silver, turquoise, cattle and sheep were evaluated in terms of lengths of silk cloth (Wicks 1992: 301, 302, 307–8). Wicks, however, says that cloth, 'did not appear as an independent standard of value in Insular societies' (Wicks 1992: 308). Reid's estimation of cloth being used as currency in eastern Indonesia as late as the eighteenth century can now be revised to take in the nineteenth century as well (Reid 1993: 95). Of related interest is an English factor whom Reid quotes as requesting in the early seventeenth century that Indian cloth be sent to the islands instead of silver reals, since the Indonesians used the coins as oraments or buried them in the ground (Reid 1993: 109).

13. Scott (1981: 24–5) comments on trade specialization in the seventeenth-century Philippines in ways similar to Lembata and notes that the, 'Cuyo Islanders wove cotton but did not grow it, and kept the inhabitants of neighboring islands in mat-weaving and salt-making subjugation.'

Chapter 8

1. The phrase is one of many examples in Austronesian languages of the use of *mata* in a compound name for the sun (cf. R. H. Barnes 1977*b*: 305). The difference in Lamaholot is that there has been a semantic shift from the sun *per se* to the season which it seems to dominate. This expression is not to be confused with *lerā mata*, the eclipse of the sun (Leemker 1893: 443). In this case *mata* is a word meaning death with a different Austronesian root. Leemker gives *kolīn*, Müller *kolhim*, as the Lamaholot for the dry season (Leemker 1893: 441; Müller 1857). Perhaps this name refers more specifically to the period when the lontar palm, *koli*, is giving abundant palm wine. Arndt (1937: 16) has *nua rerhan*, time of sun, as the name for the dry season. Lamalera's *lerā matā* is exactly paralleled by the Kédang name for the dry season *loyo matan*, where *loyo* also means sun (R. H. Barnes 1974*a*: 129).
2. Professor Gregorius Keraf once objected to my reference to the 'traditional village calendar', saying that they had no calendar until they were given the Gregorian calendar. His point I think is that the villagers lacked a formally organized calendar. Anthropology, however, commonly uses the word more loosely to refer to conventional patterns of annual time reckoning, as I do here.
3. *Nalé datā*, bad seaworms.
4. *Nalé saré*, good seaworms.
5. These priests declared that the local name for God was *Latala*, which is of course of Arabic derivation. While not doubting that the priests were speaking from experience, I must say that I have never run across the idea that Lera Wulan was subordinate to Latala, or Lahatala. Generally the two are treated as alternate names for the same thing.
6. According to Wilkinson (1932: vol. 2: 447), *serani* comes from Arabic *nasrani* and means Nazarene, i.e. Christian.
7. To demonstrate the nature of these difficulties, Arndt (1937: 90) translates *lali haka*, as a southerly direction, *héti hau*, a northerly direction. As demonstrated in Fig. 9, however, in the open sea in front of Lamalera, *lali haka* would indicate from the west toward the east and *téti hau* would indicate from the east toward the west. If, however, the reference was to passage back and forth between the upper and lower villages, the direction in terms of cardinal points would be the reverse and the proper interpretation of *téti hau* would be from above down and of *ladi haka* from below up. These last two glosses at least agree with Arndt's definitions of *hau* and *haka* (Arndt 1937: 89). Elsewhere (Arndt 1937: 106), he gives the following definitions, although he immediately warns that they are misleading, *lali*, south, *héti* (*téti*), north, *lau*, east, *raé*, west. Naïvely translated, which means inadequately at best, in Lamalera they would be west, east, south, and north, respectively. Gregorius Keraf's definitions are as follows, *lali*, west, below, *téti*, to the interior, *lau*, toward the sea, *raé*, toward the interior (Gregorius Keraf 1978: *passim*, but see 168, 205, 231, 44, 46). The only problematic definition is of *téti*, but this is taken from translations of texts and it is plain that the locations referred to are to the east. The primary meaning of *téti* is above, of *lali*, is below. For comparative consideration of problems in interpreting direction terms in Maritime South-East Asia, see R. H. Barnes (1988*b*).
8. *Āpu* is normally dew (Gregorius Keraf 1978: 37), *lolo* is above. Perhaps this phrase refers to spray blowing in the faces of the crew.

Chapter 9

1. Wintjes was a missionary in contact with Lamalera. His list of fish names was supplementary to a vocabulary he filled out using a blank list prepared for wide use by K. F. Holle (Holle 1894). Only recently have these lists been collated and published by W. A. L. Stokhof (see Stokhof 1980).

2. Gregorius Keraf says that jerking the pole when the fish nibbles the bait is called *fala*, while pulling the line up strongly once it has swallowed the bait is *kedauk*.

3. Among seaweeds are *fata biti* (crushed maize), which is dark brown, rather tough and multiple branching. Another is *faja pu* (blossom on a betel basket), which is dark brown and fleshy. *Muko lolo* (banana leaf) is bright green, flat, and transparent. *Ikã matã* (fish eye) is tear shaped with a spot in the centre and light green. *Au rabo* is like moss and is dark green. *Fafě kebingu* is a coral-like growth, which is fleshy and pale green. *Kěrogo* grows like a small cluster of mushrooms. *Aluma* is thick, fleshy, and dark green. *Lima panga* is fleshy and dark red. The seaweed should be thoroughly washed, chopped up, and then may be mixed with salt, tamarind fruit, chopped onion, chilis, and coconut gratings to make a very tasty condiment.

4. See *bělũtu*, pregnant and *lĩka*, hearth stones (Gregorius Keraf 1978: 237, 258).

5. Verheijen (1984: 51) reconstructs the Proto-Malayo-Polynesian of this plant as **tuba*. Other fish poisons, which I have not identified, are *nama fuã*, the seeds of which may be used, and *kũla*, which Gregorius Keraf (1978: 39) describes as a kind of poisonous seaweed. They pull the latter up and rub it in the tide pools.

6. *Alstonia specatbilis* (Teysmann 1874: 503) or *Alstonia scholaris* (Verheijen 1984: 45). Verheijen reconstructs the Proto-Malayo-Polynesian of *Alstonia scholaris* as **ditaq*, but has a different root, **loi*, for Proto-Florenese for *Alstonia specatabilis*.

7. *Senirã* also means the splashing of water (Oleona 1989: 55). See *senĩra*, winnow, *senirang*, related to winnowing (Gregorius Keraf 1978: 195, 205), *nira*, to fan, *dira*, to blow, to fan (Leemker 1893: 430, 449).

8. Leyn (1981: 26) mentions boats with outriggers large enough to carry ten to twelve paddlers called *berok kelaba*.

9. Nooteboom (1932: 200, 203) states that *bero* is used to indicate a type of boat on Wetar and Timor. *Sampan* is of course also widespread, but does not name a uniform type throughout the archipelago. Nooteboom's photograph 99 shows an outrigger dugout from Solor large enough to comfortably accommodate twelve men (see also Nooteboom 1932: 201–2).

10. This device is a variation of the arrangement used by boats in Lamakera, Solor, to control their steering oars. There they place a thick cross-beam, *sěpi*, across the boat in the stern. At either end of this beam stand two erect short posts, *tamui*, with narrower extensions emerging for a few inches from their tops. In the middle, a taller strong wooden cross, *madung*, stands. The rudder, in Lamakera called *uli* and larger than the steering oar of Lamalera, hangs from the wooden cross. A rope around it is tied to the *tamui*.

11. Beckering (1911: 195) commented that the people of Lamalera caught small fish in nets called *kliran*. These would have been small nets, locally woven from cotton cord. Given his spelling, however, I suspect a confusion with *kelerã*, fishing lines.

12. Beckering (1911: 195) wrote that when *béro* were used to catch fish, such as shark, the results were divided into three, of which one share went to the owner of the boat.

13. Bioluminescence may be a sheet-like diffuse glow extending over a large area of the sea surface and caused by one-celled protozoa, flickering points of light caused by minute shrimplike copepods, or glowing balls of light caused by jellyfishes. Such displays may occur at any time of year. In the Banda Sea large areas of the ocean may become luminous, looking like a snow-covered plain. 'An expanse of sea may turn milky so suddenly that it appears as if a light switch had been thrown' (US Navy Hydrographic Office 1962: 51).

14. Engbers (1906: 11) wrote that, 'In the west monsoon the breakers are so violent that it is impossible to land a boat or to put to sea. Many fishermen then leave their island even before the beginning of the bad period in order to look for better fishing water elsewhere and then stay away for some months.'

Chapter 10

1. I have been unable to discover any evidence supporting the conviction of the people of Lamalera that *pělédang* is Malay. It appears in no dictionary of Malay or Bahasa Indonesia, and in none of the vocabulary lists of eastern Indonesian Malay dialects that I have been able to consult, not even, surprisingly, Monteiro's dictionary of the Malay dialect spoken in Larantuka (Monteiro 1975; see de Clercq 1874, 1876; Donselaar 1873, 1892; van Hoëvell 1876; Voorhoeve 1983; Taylor 1983; and Steinhauer 1983). I am inclined to derive the word from Lamaholot. Wintjes (1894*b*, 1983: 276) records the phrase *tenna pledang*, i.e. *téna pělédang*, as the Lamaholot for a boat, in which *pělédang* appears to serve as an adjective. Lamaholot has a verb *lédang* which means to lean on something, to support (Arndt 1937: 7; Leemker 1893: 442), and Gregorius Keraf (1978: 260) gives a line of a song in which this verb is used to mean to sit in the boat: *bua dulo dégafunu lédã raé uring*, while sailing struggle to sit in the stern. This usage suggests interpreting *téna pělédã* as meaning a boat (type) with places for rowers to sit or support themselves while rowing, as opposed, for example, to cargo vessels which depend primarily on sails. The intention would be virtually the same as the phrase currently in use for specifying the Lamalera boat type, i.e. *téna lama faij*, boats with places for paddlers.

2. See the difficulties Malinowski has in defining the canoe owner or canoe master in the Trobriands (Malinowski 1922: 117).

3. Known as *baru* in Malay, the *fao* is called *waru* in Java, *varu* as far away as Madagascar, and *baroe* even in Tahiti. According to Burkill (1935: vol. 1: 1172–3), 'It is the fibre par excellence throughout the Pacific for all purposes'. It is commonly used to make cordage, and its water-resistant wood is often used in the Pacific and in Malaysia for making boats. Burkill describes the Malay method for preparing the fibre.

   The bark is stripped, spread out on the ground for a day or two to dry, then the fibre is separated from the useless outer layer and twisted, or plaited into a rope

   Verheijen (1984: 33) provides a useful note on the distribution of related names for this plant.

4. This statement corrects that in R. H. Barnes (1980*b*: 28) which has it that this share goes to the man who owns the house associated with the boat. I had been thrown off by the situation in respect of *kélik* (see above).

5. Family *Sphyrinidae* and *Carchardon carcharius* (Linnaeus), respectively. The white shark is *io temu io burã*, which in Lamaholot literally reads 'porpoise shark white shark' (see Appendix II).

Chapter 11

1. Leyn (1979: 20) describes *tena kora-kora* as being the type of boat used in Lamakera and Lamalera.

2. Nor does it apply to the boat type called *kalulis* on Kei Kecil which the Oxford University Expedition to Kei Kecil commissioned and filmed the construction of in 1990 (Oxford University Expedition to Kei Kecil 1994). This particular boat was internally dowelled and contained lugs on all of the planks, like the boats of Lamalera. The principal difference, however, was that the lugs were not attached to ribs. Instead a strip of palm branch was run through the holes in the lugs in a given row three times and then pulled tight and fastened.

   Leyn (1979: 30) records a mythical account of the coming of the ruling family of Lohayong, Solor, from the Moluccas. Some of the persons mentioned in this myth are known to be historical and figure prominently in Portuguese and Dutch records of the late sixteenth and early seventeenth centuries. The boat they came in was called Kalulus.

3. Coincidentally Leyn (1981: 29–32) records an account from Menanga, Solor, more mythical than legendary, concerning ritual combat and warfare between Lamakera and Lamalera, in which in the end fortune turns against Lamalera. Interestingly the grave of one of the Lamalera contingent allegedly still exists on Solor and is said to have become sacred. If people hunt in the woods near there and the animal runs past the grave, it will disappear into thin air.

4. According to Verheijen (1984: 48), the Proto-Malay root from which *kena* derives is **kenDal*. *Cordia dichotoma*, which is Verheijen's identification of **kenDal*, is used in India for boat building (Burkill 1935: vol. 1: 660; Verheijen 1984: 48). *Kena* must be distinguished from *kĕnā*, which is another favoured boat-building wood, *Pterocarpus indicus* Willd., called *angsana* or *kayu merah* in Indonesian. Verheijen derives *kĕnā*, for which he offers the Solorese version *kenaha*, from Proto-Malayo-Polynesian **naRa* (Verheijen 1984: 64). Commonly called *kusambi* in Indonesian, *Schleichera oleosa* has a strong hard wood (Burkill 1935: vol. 2: 1978). Verheijen (1984: 66) offers no Proto-Austronesian root, but suggests that forms related to *kusambi* may have resulted from a borrowing from other peoples, while he thinks that the Sika/Solor forms are of great age. He confirms that the Lamaholot name, which he has as *kabahi*, is this plant, as does van Lynden (1851a: 320). Teysmann (1874: 492) identifies *kalabai* in Alor as *Stadmannia sideroxylon*. It has given its name to a prominent town on Alor.

   Pelly (1975: 19) indicates that both *Vitex* and *Pterocarpus* are used in building Bugis boats, as is teak, *Tectona grandis*, which is unavailable for use on boats in Lamalera, except that *Kelulus* was rebuilt with commercial timbers in 1987, the first such case, and that wood was possibly teak.

5. Not mouth as I once misunderstood it (R. H. Barnes 1974b: 148).

6. This name appears to be a clear case of metathesis, as the Proto-Malayo-Polynesian root is **kabu* and the Manggarai is *kawu*, from which Lamalera *fūka* and general Lamaholot *wuka* is easily reached (Verheijen 1984: 48).

7. This technique must be very ancient, not only in South-East Asia, but elsewhere too. Casson describes the compression loop and twisting lever used not as a building device but as a structural feature in Egyptian sea-going ships as depicted in tomb murals of some time after 1579 BC. Around one end of the vessel was looped an enormous hawser, which was carried along the centre line above the deck, and looped over the ship at the other end. 'By placing a stout pole through the strands of the hawser where it passed over the deck, and twisting, one could tighten the whole harness like a tourniquet. This was the substitute for internal stiffening; twisted until it had the proper tension, the hawser kept the ends from sagging when the vessel rode heavy waves' (Casson 1971: 21; 1991: 14). Lacking a proper internal skeleton, ancient Egyptian ships were otherwise unsuited for use on the open sea.

8. Verheijen (1984: 47) gives as the Proto-Malayo-Polynesian for the various *Calamus* rattans **quay*, and notes that Lamaholot *uwa*, or *uwaj*, is a reflex of it. It is unclear to me if any of the rattans among the *Daemonorhopos* are included in the Lamaholot word.

9. According to Burkill (1935: vol. 2: 108), *aloe vera* is of African origin and has been widely spread through cultivation. The local name for this plant is *kobu éfél*, which translates literally the common Malay name *lidah buaya*, i.e. crocodile tongue.

10. This wood is often mentioned in Dutch records from the earliest times as a trade item. It is valued for construction, but also provides a red dye (Burkill 1935: vol. 1: 390–3). Verheijen has reconstructed a Proto-Malayo-Polynesian root for this word as **sepaŋ* (Verheijen 1984: 47).

11. *Grewia*, is called *kenīla* in Lamaholot. Teysmann (1874: 491) identifies it as *Grewia salutaris*. According to Verheijen (1984: 58), the Proto-Malayo-Polynesian for *Grewia* spp. and other *Tiliaceae* is **qanilaw*.

12. The gebang, variously *Corypha utan*, Lam., *Corypha elata*, Roxb., *Corypha gebanga*, Blume, is locally called *ketebu*.

13. According to Gregorius Keraf, the yard is generally made of bamboo of the type locally called *petung*, *Dendrocalamus asper*, for which Verheijen (1984: 51) has the Proto-Malayo-Polynesian root **betuŋ*. The boom is commonly made from bamboo called *au*. This plant may be *Gigantochloa scortechinii*, called *buloh aur* in Malay (Burkill 1935: vol. 1: 1069). However, as Verheijen writes (1984: 46), 'cognates of *aur* are used for different kinds of bamboo, sometimes it has a generic function'. He ascribes Proto-Malayo-Polynesian **qauR* to *Bambuseae*, without further discrimination.

14. Pelly writes that the Bugis work unit consisting of a master builder and several shipwrights and apprentices must total an uneven number, because an uneven number makes a complete unit (Pelly 1977: 90). Furthermore, a boat must be made up of an uneven number of levels (or muscles) of planks, and each of these must be made of an even number of pieces, because the sum of uneven and even numbers symbolizes harmony in the ship (Pelly 1975: 29; 1977: 97). In addition, even though provided with a piece of wood of sufficient length to make the whole keel, the master builder will still divide it into three sections for reasons that are not technical (Pelly 1975: 57).

15. Barraud says that on Tanebar-Evav, the prow of a boat is thought of as being toward above and masculine, while the stern is lower and feminine (Barraud 1979: 58).

16. Richard LeBaron Bowen was therefore wrong to write that, 'in the Indonesian islands the oculus occurs only in Hindu Bali' (Richard LeBaron Bowen 1955: 43).

17. I would like to thank P. Filomeno Abel, SJ for assistance in deciphering and translating several of these slogans, in particular, but not exclusively, those in Latin.

18. I am grateful to Mr Tetsuo Nakano, for sending me photographs of the *Holo Sapā* in 1988 and of the *Sili Ténā* in 1991, as well as the information about the slogan on the *Sili Ténā*. In response to the demand of the Raja of Adonara to know who his parents were, Paun gave the evasive answer that his mother was Dulo (to swim within the water as does a school of fish) and his father Nange (to swim on the surface), before grudgingly admitting that they were Nidi Tobin and Kifan, respectively.

Chapter 12

1. *Laba* is a chisel; *ketilo* are dowels. *Pau* means 'to feed' (see Keraf 1978: 80, 176); Leemker (1893) also gives 'to provide', 'to breed', 'to grow', and 'to tend'. There is a phrase '*pau ribu, boi ratu*', 'to feed the citizenry (*ribu–ratu*; *ribu*, thousand, *ratu*, hundred)'. *Pau* and *boi* are synonyms, although Keraf (1978: 176) says that the meaning of *boi* is not clear. The phrase has to do with providing in some public way for the people.

2. Lāma Nudek is, as Ignasius Getan Nudek has on more than one occasion pointed out to me, the clan with the traditional rights and responsibilities as master builders, although today such persons are found in several clans.

3. The *soru* is a hafted metal blade used to remove the bark of a tree before felling it.

4. He told me that he was born in 1893, thus he would have been about 27 when Bernardus Bode arrived in the village to begin intensive missionizing on the island.

5. Ritual contests involving injuries are a commonplace part of eastern Indonesian culture; see Nooteboom (1939) for Manggarai.

Chapter 13

1. Gregorius Keraf (1983) writes that these planks also provide footing for the crew when trying to pull manta ray into the boat.

2. This emphasis on odd numbers may be compared to the requirement in weaving cloth that a design be made up of an uneven number of skeins (Ruth Barnes 1989: 40).

3. A single thread, therefore, is distributed among the three bunches of thread before the

bunches are severed. That is why a rope is counted as having 99 threads, rather than, as might seem correct, 3 times 99.

4. One modernizer who was considering introducing nylon ropes in his boat told me that the advantage of nylon rope and Manila rope over locally manufactured rope is that it does not matter if the rope frays or the threads break. With their own rope, if there is an imperfection of that kind they will not get *bĕlelã*. *Bõu, mõku*, and other animals are unaffected, but *bĕlelã* they will always miss!

Chapter 14

1. Lera Fulã (Lera Wulan) is the Lamaholot name of God. I have rendered names with the *f* which is characteristic of Lamalera, rather than the normal *w* of other Lamaholot dialects. My principal source was Pamong Tomas Serani Manuk. I was accompanied to Lamamanu on this occasion by the then village head of Lamalera A, Kepala Tomas Kifan Dasion; so this information is not exclusively derived from Lamamanu.

2. At the time the mission was involved in a dispute with some of the villagers over the Catholic Junior High School and a kiosk sponsored by the Church, and several of the most prominent men in the village were currently excommunicated (Moses Beding 1982).

3. Gregorius Keraf (1983) writes that marlin, *fĕtã*, can also pull the boat rapidly, and there is also a special song used when trying to gain command of this fish: *apa dĭké e, fĕtã fara gorã! Hafiro kala ka lĕrã téna*, 'How delicious, marlin titled *fara gorã*! Allow me to harvest it in order to carry it in the boat.'

4. Fransiskus Sinu thought that they had been either four or five days at sea when I interviewed him. However, that was long after the incident and memories were faded. The sequence of events, including whether the incident with the phantom giant octopus occurred on the first as the reports have it or a subsequent night, may be taken to be uncertain.

Chapter 15

1. I have described my own single experience of being drawn into a pack of whales and boats while in a boat being pulled by an injured animal elsewhere (R. H. Barnes 1974*b*: 157).

2. They may also say *kĕloma paur lepé*, which means 'maize husk already [comes] from landward'. Professor Gregorius Keraf explained to me that *paur* derives from *pe* and *hau*, 'from the direction of the interior or land' in the following way: *pe hau (ro)* ⟹ *paur*.

3. The Japanese attacked Timor on 19 Feb. 1942.

4. In his study of whaling in the Azores, Clarke describes whalemen, alerted to the presence of whales by lookouts, running down to the boat-slip and manhandling the boats from their sheds while shouting '*Baleia, baleia!*', the meaning of which, however, is different, namely 'Whales, Whales!' (Clarke 1954: 327).

Shore whaling in the Azores was established no earlier than the 1830s by local men who had learned their whaling on ships from New England and who employed American methods, but it did not become strongly developed until the end of the nineteenth century. There is a possibility that people in the Azores may occasionally have caught whales even earlier, and it is also possible that they learned to do so from the Basques, who in the sixteenth century maintained whaling stations in Newfoundland (Clarke 1954: 287, 296; see also Tuck and Grenier 1981).

5. Rodney Needham has drawn my attention to proto-Polynesian *paLAoa, meaning 'whale', which may well be relevant (Walsh and Biggs 1966: 82).

6. In a letter of 25 June 1994, Petrus Hidang Belikolong wrote a description of these events, which I paraphrase. On 10 March the boats put to sea suddenly in response to sightings of whales (*baléo*). From Lamalera A, two boats, *Menula Belolong* and *Baka Ténã*, together har-

pooned a whale, which they killed and pulled to shore at about 4.00 p.m. From Lamalera B, there were four boats, (1) *Kebako Pukã*, (2) *Kelulus*, (3) *Kéna Pukã*, (4) *Téti Heri*. Two pairs of boats each harpooned a whale. The boats were pulled increasingly far from Lamalera by the whales, which were too wild to approach and finish off. When it was nearly evening, *Kéna Pukã* and *Téti Heri* let their whale loose. That of *Kebako Pukã* and *Kelulus* was still resisting, so these boats asked the other two boats to help, which they tried to do. The whale struck *Kéna Pukã*, breaking in a plank, but not causing much danger. When it was dark, the crew let out slack in the rope and waited until the morning. In the morning, they were even further from shore. *Kebako Pukã* advanced to harpoon the whale but the whale struck it, breaking a plank, although again there was little danger. *Kelulus* then advanced and the whale struck it, shattering planks in the bow and causing it to sink immediately. Crew members of the distressed boats called *Téti Heri*, but this boat did not want to attack because of the ferocity of the whale. *Kebako Pukã*, which was then in no great danger, approached the whale, which struck it and it immediately sank, so that there were two boats which had sunk. Everyone called, 'let the whale loose'. They cut all of the ropes and let the whale loose on Friday at midday. They tried to find a way for *Kelulus* and *Kéna Pukã* to at the same time sail and pull *Kebako Pukã*. Those in *Téti Heri* thought of their ancestors. 'Let us go ahead so that we can bring news to the village and to the boats which have turned their bows this way in order to bring provisions and water.' They let loose the rope by which they were attached to the stricken boats and went ahead. Those who remained behind later reported that during the whole of the subsequent night they were accompanied by a sea spirit. On Saturday morning, they were carried by the current to Ata Déi peninsula, east of Lamalera. Before long they were carried by the current west of Lamalera to Wai Bagan Peninsula, Solor. Saturday evening at 5.00 the villagers spotted *Téti Heri*'s sail and ordered a small boat with an outboard motor to carry provisions and water to it and to pull it to shore. *Téti Heri* brought the good news that all were well and the request that food and water be prepared for the crew of *Kéna Pukã*, *Kelulus*, and the sunken *Kebako Pukã*. That night the crew of these boats saw the lamps on Pulau Semau, a small island at the entrance of Kupang harbour. In a state of danger and knowing that they might die of hunger and thirst, they repented and prayed for help. They stripped their shirts from their bodies and stuck them in their mouths to suck, and they prepared ropes to tie their bodies to the boats. Although they prayed, they still hoped for rescue. At exactly 11.00 Sunday evening, they were met by a tourist ship in the sea near Sumba. Sunday morning they cut the rope and let *Kebako Pukã* float free and on Sunday evening the crew of the tourist ship cut the rope of *Kelulus*, in both cases because the boats were unseaworthy. Only *Kéna Pukã* was pulled by the ship to the harbour of Kupang. Monday morning at 11.00 they entered the harbour, where the captain delivered them to the Governor, who turned them over to the social office. Then they went by ship to Larantuka, where the Regent joined them for the trip to Lamalera. The village heads, the customary law elders, and the whole population waited at the beach to greet them with a customary law ceremony, 'That Which Has Disappeared is Found, He Who is Dead Lives'. During Thursday, Friday, Saturday, and Sunday, the village government and the customary law elders gathered and sat in the Bataona clearing [the centre of Lamalera B] and at the *Bao Langu* clearing above [in Lamalera A] searching for the fault and confessing the fault which caused the two boats to be lost. 'Why didn't ships see them? Is something wrong? Mouths shouted insults. The ships of Lamalera A were shoved out to sea. The paths were closed so that they could not travel. This is the customary law judgement imposed by the ancestors. The ancestors of the village and sacred stones (*Lefo Nubã*) took measures. You know. Confess and repent. Promise not to behave like that again.' After this customary law ceremony and confession of fault, the ship found them. Monday morning there was more customary law ritual and boats went to sea again to search, but the news soon arrived from Lewoleba that on Sunday evening the tourist ship had found them and that everyone was safe and in Kupang.

The fault in question concerned the behaviour of two young men of the upper village who on 1 March had been asked to take a pig to a festival in the moutains in Puor in conjunction with the installation of several village heads by the district officer, where they got drunk. On their way home they molested a young woman from Ongalere, causing a series of fights and several days of disruptions and bad language exchanged between members of Lamalera A and B. During this period of acrimony, persons from the lower village shoved some of the boats from the upper village into the sea and blocked the path to women from the upper village who wanted to go to the market. The loss of the two boats from the lower village, including the boat whose namesake brought the original ancestors from Lapan Batan, was ancestral punishment. The narrator of this account, of course, comes from the upper village. Apparently, the corporations owning *Kebako Pukã* and *Kelulus* placed tables in the boat sheds on which they put continuously burning candles and kept a vigil, hoping in vain to recover some parts of the boats, until the festival opening the fishing season in May, when they determined to rebuild the boats as soon as possible. Eventually, the vigil was ended in a ceremonial act in which the owners threw a plank into the sea and then said there is the boat before bringing the plank ashore. The tourist boat in question had been alerted to search for the boats by radio. As it happens, a member of its crew was married to a woman from Lamalera. Allegedly, while the tourist ship was searching for the lost boats, it located them on its radar, but a sea spirit kept causing the radar to go out. While the men were missing, masses were held for them by the Bishop in Kupang and the missionary in Lamalera. In 1995 people from Lamalera went by motor boat via Larantuka to Lobetobi to sacrifice a pig at the beach at Wai Otan to sort out one of the causes of the disaster that struck the boats pulled to Timor last year (see Chapter 16 for an explanation of Lamalera's involvement with Lobetobi).

7. Of course the *Téti Heri* did get into trouble in 1925 because it tried to carry seven. On 11 June 1987 the *Soge Ténã* harpooned a fourth ray late in the afternoon. They brought in only one wing and threw the rest away, which caused the crews of the other boats to grumble because they were afraid that this act would spoil the luck for all the boats.

8. The record was kept, until his death, by Yosef Bura Bataona. According to figures collected by Paulus Tapoona and conveyed to me in a letter by Father Arnoldus Dupont, the village managed to capture only 2 whales and 99 large manta rays in 1983 and 7 whales and 62 large manta rays in 1984. Mr Tetsuo Nakano has provided me with a further record of the whales taken since 1985 and some additional figures for manta ray. All of this information has been incorporated in Table 15.

9. In 1994, according to Father Arnoldus Dupont, the following fourteen boats were in service: *Demo Sapã*, *Baka Ténã*, *Menula Belolong*, *Sika Ténã*, *Kopo Paker*, *Nara Ténã*, *Horo Ténã*, *Dolu Ténã*, *Soge Ténã*, *Holo Sapã*, *Sili Ténã*, *Kéna Pukã*, *Téti Heri*, and *Jafa Ténã*. Had *Kelulus* and *Kebako Pukã* not been lost at sea in March, there would have been sixteen seaworthy boats. The list is remarkable in that it includes *Baka Ténã*, which had lain neglected and unable to put to sea for over two decades. In 1995 there was a slightly different list of fourteen active boats, *Baka Ténã*, *Menula Belolong*, *Sika Ténã*, *Kopo Paker*, *Nara Ténã*, *Horo Ténã*, *Dolu Ténã*, *Soge Ténã*, *Holo Sapã*, *Sili Ténã*, *Kéna Pukã*, *Kebako Pukã*, *Téti Heri*, and *Jafa Ténã*. There were also plans to rebuild some of the other boats.

Chapter 16

1. In November, boats from Lamalera may go to Waiwerang, Adonara, and sell fish for cash.

2. On 15 Aug. 1995 I was able to visit Lewotobi, Wai Otan, and Lewourang, meeting among others the lords of the land of Lewotobi and Lewourang. We travelled there by motor boat from Rita Ebang, Solor. We found a long stretch of wide beaches below Lewotobi. We arrived at low tide when there was only one narrow access to the shallow waters in front of the beach.

When we left a little after noon at high tide, there was little problem, but we exited the same way to face the incoming ocean swells. It seems that it is actually the lord of the land of Lewourang who is responsible for Wai Otan and with whom the men of Lamalera must deal. Lamalera received permission to use the shore at Wai Otan in return for their assistance in the war against Sikka mentioned earlier in this book. Lamakera does not have this right. When the Lamalera boats come, they must first go to the lord of the land, before they may fish. The lord of the land of Lewourang asserted that he has a right to a ray if a boat gets five, rather than the seven claimed in Lamalera, but he must divide it among the other clans. When the Lamalera boats leave, the must first go to the lord of the land to say goodbye. The *reo* trees at Wai Otan were planted by people from Lamalera when they put up poles to hang their fish. Each boat has its own spot on the beach, which another boat may not use. If so many boats come that the beach at Wai Otan fills up, they may use a beach just north of it on the other side of a tongue of lava rocks. At Wai Otan there is a stone (*nuba*) near which the boats may not be placed so close as to cast a shadow on it. They know a good deal about the Lamalera regulations concerning mess groups and cutting up and sharing the animal. They recognize that Lamalera has a prohibition on serious romantic involvement with local women while fishing there, although couples from both villages have come together by meeting in other places and eventually married.

Lewotobi fishermen harpoon rays (*bĕlelã*, *bõu*, and *mõku*) and porpoise from *sampan* and *berok*, but not whales. In Lewotobi we were shown harpoons (*kaẃé*), ropes, a lance (*belada*), and gaff (*kenaté*) manufactured in the same way and in the same form as those of Lamakera and Lamalera.

Chapter 17

1. Valentyn (1721*a*: 330) mentions whale strandings in the Moluccas 1077 and 1087, and reproduces in an etching teeth from a whale stranded in Ambon (1721*b*: facing 545). In the same place he reproduces baleen plates from a whale stranded there in 1698, which his slaves procured for him.

2. De Sá (1956: 475) gives the date 1624–5, which I have referred to in various publications. However, Dietrich has drawn my attention to an important footnote in an article by Biermann (1959: 181 n. 13), the implications of which I had missed and which dates the manuscript to 1643. This date does not of course mean that whaling did not take place in Lamalera in earlier periods.

3. 'All whales yield oil. Most of the oil is true fat, namely, a glyceride of the fatty acids. This type of oil is called whale oil. The sperm whale [including pygmy sperm whale] and the bottlenose, however, yield a solid wax, called spermaceti, and a liquid wax, called "sperm oil". Both are exclusively for industrial use and are not digestible. The spermaceti wax is contained in the cavity of the huge head and in the bones. . . . Most of the whale oil or sperm oil is contained in the blubber' (Brandt 1940: 25).

4. Crawfurd (1820: vol. 3: 446) wrote that, 'Ambergris is found in several parts of the seas of the Archipelago, and constitutes an article of the return cargoes to China. As the commodity has no name but the Arabian one Anbar, we may plausibly conjecture that the Arabs first instructed the natives in the use of it as a perfume.'

He also later wrote about ambergris that, 'That substance, supposed to be a product of the sperm whale, was probably not known to the inhabitants of the Archipelago as a perfume before they were made acquainted with it by the Arabs. This is inferred from its having no native name, and its being known only by its Arabic ones of Sahabiri and Ambar. It is stated to be cast up by the sea on the shores of some of the more easterly islands of the Archipelago, the only part frequented by the sperm whale' (Crawfurd 1856: 11).

5. Again Dietrich has drawn my attention to the implications of this passage and provided a translation, the dictionaries available to me not being competent to translate *azeite de sifa*, literally 'oil of fish oil'. An *almude* is a former liquid measure equivalent to about 32 litres.

6. According to Valentyn (1726: 121) the King of Ade Manatutu was driven out by the Portuguese. In 1680, while he was in Ambon and Banda, he became a Christian and was Christened Salomon Speelman after Commissioner Speelman.

7. According to Captain Williams of the *Thames* in 1797–8,

> Larantuca Village, on the opposite shore of Flores [from Adonara], can supply two or three ships with refreshments, such as goats, hogs, fowls, fruits of various kinds, a few buffaloes, and some turtle: fresh water may also be procured from wells here, and near the mouth of the gut [from Dutch *gat*, passage between coasts, strait]. In return for these articles, the natives will receive gunpowder in small quantities, musket-balls, glass bottles, wine-glasses, white linen cloth, and all sorts of coarse cutlery. They collect here small quantities of wax, bezoar, and ambergris, which are sent in small proas to Timor and other places, and purchased by the Chinese traders (Horsburgh 1852: 717).

8. This comment was made in a personal letter of 11 Feb. 1979. Unfortunately, I have been unable to trace these references. These are very early dates indeed, but not impossible. Hembree's premature death has meant that I cannot follow up his lead with his help. The *United States*, which made 'the first American Voyage to India', reached Aceh in November 1784, where it turned back to Madras and then Philadelphia (Snyder 1938). American vessels began calling at Sydney in 1792 (Cumpston 1964: 11). From 1802 the British no longer required licences to fish or trade in the Pacific (Cumpston 1964: 16–17), and in 1802 British ships appeared in New Zealand, where they were successful (Beale 1939: 149). For a discussion of the role of American whalers in the Dutch East Indies see Smit (1989).

9. The sources for these figures are van Lynden 1849, 1850, 1851*b*, 1852; van Capellen 1854, 1855; Fraenkel 1856, 1857. Thereafter the holdings of the Arsip National break off until 1884, when there is no longer any record kept of whale ships.

10. This is the only information I have come across indicating explicitly that the French were working in the Timor Strait. French whalers were sailing the south seas in the 1830s and 1840s and some of them seem to have reached Indonesian waters (Faivre 1953: 404–7; Lacroix 1938: 104).

11. This comment is in marked contrast to Captain William Bligh's description of the hospitality he and his men received from the dying Governor William Adrian van Este when they completed their long voyage in an open boat in June 1789 at Kupang, Timor, following the mutiny on the *Bounty*. Van Este's second in command and son-in-law, Timotheus Wanjon, even advanced Bligh the money he needed to buy a new ship (Bligh 1790: 80–2, 86). Bligh's was the first of four distressed English groups to put into Kupang between 1789 and 1792. The second was an open boat of people escaping from the prison colony at Botany Bay which crossed more than a thousand miles of ocean. They presented themselves as the shipwrecked crew of an English ship and were given financial assistance by the governor, until one of them revealed the truth. The Dutch then arrested the lot. The third was a Captain Edward Edwards who lost his ship the *Pandora*. They found the crew from Botany Bay on their arrival, and after similar assistance of the governor took them prisoner. Finally on 29 Jan. 1792 an expedition in the *Panther* and *Endeavour*, who had been attacked in New Guinea and suffered loss of life, reached Kupang, where they remained until 25 March. Amasa Delano, an American who wrote the account of this trip, testified that, 'When we landed at Timor we found the same generous hospitality, which lieutenant Bligh and captain Edwards did'. Edwards had left just before they arrived. Delano further commented, 'I cannot close my account of the hospitality of Timor, without observing, that Governor Vanjon was as attentive to us in his private and public character, and appeared to make our interest and wants his own' (Delano 1817: 103–4, 106, 109–10).

Of course between these testimonials and Wilson's comments there intervened the Napoleonic wars and the British occupations of the Dutch possessions in the Indies, including Kupang. In 1800 the British invaded Kupang, but were forced to withdraw by night, after having blown up the fort and leaving the town in ruins. They retook Kupang in 1811 and held it until they returned it to the Dutch in 1814 (Baudin 1974: 255; Rienzi 1836–7: 1: 209). Fox (1981: 376; see also Koloniaal Verslag 1850: 38) dates the British plundering of Kupang to 1797, a period when, as a consequence of the French overrunning Holland and the consequent exile of William V to England, the English were taking over the Cape of Good Hope, Ceylon, the west coast of Sumatra, and Malacca (Hall 1966: 319). According to Flinders (1814: 255), writing in April 1803, 'During the war which terminated in 1801, the communication with Batavia was interrupted, and the town taken by the English forces, an insurrection was raised by the half-caste people, and some of the troops left as a garrison were massacred, and the rest abandoned the island.' In 1800 the British failed in an attempt to take Batavia. Eventually, under Thomas Stamford Raffles, the British invaded Java in 1811, and the surrender on 17 Sept. included Timor (Hall 1966: 444, 451). According to Ormeling (1956: 1), the British occupation of Kupang (by his dating 1812–15) was shorter than of Java (1811–16). In 1814 the British largely destroyed the archive at Kupang by using it to make cartridges for an expedition to Amanuban, Timor (Heijmering 1847: 58).

12. The water was brought to the beach from inland by means of a pipe (Jukes 1847: 377). According to Horsburgh (1852: 725), 'By application to the governor, a ship may get every assistance here, and refreshments of fruit, vegetables, buffaloes, hogs, and poultry. Boats go into the river, and fill their casks above the bridge, where the water is always good, but it is sometimes brackish below it.'

13. Janet West has pointed out to me that the log, now in the Kendall Whaling Museum, Sharon, Massachusetts, of the *Adventure* under Captain J. Davis during a whaling voyage of 1844–7 records that they shipped a native of Timor on 7 June 1846 at Batugade, Timor, but that he left the ship again at Coffin's Bay, Timor, on 28 Aug. 1846.

14. Pelliot (1959: 161) identifies the 'tunny' as bonito, but denies that the whale being caught could be sperm whale, since sperm whale do not eat such fish.

15. There is no known early contact between Japan and Lembata of a kind that would be relevant to influences on whaling. When the Portuguese admiral Agostinho Lobato led an unsuccessful assault on the Dutch in the fort at Lohayong, Solor, in 1619, he had some Japanese troops with him, at the hands of one of whom he died in the course of an argument. This is the earliest, and until recently the only, evidence of individual Japanese being present in the islands in earlier centuries (Faria y Sousa 1675: 338–9; Rouffaer 1923–4: 215). The Portuguese found Japanese ships trading at Malacca when they reached there, and the Spanish also found that Japanese ships visited Manila, Jacatra (today's Jakarta), and Bantam before the Spanish conquest of the Philippines. Japanese did migrate and settle in various parts of the archipelago, and Europeans employed them as soldiers (Crawfurd 1856: 164). According to Reid (1993: 18), from about 1580 there was a brief period in which the Japanese carried on an intensive trade with South-East Asia. Between 1604 and 1635 at least 299 Japanese vessels sailed to South East Asian ports, but from 1635 Japanese were prohibited from travelling abroad on pain of death.

To my great surprise, Hens (1916: 56) said that there were some Japanese traders at Waiwerang, Adonara, as well as at Reo and Ruteng, Flores, early in the twentieth century.

Appendix II

1. There is an acknowledged unresolved problem in the identification of both *io balu* and *io sajang* as the tiger shark. Perhaps *io sajang* is the dangerous whaler shark, *Eulamia macrura*, or some similar shark.

Appendix IV

1. According to Verheijen (1984: 76 n. 76b), *kastela* applies to several very different species of plant in different Indonesian languages, of which *Ipomoea batatas* is one. It comes from Castilla, i.e. Spain.

REFERENCES

Films

BLAKE, JOHN, DAVID WASON, and R. H. BARNES 1988. *The Whale Hunters of Lamalera, Indonesia.* (John Blake, producer, David Wason, researcher, R. H. Barnes, anthropologist) Disappearing World. London and Manchester: Granada Television [first broadcast at 9:00 p.m. on 13 July 1988 on ITV Channel 3, Great Britain].

MATTHEY, HEINZ VON 1992. *Walfänger von Lamalera: Ein Bericht aus der Sundasee von Heinz von Matthey.* (Produktion von Matthey Film GmbH) Baden-Baden, Germany: Südwestfunk [first broadcast in 1992 on SW3; includes footage from Granada Television].

NHK 1992. *Shakunetsu no Umi ni Kujira o Ou (Pursuing Whales in a Broiling Sea).* (Program No. 1 in the series, *Ningen wa Nani O Tabete Kita Ka* [What Have Humans Eaten?]) Tokyo: NHK (Nihon Hoso Kyokai [Japanese Broadcasting Association]) [first broadcast at 9.00 p.m. on 19 Jan. 1992 on NHK Channel One].

OXFORD UNIVERSITY EXPEDITION TO KEI KECIL 1994. Boat-building on the Kei Islands. (Oxford University Expedition to Kei Kecil, Maluku Tenggara, Indonesia 1990) Oxford: Oxford University Expedition.

VATTER, ERNST 1963a. *Ata Kiwan ('Menschen der Berge') im Solor-Alor-Archipel (Ostindonesien)—Männerarbeiten.* (D 826/1961) Göttingen: Institut für den Wissenschaftlichen Film.

—— 1963b. *Ata Kiwan ('Menschen der Berge') im Solor-Alor-Archipel (Ostindonesien) —Frauenarbeiten.* (D 827/1961) Göttingen: Institut für den Wissenschaftlichen Film.

—— 1963c. *Ata Kiwan ('Menschen der Berge') im Solor-Alor-Archipel (Ostindonesien) —Spiel und Tanz.* (D 828/1961) Göttingen: Institut für den Wissenschaftlichen Film.

Books and Articles

ABEYASEKERE, S. 1983. Slaves in Batavia: Insights from a Slave Register. *In* Anthony Reid, ed., *Slavery, Bondage & Dependency in Southeast Asia.* St Lucia: University of Queensland Press.

AERNSBERGEN, A. J. 1909. De Missie onder de Heidenen van Oost-Flores. *Berichten uit Nederlandsch Oost-Indië voor de Leden van den Sint-Claverband* 21: 4: 254–70.

ALDERWERELT, J. DE ROO VAN 1904. Aanteekeningen over Timor en Onderhoorigheden, 1668 tot en met 1809, mee eene toelichting. *Tijdschrift voor Indische Taal-, Land- en Volkenkunde* 47: 3: 195–226.

—— 1906. Historische Aanteekening over Soemba (Residentie Timor en Onderhoorigheden). *Tijdschrift van het Koninklijk Nederlandsch Aardrijkskundig Genootschap* 48: 185–316.

ALGEMEEN OVERSICHT 1848. Algemeen oversicht van de staatkundige gesteldheid van Nederlandsch-Indië over 1839–1848. [Arsip Nasional, Jakarta, Indonesia, unpublished.]

ALMEIDA, ANTONIO DE 1945. Carne de Mamiferos Aquaticos-Tabu Alimentar dos Nativos das Colonias Portuguesas. *Boletim Geral das Colonias* 21: 48–58.

AMANUE, FRANS 1989. Rera Wulan, Wujud Tertinggi Masyarakat Lamaholot: Rera Wulan Sebagai Term Simbolik. *Buletin Candraditya* 1: 2: 43–60 [extract from Frans Amanue 1983. Rera Wulan, The Supreme Being of Lamaholot People: Its Concept and Comprehension as Gleaned from the Religious Thought and Practices of the People. (MA thesis, University of San Carlos) Cebu City, Philippines, pp. 97–116 (unpublished)].

ANDAYA, LEONARD Y. 1981. *The Heritage of Arung Palakka: A History of South Sulawesi (Celebes) in the Seventeenth Century.* (Verhandelingen van het Koninklijk Instituut voor Taal-, Land- en Volkenkunde 91) The Hague: Nijhoff.

—— 1990. *The Structure of Anthority in North Maluku in the Sixteenth Century.* (Comparative Austronesian Project Working Paper, No. 4) Canberra, Australia: Department of Anthropology, Research School of Pacific Studies, Australian National University.

—— 1993. *The World of Maluku: Eastern Indonesia in the Early Modern Period.* Honolulu: University of Hawaii Press.

ANDERSON, R. C. 1956. 'Oculi' in European Craft. *Mariner's Mirror* 42: 260.

ANDERSON, REMOLA U. 1955. 'Oculi' in European Craft. *Mariner's Mirror* 41: 80.

ANONYMOUS 1827a. Iets over de Walvisch-Vangst in de Zuid-Zee en den Indischen Oceaan. *De Nederlandsche Hermes, Tijdschrift voor Koophandel, Zeevaart en Nijverheid* 2: 1: 44–59.

—— 1827b. Iets over de Groenlandsche en Straat Davidsche Walvisch-Vangst. *De Nederlandsche Hermes, Tijdschrift voor Koophandel, Zeevaart en Nijverheid* 2: 2: 3–54.

—— 1829. Iets over de Walvisch-Vangst in de Zuid-Zee en den Indischen Oceaan. *De Nederlandsche Hermes, Tijdschrift voor Koophandel, Zeevaart en Nijverheid* 4: 1: 72–4.

ANONYMOUS 1850. The Piracy and Slave Trade of the Indian Archipelago. *Journal of the Indian Archipelago and Eastern Asia* 4: 617–28.

ANONYMOUS 1853a. Schetsen uit Nederlandsch-Indië. *Vaderlandsche Letteroefeningen of Tijdschrift van Kunsten en Wetenschappen*, Tweede Stuk voor 1853: 377–89, 465–76; 608–21.

ANONYMOUS 1853b. De militaire bezetting van Timor in 1757: uittreksel uit het algement verslag der Residentie Timor over 1851. *Tijdschrift voor Indische Taal-, Land- en Volkenkunde* 1: 332–4.

ANONYMOUS 1858. Whaling and Whaling Grounds. *Nautical Magazine* 27: 599–606.

ANONYMOUS 1910. Walvischvangst in Nederlandsch-Indië. *Tijdschrift voor Economische Geographie* 1: 156–8.

ANONYMOUS 1944. Walvischvangst in den Indischen Archipel. *Weekblad Ping Pong* 19 Oct. 1994, 1e jaargang, No. 15 [extracted in Palm 1946].

ANONYMOUS 1956. *Fundação das Primeiras Cristanades nas Ilhas de Solor e Timor, transcrito do Códice 465, existent no Fundo Geral da Biblioteca Nacional de Lisboa*, Artur Basílio de Sá, ed. (Documentação para a História das Missões do Padroado Português do Oriente, Insulínda, vol. 4) Lisbon: Agência Geral do Ultramar.

ANONYMOUS 1963. In Memoriam P. Paul Arndt, S.V.D. *Annali Del Pontificio Museo Missionario Etnologico già Lateranensi* 27: 190–2.

ANONYMOUS 1978–9. *Adat dan Upacara Perkawinan Daerah Nusa Tenggara Timur.* Kupang, Timor: Departemen Pendidikan dan Kebudayaan Pusat Penelitian dan Pencatatan Kebudayaan Daerah.

ANONYMOUS 1979–80. *Cerita Rakyat (Mite dan Legende) Daerah Nusa Tenggara Timur.* Kupang, Timor: Proyek Inventarisasi Dan Dokumentasi Kebudayaan Daerah Pusat Penelitian Sejarah Dan Kebudayaan.

ANONYMOUS 1983. *Masalah-Masalah Hukum Perdata Adat Di Kecamatan Larantuka dan Kecamatan Wulanggitang Kabupaten Flores Timur Daerah Hukum Pengadilan Negeri Larantuka Wilayah Hukum Pengadilan Tinggi Kupang.* Kupang, Timor: Directorat Jenderal Pembinaan Badan Peradilan Umum Department Kehakiman.

ARNDT, PAUL 1936–7. Déva, das Höchste Wesen der Ngadha. *Anthropos* 31: 5/6: 894–909; 32: 1/2: 195–209, 3/4: 347–77.

—— 1937. *Grammatik der Solor-Sprache.* Ende, Flores: Arnoldus Drukkerij.

—— 1938. Demon und Padzi, die feindlichen Brüder des Solor-Archipels. *Anthropos* 33: 1–58.

—— 1940. *Soziale Verhältnisse auf Ost-Flores, Adonare und Solor.* (Anthropos Ethnologische Bibliothek, vol. IV, part 2) Münster i. W.: Aschendorffschen Verlagsbuchhandlung.

—— 1951. *Religion auf Ostflores, Adonare und Solor.* (Studia Instituti Anthropos, vol. 1) Wien-Mödling: St Gabriel.

B. H. and W. B. O[ORT] 1905. Onlusten op Flores in 1904 en 1905. *Indische Militair Tijdschrift* 36: 971–94, 1149–52.

BARBOSA, DUARTE 1921. *The Book of Duarte Barbosa: An Account of the Countries Bordering on the Indian Ocean and Their Inhabitants, Written by Duarte Barbosa and Completed About the Year 1518 A.D.*, vol. 2. Mansel Longworth Dames, trans. London: Hakluyt Society.

BARLOW, COLIN and RIA GONDOWARSITO 1991. Socio-Economic Features and Potentials. *In* Colin Barlow, Alex Bellis, and Kate Andrews, eds., *Nusa Tenggara Timur: The Challenges of Development.* (Political and Social Change Monograph 12) Canberra, Australia: Department of Political and Social Change, Research School of Pacific Studies, Australian National University.

BARNES, R. H. 1972. Solorese. *In* Frank M. LeBar, ed., *Ethnic Groups of Insular Southeast Asia.* New Haven: Human Relations Area Files Press.

—— 1974a. *Kédang: A Study of the Collective Thought of an Eastern Indonesian People.* Oxford: Clarendon Press.

—— 1974b. Lamalerap: A Whaling Village in Eastern Indonesia. *Indonesia* 17: 137–59.

—— 1977a. Alliance and Categories in Wailolong, East Flores. *Sociologus* 27: 2: 133–57.

—— 1977b. Mata in Austronesia. *Oceania* 47: 4: 300–19.

—— 1980a. Marriage, Exchange and the Meaning of Corporations in Eastern Indonesia. *In* J. L. Comaroff, ed., *The Meaning of Marriage Payment.* London: Academic Press.

—— 1980b. Cetaceans and Cetacean Hunting: Lamalera, Indonesia. [Report on World Wildlife Fund Project 1428. Typescript, 82 pp.]

—— 1984. Whaling off Lembata: The Effects of a Development Project on an Indonesian Community. *IWGIA Document 48.* Copenhagen: International Work Group for Indigenous Affairs.

BARNES, R. H. 1985*a*. Tanebar-Evav and Ema: Variations within the Eastern Indonesian Field of Study. *Journal of the Anthropological Society of Oxford* 16: 3: 209–24.

—— 1985*b*. Whaling Vessels of Indonesia. *In* Sean McGrail and Eric Kentley, eds., *Sewn Plank Boats: Archaeological and Ethnographic Papers Based on Those Presented to a Conference at Greenwich in November, 1984.* (National Maritime Museum, Greenwich, Archaeological Series No. 10) Oxford: BAR.

—— 1986. Educated Fishermen: Social Consequences of Development in an Indonesian Whaling Community. *Bulletin de l'École Française d'Extrême-Orient* 75: 295–314.

—— 1987. Avarice and Iniquity at the Solor Fort. *Bijdragen tot de Taal-, Land- en Volkenkunde* 143: 2/3: 208–36.

—— 1988*a*. Ethnography as a Career: Second Thoughts on Second Fieldwork in Indonesia. *JASO* 19: 3: 241–50.

—— 1988*b*. Moving and Staying Space in the Malay Archipelago. *In* Henri J. M. Claessen and David S. Moyers, eds., *Time Past, Time Present, Time Future: Perspectives on Indonesian Culture, Essays in Honour of P. E. de Josselin de Jong.* (Verhandelingen van het Koninklijk Institut voor Taal-, Land- en Volkenkunde 131) Dordrecht, Holland and Providence, USA: Foris Publications.

—— 1989. Méi Nafa: A Rite of Expiation in Lamalera, Indonesia. *In* C. Barraud and J. D. M. Platenkamp, eds., Rituals and Socio-Cosmic Order in Eastern Indonesian Societies, Part I: Nusa Tenggara Timur. *Bijdragen tot de Taal-, Land- en Volkenkunde* 145: 4: 539–47.

—— 1993*a*. Salt Production in and near the East Flores Regency, Nusa Tenggara Timur, Indonesia. *In* Pierre Le Roux and Jacques Ivanoff, eds., *Le Sel de la Vie en Asie du Sud-Est.* Bangkok, Thailand: White Lotus.

—— 1993*b*. Lamaholot. *In* Paul Hockings, ed., *Encyclopedia of World Cultures, Volume V: East and Southeast Asia.* Boston: G. K. Hall & Co.

—— 1993*c*. Construction Sacrifice, Kidnapping and Head-Hunting Rumors on Flores and Elsewhere in Indonesia. *Oceania* 64: 2: 146–58.

—— 1993*d*. Everyday Space: Some Considerations on the Representation and Use of Space in Indonesia. *In* Jürg Wassmann and Pierre Dasen, eds., *Alltagswissen: Der kognitive Ansatz im interdisziplinären Dialog.* (11. Kolloquium [1990] der Schweizerischen Akademie der Geistes- und Sozialwissenschaften) Freiburg, Switzerland: Universitätsverlag Freiburg.

—— 1995. Time and the Sense of History in an Indonesian Community. *In* Diane Owen Hughes and Thomas R. Trautmann, eds., *Time: Histories and Ethnologies.* Ann Arbor, Michigan: University of Michigan Press.

—— n.d. The Power of Strangers in Flores and Timor. (Paper given at the Colloquium on Timor held in Lisbon in December 1989).

BARNES, R. H. and RUTH BARNES 1989. Barter and Money in an Indonesian Village Economy. *Man* 24: 3: 399–418.

BARNES, RUTH 1987. Weaving and Non-Weaving among the Lamaholot. *Indonesian Circle*, No. 42: 17–31.

—— 1989. *The Ikat Textiles of Lamalera: A Study of an Eastern Indonesian Weaving Tradition.* Leiden: Brill.

—— 1991. Boats of the Ancestors: Textile Design and Wood Carving in Lamalera,

Lembata. *Orientations: The Monthly Magazine for Collectors and Connoisseurs of Asian Art* (Dec. 1991): 71–9.

—— 1993. Change and Tradition in Lamaholot Textiles: The Ernst Vatter Collection in Historical Perspective. *In* Marie-Louise Nabholz-Kartaschoff, Ruth Barnes, and David J. Stuart-Fox, eds., *Weaving Patterns of Life: Indonesian Textile Symposium 1991*. Basel, Switzerland: Museum of Ethnography.

BARRAUD, CÉCILE 1979. *Tanebar-Evav: Une Société de Maisons Tournée vers le Large.* Cambridge and Paris: Cambridge University Press and Éditions de la Maison des Sciences de l'Homme.

—— 1985. The Sailing Boat in the Kei Islands. *In* R. H. Barnes, Daniel de Coppet, and R. J. Parkin: *Contexts and Levels: Anthropological Essays on Hierarchy.* (JASO Occasional Papers, No. 4) Oxford: JASO.

BATAONA, MANS 1974. The System of Distribution of Fish Intake in the Village of Lamalera. [No publisher.]

BATAONA, YOSEF BURA n.d. *Sejarah Lamalera.* [Unpublished.]

BAUDIN, NICOLAS 1974. *The Journal of Post Captain Nicolas Baudin Commander-in-chief of the Corvettes Géographie and Naturaliste*, Christine Cornell, trans. Adelaide: Libraries Board of South Australia.

BEALE, THOMAS 1839. *The Natural History of the Sperm Whale*, 2nd edn. London: van Voorst.

BECKERING, J. D. H. 1911. Beschrijving der Eilanden Adonara en Lomblem, Behoorende tot de Solor-Groep. *Tijdschrift van het Koninklijk Nederlandsch Aardrijkskundig Genootschap*, 2nd scr. 28: 167–202.

—— 1921. De Bevolking van de Timor-groep. *In* J. C. van Eerde, ed., *De Volken van Nederlandsch Indie*, vol. 2. Amsterdam: Elsevier.

BEDING, ALEX 1986*a*. *Seratus Tahun Gereja Katolik Lembata.* Ende, Flores, Indonesia: Arnoldus.

—— 1986*b*. *Perayaan Ekaristi Syukur Peringatan Seratus Tahun Gereja Katolik di Lamalera–Lembata 22 Juni 1986.* Ende, Flores, Indonesia: Arnoldus.

BEDING, MOSES 1982. Surat terbuka untuk umat paroki Lamalera. *Dian* 9: 21: 16.

BEMMELEN, REIN W. VAN 1949. *The Geology of Indonesia. Vol. 1A, General Geology of Indonesia and Adjacent Archipelagoes.* The Hague: Government Printing Office.

—— 1954. *Mountain Building: A Study Primarily Based on Indonesia* [sic] *Region of the World's Most Active Crustal Deformations.* The Hague: Nijhoff.

BENNETT, F. D. 1840. *Narrative of a Whaling Voyage Round the Globe from the Year 1833 to 1836*, 2 vols. London: Bentley.

BIERMANN, BENNO M. 1924. Die Alte Dominikanermission auf den Solorinseln. *Zeitschrift für Missionswissenschaft* 14: 12–48; 269–73.

—— 1959. Frei Luis de Andrada und die Solormission. *Zeitschrift für Missionswissenschaft* 43: 176–87, 262–9.

BIK, J. TH. 1864. Aanteekeningen Nopens Eene Reis naar Bima, Timor, De Moluksche Eilanden, Menado en Oost-Java, Gedaan in 1821 en 1822 met den Hoogleeraar C. G. C. Reinwardt. *Tijdschrift voor Indische Taal-, Land- en Volkenkunde* 14: 125–83.

BINTANG TIMOER 1928*a*. Lamalerap. *Bintang Timoer* 3: 11 (May): 282.

—— 1928*b*. Lebala (Poelau Lomblem). *Bintang Timoer* 4: 4 (Oct.): 47.

—— 1931. Labala. *Bintang Timoer* 7: 6: 96.

BINTANG TIMOER 1932. Lamalera (Lomblen). *Bintang Timoer* 7: 12 (June): 208.
—— 1936. Watoewawer (Lomblén). *Bintang Timoer* 12: 6 (Dec.): 96.
BIRO PUSAT STATISTIK 1981a. *Penduduk Indonesia 1980 Menurut Propinsi dan Kabupaten/Kota Madya, Hasil Pencacahan Lengkap Sensus Penduduk 1980.* Jakarta, Indonesia: Biro Pusat Statistik.
—— 1981b. *Sensus Penduduk 1980: Penduduk Propinsi Nusa Tenggara Timur, Hasil Pencacahan Lengkap.* Kupang, Timor: Statistik Propinsi Nusa Tenggara Timur.
—— 1991. *Statistik Indonesia (Statistical Year Book of Indonesia) 1991.* Jakarta, Indonesia: Biro Pusat Statistik.
—— 1992. *Penduduk Nusa Tenggara Timur: Hasil Sensus Penduduk 1990, Seri S2.16.* Jakarta, Indonesia: Biro Pusat Statistik.
BLEEKER, P. 1851. Visschen van Solor. *Natuurkundig Tijdschrift voor Nederlandsch-Indië* 2: 347–8.
—— 1852. Visschen van Solor. *Natuurkundig Tijdschrift voor Nederlandsch-Indië* 3: 490–1.
—— 1853. Bijdrage tot de Kennis der Ichthyologische Fauna van Solor. *Natuurkundig Tijdschrift voor Nederlandsch-Indië* 5: 67–70.
—— 1854. *Diagramma polytaenioïdes*, eene nieuwe soort van Solor. *Natuurkundig Tijdschrift voor Nederlandsch-Indië* 6: 376–8.
—— 1877. *Atlas Ichthyologique des Indes-Orientales Néerlandes*, 8 vols. Amsterdam: Fréderic Muller.
BLIGH, WILLIAM 1790. *A Narrative of the Mutiny, on Board His Majesty's Ship* Bounty; *and the Subsequent Voyage of Part of the Crew, In the Ship's Boat, From Tofoa, one of the Friendly Islands, to Timor, a Dutch Settlement in the East Indies.* London: George Nicol.
BLOCH, MAURICE 1989. The Symbolism of Money in Imerina. *In* J. Parry and M. Bloch, eds., *Money and the Morality of Exchange.* Cambridge: Cambridge University Press.
BLUST, ROBERT 1980. Austronesian Etymologies. *Oceanic Linguistics* 19: 1/2: 1–189.
—— 1987. The Linguistic Study of Indonesia. *Archipel*, No. 34: 27–47.
BODE, BERNARDUS 1925. Lamalera's Sterved Heidendom en Groeiende Christelijkheid. *De Katholieke Missiën* 50: 6: 113–6, 7: 129–32.
BOEKE, J. H. 1953. *Economics and Economic Policies of Dual Societies—as Exemplified by Indonesia.* New York: Institute of Pacific Relations.
BOR, L. 1663. *Amboinsche Oorlogen, door Arnold de Vlaming van Oudshoorn als Superintendent, over d'Oostersche Gewesten Oorlogaftig ten Eind Gebracht.* Delft: Bon.
BOUMAN, M. A. 1916/17. Uit Flores. *Indologenblad* 8: 112–14.
—— 1943. De Aloreesche Dansplaats. *Bijdragen tot de Taal-, Land- en Volkenkunde van Nederlandsch-Indië* 102: 481–500.
BOWEN, JOHN R. 1989. Narrative Form and Political Incorporation: Changing Uses of History in Aceh, Indonesia. *Comparative Studies in Society and History* 31: 4: 671–93.
BOWEN, RICHARD LEBARON 1955. Maritime Superstitions of the Arabs. *The American Neptune: A Quarterly Journal of Maritime History* 15: 1: 5–48.
—— 1957. Origin and Diffusion of Oculi. *The American Neptune: A Quarterly Journal of Maritime History* 17: 3: 262–91.
BOXER, C. R. 1947. The Topasses of Timor. *Koninklijke Vereeniging Indisch Instituut*, Mededeling LXXIII, No. 24.
—— 1965a. *The Dutch Seaborne Empire 1600–1800.* London: Hutchinson.

—— 1965*b*. Asian Potentates and European Artillery in the 16th–18th centuries: A Footnote to Gibson-Hill. *Journal of the Malaisian Branch of the Royal Asiatic Society* 38: 2: 157–72.

—— 1969. *The Portuguese Seaborne Empire 1415–1825*. London: Hutchinson.

BRANDT, KARL 1940. *Whale Oil: An Economic Analysis*. (Fats and Oil Studies, No. 7) Stanford, California: Food Research Institute, Stanford University.

BROEZE, F. J. A. 1977. Whaling in the Southern Ocean: The Dutch Quest for Southern Whaling in the 19th century. *Economisch- en Sociaal-Historisch Jaarboek* 40: 66–112.

BROUWER, H. A. 1939. Exploration in the Lesser Sunda Islands. *Geographical Journal* 94: 1 (July): 1–10.

BROWN, JOSEPH 1813. Report of the Resident of Timor, Joseph Brown 28th May 1813. [Raffles Collection, India Office Library, unpublished.]

BRUMUND, J. F. G. 1853. *Indiana: Verzameling van Stukken van onderscheiden Aard, over Landen, Volken, Oudheden en Geschiedenis van den Indischen Archipel*. Amsterdam: van Kampen.

BRY, JOHAN DIETERICH DE and JOHAN ISRAEL DE BRY 1600. *Der Orientalischen Indien, Vierder Theil*. Frankfurt a. M.: Richter.

BULLARD, FRED M. 1984. *Volcanoes of the Earth*, 2nd rev. edn. Austin, Texas: University of Texas Press.

BULMER, RALPH 1967. Why is the Cassowary not a Bird? A Problem of Zoological Taxonomy among the Karam of the New Guinea Highlands. *Man* 2: 1: 5–25.

BURGER, D. H. 1975. *Sociologisch Economische Geschiedenis van Indonesia*, vol. 2. The Hague: Nijhoff.

BURKILL, I. H. 1935. *A Dictionary of the Economic Products of the Malay Peninsula*, 2 vols. London: Crown Agents for the Colonies.

CÁCEGAS, LUÍS and LUÍS DE SOUSA 1678. *Historia de S. Domingos*, vol. 3. Lisbon: de Vinha.

CALLBROOKE, WILLIAM 4 May 1812. Sketches Relating to the Range of Islands Connected with the East Coast of Java. [Unpublised. Mackenzie Private Collection, vol. 82, No. 14. India Office Library, London.]

CAPELLEN, JHR. T. VAN 1854. Algemeen verslag der residentie Timor en Onderhoorigheden over het jaar 1854. [Arsip Nasional, Jakarta, Indonesia, unpublished.]

—— 1855. Algemeen verslag der residentie Timor en Onderhoorigheden over het jaar 1855. [Arsip Nasional, Jakarta, Indonesia, unpublished.]

CARCASSON, R. H. 1977. *A Field Guide to the Coral Reef Fishes of the Indian and West Pacific Oceans*. London: Collins.

CASPERSZ, J. A. 1870. Politiek Verslag der Residentie Timor over 1870. [Arsip Nasional, Jakarta, Indonesia, unpublished.]

CASSON, LIONEL 1971. *Ships and Seamanship in the Ancient World*. Princeton, New Jersey: Princeton University Press.

—— 1991. *The Ancient Mariners: Seafarers and Fighters of the Mediterranean in Ancient Times*, 2nd edn. Princeton, New Jersey: Princeton University Press.

CASTRO, AFFONSO DE 1862. Résumé historique de l'établissement Portugais à Timor, des usages et coutumes de ses habitants. *Tijdschrift voor Indische Taal-, Land- en Volkenkunde* 11: 465–506.

CHIJS, J. A. VAN DER 1879. Bijdrage tot de geschiedenis van het inlandsch onderwijs in

Nederlandsch-Indië: Het inlandsch onderwijs in de Residentie Timor in 1871. *Tijdschrift voor Indische Taal-, Land- en Volkenkunde* 25: 1–51.

—— ed., 1891. *Dagh-Register gehouden int Casteel Batavia vant passerende daer ter plaetse als over geheel Nederlandts-India Anno 1663*. The Hague: Nijhoff.

—— ed., 1892. *Nederlandsch-Indisch Plakaatboek 1602–1811, tiende deel (1776–1797)*. Batavia: Landsdrukkerij; The Hague: Nijhoff.

—— ed., 1903. *Dagh-Register gehouden int Casteel Batavia vant passerende daer ter plaetse als over geheel Nederlandts-India. Anno 1675*. The Hague: Nijhoff.

CLARKE, ROBERT 1954. Open Boat Whaling in the Azores: The History and Present Methods of a Relic Industry. *Discovery Reports* 26 (Feb.): 281–354.

CLERCQ, F. S. A. DE 1874. Het Maleisch van Timor. *Bijdragen tot de Taal-, Land- en Volkenkunde* 21: 283–90.

—— 1876. *Het Maleisch der Molukken: Lijst der meest voorkomende vreemde en van het gewone Maleisch verschillende woorden, zooals die gebruikt worden in de residentie Manado, Ternate, Ambon met Banda en Timor Koepang, benevens eenige proeven van aldaar verwaardigde pantoens, prozastukken en gedichten*. Batavia: W. Bruining.

—— 1890. *Bijdragen tot de Kennis der Residentie Ternate*. Leiden: Brill.

COLEMAN, NEVILLE 1991. *Encyclopedia of Marine Animals*. London: Blandford.

COLENBRANDER, H. T., ed., 1920. *Jan Pietersz. Coen: Bescheiden omtrent zijn Bedrijf in Indië, Tweede Deel*. The Hague: Nijhoff.

—— ed., 1923. *Jan Pietersz. Coen: Bescheiden omtrent zijn Bedrilf in Indië, Vijfde Deel*. The Hague: Nijhoff.

COMPAGNO, L. J. V., D. A. EBERT, and M. J. SMALE 1989. *Guide to the Sharks and Rays of Southern Africa*. London: New Holland.

COOLHAAS, WILLEM PHILIPPUS, ed., 1964. *Generale Missiven van Gouverneurs-Generaal en Raden aan Heren XVII der Verenigde Oostindische Compagnie, vol. 2 (1639–1655)*. The Hague: Nijhoff.

—— ed., 1968. *Generale Missiven van Gouverneurs-Generaal en Raden aan Heren XVII der Vereenigde Oostindische Compagnie, vol. 3 (1655–1674)*. The Hague: Nijhoff.

—— ed., 1975. *Generale Missiven van Gouverneurs-Generaal en Raden aan Heren XVII der Verenigde Oostindische Compagnie, vol. 5 (1686–1697)*. The Hague: Nijhoff.

—— ed., 1976. *Generale Missiven van Gouverneurs-Generaal en Raden aan Heren XVII der Verenigde Oostindische Compagnie, vol. 6 (1698–1713)*. The Hague: Nijhoff.

COORENGEL, J. G. 1867. Politiek Verlag der residentie Timor over 1867. [Arsip Nasional, Jakarta, Indonesia, unpublished.]

CORNABÉ, ALEXANDER 1771. Memorie nagelaten door het afgaande opperhoofd den koopman, Alexander Cornabé aan sijnen vervanger den E. E. Heer Barend Willem Fockens onderkoopman en aankomend opperhoofd van Timor en onderhorige Eijlanden. [Arsip Nasional, Jakarta, Indonesia, unpublished.]

CORNER, LORRAINE 1991*a*. East and West Nusa Tenggara: Isolation and Poverty. *In* Hal Hill, ed., *Unity and Diversity: Regional Economic Development in Indonesia since 1970*. Singapore: Oxford University Press.

—— 1991*b*. Health, Education and Social Services in NTT: Social Development in a Poor Province. *In* Colin Barlow, Alex Bellis, and Kate Andrews, eds., *Nusa Tenggara Timur: The Challenges of Development*. (Political and Social Change Monograph 12) Canberra, Australia: Department of Political and Social Change, Research School of Pacific Studies, Australian National University.

CORTESÃO, ARMANDO 1944. Introduction. *In The Suma Oriental of Tome Pires*, 2 vols., Armando Cortesão, ed. London: Hakluyt Society.

COUVREUR, A. J. L. 1907. Verslag van eene dienstreis benoorden Larantoeka, 18–28 April 1907; Beschrijving van het rijk Larantoeka en verslag van eene reis rond Larantoeka, 13–23 May 1907. [Algemeen Rijksarchief, The Hague, Netherlands, LeRoux Collection, No. 7, unpublished.]

CRAWFURD, JOHN 1820. *History of the Indian Archipelago*, 3 vols. Edinburgh: Constable.

—— 1856. *A Descriptive Dictionary of the Indian Islands & Adjacent Countries*. London: Bradbury and Evans.

CUMPSTON, J. S. 1964. *Shipping Arrivals and Departures, Sydney, 1788–1825*. Canberra: Roebuck.

DAKIN, W. J. 1938. *Whalemen Adventurers: The Story of Whaling in Australian Waters and Other Southern Seas Related Thereto, From the Days of Sails to Modern Times*, rev. edn. Sydney: Angus & Robertson.

DAM, PIETER VAN 1931. *Beschrijving van de Oostindische Compagnie, tweede boek*, vol. 1, F. W. Stapel, ed. The Hague: Nijhoff.

DAMPIER, WILLIAM 1906. *Dampier's Voyages*, 2 vols., John Masefield, ed. London: Richards.

DANNENFELDT, KARL H. 1982. Ambergris: The Search for its Origin. *Isis* 73: 268: 382–97.

DASION, PETRUS BAU [1979]. *Singkatan Usul Asal Dari Mojang Kami Bernama Korohama Lewohajo*. [Unpublished.]

DELANO, AMASA 1817. *Narrative of Voyages & Travels*. Boston: House.

DEMPWOLFF, OTTO 1938. *Austronesisches Wörterverzeichnis. (Vergleichende Lautlehre des Austronesischen Wortschatzes, vol. 3)*. (Beihefte zur Zeitschrift für Eingeborenen-Sprachen, No. 19) Berlin: Reimer.

DIAN 1980*a*. Lamtoro Gung Dipromosikan di NTT. *Dian* 7: 7 (24 Jan.): 15.

—— 1980*b*. Gunung Hobal Meletus dan Tanah Longsor di Pauora. *Dian* 7: 13 (24 Apr.): 8.

DIAS VIEIRA GODINHO, RAJA OESI n.d. Tjeritara pendek dari Ketoeroenan Radja di Tanah Larantoeka. *In* Couvreur 1907. Verslag van eene dienstreis benoorden Larantoeka, 18–28 April 1907; Beschrijving van het rijk Larantoeka en verslag van eene reis rond Larantoeka, 13–23 May 1907. Algemeen Rijksarchief, The Hague, Netherlands, LeRoux Collection, No. 7 [unpublished].

DIETRICH, STEFAN 1983. Flores in the Nineteenth Century: Aspects of Dutch Colonialism on a Non-Profitable Island. *Indonesian Circle*, No. 31: 39–58.

—— 1984. A Note on Galiyao and the Early History of the Solor-Alor Islands. *Bijdragen tot de Taal-, Land- en Volkenkunde* 140: 2/3: 317–34.

—— 1985. 'Religiöse' und 'säkulare' Reaktionen gegen die koloniale Verwaltung auf Flores. *In* Wolfgang Marschall, ed., *Der grosse Archipel: Schweizer ethnologische Forschung in Indonesien*. (Ethnologica Helvetica 10) Bern: Schweizer Ethnologische Gesellschaft.

—— 1989. *Kolonialismus und Mission auf Flores (ca. 1900–1942)*. Hohenschäftlarn: Renner.

—— 1992. Mission, Local Culture and the 'Catholic Ethnology' of Pater Schmidt. *JASO* 23: 2: 111–25.

DINAS PERIKANAN 1977. Laporan Tahunan 1976/77. Kupang, Timor: Dinas Perikanan Propinsi Daerah Tk. I. Nusa Tenggara Timur.

DONSELAAR, W. M. 1873. Lijstje van Rottinesche woorden in het Koepangsch Maleisch. *Tijdschrift voor Indische Taal-, Land- en Volkenkunde* 20: 357–62.

—— 1882. De Christelijke zending in de residentie Timor. *Mededeeling van wege het Nederlandsche Zendinggenootschap* 21: 269–89.

—— 1892. Woorden uit het Rottineesch, Timoreesch, Portugueesch en Hollandsch ontleend en gebruikelijk in het Maleisch te Timor Koepang. *Tijdschrift voor het Binnenlandsch Bestuur* 7: 92–101.

DORAN, E. 1981. *Wangka: Austronesian Canoe Origins*. College Station, Texas: Texas A & M Press.

DOWNS, R. E. 1955. Head-hunting in Indonesia. *Bijdragen tot de Taal-, Land- en Volkenkunde* 111: 1: 40–70.

—— 1977. Head-hunting in Indonesia. *In* P. E. de Josselin de Jong, ed., *Structural Anthropology in The Netherlands*. (Koninklijk Instituut voor Taal-, Land- en Volkenkunde, Translation Series 17) The Hague: Nijhoff.

DUMONT, LOUIS 1968. Marriage Alliance. *International Encyclopedia of the Social Sciences* 10: 19–23.

EARL, GEORGE WINDSOR 1853. *The Native Races of the Indian Archipelago: Papuans*. London: Bailliere.

EERDE, J. C. VAN 1923. Don Lorenzo II van Larantoeka. *Onze Eeuw* (Haarlem), No. 2, pp. 73–113.

—— 1929. Onpersoonlijk Ruilverkeer in den Indischen Archipel. *Feestbundel Uitgegeven door het Koninklijk Bataviaasch Genootschap van Kunsten en Wetenschappen bij Gelegenheid van zijn 150 Jarig Bestaan 1778–1928*, vol. 1. Weltevreden: Kolff.

ELLIS, RICHARD 1991. *Men and Whales*. New York: Knopf.

EL-KAZWÎNI 1868. *Zakarija ben Muhammed ben Mahmûd El-Kazwîni's Kosmographie*, Hermann Ethé, trans. Leipzig: Fues.

EMMERSON, DONALD K. 1980. *Rethinking Artisanal Fisheries Development: Western Concepts, Asian Experiences*. (World Bank Staff Working Paper, No. 423) Washington, DC: The World Bank.

ENCYCLOPÆDIA BRITANNICA 1797. Ambergrease. *Encyclopædia Britannica*, 3rd edn., vol. 1. Edinburgh: Bell and Macfarquhar.

ENGBERS, E. 1906. Walvischvangers op het eiland Lomblem. *Berichten uit Nederlandsch Oost-Indië voor de Leden van den Sint-Claverband* 18: 1: 9–13.

EYSINGA, P. P. ROORDA VAN 1841. *Handboek der Land- en Volkenkunde, Geschied-, Taal-, Aardrijks- en Stadtkunde van Nederlandsch Indië*. Amsterdan: van Bakkennes.

EZERMAN, H. E. K. 1917. Timor en onze politieke verhouding tot Portugal sedert het herstel van het Nederlandsch gezag in Oost-Indië. *Koloniaal Tijdschrift* 6: 2: 865–96, 1047–78, 1209–32.

FAIVRE, JEAN-PAUL 1953. *L'Expansion Française dans le Pacifique 1800–1842*. Paris: Nouvelles Éditions Latines.

FARIA Y SOUSA, MANUEL DE 1675. *Asia Portuguesa*, vol. iii. Lisbon: Antonio Craesbeek.

FERNANDEZ, INYO JOSEF 1977. Bahasa Lamaholot Ile Mandiri. (Tesis Sarjana, Universitas Gajah Mada) Yogyakarta, Indonesia: Universitas Gajah Mada [unpublished].

—— 1980. *Reflex Fonem-Fonem Proto Melayu-Polinesia Pada Dua Bahasa di Flores*

Timur dan Tengah. Jakarata, Indonesia: Pusat Pembinaan dan Pengembangan Bahasa, Departemen Pendidikan dan Kebudayaan.

—— 1983–4. *Relasi Historis di Bidang Fonologi Kekerabatan Bahasa-bahasa di Flores.* Jakarta, Indonesia: Pusat Pembinaan dan Pengembangan Bahasa, Departemen Pendidikan dan Kebudayaan.

—— 1988. Rekonstruksi Protobahasa Flores. [(Doctoral dissertation, Universitas Gajah Madah) Yogyakarta, Indonesia: Universitas Gajah Madah (unpublished).]

FIRTH, RAYMOND 1959. *Economics of the New Zealand Maori*, 2nd edn. Wellington, New Zealand.

—— 1966. *Malay Fishermen: Their Peasant Economy*, 2nd edn. London: Routledge & Kegan Paul. [Orig. pub. in 1946.]

FISCHER, H. TH. 1932. Der magische Charakter des Brautpreises. *Der Weltkreis* 3: 65–8.

FLACOURT, LE SIEUR DE 1661. *Histoire de la Grande Isle Madagascar.* Paris: Clouzier.

FLINDERS, MATTHEW 1814. *A Voyage to Terra Australis . . . 1801, 1802, and 1803*, vol. 2. London: Nicol.

FLORES TIMUR DALAM ANGKA 1994. Larantuka, Flores, Indonesia: Kantor Statistik Kab. Flores Timur, Propinisi Nusa Tenggara Timur.

FORMAN, SHEPARD 1977. East Timor: Exchange and Political Hierarchy at the Time of the European Discoveries. *In* Karl L. Hutterer, ed., *Economic Exchange and Social Interaction in Southeast Asia.* (Michigan Papers on South and Southeast Asia, No. 13) Ann Arbor, Michigan: University of Michigan.

FORSTER, HONORE, ed., 1991. *The Cruise of the 'Gipsy': The Journal of John Wilson Surgion on a Whaling Voyage to the Pacific Ocean 1839–1843.* Fairfield, Washington: Ye Galleon Press.

FORTH, GREGORY L. 1981. *Rindi: An Ethnological Study of a Traditional Domain in Eastern Sumba.* (Verhandelingen van het Koninklijk Instituut voor Taal-, Land- en Volkenkunde 93) The Hague: Nijhoff.

FOX, JAMES J. 1971. A Rotinese Dynastic Genealogy: Structure and Event. *In* T. O. Beidelman, ed., *The Translation of Culture: Essays to E. E. Evans-Pritchard.* London: Tavistock.

—— 1977. *Harvest of the Palm: Ecological Change in Eastern Indonesia.* Cambridge: Harvard University Press.

—— 1979*a*. The Ceremonial System of Savu. *In* A. L. Becher and Aram A. Yengoyan, eds., *The Imagination of Reality: Essays in Southeast Asian Coherence Systems.* Norwood, New Jersey: Ablex.

—— 1979*b*. 'Standing' in Time and Place: The Structure of Rotinese Historical Narratives. *In* Anthony Reid and David Marr, eds., *Perceptions of the Past in Southeast Asia.* (Asian Studies Association of Australia, Southeast Asian Publications Series, No. 4) Singapore: Heinemann.

—— 1979*c*. Figure Shark and Pattern Crocodile: The Foundations of the Textile Traditions of Roti and Ndao. *In* Mattiebelle Gittinger, ed., *Indonesian Textile.* (Irene Emery Roundtable on Museum Textiles 1979 Proceedings) Washington, DC: The Textile Museum.

—— 1981. Sailing to Kupang. *Hemisphere* 25: 6: 374–7.

—— 1983. 'For Good and Sufficient Reasons': An Examination of Early Dutch East Indies Company Ordinances on Slaves and Slavery. *In* Anthony Ried, ed., *Slavery, Bondage & Dependency in Southeast Asia.* St Lucia: University of Queensland Press.

Fox, James J. 1989. Category and Complement: Binary Ideologies and the Organization of Dualism in Eastern Indonesia. *In* David Maybury-Lewis and Uri Almagor, eds., *The Attraction of Opposites: Thought and Society in the Dualistic Mode*. Ann Arbor, Michigan: University of Michigan Press.

Fraassen, Ch. F. van 1976. Drie plaatsnamen uit Oost-Indonesië in de Nagara-Kertagama: Galiyao, Muar en Wwanin en de vroegere handelsgeschiedenis van de Ambonse eilanden. *Bijdragen tot de Taal-, Land- en Volkenkunde* 132: 293–305.

—— 1991. De positie van Luwu in Zuid- en Centraal-Sulawesi. *In* Harry A. Poeze and Pim Schoorl, eds., *Excursies in Celebes*. (Verhandelingen van het Koninklijk Instituut voor Taal-, Land- en Volkenkunde 147) Leiden: KITLV Press.

Fraenkel, S. G. F. 1856. Algemeen verslag der residentie Timor en Onderhoorigheden over het jaar 1856. [Arsip Nasional, Jakarta, Indonesia, unpublished.]

—— 1857. Algemeen verslag der residentie Timor en Onderhoorigheden over het jaar 1857. [Arsip Nasional, Jakarta, Indonesia, unpublished.]

Francis, E. 1838. Timor in 1831. *Tijdschrift voor Nederlandsch-Indië* 1: 1: 353–69, 374–400; 2: 24–53.

Francis, Peter 1993. *Volcanoes: A Planetary Perspective*. Oxford: Clarendon Press.

Fraser, Thomas M. 1960. *Rusembilan: A Malay Fishing Village in Southern Thailand*. Ithaca, New York: Cornell University Press.

Freijss, J. P. 1860. Kort overzigt omtrent het eiland Flores en deszelfs bewoners. *Tijdschrift voor Indische Taal-, Land- en Volkenkunde* 9: 505–30.

Freycinet, Louis Claude de Saulces de, ed., 1825. *Voyage autour du Monde, fait par ordre du roi, sur les corvettes du L. M. l'Uranie et la Physicienne, pendant les annés 1817, 1818, 1819 et 1820. Atlas Historique*. Paris: Pillet Ainé.

Fruin-Mees, W., ed. 1928. *Dagh-Register gehouden in 't Casteel Batavia, Anno 1624–1629*, vol. 1. The Hague: Nijhoff.

—— ed., 1931. *Dagh-Register gehouden int Casteel Batavia vant passerende daer ter plaetse als over geheel Nederlandts-India. Anno 1682*, vol. 2. The Hague: Nijhoff.

Garnaut, Ross and Peter McCawley 1980. Introduction. *In* R. G. Garnaut and P. T. McCawley, eds., *Indonesia: Dualism, Growth and Poverty*. Canberra: Research School of Pacific Studies, Australian National University.

Gebuis, L. 1939. Ontwikkeling van den Timor Archipel. *Koloniale Studiën* 23: 264–78.

Geertz, Hildred 1963. Indonesian Cultures and Communities. *In* Ruth T. McVey, *Indonesia*. New Haven, Connecticut: HRAF Press.

Gell, Alfred 1992. Inter-Tribal Commodity Barter and Reproductive Gift-Exchange in Old Melanesia. *In* Caroline Humphrey and Stephen Hugh-Jones, eds., *Barter, Exchange and Value: An Anthropological Approach*. Cambridge: Cambridge University Press.

Gennep, Arnold van 1908. Essai d'une théorie des langues spéciales. *Revue des études ethnographiques et sociologiques* 1: 327–32.

Geurtjens, H. 1921. *Uit een vreemde Wereld, of het Leven en Streven der Inlanders op de Kei-Eilanden*. 's-Hertogenbosch: Teulings.

Gibson-Hill, C. A. 1950. The Indonesian Trading Boats Reaching Singapore. *Journal of the Malayan Branch of the Royal Asiatic Society* 23: 108–38.

Gilliland, Frank 1955. 'Oculi'. *Mariner's Mirror* 41: 259.

Gimlette, John D. 1923. *Malay Poisons and Charm Cures*, 2nd edn. London: J. & A. Churchill.

GITTINGER, MATTIEBELLE 1979. *Splendid Symbols: Textiles and Tradition in Indonesia.* Washington, DC: The Textile Museum.

GLOVER, IAN 1979. The Late Prehistoric Period in Indonesia. *In* R. B. Smith and W. Watson, *Early South East Asia: Essays in Archaeology, History, and Historical Geography.* New York: Oxford University Press.

GODELIER, MAURICE 1977. *Perspective in Marxist Anthropology.* Cambridge: Cambridge University Press.

GONDA, J. 1948. The Javanese Vocabulary of Courtesy. *Lingua* 1: 3: 333–76.

GOUVERNEMENT VAN NEDERLANDSCH INDIË 1864–5. Contract tusschen het Gouvernement van Nederlandsch Indie en de verschillende singhadjies op de Solor-eilanden en den radja van Larantoeka (oosthoek van het eiland Floris), sorterende onder de residentie Timor. *Bijblad van de Nederlandsche Staats-Courant 1864–1865*: 184–6.

GRAHAM, PENELOPE 1985. *Issues in Social Structure in Eastern Indonesia.* [(M.Phil. thesis, University of Oxford) Oxford: University of Oxford (unpublished).]

—— 1987. East Flores Revisited: A Note on Asymmetric Alliance in Leloba and Wailolong, Indonesia. *Sociologus* 37: 1: 40–59.

—— 1991. To Follow the Blood: The Path of Life in a Domain of Eastern Flores, Indonesia. [(Ph.D. thesis, Australian National University) Canberra, Australia: Australian National University (unpublished).]

GREVE, W. 1884. Algemeen verslag der residentie Timor en Onderhoorigheden over het jaar 1884. [Arsip Nasional, Jakarta, Indonesia, unpublished.]

—— 1886. Algemeen verslag der residentie Timor en Onderhoorigheden over het jaar 1886. [Arsip Nasional, Jakarta, Indonesia, unpublished.]

—— 1887. Algemeen verslag der residentie Timor en Onderhoorigheden over het jaar 1887. [Arsip Nasional, Jakarta, Indonesia, unpublished.]

GRONOVIUS, D. VAN DEN DUNGEN 1836. Algemeen verslag der residentie Timor en Onderhoorigheden over het jaar 1836. [Arsip Nasional, Jakarta, Indonesia, unpublished.]

—— 1838. Algemeen verslag der residentie Timor en Onderhoorigheden over het jaar 1838. [Arsip Nasional, Jakarta, Indonesia, unpublished.]

—— 1839. Algemeen verslag der residentie Timor en Onderhoorigheden over het jaar 1839. [Arsip Nasional, Jakarta, Indonesia, unpublished.]

—— 1840. Algemeen verslag der residentie Timor en Onderhoorigheden over het jaar 1840. [Arsip Nasional, Jakarta, Indonesia, unpublished.]

—— 1842. Algemeen verslag der residentie Timor en Onderhoorigheden over het jaar 1842. [Arsip Nasional, Jakarta, Indonesia, unpublished.]

—— 1843. Algemeen verslag der residentie Timor en Onderhoorigheden over het jaar 1843. [Arsip Nasional, Jakarta, Indonesia, unpublished.]

—— 1845. Algemeen verslag der residentie Timor en Onderhoorigheden over het jaar 1845. [Arsip Nasional, Jakarta, Indonesia, unpublished.]

—— 1846. Algemeen verslag der residentie Timor en Onderhoorigheden over het jaar 1846. [Arsip Nasional, Jakarta, Indonesia, unpublished.]

—— 1847. Algemeen verslag der residentie Timor en Onderhoorigheden over het jaar 1847. [Arsip Nasional, Jakarta, Indonesia, unpublished.]

GROOT, J. P. CORNETS DE 1847. Notices historiques sur les pirateries commis dans l'archipel indien-oriental, seconde partie 1830–1835. *In* Ph. Fr. de Siebol and

P. Melvill de Carnbee, *Le Moniteur des Indies-Orientales et Occidentales (1846–47)*. Le Haye: Belinfante.

—— 1848. Notices historiques sur les pirateries commis dans l'archipel indien-oriental, quatrième partie 1841–1845. *In* Ph. Fr. de Siebold and P. Melvill de Carnbee, *Le Moniteur des Indies-Orientales et Occidentales (1847–48)*. Le Haye: Belinfante.

GROSS, M. GRANT 1972. *Oceanography: A View of the Earth*. Englewood Cliffs, New Jersey: Prentice-Hall.

GRZIMEK, BERNHARD 1973. *Grzimek's Animal Life Encyclopedia*, vol. 5. New York: Van Nostrand Reinhold.

HAAN, F. DE, ed., 1919. *Dagh-Register gehouden int Casteel Batavia vant passerende daer ter plaetse als over geheel Nederlandts-India. Anno 1681*. The Hague: Nijhoff.

HABIR, MANGGI 1984. A Migration Equation: The Flow of Workers from Indonesia to Malaysia—Often Clandestine—Comes in for Growing Scrutiny. *Far Eastern Economic Review* (Apr.): 166–70.

HAGENAAR, T. C. K. 1934 (mei). Beknopte gegevens betreffende het patrouille gebied van het detachement te Larantuka omvattende Larantoeka, Maoemere, Adonara, Soloren en Lomblen. [General State Archives of the Netherlands, The Hague, unpublished.]

HAGESTEIN, F. 1883. Algemeen verslag der residentie Timor en Onderhoorigheden over het jaar 1883. [Arsip Nasional, Jakarta, Indonesia, unpublished.]

HAKLUYT, RICHARD 1904. The Voyage and Travell of M. Caesar Ferdericke, Marchant of Venice, into the East Indies, and Beyond the Indies. *The Principal Navigations, Voyages, Traffiques & Discoveries of the English Nation*, vol. 5. Glasgow: Maclehose.

HALL, D. G. E. 1966. *A History of South-East Asia*, 2nd edn. London: MacMillan.

HANGELBROEK, J. J. 1977. Controleur in Larantoeka 1937–1938. *In* S. L. van der Wal, ed., *Besturen Overzee: Herinneringen van oud-ambtenaren bij het binnenlands bestuur in Nederlandsch-Indië*. Franeker: Wever.

HARTMANN, MAX 1935. De werkende vulkanen van het eiland Lomblèn (Solor Archipel). *Tijdschrift van het Koninklijk Nederlandsch Aardrijkskundig Genootschap* 52: 817–36.

HEERES, J. E. DE, ed., 1896. *Dagh-Register gehouden int Casteel Batavia vant passerende daer ter plaetse als over geheel Nederlandts-India. Anno 1624–1629*. The Hague: Nijhoff.

—— 1907. Corpus Diplomaticum Neerlando-Indicum, Eerste Deel (1596–1650). *Bijdragen tot de Taal-, Land- en Volkenkunde van Nederlands-Indië* 57: i–xxxii, 1–586.

HEIJMERING, G. 1847. Bijdragen tot de Geschiedenis van het eiland Timor. *Tijdschrift voor Neêrland's Indië* 9: 3: 1–62, 121–232, 243–4.

HELLMUTH, J. C. J. 1853. Geneeskundig-Topographische Schets van Lawaaijang. *Tijdschrift der Vereeniging tot Bevordering der Geneeskundige Wetenschappen in Nerderlandsche Indië* 2: 217–43.

HEMBREE, E. D. 1980. Biological Aspects of the Cetacean Fishery at Lamalera, Lembata. World Wildlife Fund Project 1428.

HENS, A. M. 1916. *Memorie van Overgave der Afdeeling Flores*, vol. 2. (Collectie Le Roux, 4) The Hague: Algemeen Rijksarchief [unpublished manuscript].

HERTZ, ROBERT 1960. The Collective Representation of Death. *In* Robert Hertz, *Death & the Right Hand*, Rodney Needham, trans. Glencoe, Illinois: The Free Press.

HESLINGA, T. 1891. Larantoeka op het eiland Flores: Ter Nagedachtenis van den Eerw. Pastoor Corn. ten Brink, Zijn werkkring op het eiland Flores. *Berichten uit Nederlandsch Oost-Indië voor de Leden van den Sint-Claverband* 3: 46–84.

HEYNEN, F. C. 1876. *Het rijk Larantoeka op het Eiland Flores in Nederlandsch Indië.* (Studiën op Godsdienstig, Wetenschappelijk en Letterkundig Gebied 8: 6) The Hague: van Gulick.

HOEBERECHTS, J. 1913. Naar Lamelara en Lewoleba. *Berichten uit Nederlandsch Oost-Indië voor de Leden van den Sint-Claverband* 25: 3: 149–63.

HOËVELL, G. W. W. C. VAN 1876. *Vocabularium van vreemde woorden, voorkomende in het Ambonsch-Maleisch, benevens korte opmerkingen over dit locaal-Maleisch en verder eenige Ambonische spreekwoorden, eigenaardige uitdrukkingen en gezegden te Ambon gebruikelijk.* Dordrecht: Blussé en van Braam.

HOEVEN, A. PRUIJS VAN DER 1867. Iets over den Bruidschat. *Tijdschrift voor Indische Taal-, Land- en Volkenkunde* 16: 277–89.

HOGENDORP, W. van 1779. Beschrijving van het Eiland Timor voorzoover het tot nog toe Bekend is. *Verhandelingen van het Bataviaasch Genootschap van Kunsten en Wetenschappen* 1: 192–214.

—— 1780. Vervolg der Beschrijving van het Eiland Timor. *Verhandelingen van het Bataviaasch Genootschap van Kunsten en Wetenschappen* 2: 405–31.

HOLLE, K. F. 1894. *Blanco woordenlijst uitgegeven op last der Regeering van Ned.-Indië ten Behoeve van Taalvorschers in den Ned.-Indischen Archipel.* Batavia: Landsdrukkerij.

HOLZINGER, ROSWITHA 1970. Die Sammlung von den Inseln Pantar und Pura im Museum für Völkerkunde zu Frankfurt am Main. *Tribus* 19: 17–45.

HORNELL, JAMES 1920a. The Outrigger Canoes of Indonesia. *Rept. No. 2, Madras Fisheries Bulletin* 12: 43–114.

—— 1920b. The Origins and Ethnological Significance of Indian Boat Designs. *Memoirs of the Asiatic Society of Bengal* 7: 3: 139–256.

—— 1923. Survivals of the Use of Oculi in Modern Boats. *Journal of the Royal Anthropological Institute of Great Britain and Ireland* 53: 2: 289–321.

—— 1934. Indonesian Influence on East African Culture. *Journal of the Royal Anthropological Institute of Great Britain and Ireland* 64: 2: 305–32.

—— 1938. Boat Oculi Survivals; Additional Records. *Journal of the Royal Anthropological Institute of Great Britain and Ireland* 68: 2: 339–48.

—— 1943. The Prow of Ships, Sanctuary of the Tutelary Deity. *Man* 43: Art. No. 103: 121–31.

—— 1946. *Water Transport: Origins and Early Evolution.* Cambridge: Cambridge University Press.

HORRIDGE, G. A. 1978. The Design of Planked Boats of the Muluccas. *Maritime Monographs and Reports, National Maritime Museum*, No. 38. Greenwhich: National Maritime Museum.

—— 1979. The Konjo Boatbuilders and the Bugis Prahus of South Sulawesi. *Maritime Monographs and Reports, National Maritime Museum*, No. 40. Greenwich: National Maritime Museum.

—— 1981. *The Prahu: Traditional Sailing Boat of Indonesia.* Kuala Lumpur: Oxford University Press.

—— 1982. The Lashed-Lug Boat of the Eastern Archipelagoes. *Maritime Monographs and Reports, National Maritime Museum*, No. 52. Greenwhich: National Maritime Museum.

—— 1986. *Sailing Craft of Indonesia*. Singapore: Oxford University Press.

HORSBURGH, JAMES 1852. *The India Directory, or, Directions for Sailing to and From the East Indies, China, Australia, and the Interjacent Ports of Africa and South America: Originally Compiled from Journals of the Honourable Company's Ships, and from Observations and Remarks, Resulting from the Experience of Twenty-One Years in the Navigation of Those Seas*, vol. 2, 6th edn. London: Wm. H. Allen.

HULLU, J. DE, ed., 1904. *Dagh-Register gehouden in 't Casteel Batavia, Anno 1656–1657*. The Hague: Nijhoff.

H[UMME], H. C. 1877. Het Islam-element in den Oost-Indischen Archipel. *Tijdschrift voor Nederlandsch-Indië*, 4th ser. 6: 81–90.

HURGRONJE, C. SNOUCK 1893. *De Atjèhers*, 2 vols. Batavia: Landsdrukkerij.

—— 1906. *The Achehnese*, A. W. S. O'Sullivan trans., 2 vols. Leiden: Brill.

JACKSON, CORDON 1978. *The British Whaling Trade*. Hamden, Connecticut: Archon Books.

JACOBS, HUBERT, ed., 1971. *A Treatise on the Moluccas (c. 1544), Probably the Preliminary Version of António Galvão's Lost História das Molucas*. Rome: Jesus Historical Institute.

—— ed., 1974. Fr. Baltasar Dias S. J. to Fr. Provincial António de Quadros S. J., Goa-Malacca, December 3, 1559. *Documenta Malucensia*, vol. 1 (1542–1577). (Monumenta Historica Societatis Iesu, vol. 109) Rome: Institutum Historicum Societatis Iesu.

—— ed., 1988. *The Jesuit Makassar Documents (1615–1682)*. (Monumenta Historica Societatis Iesu, vol. 134/Monumenta Missionum Societatis Iesu, vol. xlix: Missiones Orientales) Rome: Jesuit Historical Institute.

JAVA-POST 1910. Adonara en Lomblem. *De Java-Post* 2: 728–9.

—— 1914. Overval op Lemblen. *De Java-Post* 12: 734–5.

JENKINS, JAMES TRAVIS 1921. *A History of the Whale Fisheries*. London: Witherby.

—— 1932. *Whales and Modern Whaling*. London: Witherby.

JONES, HORACE LEONARD 1930. *The Geography of Strabo*, vol. vii. London: Heinemann.

JONG, C. DE 1978. *Geschiedenis van de Oude Nederlandse Walvisvaart, Deel Twee: Bloei en Achteruitgang, 1642–1872*. Johannesburgh, South Africa: Universiteit van Suid-Afrika.

JOSSELIN DE JONG, J. P. B. 1935. *De Maleische Archipel als Ethnololgisch Studieveld*. Leiden: Ginsberg.

—— 1977. Eastern Indonesia as a Field of Anthropological Study. *In* P. E. de Josselin de Jong, ed., *Strictural Anthropology in The Netherlands*. (Koninklijk Instituut voor Taal-, Land- en Volkenkunde, Translation Series 17) The Hague: Nijhoff. [Orig. publ. in 1935 in Dutch.]

JOSSELIN DE JONG, P. E. DE 1975. The Dynastic Myth of Negri Sembilan (Malaya). *Bijdragen tot de Taal-, Land- en Volkenkunde* 131: 2/3: 277–308.

JUKES, JOSEPH BEETE 1847. *Narrative of the Surveying Voyage of H.M.S. Fly, Captained by F. P. Blackwood, R. N. in Torres Strait, New Guinea, and other Islands of the Eastern Archipealgo During the Years 1841–1846*, vol. 1. London: Boone.

KALLAND, ARNE and BRIAN MOERAN 1992. *Japanese Whaling: End of an Era?*

(Scandinavian Institute of Asian Studies Monograph Series, No. 61) London: Curzon Press.

KANTOR STATISTIK 1992. *Penduduk Kabupaten Flores Timur: Hasil Sensus Penduduk 1990*. Larantuka, Flores, Indonesia: Kantor Statistik Kab. Flores Timur, Propinisi Nusa Tenggara Timur.

KARTHAUS, P. F. J. 1931. Memorie van Overgave van den Aftredenden Resident van Timor en Onderhoorigheden, P. F. J. Karthaus, Mei, 1931. Mit Bijlagen. Kupang, Timor. [Unpublished, Algemeen Rijksarchiv, den Hague.]

KATE, H. F. C. TEN 1894. Verslag eener reis in de Timorgroep en Polynesië. *Tijdschrift van het Koninklijk Nederlandsch Aardrijkskundig Genootschap* 11: 195–246.

KECAMATAN ATADEI DALAM ANGKA 1994. Larantuka, Flores, Indonesia: Kantor Statistik Kabupaten Flores Timur.

KECAMATAN BUYASURI DALAM ANGKA 1994. Larantuka, Flores, Indonesia: Kantor Statistik Kabupaten Flores Timur.

KECAMATAN ILEAPE DALAM ANGKA 1994. Larantuka, Flores, Indonesia: Kantor Statistik Kabupaten Flores Timur.

KECAMATAN LABATUKAN DALAM ANGKA 1994. Larantuka, Flores, Indonesia: Kantor Statistik Kabupaten Flores Timur.

KECAMATAN NAGAWUTUNG DALAM ANGKA 1985–1994. Larantuka, Flores, Indonesia: Kantor Statistik Kabupaten Flores Timur.

KECAMATAN OMESURI DALAM ANGKA 1994. Larantuka, Flores, Indonesia: Kantor Statistik Kabupaten Flores Timur.

KEMMERLING, G. L. L. 1929. De actieve vulkanen van den Ned. Ind. Archipel in 1928–1929. *Tijdschrift van het Koninklijk Nederlandsch Aardrijkskundig Genootschap* 46: 468–96.

KEMP, PETER, ed., 1976. *The Oxford Companion to Ships and the Sea*. London: Oxford University Press.

KENNEDY, RAYMOND 1955. *Field Notes on Indonesia: Flores, 1949–50*, Harold C. Conklin, ed. New Haven, Connecticut: Human Relations Area Files.

KERAF, A. SONNY 1982. Faham Tentang Kematian Dalam Masyarakat Lamalera-Lembata. *Hidup*, No. 45: 11–12.

KERAF, GREGORIUS 1978. *Morfologi Dialek Lamalera*. Ende-Flores, Indonesia: Arnoldus.

—— 1983. Counterpart's Report on the 'Economy and Social Change' Project in Lamalera, 1982. [Unpublished, in Indonesian.]

KERCHOVE, R. DE 1954. 'Oculi'. *Mariner's Mirror* 40: 241.

KLEIAN, E. R. 1891. Eeen voetreis over het oostelijk deel van het eiland Flores. *Tijdschrift voor Indische Taal-, Land- en Volkenkunde* 34: 485–532.

KLUPPEL, J. M. 1873. De Solor-Eilanden. *Tijdschrift voor Indische Taal-, Land- en Volkenkunde* 20: 378–98.

KNIPHORST, H. H. P. E. 1885. Een terugblik op Timor en onderhoorigheden. *Tijdschrift voor Nederlandsch-Indië*, NS 14: 2: 321–62.

KOHL, KARL-HEINZ 1986. Religiöser Partikularismus und kulturelle Transzendenz: Über den Untergang von Stammesreligionen in Indonesien. *In* Hartmut Zinser, ed., *Der Untergang von Religionen*. Berlin: Dietrich Reimer Verlag.

—— 1988. Ein verlorener Gegenstand? Zur Widerstandsfähigkeit autochthoner

Religionen gegenüber dem Vordringen der Weltreligionen. *In* Hartmut Zinser, ed., *Religionswissenschaft: Eine Einführung*. Berlin: Dietrich Reimer Verlag.

—— 1989. Der Elefant mit den sieben Stosszähnen: Heiratsregeln im Lewolema-Gebiet und ihre Begründung im Mythos. *In* Hartmut Zinser, Friedrich Stentzler, and Karl-Heinz Kohl, eds., *Foedera Naturai: Klaus Heinrich zum 60. Geburtstag*. Würzburg: Königshausen & Neumann.

—— 1990. Der Mythos von Tonu Wujo: Religiöse Weltsicht in Ost-Flores. *In* Bernhard Mensen, ed., *Die Schöpfung in den Religionen*. Nettetal: Steyler Verlag.

KOLONIAAL VERSLAG 1850. *Koloniaal Verslag van 1849 en 1850.*

—— 1875. *Koloniaal Verslag van 1875.*

—— 1913. *Koloniaal Verslag van 1913.*

—— 1914. *Koloniaal Verslag van 1914.*

—— 1915. *Koloniaal Verslag van 1915.*

KRUSEMAN, J. D. 1835. Beschrijving van Timor. *De Oosterling: Tijdschrift bij Uitsluiting Toegewijd aan de Verbreeding der Kennis van Oost-Indië* 2: 1: 1–41.

KRUYT, ALB. C. 1923. Koopen in Midden Celebes. *Mededeelingen der Koninklijke Akademie van Wetenschappen, Afdeeling Letterkunde*, vol. 56, series B, No. 5: 149–78.

KUMANIRENG, PIET 1990. *Himpunan Cerita Rakyat Suku Demong Pagong di Flores Timur, Nusa Tenggara Timur*. Surabaya, Indonesia: Penerbit Mingguan ASAS.

LACROIX, LOUIS 1938. *Les Derniers Baleiniers français: Un demi-siècle d'histoire de la grande pêche baleinière en France de 1817 à 1867*. Nantes: Imprimerie de Bretagne.

LANG, JOHN DUNMORE 1834. *An Historical and Statistical Account of New South Wales*, 2 vols. London: Cochrane and MᶜCrone.

LEACH, E. 1951. The Structural Implications of Matrilateral Cross-Cousin Marriage. *Journal of the Royal Anthropological Institute* 81: 23–55.

LEEMKER, H. H. O. 1893. Woordenlijstje van de Soloreesche Taal. *Tijdschrift voor Indische Taal-, Land- en Volkenkunde* 36: 421–61.

LE GENTIL, M. 1781. *Voyage dans les Mers de l'Inde fait par Ordre du Roi, a L'occasion du Passage de Vénus sur le Disque du Soleil, le 6 Juin 1761, & le 3 du même mois 1769*, vol. 2. Paris: Imprimerie Royal.

LE GOFF, J. 1980. *Time, Work, and Culture in the Middle Ages*. Chicago: University of Chicago Press.

LEGUÉVEL DE LACOMBE, B.-F. 1840. *Voyage à Madagascar et aux îles Comores (1823 à 1830)*, vol. i. Paris: Desessart.

LEUPE, P. A. 1877. Besognes der Hooge Regeering te Batavia Gehouden over de Commissie van Paravancini naar Timor 1756. *Bijdragen tot de Taal-, Land- en Volkenkunde van Nederlandsch-Indië* 25: 421–94.

LEUR, J. C. VAN 1967. *Indonesian Trade and Society: Essays in Asian Social and Economic History*. The Hague: Van Hoeve.

LÉVI-STRAUSS, CLAUDE 1949. *Les Structures élémentaires de la parenté*. Paris: Presses Universitaires de France.

—— 1969. *The Elementary Structures of Kinship*, Bell, Sturmer, and Needham, trans. London: Eyre & Spottiswoode.

LEWIS, DOUGLAS 1988. *People of the Source: The Social and Ceremonial Order of Tana Wai Brama on Flores*. (Verhandelingen van het Koninklijk Instituut voor Taal-, Lande- en Volkenkunde 135) Dordrecht, Holland and Providence, USA: Floris Publications.

LEYN, GABRIEL SUBAN 1979. Sejarah Daerah Pulau Solor. (Laporan Kegiatan Penilik Kebudayaan Kandep. Menanga: P & K Kec. Solor Timur) Menanga, Solor, Indonesia: P. & K. [unpublished].

—— 1980. Adat Istiadat Daerah. (Laporan Kegiatan Penilik Kebudayaan Kandep. Menanga: P & K Kec. Solor Timur) Menanga, Solor, Indonesia: P. & K. [unpublished].

—— 1981. Ceritera Asal-Usul yang Mengandung Sejarah dan Adat-Istiadat, Pulau Solor bahagian Timur. (Dep. P & K, Kab. Flores Timur, Kantor Kecamatan Solor Timur, Menanga) Menanga, Solor, Indonesia: P. & K. [unpublished].

LIEBNER, HORST 1993. Remarks on the Terminology of Boatbuilding and Seamanship in Some Languages of Southern Sulawesi. *Indonesian Circle* Nos. 59/60: 18–44.

LIEFRINCK, F. A. 1908. Oude Olifantstanden te Larantoeka. *Notulen van de Algemeene en Directievevergaderingen van het Bataviaasch Genootschap van Kunsten en Wetenschappen* 46: 62–4.

LIGTVOET, A. 1878. Beschrijving en Geschiedenis van Boeton. *Bijdragen tot de Taal-, Land- en Volkenkunde van Nederlandsch-Indië* 26: 1–112.

LLOYD, J. A. 1851. Memoire on Madagascar. *Journal of the Royal Geographical Society* 20: 53–75.

LOCKYER, C. 1976. Body Weights of some Species of Large Whales. *Journal du Conseil, Conseil International de l'Exploration de la Mer.* 36: 3: 259–73.

LULOFS, C. 1911. Toepassing en Resultatent van de Nieuwe Beginselen van Politiek Beleid in de Residentie Timor en Onderhoorigheden. *Tijdschrift voor het Binnenlandsch Bestuur* 40: 281–308.

LUTZ, NANCY MELISSA 1986. Authoritative Discourse: Language and Ideology in Adonara, Eastern Indonesia. [(Ph.D. thesis, University of California) Berkeley, California: Graduate Division of the University of California, Berkeley (unpublished).]

LYNDEN, D. W. C. BARON VAN 1849. Algemeen verslag der residentie Timor en Onderhoorigheden over 1848 & 1849. [Arsip Nasional, Jakarta, Indonesia, unpublished.]

—— 1850. Algemeen verslag der residentie Timor en Onderhoorigheden over het jaar 1850. [Arsip Nasional, Jakarta, Indonesia, unpublished.]

—— 1851a. Bijdrage tot de kennis van Solor, Allor, Rotti, Savoe en omliggende eilanden, getrokken uit een verslag van de residentie Timor. *Natuurkundige Tijdschrift voor Nederlandsch-Indië* 2: 317–36, 388–414.

—— 1851b. Algemeen verslag der residentie Timor en Onderhoorigheden over het jaar 1851. [Arsip Nasional, Jakarta, Indonesia, unpublished.]

—— 1852. Algemeen verslag der residentie Timor en Onderhoorigheden over het jaar 1852. [Arsip Nasional, Jakarta, Indonesia, unpublished.]

McCAY, BONNIE J. 1981. Development Issues in Fisheries as Agrarian Systems. *C & A (Culture & Agriculture): Bulletin of the Anthropological Study Group on Agrarian Systems*, No. 11: 1–8.

McCRINDLE, J. W., trans., 1879. *The Commerce and Navigation of the Erythræan Sea; Being a Translation of the Periplus Maris Erythræi, by an Anonymous Writer, and of Arrian's Account of the Voyage of Nearkhos from the Mouth of the Indus to the Head of the Persian Gulf.* London: Trübner.

MACKIE, J. A. C. 1980. The Concept of Dualism and its Applications to Indonesian Agriculture. *In* R. G. Garnaut and P. T. McCawley, eds., *Indonesia: Dualism, Growth and Poverty*. Canberra: Research School of Pacific Studies, Australian National University.

McKINNON, SUSAN 1991. *From a Shattered Sun: Hierarchy, Gender, and Alliance in the Tanimbar Islands*. Madison, Wisconsin: University of Wisconsin Press.

MACKNIGHT, C. C. 1973. The Nature of Early Maritime Trade: Some Points of Analogy from the Eastern Part of the Indonesian Archipealgo. *World Archaeology* 5: 2: 198–208.

—— 1980. The Study of Praus in the Indonesian Archipelago. *The Great Circle* 2: 2: 117–28.

MACKNIGHT, C. C. and MUKHLIS 1979. A Bugis Manuscript about Praus. *Archipel*, No. 18: 271–81.

McNAB, R. 1913. *The Old Whaling Days: A History of Southern New Zealand from 1830 to 1840*. Christchurch, New Zealand: Whitcombe and Tombs.

MALINOWSKI, BRONISLAW 1922. *Argonauts of the Western Pacific: An Account of Native Enterprise and Adventure in the Archipelagos of Melanesian New Guinea*. London: Routledge & Kegan Paul.

—— 1926. *Myth in Primitive Psychology*. New York: W. W. Norton.

MANGUIN, P.-Y. 1983. Manpower and Labour Categories in Early Sixteenth Century Malacca. *In* Anthony Reid, ed., *Slavery, Bondage & Dependency in Southeast Asia*. St Lucia: University of Queensland Press.

MARSHALL, TOM 1966. *Tropical Fish of the Great Barrier Reef*. Sydney, Australia: Angus & Robertson.

MAXWELL, ROBYN J. 1985. De rituele weefsels van Oost-Indonesië. *In* Loan Oei, ed., *Indigo: Leven in een kleur*. (Stichting Indigo, Amsterdam) Weesp: Uitgeverij Fibula-Van Dishoeck.

[MAY, J.] 1864. Zeeroof in den Indischen Archipel. *Tijdschrift voor Nederlandsch-Indië* 2: 2: 375–8.

MEILINK-ROELOFSZ, M. A. P. 1962. *Asian Trade and European Influence in the Indonesian Archipelago between 1500 and about 1630*. The Hague: Nijhoff.

MELVILLE, HERMAN 1851. *Moby-Dick; or, The Whale*. New York: Harper & Brothers.

METZNER, JOACHIM K. 1976a. Lamtoronisasi: An Experiment in Soil Conservation. *Bulletin of Indonesian Economic Studies* 30: 3: 224–34.

—— 1976b. Landschaftserhaltung und Möglichkeiten zur Intensivierung der Landnutzung durch Leucaena Leucocephala im Kabupaten Sikka, Flores. *Erdkunde* 30: 3: 224–34.

—— 1977. *Man and Environment in Eastern Timor: A Geoecological Analysis of the Baucau-Viqueque Area as a Possible Basis for Regional Planning*. (Development Studies Centre Monograph 8) Canberra: Australian National University.

—— 1982. *Agriculture and Population Pressure in Sikka, Island of Flores: A Contribution to the Study of the Stability of Agricultural Systems in the Wet and Dry Tropics*. (Development Studies Centre Monograph 28) Canberra: Australian National University.

MEULEMANS, J. 1983. Alor. *In* W. A. L. Stokhof, ed., *Holle Lists: Vocabularies in Languages of Indonesia, Vol. 6: The Lesser Sunda Islands (Nusa Tenggara)*. (Materials in Languages of Indonesia, No. 22; Pacific Linguistics Series D, No. 59) Canberra:

Department of Linguistics, Research School of Pacific Studies, Australian National University [original 1895].

MIKSIC, JOHN N. 1985. Traditional Sumatran Trade. *Bulletin de l'École Française d'Extrême-Orient* 74: 423–67.

MONTEIRO, F. 1975. *Kamus Dwi Bahasa: Dialek Melayu Larantuka (Flores)–Bahasa Indonesia*. Kupang, Timor: Fakultas Keguruan Undana, Universitas Nusa Cendana.

MOOR, J. H. 1837. *Notices of the Indian Archipelago and Adjacent Countries*. Singapore: (no publisher given).

MOULE, A. C. and PAUL PELLIOT 1938. *Marco Polo: The Description of the World*. London: Routledge.

MUDA, HUBERTUS 1989. Bentuk-Bentuk Manifestasi Wujud Tertinggi Dalam Masyarakat Ngadha, Flores. *Buletin Candraditya* 1: 2: 61–78 [extract from Hubertus Muda 1986. The Supreme Being of the Ngadha People in Flores (Indonesia): Its Transcendence and Immanence. (Doctoral dissertation, Pontificia Università Gregoriana) Rome, pp. 210–29 (unpublished)].

MÜLLER, SALOMON 1857. *Reizen en Onderzoekingen in den Indischen Archipel, Gedaan op Last der Nederlandsche Indische Regering, Tusschen de Jaren 1828 en 1836*, nieuwe uitgave, vol. 2. (Werken van het Koninklijk Instituut voor Taal-, Land- en Volkenkunde van Nederlandsch-Indië, Tweede Afdeeling, Afzonderlijke Werken) Amsterdam: Frederik Muller.

MUNRO, W. G. 1915. Nota over Lomblen (Afdeling Flores). [Unpublished.]

MUSSCHENBROEK, S. C. J. W. van 1877. Cachelot-visscherij van de Amerikanen in den Ned. Indischen Archipel. *Tijdschrift Uitgegeven door de Nederlandsche Maatschappij ter Bevordering van Nijverheid* 40: 1: 473–89, 505–32.

NEEDHAM, RODNEY 1962. *Structure and Sentiment*. Chicago: University of Chicago Press.

—— 1983. *Sumba and the Slave Trade*. (Centre of Southeast Asian Studies Working Paper, No. 31) Melbourne, Australia: Monash University.

—— 1986. Alliance. *Oceania* 56: 3: 165–80.

NIEUHOF, JOHANNES 1670. *Het Gezantschap der Neêrlandtsche Oost-Indische Compagnie aan den Grooten Tartarischen Cham, Den tegenwoodigen Keizer van China . . . Algemeene Beschryving van 'tRyk Sina*. Amsterdam: Jacob van Meurs.

NOORDUYN, J. 1983. De Handelsrelaties van het Makassaarese Rijk Volgens de Notitie van Cornelis Speelman uit 1670. *Nederlandse Historische Bronnen* 3: 96–123.

NOOTEBOOM, C. 1932. *De Boomstamkano in Indonesie*. Leiden: Brill.

—— 1939. Main tjatjing, een Manggaraisch vechtspel. *Tijdschrift voor Indische Taal-, Land- en Volkenkunde* 79: 123–5.

OLEONA, AMBROS 1989. *Tena Laja–Ola Nuâ (Teknologi Pembuatan Perahu dan Kehidupan Nelayan Lamalera)*. Lewoleba, Lembata. [Unpublished.]

OLIVER, W. H., ed., with B. R. WILLIAMS 1981. *The Oxford History of New Zealand*. Oxford: Clarendon Press.

OLLIER, C. D. 1980. The Geological Setting. *In* J. J. Fox, ed., *Indonesia: The Making of a Culture*. Canberra, Australia: Research School of Pacific Studies, Australian National University.

OMMANNEY, F. D. 1933. Whaling in the Dominion of New Zealand. *Discovery Reports* 7: 239–52.

424   References

ORMELING, F. J. 1956. *The Timor Problem: A Geographical Interpretation of an Underdeveloped Island*. Groningen: Wolters.

ORTA, GARCIA DA 1908. *Colloquies on the Simples and Drugs of India*. London: Sotheran.

OSSENBRUGGEN, F. D. E. VAN 1930. Verwantschaps- en Huwelijksvormen in den Indischen Archipel. *Tijdschrift van het Aardrijkskundig Genootschap* 47: 212–29.

—— 1935. Het Oeconomisch-magisch Element in Tobasche Verwantschapsver-houdingen. (*Mededelingen der Koninklijke Akademie van Wetenschappen, Afdeeling Letterkunde*, vol. 80, series B, No. 3) Amsterdam: Noord-Hollandsche Uitgevers-Maatschappij.

OUWEHAND, C. 1950. Aantekening over volksordening en grondenrecht op Oost-Flores. *Indonesië* 4: 54–71.

—— 1951. De Gemohin, een maatschappij op Adonara. *Bijdragen tot de Taal-, Land-en Volkenkunde* 107: 4: 379–91.

OWEN, W. F. W. 1833. *Narrative of Voyages to Explore the Shores of Africa, Arabia, and Madagascar; Performed in H.M. Ships Leven and Barracouta, under the Direction of Captain W. F. W. Owen, R.N.*, Heaton Bowstead Robinson, ed., vol. 1. London: Bentley.

PALM, W. H. G. 1946. *Walvischen en Walvischvaart*. Amsterdam: Veen.

PARRY, JONATHAN 1989. On the Moral Perils of Exchange. *In* J. Parry and M. Bloch, eds., *Money and the Morality of Exchange*. Cambridge: Cambridge University Press.

PARRY, JONATHAN and MAURICE BLOCH 1989. Introduction: Money and the Morality of Exchange. *In* J. Parry and M. Bloch, eds., *Money and the Morality of Exchange*. Cambridge: Cambridge University Press.

PEHL, BRUNO 1959. Keluarga jang katolik di Flotim. *Pastoralia* 3rd ser. 8: 87–8.

PELLIOT, PAUL 1959. *Notes on Marco Polo*, vol. 1. Paris: Imprimerie Nationale.

PELLY, USMAN 1975. *Ara, Dengan Perahu Bugisnya (Sebuah Studi Mengenai Pewarisan Keahlian Orang Ara Kepada Anak dan Keturunannya)*. Ujung Pandang, Sulawesi, Indonesia: Pusat Latihan Penelitian Ilmu-Ilmu Sosial.

—— 1977. Symbolic Aspects of the Bugis Ship and Shipbuilding. *Journal of the Steward Anthropological Society* 8: 2: 87–106.

PIGEAUD, TH. 1938. *Javanese volksvertoningen: Bijdrage tot de Beschrijving van Land en Volk*. Batavia: Volkslectuur.

—— 1967. *The Literature of Java*, vol. 1. The Hague: Nijhoff.

PIRES, TOMÉ 1944. The *Suma Oriental of Tomé Pires*, 2 vols., Armando Cortesão, ed. London: Hakluyt Society.

PISKATY, KURT 1964. *Die Katholische Missionsschule in Nusa Tenggara (Südost-Indonesien)—ihre geschichtliche Entfaltung und ihre Bedeutung für die Missionsarbeit*. (Studia Instituti Missiologici Societas Verbi Divini 5) St Gabriel-Mödling: Steyler Verlag.

POERWADARMINTA, W. J. S. 1966. *Kamus Umum Bahasa Indonesia*, 2 vols. Jakarta: P. N. Balai Pustaka.

POTT, J. G. 1908. Oude Olifantstanden te Larantoeka. *Notulen van de Algemeene en Directievevergaderingen van het Bataviaasch Genootschap van Kunsten en Wetenschappen* 46: 89.

PRINS, A. H. J. 1970. Maritime Art in an Islamic Context: Oculus and Therion in Lamu Ships. *Mariner's Mirror* 56: 327–39.

PRIOR, JOHN MANSFORD 1988. *Church and Marriage in an Indonesian Village: A Study of Customary and Church Marriage among the Ata Lio of Central Flores, Indonesia, as a Paradigm of the Ecclesial Interrelationship between Village and Institutional Catholicism.* (Studien zur Interkulturellen Geschichte des Christentums, vol. 55) Frankfurt am Main: Verlag Peter Lang.

QUIGLEY, CARROLL 1955. Certain Considerations on the Origin and Diffusion of Oculi. *The American Neptune: A Quarterly Journal of Maritime History* 15: 3: 191–8.

—— 1958. The Origin and Diffusion of Oculi: A Rejoinder. *The American Neptune: A Quarterly Journal of Maritime History* 18: 1: 25–58.

RADERMACHER, J. C. M. 1786. Korte Beschrijving van het Eiland Celebes en de Eilanden Floris, Sumbauwa, Lombok, en Baly. *Verhandelingen van het Bataviaasch Genootschap der Kunsten en Wetenschappen* 4: 143–96.

RAFFLES, WILLIAM STAMFORD 1813. Letter of 30 June 1813. [India Office Library, London.]

REID, ANTHONY 1969. *The Contest for North Sumatra: Atjeh, the Netherlands and Britain 1858–1898.* London: Oxford University Press; Kuala Lumpur: University of Malaya Press.

—— 1983. Introduction: Slavery and Bondage in Southeast Asian History. *In* Anthony Reid, ed., *Slavery, Bondage & Dependency in Southeast Asia.* St Lucia: University of Queensland Press.

—— 1987. Low Population Growth and its Causes in Pre-Colonial Southeast Asia. *In* Norman G. Owen, ed., *Death and Disease in Southeast Asia: Explorations in Social, Medical and Demographic History.* (Asian Studies Association of Australia Southeast Asia Publication Series 14) Singapore: Oxford University Press.

—— 1988. *Southeast Asia in the Age of Commerce 1450–1680, Volume One: The Lands Below the Winds.* New Haven: Yale University Press.

—— 1993. *Southeast Asia in the Age of Commerce 1450–1680, Volume Two: Expansion and Crisis.* New Haven: Yale University Press.

REINAUD, M. 1845. *Relation des voyages faits par les Arabes et les Persans dans L'Inde et à la Chine dans le IXe Siècle de L'Ere Chrétienne,* vol. 1. Paris: Imprimerie Royale.

RENARD-CLAMAGIRAND, BRIGITTE 1982. *Marobo: Une société ema de Timor.* (Langues et Civilisations de L'Asie du Sud-Est et du Monde Insulindien, No. 12) Paris: SELAF.

RESINK, G. J. 1968. The All-But-Inverted Image. *In* G. J. Resink, *Indonesia's History Between the Myths: Essays in Legal History and Historical Theory.* The Hague: W. van Hoeve.

RIDLEY, HENRY N. 1922–5. *The Flora of the Malay Peninsula,* 5 vols. London: L. Reeve.

RIEDEL, J. G. F. 1885. Timor en Onderhoorigheden in 1878 en later. *De Indisch Gids* 7: 1: 1–12.

RIENZI, G. L. DOMENY DE 1836–7. *Océanie ou cinquième partie du monde,* 5 vols. Paris: Didot.

ROUFFAER, G. P. 1910. De Ili Weroeng. *Tijdschrift van het Koninklijk Nederlandsch Aardrijkskundig Genootschap* 27: 5: 1026–8.

—— 1923–4. Chronologie der Dominikaner-Missie op Solor en Flores, vooral Poeloe Ende (ca. 1556–1638). *Nederlandsch Indië Oud en Nieuw* 8: 204–22, 256–60.

RUIBING, AALDRIK HENDRIK 1937. *Ethnologische Studie betreffende de Indonesische slavernij als maatschappelijk verschijnsel.* Zutphen: W. J. Thieme.

RUMPHIUS, GEORGIUS EVERHARDUS 1705. *D'Amboinsche Rariteitkamer.* Amsterdam: Halma.

Sá, Artur Basílio de, ed., 1956. *História de Maluco no Tempo de Gonçalo Pereira Marramaque e Sancho de Vascincellos . . . 1636. Fundação das Primeiras Cristandades nas Ilhas de Solor e Timor, 1624–25.* (Documentação para a História das Missões do Pradroada Português do Oriente, Insulíndia, vol. 4) Lisbon: Agência Geral do Ultramar.

Samely, Ursula 1991. *Kedang (Eastern Indonesia): Some Aspects of its Grammar.* Hamburg: Helmut Buske Verlag.

Santa Catharina, Lucus de 1733. *Quarte Parte da Historia de S. Domingos.* Lisbon: Academia Real.

Schare, Andrea 1990. Ernst Vatter (1988–1948): Leben und Werk, Ein Beitrag zur Geschichte der deutschsprachigen Ethnologie. [(MA thesis, Johannes Gutenberg-Universität Mainz) Mainz, Germany (unpublished).]

Schulte Nordholt, H. G. 1971. *The Political System of the Atoni of Timor.* The Hague: Nijhoff.

Scoresby, W. 1820. *An Account of the Arctic Regions with a History and Description of the Northern Whale-Fishery,* 2 vols. Edinburgh: Constable.

Scott, W. H. 1981. *Boatbuilding and Seamanship in Classic Philippine Society.* (Anthropological Papers, No. 9) Manila, Philippines: National Museum.

Seegeler, C. J. 1931. Nota van toelichting betreffende het zelfbesturende landschap Larantoeka . . . (ddo. 2 Augustus 1931). [Algemeen Rijksarchief, The Hague, formerly in the Museum voor de Tropen, Amsterdam, unpublished.]

Semmelink, J. 1864. Geneeskundig Verslag van Larantoeka (Eiland Flores) over het Jaar 1862. *Geneeskundig Tijdschrift voor Nederlandsch-Indië* 11: 57–86.

Sherman, D. George 1990. *Rice, Rupees, and Ritual: Economy and Society Among the Samosir Batak of Sumatra.* Stanford, California: Stanford University Press.

Slijper, E. J. 1979. *Whales,* 2nd English edn., A. J. Pomerans, trans. Ithaca, New York: Cornell University Press.

Smit, J. G. V. 1989. Activities of American Whalers in the Dutch East Indies, 1830–1880. [(Doctoraal Scriptie, Zeegeschiedenis, Rijks Univeriteit Leiden, 6 June 1989, (unpublished).]

Smith, R. B. and W. Watson 1979. Introduction. *In* R. B. Smith and W. Watson, eds., *Early South East Asia: Essays in Archaeology, History, and Historical Geography.* New York: Oxford University Press.

Snyder, James Wilbert 1938. The First American Voyage to India: Being Excerpts from the Log of the Ship United States from Philidelphia to Pondicherry, 1784. *Americana* 32: 2: 284–304.

Sopher, David E. 1965. *The Sea Nomads: A Study Based on the Literature of the Maritime Boat People of Southeast Asia.* (Memoirs of the National Museum, No. 5) Singapore: National Museum.

Spanoghe, J. B. 1834. Algemeen verslag der residentie Timor en Onderhoorigheden over het jaar 1834. [Arsip Nasional, Jakarta, Indonesia, unpublished.]

—— 1835. Algemeen verslag der residentie Timor en Onderhoorigheden over het jaar 1835. [Arsip Nasional, Jakarta, Indonesia, unpublished.]

[Spanoghe, J. B.] 1849a. Bijdragen tot de Kennis van het Eiland Timor en Onderhoorigheden. *Tijdschrift voor Nederlandsch-Indië* 11: 2: 307–24.

—— 1849b. Walvischvangst der Solorezen. *Tijdschrift voor Nederlandsch-Indië* 11: 2: 66–7.

—— 1850. Whale Fishing of the Solorese. *Journal of the Indian Archipelago and Eastern Asia* 4: 766–7.

SPOEHR, ALEXANDER 1980. *Protein from the Sea: Technological Change in Philippine Capture Fisheries.* (Ethnology Monographs, No. 3) Pittsburgh: Department of Anthropology, University of Pittsburgh.

SPRENGER, ALOYS 1841. *El-Masʿudīʾs* [al-Masʿudi's] *Historical Encyclopaedia, Entitled 'Meadows of Gold and Mines of Gems',* vol. 1. London: The Oriental Translation Fund.

STACKPOLE, EDOUARD A. 1972. *Whales & Destiny: The Rivalry Between America, France and Britain for Control of the Southern Whale Fishery, 1785–1825.* Boston: University of Massachusetts Press.

STAPEL, F. W., ed., 1934. Corpus Diplomaticum Neerlando-Indicum, Derde Deel (1676–1691). *Bijdragen tot de Taal-, Land- en Volkenkunde van Nederlandsch-Indië* 91: v–xix, 1–616.

—— ed., 1955. *Corpus Diplomaticum Neerlando-Indicum, Zesde Deel (1753–1799).* The Hague: Nijhoff.

STEINHAUER, HEIN 1983. Notes on the Malay of Kupang (Timor). (Studies in Malay Dialects, Part II, James T. Collins, ed.) *NUSA: Linguistic Studies of Indonesian and Other Languages of Indonesia* 17: 42–64.

STIRRAT, R. L. 1989. Money, Man and Women. *In* J. Parry and M. Bloch, eds., *Money and the Morality of Exchange.* Cambridge: Cambridge University Press.

STOKHOF, W. A. L., ed., 1980. *Holle Lists: Vocabularies in Languages of Indonesia, Vol. 1, Introductory Volume (Materials in Languages of Indonesia, No. 1).* (Pacific Linguistics Series D, No. 17) Canberra, Australia: Department of Linguistics, Research School of Pacific Studies, Australian National University.

SUTHERLAND, H. 1983. Slavery and the Slave Trade in South Sulawesi, 1660s–1800s. *In* Anthony Reid, ed., *Slavery, Bondage & Dependency in Southeast Asia.* St Lucia: University of Queensland Press.

SVENSSON, SAM 1971. *Handbook of Seaman's Ropework.* London: Adlard Coles.

SWIETEN, TH. VAN 1898. Huiselijk leven der Timorese Christenen. *Berichten uit Nederlandsch Oost-Indië voor de Leden van den Sint-Claverband* 10: 2: 68–78 (cited in Ormeling).

SYMONS, J. J. M. F. 1935. Memorie van Overgave van de onderafdeling Oost Flores en Solor Eilanden en Maomere. [Algemeen Rijksarchief, The Hague, formerly in the Museum voor de Tropen, Amsterdam, unpublished.]

TARLING, NICHOLAS 1963. *Piracy and Politics in the Malay World: A Study of British Imperialism in Nineteenth-Century South-East Asia.* Singapore: Donald Moore.

TASMAN, ABEL JANSZ. 1898. Journal or Description Drawn Up by Abel Jansz. Tasman of the Discovery of the Unknown South land in 1642. In *Abel Janszoon Tasman's Journal.* Amsterdam: Muller.

TAYLOR, PAUL MICHAEL 1983. North Moluccan Malay: Notes on a 'Substandard' Dialect of Indonesian. (Studies in Malay Dialects, Part II, James T. Collins, ed.) *NUSA: Linguistic Studies of Indonesian and Other Languages of Indonesia* 17: 14–27.

TEMMINCK, C. J. 1849. *Coup-d'oeil général sur les possessions Néerlandaises dans l'Inde Archipélagique,* 3 vols. Leiden: Arnz.

TEYSMANN, J. E. 1874. Verslag eener Botanische Reis over Timor en de daaronder

Resorteerende Eilanden Samauw, Alor, Solor, Floris en Soemba. *Natuurkundig Tijdschrift voor Nederlandsch-Indië* 34: 348–506.

TIBBETS, G. R. 1979. *A Study of the Arabic Texts Containing Material on South-East Asia*. (Royal Asiatic Society Oriental Translation Fund, NS vol. xliv) Leiden: Brill.

TIELE, P. A. and J. E. HEERES, eds., 1886. *Bouwstoffen voor de Geschiedenis der Nederlanders in den Maleischen Archipel*, vol. 1. The Hague: Nijhoff.

—— 1890. *Bouwstoffen voor de Geschiedenis der Nederlanders in den Maleischen Archipel*, vol. 2. The Hague: Nijhoff.

—— 1895. *Bouwstoffen voor de Geschiedenis der Nederlanders in den Maleischen Archipel*, vol. 3. The Hague: Nijhoff.

TIMMERS, M. 1902. Iets over de Slavernij. *Berichten uit Nederlandsch Ost-Indie voor de Leden van den Sint-Claverbond*, No. 4: 34–50.

TOWNSEND, CHARLES HASKINS 1935. The Distribution of Certain Whales as Shown by Logbook Records of American Whaleships. *Zoologica* 19: 1: 1–50.

TUCK, JAMES A. and ROBERT GRENIER 1981. A 16th-Century Basque Whaling Station in Labrador. *Scientific American* (Nov.) 245: 180–90.

TUKAN, BERNARD and JOHAN SUBAN TUKAN 1995. *Keluarga Lamaholot: Opu Lake-Opu Bine*. Larantuka, Flores, Indonesia: Komisi Pastoral Keluarga Keuskupan Larantuka.

US NAVY HYDROGRAPHIC OFFICE 1962. *Sailing Directions for Java (Except West Coast from Tandjung Tjankuang to Udjung Krawang), Lesser Sundas: South, Southeast, and East Coasts of Borneo; and Celebes*, 5th edn. Washington, DC: United States Government Printing Office.

VALENTYN, FRANÇOIS 1721a. *Omstandig Verhaal van de Geschiedenissen en Zaaken het Kerkelyke ofte den Godsdienst Betreffende, zoo in Amboina Als in alle de Eylanden, Daar Onder Behoorenden*... Derde Deel. Dordrecht and Amsterdam: Johannes van Braam, Gerard onder de Linden.

—— 1721b. *Verhandeling der Zee-Horenkens en Zee-Gewassen in en omtrent Amboina en de naby gelegene Eylande*... Derde Deel Tweede Stuk. Dordrecht and Amsterdam: Johannes van Braam, Gerard onder de Linden.

—— 1724. *Oud en Nieuw Oost-Indiën, Tweede Deel, Beschryving van Amboina*. Dordrecht and Amsterdam: Johannes van Braam. Gerard onder de Linden.

—— 1726, *Oud en Nieuw Oost-Indiën, Derde Deel, Beschryvinge van Solor en Timor*. Dordrecht and Amsterdam: Johannes van Braam, Gerard onder de Linden.

VALMY, ROBERT 1956. La Pêche rituelle des mammifères marins. *Le Revue de Madagascar* 26: 29–35.

VATTER, ERNST 1932. *Ata Kiwan: Unbekannte Bergvölker im tropischem Holland*. Leipzig: Bibliographisches Institut.

VERGOUWEN, J. C. 1964. *The Social Organisation and Customary Law of the Toba-Batak of Northern Sumatra*. (Koninklijk Instituut voor Taal-, Land- en Volkenkunde Translation Series 7) The Hague: Nijhoff.

VERHEIJEN, J. A. J. 1951. *Het Hoogste Wezen bij de Manggaraiers*. (Studia Instituti Anthropos, vol. 4) Wien-Mödling: Drukkerij van het Missiehuis St Gabriël.

—— 1984. Plant Names in Austronesian Linguistics. *NUSA: Linguistic Studies of Indonesian and Other Languages of Indonesia* 20: i–x, 1–98.

—— 1986. *The Sama / Bajau Language of the Lesser Sunda Islands*. (Pacific Linguistics,

Series D, No. 70) Canberra, Australia: Department of Linguistics, Research School of Pacific Studies, Australian National University.

VETH, P. J. 1855. Het eiland Flores. *Tijdschrift voor Nederlandsch-Indië* 17: 2: 153–84.

—— 1869. *Aardrijkskundig en Statistisch Woordenboek van Nederlandsch-Indië*, 3 vols. Amsterdam: van Kampen.

VICKERS, A. H. 1987. Hinduism and Islam in Indonesia, Bali and the Pasisir World. *Indonesia* 44: 31–58.

—— 1993. From Bali to Lampung on the Pasisir. *Archipel*, No. 45: 55–76.

VILLENEUVE G. G. DE 1888. Algemeen verslag der residentie Timor en Onderhoorigheden over het jaar 1888. [Arsip Nasional, Jakarta, Indonesia, unpublished.]

—— 1889. Algemeen verslag der residentie Timor en Onderhoorigheden over het jaar 1889 [Arsip Nasional, Jakarta, Indonesia, unpublished.]

VOORHOEVE, C. L. 1983. Some Observations on North-Moluccan Malay. (Studies in Malay Dialects, Part II, James T. Collins, ed.) *NUSA: Linguistic Studies of Indonesian and Other Languages of Indonesia* 17: 1–13.

VROKLAGE, BERNHARD 1952. Bride Price or Dower. *Anthropos* 47: 133–46.

WALSH, D. S. and BRUCE BIGGS 1966. *Proto-Polynesian Word List I*. (Te Reo Monographs) Auckland: Linguistic Society of New Zealand.

WARREN, JAMES FRANCIS 1981. *The Sulu Zone 1768–1898: The Dynamics of External Trade, Slavery, and Ethnicity in the Transformation of a Southeast Asian Maritime Sate*. Singapore: Singapore University Press.

WATSON, LYALL 1981. *Sea Guide to Whales of the World*. London: Hutchinson.

WEBB, R A F PAUL 1986. *Palms and the Cross: Socio economic Development in Nusatenggara*. (Centre for S. E. Asian Studies Monograph, No. 15) Townsville, Australia: James Cook University of North Queensland.

—— 1989. Old Lamps for New: Recent Developments in Nusa Tenggara Timur. *Sojourn: Social Issues in Solutheast Asia* 4: 2: 205–32.

WEBER, MAX 1902a. *Siboga-Expeditie I: Introduction et Description de l'Expedition*. Leiden: Brill.

—— 1902b. Iets over Walvischvangst in den Indischen Archipel. *In* M. Greshoff, ed., *Rumphius Gedenkboek (1702–1902)*. Haarlem: Koloniaal Museum.

WEBER-VAN BOSSE, A. 1904. *Een Jaar aan Boord H. M. Siboga*, tweede druk. Leiden: Brill.

WEHR, HANS 1966. *A Dictionary of Modern Written Arabic*, J. Milton Cowan, ed. Wiesbaden: Otto Harrassowitz.

WEST, JANET and R. H. BARNES 1990. Scrimshaw by William Lewis Roderick: A Whale Bone Plaque Dated 1858 Showing the Barque Adventure of London Whaling off Flores and Pulau Komba in the Indian Ocean. *Mariner's Mirror* 76: 2: 135–48.

WHEATLEY, PAUL 1961. *The Golden Khersonese: Studies in the Historical Geography of the Malay Peninsula Before A.D. 1500*. Kuala Lumpur: University of Malaya Press.

WHITE, WALTER GRAINGE 1992. *The Sea Gypsies of Malaya: An Account of the Nomadic Mawken People of the Mergui Archipelago with a Description of their Ways of Living, Customs, Habits, Boats, Occupations, etc., etc., etc.* London: Seeley, Service & Co.

WICHMANN, ARTHUR 1891. Bericht über eine im Jahre 1888–89 ausgeführte Reise nach dem Indischen Archipel. *Tijdschrift van het Koninklijk Nederlandsch Aardrijkskundig Genootschap* 8: 188–293.

WICHMANN, ARTHUR B. 1925. *Siboga-Expeditie LXVI: Geologische Ergebnisse der Siboga-Expedition.* Leiden: Brill.

WICKS, ROBERS S. 1992. *Money, Markets, and Trade in Early Southeast Asia: The Development of Indigenous Monetary Systems to AD 1400.* (Studies on Southeast Asia) Ithaca, New York: Southeast Asia Program, Cornell University.

WIGNYANTA, THOM 1979. Jagung Titi. *Dian* 7: 4: 10.

WIJNEN, R. 1863. Politiek Verslag der Residentie Timor over 1863. [Arsip Nasional, Jakarta, Indonesia, unpublished.]

WILKINSON, R. J. 1932. *A Malay-English Dictionary (Romanized)*, 2 vols. Mytilene, Greece: Salavopoulos and Kinderlis.

WINDT, NIKO VAN DEN 1936. Vijftien jaar missiewerk op 't eiland Lomblem. *De Katholieke Missiën* 61: 4: 75–8.

WINTJES, P. A. 1894*a*. Veertig dagen onder de visschers van Lamalerap op het eiland Lomblen. *Berichten uit Nederlandsch Oost-Indië voor de Leden van den Sint-Claverband* 6: 2: 27–34.

—— 1894*b*. Woordenlijst van het Soloreesch zoals het gesproken wordt te Lamalera op Lomblen. (Ingevulde Holle'se Woordenlijsten, No. 47) Jakarta: Museum Negara [unpublished, see Wintjes 1983].

—— 1895. Lamalera op het eiland Lomblen, ten jare 1894, *Berichten uit Nederlandsch Oost-Indië voor de Leden van den Sint-Claverband* 7: 3: 57–61.

—— 1983. Solor. *In* W. A. L. Stokhof, ed., *Holle Lists: Vocabularies in Languages of Indonesia, Vol. 6: The Lesser Sunda Islands (Nusa Tenggara).* (Materials in Languages of Indonesia, No. 22; Pacific Linguistics Series D, No. 59) Canberra: Department of Linguistics, Research School of Pacific Studies, Australian National University [published version of Wintjes 1894*b*].

WOUDEN, F. A. E. VAN 1935. *Sociale Structuurtypen in de Groote Oost.* Leiden: Ginsberg.

—— 1968. *Types of Social Structure in Eastern Indonesia*, Rodney Needham, trans. The Hague: Nijhoff. [Orig. pub. in 1935 in Dutch.]

YULE, HENRY, ed., 1903. *The Book of Ser Marco Polo*, 2 vols. London: Murray.

NAME INDEX

Abel, Filomeno 395
Abeyasekere, S. 17
Abū Said 387
Ade Manduta (Manatutu), King of, *see*
 Speelman, Raja Solomon
Adonara, Raja of 20–1, 29, 90, 237, 321, 378,
 382, 395
Aernsbergen, A. J. 378
al-Mas'udi, Abu'l-Hasan 'Ali 325
Alcina, Alcisco 204, 215–16
Alderwerelt, J. de Roo van 15, 387
Alexander the Great 337
Algemeen Oversicht 378
Almeide, Antonio de 340
Amanue, Frans 161, 163
Andaya, Leonard Y. 12–13, 56, 383
Anderson, R. C. 230
Anderson, Remola U. 230
Anonymous 11, 15, 31–3, 323, 332, 335–6
Arakian Léré Géré 66, 76
Arndt, Paul vii, 29, 31, 57, 65, 91, 109–10,
 115–16, 126–7, 150, 158–62, 166, 184, 228,
 258, 307, 385–6, 388–9, 391, 393
Asu 78, 116
Ata Kělaké 65, 67, 71
Atakebělaké Dasi 61
Atala 48

B., H. and W. B. O[ort] 381
Babulah Datu Sah, Sultan of Ternate 11, 379
Baha 382
Bai Palembang, Raja 51, 203
Barbosa, Duarte 99
Barlow, Colin 29, 379
Barnes, R. H. vii, ix, 12, 18, 20, 24, 32, 57,
 61–2, 81, 99, 103, 105, 109, 120–1, 123, 126,
 129, 138–9, 142, 163, 180, 182, 203, 230, 334,
 354, 383, 391, 393–4, 396
Barnes, Ruth viii, ix, 5, 31–2, 99, 105, 132,
 135–8, 207, 225, 395
Barraud, Cécile 103, 339–40, 395
Bataona, Adreanus Ubas 124–5, 246–7, 329
Bataona, Mans 194–6, 198–200
Bataona, Yosef Bura 56, 61, 82, 383–4, 398
Baudin, Nicolas 401
Beale, Thomas 330, 400
Beckering, J. D. H. 7, 16, 20–1, 39, 43, 47, 62,
 92, 100, 122, 135, 137, 147–8, 378, 381,
 384–5, 388, 392
Beding, Alex 52–3, 389
Beding, Moses 24, 396

Belafa 70
Bélé Gora 237
Belikololong, Maria Sura 351, 354
Belikololong, Petrus Hidang 295, 384, 396
Bélo 295
Bemmelen, Rein W. van 6
Benga 71
Bennett, F. D. 320, 334–5
Bernardu 118
Biermann, Benno M. 19, 382, 399
Biggs, Bruce 396
Bik, J. Th. 335
Bintang Timoer 7, 48–9, 52
Biro Pusat Statistik 23, 27, 379 80
Bishop of Kupang 398
Blake, John 32
Bleeker, P. 168, 355, 361
Blida 117
Bligh, William 400
Bloch, Maurice 343
Blust, Robert 33
Boccaro, Manuel Tavares 382
Bode, Bernardus 37, 43, 51–2, 61, 68, 118,
 123 7, 204, 244 5, 287, 300, 385, 395
Boeke, J. H. 341
Boli Léla 66
Boli, Sengaji 17
Bor, L. 13
Bossche, J. G. van den 101
Bouman, M. A. 100, 129–30
Bowen, John R. 61, 383
Bowen, Richard LeBaron 230, 395
Boxer, C. R. 12–13, 17, 57, 323, 382, 386
Brandt, Karl 399
Brink, Cornelius ten 25, 121
Broeze, F. J. A. 333
Brouwer, H. A. 6
Brown, Joseph 330
Brumund, J. F. G. 14–15, 100
Bry, Johan Dieterich de 338
Bry, Johan Israel de 338
Bullard, Fred M. 6
Bulmer, Ralph 296
Bupati 46, 381, 397
Burger, D. H. 135, 139–40
Burkill, I. H. 170, 211, 282, 362, 386–7, 394–5
Buton, King of 12

Cácegas, Luís 11, 382
Callbrooke, William 327
Capellen, Jhr. T. van 400

Carcasson, R. H. 355–6, 358–9
Caspersz, J. A. 116
Casson, Lionel 201, 221, 394
Castro, Affonson de 17, 380
Chao Ju-kua 338
Chijs, J. A. van der 12, 25, 99, 324
Chili, Sengaji 17
Civil Officer in Larantuka 101–2
Clarke, Robert 396
Clercq, F. S. A. de 13, 379, 393
Coen, Jan Pietersz 18, 19
Coleman, Neville 280
Colenbrander, H. T. 18–19
Compagno, L. J. V. 280–1
Conklin, Harold 32
Coolhaas, Willem Philippus 12–13, 17, 99
Coorengel, J. G. 16–17
Cornabé, Alexander 323
Corner, Lorraine 379
Cortesão, Armando 57
Couvreur, A. J. L. 57, 382
Crawfurd, John 4, 330–1, 387, 399–401
Cumpston, J. S. 400

Dakin, W. J. 293
Dam, Pieter van 13
Dampier, William 320–1
Dannenfeldt, Karl H. 325–6
Dasi Dasi, *see* Yosef Raja Muda
Dasion, Petrus Bau 48, 59, 61, 82, 348–9, 354, 383, 385
Dasion, Tomas Kifan 48, 396
Daté 71
Dato 142
Davis, Captain J. 401
Delano, Amasa 327, 400–1
Demon 160, 300
Dempwolff, Otto 119
Deos, Simão da Madre de 382
Dian 379
Diaz Vieira Godinho, Don Gaspar 380
Diaz Vieira Godinho, Don Lorenzo Oesi 25, 41, 47, 61, 380
Dietrich, Stefan viii, 4, 20, 30, 32, 56–7, 60, 158–60, 381, 383, 389, 399–400
Dili, Portuguese Governor of 15
district officer 398
Djaialabidin 379
Donselaar, W. M. 4, 393
Doran, E. 172
Downs, R. E. 32
Dresch, Paul viii
Dulo 237, 395
Dumont, Louis 81
Dupont, Arnoldus viii, 380–1, 398
Dutch East Indies, British Governor-General of 330

Earl, George Windsor 325, 380, 388
Ebert, D. A. 280–1
Edwards, Captain Edward 400
Eerde, J. C. van 47
El-Kazwîni 338
Ellis, Richard 339
Ema 68–9
Emmerson, Donald K. 2
Encyclopædia Britannica 327
Enderby, Charles 331
Engbers, E. 5, 35, 49, 392
Este, Governor William Adrian van 400
Eysinga, P. P. Roorda van 328, 377–8
Ezerman, H. E. K. 15

Faivre, Jean-Paul 400
Faria y Sousa, Manuel de 401
Fasã 71
Fernandez, Inyo Josef 32, 119
First Class Medical Officer 101
Firth, Raymond 1–2
Fischer, H. Th. 102
Flacourt, le Sieur de 338
Flinders, Matthew 18, 401
Flores Timur Dalam Angka 380
Forman, Shepard 140
Forster, Honore 335–6
Fortalezza, João Bautista de la 382
Forth, Gregory L. 81
Fox, James J. viii, 2, 17, 61, 151, 161, 385, 389, 401
Fraassen, Ch. F. van 56
Fraenkel, T. G. F. 334, 400
Francis, E. 20, 327–8, 388
Francis, Peter 6
Francisco, Fr. António, SJ. 382–3
Fraser, Thomas M. 1–2
Freijss, J. P. 100, 103, 389
Freycinet, Louis Claude de Saulces de 201
Fruin-Mees, W. 12

Garnaut, Ross 341
Gebuis, L. 10
Geertz, Hildred 377
Gell, Alfred 148
Gélu Bala 67
Gennep, Arnold van 296
Gési Guã Bala Bata Bala Mai, *see* Gési Raja
Gési Guã Fasa 71–2
Gési Guã Fasa, *see* Gési Raja
Gési Raja 59, 65, 270, 298, 385
Geurtjens, H. 340
Gibson-Hill, C. A. 201
Gilliland, Frank 230
Gimlette, John D. 170
Gittinger, Mattiebelle 148

Glover, Ian 377
Godelier, Maurice 342
Gonda, J. 296
Gondowarsito, Ria 29, 379
Gouvernement van Nederlandsch Indië 379
Governor of Nusa Tenggara Timur 397
Graham, Penelope viii, 32, 81, 92, 354
Gray, George 333
Grenier, Robert 396
Greve, W. 25, 51, 101, 203
Groffola, Captain 12
Gronovius, D. van den Dungen 331–3
Groot, J. P. Cornets de 15
Gross, M. Grant 155
Grzimek, Bernhard, 280

Haan, F. de 100
Habir, Manggi 381
Haga 118
Hagenaar, T. C. K. 14–15, 49, 381
Hagestein, F. 51, 203
Hairun, Sultan of Ternate 10–11, 379
Hakluyt, Richard 386
Hall, D. G. E. 11, 401
Hangelbroek, J. J. 48, 381
Hartmann, Max 7, 8, 378
Heeres, J. E. de 12, 18, 99, 201, 203, 387
Heijden, Jacob van der 12–13
Heijmering, G. 12, 324, 401
Hellmuth, J. C. J. 168, 328, 361, 378
Hembree, E. Durant viii, 281, 310, 312, 329, 376, 400
Hens, A. M. 48, 101, 116, 148, 401
Hertz, Robert 123
Heslinga, T. 25, 121
Heynen, F. C. 57
Hidang 74
Hobalt, Peter 378
Hoeberechts, J. 44, 51
Hoëvell, G. W. W. C. van 393
Hoeven, A. 103
Hogendorp, W. van 100, 323, 327, 387
Holle, K. F. 391
Holzinger, Roswitha 31
Horace 234
Hornay, António 12–13
Hornay, Jan d' 18
Hornell, James 171, 201, 204–5, 230–1
Horridge, G. A. 166, 201, 203–5, 209, 212, 214, 216–17
Horsburgh, James 20, 383, 400–1
Hughes, Diane Owen ix
Hullu, J. de 13
Hurgronje, C. Snouck 296
H[umme]., H. C. 380

Injai Chili Muda 17

Jackson, Cordon 331
Jacobs, Hubert 203, 383, 387
Java-Post 48, 379
Jenkins, James Travis 329, 336
Johannis Mura 47–8, 74
Jones, Horace Leonard 338
Jong, C. 333
Josselin de Jong, J. P. B. de 81
Josselin de Jong, P. E. de 383
Juang 70, 75
Jukes, Joseph Beete 15, 331, 335, 390, 401

Kaja Kěrofã 288
Kakang of Lamalera 41–2, 47–8, 52, 57, 74, 113, 117, 122, 305, 382–3
Kakang of Lewoleba 48
Kalland, Arne 339
Kantor Statistik 23, 27, 380
Karowe 118
Karthaus, P. F. J. 389
Kate, H. F. C. ten 238, 336
Kecamatan Atadei Dalam Angka 23
Kecamatan Buyasuri Dalam Angka 23
Kecamatan Ileape Dalam Angka 23
Kecamatan Labatukan Dalam Angka 23
Kecamatan Nagawutun Dalam Angka 11, 23, 379–80
Kecamatan Omesuri Dalam Angka 23
Kemmerling, G. L. L. 7
Kemp, Peter 216, 220, 223
Kennedy, Raymond 32, 62–4, 96, 386
Kentley, Eric ix
Keraf, A. Sonny 128–9
Keraf, Fransiskus Keraf 288, 396
Keraf, Gabriel Blido 151–2, 269, 355
Keraf, Gregorius Prafi vii, viii, 32–4, 52–4, 58, 64, 66, 76–7, 81, 87, 89, 92, 102, 114, 117, 127, 136, 145, 150–2, 158, 168, 170, 183–4, 188, 193–6, 198, 203, 207, 210–11, 217–18, 225, 228, 229, 237, 239, 243, 246, 251, 253, 256, 258–61, 263–4, 269–71, 280–1, 285, 287, 292, 294–6, 298, 307, 346–50, 355, 359–60, 362, 376, 382–5, 388, 391–3, 395–6
Keraf, Marsel Kalang 256, 355
Keraf, Petronela Ema 383
Keraf, Yosefina Sefai 351, 354
Kerak 78, 116
Kerchove, R. de 230
Kibori, Paduka Siri Sultan Kaichil, Prince Amsterdam, King of Ternate 12
Kifan 45, 395
King William I of The Netherlands 332
Kleian, E. R. 389
Kluppel, J. M. 100–1, 148, 203, 328, 381
Kniphorst, H. H. P. E. 329, 380
Kock, Captain 51
Kohl, Karl-Heinz 32, 158, 162

Koloniaal Verslag 12, 15–16, 48–9, 381, 398, 401
Korohama 54, 58–60, 65–6, 68, 71, 75, 112, 385
Korohama, Maria 351, 354
Kruseman, J. D. 148, 324, 328, 335
Kruyt, Alb. C. 102
Kumanireng, Piet 61
Kupa 124–5
Kupang, Head (*Opperhoofd*) 323
Kupang, King of 324
Kupang, Resident of, *see* Timor, Resident of
Kĕlaké (or Ata Kĕlaké) Dasi 65, 74
Kĕlaké (or Ata Kĕlaké) Muda Ama 65, 385

Labala, Raja of 21, 382
Labi So 71
Lacroix, Louis 400
Lang, John Dunmore 331
Larantuka, Controleur of 48, 381
Larantuka, Raja of 15, 20, 29–30, 41, 47, 48, 51, 57, 72–3, 90, 96, 286, 321, 379–81
Laurensus Koli Sinu 48
Le Gentil, M. 338
Le Goff, J. 343
Leach, E. 81
Leemker, H. H. O. vii, 54, 116, 228, 386, 388, 391–3, 395
Leguevel de Lacombe, B.-F. 338
Leupe, P. A. 12
Leur, J. C. van 18
Lévi-Strauss, Claude 81
Lewis, Douglas 385
Leyn, Gabriel Suban 32, 57, 392–4
Libu Lāma Mau 59, 76, 270, 298
Liebner, Horst 212
Liefrinck, F. A. 102
Ligtvoet, A. 12
Lloyd, J. A. 338
Lo Kuku 79–80
Lockyer, C. 310
Lulofs, C. 4, 20, 381
Lutz, Nancy Melissa 32
Lynden, D. W. C. Baron van 3–4, 96, 103, 135, 148, 328–9, 334, 394, 400

McCawley, Peter 341
McCay, Bonnie J. 2
McCrindle, J. W. 337
McGrail, Sean ix
Mackie, J. A. C. 341
McKinnon, Susan 61
MacKnight, C. C. 102, 148, 201, 217
McNab, R. 331
Magdalena, Augustinho da 382
Malinowski, Bronislaw 2, 55–6, 183, 393
Manguin, P.-Y. 17

Manuk, Tomas Serani 396
Marshall, Tom 281
Mary 162, 231–3, 237
Matthey, Heinz von 32
Maxwell, Robyn J. 389
[May, J.] 15
Meilink-Roelofsz, M. A. P. 13
Melang 51, 203
Melville, Herman 293
Menado, Resident of 333
Metz, G. 24
Metzner, Joachim K. 2, 139, 379
Meulemans, J. 203
Mikael Molan 47–8, 52, 113
Miksic, John N. 148
Miku 72
Moeran, Brian 339
Molan Dasi, *see* Mikael Molan
Monteiro, F. 32, 92, 126, 393
Moor, J. H. 103, 328, 387–8
Moule, A. C. 338
Muda, Hubertus 162
Mukhlis 217
Müller, Salomon 13–14, 324, 333, 391
Munro, W. G. 21, 25, 47–8, 90, 96, 101, 113, 122–3, 135, 388, 390
Musschenbroek, S. C. J. W. van 311, 336

Naga 77
Nakano, Tetsuo 395, 398
Nange 237, 395
Nara Guan 298
Nearchus 337
Neck, Jackob van 338
Needham, Rodney viii, 14–15, 19, 81, 377, 396
Nidi Tobin 395
Nieuhof, Johannes 339
Niggemeyer, Hermann 32
Nogo 68–9
Noorduyn, J. 100, 326, 387
Nooteboom, C. 171–2, 392, 395
Nudek, Ignasius Getan 395

Ola Bélu Taran 67
Oleona, Ambros vii, 151, 172, 184, 193, 196, 204, 213, 220, 230, 242–3, 248, 260, 392
Oliva, Fr. Giampaollo 382
Oliver, W. H. 331
Ollier, C. D. 6
Ommanney, F. D. 331
Ormeling, F. J. 2, 6, 389, 401
Orta, Garcia da 325
Ossenbruggen, F. D. E. 81, 102
Oudtshoorn, Arnold de Vlamingh van 13
Ouwehand, C. 31–2
Owen, W. F. W. 338
Oxford University Expedition to Kei Kecil 393

Pago 160
Pajo Kifa Ama 67
Pandai 67
Parason 118
Parry, Jonathan 343
Pati Mangun 67, 76
Paun, Captain 237, 395
Paung 72
Pehl, Bruno 96–7, 125–6
Pelliot, Paul 338, 401
Pelly, Usman 204, 212, 217, 394–5
Peni Bélã Lolo 70, 226
Pigeaud, Th. 1, 377
Pires, Tomé 99, 378, 387
Piskaty, Kurt 26
Poerwadarminta, W. J. S. 377
Polo, Marco 338
Pope, the 383
Poro, Captain 17
Portugal, King of 383
Pott, J. G. 102
Prins, A. H. J. 230
Prior, John Mansford 91, 102, 396

Radermacher, J. C. M. 100
Raffles, William Stamford 330, 401
Raja Bala Mai(k) 65
Raja of Lamakera 51, 203
Reiche, Th. 361
Reid, Anthony 16–17, 30, 103, 109, 390, 401
Reinaud, M. 325
Renard-Clamagirand, Brigitte 81
Resink, G. J. 18, 30
Ridley, Henry N. 211
Riedel, J. G. F. 15–16
Rienzi, G. L. D. 328, 401
Roderick, William Lewis 334
Rouffaer, G. P. 7, 386, 401
Ruibing, Aaldrik Hendrik 16
Rumphius, Georgius Everhardus 323, 325–6, 339

Sá, Artur Basílio de 29, 99, 399
Sai 77
Samely, Ursula 163
Samo, Kakang 286
Sande, G. A. J. van der 101
Santa Catharina, Lucus de 29, 323
Schare, Andrea 31
Schulte Nordholt, H. G. 323
Scoresby, W. 330
Scott, W. H. 204, 214, 216, 382, 390
'Second' Raja of Larantuka 57, 60
Seegeler, C. J. 23–4, 48, 57, 60, 90, 109, 304
Semmelink, J. 19, 148, 380
Sherman, D. George 342–3, 387–8, 390
Silalahi, Saddon viii

Sinu Kéfa Ama 67
Sinu Kiko 79–80
Slijper, E. J. 291
Smale, M. J. 280–1
Smit, J. G. V. 400
Smith, R. B. 378
Snyder, James Wilbert
Solé 43, 74
Solor, Queen of 13, 17, 99–100
Somi Bola Deran 58, 113, 384
Sopher, David E. 1–2
Sousa, Luís de 11, 382
Spanoghe, J. B. 324, 328
Speelman, Cornelis 100, 326
Speelman, Raja Solomon 326, 400
Spoehr, Alexander 1–2
Sprenger, Aloys 325
Stackpole, Edouard A. 334
Standing Person 384
Stapel, F. W. 12, 324
Steinhauer, Hein 393
Stirrat, R. L. 343
Stockum, van 361
Stokhof, W. A. L. 391
Strabo 337
Sutherland, H. 14, 17
Svensson, Sam 259
Swieten, Th. van 389
Symons, J. J. M. F. 24, 30

Tapoona, Paulus 398
Tarling, Nicholas 14
Tasman, Abel Jansz 13
Taylor, Paul Michael 393
Temminck, C. J. 4
Ternate, Sultan of 12–13, 379, 383
Teysmann, J. E. 386, 392, 394
Tibbets, G. R. 19, 387
Tiele, P. A. 12, 18, 203, 387
Timmers, M. 103
Timor, Assistant-Resident of 388
Timor, Resident of 15–16, 43, 47, 100, 102, 203, 324, 327, 330–1, 334–5, 381, 389
Townsend, Charles Haskins 334
Trautmann, Thomas R. ix
Tuck, James A. 396
Tukan, Bernard 386
Tukan, Johan Suban 386

Uba 75
Ula 77
U.S. Navy Hydrographic Office 10, 154–5, 321, 361, 383, 392

Valentyn, François 201, 399–400
Valmy, Robert 338

Vatter, Ernst 6, 31, 32, 56–7, 60–2, 91, 115–16, 121–3, 129, 142, 158, 160–2, 246–7, 304, 336, 385–6
Vergouwen, J. C. 387
Verheijen, J. A. J. 2, 158, 214, 257, 392–5, 402
Veth, P. J. 15, 100, 336
Vickers, A. H. 377
Villeneuve G. G. de 47, 378
Voorhoeve, C. L. 393
Vries, J. de 25
Vroklage, Bernhard 102

Walsh, D. S. 396
Wanjon, Timotheus 400
Warren, James Francis 13, 14
Warwijck, Wybrant 338
Watson, Lyall 292–3, 376
Watson, W. 378
Webb, R. A. F. Paul 379
Weber, Max 336

Weber-van Bosse, A. 383
Wehr, Hans 237, 299
West, Janet viii, 334, 401
Wheatley, Paul 387
White, Walter Grainge 1–2
Wichmann, Arthur 25, 381–2
Wicks, Robers S. 390
Wignyanta, Thom 370
Wijnen, R. 324
Wilkinson, R. J. 150, 237, 299, 390–1
William V. 401
Williams, B. R. 331
Williams, Captain 400
Wilson, John 335–6, 401
Windt, Niko van den 4, 21, 25, 49
Wintjes, P. A. 35, 42, 44, 54, 121–2, 168, 359–60, 381, 391, 393
Wouden, F. A. E. van 81

Yosef Raja Muda 41, 47, 57, 113, 122, 382
Yule, Henry 338

SUBJECT INDEX

Abo-Muã 56
abortives 112
absence of markets 139–41
Acanthurus spp. 170
accident at sea 246, 316
Aceh 30, 296, 400
administrative structure 46
Adonara 3, 12–13, 16–17, 20, 21, 25–6, 28, 29,
   31–2, 48, 50, 57, 62, 65, 88–9, 91–2, 100,
   103, 109, 115 16, 123, 131, 136, 140, 148,
   165, 173, 203, 286, 317–18, 323, 336, 379,
   381, 383, 386, 389, 398, 400–1
Adventure 334, 401
adzes 213–14, 241, 243, 247
ãé marã 108, 129
Aegialitis annulata 386
Aegialitis rotundifolia 386
Aetobatus Narinari 282
Afdeeling Larantoeka en onderhoorigheden 381
Africa 51
afterbirth 109
afternoon 158
Agena 157
aggression 1
agricultural products 138, 143
agriculturalists 5, 144
aji 274
alliance cycles 82
alliance, marriage 20, 74, 81–108, 179, 187
   variation in 81
   see also assymetric marriage alliance
alliances between descent groups 81–7
Aloe Vera, Linn. 216, 394
Alor 3–4, 12, 15–16, 21, 31, 104, 203, 320–1,
   326, 328, 332, 334–6, 379, 394
Alor language 3, 203
Alpine-Himalayan belt of volcanoes 6
Alstonia scholaris 392
Alstonia specatbilis 392
ama 114, 161
Amanuban 401
ambergris 74, 78, 100, 323, 325–9, 399–400
ambergris-hunting camels 325
ambergris shark 326
ambergris springs 325
Ambon 56, 99, 330, 399–400
American whalers 323, 400
American whaling methods 396
Amsterdam 102
amu alep 117
ana méã 110

ana-opu 82, 87, 128
ãnã-opu biné-maki 184
ãnã-opu ina-biné 184
ancestors 66–7, 102, 111, 113, 117–19, 121, 124,
   158, 161, 184, 241, 244, 248, 262, 274, 277,
   297–8, 313, 385–6, 397–8
anchor 69
'anchor' stones 64
anchorage 49
ang kotã lõlong 197
angi 153
angi Fãi Lula nãé 154
angi Fato Méã nãé 154
angi kota futu nãé 154
angi lẽfã 153
angi nadé 153
angi pãnga 154
angi tana 154
ankle ring, bronze 381
Anna & Louisa 333
Antarctic 339
Antares 157
anti-dehydration packages 133
antlers, deer 328
ants 318
Anu Fanga 43
apa bélã 157
apa bélã laké 157
apa bélã roné 157
apu 138
ãpu 391
ãpulolo 166
arã 251
ãrã 209
ãrã bélã 209, 211, 217, 243
ãrã belikãng 209–11, 216, 243
arã kélik 214
ãrã kenãti 209–11, 243
ãrã tũkã 209–10, 243
Arabic 380
Arabs 325–6, 338, 387, 399
arak 100, 103, 317
areca nuts 141, 143–4, 154, 186, 244, 247, 270
Areca catechu, Linn. 247
aref 251
areng palm, *see* sugar palm
Arenga pinnata, Merr. 216
Arenga saccharifera, Labill. 216
ari-ãmã 81–2
ari-ana, léi lima 77
armpit share 185–6

Arsip National 400
assemblage at the beach 270
assignations 90
assisted dowels 217
asymmetric marriage alliance 81, 85, 87, 344,
    348, 352–4, 386
ata marang 90, 92
ata molã 117–18, 120, 123, 182, 241, 266
ata mõlã bélã 241
ata mõlã kéni 241
ata ribu 63
Ata Déi (Standing Person) 22–3, 58, 72, 77,
    113, 177, 306, 384, 397
Ata Folo 40, 63, 70, 77, 83, 85, 87, 98, 113
Ata Gora 40, 63, 70, 72–3, 77, 83, 85, 87, 113,
    170, 240
Ata Kéi 40–1, 63, 69–70, 75–6, 83–4, 86, 113,
    131, 180
Ata Kéi, Lamamanu 69–70, 98
Ata Nila 182, 259
Atadiké! 301
Atafolo 113
Atapupu 14–15, 328, 335, 389
Atawolo 384
Atawuwur 9, 72
até 115
Atlantic 329
attachment of harpoon leader and rope 252
attack on *Sili Ténã* 51
au 255–6, 395
au rabo 392
Auckland 331
Australia 9–10, 331, 362, 386
Australian Continental Crust 6
Austronesian languages 339, 383, 391
Awé Lolo 70
axes 213, 335
Azores 396

babies 110–11
Bacau 335
back door 120
backpackers 345
backstay 218–19, 223, 228
bad deaths 120, 126, 132–3
bad seaworms period 151, 391
Bada Ilé Golé 70
Badi Langu 40–1, 63–4, 76–7, 80, 84, 86, 180
baé tabé soro 167
bafã burã 176
bafalofé, see gates, village
Bafalofé Bélã 44
Bafalofé Lefoléin 44
Bafalofé Méi Larã 44–5
Bahasa Indonesia 90, 112, 119, 230, 298, 321,
    354, 390
bai 168, 297

bai béra! 297
bai béra muri 293
bai huba menoté-angi 167
bailer 69, 267, 271
bailers 196, 199, 229, 246, 277
bailers' share 197
bailing 218
bailing pots 229
bait 276, 282, 392
Bajo Laut 69, 291
baka 385
Baka Fai 59
Baka Ténã 59, 180, 231, 266, 305, 385, 396, 398
Baka Walang 385
bako 172
balai desa 42
balast 173
Balaurin 50, 140, 177
balé 40
Balé Olé Mau 39–41, 64
baleen plates 332, 399
baleen whales 54, 69, 274, 282
baleia 307
baléo 152, 274, 306–7, 396
Bali 103, 110, 395
Bama 91
bamboo 69–70, 73, 132–3, 169, 182, 193,
    197–8, 203, 216, 218–19, 226, 243, 251,
    255–7, 309, 318–20, 324, 395
bamboo cup 266
bamboo guide for palm strips in weaving sail
    225
bamboo poles 218–19
banana tree trunk substitutes for a corpse 122,
    131–2
banana, wild 248, 385
bananas 143–6, 247–8, 288, 315, 335, 381, 389
Banda 99, 400
Banda Sea 332, 392
Bandung 83
Banggai Archipelago 56
bank 104, 388
banko 170
Bantam 401
Banten 377
banyan 39
bao 171
Bao Futung 40, 45
Bao Langu 397
bapa 112, 114
bapa, pěleba 297
baptism 112, 114, 118, 383
barafãi 150–3
barnacles, giant 168
barter 103, 137, 139, 141, 146–9, 175, 186, 315,
    325, 389
bartering 145

base of mast 219
baskets 94, 109, 143, 146, 153, 177, 267, 318,
  384
Baso Langu 63, 84
Basques 396
Basra 338
Bata, *see* Bata Bala Mai
Bata Bala Mai 65, 88, 385
Bata Fo 40, 59, 63, 67, 77, 82–4, 86, 98, 113,
  119, 180
bata nama pota apé 304
Bata Onā 39–40, 59, 60, 63–4, 66–7, 72, 73,
  76–7, 82–4, 86, 88, 98, 113, 122, 124, 180,
  241, 269, 271, 383–4
Batafor 113
Bataona 113
Batavia 18, 102, 324, 329, 331–3, 381, 401
Batavian Society of Arts and Sciences 101–2
bathing 130, 271
bathing, four day restriction on 95
battery carbon 215, 318
Batugade 401
bau 39, 382
baut 217, 227
Day of Antongil 330
Bay of Bengal 386
Bay of Bone 56
beach 35, 45–6, 65, 115–16, 124, 153, 156, 170,
  179, 184, 186, 188, 199, 206, 244, 246, 248,
  260–1, 263, 268–72, 277, 288, 295, 301–5,
  309, 318, 321, 399
Bean 320
bedi 170
Bedi Onā 40, 59, 63, 67, 68, 70, 72, 75, 77, 79,
  88, 98, 113, 170, 180, 194, 203
Beding 113
befajak 212
běfalé 228
běfaléng 227–8, 255, 275
běfānā 184, 187, 195, 365–6
běfānā bélā 183–5, 187, 193, 195, 365
běfānā kéni 184, 187, 366
befedā 168
beka 170
béket 197–8
bélā 69–70, 226
bělāda 193–4, 253, 255, 294, 296
bělāda alep 188
bělaja-petola 136
Bělaké Langu 40, 63, 76, 84, 86
belāku 184
bělaong mas 80
bělarā 117
bělarā kalipīn baa 388
bělaung 384
Bélé Gora 77
belébā 281–2

bělélā 239
bělelā 156, 196–7, 253, 255, 257, 276, 280, 282,
  284–5, 287, 309, 311, 313–15, 317, 321,
  396, 399
bělelā haring 280
bělelā lemé 280
belera, see stone seats
běléréng 239
beletu 273
beléu 219
beléu fā 219, 222
beléu uring 219, 223
Bělida Ténā 69
Bělido hir kaé 298
bělifo 94
bělik 146
bělika 170
Běliko Lolo 34, 39–41, 43, 54, 59, 63–7, 74–7,
  80, 82–4, 86, 98, 112–13, 122, 147, 170,
  217, 239, 269–70
Belikololong 113
bělīna 219, 227
bellows 251–2
bélo 295, 297
bělobeo 208–9
bélo fika 248
beloé 225
Belogili 32, 162
běloi 257
běloné 108
bělorak 266
Belu 56, 389
Belugus 43
belulung 292
bělūtu 109, 392
bělutu 72, 170
bench 384
Bengal 99
Beni Onā 79, 83, 87
běrā 217
Béra Onā 40–1, 63, 72, 74, 75, 84, 86
beragi 137
běréun 83
běréun alep 294, 308–9
Bernusa descent group 77–6
Bernusa, Pantar 77, 322, 379
béro 172–3, 176, 225, 306, 313, 392
béro baololo 172
béro kělaba 171
berok kelaba 392
běromé 309
Besi 297
bestuursassistent 381
betel 95, 138, 143, 186, 244, 247, 270, 296
  basket 212, 285
  pepper 141, 143, 154, 186, 270
běti 186

Betsimasaraka 338–40
bezoar 100, 387, 400
Bima 328
bindings 175, 205–6, 264–5, 273
bindings holding the loop at the end of the
    harpoon rope 127
bioluminescence, *see* phosphorescence
bird nests 100, 318, 326, 328
birth 109, 204
birth control 111–12
bité 263, 264–5
bité lorak 266
bītu 168
black 135
black magic 290
Black Portuguese 12–13, 323
blade 250, 294
blade of harpoon 245
Blagar 379
blood 119, 124, 241, 243–4, 246, 261–2, 277,
    299, 384–5
blubber 195, 255, 293, 309, 325, 327–8, 338,
    399
Blue-spotted Sting Ray 281
blue whale 274, 282
bō 267
boat becoming drunk 287
boat builder, *see* master boat builder
boat building 128, 135, 179, 203–43, 324, 342,
    367–70, 393–4
boat construction ceremonies 183, 241, 243
boat construction sequence 206–19
boat corporations 127, 149, 179–200, 260, 311,
    364–6
  obligations of members of 149
boat launching 204, 238, 243, 246, 248–9
boat master 125, 127, 179, 181, 183, 185, 188–9,
    194–200, 230, 244, 249, 263, 300, 305–8,
    313, 316, 364, 366, 392
boat measurements 372–5
boat names 229
boat-owning groups 179–200
boat sheds 35–8, 70, 121–5, 152, 175, 194, 230,
    244, 246, 261, 271–2, 277–8, 300, 301–4,
    318, 365, 398
boat signals for assistance 130
boat sinking at Ata Déi 384
boats 50, 115–16, 124–5, 127, 130, 149–50,
    152–3, 156–7, 165–8, 171–88, 193–4,
    198–204, 253, 259, 270–322, 326, 344–5,
    364–6, 371–5, 384, 393, 395–6, 398
  dismantled 345
  lost 308, 398
  pulled by sperm whales 142, 304–6, 396–8
  pulled under by whales 306
  sunk 290, 294
boat's centre 213

Bobu 58, 72, 152, 170, 176–8, 203
body 115
bokel ketebu 225–6
bokil arā 214
Boko Lolo 180, 233, 239–40, 266
bŏlé 263
Boleng 25, 165, 286
Boli Sapā 180, 232, 266, 314, 364
boltropes 221–2
bomak 128–9, 241
bombing fish 171
bone setter 117
Bonerate 285
bones 309
bonito 401
boom 220–2, 395
booms 182
bōpa 260–2, 265–6
bopo lari 115
Borneo 14, 172, 387
Botany Bay 400
Boto 9, 142, 146
bottlenose dolphins 328, 399
bōu 173, 196, 255, 275, 280–2, 284–6, 305, 311,
    314, 396, 399
boundary, land/sea 46
Bounty 400
bow 223, 228–9, 234–6, 243, 246, 250, 255,
    259, 267, 271, 290, 294, 395
  decorations 229–38
bowsprit, *see* stempost
Brachirus brachypterus 176
brain 245, 278, 287
brazil wood, *see* sappan wood
breakers 156, 171, 257, 271, 301, 309, 392
breech births 109
bricks 152
bride abduction 386
bride capture 90–2
bride service 96, 386
bridewealth 66, 91–2, 95–6, 102, 104, 106, 136,
    343, 349, 388
  see also marriage prestations
brine 138–9
Britain 32
British 30, 330, 398, 400
British occupation of the Dutch East Indies 401
British whalers 323, 329
Bronze Age 204
bua 265
bua ana 109
budi tree 39, 382
buffalo 76, 335, 384, 400–1
Bugis 14, 56, 103, 204, 217, 325, 328, 394–5
bui 383
Bui Pukā 58, 180, 230, 233, 239, 266, 383
Bui Pukā/Keroko Pukā 383

buna 251
buoys for harpooned whales 338
burial 121–4, 126, 130–1, 136, 142
burial of ancestral skulls 244
burning knots in wood 217
Buton 12, 148, 285
Butonese 100, 201, 328
Buyasuri 22–3
buying the currents and wind 58, 60

cactus 35, 44
Caesalpinia Sappan, Linn. 216
calcining lime, *see* lime making
calendar 150–3, 391
Calicut 386
Calotropis gigantea 44, 56
Cambodia 100, 390
Canarium communei 264
candlenut 117–18, 244, 381
candles 133
Candraditya Centre 161
cannons 41, 102, 382
canon law 108
Cape Horn 333
Cape of Good Hope 101
capital 101–2
capsizing 229, 285, 294, 297, 299, 306, 317, 388
Carchardon carcharius (Linnaeus) 393
cardinal points 163–7, 391
Caretta Caretta 199
carpentry 26, 181
carrying loads 135
cartilage 196, 198, 310
cash 106, 108, 139–41, 144, 342–3, 387, 398
cassava 153, 315
categorical confusion 61
Catholic Junior High School 396
Catholic marriage 96
Catholic mission 21, 25, 35, 42, 51–3
  see also missionaries
Catholicism 81
Catholics 53
cattle 387
caulking 198, 216, 273, 318, 328
causes of misfortune or illness 119, 123, 132, 398
caves 43, 387
Ceiba pentandra 211
Celebes 14, 100, 103, 333
celestial objects 150
Cerbon 377
ceremonial exchange, *see* exchange, ceremonial
ceremonial locations 74
ceremonies 39, 44, 62, 93, 96–7, 110, 115, 119–20, 122, 128, 175, 179, 181, 197–8, 204, 241–9, 299–300, 315, 322, 328, 340, 344, 397

annual fisheries 60, 68, 243, 268–71, 398
  to clean the mouth 287, 299
  for people lost at sea 397
  to undo funerals 142
cetacean intestines, fermenting 309
cetaceans 280
Ceylon 401
charcoal 215, 251, 318
charter myth 55–61
chest share 184–5, 365
chicken 117–18, 124, 128–9, 175, 241, 243, 245–6, 251, 262–3, 381, 400–1
  feathers 176
  head 243
  meat 241–2
children 46, 60, 73, 92, 105, 112, 114, 133, 135, 153, 186, 195, 246, 248, 270, 300–1, 317, 346–7
  carried away by currents 171
Chile 31
China 19, 230, 335, 339, 363, 387, 399
China Sea 332
Chinese 19, 328, 330, 387
Chinese imperial court 387
Chinese merchants 101, 117, 177, 200, 336, 362, 400
chisel and peg 183, 185, 195, 199, 364
chisels 241, 247, 250, 395
Christianity 231
church 35, 41, 43, 52, 124–5, 248, 298, 388–9
Church 87, 197–8, 314, 344, 348–9, 386, 396
ciguatera 361
cinnamon, wild 100
circles of obligation 105
circling water over the head 110–11
circulating connubium 81
citrus 143, 381
Citrus maxima 335
civilgezaghebber 381
clan divisions, *see* descent group divisions
clan temple, *see* great house
clan treasures 54
clans, *see* descent groups
closing the sea 130
cloth, *see* textiles
cloth money 148
clothing 94, 108, 129–30, 135, 147, 172, 273, 275, 335, 342
coastal dwellers 3, 103, 135, 138–9, 142, 148, 151, 343, 377–8
Cochin China 386
coconut-leaf roof 269
coconut oil 96, 100, 123–4, 143, 244, 326
coconut palm 239
coconuts 143–5, 147, 216, 335, 381, 383, 390
coffee 143, 146, 315, 381
coffin 127, 130, 133

Coffin's Bay 401
coiling rope 259
coils of rope 261
coins 148
colour of cloth 389
colours 135
commensality 93, 123
commercial exchanges 103
commodities 343
communications 49–51
completed life 126
compression 173, 205–7, 218
compression loop 214–15, 394
confession 120, 287, 315, 397
conical hats 273
construction principles 203–6
construction work 180
contact with whalers 336–7
contract between mountain agriculturalists and
    coastal fishermen 142
conversions between spheres of exchange 343
conviviality of markets 144
copper wire 100
copra 147
coral 138, 304
coral reefs 322
cord around edges of sections of a sail 222
cord for restraining harpoon rope 229
Cordia subcordata, Linn. 206, 217
cords 257, 264
    framing sections in the sail 220
    suspended from the yard 223
Coromandel Coast 99
corporations, _see_ boat-owning groups
corpse eating 159, 161, 163
Corypha elata, Roxb. 394
Corypha gebanga, Blume 394
Corypha utan, Lam. 182, 394
Cosmography 338
cotton 100, 111, 135–6, 141, 149, 150, 258–60,
    263–4, 390
coup of 1965: 50, 116
cows 76
craft specializations, _see_ production
    specializations
crafts 26
crew 166, 181–3, 187–9, 193–200, 244, 253,
    257, 267, 271–4, 276, 278, 283, 284–6,
    293–4, 297–8, 303, 306, 309, 313–14,
    317–18, 320–1, 344–5
crew's share 195
crown of the rope 261
crustaceans 310
cultural tourism 344
currency 390
currents 150, 153–6, 158, 166–7, 171, 177, 222,
    272–3, 287, 295, 298–9, 313, 318, 320, 384

cursing 295, 315, 398
customary law 90, 97, 103, 397
cutting timber for boats 299
cutting up fish 180, 246
cutting up ray 180
cutting up whales 38, 45, 302
cutting up whales and porpoises 188–95
cuttlefish 326
Cuyo Islanders 390
cycles of production 149
cycles of wealth objects 103
Cygnet 320

Daé Langu 40, 63, 76, 84, 86
Daemonorhopos 394
dancing 89–90, 123, 246–7
dangers at sea 307–9
dapu 243
dasi 385
Dasi Langu 40–1, 63–4, 66, 74–5, 77, 84, 86,
    98, 112, 180
Dasion 112
Dato Ténã 142, 180, 232, 266, 304
dawn 158, 247
day 158
dead souls, _see_ dead spirits
dead spirits 79, 110–11, 115, 122–3, 129, 130,
    142, 184, 244
death 42, 64, 79–80, 97, 108, 110, 116, 119,
    121–34, 142, 320, 391
    see also bad
deaths:
    in childbirth 133
    by falling from trees 123, 126
    by heart attack 316
    at sea 116–17, 126, 130–3, 171, 277, 294,
        297, 307–8, 322
    from snake bite 126
    songs 125
    in war 123
debt slavery 89, 92, 343, 379
debts 92
decline in fishery 306, 310–11, 314
decorated bows 172, 229–38
decorated stern piece of boats 137, 209–10, 217,
    243, 245, 318
decorations on harpooning platform 219
decorations on _sasalāpi_ 318
decorative strips of cloth 216, 235, 237
deer 387
Deer Island 129, 320–1
déi mega gé mo tūba ikã 283
deko tou 74
Demo Sapã 177, 180, 231, 239, 266, 290, 299,
    316, 364, 384, 398
Demon 29, 160
Demon and Paji 29, 31, 49, 160

Demon Lewo Pulo 29
Dendrocalamus asper 256, 394
depopulation 345
depression, economic 50
Dermochelys Coriacea 199
Derris elliptica 170
Derris spp. 385
descent groups 38, 55–6, 62–87, 92, 96–9, 105,
    108, 110, 119, 122, 126–7, 129, 132, 137,
    179–80, 183, 185, 187, 230, 246, 262–3,
    268–70, 298, 325, 364–6
  autochthonous 68
  class divisions within 63, 74–7, 179
  expulsion from 85, 88
  incorporation of outsiders 63
  leaders 64, 92, 130, 186–7, 200, 204, 271
  rituals 62, 244
  which have disappeared 79
development 5–6
development, physical 109–20
devil ray 173–4
Dian 93
digging the first soil at a burial 126
Dili 15, 18, 330, 335, 380
directions 150, 163–7, 391
disaster at Lapan Batan, legend of 54–61, 75,
    113, 383
dispersal of population 61
display of wealth 60
dissention within boat-owning groups 179–82,
    204, 253, 299
distaff 388
distinction between coastal and mountain
    dwellers 3–4, 15–16, 103, 135–49, 377–
    8
divers 169
dividing up whales, *see* cutting up whales
Divine Word Society 35, 51, 344, 383
division of fish 277, 299
division of provisions brought to boat 298
division of turtle 199
division of whale 292
divorce 108
dogs 110, 121, 175, 246, 316, 381
Dolu Ténā 180, 237, 266, 307, 314, 317–20, 398
Dominicans 4, 11, 382–3
Doni Nusa Léla 59, 142, 384
door of great house, regulations about 300
door posts 244
dopā 281
dopi 248
dorsal fin 195
dowels 198, 204, 213–14, 216, 217, 241, 395
dowels, large 217, 219
drain hole 172, 212, 229, 258
dreaming 115, 313
dried fish 390

dried meat 328
driftnets 282
drums, bronze 104
dry season 10, 138–9, 150–2, 155, 268, 270,
    312, 333, 389, 391
drying fish 317–18, 324
drying platforms 35, 186, 192
drying rack 300
du hopé 149
du sūsu 186
Duang Rego Pati Mangun 67, 76, 113
dugong 291, 340
Dugong dugon 291
dugouts 168, 171–2
  construction of 171
duit 390
Duli 320–2
duri 253, 296–7
Dutch 3–4, 11–14, 17, 19–21, 25, 30, 35, 39,
    47–8, 51, 91, 99, 103, 140, 148, 168, 203,
    322–5, 329, 331–2, 336, 342, 381–3,
    389–90, 393–4, 400–1
  attempted return after World War II 50
  language 297
  voyages to the Indies 338
  whaling 331–3
Dutch East Indies 330–3, 377, 390, 400–1
Dutch East Indies Company 13, 17–19, 91,
    99–100, 103, 323–4, 327, 329, 332
dyeing 135, 137–8, 385
dyes 135–6, 140–1
  chemical 135–6, 141, 143, 389
dysentery 133
D'Amboinsche Rariteitkamer 323

E. & S. & C. St Martin, N. J. de Cock, and
    C. A. Vlierboom 333
earrings 147
'ears' 196–7, 208, 245, 287
earthquake 111, 130, 388
east current 154–6, 166–7, 272, 280, 301, 313,
    318
east monsoon, *see* dry season
east wind 153–4, 165, 166, 272–3, 280, 287–8,
    298
East African coast 325
East Flores Regency, *see* Kabupaten Flores
    Timur
eating dirt 110
Ebā Onā 40–2, 63, 69, 76, 82–4, 86, 98, 113
  ancestor of brought on the back of a whale
    42
Ebang 113
ebb tides 150, 154
eclipse of the moon 157
eclipse of the sun 158, 391
edge to edge planking 173, 204

education 24–6, 50, 53, 117, 147, 181, 342–3,
    345
Eersteling 333
egg 24, 268
Egyptian ships 216, 394
éka 158
éka daé 158
elders 161, 277, 300, 314, 397
ĕlé 172, 218
ĕlé alep 184
ĕlé fana 227
ĕlé meki 227
electricity 50, 133
elephants 387
Elisabeth 293
elopement 90–1, 386
ĕlu 253, 297
ema 112, 114
ĕma fai 296–7
Ema Onã 69
emptying a sunken boat 290, 306
Emu Sia pota apé 304
enã 155
enã ba 156
enã bëliku 156
enã benak 156
enã bodo 156
enã fafĕ ferong 156
enã keperek 156
enã kĕléa 156
enã nabé dupa 156
enã odo 156
enã onã 156
enã sĕmugur 156
enã taduk 156
Ende 14–15, 19, 47, 49, 69, 100, 103, 139, 389
Endeavour 400
Endenese 14
England 332, 401
English 19, 51, 145, 390, 401
English (language) 230, 321
English whalers, *see* British whalers
eor 115
Eretmochelys Embricata 199
erosion 10
erysipelas 117, 388
Ethnological Museum of Frankfurt, Germany
    31–2
éto lata ria 176
Eulamia macrura 401
Europe 19, 230–1, 388
European clothing 89
European traders 377
Europeans 4, 10, 13, 16–20, 29, 90, 119, 125,
    325, 343, 378
evaporation pans 138
even numbers 228, 265

evening star 157
evil spirits 128, 247
exchange:
    ceremonial 20, 149, 343
    of crafts 59–60, 142
    cycles 343
    of goods in kind 141, 175, 390
    of office 59–60, 66, 75, 142
exogamy 81
    breach of 83, 87
extension to harpoon pole 255–6
extension to pole used in the surf 257
extensions to planks 209–10, 217, 219, 243
extensions to ropes 257–9
external trade 149
eyes 230

fã 265–6
fadar 184, 186, 193, 195, 263
fadar-folar 195
fafĕ 156
fafĕ kebingu 392
fai 296–7
fãi 267, 297
fai lera fulã 269
Fãi Lula nãé 154
fai mãtã 227, 229
fai matã alep 196
fai matã alep fãnã 246
Fai Bĕlolo, *see* springs, tidal
Fai Léré, *see* springs, tidal
Fai Nãé 154
faja 267
fãja 296
faja pu 392
fãjo 214–15
fala 392
false ends 207, 211
false keel 206, 277
false killer whale 255–6, 274
family associations 46
family histories 74
Family *Sphyrinidae* 393
famine 153, 246, 343
fao 176, 180, 393
Fao Pukã 79, 230
fãra 153–4, 165
fãra lĕfa 154
fãra tana 154
fãré 198
fata biti 392
father's sister's daughter marriage 88, 349
father's sister's son marriage 83, 87, 92
fato 384
fato bani 241
Fato Bélã 56
Fato Bélã Bako 384

fato bĕlang 168
fato fajo 70
fato faka 59
fato kener 241
Fato Kotekĕlema 268
fato lité 170
Fato Méã nãé 154
Fatu Boli Ama 43
faults 117–20, 123, 127–8, 181, 228, 276–7, 287, 299–300, 315, 322, 397–8
feasts 83, 108, 114, 120, 123, 126–7, 129, 146, 175, 206, 241–2, 246–7, 316, 398
feda 168
feeding sacred stones 270
feeding the boat 243, 246
fefã 208, 245
fefã bélã alang meloan 245
fefakumu 274
feki 115
feki lãki 208, 216
feki rõné 208, 216
fĕla 145
Felãdã 297
fĕli 102
festival 93, 108, 114, 123, 127, 136, 186, 217, 246–7, 263, 398
fĕta 199, 396
fĕu 207, 210
feuding 140
fevers 133
Ficus bengalensis 39
Ficus benjamina 382
Ficus religiosa 382
field knives 100
field research vii–viii
fields 70, 309
film 32
finger rings 310
fire-arms, confiscation of 20, 47, 123, 322, 335
fire sticks 241, 243
fires 10, 301, 304
firewood 135, 139
first communion 114
first cross-cousin cousin marriage 85, 87, 92, 386
    Catholic prohibition on 85, 349, 354, 386
first day a new boat goes out 245
first day of fishing season 244
first harpooning 257
first parallel cousin marriage 85
fisar 291
fish 115, 121, 122, 124, 130, 137–9, 141–6, 150, 168–71, 173–7, 181, 196–200, 204, 243, 245–7, 259, 263–6, 268–322, 324, 355–62, 392
    intestines, fermenting 309, 319–20
    line 168
    names 168, 391
    poison 170, 392
    temple 269
    traps 72, 168–70
    types 168, 282
    weights 168
Fish Heads, *see Ikã Kotã*
Fisheries Service 174
fishermen 14, 142, 152, 155, 227–8, 231, 251, 280–2, 285, 290–1, 295–6, 307, 321, 325, 381, 392
fishery 59–60, 68, 141, 180, 246, 260, 310
fishing 2, 5, 39, 118, 130, 140–1, 149, 152, 168–78, 181, 201, 203, 209, 243–4, 250, 268–88, 309–22, 324, 327, 342–3, 389
    communities 1
    gear 74, 342
    lines 173, 177, 250, 273, 321–2, 392
    pole 168, 392
    season, large scale 41
fiti-bala 102
fiti-belãu 106
flag of boats 70, 72, 240
flag of *Soge Ténã* 226
flash floods 10
flensing knives 253, 294, 297
float fishing 171
floating coral 287–8
flood, *see* inundation, legions of
Florenese 327
Flores 2, 4, 6, 10, 14–16, 19, 21, 26, 30–2, 48–9, 52, 57, 61–4, 68–71, 73, 75, 91, 100–3, 109, 116, 119, 121, 138–40, 148, 155, 160, 162, 170, 209–11, 232, 247, 291, 310, 312–13, 317, 321, 323, 327, 334, 336, 349, 379, 382, 385–7, 389, 400–1
Flores Strait 19, 155, 168, 312–13
flying fish 17, 173, 176 7, 253, 273, 275, 278
foetuses, ray 280, 314–15
folar 195
folding and wrapping palm leaf strips 225–6
folk etymology 54
fontanelle 110
Food and Agricultural Organization 173–4, 311
Food and Agriculture Organization project 24
football 89
forã 195
forehead 194
fore *léo* 229
forestay 219, 222–3
fork for resting the sail 223
forked sticks for holding fishing lines 273
forked termination to the mast poles 219, 245
frame cords of the sail 225
frame for weaving sail sections 220, 224
Fraser's dolphin 274

French 19
  occupation of Holland 401
  whalers 334, 400
Friend 339
front door 110–11, 120
fua 244
fufo 170
Fujon 113
fūka 211
Fūka Léré 40, 68, 268
Fuka Pukã 230
fūlã 109, 154, 156–8
fūlã bisak 157
fūlã géré mau 158
fūlã haka Lefotukã 158
fūlã hobing 158
fūlã kenéka 157
fūlã kukar nong 157
fūlã lali haka 158
fūlã maté 157
fulã malu 154
fūlã mitang 157
full moon 155, 158, 279–80, 282
fūlo 207, 251
fulolepã 280
funerals 111, 121, 125–31
Fung 40–1, 76
funo 156
funo pito 157
fura 153, 155–6
furã 195
fura-fãra 154
fura nalu 156
Fusu Golo 40
fūtu 197, 208, 216
fūtu-lima 216
Futung 42–3
Futung Lolo 24, 34, 38, 40, 45, 97, 172

gãda 256
Gafé Futuk 58
gaffs 253, 255, 259, 278, 285–6, 294
gēlara 116
Gali 17
galu 259
gambling 20
gaol 223
garlic 111, 176
Garuda 325
gaskets 223
gata poli ga 298
gaté 89
gates, village 43–4, 247
Gayo 383
gear 175–6, 203, 226, 250–67, 273
gebang palm 182, 219–20, 223, 250, 257,
  259–60, 263, 394
gebang palm leaf strips 223

géi ratã 114
gĕlefĕ 172, 227–8, 255, 275
gĕlefĕ fã 227
gĕlefĕ uring 227
Gĕléko Ténã 180, 184, 233, 266, 307
gĕletã 297
Gĕleteng tou! 296
gĕlĩfa 253
Geliting 15
gélo 218
gĕlõto 251
gélu 284
Gelu Gala Wutun 384
genealogies 61, 82, 87, 304
gerédo 109
Gereja hir kaé 298
Géripé 43
Germans 30
Germany 31–2
gĕroi téna 247–9
geru 218
Gési Guã Bala Bata Bala Mai, *see* Bata Bala Mai
Gési Raja hir kaé 298
gezaghebber 381
ghosts 115
giant octopus 287–8, 396
gifts 343
Gigantochloa scortechinii 255–6, 394
Gigantochloa verticillata 256
gĩli kajo 213
gills 196–7, 277
ginger 175–6, 264
Giri 379
glass bottles 400
Globicephala macrohyncus 255
Gnetum gnemon 257
Goa 380
goat, wild 387
Goat Island 129, 237, 321
goats 76, 88, 102, 108, 114, 118, 123, 129, 146,
  153, 246, 248, 263, 381
God 55, 123, 158–63, 242, 245, 273, 285, 316,
  321, 391, 396, 400
gofal ié 206
gold 100, 384
gold bracelets 102, 111
golden bench 58
golden chain 80, see also *Sora Kai*
golden earrings 80, 111, 143
golden ring 111
Golkar 174
Golok 72, 77
gongs 99–102, 343
good searworms period 151, 391
Goosebeak Whale (Cuvier's) 256, 274, 280, 291
goosebeak whales 173, 194
Goram 56, 72
Gorang 113

gouges 247
government ban on marriage festivals 93
government, village 46
governmental structure 29–31
grabbing sharks by the tail 170, 305, 309
Granada Television vii
graves 121–2, 125–7, 130, 133, 394
graveyard 41, 43, 124–6, 133
great house(s) 39–42, 62–7, 71, 74–6, 78, 95–7,
    108, 111, 113, 115, 120, 126–8, 130, 133,
    171, 175, 179–80, 185–7, 193, 241, 243–5,
    268, 270, 300, 307, 325, 329, 337, 345,
    364–6, 385
great *léo* 229
Greeks 201
Greenland 332
Gresik 377
Grewia 217
Grewia salutaris 394
grey (Risso's) dolphin 274
grief 121, 125
Groene Geuszen 13
guǎ gaté 211
guarding a corpse 123, 126–7
gudi 382
Gulf of Mexico 155
Guma Langu 40, 63, 76, 84, 86
Guna Langu 40, 63, 85, 87, 180
gunpowder 100–1, 322, 335, 387, 400
guté tenulaj 215
Gypsy 335

Hadakewa 30, 47, 49, 78, 116, 140, 177, 381
Haga Langu 40, 63, 75, 84, 86
Hainan Island 339–40
hair cutting 114, 136
hāla tree 54
Halmahera 10, 12
halo around the moon 157
Ham Bobu 384
hãmã 218, 227
hammerhead shark 199–200, 315
hangak 251, 258
hapus nu 287, 299
hapus nuté 299
hari 152
Hari Botan 160, 388
Hari Onã 40, 63, 70, 75, 83, 85, 87, 98, 113, 180
haring 130
Haring 113
harpoon measurements 254
harpoon pole rack 223, 228–9, 250, 258, 308
harpoon poles 186, 193, 195, 198, 243, 245, 250,
    255–7, 275, 279, 282, 284, 293, 308
harpoon ropes 218, 229, 243, 282, 294, 307
harpooner 186–8, 193, 195, 197–201, 208, 223,
    237, 243–4, 255, 271, 274–9, 282–4, 291,
    293–4, 303, 307–9, 313–14, 320

harpooner's assistant 229, 282, 284, 294, 303,
    308
harpooner's signals 293
harpooning:
    dugong 291
    fish 264, 270–88, 315, 318
    platform 198, 201, 211, 218–19, 222,
        245–6, 250, 256, 274–7, 283, 292–4,
        320
    porpoise 274–5, 283, 340
    ray 280–8, 309, 321
    shark 309, 324
    whales 142, 248, 289–312, 397
harpoons:
    brazil-wood 59, 142, 279
    iron 59, 89, 142, 182, 184, 193–4, 199, 201,
        245, 247, 250–67, 276, 282, 285, 289–90,
        293, 297, 307, 315, 323
    western 337
hats 273, 335
Hawaii 333
hawksbill turtle 199
hawser laid rope 259
Hayong clan 57
head of shark 199
head of sperm whale 194, 270
headhunting 15, 32, 161, 163, 382
healers 117–18, 134
health 20, 28, 117–18
heart 195
hearth stones 65
heirlooms 54–5, 60, 74, 100, 136, 325, 342
heka kemité 266
helã diké 127
helmsman 166, 207, 218, 292, 303, 314
helmsman's seat 228, 275
hēpa 216
heri téna lépé 152
Heteropcylla sp. 379
Hibiscus tiliaceus Linn. 176, 180, 220, 250, 257,
    259, 263
high tide 154–5
High Village 381
historical background, recent 47–9
histories of clans 55
history, regional 10–20, 383
hitting master builders' elbows 241–2
hoder 108, 263
hodi 390
hodi kělīfa 260
hodi kenaing 146
hodi léo 260–1
hodi talé 260
hofil 265–6
hoi kenafé 94
Holland 15, 332, 401
Holo Sapã 180, 202, 234–5, 266, 278, 314,
    360–1, 395, 398

holy stones, *see* sacred stones
holy water 242–4, 256, 261–2, 264, 269, 271,
    277, 287, 299, 316
hōmā 292
Honolulu 339
hook on forestay 222
hooks 176
hopi enā angi, see buying the currents and wind
Horo Ténā 180, 184, 236, 266, 314, 398
Horowura 62
hospital 308, 331
house building 140, 152
house of the dorsal fin 293
household associations 46, 176
houses 63–4, 90, 111, 125, 175
hūba ié 206
hull 218, 229, 243, 318
human sacrifice 382
hunger season 139, 153
Hunter 18
hunters and gatherers 2
hunting 10, 141, 149, 201, 222, 250, 268–88,
    289–322, 342
  large game 340
  ray 280–8
  whales and other cetations 289–312, 328, 338,
    344
hupā alep 117, 119
hupā tuber 117
huro 296, 297
huro menaluf héna! 297
hygiene 20

ida 219–20, 257
ideal pattern of marriage alliances 83, 97, 386
  lack of conformity to 83
identifying characteristics of sails 371
ié 206
ié fã 206
ié tūkã 206
ié uring 206
ié īnã 206
īfi 222
īfi léi 222
īfi lōlo 222
ikã 297
īkã 295
ikã aké nãé noi 217
ikã ãng 196
ikã fato feki 168
ikã gōkala 294
ikã kenéã 293
Ikã Kotã 44–5, 270
ikã lãja 193
ikã lemé 168
ikã mabok 293
ikã matã 392

ikã méã 173, 274, 280, 291
ikã pung alep 244, 271
ikã rã 208
ikat 135
īka ūk 197
īku 239
īku lãja 193, 195
Ilé Ado Wajung 7
Ilé Apé 22–3, 53, 135, 165
Ilé Belopor 8, 154
Ilé Benolo 8
Ilé Boleng 26, 280, 286
Ilé Hobal 7, 312, 379
Ilé Labalekang 7–9, 21, 39, 70, 289, 305
Ilé Lewotolo 7, 21, 26
Ilé Mandiri 280
  bird digs entrails of 73
  district 91
Ilé Mingar 21
Ilé Monyet 7
Ilé Petrus 7, 378
Ilé Wariran 7, 21
Ilé Werung 7–8
Ilé Woka 160
Ili Uyolewun 7, 21
Illanun (Iranun) 14–15
illness 117–18, 123, 125, 132–4
imperfections in a rope 262–3, 396
implements given newborn boy or girl 109
imports 136, 147
  ceremonial significance of 148–9
improper marriages 87–9
Imulolo 9
ina 114, 161
ina umã 105–6
inã–ãmã 82
Ina ama tīté beribu ilé teratu? 297
Ina ama tīté nala di ga? 297
ina-ama 158, 161, 314
ina-biné 98
incense 244
incest 119
India 99–100, 135–6, 171, 326, 380, 387, 394,
    400
Indian Ocean 230, 330, 332, 336–40
indigenous whaling in the Indian and Western
    Pacific Oceans 337–40
indigo dyeing 226
Indo-Europeans 204
Indonesia 3, 5–6, 17, 344, 379–80
Indonesian flag 318
Indonesian Primeval Continent 6
Indonesian revolution 50
Indus 337
inflorescence 150
influence of commercial whalers on indigenous
    whaling, possible 336

influenza epidemic of 1918: 50
infractions 119
injuries 133–4
    at sea 294
inner states 115
inspecting coconut oil in connection with a
    death 123, 127
Institut für Wissenschaftlichen Film, Göttingen
    32
internal dowelling 173, 393
internal structure 217
international economy 344
inundations, legends of 6, 57–8, 60
io 199
io balu 401
io bungkuri 43
io naka 199
io sajang 401
io temu 309
io temu i burã 309
io temu io burã 393
ipã 208, 216
Ipomoea batatas 402
iron 100, 250, 297, 326, 328
Islam 53
iting 193, 195
iting lango 293
Itok Kefélong Fata 268
ivory arm bands (bracelets) 92, 94, 105–7,
    146–7
ivory, *see* tusks, elephant

Jafa Langu 40, 63, 67, 77, 84, 86, 98, 180
Jafa Ténã 71, 180, 238, 266, 279, 299, 314,
    398
Jakarta 28, 83, 329, 347–8, 381, 401
Japan 31–2, 401
Japanese 30, 51, 78, 116, 401
    factory fishing ships 337
    ground 330, 334, 339
    influence on indigenous whaling 401
    invasion 50
    traders 401
    whaling 339–40
Java 14, 47, 51, 57, 99, 203, 296, 327, 330–2,
    334, 362, 379, 387–8, 390, 393, 401
Java Sea 155, 311
Javanese 14
jeer 220–3
Jesuits 4, 24–5, 35, 51, 382–3
joins in planks, *see* tenoned joints
joints of bamboo poles 243, 256
junk 201
juru 291

kã 280
kabi 219

Kabupaten Flores Timur vii, 3, 23–4, 26–8,
    381
kada 207
kada-fali 218
kafé 89
kãfé 250–1, 297
kãfé bélã 255
kãfé bĕlelang 255
kafé-gaté 89
kãfé kotekĕlema 253–5, 259, 267
kãfé kubi 254
kãfé léo 245, 276
kãfé léo bélã 253–7
kãfé léo fã 250, 253–6, 282, 284
kãfé mafang 259
kãfé munung 254–5
kãfé nodé pukã 253, 257
kãfé nodé pukã fãnã 253–5
kãfé nodé pukã mĕki 253
kãfé nomang 254–5
kãfé suka bélã 251, 253, 255
kãfé suka fã 253–5, 257, 284
kãfé suka uring 253
kaja lolo 282
Kaja Langu 40, 63, 77, 84, 86, 180
kajo kayana 264
kajo matã 217
kaka-ãri 82, 87
kakang:
    office of 30, 39, 41, 47, 59, 66
    title of 29, 381
kakang-ari 366
kala 92
kala belopor 107
kala flo 107, 322
kala ufung 107
kalabai 206
kalabai tree 153
Kalãh 387
Kalikasa 142
Kalikur 49, 237, 321, 384
Kalimantan 26
kampua 148
kapok, *see* silk-cotton (kapok) tree
Karam 296
Kawela 22–3, 48, 122
kéa 199, 297
kéa bura 199
kéa méa 199
Kebako Pukã 58, 60, 73, 180, 203, 230, 238, 240,
    266, 274, 290, 301, 308, 329, 364, 383–4,
    386, 397–8
kebalung 251
kebeku 200
Kebéla Ténã 70, 180, 229–30, 232, 239, 266,
    305–6
Kebesa Langu 40, 63, 77, 84, 86, 180

Kecamatan Leworaja 141
Kecamatan Naga Wutun 141
Kéda Langu, Bata Fo 40, 63, 77, 84, 86
Kéda Langu, Lefo Tukã 40, 63, 74, 84, 86
Kédang vii, 3, 7, 21–2, 53, 58, 61, 65, 72, 85,
　　93, 99, 101, 105, 113, 129, 135, 163, 177,
　　182, 259, 354, 384, 391
　　language 281
kedauk 392
Kediri 51, 203
kedolu 214
keel 206–10, 212, 214, 218, 243, 271, 286, 395
　　ceremony 204
　　sections 206–7, 242
kĕfaka 386
Kefaka Futu 69
Kefakal Také 70
kĕfatã 253
kefatek 92, 136
kefatek menikil 136
kefatek nai rua 106, 136
kefatek nai telu 106, 136
kefatek olung 136
kefina muko pukã 97–8, 129
kefokel 294
kefoko seba 184, 193, 195, 365
kefokot 115, 123, 129, 244
kefīna 263
Kei Islands 69, 103, 339–40
Kein 113
kĕlaba 171–2
kelabo 297
Kĕlaké Langu 40, 63–4, 67, 77, 84, 86, 98, 124,
　　180, 241, 271
kĕlapa 241–2
kelara 221
kelaru 69, 274, 328
kelaru tegel ané 282
kelata 132
kelatã lĕi 221
kelatã lōlo 221
kĕlé 82
kĕlé-kenapé 82
kelefuk tukã 110
keléla 156
kelepa 206, 266
kĕlepé 241–2
kĕlepé-kĕlapa 241
keli 170
kĕlīfa 245, 251
kĕlīfa kãfé kĕnaté 264
kĕlīfa kãfé kotekĕlema 264
kĕlīfa kãfé kubi 263
kĕlīfa kãfé léo fã 263
kĕlīfa kãfé nodé pukã 263
kĕlīfa kãfé suka bélã 264
kĕlīfa kãfé suka fã 263

kĕlīfa kãfé suka uring 264
kélik 186, 193, 208, 393
kélik lango bélã nãé 186
kelika 217
Kĕlodo Onã 63, 66, 70, 75, 77, 84, 86
kĕlōki 168
kĕloma 297
kĕloma bao pau! 298
kĕloma paur lepé 396
Kĕloré Langu 40, 63, 77, 84, 86, 180
kĕlua 170
Kelulus 180, 203, 230, 237–8, 249, 266, 308,
　　314, 394, 397–8
kelura 222, 225, 245
keluraj 170
Kema 333
Kema Langu, *see* Sinu Langu, Lāma Kéra
kemara 170
kemié 117, 244
kemité 175, 264–6
kemité bĕlã 252, 265–6
kemité fã 252, 266
kemité léo 127
kemité tūkã 252
kemité uring 252
kemui 223
kemãnu 176, 273
kena 206, 394
kĕna 394
Kéna Pukã 180, 230, 237, 266, 279, 289–90,
　　305, 308, 314, 337, 397–8
kenaing 390
kenalat 263
kenaté 198, 259, 280
kĕnaté 253
Kendall Whaling Museum 401
kenelep 226
kenema 223
kenetang 265
kéni 217
keniki 297
kenima 168
kenito 194
kenolé 157
kenolé golé fulã 157
kenãda 245
kenãjo 266
kenãti 210
kenīla 394
kepa 195
kepapa 206
kéra 267
Keraf 113
kĕrāki 219, 227
kérakotã 282
keriki kĕlada 239
kĕrogo 392

keroing 251
Kĕroko Pukan 55, 57, 385
Kĕroko Tafa-Tĕria Géré 56–7
kĕroko trees 44, 56
kĕrōnā 150–2
Kĕrongo Arakian 43
kerosene 143, 145
kĕru-baki 248
kesebō 105–7, 147, 342, 388
ketebu 182, 394
ketebu lolo 223
ketebu nubu menuré 223
ketebu riuk 223
ketilo 219, 395
ketilo ama 216
ketilo bĕrā 217
ketilo bĕropong 214
ketilo olung 217
ketipa 100–1, 136
Keto Pukă 79, 83
kettledrums, bronze 102
ketupat 248
kidnapping 13, 15, 92, 379
kidney 195
Kifa Langu 40, 63, 67, 77, 84, 86, 98, 180
Kiko Langu 63, 84, 86
Kiko Onă 79
kīlā 183, 193, 195, 364
Kila Langu, Lāma Kéra 77
killer whale oil 291, 338–9
killer whales 5, 188–9, 194, 245, 255–6, 274, 282, 290–1, 299, 305, 310, 314, 344
kiosks 140, 143, 396
knives 74, 100, 335
knots in wood 217
koba īna 288
kobu éfĕl 394
koda kiri 119
Kodi 19
koker, see *korké*, village temple
kokila bird 260
kōlé 206–7, 210, 227, 238
kolo kafak 264
kōlo loti 251
kombo 170
Konga 389
Kopo Paker 125, 180, 230, 234–5, 266, 289, 305, 308
kora kora 201, 203, 382
Kora Kora 69
Korea 339–40
korké, see village temple
Korké Ikā 269
korok 184, 199, 208, 365
kotā 207, 210
kotekĕlema 274, 295, 297–8, 328
Krofan 113

krupuk 143
Kuda Belaung (Golden Horse), *see* golden bench
kūgu 214, 257
kūla 392
kuma 281
kūmi 218, 223, 227–8
kung 280
Kupa 304
Kupā 297
Kupang 3, 18, 25, 28–9, 31, 50, 72–3, 165, 173, 201, 297, 299, 304–5, 308, 311, 322–6, 328–31, 333, 335–6, 378, 388–9, 397–8, 400–1
  archive at 401
  British attack on 398, 401
  fort at 324, 331, 401
  Japanese attack on 305, 396

laba 395
laba ketilo 183, 193, 195, 364
laba ketilo alep 241
Laba Langu, Lāma Kéra 77
Laba Langu, Tana Kĕrofa 40, 63, 75, 84, 86
Labala 8, 13, 21–2, 29, 30, 42–4, 48–9, 58, 60, 66, 75, 101, 131, 140–4, 147, 362, 384–5
Labala bay 7–8, 58, 384–5
Labatukan 22–3
Labuan Bajo 49, 69
lada 218, 243
ladder 257
lafā 263
Lafa Langu 40–1, 63, 69, 76, 84, 86
Laga Doni 273
laja 220, 365
lāja 167, 184, 197
laja fānā 167
laja mātā 220
lala 195
lala di kāmā 195
lala di kotā 195
lali 391
Lali Fata, see Lamalera B
lali haka 391
Lali Nama Papā 40–1, 43, 63, 74, 80, 84, 86, 98, 180
lāma 54
lama fa (mess group) 315
lama fa tobo 219, 227
lāma kéra 54
Lāma Kéra 34, 40–1, 63, 66–70, 77, 80, 98, 113, 180, 232
Lāma Kéra A 82–4, 86, 98
Lāma Kéra B 82–4, 86, 98
Lāma Kéra, Lamamanu 69–70
Lāma Lera, *see* Sun Plate

Lama Manuk, *see* Lamamanu
Lāma Mau clan 59–60, 68, 298, 385
Lāma Nifa 40, 63, 68–9, 77, 82– 4, 86, 98, 113, 138, 180
Lāma Nudek 40–1, 59–60, 63, 66–7, 70, 75, 77, 82–4, 86, 98, 113, 180, 239, 241, 383, 395
lama tukã (mess group) 315
lama uri tobo 227
lama uring (mess group) 315
Lamabakan 34, 39, 54, 75, 380
Lamadua 54
lamafa 297
Lamahala 11, 13, 17–18, 25, 29, 50, 54, 88, 99, 115, 178, 203, 323, 325, 336, 378–9
Lamaheku 7
Lamaholot culture 31–2, 110, 158, 161, 187, 285, 385, 388
Lamaholot language vii, 3, 33–4, 52, 54, 55, 57, 61, 118, 129, 141, 158, 161–2, 168, 179, 230, 291, 295, 346, 379
Lamaholot linguistics 31–2
Lamaholot-speaking region vii, viii, 4–5, 12, 31, 62, 114, 123, 135, 159, 324, 382
Lamakera 11, 13, 25, 29, 30, 34, 46, 50, 54, 69, 70, 75, 169–70, 198, 203, 232, 238, 274, 291, 295, 314, 316–17, 323–4, 328, 336, 343, 354, 362–3, 376–9, 382, 386, 388, 392–4
lamaléfa 298
Lamalera 35–53, 341–5
  baptisms, first in 25
  Catholicism of 5
  claim to rank 56, 59–60
  conversions to Christianity 5, 51–3
  demographic stagnation of 5, 341, 344–5
  dependency on authochthonous peoples for land 56, 60
  different kinds of 35–9
  district of 22
  economic dualism in 5, 341
  fencing of 21, 35, 43
  foundation of 54–61
  head of 3
  history of 54–61
  mixed economy of 5
  outside origin of 4
  political dominance by 5
  Portuguese references to 4
  research in, *see* field research
  social geography of 21
  variety of society of 1
Lamalera A 24–6, 35, 38–44, 46, 50, 65, 68, 70, 74–5, 79, 98, 165, 174, 194, 248, 268–70, 298, 318, 345, 380–1, 385, 391, 396–7
Lamalera B 24–6, 35–40, 42–6, 50, 65, 68, 76–7, 98, 121, 124, 165, 174, 194, 248, 268,

270, 298, 345, 380, 383, 385, 391, 397
Lamalere 54
Lamamanu 8, 38–9, 46, 68–70, 72, 77, 112, 268, 381, 396
Lamanu, *see* Lamamanu
Lambunga 91
lamps 305
lamtoro gung 379
lance 193, 253–4, 267, 294
lance owner 188
lancing 294
land and sea opposition 61
land people and sea people opposition 61
land sharing 146
land wind 154
landslide 379
Lango Bélã, Lāma Kéra 77
lango bélã pung alep 245
lango bélã, *see* great house
Lango Bélã, *see* Kĕlaké Langu
lango bélã tou 74
lango ikã bĕlifu 193–4
lango kéni 63
lango umã 105–6
Lango Fujo 40, 59–60, 63, 65, 68, 70–2, 76–7, 85, 87, 113, 194, 268, 270, 298, 386
lapa 170
Lapan Batan (*Lepã Batã*) 40–1, 54–7, 59–61, 75, 231, 234, 236, 238, 247, 383–6, 398
Larantuka 4, 10, 12, 14–19, 21, 24–6, 28–32, 42–3, 49–52, 55, 57, 73, 75, 92, 140–1, 147–8, 154, 165, 203, 297–8, 308, 317, 323, 329, 351, 378–81, 383, 389, 393, 397–8, 400
Larantuka Malay 92, 126, 392
large boats 201–40
lashed lug technique 173, 204–19
lashing 214–15
Latin 230
launching a *kora kora* across a slave 382
launching the fleet 271–2
léa 166–7
léa laja fãnã 167
léa laja meki 167
leader 245, 251–3, 255
leader rope 245
leadership in war 75
learning to harpoon 283
leather back turtle 199
Lebatukan 380
léfa 152, 154, 156, 243, 268, 271
léfa-ari 152
léfa bogel 152
léfa ceremony 270
léfa haring 115
léfa nuang 152
lefo 188, 193

lefo alep 188
lefo nubã 270, 397
Lefo Bĕlolo 381
Lefo Hajo clan 59, 65
Lefo Kumé 58
Lefo Léin 40, 44, 63, 68, 70–2, 77, 82–4, 86,
    98, 113, 194, 386
Lefo Léré 381
Lefo Séfõ 79–80, 83, 98
lefo-tana 193
lefo-tana alep 268
Lefo Tukã 39–41, 43, 59, 62–7, 72, 74–7, 82–4,
    86, 98, 112, 122, 180, 270, 385
Lefoléin 71
left 110
legã 166–7, 258
legã déké 167
legã penonu 167
Leiden 102
Lein 113
léi naké 197–8, 320
léi nolo 109
lekã 255
lekã kenãda mafang 256
lekã kenãda puã gãda 256
lekã nubã 256
lekã tĕlãkã bĕlelã 257
lekã tĕlãkã kotekĕlema 257
lekã tĕlãkã nomang 257
lekã tĕlãkã õjo bélã 257
Lekluo 160
Léla Onã 40–1, 59, 63, 66–7, 74–6, 82–4, 86,
    98, 108, 113, 180, 385
  design appropriate to 66
  extermination of 66
Léla Sapã 178, 180, 231, 240, 266, 384
lélang 274
Lelang 113
lélangaji 274
Leloba 64, 116, 121
Lembata vii, viii, 3–10, 13, 15–16, 20–3, 26–9,
    31, 40, 47–9, 53, 55–8, 62, 69–70, 78, 99,
    101, 103, 109, 114–16, 118, 122, 129, 135,
    138, 140, 142, 149, 155, 157, 159, 177–8,
    203, 237, 247, 291, 304, 321, 323, 327, 329,
    334, 336, 341, 344, 377–9, 381–4, 386, 388,
    390, 401
léo 179, 243, 245, 250, 258–63, 264, 266, 307,
    313
léo bélã 127, 229, 253, 266, 307
Leodice viridis 151
léo fã 127, 175, 229, 253, 264–5, 271, 282, 307
léo fefã 264
léo fũtu 262
léo kepur 261
léo menõlã 262
léo ũli 227, 229

Lepã-Batã 57–8
lerã 150–2, 270
Lera-Fulã 158–63, 396
lera géré 158
lera helut 158
lera léré 158
lera lodo 158
lera mata 158, 390
lerã matã 150, 390
lera maté 158
lera tree 54
lera tukã 158
Lerek Peninsula 7–8, 21, 118, 135, 142, 152,
    171, 176, 312, 378, 384
lero 158
lerong senaréng 299
Lesser Sunda Islands 377, 379
leteh leteh 201
Leti Archipelago 56
letters of Marque 330
létu lofat 129
Leucaena leucocephala 379
Levant 332
Lewohajo 384
Lewo Hajo, Lembata 58, 60, 66
Lewo Hayon 57
Lewo Hajon clan 385
Lewo Hayong 61
Lewo Leru 48
Lewo Raja 384
Lewokewe 21
Lewokukun 21, 72
Lewoleba 21–3, 28–9, 31, 49, 51–2, 70, 74, 88,
    101, 115, 116, 140–1, 165, 177, 323, 325,
    345, 380, 397
Lewolein 71, 313
Lewotala, East Flores 32
Lewotala, Lembata 8, 38–9, 40, 42–3, 47, 68,
    117, 131, 133, 154, 380
Lewotobi 50, 313, 386, 398–9
Lewotolo 22, 135, 378
Lewourang 313, 316, 398–9
Lewuka 45, 117, 142, 247
Lewuun 116
lia 176
lia méã 264
Libu hir kaé 298
lĩka 392
life 109–20, 126, 204, 228, 230, 246
life changes 109
lika 65
lima 208, 216
Lima Langu 40, 63, 74, 84, 86, 98
lima panga 392
lima pantai 29
lime 5, 135, 143, 145, 230, 233
lime making 135, 138–9, 343, 389

limes 145, 335
limpets 168
line fishing 168, 175
linen 103, 221, 335
lines in boat 212–13, 216–17, 229, 245
Lio 91, 102
lipa 129–30, 136, 148, 273, 299, 306, 309, 322
literacy 12, 380
liver 115 195, 198
Loang 8, 49, 177, 379
Lobetobi 50, 116, 170, 209–11, 280, 310–22,
      398
lock scarf 216
loda mas 80
lodging houses 345
Lodobelolong 165
Lodo Ikã 42, 79
Logan 333
loggerhead turtle 199, 314
Lohayon 57
Lohayong 4, 11–13, 18, 29–30, 57, 168, 301,
      324, 328, 361, 378–9, 382, 393, 401
Lombata, *see* Lembata
Lombok 103, 334
London 293
long lines 170–1, 282, 361
lontar palms 150, 208, 216, 239, 249, 253, 264,
      273, 391
lontar-leaf measure 214
loom, back-strap 137, 147
loop at the base of the *léo* 261, 264–5
lord(s) of the land 38–9, 41, 44, 59, 65–6, 68,
      70, 75–6, 176, 193–4, 199, 268–71, 298,
      306, 316, 321, 383, 385, 389, 398–9
lõsi 145
loss of objects at sea 299
love 90, 115
Low Village 381
low tide 154–5, 399
lower jaw 183, 185–7, 194, 196, 198–9, 364
lower village, *see* Lamalera B
luck 175, 180, 182, 204, 244, 263, 276, 279,
      289–90, 299–300
lugs 205–7, 214, 393
Luki Lefo Bala 385
Luki Lewobala 58
Luki Lokã Bua Fatu 385
Luki Point 58, 384–5
lungs 195, 198
lures 175–6
Luwuk 56
Luwuk-Bélu 56

Macao 99, 382
Macassar 148, 165, 200, 328, 362, 383, 389
Macassar ships 100
Macassarese 14, 99, 325–6, 328

mace 99
machine-woven sarongs 141
mada fũtu 197
Madagascar 338–40, 343, 393
mãdi 207, 209, 217, 227, 238–40, 243, 245
madil 217
Madras 388, 400
Madura 214
magic 117
magu 112
mahol 123–4
maize 100–1, 129, 138–9, 141–7, 153, 177, 186,
      247–8, 315, 321, 325, 343, 389
Majapahit 377
make-up crews 336, 401
Malacca 1, 11, 99, 386–7, 389, 401
Malang 51, 203
Malay 32, 377
Malay Peninsula 387
Malays 387
Malaysia 14, 27, 282, 381, 386–7, 393
male nurse 317
mallet, wooden 241, 256
Malua 379
mammals 5
Mana Langu 40, 63
Mandor Pasar 143–4
manger 115
Manggarai 148, 395
mango tree 171
mangoes 143
Manila 401
Manila rope 396
manta ray 5, 45, 152, 156, 158, 170, 173–4, 176,
      179, 192, 196–8, 251, 253, 255, 257–8, 263,
      276, 279, 281–2, 284–5, 287, 290, 292, 300,
      305, 307–22, 340, 395, 398
Mantis birostris 197, 253, 276, 281
mãnu 251
manu sili goko 65
Manuk 112
many toothed blackfish 274
mao/mau 94–6, 106
Maori 2
marginalization 1–2
Marisa 130
mark at centre of the yard 221
market networks 139–40
market official 143
markets 90, 135–49, 154, 247–9, 270, 381, 384,
      390
marking bunches of thread 261
marking cord 214
marking guage 214
marks for dowels 216–17
marlin 194, 199–200, 237, 255, 273, 396
marlin spike 223

marriage 64, 81–108, 388
  alliance, *see* alliance, marriage
  forms 386
  in a circle 87
  prestations 88–9, 94–6, 98–108, 135–6, 141,
    147, 149, 342–3, 386
  statistics 83–7, 91
  types 90–1
  see also bridewealth
mass 277, 398
mast 217–20, 223, 245, 271, 273
master boat builder 59–60, 117, 151, 173,
    181–3, 196, 199, 206, 212, 214, 241–3, 247,
    249, 298, 364, 395
master of the chisel and dowels 241
master of mice and rats 72
mat-weaving 390
mata 390
mata gapo 146, 153, 177
matã 150
matrilineality 62, 385
Maumere 49, 75, 139, 176
measurements of harpoon poles 255–7
measurements of ropes 257–9
measuring elephant tusks 105
meat 137–8, 142–6, 149, 187, 192–3, 305,
    309–10, 316
  of killer whale 290
medicine 117–18, 133–4, 176, 200, 387
Mediterranean 220, 230
Megui 386
méi 119
méi nafa 119
meka 105–6
Melanesian trade 148–9
mélo huri 75
melons 335
mélung 123, 126
mélung beléong 126
men 83–5, 87, 94, 97, 123, 132, 136–41,
    143, 149, 213, 260, 273, 286–7, 304, 309,
    313
menaka 115, 118, 160
menãmi 220
Menanga 25, 57, 394
měng 188, 193
meningo, 241
menoté 156
menstruation 109–10, 112, 154
menué 137
menula 206, 208, 223, 227, 243
Menula Belolong 180, 226, 230, 232, 240, 253,
    256, 266, 275–7, 279, 293, 304–5, 314, 364,
    372–5, 396, 398
menuli 222–3, 279
men's cloth 136
Merekpuka 7

Merina 343
mess groupings at Lobetobi 315, 399
mestizos, *see* Black Portuguese
meteorological patterns 312
meti bélã 155
meti etã 154
meti fulã 109, 154
meti fulã elã 154
meti géré 154
meti lodo 154
meti mara 154
meti marak patak 154
meti nefu 154
meti ofã 154
meti ofã bélã 155
meti peno 154
meti pělerong 155
mice 72–3, 240
midnight 158
midwives 109
migrant labour 26–7
migration 54–61
  charter 55–61
  legends 56, 74
Miku Langu 40, 63, 77, 84, 86, 180
military garrison at Larantuka 21
mimã 183, 186, 193, 364
mimã alep 183
Mindanao 14
Mingar 29, 122, 135, 145–6, 177, 295, 305
missionaries 117, 121, 129, 133, 163, 268–71,
    277, 344, 378, 380–2, 389, 391, 398
  see also Catholic mission
mītu 168
Moa 56
mobo 199
Mobula dabolus 280–1
Mobula kuhlii 275, 280–1
Moby Dick 293
moé hopé poé 107
mõfa 136
moko 104
moku 173, 255
mõku 280–2, 307, 313–15, 396, 399
mõku anamīté 281
mõku belébã 281
mõku éak 281
mõku pilifato 281
molã 262
Mola Mola [Lin.] 200
molluscs 355, 362–3
Molucca ground 330
Molucca Passage 333–4
Moluccas 11, 13, 56–7, 72, 99, 201, 203, 230,
    332, 393, 399
monetary economy 343
monetization 102, 175, 342

money 50, 103, 148, 174–5, 315, 317, 341–3,
  387–8, 390
monga/munga 139, 145
monkeys 387
monosodium glutamate 143
monsoon patterns 9
monsoons, *see* seasons
moon 109, 112, 154–63, 279–80, 282
mōrā 259
moray eels 322
Moringa oleifera Lam. 54
morning star 157, 305
mortars 99
mortise guage, *see* marking guage
mother sister's child marriage 85
mother's brother 114
mother's brother's daughter marriage 83, 87,
  92, 349, 386
motions of ray 280
mōtong tree 54
motor boats 290, 301, 320, 398
mountain dwellers 3, 101, 103, 135, 137–44,
  146–9, 153, 182, 243, 247, 249, 259, 270,
  309, 315, 325, 328, 343, 377–8, 384, 389
mouse king 73
mouth 208, 245
muko lolo 392
Muko Ténā 131, 180, 231, 239, 257, 266,
  289–90, 314, 317–19
Mulan Doro 171, 176
multiple family houses 96
munung 254
murai bird 260
murder 119, 126, 140, 203, 344
Muri Langu 40, 63, 75, 77, 84, 86, 180
Museum Negara 381
museums 101–2
mūsi 150
Musi Langu 40, 63, 85, 87, 180
musket-balls 400
Muslims 53
muting 251
myths 55–61

nā 297
nada 223, 290
nada ikā 276
naé noi 194
nafa 119
nafak 207, 210, 251
naga 214
nagat 223
Nagawutun 22–3, 26–7, 49, 379, 386
nai 390
nāké 184
nalé 151, 391
nalé datā onā 151–2, 391

nalé saré 151–2, 391
nama, *see* village plain
nama 169–70
Nama Bau Lāngu 39
nama bélā 169
nama fuā 392
nama kéni 169
names 74, 112–14, 346–7
names of boats 227
nangak onā 264
Nanzhao 390
Napoleonic wars 401
Nara Guan hir kaé 298
Nara Ténā 72, 151, 180, 183, 196, 233–4,
  238–9, 266, 297–8, 305–6, 314, 398
nasib 299
national cash economy 147, 344
National Library of Australia 334
naung 150
Nautical Magazine 334
nautilus shell 130–1, 142
Ndao 389
neap tides 155
nebo 126–31
necklaces 147
nedek 239
Nederlandsche Handel-Maatschappij 332
nefā 224–5
néfi 209, 211, 217, 243
nefu bélā 154
nefu kéni 154
negotiations about marriage prestations 99, 104
Negri Sembilan 383
nekat 225
nélu 209, 211
neolocal residence 96
Netherlands, the 29–30, 165, 297, 332, 378
Netherlands-Indies 21, 378
nets 153, 173–7, 281–2, 311, 322, 392
netting 181
new boat ceremony 243, 248–9
New England 396
New Guinea 17, 296, 332, 400
New Holland 330
new maize ceremonies 243
new moon 155
New Zealand 293, 331, 400
Newfoundland 396
newly built boats 142, 216
  exchange of food at Wulan Doni 142
Ngada 162
Nias 17
Nifak 113
night 158
nitrate of potash 387
nitun 115–16
nōbé 266

nodé 223
nodé fã 227, 229
nodé pukã 227, 229, 255
nodé uring 227–8
noder 108
nofek 193–4, 198
nofi 322
nõfi 136
nõfi bĕlaja 136
Nogo clan, Boleng, Adonara 69
Nogo clan, Lamakera, Solor 69
noloj 255
noloj kenãda nãé 255
nomang 254
non-cash economic sphere 147
non-descent means of acquiring clan
    membership 77–9
'non-interference policy' 4, 29–30
non-subsistence occupations 344
nõni lãrã 129
noon 158
Nor Futu 58
Nor Peninsula 384
North Atlantic 155, 332
North Brabant 378
North Pacific 339
Notã Ténã 131, 180, 184, 232, 239–40, 266,
    314
nua bélã 129
nua bãko 157
nua kéni 129
nua tapo 156
Nualela 24, 38, 46–7, 59–60, 66, 75, 141–4,
    170, 247, 315, 380, 384–5
nuang 168
nuang urã 150
nuba 268
nuba nara, see sacred stones
nũba 245
Nuba Lefo 41, 43
Nuba Siola 43
nubit 222
Nudek 113
nufa 170, 385
nulu fũtu 209–11, 217, 243
numbers, *see* even numbers, uneven numbers
Nuo 297
nupã 184, 194
nuro 297
nuro menaluf 293, 296
Nusa Tenggara Barat 28
Nusa Tenggara Timur 3, 14, 23, 27–9, 62, 151,
    379
Nusa Toné Tobo Baka Walang Pai 385
nutmeg 99
nylon fishing lines 173, 253
nylon rigging 249, 345, 396

o rata 96
oars 201, 267, 279
objects brought in from the outside 102
Occusi 73, 335
octopi 362
oculi 230–7, 395
odd numbers, *see* uneven numbers
odo mãdi 243
oé/oi 92
offerings, sacrificial 52, 121, 124, 160
oil 100
ojo 156
ojo bélak 156
ojo bĕlino 156
ojo éfél 156
ojo gefòket 156
ojo golo 156
ojo pĕrefa 156
Õla 297
Ola Langu 40, 63, 67, 82–4, 86, 98, 180,
    383
Ola Langu, Lãma Kéra 77
õla meting 168
old woman 57, 60
olé 153–5
Olé Onã 40, 63–4, 70, 77, 82–4, 86, 98, 113,
    180
Oleona 113
olung 96, 104–6
Ombai Strait, *see* Timor Strait
Omesuri 22–3
onã 115, 150, 195
Onã marã! 296–7
Onã néro mara héna! 296
onã-furã 195
100 Years of Religion 37, 53
Ongalere 38, 46, 398
Ongaona 24, 249, 321, 378
open sea fishing and hunting 268–88
opu 98
opu alep 98
opu pukã 85, 94–5, 99, 106, 108, 129, 132
opu-faé 98
opu-laké 82, 87, 98, 106–7, 132
opu-maki 98, 346
õrã 219–20, 245
õrã kélik 220
oranges 335
Orcinus Orca 255
orientation terms 163–7
origin of the Wulan Doni market 142
orphans 301
ossuaries 122, 125
outboard motors 174, 201, 316, 344, 397
outrigger booms 211, 217–19, 222, 228–9, 245,
    259, 271, 276, 290, 304
outrigger dugout 392

outriggers 172–3, 184, 201, 203, 218, 290, 294, 304, 392
overhunting whales 311, 333
owner of the fishing line 200
Oxford University Expedition to Kei Kecil 393
oysters 168

Pacific Ocean 6, 329–30, 332, 339–40, 393, 400
pacification 30, 322
paddles 166, 201, 250, 267, 277, 297
pafã lama 186
Pagan 390
Pagoran 378
Pahang 387
pãé 282
pãé bĕlelang 282
pãé bõu 282
Paji 29, 160
Palembang 1, 172, 387
palm wine 95, 115, 117–18, 122, 143, 145, 150–1, 174–5, 196, 200, 217, 243, 248, 261, 267, 295, 316, 318, 321, 391
Pamakayu 47, 57, 115, 160, 385
pana 280
pana léo 260
Pandai 379
Pandora 400
pano 225
pãno 253
Pantar 3, 6, 12, 16, 21, 31, 56, 77, 107, 129–30, 142, 155–6, 203, 237, 247, 278, 280, 299, 305, 308, 313, 320–2, 336, 378–9, 383
Panther 400
pao/pau 94
papaya 381
Parelvisscherij Maatschappij Djoempandang 383
pari 157
'Pasisir culture' 377
'Pasisir Literature' 377
'Pasisir period of Javanese history' 377
passenger boats 46, 141, 181, 318
passive whaling 337
patola 74, 99–100, 135–6, 147, 149, 326
patrilineality 62, 87, 179, 344, 348, 352–4
patrilocal residence 96
pattern of planking 209–12
Paugora 7, 378–9
pau kebarek 94
pau laba ketilo alep 243
pau lefo 68
Pau Léré 268
pau ribu boi ratu 395
pau soru-naku 243
pearl fishery 51, 383
pectoral fins 294
pectoral section 199–200

Peda 318
pĕlaé baléo 152
pĕlédang 179, 392
pĕlédar kenafĕ 129
Peleng Strait 56
pelepah 206, 214, 216–19, 253, 264–6, 273
pĕloru 264
penatil 223, 225
pendants on sails 226
penebo 126–7
penétã 141
Peni Banana Leaf 285
Peni Kéni 176, 360
penimafa 168
penimari 168
penis 195
pepal léo 262
peppers 139, 168, 389
Pĕrafi Langu 40, 63, 76, 84, 86, 180
pera ikã 293
perahu ayam 203
pĕrãnã 251, 264
Pĕraso Sapã 180, 231, 266
pĕratã ikã 294
peré 222
pĕreka 215
period of restriction after giving birth 109
Persia 387
Persian Gulf 337–8
person 115
person who first sees game animal 194, 196, 199–200
pésa, *see* cannon
pesisir (pasisir) societies 1, 377
Pesiwatu 125
pétã 115
petrified boats 61, 384–5
petrified people 60–1
petrified whales 268
petung 256, 395
Philadelphia 400
Philippines 14, 204, 216, 336, 382, 390, 401
Phoenician ships 216
phosphorescence 176, 392
Physeter 292
Physeter catodon 326
Physeter macrocephalus 328
pĩ 127–9, 389
pĩga 124
pigs 51, 76, 108, 110, 114, 118, 120, 123, 129, 146, 156, 246–9, 263, 335, 398, 400–1
penning of 51, 121, 381
tethering 345
pili arã 214
pilot whale 79, 194–5, 245–6, 263, 290–1, 307, 339
pineapples 143

pins 217–18
Piper betle, Linn. 247
piracy 13–20, 330, 379
pivots of the mast poles 219
plank's armpit 214
planks 173, 182, 205–6, 209–19, 243, 247, 249, 257, 273, 290, 297, 318, 327, 393
plankton 176, 280, 282, 290, 312
plantains 335
plants 367–70
plastic wool 258–9
plates 54, 69, 92–4, 102, 124, 244, 322
Pleiades 157
pod 293
Pohon Sirih 43
poi bula 106
poisoning by fish 360–1
poisonous beans 153
polyclinic 39, 42, 109, 112, 117, 124, 133, 142, 301, 304, 308
population 20–9, 379–80, 385
population growth 20–9
porcelain 74, 99–100, 124, 244, 329
porcupines 387
porpoises 5, 152, 173–4, 176, 177, 179, 184, 186, 188–95, 255, 257, 259, 274–5, 277, 281, 283, 290, 292–3, 299–300, 313–14, 322, 328, 339–40, 376, 399
Port Jackson 331
Portugal 15, 21, 24, 29, 329
Portuguese 3–4, 10–12, 14–15, 17–19, 21, 24, 29–30, 99, 124, 323–4, 378, 381–3, 387, 393, 400–1
Portuguese claims to Flores and the Solor Islands, sale of 15, 383
Portuguese Timor 17, 340, 380
posthouders 381
pot-making 59, 142, 148, 389
pots 139, 141, 143, 145, 170, 315
poverty 28–9
power to curse 85
prayer 243–4, 245, 271, 276, 292, 397
pre-Viking boats 204
pregnancy 89–91, 109, 133, 154, 204
prescribed marriage category 83, 85, 87, 349
priests, native 52, 61, 123
production specializations 1, 4–5, 60, 135–6, 141, 148, 342, 390
prohibited marriages 85
prohibition:
    at Lobetobi on eating with another boat group 315
    on addressing older persons by name 114, 346–7
    on bailer getting out of boat 246
    on contact with the sea following a death 130–1
    on cursing at Lobetobi 315
    on disembowelling a ray on the day it is caught 287
    on dyeing cloth 135
    on eating moray eels 322
    on further boats going to Lobetobi after others have already departed 317
    on going through a field being harvested 382
    on harpooner eating meat from the armpit share 186
    on harpooning game while searching for someone 130–1
    on marriages between Lefo Tukā and Léla Onā clans 67
    on speaking to anyone cutting up game 300
    on speaking to anyone harvesting rice 300
    on standing on someone's shadow 115
    on touching the eyes of fish 287
    on touching women at Lobetobi 315, 399
    on using lontar leaf for the roof of the lord of the land's temple 269
    on weaving and cloth production 5, 135, 140, 146, 343
propitiation 115
Procorpina 333
protective duty on whale oil 334
Protestants 53, 321
Pseudora Crassidens 255
Pterocarpus indicus, Willd 211, 219, 263, 394
pūa 256
puā fānā 219–20
puā méki 219–20
puā pukā 227, 229
puang (uli) léii 219
puang léi 219
puang uli 217, 227
pukā 383
Pulau Kambing 129, 237, 320–1
Pulau Rusa 129, 178, 320–1
Pulau Suangi 288
pulling the boat up the beach 186, 302–4
pumpkins 335
punaj 125
punek edā 204
pung alep 115, 244–5, 271
puo 195, 211
Puor 9, 47
puper léo 261
Puskesmas (Public Health Centre) 28
pygmy killer whale 274, 291
pygmy sperm whale 399
pygmy whales 5
python 125

race betweeen *Kebako Pukā* and a horse 329
radar 398
radio 50

raiding 13–14, 19–20, 92
rain 150–1, 161, 312, 384
rainfall 10–11, 379
rainy season, *see* wet season
Rangafak 268
ranking of sacrificial animals 76
rapo bélã 297
rattan 216, 219, 255, 394
rauk fũtu 219, 227
raw materials 149
ray meat 198, 281
rays 277–88, 292, 299, 308–22, 398–9
rebuilding boats 308, 317
record of the catch 310–12, 398
recursive complementarity 161
red 135
refrigeration 133
registration of the population 20
relationship classification 87
relationship terminology 87, 112, 346–54, 386
religion 31, 51–3, 250, 344
religious/secular authority 65
remã 158
remã tukã 158
remittances to the village 341
Reo 401
reo trees 399
repairing sails 216, 220–1
reprovisioning of ships 335
residence 96–7
resist-dyeing 135, 137, 224, 343
restriction during funeral 127–9
retribution 109
return gifts 107
réu 83, 87, 349, 354
reversal 160
reversal of marriage direction 82, 85
Rhinchodon typus Smith 200
Rhinoptera Javanica 282
Riang Kamié 385
Riang Koli 61
Riang-Roma 384
ribbontail ray 282
ribs 173, 205, 206, 217–18
ribs placed in last 173
ribu-ratu 270
rice 50, 94, 99–100, 121, 124, 129, 138, 146–7,
    196, 198, 243, 246–8, 315, 322, 325, 343,
    388–90
riding sharks 170–1, 309
rié fanã 241
rifles 101
rigging 240
right 110
    handed rope 259
    house post 241
    wing of manta ray 300

rights and distribution of fish and
    meat 183–200
right to head of a sperm whale 68, 71
Rigil Kentaurus 157
ring 183, 185, 195, 364
ring from tooth of a killer whale 290
'ring of fire' 6
rita 171
ritual:
    contests 395
    language 270–1
    violence 249
rituals, *see* ceremonies
Rium 15
roads 39, 49
'roasting' mothers after childbirth 109
Roebuck 320
roi alep 196
roi bala 92
rokã 251–2
Roman Catholic College of Goa 380
Romang 384
Rome 382
roots 117
rope ceremonies 261, 263
rope making 149, 182, 219, 259–66, 393
rope yarn 259
ropes 100, 127, 135, 141, 149, 170, 175, 179–80,
    218–20, 222, 228–9, 250–67, 271, 275,
    285–6, 289, 294–5, 301–2, 304, 308–9, 313,
    393, 397
Rorquals 291
Roti 2, 6, 24, 267, 278, 382, 385, 389
Rotinese 323, 389
Rotterdam 102, 333
rowdiness during funerals 121
rowing 152, 166–8, 222, 267, 273–5, 278–9,
    284, 292–3, 300, 302–3, 305, 318
rowing songs 273, 284, 298, 300
Royal Packet Company 100
rubber 100
rubbing:
    ambergris on boats 326–7
    coconut oil in a restricted person's hair 129
    oil on boat planks 338
    oil on sacred stones 270
    skulls on stempost 244
    skulls with oil 124
    the rope with sap 262–3
ruki 214
rukun keluarga (RK), *see* family associations
rukun tetangga (RT), *see* household associations
runners 271, 302, 304
running water, *see* water, fresh
Ruteng 401

saba 229, 294

saba uli 227, 229
saboq burā 132
Sabu 18
sacred parts of boat 244–5
sacred stones 41, 43, 52, 76, 123, 241, 244, 268, 270, 384, 397, 399
  burial of 43
sacrifice 123, 160, 241, 244, 246, 398
sādo 248
sail decorations 226
sail maker 182, 184, 196, 199, 220, 223–4, 365
sail share 184–5
sailing 222, 273, 292, 320
sailing directions 166–7
sailing stones 385
sailors 188
sails 166–7, 171–3, 182, 188, 197, 201–3, 216, 220–6, 250, 267, 271, 273–6, 278–9, 285, 288, 292, 294, 301–2, 306, 317, 365, 371
'sails' 197
St Antony's fire 117
St Peter chapel 44–5, 248, 269–71
Salayer 15
salt 5, 135–49, 153, 168, 230, 233, 247, 324, 389–90
salt making 130, 135, 138, 148, 343, 389–90
salt pans 304
saltpetre 100, 387
Samoa 333
sampan 201, 392, 399
San Francisco 333
sand 382
sandalwood 99–100, 264, 386
Sangihe 336
sapā 153, 172–3, 177, 179, 301, 306, 311
Sapium baccatum, Roxb. 382
sappan wood 216–17
Sara and Elisabeth 15
Sarabia 40
Sarapuka 8, 50, 131, 177–8
Sarawak dolphin 274
sarong 208
sasalāpi 210–11, 318
Savu 6
Savunese 15, 323
Savu Sea 155, 329
scaffold burial 122–3
Schizostachyum brachycladum, Kurz. 70, 251
Schleichera oleosa, Marr. 153, 206, 394
school fees 147, 343, 381
schooling, *see* education
schools 24–5, 88, 118
schoolteachers 181, 295, 310
schoolteaching 135
Schoutenia ovata 214, 217–18, 222, 257, 261
sea 46, 115
sea creature found inland 61

Sea of Japan 331
seafaring peoples 5
sea spirits 130, 152, 388, 398
sea swells 156
sea urchins 168
sea water 156
sea winds 153
searching for corpses 131
seasonal variation in supply of products 145
seasons 150–3, 168, 268, 270, 311, 324, 391
seasickness 273
seats 218–19, 228, 266
seaweed 168–9, 392
secondary burial 122–3
sections in the hull of the boat 226–9, 250, 253, 255, 257–9, 266
sections of cloth 390
secure incomes 175
segao 281
segara 322
sĕgépot 197
seguni 255, 274, 298
sĕlaba 168
selaga 220–1, 224
selling whale oil 336
sĕlorut 253
sĕluku 255
Semau 397
sĕmugur 227–8, 253, 275
sĕmugur bélā 227, 257
sĕmugur kéni 227, 266–7
senabi 210, 218
senai 136
sĕnaré 117
senégat 222
senia beléré 108
sĕnili 130
senirā 392
senubang 107, 388
sĕnudem 248
senuré 388
Sepia officinalis 326
serā 227, 229, 257, 259
Sérā-Gorā 56
Seram 56
Seran 56
Serani 165, 297
Sesbania grandiflora 251, 262–3
setting up the warp strands in a sail section 225
sewn planked boats 204
sexual relations 90, 95
shaddocks 335
shadow 115
sham battle 247–9, 300
shaping planks 213
shares 173–5, 180–8, 193–200, 244, 292, 299, 320, 364–6, 392–3, 399

shark fins 100, 171, 200, 328
shark harpoon 278–9
shark lines 253, 275, 278, 280
sharks 117, 119, 121, 145, 170–1, 173–4, 176,
    194, 199–200, 254–5, 259, 273, 275, 278,
    280, 283, 289–90, 294, 300–7, 309, 314–15,
    393, 401
Sharon, Massachusetts 401
sharpening stones 253, 267, 297, 299
sheath for stempost 208, 271
sheep 76
sheets 222–3
shell bracelets 107, 322
shellfish 362
    gathering 168–9
    iron 168
shields, buffalo hide 248
shortfin devil ray 255, 275
short-finned pilot whale 255, 274
shoulder cloths 136
shrimp wafers 143
sia 138
Sia Apu 77, 138, 180, 229–30, 233, 266
Siam 100
Siau 336
sibling groups to one's own 81–2, 87
siblings 366
Siboga expedition 382
sigé 92
sign of trouble at sea 288
signal fires 177–8, 304
signals that whales are present 306
signs of ownership 239
Sika Ténã 180, 184, 233, 237, 258, 266, 275–6,
    289, 305, 308
Sikka language 3
Sikka region 2, 119, 247, 399
silent trade 144
Sili Ténã 45, 51, 125, 180, 203, 237, 266, 290,
    395, 398
silk, 99, 328
    cloth 390
    shawls 101
silk-cotton (kapok) tree 171, 381
silver earrings 123
simulated harpooning exhibitions 249
Sinar Harapan 378
Singapore 100, 102, 145, 388
singing 89–90, 123, 244, 246, 300, 302
Sinu Langu, Léla Onã 40, 76, 84, 86, 180
Sinu Langu, Lãma Kéra 40–1, 63, 69, 76, 84,
    86
Sinu Sapã 180, 238, 266
Siraf 338
sister exchange 386
sisters 68, 82, 85, 89, 96–7, 177, 182, 260
sister's children 86, 136

sisters' husbands 184
Sita Langu 40, 63, 76, 84, 86
skull houses 122, 124, 244
skulls, ancestral 52, 118, 121–5, 244
slaughtering animals 75
slave trading 15
slavery 13–20, 47, 71, 89, 92, 103, 379, 388
    see also debt slavery
slaves 63, 67, 78–9, 99, 100, 103, 153, 324, 326,
    342–3, 379, 382
slogans 172–3, 230–4, 236–8, 395
small boats 171–3
smallpox 116, 331
smearing blood on objects 241, 243, 245
smells 35, 46, 318
smith 182, 184, 193–4, 250–1, 299–300
snake spirit 77
sneezing 243
soaking a new rope 262
social change 5–6
socializing 89, 146
Socotra 338, 340
Soedoe Hormat 53
Soge Paga 68–71, 75, 232, 247
Soge Ténã 70, 180, 226, 253–5, 266, 274–8,
    288–90, 306, 314, 398
sokal 139
Sola Langu 40, 63, 85
solé 90
Solé Bafalofë 43
Solor vii, 3–4, 11–13, 15, 17–18, 20, 25, 29, 31,
    47, 50, 57, 69–71, 75, 100, 103, 105, 109,
    116, 139, 148, 155, 160, 168–9, 201, 238,
    291, 312–13, 316, 318, 323–5, 327, 361,
    376, 378, 380–2, 385–7, 392–4, 397, 401
    Archipelago 24, 91, 101, 160, 201, 323,
        325–6, 329, 355, 363, 377
    fort 11, 13, 18, 57, 201, 382
    Strait 4, 25, 51, 168–9, 201, 203, 291
Solorese 11–13, 100, 323–5, 327–8
Somali coast 338
Sonbai 12
songs addressed to submerged ray 281, 286
Sonneratia acida, Linn. 383
Sonneratia caseolaris, Engl. 383
sopé utã 176
Sora Kai 58
soro 166
soru 243, 395
soul 115, 119, 204, 246, 256, 314
soul of the boat, *see* spirit of the boat 246
source of life 102
sources 31–3
South America 332
South-East Asia 230
South Pacific 332
Southeast Islands 325

Southern Cross 156–7, 305
sovereignty 30
Spain 402
Spanish 10, 11, 18–19, 401
Spanish Mackerel 282
spatial orientation 163–7
spearguns 168, 170–1, 177
special terms 295–8
speech prohibitions 293, 295–9
speeches 92
sperm whales 5, 68, 156, 188–95, 212, 234, 236,
    246, 255, 257, 259, 263, 273–5, 282,
    289–322, 325–7, 330, 334, 340, 345,
    399–401
spermaceti 188, 191, 193, 195, 309, 325, 327,
    329–30, 334, 399
spheres of exchange 341, 343
spheres of influence 30
Spice Islands 57, 330
spices 331
spindle 388
spindles 260–2, 264
spinner dolphin 274, 289
spinning thread 137
spinning-wheel 137
spinsters 104
spirit:
    of the boat 244–6
    of the fish 244, 271
    of the great house 245
    of the interior 378
    of the sea 378
spirits 115–17, 133, 300, 314, 340
    land 46
    sea 46, 116
spittle 118
splash screens 171
splashing boat with seawater so it will move 271
splitting tree trunks 213
spokesman in marriage negotiations 88, 90, 92
spool of gebang palm leaf strips 223–4
Spotted Eagle Ray 282
spout of baleen whales 291
spout of sperm whales 291
spring tides 155, 321
springs, tidal 40, 42, 69, 116–17
sprinkling water 83, 249
sprinkling with holy water 244, 247, 271, 277,
    287, 315–16
squid 362
Stadmannia sideroxylon 394
stages of the moon 157
stages of the sun 158
standing strongly, harpooner 283, 320
stars 156–7
steamships 381
steering 207

steering oar 166–7, 172, 222, 392
Stella Maris 231
stempost 206, 219, 243–6, 271
steps, stone 43
stern 218, 228, 243, 246, 250, 255, 267, 290,
    303–4, 318, 395
stern decorations 238–40, 278
sternpost 206, 218, 243
stinger, ray 198, 280–1
stockings 335
stomach contents 195
stone seats 39, 64, 65
storm winds 153–4
strait between Lembata and Pantar 320
stranding of whales 323, 339–40, 399
stranger-king theme 383
stretcher 121, 132–3
stringers 205, 218, 255
submergence of land 6
subsidy 345
subsistence economy 342, 345
substitute marks 212, 215
succession to political office 385
sugar 143, 315
sugar cane 143
sugar palm 216
sugar palm fibre 216, 273, 318
suicide 126
uılıu 62
Suku Hama, Lāma Kéra 77
suku-lāma 62
Sula Onā 40, 59, 63, 67, 77, 82–4, 86, 88, 98,
    113, 180
Sulang 113
Sulawesi 56, 100, 102, 212, 214, 332, 336, 362
sulphur 100, 387
Sulu Islands 379, 387
Sulu Sea 332, 334
Sumatra 14, 85, 148, 172, 331, 383, 387–8, 390,
    401
Sumba 6, 15–16, 19, 103, 139–40, 379, 397
Sumbawa 103, 328
sun 123, 150–2, 158–63, 198, 285, 391
Sun Plate 54–5
sunburn 273
Sunda Mountain System 6
Sunda region 6
Sunda Straits 331
sunfish 200, 289, 314–15
Sung dynasty 387
sunrise 158
sunset 158
Surabaya 1, 377
surf 257, 271, 301–3, 317–18
surnames 112–13
surplus 101, 103
surplus production 342

Sutrana 335
swallows' nests, 264
sweet potatoes 143, 247
swift 137
swimming 317
swordfish 315
swords 74, 248, 335
Sydney 331, 333, 400

tacking 222
Taenyura Lymma 282
Tahiti 393
Tahulandang 336
tāi 156
tai bĕlino 156
tai lolo dataf 156
tai lolo kesafut 156
tāi muru 130
tail fins 195
takā 150
tăka 150
Talaud 336
talé 250
talé bĕfaléng 228, 258–9, 263, 290
talé gĕlefĕ 228, 259, 263, 290
talé kenaté 259
talé kubi 259
talé léo bélā 258, 260
talé léo fā 258–9, 282
talé māda 259
talé nodé pukā fãnā 258
talé nodé pukā méki 258
talé puã pukā 258
talé suka bélā 258
talé suka bĕlelā 258
talé suka fā 257, 275, 284
talé suka uring 259
talé ura 273
tamarind 137, 168, 381, 384, 387
Tamils 171
tanã 225
Tana 'Ai 62, 385
Tana Boléng 203
Tana-Ékā 158–63
Tana Kĕrofa 40–1, 58–60, 63, 65, 75, 82–4, 86, 98, 113
tané 137, 225
Tanebar-Evav 103, 339, 395
Tanembar 326
Tanjung Suba 288
Tapobali 77, 380
tapo lolo 157
tapo pukā 157
Tapo Onã 40, 63, 70, 77, 82–4, 86, 98, 113, 180, 226
Tapon 113
tarring boats 326

Tawau 26–7, 381
tax 50, 147–8, 343
teak 137, 394
tebā 193, 195
teboōngā 196
Tectona grandis 394
tekā 217
teka-elā 228
teka nālā 227
tékél 265
tĕlākā 257
telephones 49–50
television 50
teluma 251
temaka takā 150–1, 270
temple of the lord of the land 268–9
temporary dowels 214
temporary strake 210
temu 328
temu bélā 194, 255, 274, 298, 321
temu bĕlā 255, 274, 298
temu bĕlurā 255, 274
temu burā 274
temu kebong 274
temu kebung 274
temu notong 274
temōto 238–40, 278, 318
temōto lako īku 240
téna 177, 179, 201, 209, 212, 225, 227, 247, 254, 268, 271–3, 280, 290, 303, 319, 384
téna alep 179, 186
Téna Ana 180, 184, 230, 238, 266, 280, 289, 308, 314
Téna Bĕlā 230, 232
téna kebuénga 287
téna kenafang 218
téna kepur 213, 216–17, 229, 245
téna kora kora 203
téna-laja 203
téna-laja umã 188
téna lama faij 201, 203, 226, 393
téna pĕlédā 393
téna pung alep 244
Téna Tapoona, see *Sia Apu*
téna uak nālā 228
tenané 137
tenarap 183, 185–7, 193, 195, 199, 364
Tenasserim 386
tenebe 115
tenépa 209
tenépa fā 210
tenépa uring 210
tenigi 222, 273
tenika 151
tenoned joints 206, 208, 212, 216
tenuda 267
tenūlé 137

tenutu 214
teri 256
Tĕria 56
Termanu 385
termites 318
Ternate 10–12, 201, 205, 333
Terong 11, 13, 29, 203, 323, 336, 379
terrain 6–10
téti 391
téti hau 391
Téti Heri 119, 180, 230, 234, 238, 266, 277,
    287–90, 306, 308–9, 397–8
Téti Heri disaster 119, 287–8, 398
Téti Lefo, see Lamalera A
Téti Nama Papã 39–41, 63–4, 74–7, 84, 86, 98,
    147, 180
Tetun 56
textile patterns 74, 135, 136, 143, 343, 386
textiles 5, 32, 50, 74, 79–80, 89, 92, 94, 97,
    99–100, 105–6, 117, 122, 129, 132, 135–49,
    172, 224–5, 244, 273, 306, 309, 322, 326,
    328, 342, 385, 390
Thames 19, 400
thread 93–4, 107, 118, 129, 132, 135–6, 141,
    143, 147, 149, 182, 224, 250–1, 253,
    257–60, 263, 265–6, 322, 390, 395–6
three-part circle 87
thwarts 173, 204–5, 211, 217–19, 222–3, 226,
    229, 253, 257–8, 266, 271, 273, 276
tidal spring 316
tidal wave 8, 50, 111, 142
tide pools 150
tides 109, 150, 154–5, 301–2, 313
Tidore 10, 18
tīfa sahoq 130
tiger shark 309, 401
tika 151
Tiliacene 394
tilu 196, 208, 245, 287
tilu onã 196
time marks 150
time reckoning 391
Timor 2–4, 6, 12–15, 18–19, 21, 24–5, 29, 31,
    56, 62, 70, 72, 99–100, 103, 139–40, 201,
    280, 304, 323–36, 381–2, 386–7, 389, 392,
    397–8, 400–1
    Archipelago 101
    European and American contacts with 323–
    36
    ground 330, 334
    Residency 4, 30
    Strait 155, 329–32, 334, 336, 400
    Trough 6
    visits to 51, 71–3, 173, 240, 278, 308, 329,
    336, 383
Timorese 13, 324, 326
'Timor fever' 335

'Timor-season' 334
timu 153–4, 165
timu lĕfa 154
timu olé 154
timu tana 154
'tips' 197
titi 296
Toba Batak 85, 387–8, 390
tobacco 145, 186, 247, 315
Tobi Lã Déké 384
todã ié 242
todã menula kolé 242
Togo, Africa 51
Tomini Bay 332
tongue and groove, *see* tenoned joints
tool boxes, wooden 241–2
Topasses, *see* Black Portuguese
tõpo 197–8, 320
tõpo fãnã 197
top of mast 219, 245
tõpo meki 197
Toraja 102
toro nalã 264
tortoiseshell 18, 100, 199
toto 243
toto léo 263
toto léo kepur 261
tourism 345
tourist ship 308, 397
tourists 249, 299, 341
trade 13–20, 103, 139–41, 148, 177, 259–60,
    315, 318, 323, 328, 343
    cloth 137–8
    goods 135
    partners 149
traders 327–8
trading 135, 144, 146, 203, 213
trading journey 145–9
transferring shares 181
transition between seasons 268, 324
transportation 24, 31, 39, 44, 46, 48–9, 51, 90,
    116, 133, 141, 181, 343, 345
treaty of 1859 21, 29
trepang 14
tribute 48, 51, 203
triremes 201
Trobriand Islanders 2, 55, 183, 393
trolling 168
trotlines, *see* long lines
true-false 228
trunk wife-givers 85, 129, 132, 351
Tuakwutu 386
tuba 170
tuber 115
tué 137
tufa tree 68
Tufan 113

Tufa Onã 40–1, 60, 63, 65, 68, 70, 75–6, 83–4,
86, 98, 113, 180, 194, 270, 385
tukã-hebã 136
Tukan 113
tūlé bua 137
turtle eggs 199
turtles 171, 199, 254, 279, 297, 314, 355, 362,
400
Tuscan 320, 334–5
tusks, elephant 50, 74, 88–9, 91–2, 96, 99–106,
108, 136, 146–7, 149, 301, 326, 328, 343,
386–7
tutu ina-biné fĕli 98
twins 109–10
opposite sex 109–10
twisting lever 215, 394

uaj 216
uak 226
uak kenetang 228
uak léo ūli 258
uak nãlã 228
uak puã pukã 258–9, 267, 276, 287
uak tukã 265–6
ubã futu, bara fãi 150
udép 258
ufã nolo 109
ujuk 154
ujuk Fai Nãé 154
ujuk Ilé Belopor 154
Ujung Pandang 200, 383
uk 108
ūk 174, 197–8, 263, 316
uk kajo 108
Ulchu County 339
umã 184, 187, 193, 195, 199–200, 365
ūmã 212, 217, 227, 229, 258
uma lima 105–6
umã mĕng 193, 105
unaj 255–6
underemployment 343
uneven numbers 175, 228, 253, 260, 264–5, 395
unilineal descent 81
United States 332
United States 400
uno narã 204
unseaworthy boats 130, 181
upa ikã pung alep 244
upper village, *see* Lamalera A
urbanization 344
Urfal 301
uri 109
urinating on nets 175–6
uring 265–6
Urolophus Armatus 281
utã 176–7
ūta kéda 153

Valparaiso 333
values 50, 137–9, 144–7, 196, 198, 200, 317, 335
Vatter's museum collection 31–2
vigil at beach 305, 308, 398
Viking boats 204
village head 46, 65, 90, 99, 115–16, 174, 203–4,
249, 270, 316, 397–8
village plain 39, 74
village temple 39–40, 65–6
Visaya 382
vitamin B 109, 133
Vitex, Linn. 206, 217, 219, 394
volcanic eruption 130, 379
volcanoes 6–7

wage-paying jobs 175, 181, 343
wages for the feet 198
wages for the spirit of the fish 244
Wai Bagan Peninsula 397
Wai Jaran 49
Wai Komo 165
Wai Léi 176
Wai Otan 313, 316, 398–9
Wai Teba bay 384
Waiteba 8, 50, 131, 177
Waiteba catastrophe 8, 50, 111, 130–1, 177, 312
Waibalun 26, 317
Waikomo 381
Wailolong vii, 63–4, 96, 386
Wairiang 384
Waiwejak 384
Waiwerang 28, 50, 88, 115, 140–1, 165, 173,
317–18, 325, 381, 398, 401
wall, *see* Lamalera, fencing of
Wãqwãq 19
warp in sail section 225
wars 14, 48, 73, 91, 139–40, 297, 379, 383–4,
394, 399
washing mouth 299
washing the hair 96–7
water bamboos 305
water, fresh 20, 35, 42, 116, 135, 297, 322, 335,
400–1
water pipes 42–3
water pot 266, 305
Wato Manu Peninsula 384
Wato Téna 384
Watu Bela Archipelago 56
Watuwawer 7
wave shadows 156
waves 156, 168, 257, 283, 287, 302–3, 306, 321
wax 18, 100, 326, 400
weather 151
weaving 5, 135–7, 140, 146, 342–3, 390, 395
a harpoon leader 264
leader 253
sword, design on base of 137

sword for sail making 224
swords 137, 147
the sail 221, 223–6, 260
weddings 89, 91, 94, 105, 156, 320
weeping 95
weevils 153
weft in cloth 225
weft in sail section 225
well of the boat 206, 218, 223, 229, 245–6, 266, 276–7, 290, 300, 308
west current 153–6, 166, 272, 301, 313
west monsoon, *see* wet season
west wind 153–4, 165–7, 298, 302, 318
Western Australian Museum 329
wet season 9–10, 139, 150–3, 155, 170, 273, 333, 392
Wetar 384, 392
whale:
  hunting 5, 203, 257, 268, 273
  meat 327
  oil 100, 124, 195, 244, 309, 323, 325–9, 332–4, 338, 399
  seeing imperfection in the construction of a boat 212–13, 217
  shark 200, 255, 257 8, 282, 284, 314
  ships 400
  skulls 309
  teeth 194, 310, 328, 335, 399
Whale Hunters of Lamalera 295, 390
whalebone plaque 334
whale-oil lamps 301
whaler shark 401
whales 45, 117, 121, 142, 152–3, 156, 179, 184, 186, 188–95, 198–9, 203, 213, 229, 247, 251, 259, 270, 273–5, 282, 289–340, 376, 396, 398
  attacking boats 291
  ramming boats 293, 297
  striking boats 290, 293, 296–7, 307–8
whaling, European and American 323, 329–37
whaling grounds 311, 330–2, 334
whiptail devil ray 255, 281
whirlpool 156
white cloth, placing in coffin 130, 132
white shark 199–200, 255, 309, 393
widows 146, 185, 187, 232, 270, 285, 301, 365
wife-givers 82, 85, 87, 92–3, 96–7, 103, 107, 108, 126, 129, 136, 183, 185, 346, 348, 351, 354, 365

wife-givers superior to wife-takers 107, 187
wife-takers 68, 82, 85, 87–8, 92, 97, 103, 107–8, 129, 132, 136, 183–5, 187, 346, 348, 350–1, 354
wild yams 153
William and Ann 331
winds 150–4, 166–8, 177, 206, 222, 245, 268, 272–3, 275, 278–9, 283, 285, 287, 298–9, 302, 313, 320
wine glasses 400
Witch Island 288
witchcraft 161
witches 67, 78, 115–16, 159–60, 163
Witihama 65
wives 177, 182, 260
Wolo Wutun 318, 378
Wolofeo district 91
women 83, 86–7, 91, 93–4, 97, 102, 109, 112, 123, 132–3, 135–49, 182, 184, 213, 226, 260, 263, 299, 388
  carrying meat 45–6, 135, 144, 184, 186, 192, 320
  in the sea 308–9
women's cloth 136
wooden crutch to keep sail half furled 267
wooden cyclinder for guaging diameter of rope 263
wooden pole used to support outrigger 276, 290
word substitutes 297
work songs 261–2, 304
World Bank 49
World War II 35, 77–8
woven belts 322
woven wire chains 74
wrapping 253, 263, 266
Wulan Doni 34, 59, 138, 141–6, 154, 238, 247–9, 384, 390
Wurch 389

yams 144–5, 315
yard 220–2, 395
Yogyakarta 47
youngest son inheritance 385

Zanthoxylum myriacanthum, Wall. 211